SELWYN'S LAW OF EMPLOYMENT

SELWYN'S
LAW OF EMPLOYMENT

Fourteenth Edition

NORMAN SELWYN
LLM, Dip Econ (Oxon), Barrister at Law

OXFORD
UNIVERSITY PRESS

OXFORD

UNIVERSITY PRESS

Great Clarendon Street, Oxford OX2 6DP

Oxford University Press is a department of the University of Oxford.
It furthers the University's objective of excellence in research, scholarship,
and education by publishing worldwide in

Oxford New York

Auckland Cape Town Dar es Salaam Hong Kong Karachi
Kuala Lumpur Madrid Melbourne Mexico City Nairobi
New Delhi Shanghai Taipei Toronto

With offices in

Argentina Austria Brazil Chile Czech Republic France Greece
Guatemala Hungary Italy Japan Poland Portugal Singapore
South Korea Switzerland Thailand Turkey Ukraine Vietnam

Oxford is a registered trade mark of Oxford University Press
in the UK and in certain other countries

Published in the United States
by Oxford University Press Inc., New York

British Library Cataloguing in Publication Data

Data available

Library of Congress Cataloging in Publication Data

Data available

Typeset by RefineCatch Limited, Bungay, Suffolk
Printed in Great Britain
on acid-free paper by
Ashford Colour Press Ltd, Gosport, Hampshire

ISBN 0–19–928730–9   978–0–19–928730–7

1 3 5 7 9 10 8 6 4 2

Preface

The aim of this book is to state the modern law of employment, as it affects employers and employees, in a manner which is readable, accurate and up-to-date, for the benefit of employers and employees generally, and, in particular, for lawyers, students, human resources personnel, and others who have to advise on the subject.

The inexorable march of employment law goes on. This edition includes most of the significant legislative changes which have taken place in the past two years. These include the Transfer of Undertakings (Protection of Employment) Regulations 2006, Employment Equality (Age) Regulations 2006, Asylum, Immigration and Nationality Act 2006, Equality Act 2006, Civil Partnership Act 2006, Constitutional Reform Act 2005, Disability Discrimination Act 2005, Employment Equality (Sex Discrimination) Regulations 2005, Information and Consultation of Employees Regulations 2004, Equal Pay Act 1970 (Amendment) Regulations 2004, and other minor legislative items. Also included are a number of significant decisions from UK and European courts. Several chapters have been thoroughly revised, and there has been a reorganisation of material.

At the time of writing, the Work and Families Act 2006 has just received the Royal Assent, and under its provisions regulations will be made on matters such as paternity and adoption leave, maternity and parental leave, statutory maternity pay and maternity allowance, flexible working, etc. These changes are due to take effect as from 1 April 2007.

Having been 'Tupe'd' over to Oxford University Press, I would like to thank all those who have assisted in preparing this edition for publication.

I have tried to state the law in accordance with the sources available to me as at July 2006.

Norman Selwyn
Juno@selwynfamily.co.uk

Contents

Appendices

Table of statutes

Table of statutory instruments

Table of cases

1

The Institutions of Employment Law

Advisory, Conciliation and Arbitration Service

1.1 The Advisory, Conciliation and Arbitration Service (ACAS) was placed on a statutory basis by the Employment Protection Act 1975 and continued by virtue of the Trade Union and Labour Relations (Consolidation) Act 1992 (TULR(C)A, s 247). It is charged with the general duty of promoting the improvement of industrial relations. Its work is directed by a Council, which consists of a chairman and up to nine other members appointed by the Secretary of State. Three of these are to be appointed after consultations with employers' organisations, three after consultation with workers' organisations, and three 'neutral' (usually academic) appointments are usually made. Additionally up to three deputy chairmen may be appointed. The Secretary of State may appoint two further members of the Council, after consultation with both sides of industry. Currently, the Council has 12 members. The appointments will be initially for a period of five years, and may be renewed for a further period (TULR(C)A, s 248).

1.2 ACAS will appoint its own staff, including a secretary, and will also provide staff for the Certification Officer and the Central Arbitration Committee. Although it will perform its functions on behalf of the Crown, it shall not be subject to any directions from any minister as to the manner in which it is to exercise any of those functions. It is this complete independence from government control which is a distinguishing feature of ACAS. It will make an annual report on its activities and those of the Central Arbitration Committee to the Secretary of State, which will be laid before Parliament and published.

Whenever it thinks appropriate to do so, ACAS may charge a fee for its services, and also the Secretary of State may direct ACAS to charge fees, either at a full economic cost or a specified proportion or percentage of the economic cost. However, ACAS must notify the person concerned that a fee may or will be charged (TULR(C)A, s 251A).

1.3 The function of ACAS can be examined under the following headings:

A. Advice

1.4 ACAS may, on request or otherwise, give employers, employers' associations, workers and trade unions such advice as it thinks appropriate on matters connected with or likely to affect industrial relations. General advice on this topic may also be published (TULR (C)A, s 213). ACAS has produced a number of Advisory Booklets and Advice Leaflets on a wide range of topics with the aim of giving advice to employers and employees about employment rights generally.

B. Conciliation

1.5 Where a trade dispute exists or is apprehended, ACAS may offer its assistance to the parties, either on its own volition or at the request of any party, with a view to bringing about a settlement. This may be achieved by conciliation or other means, and by the appointment, if necessary, of someone outside ACAS whose assistance may be used. Due regard will be had to the desirability of encouraging the parties to use any appropriate agreed procedures (TULR(C)A, s 210).

If there is a dispute over union recognition, ACAS may be invited to use its conciliation role. At the request of both parties, it may hold a ballot of workers involved in the dispute, and/or ascertain the strength of union membership of such workers. However, any such request may be withdrawn by either side, whereupon ACAS shall cease to take any further steps in the matter (TULR(C)A, s 210A).

1.6 It should be noted that for conciliation purposes, the definition of 'trade dispute' is the old definition (based on the Employment Protection Act 1975), now contained in TULR(C)A, s 218, not the more restricted definition (based on the Trade Union and Labour Relations Act 1974) now contained in TULR(C)A, s 244. The effect is to give ACAS a wider conciliation brief.

1.7 Conciliation officers will also be appointed for the purpose of settling by conciliation certain matters which are, or could be, the subject of proceedings before an employment tribunal under any legislation, whenever passed (TULR(C)A, s 211), provided the relevant legislation so indicates (see Employment Tribunals Act 1996, s 18). When a complaint is presented to an employment tribunal, a copy will be sent to a conciliation officer, who is an officer of ACAS, and who has a duty to try to promote a settlement without the matter having to be dealt with by the tribunal. He will intervene for this purpose if requested to do so by the claimant or the person against whom the complaint has been made (ie, the respondent), and also in the absence of such request, if he thinks he could act with a reasonable prospect of success. He may also conciliate at the request of either party in respect of a matter which could be the subject of tribunal proceedings, but before a complaint has been presented. In practice, a large number of claims made to employment tribunals are disposed of as a result of the intervention of the conciliation officer. The majority of these will be settled on the basis of the employer making some financial payment to the claimant, and the rest will be withdrawn or a private settlement reached.

A conciliation officer will exercise his functions in the following circumstances:

Equal Pay Act, s 2; Sex Discrimination Act, s 63; Race Relations Act, s 54; Trade Union and Labour Relations (Consolidation) Act, ss 64 (unjustified discipline) 68 (unauthorised or excessive deductions), 70B (obligations in relation to a collective bargaining unit), 86 (objection to paying into the political fund), 137 (refusal of employment because of union membership), 146 (action short of dismissal because of union membership or activities), 168–169 (time off work for trade union duties), 168A (time off work for union learning representatives), 170 (time off work for trade union activities), 174 (unlawful exclusion or expulsion from a trade union), 188 (failure to consult on redundancies), 190 (protective award), Sch A1 (detriment because of collective bargaining recognition); Disability

Discrimination Act, s 8; Employment Rights Act, ss 8 (itemised pay statement), 13–21 (unauthorised deductions and unauthorised payments), 28 (guarantee payments), 80G (flexible working), 92 (written reasons for dismissal), 135 (redundancy payments), Part V (detriment in employment), Part VI (time off work for public duties, retraining, ante-natal care, dependants, occupational pension trustees, employee representatives), Part VII (suspension from work on medical or maternity grounds), Part X (unfair dismissal); National Minimum Wage Act; Extension of Jurisdiction Order; Working Time Regulations; Transnational Information and Consultation Regulations; Part-time Workers (Prevention of Less Favourable Treatment) Regulations; Fixed-Term Employees (Prevention of Less Favourable Treatment) Regulations; Employment Equality (Sexual Orientation) Regula-tions; Employment Equality (Religion or Belief) Regulations; Information and Consult-ation of Employees Regulations; Transfer of Undertakings (Protection of Employment) Regulations 2006 (employee liability information); Employment Equality (Age) Regula-tions 2006.

1.8 The Employment Tribunals (Constitution and Rules of Procedure) Regulations 2004 make provision for two periods of conciliation, within which the parties will have the opportunity to reach an ACAS conciliated settlement. A tribunal hearing will not take place during the conciliation periods (other than pre-hearing reviews and case management discussions).

The 'short conciliation period' is for seven weeks, and applies to the following claims:

(a) claims made in respect of the Employment Tribunals Act, s 3 (breach of contract);

(b) the following provisions in the Employment Rights Act, ss 13–27 (failure to pay wages and unlawful deductions), s 28 (guarantee pay), ss 50, 52, 53, 55, 56 (time off work for public duties, to look for work, antenatal care, and failure to pay remuneration), s 64 (medical suspension), s 68 (maternity suspension), ss 163–164 redundancy payment);

(c) the following provisions of TULR(C)A, s 68 (deduction of unauthorised union subscriptions), ss 168–169 (time off work and payment for trade union duties), s 170 (time off work for trade union activities), s 192 (failure to pay a protective award);

(d) Transfer of Undertakings (Protection of Employment) Regulations, reg 11 (failure to pay compensation following failure to inform or consult), Working Time Regu-lations, regs 13, 14, 16 (right to be paid annual leave).

All other proceedings (except those noted below) will have a 'standard conciliation period' of 13 weeks. The short period of conciliation can be extended if the chairman of the employment tribunal thinks that, on the basis of the complexity of the claim, the standard conciliation period would be more appropriate, and the standard period of conciliation may be extended by a further two weeks if all the parties to the proceedings agree, or if a realistic proposal for a settlement is being given serious consideration, or if ACAS considers that it is probable that proceedings will be settled within the extended period.

Neither of these conciliation periods apply to claims made under the Equal Pay Act, s 2(1), Sex Discrimination Act, s 63, Race Relations Act, s 54, Disability Discrimination Act, s 8, Employment Equality (Sexual Orientation) Regulations 2003, Employment Equality (Religion or Belief) Regulations 2003, Employment Right Act, ss 47B, 103A, 105 (6A) (protected disclosure) and national security proceedings.

1.9 Anything communicated to the conciliation officer in connection with the perform-ance of his functions shall not be admissible in evidence in any proceedings before the tribunal without the consent of the party who communicated it. So far as dismissals are concerned, he shall try to promote the re-engagement or reinstatement of the claimant by the employer or by a successor or associated employer on terms appearing to him to be equitable or, if this is not possible, to try to promote a settlement on the sum to be paid by way of compensation. Apart from certain specific instances (see para 20.41), it is not possible for a person to contract out of his statutory rights, and any agreement to this effect is generally void, but this rule does not apply to any agreement reached through the intervention of the conciliation officer, and any such settlement agreed between the parties will be legally binding (Employment Rights Act 1996, s 203(2)(e)).

A conciliation officer may become involved prior to the presentation of a claim to an employment tribunal. If a person claims that he has a complaint which could be the subject of tribunal proceedings, then either he or the potential respondent could seek the services of a conciliation officer, who must then act as if an actual complaint has been lodged with the tribunal (Employment Tribunals Act, s 18(3)).

1.10 The conciliation officer does not have to advise if the terms of any proposed settlement are fair (*Clarke v Redcar & Cleveland Borough Council*). How he performs his functions is a matter for his discretion, and in the absence of bad faith, or adopting unfair methods, an agreement reached under his auspices cannot be set aside (*Slack v Greenham Plant Hire*). However, the conciliation officer must take care not to give the impression that he favours the views of one side to the dispute. Thus, if the parties have reached an agreement, he should not get involved with its merits, but merely record it on the appropriate form and obtain the parties' signatures (*Moore v Duport Furniture Products*). Indeed, an agreement reached orally between the parties under the auspices of the conciliation officer is equally binding (*Gilbert v Kembridge Fibres*).

1.11 In *Hennessy v Craigmyle & Co Ltd* the claimant was told that he would be dismissed summarily but, provided he signed an agreement which had been prepared by the concili-ation officer giving up his rights to bring a complaint before an employment tribunal, he would be treated as having been made redundant, and would be given certain monies. After taking legal advice, he signed the agreement, but subsequently brought a claim for unfair dismissal. He alleged that his consent had been obtained by economic duress, and hence was void. The argument was dismissed by the employment tribunal, the EAT and the Court of Appeal. Economic duress was a ground for avoiding an agreement only if the claimant's will was so overborne that his consent was vitiated because he had no real alternative. In this case there was such an alternative, for he could have refused to sign the agreement and taken his chance in the employment tribunal. In any case, whether economic duress exists is a question of fact for the employment tribunal to determine.

C. Arbitration

1.12 At the request of one or more parties to a trade dispute, but with the consent of all of them, ACAS may refer any matter to arbitration for settlement, either by a person appointed from outside ACAS, or by the Central Arbitration Committee. However, arbitration is not to be used unless the parties have exhausted agreed procedures for negotiation or the settlement of disputes, unless there is a special reason which justifies arbitration as an alternative to those procedures (TULR(C)A, s 212). With the consent of all the parties, ACAS may decide to publish the award. The Arbitration Act 1996 does not apply to any arbitration under this section, and thus the award is not capable of being legally enforced in a court of law.

In an effort to reduce the number of cases going to employment tribunals, and to avoid the intense legalism which is frequently found there, TULR(C)A, s 212A enabled ACAS to introduce an arbitration alternative, whereby claims for unfair dismissal (only) may, with the agreement of both parties, be heard in private by a single arbitrator. The scheme only operates when both sides have signed a COT3 (see para 1.7) or a compromise agreement (see para 20.43). The arbitrator will be appointed from a special panel of ACAS arbitrators, the actual hearing will be as informal as possible, and held in private at a convenient location. By agreeing to submit to ACAS arbitration, both parties waive their rights to raise any jurisdictional issues, eg whether time limits have been observed, whether there was or was not a dismissal, etc. A constructive dismissal case can only be heard if both parties agree that there was in fact a dismissal.

The parties will be invited to submit a written statement of their case in advance of the hearing, and will be expected to cooperate in the production of relevant documents. The arbitrator will adopt an inquisitorial approach, ie he will generally ask the questions and seek out the relevant facts, rather than leaving it to the parties to adopt the traditional adversarial approach to the case. Legal representation is not necessary. Strict legal principles and legal precedents will not be followed, but the arbitrator will take account of the general principles of fairness and good practice set out in the ACAS Code of Practice on 'Disciplinary and Grievance Procedures' and the ACAS Handbook 'Discipline at Work'. The arbitrator can make awards (which will be confidential to the parties and ACAS) identical to those which could be made by an employment tribunal (see Chapter 17). An award will generally be binding, and no appeal will be permitted, except where there is a point of EC law or the Human Rights Act 1998 is relevant, or where there is an allegation of serious irregularity.

The scheme will not be suitable for cases where there is a jurisdictional issue (eg was the applicant an employee, etc), where there are complex legal issues involved (eg was there a transfer of an undertaking), or where issues arising out of the implementation of EC law are concerned (eg Working Time Regulations, Sex Discrimination cases, etc). If issues other than unfair dismissal are revealed, these must be settled, withdrawn, or heard by an employment tribunal.

If the arbitrator recommends that the employee is re-engaged or reinstated, this order can be enforced, if necessary, by an employment tribunal. Continuity of employment will be preserved.

To date, the scheme has not been a success. In the year 2002/2003 only 23 such arbitrations were held and in 2003/2004 only seven such applications were received.

Full details of the scheme can be found in the ACAS Arbitration Scheme (Great Britain) Order 2004.

ACAS also has an arbitration scheme to deal with disputes over applications for flexible working (see para 2.134). The scheme is set out in the ACAS (Flexible Working) Arbitration Scheme (Great Britain) Order 2004 and can be used as a voluntary alternative to employment tribunal proceedings. It is claimed that the scheme will be confidential, informal, relatively fast and cost efficient. Again, the scheme has not proven to be popular.

D. Enquiries

1.13 ACAS may enquire into industrial relations generally, or in a particular industry, or in a particular undertaking. After taking into account the views of the parties, such findings may be published (TULR(C)A, s 214).

E. Codes of Practice

1.14 ACAS may issue Codes of Practice containing such practical guidance as it thinks fit for the purpose of promoting the improvement of industrial relations (TULR(C)A, s 199). Three Codes are currently in force (see Appendix D), namely:

(a) Disciplinary and Grievance Procedures;

(b) Disclosure of Information to Trade Unions for Collective Bargaining Purposes;

(c) Time Off for Trade Union Duties and Activities.

1.15 The codes are first prepared and published in draft form, and then ACAS shall consider any representations made about them (and if necessary modify them) before they are finally submitted to the Secretary of State. If he approves, he shall lay them before Parliament. If he does not approve, he will give reasons for withholding his approval. After completing the Parliamentary procedure, the code will be issued in the form of a draft by ACAS and will come into effect on a day appointed by the Secretary of State. A failure on the part of any person to observe a code shall not of itself make him liable to any proceedings, but in any proceedings before an employment tribunal or the Central Arbitration Committee the code will be admissible in evidence, and any relevant provision shall be taken into account in determining the issue (TULR(C)A, s 207) (see *Lock v Cardiff Rly Co*).

1.16 A Code of Practice may be revised or revoked with the approval of the Secretary of State (TULR(C)A, ss 201–202).

ACAS also issues a number of advisory booklets, handbooks and leaflets on many aspects of employment law, and a number of leaflets are available from the Department of Trade and Industry (see Appendix D).

Certification Officer (TULR(C)A, s 254)

1.17 The post of Certification Officer was originally created to take over certain administrative functions exercised in connection with trade unions, although nowadays he has wide powers of investigation and supervision over matters such as register of members, accounting records, elections, breaches of union rules, funds for political objects, and so on (see Chapter 22). He is appointed by the Secretary of State, and will make an annual report to him and also to ACAS. Although the staff of the Certification Officer is provided by ACAS, he is completely independent of that organisation.

Since TULRA 1974 (now TULR(C)A, s 2) the Certification Officer has kept a list of organisations which are trade unions and employers' associations within the legal definition. Since the Employment Protection Act 1975 (now TULR(C)A, s 6) he has issued certificates of independence to those trade unions which have applied, and meet the necessary criteria (see Chapter 22). He has issued a booklet entitled 'Guidance for trade unions wishing to apply for a certificate of independence'. He has taken custody of all documents held by his predecessors since 1871, and will keep these for public inspection, along with the list of trade unions and records of all applications for certificates of independence (TULR(C)A, ss 255–258). Following the abolition of the office of the Commissioner for the Rights of Trade Union Members many of the functions of that office have been transferred to the Certification Officer (Employment Relations Act 1999, Sch 6). The Certification Officer now has wide powers in respect of complaints by trade union members of alleged breaches of trade union law and trade union rules, and can now make declarations and orders on a number of matters, which may be enforced in the same manner as an order of the courts. An appeal from his decisions may be made on a point of law to the Employment Appeal Tribunal.

The Certification Officer may also strike out an application or complaint on the ground that it is scandalous, vexatious, has no reasonable prospect of success, or is otherwise misconceived, or refuse to entertain an application by a vexatious litigant (TULR(C)A, ss 256A–256AA).

Central Arbitration Committee

1.18 This body replaced the Industrial Arbitration Board (formerly known as the Industrial Court) and consists of a chairman (and deputy chairman) appointed by the Secretary of State (after consultation with ACAS) and other persons appointed from representatives of employers and workers who are experienced in industrial relations. The appointments may be for up to five years, and are renewable. The Central Arbitration Committee (CAC) will exercise its functions on behalf of the Crown, but will not be subject to directions of any kind from any ministers as to the manner in which those functions are to be exercised. CAC has a central role in the new statutory scheme for the recognition of trade unions, created by the Employment Relations Act 1999 (see Chapter 23). In performing its functions, CAC must have regard to the object of encouraging and promoting fair and efficient practices and arrangements in the workplace, although it will remain neutral on the issue of collective bargaining. CAC will continue to exercise its former statutory functions to adjudicate on claims relating to disclosure of information for collective bargaining purposes brought under TULR(C)A, s 183 (see para 23.15) and will also adjudicate on certain disputes arising out of the provisions of the Transnational Information and Consultation of Employees Regulations 1999 (see para 23.128), and the Information and Consultation Regulations 2004 (see para 23.137).

CAC also resolves disputes concerning the provision of information, consultation and participation arising from the European Public Limited Liability Company, and can act as a voluntary arbitration body following a reference from ACAS under TULR(C)A, s 212.

Employment Appeal Tribunal (Employment Tribunals Act 1996, ss 20–37)

1.19 This tribunal consists of judges of the High Court appointed by the Judicial Appointments Commission on the recommendation of the Lord Chancellor in England, and the Lord President of the Court of Session in Scotland, plus other members (appointed on the joint recommendations of the Lord Chancellor and the Secretary of State) who have special knowledge or experience of industrial relations as representatives of employers or of workers. The Employment Appeal Tribunal (the EAT) will be a superior court of record, with a central office in London, but it may sit anywhere in the country, and one or more divisions of the EAT may sit at the same time. In practice, hearings take place either in London or Edinburgh.

1.20 The jurisdiction of the EAT is as follows:

(a) to hear appeals on points of law from decisions of employment tribunals under the various statutory provisions set out in s 21 of the Employment Tribunals Act 1996, which generally cover most, but not all, of the jurisdiction enjoyed by employment tribunals (see para 1.27). In particular, it should be noted that appeals against decisions relating to the issue of improvement notices and prohibition notices go to the Divisional Court. The reason is that a breach of these notices amounts to a criminal offence, and the EAT only has specific civil jurisdiction. There have been a few cases where the relevant statutory provision has inadvertently not been included in s 21 of the Employment Tribunals Act, with the result that the EAT lacked jurisdiction to hear an appeal: see eg *Wolstenholme v Refreshment Systems Ltd (t/a Northern Vending Services)*;

(b) to hear appeals on questions of law from the decisions of the Certification Officer given under the provisions of Pt VI of TULR(C)A (restrictions on the use of trade union funds for political objects) (see TULR(C)A, s 95);

(c) to hear appeals on points of law from decisions of the Certification Officer given under TULR(C)A, s 103 (resolutions approving instruments of amalgamation) (see s 104);

(d) to hear appeals on points of law and fact from decisions of the Certification Officer given under TULR(C)A, ss 2–6 (entry on the list of trade unions, and applications for certificates of independence) (see s 9);

(e) to hear appeals on a point of law arising from a decision of the Certification Officer made under TULR(C)A, s 25 (failure of trade union to maintain register of names and addresses of members), s 31 (rights of members to have access to accounting records) and s 45C (duty to ensure that union posts are not held by certain offenders);

(f) to hear complaints of a failure to establish a European Works Council (as required by the Transnational Information and Consultation of Employees Regulations 1999, see para 23.128, and the Information and Consultation of Employees Regulations 2004, see para 23.137).

1.21 The procedure before the EAT is governed by the Employment Appeal Tribunal

Rules 1993, which were amended in 2004 in order to align procedures with those followed by employment tribunals. Thus the overriding objective of the Rules is to enable the EAT to deal with cases justly, including, so far as practicable, ensuring that the parties are on equal footing, saving expense, dealing with cases in ways which are proportionate to the importance and complexity of the issues, and ensuring that cases are dealt with expeditiously and fairly. The Rules lay down the procedure to be followed when lodging an appeal, although if a judge or Registrar thinks that an appeal has no reasonable grounds of succeeding, or is an abuse of process, he can notify the appellant accordingly, and order that no further action be taken in the matter. Further details of the procedure before the EAT can be found in Practice Direction 2004, which supersedes all previous directions.

A party may appear before the EAT in person, or be represented by a solicitor, barrister, representative of a trade union or employers association, or any other person whom he desires to represent him. Costs will normally be awarded by the EAT, although there is a power to make a costs order, if the proceedings brought by a party were unnecessary, improper or vexatious, or there has been unreasonable delay or other unreasonable conduct in bringing or conducting the proceedings. The EAT may make a costs order in favour of a litigant in person, and also make a wasted costs order against a party's representative if there has been improper, unreasonable or negligent acts on his part.

Appeals will be heard by a judge and either two or four members, so that in either case there is an equal number of persons whose knowledge or experience of industrial relations is as a representative of employers and workers respectively. With the consent of the parties, however, an appeal may be heard by a judge and one or three members. If the appeal is from a decision of an employment tribunal chairman sitting alone (see para 1.24), the appeal may be heard by the judge alone, unless the judge directs that one or more appointed member should sit also.

If a judge or tribunal chairman feels that there may be a conflict of interest because he (or a member of his family) have had some form of professional or personal connection with one of the parties, he should ensure that the full facts are placed before the parties, with an explanation. If there is a real chance of an objection, he should ascertain whether there is another judge who can hear the case (*Jones v DAS Legal Expenses Insurance Co Ltd*). For example, there is an objection to an advocate appearing before the EAT if he is also a part-time judge in that tribunal, and such action is contrary to Art 6 of the Human Rights Convention as being a violation of the right to a fair hearing (*Lawal v Northern Spirit Ltd*).

A restriction on proceedings order may be made to prevent vexatious litigants wasting court time (rr 13–17), and a restricting reporting order may be made in cases where sexual misconduct is alleged (r 23) or disability discrimination (r 23A). It is an offence, punishable by a fine not exceeding level 5 on the standard scale (currently £5,000) to act in contravention of such an order.

1.22 An appeal can only be entertained by the EAT if there is a genuine dispute between the parties (*IMI Yorkshire Imperial Ltd v Olender*) and appeals should not be pursued with other ulterior motives (*Baker v Superite Tools Ltd*). A further appeal will lie on a point of law to the Court of Appeal or, in Scotland, to the Court of Session, and a final appeal will lie to the House of Lords. At any time, however, a tribunal or court can refer a case to the European Court of Justice in Luxembourg, if a question arises as to the application of European law (see para 1.66).

Employment tribunals

1.23 The constitutional basis for employment tribunals can be found in the Employment Tribunals (Constitution and Rules of Procedure) Regulations 2004, which apply to England, Wales and Scotland. A Central Office of Employment Tribunals (COET) has been set up in London, with offices throughout the country. An employment tribunal is an inferior court, exercising the judicial powers of the state for the purpose of the Contempt of Court Act 1981, s 19, and contempt of court proceedings may be brought if there is an attempt to pervert the course of justice or any other breach of the Act (*Peach Grey & Co v Sommers*).

1.24 An employment tribunal consists of a legal chairman and two lay members. The chairman can be either a barrister or solicitor, and may be full-time or part-time. The lay members, who are all part-time, are selected from a panel drawn up after consultation with representatives of employers' organisations and trade unions. There is also a self-nomination procedure, designed to attract women, ethnic minorities, and persons with disabilities. At an actual hearing, there will always be a representative from each side of industry, although a chairman can sit with one lay member only if both parties to the dispute agree. Each member of the employment tribunal has an equal vote, and although decisions can be reached by a majority vote, in practice it appears that, despite the some-what diverse backgrounds, 96% of all decisions reached are unanimous. In the remaining cases, the 'wingmen' are just as likely to unite in outvoting the legal chairman as the latter is likely to have the support of one or the other member. In cases of sex discrimination, it is desirable to have one member of either sex, and in race discrimination cases, a member who has special experience of race relations, but there is no absolute legal requirement that an employment tribunal should be so composed (*Habib v Elkington & Co Ltd*). A tribunal chairman or member should not have any connection with any of the parties who appear before them, nor with any of the witnesses (*University of Swansea v Cornelius*). However, the fact that the chairman or members know an advocate who appears before them should not cause any problem.

Although, generally speaking, an employment tribunal will consist of a chairman and two members, in the following circumstances a chairman may sit alone (Employment Tribunals Act, s 4). These are:

(a) the following complaints made under TULR(C)A, ie s 68A (unauthorised or excessive deductions of trade union subscriptions), s 87 (unauthorised deduction of contribution to a political fund), ss 161, 165, 166 (application for interim relief etc), s 192 (failure by employer to pay a protective award);

(b) a complaint under the Pension Schemes Act 1993, s 126;

(c) proceedings brought under the following provisions of the Employment Rights Act 1996, ie s 11 (failure to give written statement of terms and conditions), s 23 (unauthorised deductions from wages), s 34 (failure to make a guarantee payment), s 70 (failure to pay remuneration following suspension on medical grounds), ss 128, 131, 132 (application for interim relief etc), s 163 (right to or amount of redundancy payment), s 170 (reference following an application to the Secretary of State for a redundancy payment), s 188 (rights of employee on employer's insolvency), s 206(4) (appointment of an appropriate person where there is no personal representative of a deceased employee);

(d) complaints brought under the Transfer of Undertakings (Protection of Employment) Regulations 2006, reg 11(5) (failure to pay compensation in pursuance of an order made following a failure to consult on a transfer);

(e) complaints made under the National Minimum Wage Act 1998, s 11 (failure to allow access to records), s 19 (appeal by an employer against an enforcement notice), s 22 (appeal against a penalty notice);

(f) proceedings brought under the provisions of the Employment Tribunals Extension of Jurisdiction (England and Wales) Order 1994 and Employment Tribunals Extension of Jurisdiction (Scotland) Order 1994 (breach of contract claims);

(g) proceedings in which the parties give their written consent to be heard by a chairman alone;

(h) proceedings in which the person against whom they are brought does not contest the case.

1.25 However, in any of the above circumstances, the chairman may at any stage decide to have the case heard by a full tribunal:

(a) where there is a likelihood of a dispute arising from the facts;

(b) where there is a likelihood of an issue of law arising;

(c) having taken into account the views of any of the parties;

(d) where there are other proceedings which might be heard concurrently and which do not come within the above categories which enable a chairman to sit alone.

1.26 If the chairman decides to hear the case sitting alone, he is under a continuing duty to keep that decision under review. Thus, if it becomes evident that the parties intend to call a number of witnesses, this would be a clear indication that the claim should be heard by a full tribunal (*Clarke v Arriva Kent Thameside Ltd*). Indeed, a chairman should not sit alone, even if all the parties agree to him so doing, where there is a likelihood of a dispute on the facts (*Sogbetun v Hackney London Borough*).

1.27 The jurisdiction of employment tribunals is as follows:

(a) Equal Pay Act 1970, s 2 – breach of equality clause in contracts of employment;

(b) Employment Agencies Act 1973, s 3 – application by the Secretary of State for a prohibition order;

(c) Health and Safety at Work Act 1974, s 24 – appeals against prohibition or improvement notices;

(d) Local Government (Compensation) Regulations 1974 – compensation payments for loss of office on reorganisation;

(e) Sex Discrimination Act 1975, s 63 – complaints of unlawful sex discrimination; s 68 – appeals against non-discrimination notices; s 72 – EOC enforcing provisions relating to discriminatory advertisements;

Relations Act 1976, s 54 – complaints of race discrimination; s 59 – appeals against non-discrimination notices; s 63 – enforcing provisions relating to discriminatory advertisements; s 64 – applications by CRE prior to county court action;

(g) Safety Representatives and Safety Committees Regulations 1977 – time off work with pay for safety representatives;

(h) Transfer of Undertakings (Protection of Employment) Regulations 2006 – failure to inform or consult with trade unions or employee representatives, failure to pay compensations, failure to provide employee liability information;

(i) Industrial Training Act 1982, s 12 – appeals against assessment of industrial training levies;

(j) Occupational Pension Schemes (Disclosure of Information) Regulations 1986 – consultation requirements for independent trade unions;

(k) Sex Discrimination Act 1986, s 6 – complaints of discriminatory collective agreements;

(l) Trade Union and Labour Relations (Consolidation) Act 1992 – complaints of unjustified discipline; s 68A – unauthorised check-off; s 87 – unauthorised deduction from wages for political fund; s 137 – refusal of employment on grounds of union membership or non-membership; s 138 – refusal of employment agency to offer employment on grounds of union membership or non-membership; s 145A – offer of inducement relating to trade union membership or activities; s 145B – offer of inducement relating to collective bargaining; s 146 – detriment on grounds of trade union membership or non-membership; s 161 – application for interim relief; s 168 time off work for trade union duties; s 168A – time off work for union learning representatives; s 169 – failure to pay for time off work for trade union duties or learning representatives; s 170 – failure to permit time off work for trade union activities; s 174 – wrongful exclusion or expulsion from a trade union; s 189 – failure to arrange for the election of trade union or employee representatives and failure to consult on redundancies; s 192 – failure to pay the protective award; s 238 – dismissal in connection with other industrial action; s 238A – dismissal of participants in official strike action; Sch A1 Pt IX – demand for costs by appointed person;

(m) Pension Schemes Act 1993, s 126 – complaint of failure by the Secretary of State to make payments on an employer's insolvency;

(o) Employment Tribunals Extension of Jurisdiction Order 1994 – breach of contract claim;

(p) Disability Discrimination Act 1995, s 8 – complaints of unlawful discrimination on disability grounds;

(q) Employment Rights Act 1996, s 11 – reference relating to failure to give s 1 statement or s 8 itemised statement; s 23 – unlawful deductions or unlawful payments from wages; unlawful deductions or unlawful payments from cash shortages; s 34 – guarantee payments; s 48 – protection from detriment in health and safety cases, Sunday working for shop and betting workers, working time cases, trustees of occupational pension schemes, employee representatives, time off work for study or training, protected disclosures, leave for family or domestic reasons; s 51 – time off work for public duties, jury service; s 54 – time off work to look for work or retraining; s 57 – time off work for antenatal care; s 57B – time off work to care for dependants; s 60 – time off work for pension trustees; s 63C – time off work for employee representatives; s 70 – remuneration on suspension on medical grounds or maternity grounds; s 80 – preventing or postponing paternity leave; s 80 H – failure to comply with flexible working procedures; s 93 – failure to give written reasons for dismissal; s 111 – complaint of unfair dismissal; s 128 – application for interim relief; s 163 reference for redundancy payments; s 170 – reference of Secretary of State's liability on employer's insolvency; s 177 – application for payments by certain office holders; s 188 – payments to be made on an employer's insolvency;

(r) Health and Safety (Consultation with Employees) Regulations 1996 (time off work with pay for employee safety representatives);

(s) Working Time Regulations 1998;

(t) National Minimum Wage Act 1998, s 11 – failure by employer to produce records, failure to permit worker to inspect records and copy them or to be accompanied; s 19 – appeals from enforcement notices; s 20 – complaint by enforcement officer in respect of unlawful deduction from wages; s 22 – appeals against financial penalties; complaint of detriment;

(u) Employment Relations Act 1999, s 10 – right to be accompanied at disciplinary hearings;

(v) Transnational Information and Consultation with Employees Regulations 1999;

(w) Part-time Workers (Prevention of Less Favourable Treatment) Regulations 2000;

(x) Fixed-Term Employees (Prevention of Less Favourable Treatment) Regulations 2002;

(y) Flexible Working (Procedural Requirements) Regulations 2002;

(z) Employment Equality (Religion and Belief) Regulations 2003;

(aa) Employment Equality (Sexual Orientation) Regulations 2003;

(ab) Disability Discrimination (Blind and Partially Sighted Persons) Regulations 2003;

(ac) Employment Equality (Age) Regulations 2006;

(ad) Information and Consultation of Employees Regulations 2004 (time off work, detriment and dismissal).

Employment tribunals have jurisdiction to apply EC law to claims made under UK law, ie as laid down in specific UK legislation (eg SDA, RRA, etc). But there is no jurisdiction to hear or determine 'free-standing' claims based on the Treaty of Rome or an EC Directive, outside the domestic statutory framework (*Biggs v Somerset County Council*). Also, there is no jurisdiction to hear '*Francovitch*' style claims (*Secretary of State for Employment v Mann*).

1.28 The procedure before employment tribunals is governed by the Employment Tribunals (Constitution and Rules of Procedure) Regulations 2004. These regulations provide for the making of claims, appearance by respondents, case management, further particulars, witness attendance orders, pre-hearing review, procedure at the hearing, applications for review, award of costs, extension of time, joinder of parties, and other miscellaneous matters. Generally speaking the tribunal has a wide discretion in operating its procedures, and its decision can only be challenged on appeal where the discretion was wrongly exercised because of a mistake of law, a disregard of principle, a misapplication of the facts, or the tribunal took into account irrelevant matters or failed to take into account relevant matters, or where the decision was outside the generous ambit within which a reasonable disagreement is possible (*Noorani v Merseyside TEC Ltd*) (see Chapter 20).

1.29 The jurisdiction of an employment tribunal is territorial. Save where there is an express provision to the contrary, a claimant must be employed in Great Britain (see para 2.112). If he is employed exclusively outside Great Britain, the tribunal has no jurisdiction to hear a complaint (but see *Serco Ltd v Lawson*, para 2.111). If the respondent is a company registered in Great Britain, it is resident here even though it carries on business elsewhere (*Odeco (UK) Inc v Peacham*), and it may carry on business in Great Britain even though it has no registered office here (*Knulty v Eloc Electro-Optick and Communicatie BV*).

1.30 Legal aid is not available in England and Wales, but Scottish ministers took the view that a denial of legal aid may amount to a violation of the right to a fair hearing, contrary to Art 6 of the European Convention on Human Rights (see para 1.97). Thus legal aid will be available in Scotland, where (a) the applicant is unable to fund or find alternative representation elsewhere, (b) the case is an arguable one, and (c) the case is too complex to allow the applicant to present it to a minimum standard of effectiveness.

A. Claims for breach of contract

1.31 Under the Employment Tribunals Extension of Jurisdiction (England and Wales) Order 1994, and the Employment Tribunals Extension of Jurisdiction (Scotland) Order 1994, employment tribunals have jurisdiction to hear claims for damages for breach of a contract of employment, or any other contract (subject to certain exceptions, see below) connected with employment, including a claim for a sum due under such a contract, and a claim for the recovery of a sum in pursuance of any enactment relating to the terms or performance of such a contract. The claim must be outstanding on the termination of the employee's employment, which is the moment in time when the employee ceases to work for the employer (*Miller Bros & FP Butler Ltd v Johnston*), and the maximum award which can be made in respect of any number of claims is £25,000. The claim must be brought within three months from the effective date of termination of the contract of employment (or within three months from the last day when the employee worked in the employment which has been terminated) with the usual extension of time if it was not reasonably practicable to bring the claim within that time (see also para 20.2). There is no requirement that the employee should have been employed for any particular period of employment before bringing a claim under the Order.

1.32 Once an employee has lodged such a claim, the employer may lodge a counterclaim in respect of breach of contract by the employee, within six weeks (or, if not reasonably practicable to do so, within such further time as the employment tribunal considers to be reasonable). The counterclaim is not limited by the amount of the original claim, and may be continued irrespective of what happens to the original claim, as long as it has been presented before the employee's claim has been settled or withdrawn. Indeed, if the employee's breach of contract claim fails because it was not presented within the appropriate time limits, the employer's counterclaim, validly presented, can still proceed (*Patel v RCMS Ltd*).

1.33 Neither the employee nor the employer can bring a claim or counterclaim in respect of:

(a) damages for personal injuries;

(b) breach of a term requiring the employer to provide living accommodation for the employee, or a term imposing an obligation on either of them in connection with the provision of living accommodation;

(c) a term relating to intellectual property;

(d) a term imposing an obligation of confidence;

(e) a term which is a covenant in restraint of trade.

1.34 One effect of the Order is to give an alternative route for claims (other than the above exceptions) which would otherwise have to be brought in the county court, although it should be noted that there are a number of differences in the respective jurisdictions and procedures (see para 8.3). Another effect of the Order is to enable employment tribunals to deal with matters which hitherto were not within the scope of the Wages Act 1986 (now Employment Rights Act 1996, ss 13–22, see para 8.4), in particular claims for payments in lieu of notice, holiday pay, advances etc. Again, there are differences between the Order and the Act, and it will be necessary to scrutinise the nature of a claim very carefully in order to bring it under the appropriate heading.

1.35 However, there appears to be a further development which needs to be considered. A claim for constructive dismissal (see para 17.24) is essentially based on a claim for breach of contract (breach of an implied term of respect etc). There thus appears to be no reason why such a complaint could not be brought under the Order, rather than under the provisions of the Employment Rights Act 1996. The advantage to the employee of using this route is that he does not need to have the requisite one year continuous employment. However, the remedy is likely to be limited to an award of damages to reflect the lawful notice period.

1.36 If a claimant is successful in recovering £25,000 under the provisions of the Order, he cannot recover any excess of that amount by instituting subsequent High Court proceedings in respect of a wrongful dismissal claim (*Fraser v Hlmad Ltd*).

Industrial training boards

1.37 The Industrial Training Act 1982 enables the minister to set up training boards in any industry in order to provide for industrial and commercial training of persons who are over school-leaving age. A board will consist of a chairman, with an equal number of persons from either side of industry, educational representatives and additional persons appointed by the Secretary of State, although only the employers' representatives may vote on the imposition of a levy. A board may provide courses for training purposes, or approve courses run by other institutions, and has wide powers relating to the making or recommendations for training, laying down training standards, and to assist persons to find facilities for being trained for industry. It can pay fees, maintenance allowances, and make grants or loans to organisations providing courses or other facilities which are approved by the board. At the present time, seven such boards are still in operation.

1.38 To meet its expenses a board may impose a levy on employers in the industry, which is assessed by reference to a percentage of the payroll. For this purpose a board may require employers to furnish returns and information, and keep and produce records (eg, see Industrial Training Levy (Construction Board) Order 2005). An employer who has been assessed for a levy may appeal to an employment tribunal which may rescind or reduce or increase it as the tribunal determines (see Employment Tribunals (Constitution and Rules of Procedure) Regulations 2004, Sch 3).

Equal Opportunities Commission

1.39 The Sex Discrimination Act 1975 established the Equal Opportunities Commission (EOC), consisting of between eight and 15 members. It will work towards the elimination of discrimination on grounds of sex, generally promote equality of opportunity between men and women, keep the Sex Discrimination Act 1975 and the Equal Pay Act 1970 under review, and, where necessary, draw up and submit proposals for amendments, and review the relevant statutory provisions relating to health and safety at work in so far as they require different treatment for men and women. The Commission also has power to draw up codes of practice giving practical guidance on ways to eliminate discrimination and promote equality of opportunity between men and women. Such codes will have the same standing as those issued by ACAS. A code entitled 'For the elimination of sex and marriage discrimination, and the promotion of equality of opportunity in employment' has been approved and a code on equal pay is also in force. The EOC may carry out formal enquiries (see Chapter 4) and can give financial or other support to actual or potential claimants.

Commission for Racial Equality

1.40 The Commission for Racial Equality (CRE) was established by the Race Relations Act 1976, and consists of between eight and 15 members. It will work towards the elimination of racial discrimination, promote equality of opportunity and good relations between persons of different racial groups, and keep under review the workings of the 1976 Act and, where necessary, draw up and submit proposals for its amendment. The CRE has issued a code of practice entitled 'For the elimination of racial discrimination and the promotion of equality of opportunity in employment'. The CRE may give financial or other assistance to any organisation which has for its objects the improvement of community relations, undertake or promote research or educational activities and has like powers of holding enquiries and giving assistance to claimants as the EOC.

Disability Rights Commission

1.41 The Disability Rights Commission (DRC) was created by the Disability Rights Commission Act 1999, with powers and functions similar to the CRE and EOC. The Commission will work towards the elimination of discrimination against disabled persons, promote the equalisation of opportunities, take such steps as it considers appropriate with a view to encouraging good practice in the treatment of disabled persons, and keep the working of the Disability Discrimination Act 1995 under review. The Commission may make proposals or give advice to the Minister, or any other Government agency or public authority as to the practical application of any law, and undertake (or arrange for support of) the carrying out of research or the provision of advice or information.

1.42 The Commission has issued a Code of Practice (which has the same status as codes prepared by ACAS etc) entitled 'For the elimination of discrimination in the field of employment against disabled persons or persons who have a disability', which is designed to give practical guidance to employers and other service providers. The Code is frequently referred to by the courts and employment tribunals (see eg *H J Heinz Co Ltd v Kenrick*). The Commission may also give assistance to persons who propose to bring claims for unlawful discrimination, may carry out formal investigations, and issue non-discrimination notices.

Commission for Equality and Human Rights

1.43 The Equality Act 2006 has created a new institution, called the Commission for Equality and Human Rights (CEHR) which will take over the existing functions of the Equal Opportunities Commission, the Commission for Racial Equality, and the Disability Rights Commission, but with additional responsibilities and wider powers.

Basically, the CEHR has the fundamental duty to create a society in which:

(a) people's ability to achieve their potential is not limited by prejudice or discrimination;

(b) there is respect for and protection of each individual's human rights;

(c) there is respect for the dignity and worth of each individual;

(d) each individual has an equal opportunity to participate in society; and

(e) there is mutual respect between groups based on understanding and valuing of diversity and on shared respect for equality and human rights.

1.44 The CEHR will have wider functions than its predecessors, and will draw up a strategic plan showing the activities to be undertaken in pursuance of its statutory powers. In addition to taking over the work of the existing Commissions, the CEHR will assume responsibility for promoting understanding of the importance of equality and diversity, and work towards the elimination of unlawful discrimination in the areas of race, sex, religion or belief, sexual orientation, sexual reassignment, age, disability, as well as the promotion of human rights. It will promote good relations between and within different groups, encourage good practice in the area of relations between different groups, and work towards the elimination of prejudice, and hatred of and hostility towards members of groups. It will monitor the effectiveness of equality and human rights enactments, give advice to the government, and make recommendations. It will issue (and revise, where necessary) Codes of Practice, which must be approved in draft by the Secretary of State, and be subject to the negative approval parliamentary procedure.

1.45 The CEHR can make enquiries into matters relating to its duties in respect of equality and diversity, human rights, disabilities and groups. It can make grants and carry out investigations. If, following an investigation, it is satisfied that a person has committed an unlawful act, it can issue an unlawful act notice, which may be followed by requiring that person to prepare an action plan for the purpose of avoiding repetition or continuance of the unlawful act. As an alternative, the Commission may enter into a legally enforceable agreement whereby the person concerned undertakes not to commit (or prepare to commit) an unlawful act, and in return the Commission undertakes not to proceed with an investigation or issue an unlawful act notice.

Health and Safety Commission

1.46 The Health and Safety at Work etc Act 1974 established the Health and Safety Commission to take over the general supervision of the promotion of health and safety at work. The Commission consists of a chairman, three members representing employers' organisations, three members representing trade unions, and three other members appointed after consultation with local authorities and other interested parties. The duty of the Commission is to do such things and make such arrangements as it considers appropriate:

(a) to assist and encourage persons concerned with matters relevant to any of the general purposes of Part I of the Health and Safety at Work etc Act 1974 to further those purposes. Since the bulk of the Act is contained in Part I, this is the widest possible duty of the Commission;

(b) to make such arrangements as it considers appropriate for the carrying out of research, the publication of results, the provision of training and information in connection therewith, and to encourage research and the provision of training and information by others;

(c) to make arrangements for securing that government departments, employers, employees, employers' organisations and trade unions are provided with an information and advisory service;

(d) to submit proposals for the making of regulations.

1.47 The Commission must report from time to time to the Secretary of State (who retains overall responsibility), act in accordance with proposals approved by him, and give effect to any directions made by him.

1.48 The enforcement and day-to-day supervision of the Act is in the hands of the Health and Safety Executive. This consists of three persons; the Director is appointed by the Commission with the approval of the Secretary of State, and two assistant directors appointed by the Commission with the approval of the Secretary of State after consultation with the Director. The powers of the Executive are wide. Generally, it must exercise on behalf of the Commission such of the Commission's functions as the Commission directs, and give effect to any direction given to it by the Commission, but the Commission may not direct the Executive to enforce any statutory provision in any particular case. At the request of any Minister of the Crown, the Executive must provide him with information concerning activities in which he has an interest, and provide him with advice on such matters.

1.49 In particular, the Commission may direct the Executive or authorise any other person to hold an enquiry into any accident, occurrence, situation or other matter, and regulations have been published concerning the conduct of such enquiries or investigations.

Low Pay Commission

1.50 This body, which consists of a chairman and eight other members appointed by the Secretary of State, was put on a statutory basis by the National Minimum Wage Act 1998, and is responsible for recommending to the Secretary of State the level of the national minimum wage. Before making regulations establishing the national minimum wage, the Secretary of State will refer the following matters to the LPC, ie:

   (a) what single hourly rate should be prescribed as the national minimum wage;

   (b) what shall be the pay reference period;

   (c) what methods should be used for determining the hourly rate at which a person is remunerated;

   (d) whether persons under the age of 26 should be excluded from the right to a national minimum wage, or be entitled to a different hourly rate;

   (e) whether any other persons should be excluded, and if so, what hourly rate should be prescribed.

The role of the government

1.51 The responsibility for employment law issues is shared by a number of government departments, including the Department of Trade and Industry, the Department for Transport, the Department for Communities, the Department for Work and Pensions, and so forth, each headed by a Secretary of State. Within these departments, junior ministers deal with a wide range of issues, such as employment relations generally, employment tribunals, ACAS and CAC, health and safety, race, sex and disability issues, job action programmes, maternity, paternity and adoption matters, pensions, work permits, adult and youth training, and so on.

1.52 The Secretary of State has power to issue Codes of Practice (TULR(C)A, s 203), and codes have been issued on Picketing, Industrial Action Ballots and Notice to Employers, and Access to Workers during Recognition and Derecognition Ballots. It is of interest to note that whereas codes of practice issued by ACAS, EOC, CRE and DRC are admissible before employment tribunals, those issued by the Secretary of State and DRC are also admissible in the courts.

Supreme Court

1.53 The Constitutional Reform Act 2005 has paved the way for the abolition of the House of Lords as the highest court of appeal, with its powers and functions being transferred to a new Supreme Court. Earlier decisions of the House of Lords will, of course, still be binding on lower courts and tribunals. The Supreme Court is expected to come into existence in 2009.

The impact of the European Union

1.54 As from 1 January 1973, the United Kingdom became a member of the European Union, and by the European Communities Act 1972 (s 2) all obligations arising out of the various treaties which set up the EU are to be given legal effect in this country without further enactment. European law is thus of particular importance in the study of domestic employment law, for it will override domestic provisions. In order to understand European Union law, we must examine the treaties, the institutions and the nature of the legal rules which take effect.

A. Treaty of Rome

1.55 This Treaty was signed in 1957 by the original six founding states (France, West Germany, Italy, Belgium, the Netherlands and Luxembourg). The UK, Ireland and Denmark acceded to the Treaty in 1973, Greece in 1981, Spain and Portugal became full members in 1992 and Austria, Finland and Sweden joined in 1995. The original Treaty required unanimity between all the member states before laws could be passed. So far as is relevant, Art 140 of the Treaty stated that one of the objects of the Community was to harmonise laws relating to 'employment, labour law and working conditions, basic and advanced training, social security, protection against occupational accidents and diseases, occupational hygiene, law of trade unions, and collective bargaining between workers and employers'.

1.56 In 1986, the Single European Act was signed in The Hague and Luxembourg, making certain amendments to the Treaty of Rome, and further amendments were made by the Treaty of Nice in 2001. A system of 'qualified majority voting' has been introduced before approval can be given to certain proposals. Each member state has been allocated a certain number of votes. Germany, Italy, France and the UK each have 29 votes, with the other member states having progressively fewer. A qualified majority decision requires the support of 232 votes out of a total of 321 (ie, a two-thirds majority). The significance is that qualified majority voting can be used to give approval to proposals relating to health and safety matters in the working environment made under Art 138 of the Treaty (see Chapter 11).

B. The Maastricht Treaty

1.57 In 1992 the Treaty of European Union (the Maastricht Treaty) was signed, expanding the scope of the Community's existing responsibilities, and introducing new policy areas. The ultimate aim is to create European citizenship, a single currency as part of economic and monetary union, a common foreign policy and a common defence policy. The concept of 'subsidiarity' was also introduced so that matters which could more usefully be dealt with at local or national level would not be the subject of Community action unless there was no other way the objectives could be achieved.

C. Treaty of Amsterdam

1.58 Originally, the UK Government opted out of certain social policy provisions which were contained in the Single European Act of 1986, set out in the Social Rights Charter in 1989, and implemented by a protocol to the Maastricht Treaty in 1991, as the 'Social Chapter'. However, by the Treaty of Amsterdam in 1997 the new UK Government announced its acceptance of the Social Chapter, and measures to implement directives so far approved have recently been introduced (see paras 1.70–1.90).

1.59 The Treaty of Amsterdam also brought about a renumbering of the Articles of the Treaty of Rome. Thus, freedom of movement is now Art 39 (formerly Art 48); the principle of equal pay for equal work is now Art 141 (formerly Art 119), and so on.

D. Expansion of the EU

1.60 At the meeting in Copenhagen in 1993, the EU adopted criteria for other states to become members of the Union. The conditions were stable institutions guaranteeing democracy, the rule of law, human rights, and respect for and protection of minorities, a functioning market economy and the ability to take on the obligations of political, economic and monetary union. As a result, a further 10 countries joined the European Union in 2004, ie Cyprus, Czech Republic, Estonia, Hungary, Latvia, Lithuania, Malta, Poland, Slovak Republic and Slovenia. It is expected that Romania, Croatia and Bulgaria will join in 2007, while, for the moment, the application from Turkey to join is being delayed. A new constitution for the European Union was proposed so as to take into account the recent enlargement, but following its rejection by France and the Netherlands in referenda, its future is currently uncertain.

E. EU institutions

Council of Ministers

1.61 This is the supreme policy-making body of the EU. Each meeting of the Council is attended by a minister from each member state. Usually, this will be the respective prime ministers or foreign secretaries, but sometimes, when specific detailed proposals are being discussed, the respective 'portfolio' ministers will attend. One member of the Council will hold the presidency for six months and then the position rotates. The Council is assisted by a Secretariat (comprising a staff of some 2,000) and preparatory work for the meetings is undertaken by frequent meetings of senior civil servants from the respective countries, known as the Committee of Permanent Representatives (Coreper).

The Commission

1.62 This is sometimes described as being the 'bureaucracy' of the Union, but perhaps a more accurate description would be the 'engine room'. There are 24 commissioners, plus a President. However, although appointed by their respective countries, commissioners are totally independent of them. Each commissioner has certain departmental responsibilities and is assisted by a cabinet and directorate general. Decisions are taken on a collegiate basis.

1.63 The Commission has the responsibility of initiating and drafting proposals for approval by the Council. It acts as a mediator between states, and as a 'watchdog' to ensure that EU rules are being observed. Indeed, if the Commission considers that a member state is failing to comply with an EU law, it can take enforcement action by referring the alleged breach to the European Court of Justice for a ruling (see para 1.94).

European Parliament

1.64 This body sits in Strasbourg and Brussels and currently consists of 732 members of the European Parliament (MEPs) elected directly from each member state. It can express an opinion to the Council of Ministers on proposals which emanate from the Commission, can submit questions to both institutions, and can, as a final sanction, dismiss the Commission on a vote of censure passed by a two-thirds majority. The Single European Act introduced a co-operation procedure, whereby the views of the Parliament must be established prior to the Council of Ministers reaching a common position on any particular proposal.

European Court of Justice

1.65 This Court sits in Luxembourg, and comprises 25 judges and eight advocates general. Appointments are made for six years. The Court gives rulings on the interpretation of European law, either on a reference from the Commission, at the request of the courts of a member state or on a claim brought by an individual person or corporation in a member state. Once it has given its ruling the matter is then referred back to the courts of the member state for compliance.

European Union law

1.66 For the purpose of this book, the law of the European Union consists of (a) Articles of the Treaty of Rome, (b) Directives passed by the Council of Ministers, (c) Recommendations, and (d) Decisions of the European Court of Justice. It must be borne in mind that any common law or statutory rule which is contrary to European law is void, and if there is any conflict between European law and UK law, the former is to be applied. Indeed, if, in any preliminary proceedings, it appears that the sole obstacle towards granting interim relief is a rule of national law which is in conflict with European law, that national law has to be set aside (*R v Secretary of State for Transport, ex p Factortame (No 2)*). Further, the UK courts have now held that an organisation (*R v Secretary of State for Employment, ex p Equal Opportunities Commission*) or a private individual (*R v Secretary of State for Employment, ex p Seymour-Smith and Perez*) can bring an action for a declaration that UK law does not correctly implement EU law.

A. Articles of the Treaty

1.67 If an article of the Treaty of Rome is clear, precise, unconditional, requires no further implementation, and does not give any discretion to member states, it is directly applicable and becomes an integral part of the law of member states (*Defrenne v Sabena*). For example, Art 141 (formerly 119) of the Treaty of Rome provides 'Each Member State shall ensure and maintain the application of the principle that men and women should receive equal pay for equal work . . .'. This article has been invoked in a number of cases, and has been held to confer a distinct legal right on an individual, which can be enforced in national courts, in addition to any legal right conferred by national law (*Garland v British Rail Engineering Ltd*). Similarly, Art 39 (formerly 48) of the Treaty provides that member states shall ensure the free movement of workers within the Community without discrimination as regards employment, remuneration and other conditions of work and employment, and this too has a direct legal effect (*Van Duyn v Home Office (No 2)*). Thus if a national of a member state wishes to obtain employment in the United Kingdom, he does not need a work permit, and he must be given equal access to social security benefits, holidays, equal pay, etc.

B. Directives

1.68 A Directive, passed by the Council of Ministers, is binding as to the result to be achieved, but the national authorities are given a choice of form and methods. However, as Directives are binding on member states, it is the duty of those states to implement them, and if the state fails to do so, an individual may seek to enforce the terms of the Directive against a state in its capacity as an employer (*Marshall v Southampton and South West Hampshire Area Health Authority*). For this purpose, 'the state' includes any body which is an emanation of the state (eg a nationalised industry) or which provides a public service under the control of the state. In other words, a state cannot take advantage of its own failure to comply with European law (*Foster v British Gas*).

In *Doughty v Rolls-Royce plc* the Court of Appeal laid down three criteria to be applied in considering whether or not any particular body is 'an emanation of the State', following principles laid down by the European Court in *Foster v British Gas*. These are:

(a) whether the entity was made responsible, pursuant to a measure adopted by the state, for providing a public service;

(b) whether the service it provided was under the control of the state; and

(c) whether it possessed or claimed to exercise any special powers.

Thus, although Rolls Royce was 100% owned by the state, it was a commercial undertaking rather than a state body for the purpose of enforcing the provisions of a Directive.

1.69 In strict legal theory, a Directive is not enforceable against a non-state body or a private individual. Thus, if there are no national rules on a subject, it is not permissible to rely on the provisions of a Directive as the basis of a claim. However, the European Court of Justice has gone a great deal further in two recent cases. In *Dekker v Stichting Vormingscentrum voor Jong Volwassenen (VJV-Centrum) Plus* (see para 4.64), it was held that it is permissible to rely on the provisions of a Directive in order to interpret national law, and in particular those provisions of national law which were designed to implement a Directive. Thus the European Court will interpret national law in the light of the language and aims of the Directive. In *Marleasing SA v La Comercial Internacional de Alimentación*, the Court went still further. They stated 'It follows from the obligation on member states to take all measures appropriate to ensure the performance of their obligation to achieve the results provided for in Directives, that in applying national law, whether it was a case of provisions prior to or subsequent to the Directive, the national court called on to interpret it was required to do so as far as possible in the light of the wording and purpose of the Directive in order to achieve the result sought by the Directive.'

Finally, in an historic decision, the European Court has stated that if a member state fails to take the necessary steps to achieve the results required by a Directive, an individual who suffers damage thereby may sue the state for the loss suffered which results from that failure. In *Francovich v Italy*, the Italian Government had failed to implement EC Directive 80/987 on the protection of employees on an employer's insolvency. In consequence, an employee was unable to recover wages owed to him following his employer's insolvency, and he sued the Italian Government for compensation. It was held that his claim could succeed as long as three conditions were satisfied. These were that: (a) the result required by the Directive includes the conferring of rights for the benefit of individuals, (b) the contents of those rights may be determined by reference to the provisions of the Directive, and (c) there is a causal link between the breach of the obligation of the state and the damage suffered by the person affected.

Since these three conditions were met, the claim succeeded. However, the European Court appeared to suggest that a claim could be made not only when a member state fails to implement the terms of a Directive, but also when it incorrectly implements a Directive. Further, national courts are the appropriate forum for such claims, without the necessity of seeking a remedy in the European Court. However it should be noted that in *R v Secretary of State for Transport, ex p Factortame*, the Advocate-General expressed the view that such liability would only arise if the breach was 'manifest and serious', which suggests that inadvertent or unwitting breaches of European law may not necessarily attract such a remedy.

Thus, although Directives are addressed to member states, and can be enforced by intended beneficiaries against the state, there now appears to be an interesting remedy against a state which fails to implement or incorrectly implements a Directive by persons who suffer damage thereby.

It should be noted that '*Francovich*' style claims arising from an alleged failure by a state properly to implement a Directive must be brought in the High Court, not an employment tribunal (*Secretary of State for Employment v Mann*).

In a recent decision (*Brasserie du Pecheur SA v Germany*), the European Court of Justice gave guidance on the principles and approach to be adopted when national courts deal with *Francovich* type claims. The three issues considered were liability, damages and retrospection.

So far as liability was concerned, the Court stated that there was no difference in principle between those EU rights which were directly or indirectly applicable. Thus a right arising out of the Treaty (eg Art 141) or a right against a state body by a state employee (*Foster v British Gas*) is to be treated in the same way as those rights which were indirectly applicable (*Marleasing SA v La Comercial Internacional de Alimentación*). Further, the state was to be considered as a single entity, and thus it did not matter if the breach was attributable to the executive, the legislature or the judiciary.

If the EU rule confers a wide discretion (as do most Directives), it must be established that it was intended to confer rights on an individual. If so, the next question to answer is whether the breach was 'sufficiently serious' in that there was a manifest and serious disregard of the discretion. This is for the national courts to decide, taking into account the clarity and precision of the rule that has been breached, the measure of the discretion given to national authorities, whether the breach was voluntary or involuntary, whether any error of law was excusable or inexcusable, whether it was caused or contributed to by any position taken by an EU institution, and the general adoption or retention of national measures which are contrary to EU law. A breach will be sufficiently serious if it has continued despite a judgment finding that there has been a breach, or where there has been a previous legal ruling from the ECJ making it clear that there has been an infringement.

So far as damages are concerned, the Court stated that national rules must not make it impossible or extremely difficult for an individual to obtain reparation, and damages awarded must be commensurate with the loss suffered. The criteria should not be less favourable than those applicable to similar claims based on domestic law. However, a national court is entitled to enquire into the steps taken by a complainant to mitigate the loss, in particular having regard to available legal remedies.

Finally, so far as retrospection was concerned, the ECJ was of the opinion that the main issue was whether the breach was sufficiently serious. If it was, then there was no temporal limit on the effect of an ECJ judgment. However, claims could be subjected to substantive and procedural limitations imposed by national law, which could take into account principles of legal certainty by applying time limits on claims.

1.70 Currently, there are a number of Directives in force which have a particular bearing on employment law, and which have been implemented by UK legislation.

Directive 75/117/EEC (Equal Pay)

1.71 This states that the principle of equal pay means, for the same work or for work to which equal value has been attributed, the elimination of all discrimination on grounds of sex with regard to all aspects and conditions of remuneration. Member states shall take the necessary measures to ensure that provisions appearing in collective agreements, wage scales, wage agreements or individual contracts of employment which are contrary to the principle of equal pay shall be declared null and void or may be amended. The Equal Pay Act 1970 and the Equal Pay (Amendment) Regulations 1983 implement this Directive.

Directive 76/207/EEC (Equal Treatment)

1.72 This states that men and women shall be entitled to equal treatment as regards access to employment, including promotion, and also to vocational training and working conditions. There shall be no discrimination on grounds of sex, either directly or indirectly by reference to marital or family status. To comply with this Directive, reference may be made to the Sex Discrimination Acts of 1975 and 1986. Equal access to occupational pension schemes is now provided for in the Pension Schemes Act 1993, and equal benefits will come within the provisions of the Pensions Act 1995. The dismissal of a transsexual for a reason relating to a sex change is precluded by the Directive (see *P v S* para 4.36).

Directive 75/129/EEC (Collective Redundancies)

1.73 This Directive requires employers to consult with workers' representatives before making collective redundancies, and also requires that prior notification be given to the competent public authorities. The provisions of TULR(C)A, ss 188–194 (as amended) are designed to meet this Directive.

Directive 77/187/EEC (Acquired Rights)

1.74 This Directive provides for the safeguarding of the rights of employees when their employment is transferred from one employer to another. The transferor and transferee are also required to consult with employees' representatives about the consequences of the transfer. The Transfer of Undertakings (Protection of Employment) Regulations 2006 implement the Directive.

Directive 79/7/EEC (Equal Treatment in Social Security Matters)

1.75 This Directive requires that there should be no discrimination on grounds of sex (either directly or indirectly by reference to marital or family status) in the scope of social security schemes (ie sickness, invalidity, old age, occupational accidents and diseases, and unemployment benefits), the conditions of access thereto, contributions, the calculation of benefits (including benefits for spouses and dependants) and the duration of benefits. However, excluded from this Directive are benefits which arise from the determination of pensionable age. At the present time, women are permitted to receive the state pension at 60, whereas men receive it when they are 65 although the Pensions Act 1995 makes provisions for the progressive equalisation of state pensions at age 65 for both sexes, and this is permissible under the Directive. Other social security legislation has been passed to conform to its provisions.

Directive 86/613/EEC (Equal Treatment in Occupational Pension Schemes)

1.76 This Directive requires that there shall be no discrimination between men and women in access to and benefits from occupational pension schemes. The Social Security Act 1989 was designed to implement the Directive, but further problems have arisen as a result of the decision in *Barber v Guardian Royal Exchange Assurance Group* (see para 4.72).

Directive 86/613/EEC (Equal Treatment for Self-employed)

1.77 This Directive requires that the laws of member states relating to self-employment shall not contain any discriminatory provisions, that there shall be protection for self-employed persons and their wives during pregnancy and motherhood, and that discrimination does not arise from the establishing of businesses or other self-employed activities.

Directive 80/987/EEC (Employers' Insolvency)

1.78 This Directive requires member states to guarantee the payment of certain outstanding claims due to an employee when his employer becomes insolvent, subject to certain limits. The provisions of the Insolvency Act 1986 meet the terms of this Directive.

Directive 91/533/EEC (Proof of Employment Relationship)

1.79 This Directive requires employers to inform employees on the terms and conditions which apply to the employment relationship. It has been given effect by the ERA, ss 1-10.

Directive 93/104/EEC (Working Time)

1.80 This Directive concerns aspects of the organisation of working time, with compulsory rest periods, and a maximum working week of 48 hours. This Directive was passed under the provisions of Art 139 of the Treaty of Rome, which permits health and safety matters to be passed by a qualified majority vote. The lawfulness of this Directive was challenged by the UK Government (*United Kingdom v EU Council*) but the ECJ held that it was properly a health and safety matter, and in consequence, the Working Time Regulations 1998 were introduced.

Directive 94/45/EC (European Works Councils)

1.81 This Directive requires works councils to be set up in Community-scale undertakings, ie an undertaking with at least 1,000 employees in a member state and at least 150 employees in at least two member states. The Transnational Information and Consultation of Employees Regulations 1999 implement this Directive.

Directive 94/33/EC (Protection of Young People at Work)

1.82 This Directive has been implemented by various provisions, eg Management of Health and Safety at Work Regulations, Working Time Regulations etc.

Directive 96/34/EC (Parental Leave)

1.83 Men and women have an individual right to parental leave on the grounds of the birth or adoption of a child to enable them to take care of that child, for at least three months, until the child reaches the age of eight. The right is 'non-transferable' ie either a man or woman can take leave in respect of a child, but not both of them, and not alternatively. The Directive leaves it to member states to decide the details of how the scheme for parental leave should be implemented, eg on a full-time or part-time basis, in a piecemeal way, or in the form of a time credit system. There is to be protection against dismissal for applying for or taking parental leave, and, at the end of the leave, workers will have the right to return to their old job, or to a similar or equivalent job. The Directive also requires states to provide that workers are to be permitted to take time off work in the event of *force majeure* for urgent family reasons in cases of sickness or accident. This Directive has led to the new provisions on parental and paternity leave (see paras 6.57, 6.76) and time off work to care for dependants (see para 7.27).

Directive 97/81/EC (Part-time Work)

1.84 This Directive requires the removal of less favourable treatment in respect of part-time workers. It has been implemented by the Part-time Workers (Prevention of Less Favourable Treatment) Regulations 2000.

Directive 96/71/EC (Posted Workers)

1.85 This Directive requires that workers who move from one EC country to another are treated no less favourably than the employees of the host country. The Directive has been implemented by various provisions in the Employment Rights Act.

Directive 99/70/EC (Fixed-term Workers)

1.86 This Directive applies the principle of non-discrimination to employees who are in fixed-term employment, and requires that action be taken to eliminate the abuse of successive fixed-term contracts. The Fixed Term Employees (Protection of Less Favourable Treatment) Regulations 2002 implement this Directive.

Directive 97/80/EC (Burden of Proof)

1.87 This Directive requires that if a person claims that s/he has suffered direct or indirect discrimination, it shall be for the respondent to prove that there has been no breach of the principle of equal treatment. The Directive has been implemented by the Sex Discrimination (Indirect Discrimination and Burden of Proof) Regulations 2001.

Directive 2000/78/EC (Equal Treatment in Employment and Occupation)

1.88 This Directive requires that there shall be no discrimination in employment on grounds of religion or belief, disability, age or sexual orientation. These matters are dealt with generally by the Sex Discrimination Act, Disability Discrimination Act, Employment Equality (Sexual Orientation) Regulations 2003, Employment Equality (Religion or Belief) Regulations 2003, Disability Discrimination Act 1995 (Amendment) Regulations 2003 and the Employment Equality (Age) Regulations 2006.

Directive 2000/43/EC (Equal Treatment between Persons Irrespective of Racial or Ethnic Origins)

1.89 This Directive requires that there shall be no direct or indirect discrimination based on racial or ethnic grounds. Its provisions are covered by the Race Relations Act.

Directive 2002/14/EC (Information and Consultation)

1.90 This Directive required employers of a certain size to give information about the conduct of the undertaking. It is implemented by the Information and Consultation of Employees Regulations 2004.

1.91 A number of other Directives relating to health and safety at work have also been passed by the Council of Ministers, and these will be referred to in Chapter 11.

C. Recommendations

1.92 A Recommendation made under Community law has no binding effect, and cannot be relied upon to enforce a legal right in a national court. However, in *Grimaldi v Fonds des Maladies Professionnelles*, the European Court of Justice held that national courts are bound to take Recommendations into account when determining disputes which are referred to them, in particular when they clarify the interpretation of laws passed to implement them, or when they are designed to supplement binding Community measures.

1.93 Recommendations have been made on such topics as the employment of disabled persons, hours of work and holidays generally, flexible retirement, vocational training for women and sexual harassment.

D. Decisions of the European Court of Justice

1.94 The Court has jurisdiction under Art 234 (formerly 177) of the Treaty of Rome to give rulings concerning the interpretation of the Treaty or Regulations or Directives made by the Council of Ministers. A member state may be taken to the Court by another state or by the European Commission (see *EC Commission v United Kingdom*, para 18.65). A UK court may, but is not bound to, make a reference to the Court if it is necessary to enable a decision to be made (see *Macarthys Ltd v Smith*, para 5.47). Once the Court has given its opinion, the matter is referred back to the national court for the application of the opinion to the facts of the case (see *Jenkins v Kingsgate (Clothing Productions) Ltd*).

1.95 It should be noted that there are no specified time limits for bringing a claim under European law, as the provisions of the Treaty of Rome came into force upon accession (see *Stevens v Bexley Health Authority*). Time will start to run against a state body from the day the state makes good its failure to comply with the objectives laid down in the Directive (*Cannon v Barnsley Metropolitan Borough Council*). However, the European Court may, when giving a ruling, indicate that this shall only apply to claims lodged at the date of the ruling (*Barber v Guardian Royal Exchange*).

1.96 However, if a person is seeking to enforce a private right which has come to light as a result of the interpretation of EC law by the ECJ, national domestic procedures relating to time limits must be adhered to. Thus in *Biggs v Somerset County Council* the applicant was a teacher who worked for 14 hours per week. She was dismissed in 1976 but, relying on the House of Lords' decision in *R v Secretary of State for Employment, ex p Equal Opportunities Commission* (which held that the 'hours' requirement was discriminatory and contrary to the EC Equal Treatment Directive), brought a claim for unfair dismissal in 1994. It was held that her claim was out of time. She was not seeking to enforce a Community right (there is no EC right to be unfairly dismissed), and there is no separate procedure for bringing claims under EC law (see also *Setiya v East Yorkshire Health Authority* and Chapter 20).

Human Rights Act 1998

1.97 In order to prevent a re-occurrence of the horrors and atrocities which took place before and during the Second World War, the European Convention for the Protection of Human Rights and Fundamental Freedoms was signed in 1950. Many European countries subsequently incorporated the Convention into their domestic law, but UK citizens who wished to assert a Convention right were forced to petition the European Court of Human Rights in Strasbourg. The UK Government would always give effect to any ruling from that court, but the Convention itself was not enforceable in UK courts.

1.98 Despite the financial and practical difficulties involved in pursuing a claim under the Convention, some notable decisions were given against the UK Government in circumstances where the ordinary legal system could not or would not provide a remedy. For example, in *R v Admiralty Board of the Defence Council, ex p Lustig-Prean*, the Court of Appeal refused to interfere with a decision to discharge the applicant from the Royal Navy on the ground that he was a homosexual, and he thus brought proceedings in the European Court of Human Rights. That Court held (*Lustig-Prean v United Kingdom*) that a decision to discharge homosexuals from the armed forces on grounds of their sexual orientation was a violation of their right to respect for their private lives, and thus was contrary to Art 8 of the Convention. The outcome was the lifting of the ban on homosexuals and lesbians joining or staying in the armed forces. A similar outcome was reached in three other cases (see *Smith v United Kingdom*).

1.99 The Human Rights Act 1998 is designed to give effect to the rights and freedoms guaranteed under the Convention, by effectively incorporating it into UK law. At this stage, however, the precise effect of the Act is unpredictable, for while in theory it could have far-reaching implications for all branches of the law, much will depend on the approach taken by the judiciary, and the extent to which judicial ingenuity will be exercised.

1.100 The Act came into force in October 2000. Its basic provisions may be summarised as follows:

(a) A court or tribunal determining a question which has arisen in connection with a Convention right must take into account any judgment, decision, declaration or advisory opinion of the European Court of Human Rights. But although it is mandatory to take these into account, the court or tribunal is given a discretion whether to follow that decision etc (see *Kleinwort Benson Ltd v Glasgow City Council*). It has long been recognised that the Convention is a 'living instrument', and a previous decision of the Court need not be followed if it is out of step with current practices and opinions, or if it is unpersuasive. Further, the Court itself developed the doctrine of 'the margin of appreciation' which recognised the relatively restrained scrutiny of national law.

(b) So far as it is possible to do so, primary and subordinate legislation must be read and given effect in a way which is compatible with Convention rights. Thus, if a court or tribunal has a choice to interpret a statute in two ways, one of which is compatible with the Convention and one not, the former interpretation must prevail (see *Marleasing*, para 1.69). This obligation arises whenever the statutory provisions was passed. But if a statute has only one possible meaning, effect must be given to it accordingly.

(c) If a court (not a tribunal) is satisfied that a provision in primary legislation is incompatible with a Convention right, it may make a declaration of incompatibility, although before doing so it must give the Crown notice of such intention, so as to enable the Crown to be joined as a party to the proceedings. Such a declaration does not affect the validity of the provision in question, nor is it binding on the parties to the proceedings but, once made, doubtless Parliament will consider taking steps to ensure compliance with the Convention.

(d) It is unlawful for a public authority to act in a way which is incompatible with a Convention right. There is some uncertainty as to which bodies are 'public authorities', which will doubtless be the subject of case law, but courts and tribunals are certainly within the meaning of the term. A person aggrieved by such an act may bring proceedings in an appropriate legal venue, and certain remedies, including compensation, are available.

1.101 So far as the law of employment is concerned, there are a number of possible implications arising from the Act. An employee cannot lodge a claim in an employment tribunal based directly on a Convention right, but in any claim brought in a tribunal based on domestic law, the tribunal will take those rights into account, unless prohibited from so doing by domestic law. At this stage, it is not possible to anticipate the effect of the Act on employment law claims, and it should also be borne in mind that some of the rights are hedged with qualifications, but the following Articles of the Convention may well be relevant:

(a) Article 6. In the determination of a person's civil rights and obligations, everyone is entitled to a fair and public hearing within a reasonable time by an independent and impartial tribunal established by law. Thus in *Somjee v United Kingdom* three claims before an employment tribunal and the Employment Appeal Tribunal took more than seven years to be resolved. The European Court held that this violated Art 6 of the Convention. If a person is charged with misconduct before a public body, this is a determination of his civil rights, and the protection in Art 6 applies. Thus he is entitled to have a fair hearing, ie, to know in good time the nature of the charges, be given adequate time to prepare his case, to question witnesses, and to call evidence, etc (*R v Securities & Futures Authority Ltd, ex p Fleurose*). It was suggested in *Smith v Secretary of State for Trade and Industry* that the independence of employment tribunals themselves was in doubt, because the Secretary of State exercised control over the appointment, tenure and pay of lay members, but subsequently changes were made in these matters which allayed the fears of any conflict of interest or lack of impartiality, and it has now been accepted that employment tribunals are impartial and independent within the meaning of Art 6 (*Scanfuture UK Ltd v Secretary of State for Trade and Industry*). It has been held that there is an objection to an advocate appearing before the Employment Appeal Tribunal if he is also a part-time judge of that Tribunal, because there was a real possibility that lay members who had sat with him in that capacity might subconsciously be biased in favour of submissions made in his capacity as an advocate (*Lawal v Northern Spirit Ltd*). On the other hand, s 40 of the Health and Safety at Work Act (see para 11.93), which reverses the burden of proof which would ordinarily apply in criminal proceedings, did not violate Art 6. Balancing the fundamental rights of the individual with the general interests of the community in ensuring health and safety at work, the reversal was justified as necessary and proportionate, and therefore compatible with the Convention (*Davies v Health and Safety Executive*).

(b) Article 8. Everyone has the right to respect for his private and family life, his home and his correspondence. This right is subject to certain qualifications, ie when the interference is by a public authority in accordance with the law, and is necessary in a democratic society in the interests of national security, public safety or the economic well-being of the country, for the prevention of disorder or crime, for the protection of health or morals, or for the protection of rights and freedoms of others. In *McGowan v Scottish Water* the employer obtained evidence through covert surveillance that the employee had been falsifying his time sheets. He claimed that he had been unfairly dismissed, arguing that his right to respect for his private life under Art 8 of the Convention had been breached. His claim was dismissed by the EAT. The interference with his rights was justified under Art 8(2), in that the employer's actions were 'in accordance with the law and necessary for the prevention of disorder or crime . . .'.

The right to respect for private life includes the right to privacy with respect to a person's sexual orientation. The European Court in *Smith v United Kingdom* held that to discriminate against a person on grounds of his/her sexual orientation was a violation of Art 8 of the Convention, and this has now been transposed into UK law by the Employment Equality (Sexual Orientation) Regulations 2003 (see para 4.27).

An employee has a reasonable expectation of privacy in respect of private telephone calls. In *Halford v United Kingdom* the employee was a senior police officer who alleged that her employer had tapped a private work telephone, in order to obtain details of a claim for sex discrimination she was pursuing. The European Court of Human Rights held that as she had not been given any prior indication that her telephone calls were liable to interception, there had been a breach of Art 8.

The right to privacy in respect of correspondence clearly includes unauthorised monitoring by employers of telephone calls, e-mail communications, and the use of the internet at the workplace. An employer must therefore seek to justify any such interference by relying on one of the qualifications mentioned above, or by notifying employees that such interception may take place at any time. The position is further clarified by the Telecommunications (Lawful Business Practice) (Interception of Communications) Regulations 2000, designed to ensure compliance with the Telecommunications Data Protection Directive (EC 97/66), which permits the interception and monitoring of telephone calls, e-mail communications etc, for certain specified purposes (see para 10.46). However, Art 8 of the Convention does not apply in respect of the commission of a criminal offence in a public place (*X v Y*).

There are a number of other possibilities arising out of Art 8, including the lawfulness of mandatory medical examinations, confidentiality of medical reports, etc. It is unlikely that any remedy will exist in cases where an employee has given his consent to such action, or where there is a contractual power to do so, and the qualifications to Art 8 must always be borne in mind.

(c) Article 9. This Article provides for the right to freedom of thought, conscience and religion, but it is subject to the same qualifications as are found in Article 8, relating to the limitations imposed in the interests of national security, public safety, economic well-being of the country, preventing disorder or crime, protecting health and morals, and protecting the rights and freedoms of others. Thus in *Ahmad v United Kingdom* the employers refused to permit a devout Muslim to take 45 minutes off work every Friday in order to pray at the local mosque. Instead, they offered to reduce his working hours from a five-day week to four and a half days. He refused this offer, arguing that he would suffer a loss of pay and benefits if he accepted, and resigned, claiming that he had been constructively dismissed. His claim was dismissed by an employment tribunal, and an appeal to the European Court of Human Rights was rejected. By offering to reduce his working hours to enable him to attend the local mosque in his own time the employers had not infringed his right to practise his religion. Similarly, in *Stedman v United Kingdom* a woman's contract of employment required her to work on Sundays. She refused to do so, and was dismissed. She claimed that the dismissal was in breach of Art 9 of the Convention, but it was held that it was her refusal to comply with her contractual obligations, not her religious beliefs, which led to her dismissal.

(d) Article 10. This Article provides that everyone has the right to freedom of expression, including the freedom to hold opinions and receive and impart information and ideas without interference by a public authority. Again, the exercise of such freedoms may be limited by such formalities, conditions, restrictions or penalties as are prescribed by law, and are necessary in a democratic society, in the interests of national security, territorial integrity or public safety, for the prevention of disorder or crime, for the protection of health or morals, for the protection of the reputation of others, for preventing the disclosure of information received in confidence, or for maintaining the authority and impartiality of the judiciary.

Thus freedom of speech is covered by the Convention, but hedged with a number of well-recognised limitations. In *Ahmed v United Kingdom*, the Local Government Officers (Political Restrictions) Regulations 1990 restricted the political activities of certain categories of local government officials. The applicant, who was a solicitor employed by one local authority, wished to stand as a candidate in the local elections in another area, but was obliged to withdraw his candidature. He claimed that his rights to freedom of expression had been infringed, but the European Court of Human Rights dismissed his claim. The restrictions imposed were 'prescribed by law', and they pursued a legitimate aim of aiming to ensure effective political democracy at the local level. The Court also applied the doctrine of 'margin of appreciation', ie leaving it to the contracting state to assess whether pressing social needs existed. In this case, the regulations had been passed following a thorough enquiry, and were a valid response by the legislature.

It could be argued that a requirement to follow a particular dress code potentially violates the right to freedom of expression, although a rule which applies to both men and women, and is designed to enforce a common standard of conventionality is not discriminatory on grounds of sex (*Smith v Safeways plc*) and rules which are unlikely to come within the scope of the Convention. In *Kara v United Kingdom* the Commission of Human Rights dismissed a claim by a male transvestite who wore female clothing at work, holding that a requirement to wear appropriate clothing was in accordance with the law and appropriate.

(e) Article 11. This states that everyone has the right to freedom of assembly and to freedom of association with others, including the right to form and join trade unions (see *Wilson v United Kingdom*, para 21.41) for the protection of their interests. Again, there are the usual qualifications to this right, and, in addition, the Convention permits the imposition of lawful restrictions on the exercise of these rights by members of the armed forces, the police, and the administration of the state.

Freedom of assembly and freedom of association also implies a freedom not to assemble or associate. In *Young, James and Webster v United Kingdom* it was held that a requirement to join a trade union which did not exist when workers were first employed (with the threat of a dismissal if there was a failure to do so) amounted to an interference with freedom guaranteed under Art 11. It was wrong to compel someone to join an association contrary to their convictions.

It is not thought that the provisions of the Trade Union and Labour Relations (Consolidation) Act 1992, with its stringent provisions and limitations on strike and other industrial action offend against the Convention, because ballotting, industrial action notices, etc are prescribed by law, and it could be argued that these rules are necessary in a democratic society. It has been suggested that the restriction on the number of pickets contained in the Code of Practice on Picketing (see para 23.101) is capable of being challenged, on the ground that there is no such restriction on any other form of public demonstration. However, Codes of Practice are not law, and a violation does not automatically lead to a breach of the law.

2

The Nature of a Contract of Employment

Parties to a contract of employment

2.1 The complex form of modern industrial and commercial organisation enables people to work under a variety of legal arrangements which may be entirely satisfactory to all concerned, but which are difficult to rationalise into well-defined categories necessary for the purpose of legal analysis. Legal rights and responsibilities are frequently at the mercy of verbal distinctions, for modern terminology does not assist in the process of drawing precise lines between different economic relationships. The nineteenth-century concept of 'master and servant', though somewhat servile by today's standards, at least had the merit of elegant simplicity.

2.2 It is undoubtedly true that the courts have generally taken policy considerations into account when trying to devise 'tests' for determining into which category a particular person will fall. The fact that there is an inadequate statutory definition, coupled with inconsistent legal decisions based on different criteria which are adopted in order to achieve a particular end result means that there is confusion and uncertainty in what is, after all, a fundamental feature of employment law. The modern trend is to widen the scope of the law by extending legal rights to 'workers', but the 'economic man' refuses to be placed in neat legal pigeon-holes.

A. Employers

2.3 In this book we shall be dealing mainly with the legal relationship which exists between the employer and his employees, and, to a limited extent, between the employer and his workers (see para 2.16 for the definition of 'worker'). These terms are bland enough to state, but give rise to considerable problems in practice. The employer is usually a readily identifiable entity, and may be defined as any person, partnership, corporate body or unincorporated association who (or which) employs one or more persons under a contract of employment, although this definition is not particularly helpful. In the building industry, for example, an 'employer' is the term used for someone who 'engages' a main contractor, whereas he ought properly to be described as 'the client'. Frequently, the 'acts' of the employer are in reality done by various levels of management, who are themselves employees, yet it is 'the employer' who will be called to account (eg *Courtaulds Northern Textiles v Andrew*). If the employer is an unincorporated association, a person employed by it will be employed by the members of the management committee for the time being (*Affleck v Newcastle Mind*). A co-operative, on the other hand, might be an association of self-employed persons (*Addison v London Philharmonic Orchestra Ltd*).

Associated employer

2.4 Certain legal consequences may flow from the fact that an employer is part of a group of employers, provided the respective employers are 'associated employers' in the legal sense. ERA, s 231 states that two employers shall be treated as being associated if

(a) one is a company, of which the other (directly or indirectly) has control, or

(b) both are companies of which a third person (directly or indirectly) has control (*Spanlite Structures Ltd v Jarrett*).

2.5 Companies in this connection, means limited companies, not other forms of statutory bodies corporate (*Hasley v Fair Employment Agency*). But the definition covers companies which are incorporated under foreign law (*Hancill v Marcon Engineering Ltd*) and a partnership of companies (*Pinkney v Sandpiper Drilling Ltd*). The hardship which would otherwise be caused to employees in the public sector who are not employed by companies as defined has been somewhat mitigated by special legislation covering local government employees (Redundancy Payments (Local Government) (Modification) Order 1983, and continuity has been preserved for teachers in schools run by local government authorities and health service employees (ERA, s 218(7)–(10) (see para 13.38).

2.6 'Control' is a legal, not factual concept, and is determined by the number of votes attached to shares which can exercise control of a company in general meeting (*Secretary of State for Employment v Newbold*). De facto control, ie, how the company is run in practice, is not sufficient (*Washington Arts Association Ltd v Forster*). A negative control, ie a 50% shareholding, is not sufficient (*Hair Colour Consultants v Mena*). It has been suggested that control by a person may be exercised by a group of persons, provided that in fact they act as one (*Zarb and Samuels v British and Brazilian Produce Co (Sales) Ltd*), but this point has been seriously doubted (*South West Launderettes Ltd v Laidler*), and there are a number of conflicting decisions on this point (compare *Russell v Elmdon Freight Terminal Ltd* with *Tice v Cartwright*).

2.7 There are a number of legislative provisions where the fact that two employers are associated employers in the legal sense is important (see, in particular, para 13.38).

(a) An employer who is taken into the employment of another employer, who, at the time of the change, is an associated employer, will find that his period of employment is continuous, and the change does not break continuity (ERA, s 218(6)). If there is a gap between the two employments, continuity may be preserved by the provision of ERA, s 212 (*Bentley Engineering Ltd v Crown and Miller* see para 13.20).

(b) The definition of redundancy contained in ERA, s 139(1) (see para 18.12) is extended so that the business of associated employers shall be treated as one business.

(c) An offer of re-engagement in redundancy situations, made under the ERA, ss 138 or 141, can be made by an employer or an associated employer (ERA, s 146).

(d) Independent advice given by a lawyer on a compromise agreement must not be given by a lawyer who is employed by or acting for the employer or an associated employer (ERA, s 203(3B)).

(e) The reference in TULR(C)A, s 182(1) to the disclosure of information for collective bargaining purposes (see para 23.15) exempts information communicated in confidence by an associated employer.

(f) An equal pay claim may be made if a comparator is employed by an associated employer (Equal Pay Act 1970, s 1(6), see *Scullard v Knowles*).

(g) An employee may be able to count employment with an associated employer for the purpose of obtaining the higher rate national minimum wage (National Minimum Wage Regulations, reg 13(2)).

2.8 But if the statute does not refer to an associated employer, then clearly no duty is imposed. Thus, there is a requirement for an employer to consult on redundancies if more than 20 employees are to be made redundant at the same establishment; several associated employers can therefore each make 19 employees redundant without involving the duty to consult (*E Green & Son (Castings) Ltd v Association of Scientific, Technical and Management Staffs*). Employees of associated employers cannot be aggregated to pass the threshold of 20 employees in order to create a bargaining unit for the purpose of statutory recognition procedures (*GPMU v Derry Print Ltd*).

B. Directors

2.9 A person who is a director of a limited company is not an employee of that company by virtue of his directorship, but he will be an employee if he has a service contract with the company, which can be express or implied. Every company must keep a copy of every written service agreement, or a written memorandum of a service agreement which is not in writing (Companies Act 1985, s 318). As a director, he can be voted out of office at any time by a simple majority of shareholders' votes at a general meeting of the company, but as an employee he will have all the protections afforded either by his service agreement or the rules of modern employment law. However, a company may not give a director security of employment for more than five years, unless the arrangement has been approved by a resolution of the company in general meeting (Companies Act 1985, s 319).

2.10 A service contract between a company and a director can be either express or implied. In the absence of a written agreement or memorandum, it must be ascertained if the person concerned worked as a director, and only occasionally worked in the capacity as an employee, or if he kept regular working hours, or worked full-time, and spent only short or insignificant periods on his duties as a director (*Folami v Nigerline (UK) Ltd*). Thus, if remuneration is by way of director's fees, rather than by a salary, if tax and national insurance contributions are not paid on the remuneration, and if there is an absence of a service agreement as required by s 318 of the Companies Act, it is unlikely that a director will be regarded as an employee of the company (*Parsons v Albert J Parsons & Sons Ltd*). It is also possible for the law to change a person's legal status in accordance with the circumstances. In *Road Transport Industry Training Board v Readers Garage Ltd* the question was whether an industrial training levy could be assessed on the earnings of a controlling director who also worked as an employee, and the court held that if there was a contract of service implied between him and the company, the employment tribunal must assess how much of his drawings from the company were in respect of that service, and assess the levy on that amount. Any sum he received in his capacity as a director would not be assessed for levy purposes.

2.11 Technically, a limited company is a separate legal entity, distinct from the persons who control it. It follows that in legal theory there is no reason why a sole shareholder of a company cannot be regarded as an employee of the company. Thus in *Lee v Lee's Air Farming Ltd*, Lee owned all the shares in a company bar one. He was killed while piloting an aircraft, and it was held that his widow was entitled to benefit under a New Zealand statute which dealt with workmen's compensation. However, this dichotomy does not always apply in respect of UK employment law, because a person who is a controlling director in fact controls the company, rather than the company controlling him. Thus in *Buchan v Secretary of State for Employment* the applicant had a 50% shareholding in a private company. He worked for the company on a full-time basis, was in receipt of an annual salary, paid tax and national insurance contributions, and was entitled to five weeks' holiday each year. However, he did not have a written service agreement. When the company went into liquidation, he applied to the Secretary of State for arrears of wages, a redundancy payment and a payment in lieu of notice. An employment tribunal dismissed his claim, holding that he was not an employee, and the decision was upheld by the EAT. A controlling shareholder cannot be an employee for the purpose of the ERA because he is able to prevent his own dismissal, and the EAT thought that it would be inconsistent with the purpose of the Act to extend its protection to a person who could not be dismissed from his employment. It followed that if he had no remedy against the company over which he had control, he cannot have any claim against the guarantor of the company's liability, ie the Secretary of State. The appointment of a receiver did not alter the applicant's status; if he was not an employee before the receiver was appointed, he did not become one after that appointment. The EAT thus distinguished *Lee v Lee's Air Farming Ltd*, on the ground that that case involved a claim for compensation under insurance arrangements.

2.12 There are a number of legal decisions by the EAT which confirm the approach taken in *Buchan*, including the Scottish EAT in *Fleming v Secretary of State for Trade and Industry*, although it was stressed that there was no rule of law involved in such a finding, the issue being one of fact. If a limited company is indeed a distinct legal entity, logic would suggest that in law it is separate from its directors, even if in practice the latter does control the former. Indeed, in *Secretary of State for Trade and Industry v Bottrill* the Court of Appeal disagreed with the reasoning in *Buchan* and held, on the special facts of the case, that a managing director who was also the sole shareholder of a limited company was an employee, and entitled to recover redundancy and other payments from the Secretary of State when the company went into liquidation. The decision in *Bottrill* was followed in *Sellars Arenascene Ltd v Connolly* where it was held that a position as a controlling shareholder was not incompatible with the status of an employee.

C. Business consultants

2.13 A person who works in a consultancy or advisory capacity is capable of being an employee, depending on the legal and factual arrangements which are made. In *Bromsgrove Casting and Machining Ltd v Martin*, the applicant was a managing director of a company. He ceased to hold office, but continued to work as a director and consultant. There was no provision as to the number of hours to be worked, and his salary was unchanged. He was then dismissed, and he brought a complaint of unfair dismissal. It was held that in his capacity as a consultant, he was retained, not employed. His employment only came into being when he was actually called upon to give advice. Therefore, the employment tribunal should have enquired into the number of hours he was normally required to give advice, to see whether or not his contract was for the requisite number of hours per week in order to qualify for protection from unfair dismissal (NB: this is no longer a prerequisite for such a claim).

D. Partners

2.14 A partner is a self-employed person in business who is remunerated by taking a share of the profits. Cases can be found where 'salaried partners' are known to exist. This is clearly a contradiction in terms. Architects and dentists frequently engage 'associates', and may make contractual arrangements which suit all concerned, but in law such persons, however designated, are probably employees. However, the contract of engagement may specify to the contrary. A junior partner, however, is a partner with (usually) a lesser share of the profits and/or a smaller say in the conduct of the partnership business. The modern vogue for co-partnership and profit-sharing schemes may well throw up further problems in the future, for although the mere fact of sharing profits is not evidence that a partnership exists (Partnership Act 1890, s 3), it could together with other relevant circumstances, lead to that conclusion (see *Glasgow v Independent Printing Co*).

2.15 If an employee is employed by a partnership, which ceases to trade, he may be able to recover a redundancy payment from the National Insurance Fund if he can show that he has taken all reasonable steps to recover the payment (ERA, s 166). But in order to obtain arrears of pay, notice money, holiday pay and compensation for unfair dismissal under s 182 of ERA, he would have to show that the employer is insolvent, which means that each and every one of the partners must be adjudged bankrupt. As long as there is a partner who is solvent, it is from such a person that the employee must first seek payment (*Secretary of State for Trade and Industry v Forde*).

E. Workers

2.16 Consider the term 'worker'. This can mean 'anyone who works for a living', and would thus include all from a managing director of a large public company to a machine operator in an engineering factory; a bookmaker's clerk on a race track to a surgeon in a hospital. Nowadays it is surely a mistake to use the term with a socio-economic undertone. On the other hand, the term 'workman' has, in the past, been given a more precise legal meaning, though it appears to be falling into legislative disuse as legal rights are given a wider scope.

2.17 Whatever the currently acceptable meanings of these terms may be, it is clear that the law can place within its ambit anyone it wishes. Thus there are two main definitions of the term 'worker' currently in use, with some minor variations in particular circumstances.

2.18 Section 296 of the Trade Union and Labour Relations (Consolidation) Act 1992 provides that a worker is an individual who works or seeks to work

(a) under a contract of employment, or

(b) under any other contract whereby he undertakes to do or perform personally any work or services for another party to the contract who is not a professional client of his, or

(c) is in employment under or for the purposes of a government department (otherwise than as a member of the armed forces) in so far as such employment does not come within (a) or (b) above.

2.19 At the same time, ss 224(6) and 235 of the Act define a contract of employment, for the purpose of the secondary action provisions (see para 23.71) and the balloting provisions (see para 23.47) as including a contract under which one person personally does work or performs services for another.

2.20 Section 230 of the Employment Rights Act 1996 (ERA) defines the term worker in similar, but not identical terms, ie an individual who has entered into or works under (or worked under)

(a) a contract of employment, or

(b) any other contract whereby the individual undertakes to do or perform personally any work or services for another party to the contract whose status is not by virtue of the contract that of client or customer of any profession or business undertaking carried on by the individual.

(The reason the definition does not deal with Crown employment is because there are other specific provisions which take effect, ie ss 191–192).

But when the terms 'shop worker' or 'betting worker' are used in this Act (see Chapter 8) they refer to employees, not workers!

2.21 The Trade Union and Labour Relations (Consolidation) Act deals with the rights of workers and employees. Part II of the Employment Rights Act, which deals with deductions from wages etc (see Chapter 8) applies to workers, as do the protected disclosure provisions contained in Pt IVA of the Act (see Chapter 10), albeit with a somewhat extended definition of the term (see s 43K). The National Minimum Wage Act 1998, the Working Time Regulations 1998, and the Part-time Workers (Prevention of Less Favourable Treatment) Regulations 2000 all apply to workers. The result is that when the term 'worker' is used, certain employment rights are extended to cover a wider group of persons, in line with the trend in modern employment law.

2.22 A 'worker', for some purposes, may have rights which are identical to those enjoyed by an employee, even though he is clearly not an employee, and is self-employed. Thus in *Flynn v Torith Ltd* the applicant worked as a self-employed joiner on a building site. He claimed he was entitled to holiday pay under the Working Time Regulations. The EAT noted that the regulations applied to 'a worker', which is defined as being an individual who works under '. . . any other contract . . .' whereby the individual undertakes to do or perform personally any work or services for another party to the contract. . . .'. The phrase 'any other contract' in reg 2(1) in those regulations was wide ranging, and included persons who worked under a contract to provide services or perform work for another, other than under a contract of employment. The only exception to reg 2(1) is an individual carrying on a profession or business undertaking of which the other party was a client. Thus the claimant was entitled to holiday pay.

2.23 The Equal Pay Act, Sex Discrimination Act, Race Relations Act, and the Disability Discrimination Act all apply to anyone who is employed under a contract of service or of apprenticeship or a contract personally to execute any work or labour. Thus these Acts apply to employees and self-employed persons.

2.24 Various groups are excluded from some (but not all) legal rights for reasons of policy, eg mariners and share fishermen, and there are a few groups who are outwith the protection of employment law altogether, eg office holders (see para 2.51). Thus a Church of England clergyman is not a person whose rights and duties are defined by contract (*Housman v Bishop of Ely* but see para 2.56).

F. Employees

2.25 The term 'employee' is defined in ERA, s 230 as an individual who enters into or works under (or, where the employment has ceased, worked under) a contract of employment, which is a contract of service or apprenticeship, whether express or implied, and (if it is express) whether oral or in writing. The definition in TULR(C)A, s 295 is similar. Since the term 'employee' is narrower than the term 'worker' it follows that most of the rights contained in ERA are limited to employees, apart from certain specific provisions, eg, ss 43A–43K, see para 10.70). Thus all employees are workers, but not all workers are employees (*Broadbent v Crisp*).

2.26 An employee, though easy to define, is not so easy to describe, for the relationship between A (the employer) and B (the employee) is complicated by the fact that there is also a relationship between B and the state. It is possible that a person can be an employee for one purpose, but not an employee for another. Thus in *Challinor v Taylor* a taxi driver was the night driver of a cab which was used during the day by the owner. The latter paid for the fuel, insurance and maintenance of the car, and took 65% of the gross takings. He also paid the cost of the employer's contribution towards the driver's national insurance stamp. The driver, however, was assessed for income tax purposes as a self-employed person under Schedule D. The owner sold the taxi and the driver was thus redundant. It was held that he was not an employee, and therefore not entitled to a redundancy payment.

2.27 There is no reason in principle why an employee cannot have more than two employers, and, provided he is within the appropriate protection of the law, pursue his legal remedies against either of them. Indeed, it is possible for an employee to have two contracts of employment with the same employer, so that if he is dismissed from his employment under one contract, he may pursue his remedy whilst still leaving the other contract subsisting (*Throsby v Imperial College of Science and Technology*).

Distinction between employees and self-employed persons

A. Contract of service

2.28 The basic division for our purposes is between those who are employed persons and those who are self-employed, and the distinction between these categories is that the employed person works under a contract *of* service, whereas the self-employed person works under a contract *for* services. Again, it is easy to state this distinction, but in practice it has proved difficult to draw it, and over the years the courts have developed a number of tests designed to produce a given result. Fundamentally, for the relationship of employer/ employee to exist, there must be a contract of employment, either express or implied. It follows that if there is no contract of any sort between the parties, there cannot be a contract of employment, and the fact that a worker is taxed as an employee under IR 35 or pays Class 1 national insurance contributions is irrelevant (*O'Murphy v Hewlett Packard Ltd*).

Control test

2.29 An important criterion for determining whether or not the relationship of employer/ employee exists is the extent to which a person is under the direction and control of the other party with regard to the manner in which the work is done (*Narich Pty Ltd v Payroll Tax Comr*). Indeed, in the nineteenth century control was regarded as the sole determining factor. Thus if the employer could tell the employee not only what to do, but how to do it, then a contract of service existed (*Yewens v Noakes*). In modern conditions the application of such a test is clearly unreal. An employee may be highly skilled and qualified, and employed specifically because he has professional training and competence, so that the employer is frequently unable (as well as being unwilling) to instruct the employee as to how the work is to be done. Despite this difficulty, some modern decisions have added to the control test a refinement which looks for *the right to control* as being the determinant factor (*Gibb v United Steel Companies Ltd*), or even the existence of the right to control, even though this is seldom if ever exercised in practice. It is clear that the greater the degree of control which is exercisable by the employer, the more likely it will be that the contract is one of service (*Whittaker v Minister of Pensions and National Insurance*), but 'the greater the skill required for an employee's work the less significant is control in determining whether the employee is under a contract of service' (*Beloff v Pressdram*).

2.30 But the exercise of a degree of control is not conclusive. In *Hitchcock v Post Office*, the applicant ran a sub-post office as part of a shop he owned. Although the Post Office exercised control over many of its activities, it was held that this was because of the need to ensure financial control and security, rather than being a control over managerial functions. Consequently, the sub-post master was not an employee of the Post Office.

Organisational test

2.31 In *Stevenson, Jordan and Harrison Ltd v MacDonald and Evans*, Denning LJ suggested a more up-to-date test. 'Under a contract of service', he said, 'a man is employed as part of the business and his work is done as an integral part of the business'. This 'organisational' test has certain advantages, particularly in relation to skilled employees who are 'integrated' into an enterprise, eg doctors, nurses etc, in respect of whom the control test is inappropriate. In *Whittaker v Minister of Pensions and National Insurance* a trapeze artiste broke her wrist as a result of a fall in her act. It was held that she was an integral part of the circus business and thus an employee for the purpose of claiming industrial injuries benefit.

Multiple test

2.32 But these problems are too complex to be capable of being resolved by the application of any single simple test, and the courts nowadays will look at all the surrounding features, thus applying what is in fact a multiple test. Certainly the power of selection, the payment of wages, national insurance stamps, income tax, holiday monies and pensions, and the power to suspend and dismiss are all relevant features which need to be taken into account. In *Ready Mixed Concrete (South East) Ltd v Minister of Pensions and National Insurance* a firm dismissed its drivers, sold all the lorries to them and re-employed them under a contract which contained obligations capable of leading to the conclusion that they were both employed and self-employed persons. The drivers had to wear the company's uniforms, place their lorries at the company's disposal for a certain number of hours, only use them for the company's business, obey the orders of the foreman, and sell the lorries back to the company at an agreed current market valuation. On the other hand, the drivers had to maintain the lorries at their own expense and pay all running costs. In addition, they could employ a substitute driver, and could own more than one lorry. They paid their own income tax and national insurance contributions, had no set hours or meal breaks, and made their own decisions as to how to drive the lorries and which routes to take. MacKenna J held that there were three conditions necessary to establish that a contract of service existed. The first was that the employee agreed to provide his own work and skill in the performance of a service for his employer, the second was that there must be some element of control exercisable by the employer, and the third was that the other terms of the contract must not be inconsistent with the existence of a contract of employment. The fact that the drivers could (and did) employ a substitute was clearly crucial in deciding that they were self-employed haulage contractors.

2.33 Mutuality of obligation and control are the irreducible minimum legal requirements for the existence of a contract of employment (*Montgomery v Johnson Underwood Ltd*), together with an irreducible level of personal service (*MacFarlane v Glasgow City Council*). As a general principle, it can be said that if a person is not contractually bound to perform the contract personally, he is not an employee. It is what is stated in the contract that will determine this, not what actually occurs in practice. If there is a clear contractual term that a person is self-employed, and could employ someone else to do the work if necessary, then it is not necessary to look at what happened in practice unless there has been a variation of the term or the term can be said to be a sham (*Staffordshire Sentinel Newspapers Ltd v Potter*). But the fact that the contract permits an applicant to have a limited ability to delegate performance to another person is not conclusive. In *MacFarlane v Glasgow City Council* the applicant was a part-time lecturer. If he was unable to take a class he could arrange for someone else to do so, but that person had to be chosen from a register held by the local authority, and sometimes the local authority organised a replacement. It was held that the applicant was an employee.

2.34 More recently the entrepreneurial test seems to be the dominating feature. The problem is looked at from a self-employed person's point of view, and the question asked 'Is he in business on his own?' Again, no exhaustive list of considerations can be formulated. Does he provide his own equipment? Hire his own helpers? Is there any degree of financial responsibility for investment or degree of risk? Does he undertake any other sort of commission, business or employment? Is there any opportunity to profit from sound management? These questions were raised in *Market Investigations Ltd v Minister of Social Security*, where a company employed women on a part-time basis to do market research. They could work as they chose, but according to a set pattern. It was held that the women were employees, and not employed in business 'on their own'. The more unskilled and untrained a person is, the less likely it will be that the employment tribunal will hold that he is running his own business. In *Airfix Footwear Ltd v Cope* the applicant was a home-worker making heels for shoes manufactured by the respondent company. She was provided with the necessary equipment and material, and worked in accordance with instructions given to her. The EAT upheld a finding that she was an employee. On the other hand, in *Argent v Minister of Social Security* an actor taught drama on a part-time basis at a school. It was held that he was a self-employed lecturer.

2.35 In *Withers v Flackwell Health Football Supporters' Club*, the EAT stated that difficult cases could be resolved by using industrial, rather than legal, terminology. Hence, the person could be asked a simple question, 'Are you your own boss?'

2.36 This pragmatic approach was taken even further in *Davis v New England College of Arundel*, where the claimant was engaged as a lecturer on a yearly renewable contract. He specifically asked to be treated as being self-employed as he wished to retain that status for income tax and national insurance purposes. He was not re-engaged, and claimed that he had been unfairly dismissed. It was held that to determine whether or not he was an employee, the matter had to be looked at objectively. His request to be treated as being self-employed, and the fact that the college so regarded him, did not alter the nature of the contractual relationship between him and his employer. In reality, he was an employee of the college, and hence he was entitled to bring a claim. It is the essence of the arrangement, rather than the form, which is the determinant factor (*Tyne and Clyde Warehouses Ltd v Hamerton*).

2.37 The difficulties inherent in such cases can be seen in *Massey v Crown Life Insurance Co* where the claimant was an employee of the respondents. It was then agreed that he should be treated as being self-employed, and a new agreement to this effect was signed. Although his actual duties were identical, the claimant was taxed under Schedule D, and paid self-employed insurance. He was then dismissed, and claimed unfair dismissal. It was held that he was employed under a contract for services. While the parties cannot alter the nature of their relationship by putting a different label on it, where the situation was in doubt, or was ambiguous, an agreement which stipulated the nature of the relationship affords strong evidence of what it is. In this case, there was a genuine attempt to change the legal situation to that of an independent contractor. There was no attempt to deceive the Inland Revenue. It was a genuine agreement to enable the applicant to be treated as being self-employed. Consequently, he could not claim that his dismissal was unfair. The Court of Appeal distinguished the case of *Ferguson v John Dawson & Partners Ltd* (see para 2.46) on the ground that in the latter case there was little evidence as to what the actual contract was.

2.38 In truth, before a clear and satisfactory answer can be given to the question 'Who is an employee?' we may well need to pose a second one, namely, 'For what purpose is the question being asked?' A part-time lecturer may well be a self-employed person for income tax purposes but an employee in relation to national insurance contributions, and he may well be an employed person (using the 'organisational test') if the issue was raised as to the vicarious liability of his employer for wrongful acts committed by him during the course of his work. The pragmatic approach adopted by the courts is to say that the matter is a question of fact, to be determined by the evidence in each case. For example, in *Maurice Graham Ltd v Brunswick* a company engaged self-employed brick-layers, who paid their own income tax and were responsible for their own national insurance contributions. The company was convicted of breaches of the Construction (Health and Welfare) Regulations 1966, and argued on appeal that those regulations only applied to 'employees', not independent contractors. It was held that though the outward arrangement gave the appearance of a worker being an independent contractor, this was not conclusive. The company controlled and supervised the men, and supplied them with the necessary equipment and materials, and the court refused to disturb the convictions.

2.39 The rule that no single factor can, by itself, be conclusive, is illustrated by the decision of the EAT in *City and East London FHS Authority v Durcan*. The claimant ran his own dental practice on a self-employed basis. Once each week, he worked on a rota at a local hospital, providing emergency services. He was paid a fixed fee, made his own arrangements for tax and national insurance, and, if he was unable to attend, he had to make arrangements for a replacement. When the hospital trust sought to reduce the number of hours worked, he claimed that he had been constructively and unfairly dismissed. The respondents resisted the claim, arguing that he was self-employed. The EAT noted that the claimant used the hospital's premises, equipment and medicines, but, on the other hand, he was not subject to any form of control as to how the work was to be done. The fact that he had to provide a replacement if he was unable to attend was not fatal to the existence of an employment contract, because the replacement had to be on an approved list, and this was not inconsistent with the modern trend towards job-sharing. It was true that the claimant did not enjoy the usual benefits of employment status, including sick pay, holiday pay, and notice rights, nor did he have the right to pursue any grievance procedure or take advantage of any disciplinary procedure. He had to treat any patient who attended for treatment, but his remuneration was not dependent on the number of patients who attended, and thus there was no risk of profit or loss from his working activities. The label attached to the relationship was not determinative of the worker's legal status, although it could tip the balance if all the relevant factors were evenly balanced. Mutuality of obligation is an important factor, but again not conclusive. Nor was it relevant that he worked only for a limited number of hours each week, because since the removal of the eight hour per week qualification, employment tribunals will increasingly be called upon to determine the legal status of workers who only work for a few hours each week. Taking into account all the considerations, the EAT refused to disturb the decision of the employment tribunal that the claimant was an employee, and was therefore entitled to pursue his claim.

2.40 A completely different approach was taken by the House of Lords in *Carmichael v National Power plc*, where the claimant was offered employment as a tour guide 'on a casual as required basis'. She performed work as and when it arose, but she was not obliged to take the work, and the company were not obliged to provide work and did not guarantee that work would be available. She was paid for the hours worked, and tax and national insurance contributions were deducted. She requested a statement of terms of employment under ERA, s 1 and when this was refused, she complained to an employment tribunal. The House of Lords held that she was not an employee. There was no obligation for the company to provide the work, and the claimant was not obliged to take it when offered. Thus there was an absence of the irreducible minimum of mutual obligation necessary to create a contract of employment.

2.41 An employment tribunal should therefore take the following factors into account, and make its determination accordingly:

(a) the contractual provisions (*BSM (1257) Ltd v Secretary of State for Social Services*);

(b) the degree of control exercised by the employer (*Global Plant Ltd v Secretary of State for Health and Social Security*);

(c) the obligation on the employer to provide work (*Nethermere (St Neots) Ltd v Gardiner*);

(d) the obligation on the employee to do the work (*Ahmet v Trusthouse Forte Catering Ltd*);

(e) the duty of personal service (*Ready Mixed Concrete Ltd (South East) v Minister of Pensions and National Insurance*);

(f) the provision of tools, equipment, instruments, etc (*Willy Scheidegger Swiss Typewriting School (London) Ltd v Minister of Social Security*);

(g) the arrangements made for tax, national insurance, VAT, statutory sick pay (*Davis v New England College of Arundel*);

(h) the opportunity to work for other employers (*WHPT Housing Association Ltd v Secretary of State for Social Services*);

(i) other contractual provisions, including holiday pay, sick pay, notice, fees, expenses, etc (*Tyne and Clyde Warehouses Ltd v Hamerton*);

(j) the degree of financial risk and the responsibility for investment and management (*Market Investigations Ltd v Minister of Social Security*);

(k) whether the relationship of being self-employed is a genuine one, or whether there is an attempt to avoid modern protective legislation (*Young & Woods Ltd v West*);

(l) the number of assignments, the duration of the engagement, and the risk of running bad debts (*Hall v Lorimer*);

(m) the presence or absence of mutuality of the obligation to provide or do the work (*Carmichael v National Power plc*).

2.42 No single factor, by itself, is conclusive, and all the relevant circumstances must be considered. As long as the employment tribunals take these into account, their decision is a question of fact, not law, and their findings (either way) cannot normally be challenged (*O'Kelly v Trusthouse Forte plc* and see *Hall v Lorimer*) unless they took a view on the facts which would not reasonably be sustained (*Lee Ting Sang v Chung Chi-Keung*). However, if there is a written contract which determines the relationship between the parties, the interpretation of that contract is a question of law, which can be considered on appeal (*Davies v Presbyterian Church of Wales*).

B. Why the distinction is important

2.43 There are a number of reasons for stressing the importance of this distinction between a contract of service and a contract for services, although recent decisions are tending to minimise this importance.

Tax reasons

2.44 Under the Social Security Contributions and Benefits Act 1992 an employer must pay secondary Class 1 contributions in respect of employed earners (the primary contribution being made on an earnings-related basis by the employed earner – which term includes an office holder). Self-employed earners pay a flat-rate Class 2 contribution, and in addition a Class 4 contribution based on the gains or profits derived which are chargeable to income tax under Schedule D (see *Lane v Shire Roofing Co Ltd*). The employer does not need to deduct PAYE income tax under Schedule E in respect of his self-employed independent contractors (who must make their own arrangements under Schedule D), and he need not pay a levy for industrial training purposes. An independent sub-contractor may have to charge VAT on services supplied, which would not be so if he were an employee. But it must be stressed that it is the substance of the relationship which will count, not the form. Thus if a person is an employee in the legal sense, the employer's obligations will arise despite any artificial attempt or arrangements made to avoid such duties (*Pennington v Minister of Social Security*). Nor does the fact that a person pays his own insurance stamps and is responsible for his own income tax payments necessarily mean that he is a self-employed person. In *Jennings v Westwood Engineering Ltd* the applicant was offered employment. He was told that he could work at a lower rate of remuneration on PAYE, or at a higher rate, paying his own tax and insurance, and he chose the latter option. It was held that he was employed under a contract of employment nonetheless. Conversely, in *President of the Methodist Conference v Parfitt*, the fact that the applicant paid Class 1 national insurance and was taxed under Schedule E did not per se make him an employee.

2.45 One of the more intractable industrial problems which caused concern some years ago was the existence of the 'lump', ie self-employed sub-contractors in the building industry. In *Construction Industry Training Board v Labour Force Ltd* when main contractors required labour they would contact Labour Force Ltd who would supply the men at agreed rates. The main contractor could dismiss the men but never paid them, and merely told Labour Force Ltd the number of hours each had worked. Labour Force Ltd paid the men on this basis, but the men agreed that they were self-employed, and agreed to be responsible for their own income tax, national insurance and holiday pay. It was held that there was no contract of any kind between the main contractors and the men, and further that there was no contract of service between

Labour Force Ltd and the men, and consequently Labour Force Ltd were not liable to pay industrial training levy (which would be normally calculated on a percentage of the payroll).

2.46 The Court of Appeal has also indicated that it is concerned with the realities of the situation, rather than the form of the arrangement. In *Ferguson v John Dawson & Partners Ltd*, a builder's labourer agreed to work on the 'lump', or as the court found, as a 'self-employed labour only sub-contractor'. He was seriously injured as a result of the employers' failure to provide a guard rail on a roof, and he sued for this breach of statutory duty. He could only succeed if he could show that he was an employee, and, by a majority, the Court upheld this contention. Megaw LJ agreed that the 'lump' arrangement was a mere device, capable of being put to advantage by each side, but which did not affect the strict legal relationship between the parties. Dissenting, Lawton LJ thought that there was no reason in law why a man could not sell his labour without becoming the employee of the other party. Also, he thought that it was contrary to public policy to allow a man to claim that he was self-employed for the purposes of evading taxation, but an employee for the purpose of claiming compensation.

Certainly, where health and safety issues are being considered, there is a policy reason which leans towards holding that injured workmen are employees as opposed to self-employed specialist sub-contractors, and tax and other such considerations are less significant than those features which would lead to the conclusion that a contract of service exists. The responsibility for overall safety is an important factor to be taken into account (*Lane v Shire Roofing Co (Oxford) Ltd*).

2.47 The alleged problems caused by the 'lump' illustrate the difficulties in trying to squeeze 'the economic man' into tight legal compartments, for in the building industry there are large numbers of 'genuine' self-employed independent contractors who provide invaluable services, and no satisfactory way has been devised whereby the one can be distinguished from the other. Since one of the problems raised by the 'lump' was income-tax avoidance, the Finance Act 2000 provided that an employer in the construction industry must deduct at source 25% of the income price (excluding the cost of materials) of sub-contractors, which at least ensures that income tax liability is met by such persons. The 'genuine' sub-contractor may apply for a tax exemption certificate, provided he meets certain stringent requirements.

Liability issues

2.48 An employer will not normally be vicariously liable for the tortious acts (civil wrongs) committed by independent contractors (though there are certain exceptions to this rule) whereas he would be so liable for torts committed by his employees in the course of their employment which cause injury or damage to third parties (see Chapter 10). Two contrasting cases will illustrate this point. In *Hillyer v St Bartholomew's Hospital* the plaintiff selected a consultant who negligently performed an operation. It was held that the hospital was not liable, because the consultant was an independent contractor who was merely using the facilities of the hospital. On the other hand, in *Cassidy v Ministry of Health*, a resident surgeon operated negligently on the plaintiff, and it was held that the hospital board, as the employer, was liable.

Health and safety issues

2.49 An employer owes a duty at common law to his employees to take reasonable care for their safety, whereas these duties do not normally apply with respect to his independent contractors, although again, there are exceptions. Thus in *McArdle v Andmac Roofing Co* the claimant worked for one of several subcontractors who were employed on converting a building at a holiday camp, who were all under the direction of Pontins (Contractors) Ltd. The latter had made no arrangements for safety precautions with the sub-contractors, and as a result, the claimant suffered severe injuries when he fell off a roof. It was held that the main contractors (Pontins) assumed the responsibility of co-ordinating the work, and were therefore under a duty to ensure that reasonable safety precautions were taken for all those who were working on the job, even though they were not the employers of those who were working. The duties owed by the employer to his employees under the Health and Safety at Work etc Act 1974 are more extensive than those owed to independent contractors (see Chapter 11). In practice this may mean that a self-employed person who is injured whilst at work may be unable to claim any compensation from the employer, and additionally will be unable to claim industrial injuries benefit and/or sick pay.

Statutory rights

2.50 Many statutory rights apply only to employees, not to workers. For example, an employee is entitled to all the rights contained in the Employment Rights Act, including a written statement of terms of employment, itemised pay statement, maternity, paternity, parental and adoption rights, guarantee pay, medical suspension pay, time off work, unfair dismissal, redundancy rights, etc. Despite the appellation, shop workers and betting workers are employees! The Flexible Working Regulations, Fixed-term Employees Regulations, Transfer of Undertaking Regulations, etc apply to employees, as does the Health and Safety at Work Act and many regulations issued thereunder. A court may be able to make an attachment of earnings order whereby an employer is obliged to make certain deductions from the earnings of an employee, which would not be possible if the person concerned was a (self-employed) worker. On the other hand, the protection of wages and the public interest disclosure provisions of ERA apply to workers (which includes employees), as do the Part-Time Workers Regulations, Working Time Regulations, the various pieces of discrimination legislation, the National Minimum Wage Act and parts of the Trade Union and Labour Relations (Consolidation) Act.

Other categories of parties to a contract of employment

A. Office holders

2.51 A special category of persons exists who are technically known as office holders. They are not employed by virtue of a contract of employment, and therefore have certain privileges attached to their position. A judge, for example, holds office during good behaviour and may only be dismissed on a resolution passed by both Houses of Parliament. A magistrate is also an office holder (*Knight v A-G*). However, some office holders may also have a contract of employment, eg a stipendiary reader in the Church of England (*Barthorpe v Exeter Diocesan Board of Finance Ltd*). In *102 Social Club and Institute v Bickerton*, a club secretary was paid an honorarium of £225 per year. The EAT held that the employment tribunal should consider whether the money was paid by way of a salary for services rendered, or whether it was an honorarium for work done as a member of the club in his capacity as an office holder. In the former case only would he be regarded as being an employee.

2.52 In *Lincolnshire County Council v Hopper* the council appointed the claimant as a registrar. The council also paid her remuneration, determined her hours of work, and made provision for her pension. However, the Registration Services Act 1953 stated that a registrar holds office during the pleasure of the Registrar General. It was held that the claimant was an office holder, not an employee. The council did not have the power to dismiss the claimant, which is an essential element of an employment relationship.

2.53 Regular earnings received by an office holder are more akin to remuneration for work done than by way of honorarium for tenure of office. Thus his claim for the money is closely analogous to a claim for a salary due under a contract of employment. It follows that the office holder must be willing and able to render the services required of him, and that if he refuses to perform his duties (as a form of industrial action) his paymaster is entitled to withhold the relevant part of his remuneration (*Miles v Wakefield Metropolitan District Council*).

2.54 In *Johnson v Ryan*, the EAT held that there were three categories of office holders, namely:

(a) an office holder whose rights and duties are defined by the office they hold, and not by any contract (such as a police officer);

(b) persons who have the title of office holder, but who are in reality employees with a contract of service; and

(c) workers who are both office holders and employees, such as company directors.

2.55 Indeed, there is a fourth category of office holder, namely a worker who is not necessarily an employee. In *Perceval-Price v Department of Economic Development*, the Northern Ireland Court of Appeal held that full-time holders of judicial posts in tribunals were 'workers' for the purpose of Art 141 of the Treaty of Rome, and hence provisions in domestic law which provided that statutory officers were not to be regarded as employed under a contract of service had to be disapplied. So far as EU law is concerned, the criterion was the existence of an employment relationship, regardless of the legal nature of that relationship and its purpose.

There is little doubt that the categories of people who nowadays could properly be described as 'office holders' is declining, because formerly the offices in question were attached to incorporeal hereditaments, and many such titles are nowadays largely obsolete. In *R v BBC, ex p Lavelle*, Woolf J commented: 'The distinctions which previously existed between pure cases of master and servant and cases where a person holds an office are no longer clear.'

A useful summary of the legal position of office holders can be found in *Percy v Church of Scotland Board of National Mission*.

B. Ministers of religion

2.56 It has long been thought that ministers of religion had few (if any) employment rights, as they were not employed under a contract of employment, having regard to the spiritual nature of their work (*President of the Methodist Conference v Parfitt*). Thus in *Diocese of Southwark v Coker* it was held that an assistant curate was the holder of ecclesiastical office, and not a person whose rights and duties were defined by a contract of employment. But this type of simplistic reasoning was rejected by the House of Lords in *Percy v Church of Scotland Board of National Mission*, where the claimant was appointed as an ordained minister. It was alleged that she had an affair with a married elder of the parish. She was suspended from her duties, pending preparation for a disciplinary hearing. Eventually she was counselled to resign and demit her status as a minister. She brought proceedings in an employment tribunal, alleging unfair dismissal and that she had been discriminated against on grounds of sex, arguing that in similar circumstances the church would not have taken such action against a male minister known to have had an extra-marital relationship. Her claim was dismissed by an employment tribunal, on the ground that having regard to the essentially religious nature of her duties she was not employed under a contract of employment as defined in the Employment Rights Act and the Sex Discrimination Act. The decision was upheld by the EAT and Court of Session, but the House of Lords found in her favour on the sex discrimination point.

It was held that there was an offer and acceptance of a church post for a specific period, with detailed provision for the claimant's duties, remuneration, travel expenses, holidays and accommodation. As such, there was clearly an intention to create legal relations. Further, the claimant was employed under a contract 'personally to execute any work or labour' as defined in s 82(1) of the Sex Discrimination Act, and hence her claim for sex discrimination could proceed.

It is important to note that although the claimant originally claimed unfair dismissal, this matter was not pursued on appeal to the House of Lords, and the decision only applies to those legislative provisions which define 'employment' in a manner similar to the Sex Discrimination Act, s 82(1). The question as to whether or not ministers of religion can be regarded as being 'employees' for the purpose of the Employment Rights Act and other legislative provisions must still be regarded as being open.

C. Crown employees

2.57 The precise legal nature of the relationship between the Crown and civil servants has long been a moot point, but it now appears that since such arrangements have an intention to create legal relations, a contract of employment exists, enforceable by private law remedies (*R v Lord Chancellor's Department, ex p Nangle*). The provisions of the Equal Pay Act 1970 (see s 1(8)), the Race Relations Act 1976 (see s 72(2)) and the Sex Discrimination Act 1975 (see s 85(2)) do apply to the Crown. Most of the provisions of the Employment Rights Act 1996 apply to Crown employees, except those relating to rights to minimum periods of notice, redundancy payments, Sunday working for shop and betting office workers, and rights on insolvency! There are restrictions on the disclosure of information based on grounds of national security, but a Minister can no longer exclude the rights of certain employments on that ground (Employment Relations Act 1999, Sch 8). The provisions of TULR(C)A similarly apply, except the power of the court to make an order against an employer in respect of a failure to ensure that a check-off arrangement excludes a payment to the political fund of a trade union (s 87), failure to comply with a declaration of the Central Arbitration Committee requiring an employer to disclose information for collective bargaining purposes (s 184), and the procedure for consulting with trade unions on redundancies (ss 188–194).

2.58 Members of the staff of the House of Commons have been accorded the same statutory protection in most fields as that enjoyed by Crown employees by virtue of ERA, s 195, with the House of Commons Commission (or Mr Speaker) being the employer. Staff employed by the House of Lords also have a similar full range of protections, except in relation to time off work for public duties connected with political activities and other minor exceptions (see ERA, s 194 and TULR(C)A, s 277).

2.59 However, where a person holds any office or employment under the Crown, which does not constitute a contract of employment, those terms shall be deemed to be such a contract for the purpose of the law relating to the liability in tort of any person who commits an act which induces another to break a contract, or interferes with the perform-ance of any contract (or induces the interference), or consists of a threat that a contract will be broken, or its performance interfered with. In other words, Crown servants will be deemed to have contracts of employment for the purpose of tort liability arising out of industrial action, unless the protections of TULR(C)A, s 219 apply.

D. Armed forces

2.60 Various provisions in the Employment Rights Act apply to members of the naval, military or air forces of the Crown. These include written particulars, antenatal care, suspension on medical and maternity grounds, rights to maternity leave of absence, written reasons for dismissal, and unfair dismissal. The Sex Discrimination Act, Equal Pay Act and Race Relations Act also apply, but nothing is to be rendered unlawful if it was done for the purpose of ensuring combat effectiveness. Although there is a general rule that a member of the Armed Forces should go through service redress procedures before complaining to an employment tribunal, this is no longer always so (see Race Relations (Complaints to Employment Tribunals) (Armed Forces) Regulations 1997, Equal Pay (Complaints to Employment Tribunals) (Armed Forces) Regulations 1997, and Sex Discrimination (Complaints to Employment Tribunals) (Armed Forces) Regulations 1997).

E. Health service employees

2.61 Employees of the National Health Service or Health Trusts have the full range of employment protection rights (now including the right to redundancy payments, see National Health Service and Community Care Act 1990, s 60).

F. Police

2.62 A person is employed in the police service if he serves as a member of any constabu-lary maintained by virtue of an enactment, or in any capacity by virtue of which he has the powers or privileges of a constable. This includes special constables, but not police cadets

(*Wiltshire Police Authority v Wynn*), nor prison officers, who are now 'workers' for the purpose of ERA and TULR(C)A (see Criminal Justice and Public Order Act 1994, s 126(1)). Otherwise, policemen, even though they may be engaged under a contract of employment in the police service, have few employment law rights. Thus, they are not entitled to an itemised pay statement, guarantee pay, rights under the Working Time Regulations, protection for employee representatives, rights in protected disclosure cases, leave for domestic reasons, time off work for public duties, time off work as an employee representative, suspension from work on medical or maternity grounds, right to return to work after childbirth, written reasons for dismissal, and unfair dismissal (except in health and safety cases), even in respect of conduct which occurs when he is not exercising the privileges or powers of a constable (*Home Office v Robinson*). Nor can they claim in respect of unlawful deductions from wages (*Metropolitan Police Comr v Lowrey-Nesbitt*). A policeman does have the right to have written particulars of his terms and conditions of employment, minimum periods of notice, and redundancy pay.

2.63 A policeman is deemed to be employed by the chief constable or the police authority for the purpose of the Sex Discrimination Act (s 17) and the Race Relations Act (s 76A) in respect of any act done by him, or the authority in relation to discrimination in employment, but not acts committed outside the course of employment (*Waters v Metropolitan Police Comr*). The Police (Health and Safety) Act 1997 applies the provisions of the Health and Safety at Work etc Act 1974 (see Police (Health and Safety) Regulations 1999) to holders of the office of constable (ie police, including police cadets), even though they are not employed under a contract of employment. For this purpose, the Chief Officer shall be treated as a corporation sole or distinct juristica (Serious Organised Crime and Police Act 2005, s 158). The Police Federation is to be treated as a recognised trade union for the purpose of appointing and consultation with safety representatives.

2.64 A policeman cannot be dismissed without a proper hearing in accordance with the rules of natural justice (*Ridge v Baldwin*) (see Police Act 1996, ss 84–85), and, in the event of wrongful dismissal, he has the right to be reinstated. Police cadets are persons training to become policemen, and are not employees (*Wiltshire Police Authority v Wynn*).

G. Those employees with special legal status

2.65 Over the years a number of different groups of employees had additionally acquired a special legal status which overrode the existence of their contracts of employment (see, eg *McClelland v Northern Ireland General Health Services Board*), but 'status' relating to a person's occupation is now in decline, and in this sense it may be truly said that in employment law, 'there is a movement from status to contract'. Thus registered dock workers no longer enjoy the special protection which they had under the dock labour scheme (see Dock Work Act 1989), and tenure for all university staff appointed or promoted after 20 November 1987 has been abolished (Education Reform Act 1988, s 203). In respect of university academic staff appointed prior to that date, regard must be had to the terms of their appointment. If these state that dismissal is only possible for 'good cause' then it is not possible to dismiss for any other reason, eg redundancy (*Pearce v University of Aston in Birmingham*).

2.66 On the other hand, there are many groups of workers who have special protections and advantages by virtue of their situation, including pregnant women, trade unionists, safety representatives etc, and in this respect, therefore, 'status' still retains a certain significance.

H. Temporary employees

2.67 A temporary employee has all the rights of any other employee as long as he has the appropriate length of service. An exception here is to be found in ERA, s 106, which states that if an employee is employed on a temporary basis in order to replace a woman who has been given maternity leave or adoption leave or to replace someone suspended on medical grounds, and the latter returns to work, the dismissal of the temporary employee will amount to some other substantial reason for the dismissal, but without prejudice to the rule that the employer must still show that he acted reasonably in dismissing the employee. It is essential that the employee has been informed in writing that the employment will be terminated when the absent employee returns to work. However, since it is unlikely that the temporary employee will have obtained the one-year qualifying period of employment, s 106 has little value. Also, in *Dean v Polytechnic of North London*, Sir John Donaldson thought that the temporary nature of the employment could well amount to 'some other substantial reason' so as to justify a dismissal, though the employment tribunal would have to be convinced that the employer had acted reasonably in the circumstances.

2.68 If a temporary worker is taken on with the expectation that, assuming all goes well, s/he will be made a permanent employee, it is probable that a contract of employment will retrospectively be implied, so as to enable the employee to obtain continuity from the date when the engagement first began. This is so even though the original engagement was made on the clear understanding that no contract of employment came into existence (*Royal National Lifeboat Institution v Bushaway*).

I. Part-time workers

2.69 The Part-time Workers (Prevention of Less Favourable Treatment) Regulations 2000 (as amended) are designed to implement EC Directive 97/81/EEC, and to ensure that part-time workers are to be treated no less favourably, in relation to terms and conditions of employment, than a comparable full-time worker whether or not the latter is on a permanent or fixed-term contract. However, less favourable treatment will not be unlawful if it is objectively justified.

2.70 Hitherto, any rights enjoyed by part-time workers were inextricably bound up with claims of sex discrimination, on the basis that since the majority of part-time workers were women, any less favourable treatment which occurred was because of their sex (eg *R v Secretary of State for Employment, ex p Equal opportunities Commission*). The Part-Time Workers (Prevention of Less Favourable Treatment) Regulations 2000 will undoubtedly go some way towards the elimination of such claims. But the regulations only apply to direct discrimination, which is capable of being justified, whereas the Sex Discrimination Act applies to direct and indirect discrimination, and only the latter is capable of being justified. The part-time worker will always have to find a full-time comparator for the purpose of showing less favourable treatment, whereas under the Sex Discrimination Act, the search is for a person of the opposite sex.

2.71 The regulations apply to 'workers', not just employees. A worker is an individual who has entered into or works under (or worked under):

(a) a contract of employment;

(b) any other contract, whether express or implied, whereby the individual undertakes to do or perform personally any work or services for another party to the contract whose status is not by virtue of the contract that of a client or customer of any profession or business undertaking carried on by the individual.

2.72 In other words, a worker is anyone who works for another person (not necessarily under a contract of employment) other than in a professional or business relationship. Only genuinely self-employed persons are excluded from the regulations.

2.73 A part-time worker is defined as one who is paid wholly or in part by reference to the time he works and, having regard to the custom and practice of the employer in relation to workers employed by the worker's employer under the same type of contract, is not identifiable as a full-time worker. Conversely, a full-time worker is a worker who is paid wholly or in part by reference to the time he works and, having regard to the custom and practice of the employer in relation to workers employed by the worker's employer under the same type of contract, is identifiable as a full-time worker.

2.74 In order to avoid being subjected to less favourable treatment, the part-time worker must be able to compare his treatment with that given to a full-time worker. This involves finding the comparator. A full-time worker will be comparable if:

(a) both workers are employed by the same employer under the same type of contract, and engaged in the same or broadly similar work, having regard, where relevant, to whether they have a similar level of qualifications, skills and experience, and

(b) the full-time worker works or is based at the same establishment as the part-time worker or, where there is no full-time worker working or based at that establishment, works or is based at a different establishment and satisfies the above requirements. A part-time worker, whether permanent or on a fixed-term contract, can compare himself with a full-time permanent worker or worker on a fixed-term contract.

2.75 In *Matthews v Kent & Medway Towns Fire Authority* the House of Lords held that part-time firefighters could compare themselves with whole-time firefighters. The term 'the same type of contract' should not be read in an over precise way, thus allowing employers to take part-timers outside the scope of the regulations by setting different terms for them. Further, to decide whether the work is 'the same or broadly similar', a tribunal should look at the similarities in the work, rather than at the differences.

2.76 A full-time worker who becomes a part-time worker can compare his treatment with the way he was treated when he was full-time. A worker who has had a period of absence (which cannot exceed more than 12 months) and then returns to work at the same job or to a job at the same level but with fewer hours can compare his treatment with the way he was treated prior to his absence.

2.77 A part-time worker has the right not to be treated by his employer less favourably than a full-time worker is treated, as regards the terms of his contract, or be subjected to any detriment by any act, or deliberate failure to act, of his employer (reg 5). However, this right only applies if the treatment is on the ground that the worker is a part-time worker, and cannot be justified on objective grounds. A pro rata principle must be applied unless it is inappropriate to do so. Thus, where a comparable full-time worker is entitled to receive pay or any other benefit, a part-time worker is entitled to receive not less than the proportion of that pay or benefit that the number of his weekly working hours bears to the number of weekly working hours of the comparable full-time worker.

2.78 If a part-time worker considers that he is receiving less favourable treatment than a full-time worker (bearing in mind the pro rata principle) he may request from his employer a written statement giving particulars of the reasons for the treatment. The employer shall provide the statement within 21 days, but if, in subsequent tribunal proceedings, the tribunal finds that the employer deliberately and without reasonable excuse omitted to provide the statement or finds that the written statement is evasive or equivocal, the tribunal may draw any inference which it considers to be just and equitable to draw, including an inference that the employer has infringed the right in question (reg 6).

2.79 It is thus clear that as a matter of principle, part-time workers must be paid the same rate of pay as comparable full-time workers. Contractual sick pay, maternity pay, access to pension schemes, access to training, holiday entitlement, etc must all be no less favourable, on a pro rata basis. Statutory rights, such as time off work (see Chapter 7) apply. Any different treatment, eg on redundancy selection, or severance payments, must be capable of being justified (*Barry v Midland Bank plc*). Thus to select an employee for redundancy because of his part-time status is to treat the employee less favourably, and is likely to be an unfair dismissal (*Hendrickson Europe Ltd v Pipe*). But if a part-time worker works overtime, he will not be entitled to any overtime premium which a full-time worker receives until he works the normal standard working hours of the full-time worker. Also, since a part-time worker is not required to pay national insurance contributions if his or her wages are below the lower earning limit, this may result in the exclusion from the right to receive statutory maternity pay and statutory sick pay.

2.80 A worker has the right not to suffer a detriment because he brought proceedings under the regulations, or requested a written statement, or gave evidence or information in connection with such proceedings brought by any worker, or otherwise did anything under the regulations, or alleged that the employer had infringed the regulations, or refused to forgo a right conferred by the regulations, or because the employer believed that the worker has done or intends to do any of these things. It will also be an automatic unfair dismissal to dismiss an employee (but not a worker) on any of those grounds (reg 7).

2.81 A worker may lodge a complaint to an employment tribunal that his rights under the regulations have been violated (within the usual time limits: see Chapter 20). The burden will be on the employer to identify the grounds for any less favourable treatment or detriment. The tribunal can make the usual awards (declaration, compensation, and recommendation) but not compensation for injury to feelings. The claimant is under a duty to mitigate the loss, and the rules on contributory conduct apply.

2.82 The regulations provide that so far as the police are concerned, the holding of an office of constable or police cadet (otherwise than under a contract of employment) shall be treated as being employment under a contract of employment. The regulations also apply to Crown employment, members of the armed forces, staff of the House of Lords and House of Commons, but not, apparently, to an individual in his capacity as the holder of a judicial office if he is remunerated on a daily fee-paid basis (it is submitted that this latter exclusion is capable of being challenged, there being no such provision which permits such derogation in EC Directive 97/81/EEC).

2.83 A set of guidance notes has been issued to assist in compliance with the regulations. Basically, these suggest that, unless there is some objective justification, part-time workers should receive the same treatment as full-time comparable workers, when considering hourly rates of pay, contractual sick pay and maternity pay (applied pro rata), access to pensions schemes, training, holiday entitlement, contractual maternity and parental leave, career breaks, selection for redundancy, etc. Less favourable treatment may be objectively justified if he intended to achieve a legitimate objective, is necessary to achieve that objective, and it is an appropriate way of doing so,

J. Probationary employees

2.84 The essence of a probationary appointment is that the employer retains the right not to confirm the appointment after a specified period, particularly on the grounds of capability. The majority of the tribunal in *Donn v Greater London Council* thought that the tests which are applied to a probationary employee are not necessarily the same as those which apply to a confirmed appointment, and a decision not to retain a probationer may be justified even though a similar decision made with respect to a fully established employee may not be justified. This view has been followed on a number of occasions (eg *Hamblin v London Borough of Ealing*), for a probationary employee must know that he is on trial, and must therefore establish his suitability for the post. The employer, however, must give the employee a proper opportunity to prove himself, and give a warning if the required standards are not being met (*Post Office v Mughal*). A probationary employee is still an employee, and is therefore entitled to have appropriate guidance and advice (*Inner London Education Authority v Lloyd*).

2.85 Certainly, if the probationary period is less than one year, few problems will arise, but a longer probationary period could create difficulties. In *Weston v University College, Swansea* the applicant was appointed as a lecturer for the probationary period of three years. At the end of this time he was not placed on the permanent staff. It was held that he was entitled to pursue his complaint in respect of his alleged unfair dismissal, for his contract was not for a fixed term. The employer must still show that he acted reasonably in dismissing a probationer, and that the reason was within the statutory requirements, and it is submitted that if a different test is to be applied, the employer must show a valid reason why a probationary period of such a length of time is required in order to establish the suitability of the employee for the post in question.

2.86 If an employee is told that his appointment is subject to a probationary period of a certain length of time, this does not give him a legal right to be employed for that length of time, and the employer may lawfully dismiss him before that period has expired (*Dalgleish v Kew House Farm Ltd*) as long as he is given his correct contractual notice (*Fosca Services (UK) Ltd v Birkett*).

K. Trainees

2.87 Section 230 of ERA defines a contract of employment as 'a contract of service or apprenticeship, whether express or implied, and (if it is express) whether it is oral or in writing'. It is clear, therefore, that a trainee can be employed under a contract of employment, and this includes, for example, an articled clerk employed by a solicitor (*Oliver v JP Malnick & Co*). However, not all such trainees are so employed. In *Wiltshire Police Authority v Wynn*, it was held that police cadets are not employees, but persons who are training to become policemen. During their training, even though they are being paid, they are not employed under a contract of employment. Similarly, in *Daley v Allied Suppliers Ltd* a young black girl was working on a Youth Opportunities scheme operated by the respondents. She alleged that she had been discriminated against on the ground of race, but it was held that the Race Relations Act was not applicable, as she was not a person employed within the meaning of s 4 and s 78 of the Act.

2.88 Indeed, the fact that young people on work experience courses are not employees has caused some concern, particularly in relation to their health and safety, for many of the duties owed by an employer are only owed to employees. Consequently the Health and Safety (Training for Employment) Regulations 1990 apply the provisions of the Health and Safety at Work etc Act 1974 to youth trainees as if they were employees.

2.89 A youth training scheme is a tripartite relationship between the individual, the employer and the training provider. Generally, the employer agrees to employ the trainee for the term of the training, and although the training is provided by a third party, the employer has somewhat wider responsibilities to the trainee than to an ordinary employee. Such arrangements, generally referred to as 'Modern Apprenticeship Agreements', are capable of amounting to a traditional contract of apprenticeship, because they secure wages for the apprentice during the period of apprenticeship, they provide training to enable the apprentice to obtain skills and give status in the labour market on successful completion of the training (*Flett v Matheson*).

L. Civil partnerships

2.90 A civil partnership is a relationship which has been entered into by two persons of the same sex which is formed when they register as civil partners under the provisions of the Civil Partnership Act 2004. So far as the law of employment is concerned, a civil partnership is to be treated in the same way and to the same extent as a married relationship. Hence, the provisions in s 3 of the Sex Discrimination Act prohibiting unlawful discrimination against married persons apply equally to persons who have formed a civil partnership. Provisions in the Paternity and Adoption Leave Regulations, Statutory Maternity Pay Regulations, Flexible Working (Eligibility etc) Regulations and the Employment Equality (Sexual Orientation) Regulations have also been amended to apply to persons who have entered into a civil partnership in the same manner as they apply to married persons (Civil Partnership Act 2004 (Amendments to Subordinate Legislation) Order 2005).

M. Apprentices

2.91 A contract of apprenticeship is an agreement whereby the apprentice binds himself to his employer in order to learn a trade, and the employer on his part agrees to teach and instruct him. The contract must be in writing, signed by the parties, and cannot be terminated by the employer except for grave misconduct (such as theft) or a refusal to attend to his duties. However, it appears that there is no longer any need for a formal apprenticeship agreement to be entered into; to give a statement of terms and conditions which described a person as an 'apprentice sheet metal worker' was sufficient to create a contract of apprenticeship in *Wallace v C A Roofing Services Ltd*, and it was not possible to terminate that contract on grounds of redundancy. An apprentice who is wrongfully dismissed may claim by way of damages not only his immediate loss, but a sum representing the value of his loss of future prospects as a qualified person (*Dunk v George Waller & Son Ltd*). Also, since an employer is, in one sense, *in loco parentis* to an apprentice, a certain latitude must be shown in respect of minor lapses in conduct. For example, in *Shortland v Chantrill*, an apprentice was criticised by a managing director about his work, and he retorted 'You couldn't have done any fucking better'. For this, he was dismissed. It was held that the dismissal was unfair; one isolated step of impudence did not warrant the termination of an apprenticeship which had only ten months to run.

2.92 An apprentice is employed for the duration of the apprenticeship, and may not be dismissed until it expires (other than for good cause). An apprenticeship differs from a contract of employment in that it is not terminable on notice, and, if there are provisions in the agreement which are inconsistent with the employer's normal terms and conditions of employment, it is the apprenticeship agreement which must prevail. In particular, an employer cannot dismiss an apprentice for reason of redundancy (*Whitely v Marton Electrical Ltd*).

2.93 But although a contract of apprenticeship is essentially a common law concept, with the old (ie pre-1971) remedies still applying, an apprentice is also within the protection of the new laws. This could cause a certain conflict. For example, in *Finch v Betabake (Anglia) Ltd* the claimant was an apprentice motor mechanic. The employers received a report from an ophthalmic surgeon that the apprentice could not continue to work at that job without undue danger to himself and to other employees. Consequently, he was dismissed. It was held that the fairness of the dismissal had to be determined under ERA, s 98(4) (see Chapter 17). The fact that the employers may have been in breach of the apprenticeship agreement did not mean that the dismissal was unfair. The circumstances which could justify the dismissal of an apprentice were very limited, but in the instant case, the employers acted fairly and reasonably.

2.94 If, on the expiry of an apprenticeship agreement, the apprentice is not re-employed, he has not been dismissed for reason of redundancy (*North East Coast Shiprepairers v Secretary of State for Employment*).

N. Those under the age of 18

Minors

2.95 A contract of employment entered into by a minor (ie a person under the age of 18) is a valid agreement provided that on the whole it is substantially for his benefit.

Otherwise, it will be void. Even though the contract contains terms which are onerous or detrimental to his interests, one must look at the effect of the whole agreement. In *De Francesco v Barnum* a 14-year-old girl bound herself by an apprenticeship deed to the claimant in order to become a professional dancer. She agreed not to marry during this time, and to perform engagements only with the plaintiff's permission. The claimant was under no obligation to provide engagements, but when he did, the pay was somewhat ungenerous. It was held that the deed was void, for it was totally unreasonable, and was not in the interests of the girl. In contrast, we can consider *Clements v London and North-Western Rly Co*, where a boy entered into the defendants' employment on terms which excluded his right to sue under the Employers' Liability Act 1880, in respect of injuries suffered during his employment. Instead, he was covered by the company's own insurance scheme, which had a wider range of protection, though the benefits were somewhat lower than the State scheme. It was held that on the whole the contract was to his advantage and was therefore binding.

2.96 Cases on this subject illustrate somewhat graphically the changing social scene. In *Denmark Productions Ltd v Boscobel Productions Ltd* a contract by four infant members of a pop group to employ a manager was held to be binding, and in *Chaplin v Leslie Frewin (Publishers) Ltd* the son of a famous film star contracted to assign to a firm of publishers a book containing his life story. This too, was held to be binding, as it conferred a financial benefit on him.

Young persons

2.97 A young person is any person who has not attained the age of 18, and therefore includes children of any age. This is not to be confused with a young worker (a term used, for example, in the Working Time Regulations 1998), which refers to a person who has attained the age of 15 but not the age of 18 and who is over compulsory school age.

2.98 Special protection is given to young persons by the Management of Health and Safety at Work Regulations 1999. Before employing a young person, the employer must make a risk assessment, taking into account his inexperience, lack of awareness of risks and immaturity, the fitting and layout of the workplace, exposure to physical, biological and chemical agents, the way work equipment is handled, the organisation of the processes, the extent to which health and safety training is provided, and the risks from certain dangerous processes. Employers must ensure that young persons are protected at work from any risks to their health and safety which are a consequence of their lack of experience, absence of awareness of risks and lack of maturity. Special provision has been made for young workers in the Working Time Regulations 1998 (see para 7.47).

Children

2.99 The Children (Protection at Work) Regulations 1998–2000 deal with the employment of children below the minimum school leaving age, and amend the provisions of the Children and Young Persons Acts 1933 and 1963 and the Children and Young Persons (Scotland) Act 1937, in order to implement the requirements of Directive 94/33/EC on the Protection of Young Persons at Work.

The general principle is that a child under the age of 14 may not be employed in any work, other than as an employee of his parent or guardian in light agricultural work or horticultural work on an occasional basis. However, children over the age of 13 may be employed in categories of light work specified in local authorities' byelaws. Light work is defined as being work which does not jeopardise a child's safety, health, development, attendance at school or participation in work experience. Children have the right to have a two-week break from any employment in school holidays. Local authorities have the power to prohibit the employment of children who are employed in a manner which may be prejudicial to their health, or render them unfit to obtain the benefit of full-time education, and they may impose restrictions on such employment (Education Act 1996, s 559).

The above legislation, together with the Children (Performances) Regulations 1968 extend controls on the employment of children in performances, including sport, advertising and modelling. A licence may be obtained from any justice of the peace if it is proposed to take a child abroad for these purposes.

Further information about the new rules can be obtained from the education welfare office of a local education authority. Local authorities have the power to prohibit the employment of children who are employed in a manner which may be prejudicial to their health, or render them unfit to obtain the benefit of full-time education, and they may also impose restrictions on such employment (Education Act 1996, s 559). A child may not be employed in an industrial undertaking or on a sea-going boat, unless the undertaking or boat is one in which only members of the child's family are employed (Employment of Women, Young Persons, and Children Act 1920, ss 1–3). A child may not be employed in a factory (Education Act 1918, s 14) nor employed underground in a mine, except for the purpose of receiving prescribed instruction (Mines and Quarries Act 1954, s 124). A child may not be required to lift, carry or move anything so heavy as to be likely to cause injury.

2.100 School children may be employed for work experience from the beginning of the school term preceding the start of the school year in which they become entitled to leave school (Education (Work Experience) Act 1973, s 1, as amended).

O. Domestic servants

2.101 A domestic servant is an employee, and provided she has the requisite periods of continuous employment, may claim appropriate statutory rights. She may claim redundancy payment, for employment in a private household is deemed to be a business like any other. However, this does not apply if she is a close relative of the employer (see para 18.60). Nor do the special rules relating to the transfer of a business apply, except where the head of the household dies, for here there may be a transfer to the new head of the household for redundancy purposes (see ERA, s 175 and *Ranger v Brown*). The Race Relations Act 1976 does apply to employment for the purpose of a private household, but under the Sex Discrimination Act 1975 (as amended in 1986) the sex of a person may be 'a genuine occupational qualification' (see para 4.78) if the employment is in a private home.

P. Foreign employees

2.102 A person who is not a national of a member state of the European Economic Area (ie European Union, Iceland, Liechtenstein and Norway), or who is not a Commonwealth citizen with the right of abode, must obtain the necessary permission to take up employment in the United Kingdom, otherwise the employment will be illegal. The Immigration Rules currently in force detail a number of different categories of workers who may be granted entry clearance to enter this country for specified periods of time, with or without work permits, and the conditions which will be attached thereto if they wish to take up employment. A consideration of these matters is outside the scope of this book, but information can be obtained from either the Home Office or the Overseas Labour Services section of the Department of Education and Employment.

2.103 The illegality of the employment has three potential consequences. In the first place, a person who is employed under an illegal contract cannot acquire any legal rights under that contract. Thus he will have no employment protection rights at all (*Sharma v Hindu Temple*, but see para 3.6). Additionally, if the contract was legal at one time, periods when the contract became illegal will not count towards continuity of employment, and will also break continuity (*Bamgbose v Royal Star and Garter Home*).

2.104 Second, the Immigration, Asylum and Nationality Act 2006, s 15 provides that the Secretary of State may apply for a penalty notice against a person who employs an adult who is subject to immigration control, and:

(a) who has not been granted leave to enter or remain in the United Kingdom, or

(b) whose leave to enter or remain has expired, or is invalid, or

(c) who is subject to a condition prohibiting employment.

The amount of the penalty notice will be prescribed by regulations. The employer may object to the penalty notice, and the Secretary of State may cancel, reduce, increase or confirm it. In the alternative, an appeal against the penalty notice may be made to a county court (or sheriff's court).

The Secretary of State will issue a Code of Practice, specifying the factors to be considered in determining the amount of the penalty notice. The Code will also give advice on how to avoid a penalty under s 15, or an offence under s 21, without contravening the Race Relations Act.

Third, it is also a criminal offence to employ an adult who is subject to the above immigration controls, an offence punishable on indictment with a maximum of two years' imprisonment, or a fine, or both, and on summary conviction to 12 months' imprisonment (six months in Scotland) or a fine, or both (s 21). Where an offence is committed by a body corporate, any director, manager, secretary or similar officer (or person purporting to act as such) will be jointly liable, if the offence was committed with his consent, or connivance, or attributable to any neglect on his part. The above offence does not apply if the employee was an asylum seeker who has been given written permission to work, or an asylum seeker who had permission to work before appealing against a refusal to grant asylum. It will be a defence for the employer to show that before the employment began, he was shown a document which related to the employee, and which was of a description specified in an order made by the Secretary of State. The documents which are acceptable are set out in the Immigration (Restrictions on Employment) Order 2004, and basically consist of secure documents, which are either a UK or EEA passport, national identity card or UK residence permit, or the originals of certain other documents which will confirm that the holder is entitled to take the employment in question. A copy of the document must be kept for the duration of the employment and for a further six months after it ends.

2.105 The purpose behind the legislation was to try to limit the number of foreign nationals working here illegally. However, the requirement that before permitting a person to commence employment, the employer must ask certain questions and seek confirmation of nationality or status raises issues of race discrimination (*Dhatt v McDonalds Hamburgers Ltd*). The CRE has issued guidelines for employers which contain a number of 'good practice recommendations'.

2.106 If the employment of a foreign worker is perfectly legal, then he will have all the employment protection rights which are applicable to his case, in the same manner as a UK or EU national, apart from being able to obtain employment in certain official posts.

Q. Posted workers

2.107 A posted worker is a worker who is sent from one EU member state to another state on a temporary basis in order to carry out some work in that other state. EC Directive 96/71/EC is designed to ensure that employers do not acquire a competitive edge by paying workers less favourable terms and conditions than the worker would otherwise earn according to the laws and practices in that other member state. They can, however, retain any terms and conditions which are more favourable under their existing contracts. It was not necessary for the UK to pass specific legislation to implement the Directive, although various minor amendments were made to a number of statutes which had previously limited the application of employment rights to persons who ordinarily work in the United Kingdom. With the removal of those limits, posted workers have the full range of appropriate rights.

R. Working abroad

2.108 An employee may be required to work outside the United Kingdom either permanently or on a temporary basis. The requirement will stem from an express term of the contract of employment, or by virtue of an implied term, when it is 'obvious' from the nature of the job and/or the employer's business.

2.109 If the employee is required to work outside the United Kingdom for more than one month, then, in addition to the matters which need to be contained in the written statement of terms and conditions given under ERA, s 1, the statement must:

(a) state the period for which the employee is to work outside the United Kingdom;

(b) state the currency in which remuneration is to be paid;

(c) give details of any additional remuneration paid and/or any extra benefits provided by reason of the requirement to work outside the United Kingdom; and

(d) specify any terms and conditions relating to the employee's return to the United Kingdom (s 1(4)(k)).

These details must be provided before the employee leaves the United Kingdom.

2.110 The parties can decide for themselves whether the contract will be governed by UK law or by the law of another country, although this cannot deprive the employee of the right to claim under the laws of the country in which he works. Otherwise the Contract (Applicable Law) Act 1990 provides that the contract will be governed by the law of the country in which the employee habitually carries out his duties. If this cannot be ascertained with certainty, the law to be applied will be the law of the country in which the employer's business is situated. Further, the Civil Jurisdiction and Judgments Act 1982 provides that if the employer is domiciled in a member state of the European Union, he can be sued in the courts of that state or in the courts of the state where the employee habitually carries out his work.

2.111 Originally, ERA, s 196 excluded employees who 'ordinarily work outside the United Kingdom' from various employment rights, including the right not to be unfairly dismissed. However, that provision was repealed in 1999, and not replaced, with the result that some confusion remained in respect of such rights. The courts then devised various tests to determine whether UK courts and tribunals had jurisdiction to hear claims under UK law, including the 'base' test (*Todd v British Midlands Airways Ltd*) and the 'substantial connection' test (*Jackson v Ghost Ltd*), but these were rejected by the House of Lords in *Serco Ltd v Lawson* (see para 17.4). It appears from this case that there are three principal factors which must be taken into account. These are (a) whether the employer is based in the United Kingdom; (b) whether the employee is working abroad for the purpose of a business in the United Kingdom, and (c) whether the employee is employed by an employer who is operating within an extra-territorial enclave of a foreign country.

2.112 Different rules apply to discrimination cases. The employment provisions of the Race Relations Act apply in respect of discrimination on grounds of colour, race, nationality, or ethnic or national origins to an employee if he does his work wholly or partly in Great Britain. Further, these provisions apply to a case involving discrimination on grounds of race, or ethnic or national origins, or harassment where the employee does his work wholly outside Great Britain, and:

(a) the employer has a place of business at an establishment in Great Britain;

(b) the work is for the purpose of the business carried on at that establishment; and

(c) the employee is ordinarily resident in Great Britain at the time when he applies for or is offered the employment, or at any time during the employment (s 8).

Identical provisions can be found in the Disability Discrimination Act (s 68), the Employment Equality (Religion or Belief) Regulations 2003 (reg 9), the Employment Equality (Sexual Orientation) Regulations 2003 (reg 9), and the Employment Equality (Sex Discrimination) Regulations 2005 (reg 11). However, no such provisions are to be found in equal pay cases, and if an employee works wholly outside Great Britain, such claims cannot succeed in this country (*Bryant v Foreign and Commonwealth Office*).

2.113 Any period spent working abroad will count for the purpose of computing the period of continuous employment (ERA, s 215(1)), but will only count for redundancy purposes if national insurance contributions are made in respect of such periods (ERA, s 215(4)). However, weeks of overseas employment do not break continuity for redundancy purposes, but the start of any such period will be postponed by seven days for each week that does not thus count.

2.114 There is no implied term that an employer will provide personal accident insurance for the benefit of a person who is required to work abroad. Nor is the employer obliged to give specific advice on special risks, or to advise the employee to take out his own personal accident insurance (*Reid v Rush & Tompkins Group plc,* and see para 10.33). Nor can a duty in tort be imposed to expand contractual duties.

S. Offshore employment

2.115 Offshore employment is defined as employment for the purposes of activities: (a) in the territorial waters of the United Kingdom; or (b) connected with the exploration of the seabed or subsoil, or the exploration of their natural resources, in the United Kingdom sector of the continental shelf; or (c) connected with the exploration or exploitation, in a foreign sector of the continental shelf, of a cross-boundary petroleum field (ERA, s 201; TULR(C)A, s 287).

2.116 Orders have been made extending the provisions of various employment legislation to offshore employment, including the Employment Rights Act 1996 (except time off work for public duties), Sex Discrimination and Race Relations Acts, Equal Pay Act 1970, National Minimum Wage Act 1998 and Trade Union and Labour Relations (Consolidation) Act 1992. Employment in the Frigg Gas Field comes within the scope of the various Acts if the employer is a British company, or has a place of business in Great Britain from which the activities are directed.

T. Retainers

2.117 A person who is retained for employment is not an employee merely because he is 'on call' even though he is paid during that time. Employment involves work or other activity carried out for the employer. In *Suffolk County Council v Secretary of State for the Environment* it was held that a retained fireman, who was permanently on call, was not an employee, for a contractual obligation to remain on call within a prescribed area did not constitute employment. His hours of work only began when he was on duty following a call.

However, a different result was reached in *British Nursing Association v Inland Revenue (National Minimum Wage Compliance Team)*, where the employers provided a 'bank' of nurses for emergency duties. A booking system operated a 24-hour service. During the day, nurses could be contacted at the employer's premises, but at night they had to be contacted at their homes. The National Minimum Wage Compliance Team took the view that those nurses engaged on the night shift were entitled to a minimum hourly rate for all hours they were on duty, but the employers argued that the nurses were not actually working during their shift. Although they were required to be available to take telephone calls, they could spend their shift doing other activities, such as watching television or reading, etc. It was held that the nurses were entitled to the national minimum wage for all the hours they were on duty. They had to hold themselves ready to answer the telephone, they could not pick and choose the times at which they had to answer the telephone, and there was a continuing obligation throughout the night to be available.

Types of contracts of employment

A. Fixed-term contracts

2.118 A fixed-term contract is a contract of employment for a specified period of time, ie, with a defined beginning and a defined end (*Wiltshire County Council v National Association of Teachers in Further and Higher Education and Guy*). As a general rule, such a contract cannot be terminated before its expiry date except for gross misconduct or by mutual agreement (*Lyritzis v Inmarsat*). However, a contract can still be for a fixed term if it contains within it a provision enabling either side to terminate it on giving notice before the term expires (*Allen v National Australia Group Europe Ltd*). A contract of apprenticeship is a classic example of a fixed-term contract (*Wallace v CA Roofing Services Ltd*).

The Fixed-term Employees (Prevention of Less Favourable) Treatment Regulations 2002

2.119 These regulations implement the Fixed-term Workers Directive (1999/70/EC). The regulations apply to employees (not workers) and are designed to introduce the principle of non-discrimination between those working on fixed-term contracts and comparators who are permanent employees. The main beneficiaries of the regulations will be employees who are employed in order to cover for employees who are on statutory periods of absence (maternity leave, adoption leave, parental leave, etc), those employed in periods of peak demand, those who are employed on contracts to carry out specific tasks, eg setting up a database, teachers in higher education, senior staff employed in the health service, etc.

2.120 A fixed-term contract is defined as being a contract of employment that, under its provisions determining how it will terminate in the normal course, will terminate (a) on the expiry of a specific term, or (b) on the completion of a particular task, or (c) on the occurrence or non-occurrence of any specific event other than the attainment by the employee of any normal and bona fide retiring age.

2.121 The regulations do not apply to agency workers, or to those working under a contract of apprenticeship, or on government training schemes, or doing work experience not exceeding one year as part of a higher education course.

2.122 The regulations do not provide for permanent employees to have the right to compare themselves with fixed-term employees, and so it is possible to treat the latter more favourably than the former, provided, of course, that no other aspect of employment law is infringed, such as sex discrimination etc.

Terms not less favourable

2.123 A fixed-term employee has the right not to be treated by his employer less favourably than a comparable permanent employee with regard to the terms of the contract, including any period of service qualification relation to a particular condition of service, the opportunity to receive training, or the opportunity to secure permanent employment in the establishment. He will also have the right not to suffer any other detriment by any act (or deliberate failure to act) of his employer. However, this right only applies if the treatment in question is on the ground that the employee is a fixed-term employee, and the treatment is not justified on objective grounds. The comparable permanent employee must be employed by the same employer at the same establishment (other locations can be considered if there is no-one appropriate at the same establishment) and be an employee who is engaged on the same or broadly similar work, having regard to whether they have a similar level of qualifications and skills. A hypothetical comparator will not suffice. An employee is not a comparable permanent employee if his employment has ceased.

2.124 Terms which must be no less favourable include pay and pensions. Where appropriate, a 'pro rata' principle is to be applied, which means that the fixed-term employee is entitled to such proportions of pay or other benefits as is reasonable bearing in mind the length of his contract of employment and the basis on which pay or other benefits is offered. An employee on a fixed-term contract of three months or less has the right to receive statutory sick pay, and, after one month's continuous employment is entitled to a week's notice if the contract is terminated, and also has the right to receive guarantee payment and payment on medical suspension. But the non-renewal of a fixed term contract does not, by itself, amount to less favourable treatment (*Department for Work and Pensions v Webby*).

2.125 It is, however, possible to justify the unequal treatment on objective grounds. According to a DTI Guide to the Regulations, in order to be objectively justified, the unequal treatment should be aimed at achieving a legitimate business objective, be necessary to achieve that objective, and be an appropriate way of achieving it. If the treatment by an employer of a fixed-term employee is less favourable than the treatment meted out to a comparable permanent employee, it will amount to objective justification if, taken as a whole, the terms and conditions of a fixed-term employee are at least as favourable as those which apply to a comparable permanent employee. Thus it is permissible to take a 'package' approach, as opposed to a term-by-term approach (as in equal pay cases). Higher salaries, or more holidays, etc can compensate for the lack of other benefits such as pensions, provided that the package as a whole is equivalent to or better than that of a permanent employee.

2.126 A fixed-term employee has the right to be informed of any permanent suitable vacancies, and may bring a claim in respect of the employer's failure to do so within three months from the date on which other individuals, whether employees or not, were informed of the vacancy.

The four-year rule and other rights

2.127 Where there is a fixed-term contract or a succession of such contracts which result in the employee being employed for four years or more, the contract will be deemed to be a contract of indefinite duration (unless there is objective justification when the contract was made or renewed), and the minimum period of notice provisions of ERA, ss 86–91 will apply (see para 15.4). He also has the right to request a written statement from his employer either giving reasons why his contract remains fixed-term beyond the four-year limitation period, or confirming that it has become open-ended.

2.128 However, there are two ways in which the four-year rule is restricted. The first is that in determining whether or not a fixed-term employee has been continuously employed, the definition of continuous employment is that contained in ERA, ss 210–219 (see Chapter 13). In particular, if a week's absence from work is not covered by s 212(3) (see para 13.18) continuity of employment will be broken. Thus if there is a gap of more than one week between successive fixed-term contracts, such contracts cannot be turned into a permanent contract under the four-year rule. The situation revealed in *Booth v United States of America* (see para 13.2) remains unaffected. The second limitation is that when computing the four-year period, any period of continuous employment falling before 10 July 2002 is to be disregarded.

2.129 The requirement which permits an employee to opt out of his right to receive a redundancy payment is repealed, although contracts which were in force prior to the commencement of the regulations are able to retain this waiver during their term (see para 18.60).

2.130 A fixed-term employee will have the right to request in writing from his employer a written statement giving particulars of the reasons for any less favourable treatment, and the employer must reply within 21 days of the request. An identical right exists for an employee who considers that his contract is one of indefinite duration under the four-year rule (above) to make a similar request for confirmation that the contract is to be so regarded. There is no remedy if the employer fails to comply with either of these requests, but if, in proceedings before an employment tribunal to enforce the fixed-term employee's rights under the regulations, it is shown that the employer deliberately and without reasonable excuse omitted to provide the written statement, or that it was evasive or equivocal, the tribunal may draw an inference that the employer has infringed the right in question. If an employee considers that he is a permanent employee under the four-year rule, he may present an application to an employment tribunal for a declaration to that effect, but he cannot do so unless he has previously requested a statement from his employer, and the employer has failed to provide one. He must also still be employed by the employer.

2.131 An employee has the right not to suffer a detriment, or be dismissed, because he did an act under the regulations, and may also bring a claim alleging unequal treatment contrary to the regulations. The claim must be brought within three months of the alleged infringement, although the tribunal can consider a complaint which is out of time if it considers that it is just and equitable to do so. If the employment tribunal finds in his favour, it may make a declaration as to the rights of the complainant and the employer, award compensation, and make a recommendation that the employer takes steps to obviate or reduce the adverse affects complained of. The compensation award shall be that which the tribunal considers to be just and equitable, and may include the loss of benefits and reasonable expenses. However, if the claim is based on less favourable treatment, there can be no award in respect of injured feelings.

There are two further significant points to bear in mind when dealing with a fixed-term contract.

Continuity rules

2.132 In respect of a fixed-term contract of short duration, the normal continuity rules apply on renewal (see Chapter 13), including the statutory presumption in favour of continuity (ERA, s 210(5)). This may enable an employee whose employment was intended to be temporary to obtain various employment protection rights in appropriate circumstances. The normal rules about giving statutory notice do not apply when the contract period expires, except where an employee has been employed under a fixed-term contract of one month or less, and has actually been employed for three months or more (ERA, s 86(4)).

Expiry of the fixed term

2.133 If a fixed-term contract is not renewed on expiry, that will not amount to a dismissal at common law, because the contract has been terminated automatically by effluxion of time. However, non-renewal under the same contract will be a dismissal for the purpose of ERA. Whether the dismissal was fair or unfair will be determined by whether or not the employer can show that he acted reasonably in not renewing the contract. If the contract is terminated prior to the expiry of the fixed term, the employee will have the normal rights in respect of breach of contract (see Chapter 15), and the employer will be liable to pay the employee for the rest of the term, subject to the employee's duty to mitigate against his loss. He will also have the right to claim unfair dismissal, provided he has been employed for the requisite period of continuous employment. However, if the contract is terminated by mutual agreement, no dismissal has taken place (*Lyritzis v Inmarsat*), although a mutual acknowledgement that the contract will terminate on the fixed date will be a dismissal nonetheless (*Thames Television v Wallis*). Nor will there be a dismissal for redundancy payment purposes if the employee is employed under a new contract which takes effect within four weeks of the expiry of the old (ERA, s 138(1)). A dismissal will take place if the new contract is substantially different from the old (ERA, s 138(2–6)), but the right to obtain a redundancy payment will be lost if the employee unreasonably refuses an offer on the same or different terms (ERA, s 141).

B. Flexible working arrangements (ERA, ss 80F–80I)

2.134 In recent years there appears to have developed a greater interest in finding alternatives to conventional full-time and part-time employment, partly with a view to trying to avoid legal responsibilities (which has had a very limited success) but mainly due to the genuine need of employers and employees for new-style flexible working arrangements, which can, in certain circumstances, be commercially advantageous to both sides. Flexitime itself has had a long history, but new arrangements, such as job-sharing, performance contracts, zero hours contracts, annualised hours contracts, home-working, etc, are now being used with greater frequency. However, because statutory rules were not designed to deal with these arrangements, legal disputes arising out of them had to be dealt with by the use of a certain amount of judicial creativity (see *Chief Constable of Avon and Somerset v Chew*).

The Employment Act 2002

2.135 The Employment Act 2002 gave a new right for an employee to request flexible working arrangements, by inserting new ss 80F–80I into the Employment Rights Act 1996. However, there is no actual right to work flexibly. The Act only lays down a procedure whereby an application for flexible working may be made to an employer, which must be considered fairly by him. A remedy may only arise on an application to an employment tribunal if it can be shown that the employer has failed to follow the statutory procedure, or has based his decision on incorrect facts. The relevant rules are laid down in the Flexible Working (Procedural Requirements) Regulations 2002, and the Flexible Working (Eligibility, Complaints and Remedies) Regulations 2002.

Application for flexible working

2.136 The application may be made by a 'qualifying employee' ie an employee:

(a) who has been continuously employed for not less than 26 weeks;

(b) is the mother, father, adopter, guardian or foster parent of a child, or who is married to or the partner of such a person;

(c) has or expects to have responsibility for the upbringing of that child.

(The Work and Families Act 2006 will extend the right to apply for flexible working to employees who care for sick or elderly relatives).

2.137 The application must be made before the fourteenth day before the day on which the child reaches the age of six or, if the child is disabled, eighteen.
The application may relate to a change of:

(a) the hours the employee is required to work;

(b) the times the employee is required to work;

(c) the place where the employee is required to work;

(d) such other aspects of the employee's terms and conditions of employment as may be specified in regulations.

2.138 The application, which must be in writing, must specify the change applied for, the date from which the proposed change will be effective, explain what effect, if any, the change will have on the employer's business and how such effect may be dealt with, and explain how the employee meets the requirements in relation to the child.

2.139 If the employer agrees to the application, he will notify the employee of the contract variation agreed to, and the date from which the variation is to take effect. Otherwise, he must hold a meeting with the employee within 28 days to discuss the matter. The time and place of the meeting must be convenient to both parties. The employer must give notice of his decision within 14 days. If the application is accepted, it will operate as a variation of the terms and conditions of employment of the employee's contract, which will be binding until and unless there is a further agreed variation. If the application is refused the employer must state his reasons, and provide for a right of appeal, which must be heard within 14 days, and a decision given within a further 14 days. The employee has the right to be accompanied at the original hearing and the appeal hearing by a fellow employee, who may address the hearing and confer with the employee. The companion is entitled to take time off work with pay for this purpose, and there are the usual sanctions if the employer fails to permit a companion to attend the hearing or the appeal hearing.

2.140 The employer will be under no duty to consider the application where the employee notifies him that it has been withdrawn, or if the employee fails without reasonable cause to attend a meeting more than once, or refuses without reasonable cause to provide the employer with further information needed in order to assess whether the contract should be varied.

2.141 The employer may refuse the request only for one of the following reasons:

(a) the burden of additional costs;

(b) the detrimental effect on ability to meet customer demand;

(c) the inability to re-organise work among existing staff;

(d) the inability to recruit additional staff;

(e) the detrimental impact on quality;

(f) the detrimental impact on performance;

(g) the lack of work during the periods when the employee proposes to work;

(h) the planned structural changes;

(i) other grounds which the Secretary of State may specify from time to time.

2.142 If the employer and employee are unable to reach an amicable agreement on the application for flexible working, then, if both parties agree, resort may be had to the ACAS Arbitration Scheme (see para 1.12). By so doing, the employee waives the right to present a claim to an employment tribunal. The decision of the arbitrator will be final. Otherwise, the employee may make a claim to an employment tribunal, on the ground that the employer has failed to comply with the procedural requirements as set out in the regulations, or has rejected the application on a ground that is not one of the above permitted reasons for refusal, or has based his decision to reject the application on incorrect facts. It should be noted that the tribunal's role is merely to verify whether the employer has followed the correct procedure and to examine any disputed facts. The tribunal does not have the power to question the commercial validity of the employer's decision, nor can it substitute its own judgment on the business reasons for those of the employer. But the tribunal is entitled to look at the ground asserted by the employer as the reason why he did not grant the application, and to ascertain if it was factually correct. This may involve an examination of the evidence as to the circumstances surrounding the application, the effect of granting it, whether there would be any potential disruption, and the attitude of customers and other members of staff (*Commotion Ltd v Rutty*). If it finds the complaint to be well-founded, the tribunal must make a declaration, and may make an order requiring the employer to reconsider the application. An award of compensation may be made, of such amount as the tribunal thinks just and equitable, up to a maximum of eight weeks' pay (not capped). The employee may also bring a complaint if there is a breach of his right to be accompanied at the hearing or the appeal hearing, for which the remedy is an award of compensation up to a maximum of two weeks' pay (subject to the statutory maximum).

2.143 There is the usual protection against an employee suffering a detriment because an application for flexible working was made, and it will be automatically unfair to dismiss an employee for a reason relating to any such application.

C. Secondment of employees

2.144 Occasionally, an employer will second an employee to another employer, either for a specific task or for a specific period of time. This arrangement can give rise to a number of legal problems, eg: (a) which employer is to accept liability if the seconded employee injures a third party; (b) which employer will be liable if the employee suffers an injury; and (c) the status of the seconded employee during the period of secondment and after it has concluded.

Liability if the seconded employee injures a third party

2.145 As a general principle, it can be stated that if a skilled employee, together with complex or valuable machinery, is loaned to another employer, the original employer will still be liable if the employee's actions cause injury or damage to a third party. For example, in *Mersey Docks and Harbour Board v Coggins & Griffiths (Liverpool) Ltd*) the harbour board loaned a crane and driver to a firm of stevedores, the latter being responsible for paying the driver's wages. Because of the driver's negligence, there was an accident. It was held that the harbour board was the driver's employer for the purpose of being held vicariously liable for the driver's negligence, for they had failed to discharge the burden of showing that the driver was no longer their employee.

2.146 A contrary conclusion was reached in *Arthur White (Contractors) Ltd v Tarmac Civil Engineering Ltd*, where a crane and driver were hired out. Under the contract, which was the standard form used in the plant hire industry, the driver was stated to be under the direction and control of the hirer, and for all purposes was to be regarded as the employee of the hirer. It was held that as between the main employer and the hirer, the latter was liable for the damage which resulted from an accident due to the driver's negligence. In other words, the two employers had, as between themselves, come to a contractual arrangement as to their respective legal liability (see also *Hawley v Luminar Leisure Ltd*, para 10.98).

2.147 But dual vicarious liability is legally permissible. The idea that when an employee is seconded to work for another employer, liability for his negligent act must rest with one employer or the other is a notion with no intrinsic justification. The core question is, who is entitled, or indeed obliged, to give orders as to how the work should be done or not done? If there is evidence of some form of dual control, then it would not be impossible to hold that both employers should share liability equally (*Viasystems (Tyneside) Ltd v Thermal Transfers (Northern) Ltd*).

Liability if the seconded employee injures himself

2.148 If the seconded employee is injured, there is a strong likelihood that it will be the temporary employer who will be responsible. In *Garrard v AE Southey & Co and Standard Telephones and Cables Ltd* the claimant was loaned by his employers (the first defendants) to the second defendants to carry out some electrical work. The foreman of the second defendants not only told the claimant what to do but also specifically controlled the way he was to do his work. The claimant was injured, and sued both employers for common law negligence. It was held that the temporary employer was liable, as they were his employer for the purpose of ensuring his safety at work. The court drew a distinction between those cases where a complicated piece of equipment and/or a skilled employee was loaned, and where an unskilled or semi-skilled workman is loaned on his own. In the former case, it may be easier to infer that the general employer does not intend to part with control over a complex and valuable piece of machinery, but if labour only is loaned, it is easier to infer the transfer of the rights of the general employer to the temporary employer.

Status of the seconded worker during, and after, the period of employment

2.149 A third problem concerns the status of the employee who has been seconded. Is he an employee of the original employer, or of the employer to whom he has been seconded? What are his continuity rights if either employer terminates the contract? Is there an impact on the employment contract by virtue of the Transfer of Undertakings (Protection of Employment) Regulations? What is his pension position during the period of secondment? Some of these questions were raised in *Astley v Celtec Ltd*, but the answers given were somewhat inconclusive.

2.150 What is the position of an employee who has been seconded to work abroad? It is now established that an employee working in another country may, in some circumstances, be able to bring a claim under UK employment legislation (see *Serco Ltd v Lawson*, para 17.4), but the position of seconded employees is not clear. Two problems are apparent, namely (a) who will be the employer against whom a claim is to be made, and (b) will the UK employment tribunals have jurisdiction to deal with a claim made by an employee who once worked in the United Kingdom, but who is then seconded to work abroad? It is a truism to state that each case will have to be determined on its own facts, but the trend is toward permitting such actions wherever possible (eg, see *Crofts v Cathay Pacific Airways Ltd*).

2.151 An allied problem arises if an employee takes a 'career break'. If the employee is expected to resign, continuity of employment is likely to be broken (*Curr v Marks and Spencer Ltd*), but if he is on some form of leave absence, continuity will be preserved by virtue of ERA, s 212(3)(c) (see para 13.23).

D. Agency workers

Employment agency or employment business?

2.152 An employer may turn to an agency to provide him with staff for a specific purpose or definite or indefinite period of time. The Conduct of Employment Agencies and Employment Businesses Regulations 2003 set out the minimum standards which govern the conduct of the private recruitment industry. Generally, such agencies must comply with the legislation on equal opportunities, equal pay, health and safety, national minimum wage, working time, etc. The DTI has produced a Guidance Note clarifying various issues.

An employment agency undertakes to find work for a work seeker, and once the worker is suitably placed, the agency will drop out of the picture, having obtained a fee from the worker's employer for its services.

On the other hand, an employment business is an organisation which supplies workers to hirers, often on a temporary basis (the term 'worker' is used in a neutral sense). The worker will do work for the hirer, but as a general rule the employment relationship is with the employment business, and it is the business which pays the worker his wages. The terms of the contract between the employment business and the worker shall specify in writing whether the worker is employed by the employment business under a contract of service or apprenticeship, or a contract for services, and, in any case, other terms and conditions relating to remuneration, notice, annual leave, etc.

Where the worker is supplied by an employment business

2.153 The main legal problem which arises is the status of the worker when supplied by an employment business. Is he an employee of the employment business (*McMeechan v Secretary of State for Employment*); an employee of the client (*Dacas v Brook Street Bureau*); or an employee of neither (*Bunce v Postworth Ltd*)?

2.154 In view of some difficult (and possibly irreconcilable) decisions it is trite to observe that it all depends on the facts of each case. The label put on a contract is only determinative of the relationship between the parties if, having considered all the relevant factors, there is still some doubt or ambiguity about the worker's true status. Thus if the evidence points clearly to the worker being an employee, the fact that the contract states specifically that it does not give rise to a contract of employment is not conclusive. In *McMeechan v Secretary of State for Employment*, the claimant worked for an employment business under a series of temporary contracts. The terms of his engagement specifically stated that he was self-employed, but he was paid on a weekly basis when he worked, and tax and national insurance contributions were deducted. The agency became insolvent, and the claimant sought to recover from the National Insurance Fund (under ERA, s 182) a payment in respect of wages owed to him from his last assignment. In allowing his claim, the Court of Appeal drew a distinction between the general terms of engagement which exist with the employment business, and the specific engagements which a worker undertakes. In respect of the latter, a single engagement was capable of giving rise to a contract of employment, even though the worker might not be entitled to employee status under his general terms of engagement.

2.155 Mutuality of obligation is important, as is the right to control what the worker does and how he does it (*Motorola Ltd v Davidson*). In particular, it appears that regard may be had to the length of time the worker works for the client, and the dealings between the parties during that time. Thus it is possible for an implied contractual relationship to have arisen, taking into account such factors as the day-to-day control exercised by the client over the agency-supplied worker, the communications between the parties, the length of time the arrangement has lasted, and so on. In *Dacas v Brook Street Bureau (UK) Ltd* an agency provided a worker who cleaned for a local authority for six years until her employment was terminated. She claimed unfair dismissal against the agency and the local authority, but an employment tribunal found that she was an employee of neither. She then appealed against the agency. The Court of Appeal held that she had little contact with the agency and could not be its employee. However, it was stated obiter that in view of the length of time the arrangement had lasted, the tribunal ought to have considered the possibility that an implied contract of employment with the local authority had come into existence.

Thus *Dacas* has extended the circumstances in which a contract of employment may be implied (*Cable & Wireless plc v Muscat*). Indeed, the fact that the employee is paid by the agency (who is then reimbursed by the end user), is not conclusive as to the employment relationship. In *RNLI v Bushaway* (see para 2.157) it was held that if an employee is paid through the agency while on a temporary contract this does not mean that the employee is not paid by the end user, and thus an implied contract of employment can still come into existence with the end user.

Further, if the end user (client) integrates the agency worker into its own organisation, and treats him on a day-to-day basis in the same way as it treats its own employees, the arrangement is capable of becoming an implied contract of employment (*Franks v Reuters Ltd*). However, if there is no kind of contract whatsoever between the worker and the client, the relationship of employer/employee cannot exist. Thus in *Hewlett Packard Ltd v O'Murphy* a computer specialist set up his own limited company which then contracted with an employment business, which in turn provided his services to the respondent company. Even though the arrangement lasted for some years, and the worker was under the respondent's control so far as performance and discipline were concerned, the strict position was that there was no contractual nexus between the worker and the respondents. Hence a claim for unfair dismissal against the respondents failed.

2.156 The presence or absence of mutuality is a significant factor to be considered. In *Bunce v Postworth Ltd (t/a Skyblue)* the claimant registered for work with Postworth, an employment business. The written agreement described the claimant as 'an associate', and stated that it was a contract for services and not intended to give rise to a contract of employment. Postworth were not obliged to obtain work for the claimant, and in turn the claimant was not obliged to accept work offered. When he accepted work, he was obliged to accept the directions, supervision and instructions of any person in the client organisation to whom he was responsible, and to conform to the client's normal hours of work, and rules and regulations. Postworth paid the claimant's wages and holiday pay, but not sick pay. Over a period of one year, the claimant accepted 142 assignments, most of which were with the same client. However, after complaints were received about the quality of his work, Postworth informed him that the arrangement was terminated. His claim for unfair dismissal was rejected by the employment tribunal, the EAT and the Court of Appeal. So far as Postworth were concerned, there was an absence of control. So far as the client was concerned, there was an absence of mutuality. For the claimant, it had been argued that he had an 'umbrella' contract, which covered all the separate arrangements made with Postworth, but the argument was dismissed by the Court of Appeal, who pointed out that the very detailed provisions in the contract left no room for implying an overall contract. Further, the fact that the claimant worked for more than one end user was fatal to the 'umbrella contract' argument.

2.157 An employee who is supplied by an agency on a temporary appointment, and who is then taken on as a full-time employee has continuity of employment from the date his temporary appointment commenced (*RNLI v Bushaway*).

E. Casual workers and global contracts

2.158 There are some workers who are employed on short-term periodic contracts, with various breaks in between, whose status has been the subject of a number of judicial decisions. If the employer is under no obligation to provide work, and if the worker is under no obligation to accept an offer of work, a contract of employment cannot exist. This is so even though during actual periods of working, tax under schedule E and national insurance contributions are deducted, for administrative reasons (*Stevedoring & Haulage Services Ltd v Fuller*). Attempts have been made to treat such workers as being employed under one 'global contract' but with very limited success. A global contract cannot exist unless there is an irreducible minimum of obligations to offer and accept work existing between the parties (*Clark v Oxfordshire Health Authority*), and it cannot be brought into existence merely by counting together a number of individual contracts which may have subsisted over a period of time (*Hellyer Bros Ltd v McLeod*). In particular, where the terms upon which casual work is offered and accepted expressly negate mutuality of obligations, eg if the employment is specifically stated to be for an 'ad hoc or casual basis' or 'as and when required', there can be no global or overarching contract. The courts will not invent an implied term which specifically overrides the express term (*Stevedoring & Haulage Services Ltd v Fuller*).

In *Carmichael v National Power plc* the appellant was engaged as a guide at a power station. She was paid for the number of hours worked, and had tax and national insurance deducted. Her contract stated that she was employed 'on a casual and as required basis'. The Court of Appeal held that, on the facts of the case, there was an implied term that the employer would offer her a reasonable amount of work, and that if so offered, she would carry out a reasonable amount of work. Thus it was held that a contract of employment existed. However, the House of Lords disagreed, and held that she was not an employee. The absence of mutuality of obligation will frequently by determinative of the matter, for if a person is not obliged to offer work, and the other party is not obliged to accept the work when offered, there is an absence of the irreducible minimum of mutual obligation necessary to create a contract of employment. It would therefore appear that the fact that a contract is repeated does not create a global contract of employment.

F. National security (ERA, s 193)

2.159 The provisions relating to protected disclosures (ERA, ss 43A–43L) do not apply in relation to employment for the purposes of the Security Service, the Secret Intelligence Service or the Government Communications Headquarters. If a complaint is made under TULR(C)A, s 146 (detriment for trade union membership, see para 21.42) or ERA, s 111 (unfair dismissal, see Chapter 17) and it is shown that the action complained of was taken for the purpose of safeguarding national security, the employment tribunal shall dismiss the complaint. The former power of a Minister of the Crown to issue a conclusive certificate that the act was done on the grounds of national security has been repealed, and staff in the security and intelligence services, as well as other Crown employees, may present claims to an employment tribunal in the normal way. However, in such cases, a specially constituted employment tribunal will be convened, with special powers and procedures to ensure that secrecy and confidentiality is maintained (see Employment Tribunals (Constitution and Rules of Procedure) Regulations 2004, regs 10–12; Employment Tribunal (Amendment) No 2 Regulations 2005; Employment Appeal Tribunal (Amendment) Regulations 2005).

Although the Employment Tribunals Act 1996, s 10 provides that if, on an unfair dismissal claim, it is shown that the action complained of was taken for the purpose of safeguarding national security, the employment tribunal shall dismiss the complaint, it is still necessary for the employer to prove that the action was for the purpose of national security. Thus, although the action taken may be analogous with 'some other substantial reason' the employment tribunal must still go on to consider the fairness or otherwise of the decision to dismiss (*B v BBA*).

Employment law remedies

A. Common law remedies

2.160 Although most of the cases involving employment law are brought in employment tribunals, there has been a small resurgence in recent years of claims seeking the old common law remedies. Thus actions may still be brought for wrongful dismissal (see para 16.6), and also for damages based on a failure by the employer to follow contractual disciplinary procedures, the measure of damages being the loss suffered by the employee as a result of that failure (*Boyo v Lambeth London Borough Council*). Also, an application may be made for an injunction to restrain an employer from purporting to act in breach of a contractual disciplinary procedure (*Jones v Lee and Guilding*) and, somewhat rare, an action seeking specific performance of the contract (*Powell v London Borough of Brent*). These matters will be explored in Chapter 10 (and see *Jones v Gwent County Council*).

2.161 If an employer acts unfairly towards an employee in such a way that the employee has acquired a cause of action at common law prior to, and independent of, a subsequent dismissal (whether fair or unfair, or whether constructive or not), the common law action is not barred by the fact that the employee has brought a statutory unfair dismissal claim (*Eastwood v Magnox Electric plc*).

B. Public law remedies

2.162 An application may be made for judicial review, seeking to ensure that a public body carries out its public duties in a manner consistent with the legal requirements. Generally speaking, there are three grounds on which judicial review may be granted: (1) where the public body has acted illegally, ie contrary to the legal rights and duties of the parties; (2) where the public body has acted irrationally, ie where the decision arrived at was so outrageous that no sensible body or person acting responsibly could have reached that decision; and (3) where there has been a procedural impropriety, ie a failure to act with procedural fairness (*Council of Civil Service Unions v Minister for the Civil Service*, per Lord Diplock).

2.163 Attempts have been made by employees in the public sector to establish legal rights based on such principles, but with mixed success. The claim must be brought within the procedure laid down in the Civil Procedure Rules (judicial review) and the remedy is not generally available if a remedy based on contractual principles would suffice. There must be a further element of a public right or the enforcement of a public duty (*R v East Berkshire Health Authority, ex p Walsh*). The public law remedies sought will be judicial review, prohibition and a declaration.

2.164 In *McLaren v Home Office*, Woolf LJ suggested that there are four general principles which apply when an employee of a public body is proposing to proceed by way of judicial review: (1) in relation to personal claims against an employer, an employee of a public body is in the same situation as other employees; (2) however, if there exists some disciplinary or other body established under the Royal prerogative or a statute to which disputes can be referred, judicial review may be the appropriate remedy; (3) if an employee of a public body is adversely affected by a decision of general application, judicial review of that decision may be sought (see *R v Secretary of State, ex p Council of Civil Service Unions*); (4) if disciplinary procedures are of a domestic nature, judicial review will not be sought.

2.165 However, if a person is seeking to enforce a private right which has a public law element, he can pursue his claim through the normal procedure of issuing a writ, and is not required to seek redress by means of judicial review (*Roy v Kensington and Chelsea and Westminster Family Practitioner Committee*). This is of particular importance if the public law issue is raised after the time for applying for judicial review has lapsed (*Doyle v Northumbria Probation Committee*).

2.166 In Scotland, however, for historical reasons, the situation is slightly different. Scots law does not depend on a distinction between public and private law, but the court will accept jurisdiction by way of judicial review to regulate the process by which decisions are taken by a person or body to whom a power has been delegated by statute, agreement or other instrument, in order to ensure that the person or body does not exceed or abuse that power. But there must always be a tripartite relationship between the person or body to whom the power has been delegated, the person or body by whom it has been delegated, and the person for whose benefit the power is to be exercised. Strict contractual rights, such as those which exist between employer and employee, are not amenable to judicial review (*West v Secretary of State for Scotland*), whether they occur in the public or the private sector. Thus where a local authority suspended a senior employee, it was exercising a power derived from the contract of employment, rather than from a statutory grant (*Blair v Lochaber District Council*).

3

The Formation of a Contract of Employment

The contract of employment

3.1 A contract of employment can be entered into formally or informally. It can emerge as a result of interviews, negotiations, exchange of letters, or a casual conversation at the factory door. It can be made orally or in writing, although apprenticeship deeds and articles for merchant seamen by definition must be written. But essentially it is a contract like any other contract, and in principle subject to the general contractual rules of the common law. The normal canons of legal construction must be applied (*Hooper v British Railways Board*).

3.2 However, traditional legal reasoning based on the law of contract does not always sit comfortably with the expansion of workers' rights which has occurred over the past few decades, partly because of the acknowledged inequality of bargaining power between the parties, but also because a contract of employment involves a continuing relationship, unlike most other forms of contracts which are generally single transactions. In the world of employment, the parties have to live together and work together over a period of time. There has to be an element of trust and confidence. If there are areas where strict adherence to contractual rights can produce inequitable results, traditional contract doctrines may be circumvented. Consequently, the courts have thus developed and expanded the doctrine of the implied term of trust and respect which is sometimes used to override strict contractual obligations, on the basis that the exercise of contractual powers by management is subject to that power being exercised reasonably and not in an unconscionable manner. Thus issues such as discretionary bonuses (*Clark v BET plc*), non-contractual share options (*Mallone v BPB Industries Ltd*), implementation of mobility clauses (*United Bank Ltd v Akhtar*), payment of non-contractual national pay rates (*Glendale Managed Services v Graham*), capricious or inequitable favouritism in non-contractual pay awards (*FC Gardner v Beresford*) etc are well outside traditional contractual doctrines. Equally, the exercise of strict contractual rights which have the effect of depriving an employee of valuable benefits may also be frustrated by the use of the implied term doctrine (*Aspden v Webbs Poultry*). And in *Dacas v Brook Street Bureau (UK) Ltd* (see para 2.155) the Court of Appeal suggested that there could be an implied contract of employment, brought about by dealing by the parties over a period of time. The law of contract, when applied to employment situations, is not static.

3.3 There must be an offer of employment, and an acceptance of that offer. In *Wishart v National Association of Citizens' Advice Bureaux Ltd*, the claimant was offered a job 'subject to the receipt of satisfactory references'. The defendants received references from the claimant's existing employer which indicated that he had been absent from work through illness for a considerable number of days, and consequently the offer was withdrawn. The claimant sought an interlocutory injunction to restrain the defendants from appointing anyone else to the post and requiring them to provide him with the job in question. The injunction was granted by a deputy High Court Judge, but on appeal the decision was reversed by the Court of Appeal. On the facts, there was a conditional offer of employment, and the only obligation on the defendants was to consider the references in good faith. Whether or not the references were satisfactory was a subjective matter. The Court of Appeal suggested that it was possible to make a conditional offer of employment subject to something which could be objectively determined, eg the passing of a medical examination, but that did not apply in this case.

3.4 Of interest in connection with 'job offers' is the new scheme arising from the Police Act 1997, ss 112–127, whereby the Secretary of State may issue certificates on application which will detail an individual's criminal record, or the absence of any such record (see para 4.250). Thus an employer would be able to discover certain relevant information prior to offering employment. Enhanced criminal records covering applicants who apply for certain sensitive posts (care of children or working with vulnerable adults) are also available.

3.5 If an employer makes an offer of employment, which is accepted, and before the date of performance the employer withdraws the offer, the disappointed employee is entitled to damages for breach of contract. These will usually be assessed according to the loss suffered, ie the lawful notice the putative employee would have been entitled to receive had he commenced the employment, less any mitigation of the loss, unless there is a collateral contract (see para 3.15). Further, such a claim for lawful notice may be brought in the employment tribunal under the provisions of the Employment Tribunals Extension of Jurisdiction Order (see para 1.31) which permits employment tribunals to hear claims arising or outstanding 'on the termination of the employee's employment', even though, as in this case, the employment had not commenced! The phrase has to be construed as meaning 'on the termination of the employee's contract of employment' (*Sarker v South Tees Acute Hospitals NHS Trust*).

3.6 In addition, there must be an intention to create legal relations (see *R v Lord Chancellor's Department, ex p Nangle*), consideration (but this doctrine does not apply in Scotland) and the absence of vitiating elements (mistake, misrepresentation, illegality, etc). The consideration for the contract is that the employee agrees to work for the employer in return for remuneration. Thus a person who does voluntary work cannot benefit from legal employment rights because he is not employed under a contract of employment (*Melhuish v Redbridge Citizens Advice Bureau*), there being no consideration for his services (*South East Sheffield Citizens Advice Bureau v Grayson*). Thus if an employee is seeking to rely on, or enforce, or found a claim on a contract of employment, that contract must not be tainted with illegality, for it is contrary to public policy to claim statutory protection in respect of an illegal contract, eg when seeking compensation for unfair dismissal or a redundancy payment. But if the protection or remedy sought does not involve relying on or enforcing the contract of employment, the illegality of that contract is not a bar to a claim. Thus, a person may claim sex or race discrimination even though the contract is prima facie illegal (*Leighton v Michael* and see *Hall v Woolston Hall Leisure Ltd*, para 3.7), but if the contract is central to the claim, eg in unfair dismissal complaints, and is tainted with illegality, it will be unenforceable (*Johal v Adams*). In *Cole v Fred Stacey Ltd*, the employee was given an additional payment which was not taxed as income. He was subsequently made redundant, but it was held that he was not entitled to a redundancy payment, as the contract was illegal and unenforceable, being a contract to defraud the Revenue (see also *Tomlinson v Dick Evans U Drive Ltd*). In *Rastegarnia v Richmond Design* the applicant (who came from Iran) had been granted a work permit for a specific job. Without obtaining permission from the Department of Employment he changed his job and went to work for the respondents. He was subsequently dismissed, but his claim for unfair dismissal was rejected. His employment was unlawful, and he could not obtain any legal rights thereunder.

3.7 An asylum seeker who is working in breach of the immigration rules and who deceives his employer about his immigration status cannot enforce a contract which is consequently illegal, and the employment tribunal has no jurisdiction to hear a claim based on that illegal contract (*Vakante v Governing Body of Addey and Stanhope School*). But if, on a complaint of unlawful discrimination, it is discovered that the contract of employment is tainted with illegality, it is still possible for an employment tribunal to make an award in respect of injury to feelings, although no compensation can be awarded for loss of earnings, since that would offend against the principle that the court will not enforce an illegal contract (*Hall v Woolston Hall Leisure Centre Ltd*).

3.8 If the terms of the contract are designed to avoid or postpone the proper payment of income tax, then the contract is illegal, and it matters not that the parties are unaware of the illegality. In *Salvesen v Simons* the employee was employed as a farm manager. He requested that his remuneration be paid in two parts – £10,000 as a salary, and £2,200 as a management fee to be paid into a firm which he owned. This enabled him to claim business expenses and defer payment of any income tax due on the management fee. A new owner took over the farm, and refused to continue the arrangement. The employee resigned, and claimed constructive dismissal. His claim succeeded before the employment tribunal, but the decision was reversed by the EAT. Ignorance of the illegal nature of the agreement did not prevent the application of the maxim *ex turpi causa non oritur actio* (no legal rights can arise out of wrongful dealings).

3.9 The fact that the employer makes an occasional tax-free payment to the employee does not render the contract illegal for this is not part of the remuneration as defined in the contract of employment (*Annandale Engineering v Samson*). Nor is a legitimate tax avoidance scheme unlawful, provided it is a proper method of reducing liability for tax and national insurance contributions, and has been (or would be) disclosed to the Inland Revenue (*Lightfoot v D & J Sporting Ltd*).

3.10 However, a fraud or dishonesty against an employer by an employee, whilst it may be grounds for dismissal, does not make the contract inherently illegal so as to make it void ab initio (*Broaders v Kalkare Property Maintenance Ltd*).

3.11 Nor will the contract be unenforceable for illegality if the employee does not receive any benefit from the illegality. In *Hewcastle Catering Ltd v Ahmed* the employers devised a scheme to avoid paying VAT, and gave certain instructions to the employees to facilitate the scheme. The employees did not receive any direct benefit. Following investigations by the Customs and Excise, the employers were prosecuted, and the employees were called as prosecution witnesses. They were subsequently dismissed, and claimed that the dismissals were unfair. The employers argued that the contracts of employment, being tainted with illegality, were unenforceable, but this claim was rejected by the employment tribunal, the EAT and the Court of Appeal. The employers had involved the employees in the fraud, but the employees did not benefit from it and were not essential parties to it. It would be contrary to public policy to deny the employees compensation when the employers had involved them in the fraud and dismissed them because they gave evidence in criminal proceedings taken against the employers.

3.12 For an employee to have certain statutory rights, he must be continuously employed under a legal contract of employment, and any period wherein the contract becomes illegal cannot be relied upon in counting towards that continuity. Thus a period of time prior to the illegality, when the contract was legal, is lost, and continuity can only be reckoned from the date when the contract became legal (*Hyland v J H Barker (North West) Ltd*). As already noted (see para 2.103), periods of employment when a foreign national is working in breach of immigration rules will render the contract unenforceable for illegality (*Bamgbose v Royal Star and Garter Home*).

3.13 If the alleged illegality lies in the performance of the contract, then a distinction must be drawn between the cases where the contractual obligation is to do an act which is unlawful, and those where the obligations are capable of being performed lawfully, but which were in fact performed by unlawful means. In *Coral Leisure Group Ltd v Barnett*, the claimant was dismissed from his post as a public relations executive. He alleged that part of his duties was to keep rich punters happy by obtaining for them, among other things, the services of prostitutes. It was held that the fact that an immoral or unlawful act was committed during the course of the employment did not render the contract void, unless it was entered into with the object of doing that unlawful or immoral act, or the contract itself (as opposed to the mode of performance) was prohibited by law.

3.14 But the contract will only be void if the party seeking to enforce it was aware of the illegality. If it can be shown that the employee was not a party to the illegality, or did not know about it, he can still rely on the contract as an innocent party (*Davidson v Pillay*). The test is not whether the employee ought to have known of the illegality, but whether he actually did know (*Corby v Morrison (t/a The Card Shop)*). Thus if an employee is paid part of his wages in cash as a tax-free payment, the essential question to ask is, has the employee knowingly been a party to a deception on the Revenue (*Newland v Simons and Willer (Hairdressers) Ltd*)?

Collateral contracts

3.15 At common law, when an employer terminates the contract of employment, the only remedy for the employee is to claim money for the period of notice to which he is entitled (see para 15.2). However, if the employer promises that the contract will subsist for a certain period of time, this may be a collateral contract to the main contract, and the employee may be able to claim damages for a breach of that collateral contract. In *Gill v Cape Contracts Ltd* the claimant gave up his job in Belfast to go to work for the defendants in the Shetlands. He was told that the work would last for at least six months, but the defendants repudiated the contract before he could start work. It was held that the plaintiff was entitled to damages for a breach of contract by the defendants, who had made representations which had been acted on by the claimant to his detriment. These representations formed a collateral contract to the main contract of employment.

Terms and conditions

3.16 It is usual to speak of the 'terms and conditions of employment' which are part of every contract of employment, although no attempt ever appears to have been made to define or delineate this expression (but see *Cory Lighterage v Transport and General Workers' Union* and *Universe Tankships v ITWF*). It is submitted that the terms of the employment are bilateral, ie they are part of the agreement made between the employer and employee, whereas the conditions of employment are unilateral instructions which are laid down by the employer. The result is that a change in the terms can only be made by an express or implied agreement to that effect, whereas a condition can be changed by the employer unilaterally at any time (see *Cadoux v Central Regional Council*) on giving reasonable notice.

3.17 For a contract of employment to come into existence, there must be certainty as to the commitment entered into. In *Judge v Crown Leisure Ltd* an employer made a promise to the claimant at a staff Christmas party that the employee would be put on roughly the same level of remuneration as other managers. This was held not to be legally enforceable. The words used were too vague to amount to a contractual commitment.

3.18 If an employer has a code of practice, or issues a policy statement, such documents do not necessarily constitute employment terms. In *Wandsworth London Borough Council v D'Silva* the local authority issued a code of practice on staff sickness, to which they proposed to make changes unilaterally. The employment tribunal and the EAT held that the relevant provisions of the code were contractually binding and the employers could not alter them unilaterally, but the decision was reversed by the Court of Appeal. The code merely set out good practice which management intended to follow, but did not constitute contractual requirements. Similarly, an equal opportunities policy was a mere statement of policy in generalised terms, and did not give rise to contractual obligations (*Grant v South-West Trains Ltd*). In *Pendragon plc v Jackson* the employer inserted a clause into a share option scheme which stated that the scheme was non-contractual. It was held that the employee had no legal entitlement to any benefits under the scheme. The employers had discharged the burden of proof to show that the scheme was not intended to create a legally binding contract.

3.19 But although a policy or practice set out in a staff manual may not be contractual, if it is relied upon by an employee, it cannot be changed unilaterally to his detriment, because that would be a breach of the implied term of trust and confidence (*French v Barclays Bank plc*).

3.20 Terms of employment can be found in express or implied agreements, collective agreements, and various statutory provisions; conditions of employment are usually contained in works rules, disciplinary and grievance procedures and job descriptions. Care should be taken not to place a term or condition in the wrong category. For example, it may be a term of a contract that an employee shall be entitled to six weeks' holiday per year; it will be a condition that he shall take those holidays at particular times of the year. A term will specify the number of hours he shall work; a condition will instruct him as to when he shall work those hours. A term will specify his employment duties; a condition will lay down how he shall perform those duties. The fact of payment is a term; the mode of payment is a condition.

A. Interpretation of terms

3.21 Under the modern law of employment, contractual terms must be applied reasonably, not literally. In *United Bank Ltd v Akhtar*, the claimant was subject to a clause in his contract which required him to work anywhere in Great Britain. On 5 June he was informed that as from 8 June he would be required to transfer from Leeds to a branch in Birmingham. He requested that the transfer be delayed for three months, because of his wife's illness, and also the impending sale of his house. This request was refused. He then asked if he could take 24 days' leave due to him to enable him to sort out his affairs, and he offered to commence work in Birmingham on 10 July, but he received no reply to this request. His pay was then stopped as from 5 June, so he resigned, and claimed he had been constructively dismissed. His claim succeeded. There was an implied term in his contract that the employers would give reasonable notice if they wished to exercise their rights under the mobility clause.

3.22 Similarly, an employer may still be acting fairly even though he dismisses an employee in circumstances which amount to a breach of contract by the employer, for statutory rights and obligations exist concurrent with, but are sometimes different from, those which exist at common law (see *Hooper v British Railways Board*).

3.23 In *Farrant v Woodroffe School* the claimant was employed as a laboratory technician at a school. Following a reorganisation of technical support services he was required to transfer from the science department where he worked and divide his time between other departments. He refused to accept the new job description and was dismissed. The dismissal was held to be fair. The employers had given him ample warning of the proposed change, had fully consulted with him, and thus had acted reasonably in the circumstances in dismissing him. The lawfulness of the instruction is not by itself determinative of the fairness of a dismissal.

3.24 Where the terms of a contract of employment are ambiguous, it is open to the courts to look at the practice adopted by the parties, and to attach considerable importance to it as indicating the proper interpretation of contractual terms (*Dunlop Tyres Ltd v Blows*).

B. Express terms

3.25 At the conclusion of the negotiations the parties may have expressly stated the terms which form the basis of the contract. These terms may deal with wages, salaries, commissions, bonuses, hours of work, the nature of the duties, holidays, overtime, sick pay, pension schemes and so on. The task of the courts and tribunals is to interpret the meaning of such express terms in a manner consistent with industrial realism. Thus in *Cole v Midland Display Ltd* the employee was a manager employed on a 'staff' basis. He refused to do overtime without pay, and his subsequent dismissal was held to be fair. The essence of being employed as 'staff' meant that he was guaranteed his wages whether there was work or not, and during sickness. In return, 'staff' are apparently required to work reasonable overtime without pay if required to do so.

3.26 On the other hand, in *Redbridge London Borough Council v Fishman*, the employee was appointed as a teacher in charge of a resource centre. Gradually, she was asked to teach more and more, and eventually dismissed when she refused. Her dismissal was held to be unfair. A headteacher could require teachers to do work other than that for which they were engaged, provided that such requests were reasonable. In this case, the teaching was ancillary to her main job, which was as a director of the resource centre. Consequently, the headmaster's instructions went beyond the strict contractual obligations of the employee, and were therefore unreasonable.

3.27 Although it may be permissible to refer to statements made in a job advertisement to ascertain the terms of a contract (*Tayside Regional Council v McIntosh*), such statement cannot override the express terms. In *Deeley v British Rail Engineering Ltd*, the employers advertised for a 'Sales Engineer (Export)'. The claimant applied for the job and was appointed, but his contract was for a 'Sales Engineer'. It was held that there were no grounds for implying the word 'Export' into his contract.

3.28 If there is an express term in the contract which permits an employee to have short-term or long-term sickness benefits, or there is in force a permanent health insurance scheme, the employer cannot bring these to an end by dismissing the employee (*Adin v Sedco Forex International Resources Ltd*), and it is probable that there is also an implied term that the employer will not dismiss an employee who is off work sick while covered by such a scheme (*Aspden v Webbs Poultry and Meat Group (Holdings) Ltd*). If the employer has the right to terminate the scheme without prior notice, benefits under the scheme will continue until the employee is notified of the change (*Bainbridge v Circuit Foil UK Ltd*).

3.29 An express term may be used to negate a liability. In *Petrie v MacFisheries Ltd* the employers posted a notice stating that half pay for sickness would be paid as an act of grace by the company to all employees with over six months' service. All the employees knew of the position and the company acted on it consistently. It was held that the company was not bound to make payments when employees were off sick.

3.30 If an employer provides facilities for his employee's property (eg car parks, cloak-rooms, etc) he cannot restrict his liability for death or personal injury resulting from negligence, and he may only be able to restrict or exclude his liability for damage to the employee's property by a term in the contract which is reasonable in the circumstances (Unfair Contract Terms Act 1977, s 2).

3.31 If the employee is in breach of a contractual term this will be ground for dismissal. Equally, if the employer is in breach, the employee may accept the breach and bring a claim for constructive dismissal (see Chapter 17). In either event, the fairness or unfairness of the dismissal has to be determined in accordance with established legal principles, though clearly the breach of a contractual term must be regarded with greater seriousness than the breach of a non-contractual term. In *Martin v Solus Schall*, the claimant signed a contract which included a clause stating 'you will be expected to work such overtime as is necessary to ensure continuity of service'. This was held to be a contractual obligation, and on the facts his dismissal for refusing to do overtime was fair.

3.32 Whether a breach by the employer of a term in a contract is so fundamental as to amount to a repudiatory breach will depend on the nature of the breach and the circumstances which gave rise to it. Thus, if there is a non-payment of agreed wages, or an interference by the employer with a salary package, a distinction must be drawn between the employer's failure to pay, or his delay in paying, and his deliberate refusal to do so. A unilateral reduction in pay diminishes the value of the employee's remuneration, and undermines the whole foundation of the contract of employment. But if the failure to pay is a result of temporary fault in the employer's technology, or a simple accounting error or mistake, or due to accident or illness etc, it would be open to the court to hold that the breach did not go to the root of the contract although this may amount to a 'deduction' under ERA, s 13 (see *Elizabeth Claire Care Management v Francis*, para 8.20). A repeated or persistent failure or delay, or one which was unexplained, might lead the court to hold that the breach was indeed repudiatory (*Cantor Fitzgerald International v Callaghan*).

3.33 At one time it was thought that a breach of contract by an employee amounted to a 'constructive resignation', but this view is now regarded as being incorrect (see *London Transport Executive v Clarke*, para 17.52). The legal position is that the employer may 'accept' the breach or not, as he wishes. If he does accept the breach, he dismisses the employee, and the fairness of the dismissal must be justified in accordance with the usual principles (see Chapter 17).

3.34 A strike by an employee is a breach of contract, as is a refusal to perform contractual duties. Either of these events gives rise to legal consequences, including the right of the employer to deduct a sum of money from the wages or salary of the employee, calculated on a proportional basis (*Sim v Rotherham Metropolitan Borough Council*).

C. Implied terms

3.35 Occasionally the courts and tribunals are prepared to imply a term into the contract in circumstances where the parties did not expressly insert a term to meet a particular contingency. The theory adopted was that the term in question was so obvious that the parties did not see the need to state it expressly. Clearly, a certain amount of judicial hindsight is required in order to imply a term after a dispute has arisen, and there is frequent room for disagreement on whether or not the court was correct in making its assumptions. However, in *Mears v Safecar Security Ltd*, the Court of Appeal held that the correct approach was to consider all the facts and circumstances before implying a term into the contract, including the way the parties had carried out the contract since it was formed. There is no presumption either way about an implied term. For example, in *O'Grady v M Saper Ltd* the employee claimed his wages for a period in which he had been off work through sickness. He had been away sick before, and had not received any wages. Indeed, he never asked for them nor expected them, until he saw an item in a newspaper which led him to believe that he might be able to claim. It was held that there was an implied term that he would not be paid.

3.36 The original justification for the implied term theory was the need to give business efficacy to the contract, but there is now a much wider approach, implying terms which are a necessary incident of a definable category of contractual relationship. In *Scally v Southern Health and Social Services Board*, the claimant was a doctor, whose terms and conditions of employment were to be found in a statutory scheme. This scheme gave doctors the right to purchase added years of pension entitlement, but this valuable right had to be exercised within certain time limits. The claimant was never informed about the scheme, and so he failed to exercise his option to purchase the added years pension. When he did discover the existence of the scheme, he was outside the time limits. He claimed that his employers had broken an implied term of the contract by failing to take reasonable steps to bring to his notice his right to enhance his pension entitlement by the purchase of added years. The House of Lords unanimously upheld his claim. It was noted that the terms of the contract had not been negotiated with the individual employee, but were negotiated with a representative body or otherwise incorporated by reference. The contract thus contained a valuable right for the employee, but this was contingent on him taking action to avail himself of the benefit. He could not be expected to do this unless the term was drawn to his attention. There was an implied term, therefore, that the employer could take reasonable steps to bring the provisions of the pension scheme to the employee's attention, so that he could enjoy its benefits if he so wished.

3.37 But there is no implied term in a contract of employment that an employer will take reasonable care for the economic well-being of an employee. In *Crossley v Faithful and Gould Holdings Ltd* a senior employee wished to resign his employment due to ill-health. His employer did not advise him that if he did so he would lose entitlements under a permanent health insurance scheme, and he claimed that there was an implied term that his employer should have warned him about the effect of his retirement on his entitlement to that benefit. The Court of Appeal dismissed his claim. The claimant was a senior employee who should have been familiar with the terms of the insurance scheme, and he also had access to expert advice. It would impose an unfair and unreasonable burden on employers to imply a term that they should assume responsibility for financial advice in relation to benefits accruing from employment. The Court of Appeal noted that in *Scally's* case the House of Lords set out three strict criteria which had to be satisfied before placing a duty on an employer to inform employees of contractual benefits, one of which was that the employee cannot reasonably be expected to be aware of the particular term. This criteria was not satisfied in the instant case.

3.38 It is not possible to imply terms which are too vague or unpredictable to be given efficacy, or to which the parties would not have agreed had the matter been drawn to their attention (*Lake v Essex County Council*). Thus, in *Cresswell v Board of Inland Revenue*, staff employed by the Inland Revenue habitually carried out their tasks by dealing manually with files and records. The Inland Revenue introduced a programme of computerisation, and the claimant alleged that in so doing there was a breach of contract, arguing that there was an implied term that he could not be required to perform tasks or carry out functions in a manner other than that which they had habitually used by custom and practice. He sought a declaration that he could not be required to operate computerised systems. It was held that the employers were not in breach of the contract by requiring employees to use computer systems. An employee is expected to adapt himself to new methods and techniques introduced in the course of his employment. It is a question of fact whether the retraining involved the acquisition of such esoteric skills that it would not be reasonable to expect the employee to acquire them. Nowadays, it is not unusual to ask an employee to acquire basic skills such as retrieving information from a computer or feeding information into one. However, the employer must be expected to provide any necessary training for the acquisition of these skills.

3.39 Recent cases have established that there is an implied term that an employer will treat the employee with respect and trust, and will not treat an employee in an arbitrary or vindictive manner. Thus, falsely to accuse an employee of theft (*Robinson v Crompton Parkinson Ltd*), unreasonably to deny an employee an increase in remuneration which had been granted to other employees (*FC Gardner Ltd v Beresford*) and, in the case of a large firm, to refuse to give an employee time off work to deal with a domestic emergency (*Warner v Barbers Stores*), have all been held to amount to conduct by the employer which could constitute a breach of the implied term that the employer should treat an employee fairly and reasonably.

3.40 It may be possible to imply a term by reference to the practices of the industry and/ or the national agreements which are in force. For example, in *Stevenson v Teesside Bridge and Engineering Ltd* a steel erector's employment was governed by the national agreement for the time being in force in the industry. Although there was no express term in his contract stating that he was expected to work away from home, this was clearly envisaged, for the national agreement made provision for lodging allowances, travelling expenses, etc. The court held that there was an implied term in his contract that he could be sent anywhere to work, for it was recognised that in the construction steel industry, where sites are, by their very nature, scattered around the country, employees know that mobility is a feature of their employment.

3.41 There is an implied term that the employer will not prevent the employee from performing his contract of employment, or delay or hinder him so as to prevent him from earning his full remuneration, but the employer is entitled to take steps which may improve that performance, and to see that the work is done in a proper manner, for example, by engaging time and motion experts (*Davies v Richard Johnson & Nephew Ltd*). If an employee is contractually obliged to do overtime without pay, there is an implied term that the requirements of overtime will always be reasonable, and would not be excessive (*Gilbert v Goldstone Ltd*). On the other hand, if a contract of employment is silent on the actual place of work, it may be necessary to imply a term to give that contract business efficacy. In *Jones v Associated Tunnelling Co Ltd* it was held that there was an implied term that the employers were entitled to require the employee to work anywhere within a reasonable daily commuting distance from his home.

3.42 There is also an implied term that the employer will not conduct his business in a fraudulent and dishonest manner so as to cause damage to the employees' reputation and consequently place them at a disadvantage in the labour market (*Malik v BCCI SA*). However, a claimant must be able to show that the failure to obtain fresh employment was because of the stigma (*BCCI SA v Ali (No 3)*).

3.43 The original basis for the implied term theory was that it is the courts' (or tribunals') view about a provision that was 'obvious' where the contract was silent. In *Shell UK Ltd v Lostock Garage Ltd*, Lord Denning suggested that if a contract of employment did not define the obligations of the parties, the courts (or tribunals) should ask what would be reasonable in the general run of such cases, and then say what the obligation shall be. This view was followed in *Pepper and Hope v Daish* (see para 17.36) and appears to have general accpetance, even though there is a fundamental difference between importing into a contract an implied term which is 'obvious' and one which is 'reasonable'. Recently, the EAT has expressed the view that there is an implied term that the employer will not conduct himself in a manner likely to destroy or seriously damage the relationship of confidence and trust between the employer and employee, and if the conduct has that effect, then the question of whether there has been a reasonable and proper cause for the behaviour must be considered. If such reasonable and proper cause could not be shown, the employer would be acting in a manner which no reasonable employer would adopt. Thus to offer a particular benefit to the entirety of one class of employees bar one is capable of being an act calculated to seriously damage or destroy the trust and confidence between the employer and that employee (*BG plc v O'Brien*). If it is done without reasonable and proper cause, it would be a breach of the employer's obligation of fair dealing (*Johnson v Unisys Ltd*). But if the employer had reasonable and proper cause to act in the manner he did, then even though there are adverse consequences to the employee, there is no breach of the implied duty of trust and confidence (*Hilton v Shiner Ltd*).

3.44 The implied term of trust and respect is both positive and negative, in the sense that it may require the employer to do something, as opposed to refrain from doing something. Thus there can be a breach of the term if an employer decides not to offer an employee a new contract, or a variation of the old one. There is an obligation to treat employees in a fair and even-handed manner (*Transco plc v O'Brien*).

3.45 The contracts of employment of professional employees do not always detail the contractual obligations, and these may be defined by reference to the nature of the profession, and the obligations incumbent on those who follow that profession (*Sim v Rotherham Metropolitan District Council*).

3.46 There is no implied term that an employer will look after the employee's property (clothes, car, etc) which are left on the employer's premises (*Edwards v West Herts Group Hospital Management Committee*), though there is an obligation under the Workplace (Health, Safety and Welfare) Regulations 1992 for employers to provide suitable and sufficient accommodation for clothing which is not worn during working hours, and if there is a statutory obligation to do something, a failure to comply with that requirement will amount to a breach of an implied term (*W A Goold (Pearmak) Ltd v McConnell*: see para 11.78). Nor is there an implied term that an employee will be entitled to work overtime if the employer is not contractually obliged to provide overtime (*McClory v Post Office*).

3.47 There is no implied term that the employer will provide personal accident insurance for the benefit of an employee who is required to work abroad, or that the employer should give specific advice on special risks, and advise the employee to take out personal accident insurance (see *Reid v Rush & Tompkins Group plc*, para 10.33). Nor can a duty in tort be imposed to enlarge on contractual duties.

If there is no agreement on the matters which should be included in the written statement which has to be given to employees under the provisions of s 1 of the Employment Rights Act 1996, then it may not be possible to rely on an implied term concerning matters which ought to be, but are not, set out in the statement (eg whether an employee is entitled to accrued holiday pay on a pro rata basis, see *Morley v Heritage plc*, but see now Working Time Regulations, para 7.47).

3.48 It is clear that if an employer breaks an express term of the contract, the employee may 'accept' the breach, resign from his employment, and claim that he had been 'constructively' dismissed (see para 17.24). This is equally true in the case of a breach of an implied term, and in particular when the conduct of the employer amounts to a breach of the implied term of mutual trust and confidence which must exist between the parties (*Post Office v Roberts*). These developments will be considered in detail in Chapter 17.

3.49 A term can only be implied into a contract of employment if it would have existed at the time the contract was made. Thus, generally speaking, it is not possible to imply a term when there is a changed situation (*Casson Beckman & Partners v Papi*). Nor can an implied term be used to override an express term, although it may be used as a means of qualifying or explaining an express term (*Stevedoring & Haulage Services Ltd v Fuller*).

3.50 It is not possible to predict when the courts or tribunals will imply a term into a contract. Thus in *Ali v Christian Salvesen Food Services Ltd* individual contracts of employment were varied by a collective agreement. Certain topics had been omitted, and the employment tribunal refused to fill in the gaps. The decision was reversed by the EAT, using implied terms, but that decision was itself reversed by the Court of Appeal. If there were omissions in a collective agreement, the inference is that the topic was too complex or controversial for discussion or agreement, and it is not for the judiciary to speculate on what might have been agreed.

D. Statutory terms

3.51 Superimposed on all contracts of employment are a number of statutory terms. These are in addition to a considerable number of statutory 'rights' which have been created by various legislative provisions. Thus the Equal Pay Act 1970 imports an equality clause into contracts of employment, minimum wages for appropriately qualified persons are guaranteed by the National Minimum Wage Act 1998 and various employment rights are contained in the Employment Rights Act 1966 and various regulations, etc. These statutory terms may be improved upon by agreement between the parties, but any attempt to oust them will be of no effect.

E. Collective agreements

Express incorporation of the terms of a collective agreement

3.52 A collective agreement is an agreement made between an employers' association, or a single employer, on the one hand, and a trade union on the other, which, as well as laying down the procedure which will govern the relationship between the signatories will also provide for the terms and conditions of employment of those covered by the agreement. There are currently about 8,500,000 employees who are members of trade unions, and many of these, but not all, will doubtless be covered by such agreements, as well as an unknown number of non-trade unionists in respect of whom their employer will apply the terms of a relevant collective agreement. There are, however, a number of different situations to consider. There can be a national or federation agreement, made between an employers' association and a trade union, on the conclusion of which the individual employers who are members of the association will start to apply its provisions to their employees. There is no rule of law which requires this, only the practice of industrial relations. The terms of the agreement will be binding in law on the individual employer and the employee if, and only if, they are expressly or impliedly incorporated into the individual contract of employment. The same rule applies to a local or plant agreement, which is usually made between a single employer and a trade union. Also, there are some employers who, though not members of the employers' association, voluntarily undertake to observe the terms of a negotiated agreement.

3.53 Certain terms contained in a collective agreement govern the relationship between the trade union and the employer. Other terms are designed to benefit individual employees, and this becomes part of the contract of employment (*National Coal Board v National Union of Mineworkers*). These latter terms are said to have a 'normative' effect. In *Alexander v Standard Telephones and Cables plc*, the claimant was employed on the basis of the terms contained in a collective agreement. The agreement contained a redundancy procedure, which stated that LIFO ('last in, first out') would be the basis of selection in the event of compulsory redundancies. The company wished to select on the basis of skills and flexibility, and the claimant sought an injunction to prevent this. The application failed, but it was suggested that there was an arguable case that the terms of the collective agreement formed part of his contract of employment. Any remedy for breach of that contract would lie in an action for damages and the case was sent for trial on that basis (see para 3.57).

3.54 The authority of a trade union to enter into agreements which will be binding on its members vis-à-vis their employers stems either from express authority, implied authority, or by virtue of the law of agency. Express authority will normally arise when a trade union (or an authorised official) is asked or is invited to negotiate on a specific issue which affects its members. Implied authority arises when a union negotiates nationally or locally on matters which affect all members (eg wage increases), and usually be inferred from the conduct of the parties and the circumstances of the case. Under the law of agency, a union would need ostensible or apparent authority to negotiate with an employer or employers. The mere fact that an employee is also a member of a trade union does not necessarily mean that the union has that authority (*Burton Group Ltd v Smith*), although nowadays the courts appear to be more willing to accept that a trade union official (or shop steward, in appropriate circumstances) has apparent or ostensible authority to negotiate a revision of terms and conditions of employment (*Harris v Richard Lawson Autologistics Ltd*).

3.55 The 'normative' terms of a collective agreement may be incorporated into the individual contract of employment by an express provision to this effect. For example, employment may be undertaken on the basis of 'union rates of pay', or 'union conditions'. It is at least arguable that the former term refers solely to the wages rates clauses in the collective agreement, whilst the latter term may be somewhat wider, and may include other provisions. In *Jewell v Neptune Concrete Ltd*, the employee's written particulars stated that his rate of wages was to be based on the national agreement. It was held that this did not, by itself, incorporate the working rule agreement's lay-off provisions into his contract of employment. Employees who work for public bodies are normally engaged on the basis of the appropriate scale laid down by the negotiating bodies and the only scope for individual bargaining may be on the precise point of entry into the scale for salary purposes. Thus in *Knox v Down District Council* the Northern Ireland Court of Appeal were prepared to incorporate into the employee's contract of employment a car assisted purchase scheme which had been negotiated by the National Joint Council, the terms of which were expressly incorporated into his contract. In *National Coal Board v Galley*, the defendant was employed on the basis of 'the national agreements for the time being in force'. These agreements required him to do a certain amount of overtime, and when he refused to do a Saturday morning shift it was held that he was in breach of his contract.

3.56 Frequently the terms of a collective agreement will be expressly incorporated into the individual contract by means of the statement given to the employee under ERA, s 1. In *Camden Exhibition and Display Ltd v Lynott* notices issued to the employees stated that their hours of work, wages, etc, would be in accordance with the working rule laid down by the National Joint Council for the industry. Rule 6 of this agreement stated that 'Overtime required to ensure the due and proper performance of contracts shall not be subject to restriction, but may be worked by mutual agreement and direct arrangement between the employer and operatives concerned.' Workmen who were dissatisfied with a wage award decided to cease overtime working. It was held that r 6 was a term of the contracts of employment of each employee. However, its effect was obscure. Lord Denning thought that it meant that the workmen would not collectively impose an overtime ban, but Russell LJ thought that the rule did not import into the contract of any individual an agreement not to limit overtime save for a reason special to himself.

3.57 To determine whether or not the terms of a collective agreement can be incorporated into an individual's contract of employment, regard must be had to the contractual intentions of the parties. In *Alexander v Standard Telephones and Cables plc*, the claimant was given a statement of written particulars, issued under ERA, s 1. This stated that the basic terms and conditions of employment were in accordance with and subject to the provisions of a plant agreement negotiated by his employers and a trade union. One of the terms of the collective agreement provided that in the event of redundancy, selection will be on the basis of service with the employers. When the company wished to make a number of employees redundant, it was decided to retain employees whose skills and flexibility were best suited to the circumstances. The trade union insisted that selection should be on the basis of length of service. After negotiations broke down, the employers went ahead with their proposals, and the claimant was one of those dismissed. He sought an interlocutory injunction to restrain the employers from terminating his employment without applying the principles of collective agreement, but this was refused. He also claimed damages for breach of contract, arguing that he would have continued in his employment until retiring age.

His claim for damages was dismissed. The only relevant document applicable to the claimant's employment was the written statement issued under ERA, s 1. This had to be construed in accordance with the relevant contractual principles. The statutory statement did not deal with redundancy matters, and therefore it did not incorporate the terms of the collective agreement into his contract of employment. The collective agreement itself, not being a contract, could be incorporated into the individual contract of employment if there was a cogent indication that this was intended. However, the clauses in question had to be considered in the context of a joint consultation scheme of a procedure agreement, and it was not sufficiently cogently worded to support the inference of incorporation into the individual contract of employment.

A contrary view was taken by the Court of Session in *Anderson v Pringle of Scotland Ltd*, where the claimant's terms and conditions of employment were in accordance with the agreement made between the employer and a trade union. This agreement contained, inter alia, a redundancy procedure which provided that selection for redundancy was on the basis of last in first out (LIFO). When the employers decided to make a large number of employees redundant, they decided not to follow that procedure, but to use a selective scheme. The claimant would not have been selected under LIFO because of his long service, but he was to be chosen for redundancy under the selective scheme. He sought an injunction to prevent the employers from selecting for redundancy on any basis other than LIFO. The court granted the injunction. It was decided that the relevant terms of the collective agreement made between the employers and the trade union had been incorporated into the contracts of employment of the individual employees. Further, although the injunction would appear to have the effect of enforcing the performance of a contract of employment – which is not normally permissible (see Chapter 10) – in this case there was no loss of trust or confidence in the employee, for the issues were the mechanics of dismissal rather than the principles of dismissal. While it might be difficult for the employer to abide by the LIFO selection system, it was not unfair to hold them to the agreement they had made (see also *Edinburgh Council v Brown*).

The terms of the collective agreement must be suitable for incorporation into the individual contract of employment. In *Griffiths v Buckinghamshire County Council* a redundancy procedure agreement negotiated between the employers and a trade union recommended that 12 months' notice should be given of impending redundancies. It was held that this was advisory in nature, and was a procedural, not a contractual obligation. Equally, a statement made in a collective agreement that the employer will not institute a compulsory redundancy programme is aspirational, and not intended to be incorporated into any individual's contract of employment (*MG Rover Group Ltd v Kaur*).

3.58 Once the terms of a collective agreement are incorporated into the individual contract of employment, they are part of that contract, and cannot be unilaterally altered. In *Robertson v British Gas Corpn*, the employee was appointed as a gas meter reader/collector, his letter of appointment stating that an incentive bonus scheme would apply. The terms of this scheme were negotiated between the employers and a trade union. Subsequently the employers gave notice to the trade union to terminate the scheme, and no new scheme was negotiated. The employee brought an action for arrears of pay. It was held that the letter of appointment was a binding contract, which gave the right to an incentive bonus scheme. Although the collective agreement had no legal force as between the signatories, it was incorporated into the employee's contract, and the employers could not terminate the scheme unilaterally.

3.59 A different result was reached in *Airlie v Edinburgh District Council*, where the employers entered into a collective agreement with trade unions representing workers in the direct labour organisation which contained, inter alia, a bonus scheme. The scheme was incorporated into the individual contract of employment, but a clause permitted the employers to alter it after consultation with the unions. When the department was making a loss, the employers wanted to alter the scheme. The unions agreed that alterations had to be made, but there was a failure to reach agreement. Nonetheless, the employers modified the scheme, which resulted in a reduction in the wages of the employees concerned. It was claimed that an unlawful deduction had been made from wages, but the claim was dismissed by an employment tribunal and the EAT. The employers had properly consulted the unions about the changes, but there was nothing in the scheme which required the agreement of either the employees or the trade unions concerned.

3.60 Indeed, the fact that the collective agreement contains a clause to the effect that its terms are binding in honour only does not affect the legal enforceability of those terms which are expressly or impliedly incorporated into the individual contract (*Marley v Forward Trust Group Ltd*). However, a distinction must always be made between contractual terms, which are bilateral in effect, and rules, which are unilateral. The latter do not have a legally binding effect (*Cadoux v Central Regional Council*).

Implied incorporation of the terms of a collective agreement

3.61 It is equally possible to incorporate the terms of a collective agreement into an individual contract of employment by implication. In certain types of employment it will be 'assumed' that employees are employed on the basis of union/management agreements. Thus, in *MacLea v Essex Line Ltd*, the plaintiff took a job as a seaman, and the court implied into his contract the contents of an agreement made by the National Maritime Board, which was the negotiating forum for the industry. In *Wilton Ltd v Peebles* employers had paid to their employees for 20 years the annual pay increases negotiated by a national agreement made between the trade unions and the employers' trade association, and the EAT confirmed that, despite the absence of any written terms of employment or oral agreement as to pay, there was an implied term that the wages of employees were to be those stipulated in the national agreement.

3.62 If a contract of employment (or the written particulars which evidence that contract) states that pay will 'normally be in accordance with' nationally negotiated rates, 'as adopted from time to time' or if there is collective agreement which has not been specifically incorporated into the individual contract, then there is an implied term that the employer will inform the employee if and when there is a departure from the normal situation. An employee is entitled to assume that such national rates will be applied unless he is informed to the contrary (*Glendale Managed Services v Graham*).

3.63 The terms of a collective agreement can also be incorporated into an individual's contract of employment by virtue of custom and practice, provided the custom and practice is reasonable, certain and notorious. In *Henry v London General Transport Services Ltd*, the employers, in preparation for a management buy-out, entered into negotiations with a trade union over changes to the employees' terms and conditions of employment. These negotiations resulted in a framework agreement which set out new and less advantageous terms and conditions, including reduced rates of pay. After holding workplace meetings, the union informed the employer that the majority of the staff affected had consented to the new terms, and these were subsequently put into effect. A number of dissident employees brought claims in an employment tribunal alleging unlawful deductions from wages (see Chapter 8). It was held that the tradition of collective bargaining between the employer and the trade union was sufficient to enable fundamental changes to be made in the employees' contract of employment, by virtue of custom and practice.

3.64 If the employers are not members of the employers' association, there is little scope for the implied incorporation of the terms of an industry-wide collective agreement into the individual contract of employment. There would have to be strong evidence to indicate that the agreement had been so incorporated by way of custom and practice (*Hamilton v Futura Floors Ltd*).

Changing the terms of a collective agreement

3.65 Terms which are incorporated into the contract of employment as a result of a collective agreement remain part of that contract until or unless they are changed either by agreement with the employees concerned or under a specific right contained in the contract. The trade union is not, per se, an agent of its members with authority unilaterally to negotiate a variation. Thus, in *Lee v GEC Plessey Telecommunications*, the employers had reached an agreement with trade unions in 1985 which gave enhanced redundancy terms to its employees. In 1990 they purported to withdraw those terms, but, following objections from the unions, negotiations took place on revised terms. An agreement appeared to have been reached which enabled the employers to withdraw the enhanced redundancy payments and substitute less favourable terms, but this was on the basis that there would be no further redundancies in the future. However, redundancies were announced, and individual employees brought an action for a declaration that the attempt to vary the enhanced redundancy terms was ineffective. Their claim succeeded in the High Court. It was not necessary to give fresh consideration every time a new collective agreement was reached, for a continuation by the workforce in their employment was a value attributed to the employer. Although the employers could unilaterally determine the collective agreement, this would not be effective to change the terms contained in the individual contracts of employment. Nor were the trade unions acting as agents for their members when they attempted to negotiate the change. They were acting in a collective manner, not on behalf of each individual.

3.66 Another example is *Burke v Royal Liverpool University Hospital NHS Trust* where the claimant was employed as a domestic worker. Her terms and conditions of employment were regulated by a Whitley Council agreement. In order to assist the trust in submitting a competitive tender, the two recognised trade unions agreed to less favourable terms and conditions than those previously enjoyed. The tender was successful, the lower wage rates were put into effect, but the claimant made a complaint under the protection of wages provisions of the ERA, claiming that an unlawful deduction had been made to her wages. An employment tribunal held that the agreement made between the unions and the trust constituted a collective agreement which has the effect of incorporating the new terms and conditions into the claimant's contract of employment. An appeal against this decision was dismissed. The claimant had signed the new contract, the consideration for her agreement to accept a reduction in her wages was the greater sense of security of employment, and the agreement was capable of being incorporated into her contract of employment.

3.67 If an agreement states that its terms can be changed after consultation, that does not require the agreement of the parties, and provided the consultation is carried out in good faith, changes can be made unilaterally (*Airlie v Edinburgh District Council*, para 3.59).

Collective agreements and non-unionists

3.68 Just as the terms of a collective agreement may be binding on a non-federated employer who assents to it, so also will those terms apply to a non-unionist if his contract of employment states so expressly. In the absence of such express incorporation, the collective agreement will not apply. In *Singh v British Steel Corpn*, the employee's contract stated that he was to work a 15-shift system over a five-day week. He resigned from his trade union, and instructed his employers to cease paying the union subscription under a check-off agreement. The union then negotiated a new agreement with the employers which provided for a 21-shift system over a seven-day week, but the employee refused to agree to this, and was dismissed. It was held that there was nothing in his contract which permitted a change in the system of working, either by the employers unilaterally or by means of a collective agreement. The tribunal thought that while he was a member of the union he was bound by such agreements because it was his negotiating body, but when he left, he ceased to be bound. The union and the employers had no power to vary the terms of his agreement without his consent.

3.69 There is clearly less scope for the implied incorporation of the terms of a collective agreement into the contracts of employment of non-unionists. In *London Passenger Transport Board v Moscrop* a collective agreement provided that on a disciplinary charge, an employee could take with him a trade union official. The claimant was a member of another union which had not been a party to the agreement, and he wished to be accompanied by an official of his own union. It was held that the terms of the agreement were not necessarily applicable to employees who were not members of the signatory union. In *Singh v British Steel Corpn* (above) it was equally held that there was no implied term of his contract that as a non-union member he would be bound by union agreements.

Backdating agreements

3.70 A further problem can arise when the terms of a collective agreement are backdated. As a general rule, it would seem that there is no implied term in a contract of employment that a wage award can be backdated, although this may come about by an express agreement to that effect. However, an express agreement cannot override the statutory position. In *Leyland Vehicles Ltd v Reston* the claimant was made redundant in February, and received his redundancy payment calculated on the basis of the wages he was then receiving. In April a new wage agreement was negotiated with the union, and this was backdated to January. The claimant contended that his redundancy pay should be calculated so as to take account of the increase in his wage rate, but his claim was dismissed by the EAT. Section 225 of ERA refers to the amount of pay actually payable at the calculation date. It does not include increases made by agreement concluded after the employment has ended, even though the agreement provided for the backdating of the increase. The payment of a backdated wage increase to employees who have left the firm is usually a matter to be considered on an *ex gratia* basis.

Conflicting collective agreements

3.71 A difficulty sometimes arises when there is an overlap between the national agreement and a local agreement which covers the same or similar ground. In *Clift v West Riding County Council* the claimant was paid less by virtue of a local agreement than he would have received on the basis of a national agreement. It was held that since the local agreement was later in time, its terms prevailed. But 'the latest agreement prevails' doctrine is not a rule of law, as *Gascol Conversions Ltd v Mercer* demonstrates. Here, a national agreement provided that the working week should be 40 hours, and overtime worked as necessary. It also stated that if the national agreement was at variance with any local agreement, the national agreement was to prevail. A subsequent local agreement provided that the working week should be 54 hours. The employee was made redundant, and the question arose as to whether his redundancy payment was to be calculated on the basis of a normal working week of 40 hours or one of 54 hours. The Court of Appeal held that the employee was employed on the basis of the national agreement, and though it was at variance with the local agreement, its terms took precedence.

Which terms are employment terms?

3.72 Another difficulty is to determine which terms of a collective agreement are to be incorporated into the individual contract of employment. Clearly, there are many terms which are capable of such incorporation, such as wage rates, hours, overtime payments, travel allowances, and so on. Equally, there are other terms which govern the relationship which is to exist between the signatories, and have no relevance to the individual contract of employment. For example, in *Gallagher v Post Office*, the defendants recognised two trade unions for negotiating purposes, and informed their employees that they were entitled to join either union. Recognition was then withdrawn from one union, and the claimant alleged that this constituted a breach of contract. It was held that there was no term, express or implied, that the Post Office should continue to recognise the union to which the claimant belonged. Any statement about recognition was purely informative, and not part of the contract of employment of any individual employee.

3.73 Some difficulty has been experienced in the past with the 'no strike' clause, or the procedural aspects of settling disputes. In *Rookes v Barnard*, this clause was held to have been incorporated into the contracts of employment of the employees, but as the point was conceded rather than argued, the case adds little to our knowledge of the subject. A great deal may well turn on the precise wording of the agreement. Supposing this states 'the union will not call a strike until the procedure for settling the dispute is exhausted'. This is an obligation on the union, and is not part of the contracts of employment of the employees. Supposing the agreement states 'the employees will not go on strike until the procedure for settling the dispute is exhausted'. This term is clearly capable of being so incorporated. However, by TULR(C)A, s 180, the incorporation of such a clause will not be binding unless:

(a) the collective agreement is in writing;

(b) it expressly states that the terms are to be incorporated into the individual contract;

(c) a copy of the collective agreement is reasonably accessible to the employees concerned;

(d) the agreement is made by an independent trade union; and

(e) the individual contract of employment expressly or impliedly incorporates the terms of the collective agreement.

However, it must be borne in mind that a strike, whether in breach of a collective agreement or not, is always a breach of contract at common law, so that the effect of s 180 must be minimal.

F. Custom as a source of employment terms

3.74 It is sometimes argued that terms of employment can be found in those practices which are customary in a particular industry or local area, or even within a single firm. Support for this view can be gleaned from the case of *Sagar v Ridehalgh*, where a deduction from the wages of a cotton weaver for bad workmanship was upheld by virtue of the existence of a long-standing custom of the trade which, apparently, was well known. But a custom, to be upheld, must be long-established, reasonable, certain, not contrary to law, and must be strictly proved. In *Hardwick v Leeds Area Health Authority* the claimant was dismissed after exhausting her period of sick pay, which was an entitlement of two months on full pay and two months on half pay. This was in accordance with the normal practice of the Health Service. It was held that such an automatic rule, whereby an employee could be dismissed irrespective of the circumstances, was totally outmoded and unreasonable, and the dismissal was held to be unfair. In *Singh v British Steel Corpn* (para 3.68) the fact that the claimant had considered himself in the past to be bound by trade union agreements was not sufficient evidence to establish a custom to that effect. Moreover, in *Gascol Conversions v Mercer* (para 3.71) the court stated that if the parties had reduced the contract to writing, it is not permissible to say that they intended something else, and thus it would appear that a custom cannot override a written statement of the terms of employment.

3.75 This point has considerable implications when, as sometimes happens, an appeal is made to 'custom and practice' as a basis of employment terms. It is true that in *Heaton's Transport Ltd v Transport and General Workers' Union* the House of Lords upheld custom and practice as being the basis of the authority of a shop steward to initiate action on behalf of a trade union, but this was a case where the union rule-book was silent on the point. However, it might be easier to argue that 'custom and practice' can override the terms of a collective agreement which has been incorporated into an employment contract (see *Parry v Holst & Co*, para 3.100). It is also arguable that a 'custom' is different from a 'practice'. The former has a legal significance which the latter does not possess. In *Spencer*

Jones v Timmens Freeman, it was a 'common practice' in the hairdressing trade for shops to be open on Saturday afternoons, but this did not make it a custom.

3.76 Clear and compelling evidence is required to establish that a custom and practice exists (*Henry v London General Transport Services Ltd*). In *Samways v Swan Hunter Shipbuilders Ltd* the claimant, who was originally employed as a labourer, was appointed as a chargeman over a gang, and was given an additional £4 per week allowance. The company then informed him that owing to a reduction in production, it was necessary to withdraw the allowance, and he was offered employment as a labourer. It was held that this constituted a dismissal for reason of redundancy, as there was a reduction in the requirements of the company for chargemen. An argument by the company that by virtue of custom and practice chargemen's allowances were temporary payments for additional responsibility so long as this lasted was rejected by the tribunal, who thought that the 'allowance' was in fact remuneration. That other men had, in the past, reverted from the job of chargeman to their former positions was not sufficient to establish a custom, for their conduct could be explained on the ground that they wanted to keep their job with the firm, and it did not follow that they were contractually bound to do so.

3.77 It may be possible to claim sick pay if there is a local custom to this effect which can be proven to exist (*Scott v Pattison*).

3.78 It is submitted that with the increasing formalisation of contracts of employment, the scope for custom and practice as a source of employment terms has decreased, and indeed there is very little by way of modern legal authorities which could indicate that 'custom and practice' have any relevance in modern employment law. For example, in *Quinn v Calder Industrial Materials Ltd*, a policy document was issued to all member companies of a group holding company, which contained guidelines on additional redundancy payments. The document had not been formally communicated to the employees or their trade unions, although its terms were generally known. Indeed, enhanced redundancy payments based on the document had been made on four occasions, although a decision to do so had to be made by higher management on each such occasion. When the claimant was made redundant, he was not given any enhanced redundancy payment, and he contended that the employers were in breach of their contractual obligation. He argued that his entitlement to enhanced payments had been incorporated into his contract through custom and practice. His claim failed. Factors to be taken into account include whether management had drawn the attention of employees to the policy, whether it had been followed without exception for a substantial period, and whether employees had a genuine expectation that the terms of the policy would be applied to them. In the circumstances, it was not possible to infer that the policy document had achieved the status of a contractual obligation.

G. Works/staff rules

3.79 Some employers issue booklets or post notices containing the rules of the workplace, and the legal significance of these is still being explored. Such rules can either be part of the contractual terms or unilaterally imposed instructions, a distinction which is important because in the former case, they can only be changed by mutual assent and agreement, whereas in the latter case, the employer may, at any time and on reasonable notice, change them (see *Cadoux v Central Regional Council*) and substitute new instructions or impose new obligations, and a failure by the employee to obey would be a breach of his duty to follow all lawful and reasonable orders.

3.80 Thus a code of practice to be invoked in cases of long-term sickness (*Wandsworth London Borough Council v D'Silva*) and an equal opportunities policy (*Grant v South Western Trains Ltd*) were statements of policies in general terms, and not contractual documents (but see *French v Barclays Bank plc*, para 3.19).

3.81 The fact that the change bears hard on a particular individual does not justify an inference that the employer has acted in such a way as to repudiate the contract of employment. In *Dryden v Greater Glasgow Health Board*, the claimant was a heavy smoker, and was accustomed to smoking cigarettes in areas of the hospital where she worked set aside for this purpose. The employers decided to ban smoking throughout the hospital and, after extensive consultations, imposed a smoking ban. The claimant decided that she could not continue to work without smoking, and resigned her employment. She claimed that she had been constructively dismissed. It was held that 'the right to smoke' was not a customary term nor an implied term of the contract, and the employers had not acted in such a way as to frustrate the employee's ability to perform her contract. In *Secretary of State for Employment v Associated Society of Locomotive Engineers and Firemen*, railwaymen proposed to engage in a work-to-rule campaign. If the rule book, by which they were working, was a part of their contracts of employment, then, by adhering to it, albeit strictly, they could hardly be said to be breaking their contracts. However, one of the rules stated that employees should 'make every effort to facilitate the working of trains and prevent unavoidable delay', which would clearly prohibit any deliberate attempt to interpret the rules in such a way as to achieve disruption of services, and to that extent there was clearly a breach of contract on either view of their legal significance. But Lord Denning held that the rules were 'in no way terms of his (ie the individual railwayman's) contract of employment. They were only instructions to a man on how he was to do his work.' It will clearly be an implied term of his contract of employment that he will interpret those rules reasonably.

3.82 In *Peake v Automotive Products* it was held that the contents of a rule book were non-contractual administrative arrangements for running the factory. If this view is correct, then works rules are non-negotiable instructions laid down by the employer. They may deal with all manner of subjects, including the method of performing the work, safety policy, disciplinary matters, concessions and privileges, and so on. A breach of the rules may lead to appropriate penalties. In *Blake v Berkel Auto Scales Co Ltd* an employee was summarily dismissed for a serious breach of the company's rules, and the dismissal was held to be fair. Indeed, a rule may be enforced even though the employee is in no way blameworthy. In *Jeffries v BP Tanker Co Ltd* the company had a rule that an employee with a history of cardiac disease should not be employed at sea as a radio officer, and an employee who had had two heart attacks was held to have been fairly dismissed, even though he had made an excellent recovery. The rule in this case was more in the nature of company policy.

3.83 But this does not mean that an employer can lay down rules and act on them in an autocratic manner, for the courts and tribunals will use the test of reasonableness to circumscribe management prerogatives. The rules must be clear and unambiguous; their contents must be made known to the employees, and reasonable in the circumstances. Thus in *Talbot v Hugh H Fulton Ltd* an employee was dismissed for having long hair, contrary to the works rules. It was held that this would only be reasonable if there was a safety hazard, and if the exact length which was acceptable was made known. Presumably the rule should have applied to female employees as well, otherwise it would have been an act of prejudice against modern styles worn by young persons.

3.84 There may be circumstances when some aspects of the works rules can be regarded as contractual terms, despite their unilateral nature. In *Briggs v Imperial Chemical Industries Ltd* the claimant was employed as a process worker at a cyanide plant. The employers decided to pull the plant down and build another one, and consequently he was asked to work elsewhere in the firm as a process worker. He refused and claimed that he was entitled to a redundancy payment. The Divisional Court dismissed his appeal from an employment tribunal finding that he was not entitled. His terms of employment were governed by the statement given under ERA, s 1 (see para 3.102), which stated that his pay would vary with the job he was performing, and clearly this contemplated that he could be transferred from one job to another. Also, he had been issued with a booklet containing the works rules of the factory, r 17 of which stated 'You must accept the right of management to transfer you to another job with a higher or lower rate of pay, whether day work, night work or shift work.' The court held that r 17 was a term of his employment, but this is probably because there was some implied (if obscure) reference to the works rules in his contract of employment. It would seem to follow that if the contract makes express reference to the works rules as being part of the contract of employment, they will more readily be regarded as part of the contractual terms. In *Singh v Lyons Maid Ltd* it was a requirement of the company that employees should not wear beards; this was in order to maintain the company's high standards of hygiene. The applicant knew of this rule, but nonetheless grew a beard in accordance with his religious beliefs. The dismissal was held to be fair. He had refused to obey a contractual term which the employers felt to be fundamental and which did not appear to be unreasonable.

3.85 At this stage it can only be said that the legal significance of the rules is a question of fact, to be determined by the circumstances of each case. For example, if the company's rule permits security guards to search employees before they leave the premises, will a refusal to be searched amount to a breach of an express term of the contract, or will it amount to a breach of the duty to obey a lawful (and reasonable) order? If a company does not have such a 'search' policy, but wishes to introduce one, can it be done unilaterally, or must the consent of each individual employee be obtained? Would a refusal to agree to be searched amount to 'some other substantial reason' for dismissal, by analogy with *R S Components Ltd v Irwin* (see Chapter 19). In *Trotter v Grattan plc*, the employer, with the support of trade unions, introduced a random body search policy, in order to minimise thefts from the premises. The claimant objected to the policy and resigned, claiming constructive dismissal. An employment tribunal held that this was a unilateral variation of the claimant's contract and amounted to a breach of the implied term of trust and confidence, entitling the claimant to resign. However, it went on to hold that the dismissal was for 'some other substantial reason', and in the circumstances, fair.

Other aspects of the contract of employment

A. Disciplinary and grievance procedures

3.86 It is generally a condition of the contract that the employment is subject to the disciplinary and grievance procedures which are in force from time to time. These procedures are unilateral in the sense that it is the employer's responsibility to draw them up, with the co-operation of the employees and/or any relevant trade union if possible, without such assistance if necessary. Some form of incorporation into the individual contract of such conditions is also desirable, especially if these procedures are contained in a collective agreement, for this will then avoid the problems of incorporation so far as non-unionists are concerned.

3.87 But if a disciplinary procedure is incorporated into the contract, it must be adhered to, and a failure may attract the usual legal remedies. In *Jones v Lee and Guilding*, the claimant was dismissed from his post as headmaster of a Roman Catholic school after he had divorced his wife and remarried. His conditions of tenure stated that before any decision to dismiss a teacher was taken, the teacher had a right to be heard and to be represented before the local education authority. This procedure had not been followed, and the Court of Appeal granted an injunction restraining the school managers from purporting to dismiss the claimant without a hearing being held by the local education authority. In *Gunton v London Borough of Richmond* the claimant was given one month's notice of dismissal, though the disciplinary procedure, which was conceded to be part of his contract of employment, had not been fully implemented. The Court of Appeal held that his damages for wrongful dismissal should be limited to the loss he had suffered, which was assessed by reference to a reasonable period it would have taken the employer to implement the disciplinary procedure. (The decision was followed, albeit with some reluctance, by another division of the Court of Appeal: see *Boyo v Lambeth London Borough Council*.)

3.88 Disciplinary procedures, discussed in Chapter 12, are designed to ensure that the employee is given every possible opportunity to put right any conduct which is likely to be the subject of critical appraisal; to this extent, the object of the procedure is corrective rather than punitive. Grievance procedures are designed to ensure that the individual employee has a proper outlet for such complaints that he may have, so as to prevent an employee from nursing a grievance.

3.89 With a view to further encouraging employers and employees to use appropriate procedures in order to resolve disputes, new statutory dismissal, disciplinary and grievance procedures have been imported into every contract of employment by the Employment Act 2002 and the Employment Act 2002 (Dispute Resolution) Regulations 2004, although not as contractual terms. These procedures are minimum standards, and do not supplant existing procedures which are not inconsistent with the statutory scheme. A failure to follow the statutory dismissal and disciplinary procedure will have certain adverse consequences for the employer, and could lead to a finding that a dismissal is automatically unfair (irrespective of the actual merits of the case). Equally, an employee who fails to use the statutory grievance procedure may find that his complaint will not be entertained by an employment tribunal (see Chapter 12).

B. Job description

3.90 A modern practice is to draw up and give to an employee a job description document, detailing the nature of his duties. Again, this should be a unilateral document, and should be specific enough to identify the employee's tasks, yet general enough to enable variations to take place within the context of the contract. The ambit of contractual obligations is not the same as the ambit of the duties which an employee in fact performs. This is especially true in small firms, where greater flexibility is needed, and thus the former may be wider than the latter (*Glitz v Watford Electric Co Ltd*). An employer may be able to change the job description provided the proposed work is still within the contractual obligations.

3.91 The fact that a job description contains a flexibility clause does not give the employer carte blanche to change the fundamental nature of the employee's work. Any job change without the employee's assent must be qualified by the requirement that the change must be reasonable, and within the scope of the employee's contract (*Land Securities Trillium Ltd v Thornley*).

C. Variation of contractual terms

3.92 The terms of the contract of employment may only be varied with the consent of both parties, and there is no power which enables one side to act unilaterally, unless the contract unambiguously provides for a unilateral variation (*Security Facilities Division v Hayes*, and see para 3.98). It follows that a unilateral variation which is not accepted amounts to the repudiation of the contract. Thus if an employee is demoted, this will be repudiatory conduct by the employer, and a consequent resignation by the employee will be an acceptance of the repudiation and hence is, in law, a dismissal by the employer (see *Marriott v Oxford and District Co-operative Society (No 2)*). But if, subsequent to the variation, the employee stays on with the firm for a considerable length of time, it is likely that he will be regarded as having accepted the change, and the modified contract will be in existence. Where an employee protests about the change, but continues with the employment, it is a question of fact in each case as to whether or not he has accepted it (albeit under protest). If an employee continues to work under revised terms and conditions, albeit under protest, for a considerable length of time, it will be extremely difficult to conclude other than that he has accepted the revised terms (*Henry v London General Transport Services Ltd*).

3.93 The employer unilaterally varies the contract if he insists that the employee performs duties other than those contained in the contract, as in *Dwyer v Superguard Ltd*, where the applicant was engaged as a telephonist-typist. Typing work declined, and she was under-employed. She was asked to take on other work, splitting invoices, but she refused and was dismissed. This was held to be unfair, for her contract could only be varied with her consent. However, such a situation could be dealt with in future cases either by stating in the contract an obligation 'to perform such other duties as may be assigned from time to time', or by declaring a redundancy situation and making an offer of alternative employment.

3.94 An employer has no right unilaterally to vary the terms of a contract of employment, eg by reducing wages or salaries (*Miller v Hamworthy Engineering Ltd*), and if he does so, the employee is entitled to a common law remedy for the whole of the time the employer is in breach, and not merely for the period of notice which the employer could lawfully give to terminate the contract. In *Rigby v Ferodo Ltd* the claimant's wages were £192 per week, and his contract of employment terminable by 12 weeks' notice. As a result of a financial crisis, the employers tried to get the trade unions to agree to wage reductions, but the unions refused to agree. The employers then unilaterally reduced the plaintiff's wages by £30 per week. The claimant continued to work at the lower rate, but issued a writ claiming damages for breach of contract. The House of Lords upheld his claim. The employers had unilaterally repudiated the contract, but the employee had not accepted that repudiation, and thus the contract had not been terminated by the reduction in wages. Thus the employee was entitled to damages for the breach of contract for the whole of the period of the breach, and not for the period after 12 weeks when the employers could have lawfully terminated the contract. Whether a shop steward has apparent or ostensible authority to negotiate changes in terms and conditions of employment is a question of mixed fact and law, to be resolved according to the facts of each case (*Harris v Richard Lawson Autologistics Ltd*).

3.95 An employee has been 'dismissed' for the purpose of ERA, s 95(1) even though he remains in employment! Thus in *Alcan Extrusions v Yates* the employers wished to impose a new working pattern system, which had the effect of reducing the employees' earnings. After negotiations with trade unions had failed, the new pattern was unilaterally imposed. Employees sent a pro forma reply to the employers, stating that they would work the new system under protest, reserving their rights to claim unfair dismissal and/or redundancy payments. They subsequently lodged claims with an employment tribunal, who held that they had been dismissed. The decision was upheld by the EAT. Where an employer unilaterally imposes radically different terms of employment, that could amount to a dismissal if the changes constitute a very substantial departure from the old contract. In this case, the old contract had been removed, and a new, substantially inferior, contract had been substituted.

3.96 But a contract of employment cannot remain static over the years, and some element of change is inevitable. In strict law, a variation must be mutually agreed by both sides, but if an employee refuses to accept such a change, this does not mean that he can exercise a power of veto over any new proposal. Ultimately, the employer retains an equal right lawfully to terminate the contract. In *Grix v Munford Ltd* the employee was dismissed when she refused to work a new shift system at a service station, which the employers had claimed was necessary on the grounds of efficiency and financial expediency. The employment tribunal, in holding that the dismissal was fair, gave some guidelines on the approach which employers should adopt in these circumstances. They should consult fully and properly with the employee, and they must give reasonable and due consideration to any objections or alternative suggestions. It is also necessary to prove that the change is necessary, and thus amounts to 'some other substantial reason' should a dismissal prove to be necessary. It is not necessarily unfair to dismiss an employee who refuses to obey an order which is outside the terms of his contract, for the test is focused on the reasonableness of the employer's actions, not whether the employer was in breach of the contract (*Farrant v Woodroffe School*). In *Bowater Containers Ltd v McCormack*, the claimant was a supervisor. After a reorganisation, it was decided that another small section should come under his supervision. He refused to take on these additional duties, as he maintained that he was not contractually obliged to do so. His dismissal was held to be unfair by the employment tribunal, but the decision was reversed by the EAT. The reason for the dismissal, ie consequent on the reorganisation, was some other substantial reason and, in the circumstances, the employers had acted reasonably.

3.97 Thus if the employer wishes to vary the contract, and the employee refuses to accept the variation, the employer must give notice to terminate the contract (*Rigby v Ferodo Ltd*). This will, of course, amount to a dismissal, and would normally give the employee a right to bring a claim for unfair dismissal. In such proceedings, the employment tribunal may make a finding as to the advantages to the employers of the proposed changes, and whether it was reasonable for them to implement them by terminating the contract and offering a new one. The question then becomes, have the employers acted reasonably in dismissing the employee for his refusal to enter into the new contract (*Chubb Fire Security Ltd v Harper*)? To answer this question, the nature of the new offer, the advantages to the employer, and the method of handling the situation, the incentives offered, etc all become relevant considerations (*Hollister v National Farmers' Union*). The dismissal will be fair if the offer is one which a reasonable employer would make in the circumstances (*Richmond Precision Engineering Ltd v Pearce*). The employment tribunal should not look solely at the advantages and disadvantages of the new contract from the employee's point of view, but should also consider and take into account the benefits to the employer in seeking to impose the change (*Catamaran Cruisers v Williams*).

3.98 However, the express terms of the contract may permit substantial variations, and if this is so, the other party is bound to accept, whether he agrees in principle or not. The terms may expressly permit a change in the location of employment, or the duties of the employee, or any other relevant matter. In *Bex v Securicor Transport Ltd* it was a condition of the employee's contract that the nature of his work could be changed by the company. When they appointed him to another position, which he regarded as a demotion, he resigned. It was held that as the employers were expressly entitled to require the employee to serve the company in any capacity, there had been no breach of contract by the employer, and consequently his resignation did not amount to a dismissal. He had the choice of carrying out his contract, or resigning.

3.99 An implied variation, accepted by both sides, may be inferred from the parties' conduct. In *Armstrong Whitworth Rolls v Mustard*, when the employee was engaged, his hours were fixed by a national agreement, and he worked an eight-hour shift for five days per week. One of his workmates left, and he was asked to work twelve-hour shifts for five days per week. This arrangement continued for seven years, and when he was eventually made redundant, it was held that his redundancy payment was to be based on a normal working week of 60 hours. Although there was no express mutual agreement to vary his hours, such agreement could clearly be inferred from the conduct of the parties.

3.100 A contract may also be varied by virtue of the terms of a collective agreement. In *Parry v Holst* the claimant's employment was expressly governed by the terms of the Working Rule Agreement of the Civil Engineering Construction Conciliation Board, Clause XD (f) of which provided that 'At the discretion of the employer, an operative may be transferred at any time during the period of his employment from one job to another'.

The employee's work in South Wales came to an end, and his employers asked him to work in Somerset. He refused, and claimed a redundancy payment. It was held that he was not entitled. His employment was subject to the Working Rule Agreement, which provided for travelling and shift allowances, and there was nothing unusual about the employers' request. However, if the proposed transfer had been so unreasonable that it could be said to be outside the contemplation of the parties to the contract, then the literal application of Clause XD (f) would be precluded. Also, it was suggested that the Clause would not apply if there was a custom and practice of a particular company which would have the effect of varying the way the rule operated. None of these considerations applied in this case, and the application for a redundancy payment was rejected.

3.101 Where a variation of an existing contract is based on a change brought about by a revised collective agreement, the change will only be binding on individual employees if it is accepted by them, or if they were collectively represented at the time the change was agreed (*Land and Wilson v West Yorkshire Metropolitan County Council*). Thus employees who are not union members, or who are members of another union, are not necessarily bound by the change. But if the collective agreement is expressly incorporated into the individual's contract, or if the union has authority to negotiate a change, the variation will bind (*Nelson and Woollett v Post Office*).

D. Written particulars of the contract of employment

3.102 Section 1 of the Employment Rights Act 1996 provides that no later than two months after the commencement of employment, the employer shall give to the employee a written statement containing the following information:

(1) (a) the names of the employer and employee;
   (b) the date when the employment began;
   (c) the date on which the employee's period of continuous employment began, taking into account any employment with a previous employer which counts towards continuity;

(2) as at a specified date, not more than seven days before the statement is given:
   (a) the scale or rate of remuneration, or the method of calculating remuneration;
   (b) the intervals at which remuneration is paid;
   (c) any terms and conditions relating to hours of work;
   (d) any terms and conditions relating to:
       (i) entitlement to holidays, including public holidays, and holiday pay (being sufficient to calculate the entitlement, including accrued holiday pay on the termination of employment);
       (ii) incapacity for work due to sickness or injury, including any provision for sick pay;
       (iii) pensions and pension schemes;
   (e) the length of notice the employee is obliged to give, and entitled to receive to determine the employment;
   (f) the title of the employee's job;
   (g) if the employment is not intended to be permanent, the period for which it is expected to continue; if it is for a fixed term, the date when it is to end;

(h) either the place of work or, where the employee is required or permitted to work at various places, an indication of that, and of the address of the employer;

(j) any collective agreement which directly affects the terms and conditions of employment; where the employer is not a party to the agreement, the persons by whom they are made;

(k) where the employee is required to work outside the United Kingdom for more than one month:

(i) the period for which he is to work outside the United Kingdom;

(ii) the currency in which remuneration is to be paid while so working;

(iii) any additional remuneration payable to him, and any benefits to be provided by reason of his working abroad; and

(iv) any terms and conditions relating to his return to the United Kingdom.

3.103 So far as the above matters are concerned, it should be noted that:

(a) if there are no particulars to be entered under any of these headings, that fact should be stated;

(b) the written statement may refer the employee to the provisions of some other document which he has a reasonable opportunity of reading in the course of his employment, or which is made reasonably accessible to him in some other way, in respect of sick pay and pension schemes;

(c) all the above particulars shall be given in one document (known as the principal statement) except terms and conditions relating to sickness, pensions, length of temporary or fixed term contracts, collective agreements and details given to employees who are to work outside the United Kingdom. These terms may be contained in a separate document or documents;

(d) the statement shall be given to the employee notwithstanding that his employment has ended before the end of two months from its commencement.

3.104 In addition to the matters required to be given by s 1, s 3(1) requires that the statement shall include a note:

(a) specifying any disciplinary rules applicable to the employee or referring him to the provisions of a document which is reasonably accessible to him specifying such rules;

(b) specifying any procedure applicable to the taking of disciplinary decisions relating to the employee, or a decision to dismiss him, or referring to the provisions of a document which is reasonably accessible to him and which specifies such procedure;

(c) specifying (by description or otherwise) a person to whom the employee can apply if dissatisfied with any disciplinary decision relating to him, or any decision to dismiss him.

3.105 However, the above s 3 requirements do not apply to rules, disciplinary decisions, decisions to dismiss, grievances or procedures relating to health and safety at work. It should further be noted that the exemption from the requirements of s 3(1) which used to operate in favour of small employers, ie where the number of employees did not exceed 20, was repealed by the Employment Act 2002.

3.106 Sections 7A and 7B of ERA (inserted by the Employment Act 2002) provides that the employer meets his obligation under s 1 and s 3 if he provides a written contract of employment or letter of engagement which provides the s 1 and s 3 information (except sick pay, pension schemes, notice entitlement, periods of non-permanent employment, collective agreements and the details relating to work outside the United Kingdom).

3.107 If there is any change in the matters specified in the written particulars, the employer shall give, within one month of the change, the relevant particulars (s 4(1)).

3.108 It is not necessary to give written particulars to an employee if his employment continues for less than one month.

3.109 It must be borne in mind that the statement given by virtue of s 1 is not necessarily a contract, and is not conclusive evidence of that contract (*System Floors (UK) Ltd v Daniel*). But it certainly helps to establish what those contractual terms were, and a failure by an employer to provide such a statement may well lead an employment tribunal to draw adverse presumptions against that employer in subsequent litigation, should the terms of the contract be in dispute.

3.110 If an employer does not provide the written statement under s 1, or if it is incomplete, the employee can require a reference to be made to an employment tribunal to determine what particulars ought to be included in such a statement. But this power only extends to matters which should be in the statement in accordance with the above statutory requirements. The tribunal has no power to amend or rewrite a contract of employment merely because there is some misunderstanding about its meaning (*Construction Industry Training Board v Leighton*).

3.111 An employment tribunal may only state those terms which have been agreed. They cannot remake the contract and insert terms which should have been agreed. 'Mandatory' terms can be determined by looking at all the evidence, including the express, implied and statutory terms. If there has been no agreement on the 'non-mandatory' terms, the employment tribunal should record this (*Eagland v British Telecommunications plc*). There is no power to invent terms which have not been agreed, except, perhaps, terms which are necessarily imposed by law, eg reasonable notice.

3.112 The Employment Act 2002, s 38 provides for various sanctions to be applied when an employer fails to give the written statement under ERA, s 1 or the statement of changes under s 4(1) in respect of proceedings brought relating to a claim by an employee under any jurisdiction listed in Sch 5 (see Chapter 12). If, in respect of such proceedings, the employment tribunal finds in favour of the employee, but makes no award in respect of the claim, and, at the time proceedings were begun the employer was in breach of his duty to give a written statement of employment particulars or particulars of change, the tribunal must make an award of the minimum amount of two weeks' pay, and may, if it considers it just and equitable in all the circumstances, award the maximum amount of four weeks' pay. Equally, if the employment tribunal does make an award in respect of the claim, it must increase the award by two or four weeks' pay. In either case, these awards need not be made if there are exceptional circumstances which would make the award or increase unjust or inequitable. It must be borne in mind that the Employment Act 2002, s 38, does not give employees a free-standing claim to compensation for incomplete or inaccurate written particulars. It only applies when a claim is being brought under one of the jurisdictions set out in Sch 5 to the Act (see Chapter 12). A reference under ERA, s 11 (above) is not specified in Sch 5, and therefore does not, by itself, give rise to any claim for compensation.

The week's pay is calculated in accordance with ERA, ss 220–224 (see Chapter 14), with the statutory maximum to be applied.

E. Itemised pay statement (Employment Rights Act 1996, ss 8–10)

3.113 Every employee has the right to be given by his employer an itemised pay statement, giving particulars of the gross amount of wages or salary, the amount of any variable or fixed deductions, and the purposes for which they are made, the net wages or salary payable and, where the net amount is paid in different ways, the amount and method of each part-payment. A pay statement need not contain separate particulars or fixed deductions as long as the aggregate amount of all deductions is stated, and the employer had given to the employee a standing statement of fixed deductions which contains all the relevant details. Such standing statement must be reissued every 12 months.

3.114 If an employer fails to give an itemised pay statement, the employee may require a reference to be made to an employment tribunal, to determine what particulars ought to be included in such a statement. But where the tribunal finds that the employer has failed to give an employee any itemised pay statement, or that it does not give the required particulars concerning deductions, the tribunal shall make a declaration to that effect (*Coales v John Wood & Co*) and, if there have been any unnotified deductions from the employee's pay within 13 weeks preceding the date of the application for the reference to the tribunal, then the tribunal may award that the employer shall pay to the employee the aggregate of the deductions made. However, no application for a tribunal reference can be made more than three months after the employment has ceased. The requirement to give an itemised pay statement does not apply to employees who work outside Great Britain, share fishermen or merchant seamen.

F. Holidays

3.115 It will be recalled (see para 3.102) that the written statement to be given to employees under ERA, s 1 shall include any terms and conditions relating to entitlement to holidays, including public holidays and holiday pay, the particulars being sufficient to enable the employee's entitlement to be precisely calculated, including any entitlement to accrued holiday pay on the termination of the employment. Under the provisions of the Working Time Regulations 1998, all workers are entitled to a minimum period of four weeks' holiday each year (see para 7.63). Other than the provisions contained in the contract (or the written statement if used as evidence of the contract), there is no legal entitlement to bank or public holidays, and these may be used to discharge the employer's liability under the Working Time Regulations. Under the regulations, accrued holiday pay is payable on termination of the employment, but if the worker's entitlement is in excess of the statutory entitlement, then on termination of employment there may be problems in calculating the contractual entitlement (*Taylor v East Midlands Offender Employment*).

G. Occupational pension schemes

3.116 The Occupational Pension Schemes (Disclosure of Information) Regulations 1986 require an employer who runs an occupational pension scheme to disclose automatically certain information to members and beneficiaries, including details of the scheme, rights of leavers, amount of pension payable to a new pensioner, and options available to persons on the death of a member or beneficiary. Other information is to be disclosed on request, including trust deeds and rules, benefit statements, the trustees' annual report and the actuarial valuation report.

3.117 The persons entitled to this information include current members and deferred pensioners, prospective members and their spouses, and recognised independent trade unions (except that the latter are not entitled to benefit statements).

4

Discrimination in Employment

4.1 The law designed to prevent unlawful discrimination in employment dates from the passing of the Sex Discrimination Act 1975. The following year the Race Relations Act was passed, and the Disability Discrimination Act was passed in 1995. All three Acts have been substantially amended, partly as a result of two EU Directives (2000/43/EC and 2000/78/EC), and partly because of defects in the legislation revealed by litigation. Additional provisions can be found in various regulations which have been passed, dealing with, in particular, unlawful discrimination on grounds of sexual orientation, gender reassignment, civil partners, religion and belief. Legislation outlawing discrimination on grounds of age will come into force in 2006.

4.2 In some respects the various statutory provisions contain similar concepts and wording, with the result that the courts and tribunals will interchange legal decisions by adopting a decision made under one Act when interpreting provisions in another Act. However, in some respects there may be a divergence of approach (see, eg, *Jones v Post Office, Harrold v Wiltshire Healthcare NHS Trust*, and *Metropolitan Police Comr v Harley*). In particular, there are small but perhaps significant differences in the wording of the respective Acts, which may lead to different results, particularly when interpreting the Disability Discrimination Act (*Rowden v Dutton Gregory*, and see *Liversidge v Chief Constable of Bedfordshire Police*). It is expected the Equality Act 2006 will lead to a general harmonisation of the law.

4.3 The Sex Discrimination Act 1975 has been amended on a number of occasions, more recently by the Sex Discrimination (Indirect Discrimination and Burden of Proof) Regulations 2001, Employment Equality (Sexual Orientation) Regulations 2003, the Employment Equality (Sex Discrimination) Regulations 2005, and the Civil Partnership Act 2004. The main changes are incorporated into the text, but at this stage the following changes should be noted:

(a) In the definition of indirect discrimination, 'detriment of a considerably larger proportion of women', has been replaced by 'putting women at a particular disadvantage when compared with men, and cannot be shown to be a proportionate means of achieving a legitimate aim'. This change may significantly reduce the number of cases where statistical evidence is required.

(b) The definition of 'harassment' has been strengthened, to include conduct which is related to a person's sex, but is not, in itself, of a sexual nature.

(c) Harassment because of gender reassignment will now cover the reassignment of the person, not just their gender.

(d) There is an express reference to discrimination on grounds of pregnancy and the taking of maternity leave. The 'small firm' exemption contained in the Maternity and Parental Leave Regulations, reg 20 (see para 6.39) will be repealed in 2007.

(e) Changes have been made to the genuine occupational qualification provisions when gender reassignment applies.

(f) The Sex Discrimination Act will apply to persons who work wholly outside Great Britain in certain specified limited circumstances.

(g) There will be an eight-week time limit for employers to respond to the EOC questionnaire.

(h) Discrimination on the grounds of sexual orientation and gender reassignment is now prohibited.

(i) Persons who have entered into a civil partnership are to be treated in the same way as a married couple (Civil Partnership Act 2004 (Amendments to Subordinate Legislation) Order 2005).

Sex discrimination

4.4 Although it was generally considered that the Sex Discrimination Act 1975 was designed to prevent unlawful discrimination against women, its provisions apply equally to the treatment of men (s 2). But no account shall be taken of special treatment afforded to women in connection with pregnancy or childbirth. Further, it is unlawful to discriminate against a married person of either sex on the ground of that person's marital status. Thus, it is permissible to discriminate against a single person of either sex, but not in favour of such a person, because that would amount to discrimination against a married person. Thus if a firm wishes to offer cheap mortgage facilities to its staff, then if these facilities are made available to married men, they must be equally made available to married women (*Sun Alliance & London Insurance Ltd v Dudman*). But it is permissible to exclude single persons of either sex from the scheme, and it is permissible to discriminate between married and unmarried couples (*Bavin v NHS Trust Pensions Agency*) although this would not apply if the unmarried couple have registered under the Civil Partnership Act 2005.

As we shall see (para 4.27) the discrimination provisions apply to persons of a particular sexual orientation (ie homosexuals and lesbians) and to persons who have had a gender reassignment (para 4.36).

4.5 The Act does not permit 'affirmative' or 'positive' action designed to give priority to persons of either sex (other than single sex training permitted under ss 47–48: see para 4.52) and indeed such positive discrimination has been held to be contrary to the Equal Treatment Directive (76/207/EEC). In *Kalanke v Freie Hansestadt Bremen*, a man successfully claimed unlawful discrimination because he was passed over for promotion when an equally qualified woman was given the post, pursuant to a law which provided that women were to be preferred to a male candidate if their qualifications were equal.

4.6 However, this case was distinguished by the ECJ in *Marschall v Land Nordrhein-Westfalen*, where it was held that where there are fewer women than men in a particular post in public service, legislation can provide for preferential treatment for women, if there is a saving clause which guarantees that women are not to be given priority if there was a reason specific to an equally qualified male candidate which would tilt the balance in his favour. In other words, if a rule does not guarantee absolute and unconditional priority to women, it does not go beyond the limits of the Directive. Positive discrimination is not allowed if a member of the under-represented sex has qualifications for the post which are inferior to those who would otherwise be appointed (*Abrahamsson and Anderson v Fogelqvist*) but a target scheme for recruitment, selection and promotion is not precluded by EC law, if the scheme does not ensure that women were automatically and unconditionally offered preferential treatment over men (*Badeck v Hessischer*). Thus positive discrimination is unlawful, but positive action may be encouraged (*EFTA Surveillance Authority v Kingdom of Norway*).

A. What constitutes discrimination?

4.7 The test for determining whether or not an act was discrimination is objective, not subjective. In other words, regard must be had to what was done, not the reasons or motives behind what was done. The question to be asked is 'would the complainant have received the same treatment from the defendant but for his or her sex'? In *James v Eastleigh Borough Council*, Mr and Mrs James were both aged 61. The local authority adopted a policy whereby children under three years of age, and members of the public over pensionable age, were permitted free entry into the local swimming pool, whereas everyone else had to pay the 75p entrance fee. Mr James complained that he had been discriminated against because of his sex, as he was required to pay an admission fee, whereas his wife was not. The House of Lords upheld his contention. Lord Bridge stated that the purity of the discriminator's subjective motive, intention or reason for discriminating cannot save the criterion applied from the objective taint of discrimination on grounds of sex. Lord Ackner stated that the reason why the local authority adopted its particular policy (ie to benefit state pensioners) cannot affect the fact that men were treated less favourably than women.

4.8 Part II of the Act prohibits unlawful discrimination in employment, which is defined as 'employment under a contract of service or apprenticeship or a contract personally to execute any work or labour'. This definition is wider than the relationship of employer/employee, and can include self-employed persons (*Quinnen v Hovells*, see para 5.4), but there must be a personal obligation to perform that work or labour, and that performance must be the dominant purpose of the contract (*Mingeley v Pennock and Ivory*).

4.9 So far as discrimination in employment is concerned, there are a number of circumstances to consider.

Direct discrimination (s 1(1)(a))

4.10 This arises where a person of one sex is treated less favourably than a person of another sex, and the sex of that person is the reason for the less favourable treatment. Thus to refuse to employ a woman because 'it is a man's job' would be an example of direct discrimination (*Batisha v Say*), but if the unfavourable treatment has nothing to do with the sex of the person concerned, there is no direct discrimination (*Moberly v Commonwealth Hall (University of London)*). A comparison of the cases of persons of different sex or marital status must be such that the relevant circumstances in the one case are the same, or not materially different, in the other. Thus in *Thorn v Meggitt Engineering Ltd* a woman was refused employment as a radial driller because she was neither tall nor strong enough, and it was held that no direct discrimination had occurred.

4.11 A person can discriminate directly even though he is unaware that he is doing so. It can happen because of an inbuilt prejudice or as a result of making a stereotype assumption (*Skyrail Oceanic Ltd v Coleman*). But the treatment afforded must be less favourable, and the fact that it is different does not mean, per se, that it is less favourable. This is a question for the tribunal to determine (*Law Society v Bahl*). Nor does it depend on whether the claimant thinks that the treatment has been less favourable, for the test is an objective one. For example, some employers may decide to lay down different rules relating to dress or appearance for men and women, and the question will then arise as to whether or not such rules constitute sex discrimination. Thus in *Schmidt v Austicks Bookshops Ltd*, the owner of a bookshop had a rule which forbade female employees wearing trousers, and obliged them to wear overalls. Male employees were forbidden to wear T-shirts. A female employee refused to comply with the rule forbidding trousers, and she was dismissed. It was held that as there were rules governing the appearance of both male and female employees, so that they were both restricted as to clothing, the appellant had not been unlawfully discriminated against. Further, the requirement that she should wear overalls was not sufficiently serious or important so as to constitute a detriment within the meaning of s 6(2)(b). In *Burrett v West Birmingham Health Authority* male and female nurses were required to wear a uniform. Female nurses wore a starched cap, which had no practical or hygienic purpose. The claimant found the wearing of this cap demeaning and undignified, and when she refused to wear one, she was transferred to another department where she had less opportunity to work overtime. She claimed that she had been unlawfully discriminated against, but her claim was dismissed. The fact that there was a different uniform for men and women did not constitute less favourable treatment. The fact that she thought she had been treated less favourably was irrelevant, for the test under s 1(1)(a) was not subjective, but was for the employment tribunal to decide (see also *Stewart v Cleveland Guest (Engineering) Ltd*).

4.12 The approach adopted in the above cases was confirmed by the Court of Appeal in *Smith v Safeway plc*, where a male assistant who worked in the delicatessen department was dismissed because his ponytail hairstyle breached the company's rule that hairstyles should not be unconventional, and should not be permitted to grow below collar length. His claim for sex discrimination was dismissed by an employment tribunal, who held that a retail store was entitled to have a dress and appearance code, and that such a code did not have to make identical provision in relation to men and women. A majority of the EAT allowed his appeal, but the decision of the employment tribunal was restored by the Court of Appeal. A code governing the appearance of male and female employees, which laid down conventional standards, and was even-handed in its approach, was not discriminatory on grounds of sex. There is a distinction between discrimination between the sexes (which may be permissible) and discrimination against one or another of the sexes, which is forbidden by the Act.

4.13 Unreasonable behaviour does not, by itself, equate with unlawful discriminatory behaviour. In *Law Society v Bahl* it was stated that all unlawful discriminatory behaviour is unreasonable, but not all unreasonable treatment is discriminatory. Similarly, all racist language is offensive, but not all offensive language is racist. The fact that the victim of such treatment is a woman (or a man) or a member of a particular race or colour or nationality etc says nothing about the grounds for the perpetrator's actions. The Burden of Proof Regulations, which apply to race and sex discrimination claims may be raised in such circumstances, and adverse conclusions brought in the absence of a proper explanation, but if the hostile action has nothing to do with race or sex, no unlawful discrimination has occurred.

4.14 Discrimination can take place even though the act is done with the best of motives, and in the best interests of the person concerned. In *Grieg v Community Industry*, the claimant and another woman were appointed to two jobs, which involved working with men. The other woman failed to turn up for work, and so the claimant was not allowed to start work, as in the past there had been problems with one woman working with an all-male team. It was held that this constituted direct discrimination; the motive of the employers was irrelevant.

4.15 Section 5(3) provides that a comparison of the cases of persons of different sex or marital status under ss 1(1) and 3(1) must be such that the relevant circumstances in the one case are the same, or not materially different, in the other. Those 'relevant circumstances' must be judged objectively. In *Bullock v Alice Ottley School* the employers decided to establish a common retiring age for all members of their staff irrespective of sex. Teaching, administrative and domestic staff had to retire at 60, and gardeners and maintenance staff at 65. The higher retirement age of the latter group was necessary because of the difficulty in obtaining such personnel, and the need to keep them in employment as long as possible. The claimant was required to retire when she became 60, and she claimed she had been discriminated against on grounds of sex, because all the gardening and maintenance staff, who stayed on until 65, were men. An employment tribunal dismissed her complaint holding that it was not discriminatory to have differing retiring ages for persons in different groups provided it was applied irrespective of sex. The EAT reversed the decision, holding that the 'like for like' comparison had to be made in respect of all the staff, not separate groups. On a further appeal, the Court of Appeal restored the decision of the employment tribunal. The conclusion that everyone employed by the same employer had to have the same retiring age was one which could not be accepted. The comparison between the claimant (who was domestic staff) and the maintenance and gardening staff could not be made, since there were special difficulties in recruiting the latter which justified the later retiring age. The 'relevant circumstances' in s 5(3) had to be those circumstances which were relevant to the comparison.

4.16 To establish direct discrimination, a tribunal should first attempt to identify an actual comparator, in order to compare the treatment of the claimant with that afforded to another person of the same sex (or race, when appropriate). The actual comparator's situation should be, in all material respects, identical to the claimant's. Where there is no actual comparator, the tribunal must create a hypothetical comparator, which can only be done by a careful drawing of inferences from all the available evidence (*Shamoon v Chief Constable of the Royal Ulster Constabulary*).

4.17 If an employer has a rule which applies equally to men and women, no apparent discrimination exists, but this will not be so if the rule in question affects pregnant women. Thus in *Brown v Rentokil Ltd* the employers had a rule which stated that any employee who was absent from work because of sickness for more than 26 weeks would be dismissed. The claimant had a series of pregnancy-related illnesses, and was dismissed after 26 weeks' absence. The ECJ held that it was contrary to the Equal Treatment Directive to dismiss a woman at any time for absence owing to pregnancy or pregnancy-related illnesses even though a man absent for that period would also be dismissed.

Indirect discrimination (s 1(2)(b))

4.18 The new definition of indirect discrimination, contained in s 1(2)(b) of the Act, (as inserted by the Sex Discrimination (Indirect Discrimination and Burden of Proof) Regulations 2001 and the Employment Equality (Sex Discrimination) Regulations 2005), is as follows.

A person discriminates against a woman if:

(a) he applies to her a provision, criterion or practice which he applies or would apply equally to a man, but
  (i) which puts or would put women at a particular disadvantage when compared with men,
  (ii) which puts her at that disadvantage, and
  (iii) which he cannot show to be a proportionate means of achieving a legitimate aim.

4.19 One important distinction between direct and indirect discrimination is that so far as direct discrimination is concerned, there is no defence of justification, whereas in indirect discrimination, justification may be raised as a defence if it is a proportionate means of achieving a legitimate end. If an employer wishes to raise the defence of justification in a claim for indirect discrimination, the employment tribunal should not adopt the test of 'the range of reasonable responses' which is used in unfair dismissal claims. Rather, the tribunal should make its own judgment, upon a fair and detailed analysis of working practices and business considerations involved, as to whether the 'policy, criterion or other practice' at issue is reasonably necessary (*Hardys and Hanson plc v Lax*).

4.20 The original wording of the Act stated that there had to be a requirement or condition with which the proportion of women who can comply is smaller than the proportion of men, and it was to the woman's detriment that she could not comply. The phrase 'provision, criterion or practice' is considerably wider in its effect, and a number of earlier decisions are thus no longer relevant. A claimant would now need to show that the provision, etc placed her at a particular disadvantage. This means that it will rarely be necessary in the future to rely on statistics to ascertain whether or not there is indirect discrimination, as long as it can be shown that the provision, etc is disadvantageous to this particular claimant. Evidence on this may come from experts or other witnesses, but an employment tribunal will make an objective assessment on whether a particular claimant was put at a disadvantage by the provision, etc, and whether or not by applying that provision, etc the employer was adopting a proportionate means of achieving a legitimate aim.

4.21 Thus a provision which requires a woman to work overtime, or a refusal to permit her to return to part-time work as oppose to full-time work (*Home Office v Holmes*), or a refusal to permit her to work from home (*Lockwood v Crawley Warren Group Ltd*), etc, could all amount to a provision, etc which could put a woman at a disadvantage (eg because of child-minding difficulties, etc) which would amount to indirect discrimination unless the employer can objectively justify such a provision, etc. In *London Underground Ltd v Edwards* the claimant was employed as a train driver, generally working from 8.00am until 4.00pm. As part of a cost saving plan, the employer introduced a new shift system, which required her to commence work at 4.45am. As she was a single mother with a young child, she was not prepared to work the new system, and she resigned, claiming indirect sex discrimination. The EAT held that the employment tribunal had been entitled to take into account their common knowledge that a proportionately larger number of women have childcare responsibilities than men, and thus indirect discrimination was made out. Having regard to her length of service (10 years) and the fact that the demands of her family would lessen in the future, the employer should have made arrangements to accommodate her personal requirements. Thus the defence of justification was not made out (under the new provisions, it would doubtlessly have been held that there was a disadvantage to the claimant, and the method adopted by the employer was not a proportionate means of achieving a legitimate aim).

4.22 The test of justification does not permit an employer to argue that there is a margin or discretion in the way he treats a woman (eg, on an application for job sharing). Nor is the test akin to that of the unfair dismissal standard of the range of reasonable responses. The principle of proportionality requires the tribunal to take into account the reasonable needs of the business, but it is for the tribunal to make its own judgment on whether the discriminatory provision, etc is objectively justified (*Hardys & Hanson plc v Lax*).

4.23 However, objective justification *is* possible. In *Briggs v North Eastern Education and Library Board* the Northern Ireland Court of Appeal took the view that a contractual provision which was imposed on a teacher that she should assist in the taking of school games outside school hours was a requirement which was justified irrespective of a person's sex or marital status. A balance must be drawn between the discriminatory effect of the provision and the reasonable needs of the employer, objectively determined (see also *Bilka-Kaufhaus v Weber von Hartz*). Further, economic factors, such as cost, can be weighed in the balance in assessing proportionality (*Cross v British Airways*).

Victimisation (s 4(1))

4.24 It is also unlawful to victimise a person because he/she has:

(a) brought proceedings under the Act, or the Equal Pay Act 1970, or

(b) given evidence or information in connection with proceedings under either Act, or

(c) done anything (in relation to either Act) to the discriminator or any other person, or

(d) has made allegations of a contravention of either Act.

However, there is no victimisation if the treatment of a person is by reason of any allegation made by him if the allegation is false and not made in good faith (*Cornelius v University College of Swansea*).

4.25 In order to establish that a person was victimised, it must be shown that s/he did one of the protected acts (above), that s/he was treated less favourably, and that the reason for the less favourable treatment was the doing of the protected act (*Aziz v Trinity Street Taxis Ltd*). But if a person claims that s/he was victimised because s/he made a complaint in respect of something which took place outside working hours, this cannot be within s 4(1)(d), because it is not in respect of an act by the employer which was in contravention of the Act (*Waters v Metropolitan Police Comr*). If an employer makes an honest and reasonable attempt to compromise proceedings in a dispute with employees, by trying to persuade them to settle those proceedings, this does not amount to victimisation (*Derbyshire v St Helens Metropolitan Borough Council*).

4.26 Earlier cases had held that there could be no claim for sex discrimination in respect of acts which took place after the employment had ended, although the European Court held that this did not apply in respect of the victimisation provisions, because the Equal Treatment Directive would be undermined if an employer could take discriminatory action after the employment had ceased (*Coote v Granada Hospitality Ltd*). However, the House of Lords held in *Rhys-Harper v Relaxion Group plc* that such a claim could succeed if there was a substantial connection between the post-termination act and the earlier employment. This position has now been confirmed by s 20A of the Act, which provides that it is unlawful for a person to discriminate against a woman by subjecting her to a detriment where the discrimination arises out of and is closely connected with her previous employment.

Discrimination on grounds of sexual orientation

4.27 The Employment Equality (Sexual Orientation) Regulations 2003 came into force in December 2003, and generally implement the relevant provisions of the EC Equal Treatment Framework Directive 2003/78. Protection is given to job applicants, persons in employment (including employees, workers and persons who are genuinely self-employed). Also within the scope of the regulations are former employees, if discrimination or harassment arises out of or is closely connected with the employment relationship (see *Relaxion Group plc v Rhys-Harper*, para 4.26). Anyone who works wholly or partly in Great Britain is covered, as are employees who work wholly outside Great Britain if the employer has a place of business in Great Britain and the work is for the purpose of the business carried on there.

4.28 Sexual orientation is defined as a sexual orientation towards persons of the same sex, of the opposite sex or of the same sex and of the opposite sex. It does not cover particular sexual practices or fetishes, eg sado-masochism or paedophile activities etc.

4.29 Generally speaking, the regulations mirror existing discrimination legislation, including direct and indirect discrimination and harassment. Direct discrimination occurs if a person treats another person less favourably on the ground of sexual orientation. It is anticipated that this phrase will be interpreted in line with decisions on race discrimination, ie any reason for an action which is based on sexual orientation, whether it be the orientation of the person affected or some other person (*Showboat Entertainment Centre Ltd v Owens*). However, there are two 'genuine occupational qualifications' which may be raised as a defence. The first is where the nature of the employment is such that being of a particular sexual orientation is a genuine and determining occupational requirement, and it is proportionate to apply that requirement in the particular case. The second applies to employment for purposes of an organised religion, where there is a requirement as to sexual orientation in order to comply with the doctrine of the religion, or to avoid conflicting with the religious convictions of a significant number of the religion's followers.

4.30 Indirect discrimination may occur when a 'provision, criterion or practice' is applied which puts persons of a particular sexual orientation at a disadvantage when compared with other persons. For example, to advertise a job as being suitable for a married couple would be indirectly discriminatory of homosexual partners, since they cannot marry. Technically speaking, a 'civil partnership' is not a 'marriage', but in effect it is to be treated as such (see para 2.90).

Harassment and sexual harassment (s 4A)

4.31 There are now three forms of harassment to consider.

A person subjects a woman to harassment if:

(a) on the grounds of her sex, he engages in unwanted conduct that has the purpose or effect of violating her dignity, or creating an intimidating, hostile, degrading, humiliating or offensive environment for her; or

(b) he engages in any form of unwanted, verbal, non-verbal or physical conduct of a sexual nature that has the purpose or effect of violating her dignity, or of creating an intimidating, hostile, degrading, humiliating or offensive environment for her; or

(c) on the grounds of her rejection or submission to the above unwanted conduct he treats her less favourably than he would treat her if she had not rejected, or submitted to, the conduct.

The first form of harassment refers to any conduct which has the unwanted purpose or effect, the second form of conduct refers to unwanted conduct of a sexual nature, and the third form will apply when there is less favourable treatment as a result of rejection or submission to the conduct in question.

Conduct shall be regarded as having the effect mentioned above in (a) and (b) only if, having regard to all the circumstances, including the particular perception of the woman, it should reasonably be considered as having that effect. So far as (c) is concerned, this will be a question of fact for the tribunal to determine.

Conduct is 'unwanted' in the sense of being 'unwelcome' or 'uninvited' (*Insitu Cleaning Co Ltd v Heads*). A single incident can give rise to harassment (*Bracebridge Engineering Ltd v Darby*). Non-sexual conduct would only give rise to liability if it was because of a woman's sex, but the fact that similar treatment is metered out to men and women is irrelevant if the conduct is of a sexual nature (*Driskel v Peninsula Business Services*).

4.32 Compensation for sexual harassment must reflect the degree of hurt suffered, and a sensible assessment made of the injury to the woman's feelings, looked at objectively, ie with reference to what any ordinary reasonable woman would feel, and also subjectively, with reference to the particular individual (*Snowball v Gardner Merchant Ltd*). If a woman's actions are provocative, it can hardly be said that she has suffered injury to her feelings (*Wileman v Minilec Engineering Ltd*). However, in recent years substantial sums have been awarded where serious harassment has taken place.

4.33 It should be borne in mind that sexual harassment can be harassment of men as well as of women and includes harassment on grounds of sexual orientation.

4.34 If an employer has reason to believe that sexual harassment is taking place, it is incumbent upon him to investigate the matter, and to take some action if necessary, without waiting for a formal complaint to be made. A failure to do so could well amount to a breach of the implied term of trust and confidence (*Reed and Bull Information Systems Ltd v Stedman*).

4.35 It must also be borne in mind that an allegation of sexual harassment (as with allegations of other acts of sex discrimination) may be met with certain defences, in particular (a) that the act was not done within the course of employment (see *Tower Boot Co Ltd v Jones*, para 4.87), and that (b) the employer took such steps as were reasonably practicable to prevent an employee from doing the act complained of (see para 4.89). If an act of sexual harassment (or sexual assault) takes place outside working hours, or during a visit to the employee's home outside working hours (*HM Prison Service v Davies*), the employer will not be vicariously liable, for the act was not committed in the course of employment (*Waters v Metropolitan Police Comr*) (but see *Chief Constable of Lincolnshire v Stubbs*, para 4.83).

Discrimination on grounds of gender reassignment

4.36 Discrimination against a person because of a gender reassignment is discrimination based on the sex of the person concerned, and hence falls to be considered under the Equal Treatment Directive. In *P v S* a male employee informed his manager that he was going to have a gender reassignment. After having the necessary operations, she was not permitted to return to work, and was dismissed. On a claim for sex discrimination the employment tribunal referred the issue to the European Court, who held that the Equal Treatment Directive cannot be confined to the fact that discrimination had to be between one sex and another. The Directive was an expression of the fundamental principle of equality, and its scope applied to discrimination based on the sex of the person concerned. Thus, in this case, the claimant was treated unfavourably by comparison with persons of the sex to which he or she was deemed to belong before undergoing the gender reassignment. To tolerate such discrimination would be tantamount to failing to respect the dignity and freedom to which persons are entitled, and which the court felt it had a duty to safeguard.

4.37 The problem, of course, is that the Directive only applies to public bodies, and to bring the private sector within the scope of the decision in *P v S* required legislation. Consequently, the Sex Discrimination (Gender Reassignment) Regulations 1999 were passed, and amended the Sex Discrimination Act by inserting new ss 2A and 7B. The regulations define gender reassignment as being '. . . a process which is undertaken under medical supervision for the purpose of reassigning a person's sex by changing physiological or other characteristics of sex, and include any part of such process'. Section 2A now makes it unlawful directly to discriminate by treating a person less favourably on the ground that he intends to undergo, is undergoing, or has undergone a gender reassignment. If a person is absent from work as a result of undergoing treatment for gender reassignment, he is not to be treated less favourably than he would have been if the absence was due to sickness or injury, or some other cause, and, having regard to the circumstances of the case, it is reasonable for him to be treated no less favourably.

4.38 There are a number of exceptions to the protections afforded by the gender reassignment provisions. It will not be discriminatory in the arrangements made (s 6(1)(a)), or to refuse a person employment (s 6(1)(c)) if there is a supplementary genuine occupational qualification for the job (see para 4.81). Nor is a refusal to afford access to opportunities for promotion or transfer (s 6(2)(a)), or a dismissal (s 6(2)(b)), discriminatory (s 7B).

Harassment on grounds of gender reassignment (s 4A(3))

4.39 A person (A) subjects another person (B) to harassment if:

(a) on the ground that B intends to undergo, is undergoing or has undergone gender reassignment, A engages in unwanted conduct that has the purpose or effect of violating dignity, or creating an intimidating, hostile, degrading, humiliating or offensive environment for B, or

(b) on the ground of B's rejection or submission to the above unwanted conduct, A treats B less favourably than he would have done had B not rejected or submitted to the conduct.

Conduct shall be regarded as having the effect mentioned only if, having regard to all the circumstances, including the particular perception of B, it should reasonably be considered as having that effect.

4.40 It should be noted that once a person has undergone gender reassignment and obtained formal recognition under the Gender Recognition Act 2004, that person is entitled to be treated in all respects as a person of the acquired gender. This is reflected in the new provisions relating to genuine occupational qualifications, see para 4.78.

B. Unlawful discrimination

4.41 There are five types of unlawful discriminatory acts which may be committed against a person in relation to employment at an establishment in Great Britain.

The arrangements a person makes for the purpose of determining who shall be employed (s 6(1)(a))

4.42 The arrangements must ensure that job opportunities are available to all, irrespective of sex. However, an advertisement which indicates an intention to discriminate is not, by itself, discriminatory against any particular person (see *Cardiff Women's Aid v Hartup*, para 4.127). Only the EOC can bring an action in respect of discriminatory advertisements, under s 38 of the Act (para 4.83) not an individual.

4.43 Even if an advertisement in itself is non-discriminatory, an unlawful act may be committed if subsequent events disclose an intention to discriminate. In *Brennan v JH Dewhurst Ltd*, a girl applied for a job as a butcher's assistant. She was interviewed by the branch manager, who made it clear that he had no intention of employing a woman in the job. However, the district manager, who had the responsibility for making the appointment, decided that the vacancy need not be filled. The EAT held that the interview by the branch manager, which was a 'first filter' arrangement, operated so as to discriminate against the girl, even though it was not made for that purpose.

4.44 Questions which are asked at interviews are also part of the employment arrangements, as can be seen from *Saunders v Richmond-upon-Thames Council*, where a woman applied for a job as a professional golfer. She was confronted with questions which were not put to male applicants, and which were concerned with the ability of a woman to do the job in question ('Are there any other woman golf professionals?', 'Are you blazing a trail?', etc). It was held that to put certain questions to women applicants which are not put to men does not necessarily make those questions an indication that the employer intends to discriminate. Clearly, an employer may wish to put certain questions to a woman which may be more pertinent in her case (eg 'do you intend to have children?' or 'who will look after the children if they are off school sick?' etc), and which are capable of indicating an intention to discriminate on the ground of parenthood rather than sex.

4.45 A similar problem may arise at some future date over the use of application forms, for it could be argued that some of the questions which are directed to finding out factual information (eg sex, marital status, number of children, etc) are discriminatory in that they have no bearing on the employment situation. On this point there is no direct decision.

4.46 It may amount to sex discrimination to insist that a woman's job is not suitable for job sharing (*Cast v Croydon College*).

4.47 It is also unlawful for an employer to subject to harassment a woman whom he employs, or who has applied for employment.

The terms on which a person offers employment to another (s 6(1)(b))

4.48 If an employer makes an offer of employment to a woman on terms which are less favourable than those offered to a man, then clearly an act of discrimination has occurred. This does not apply to any provision for the payment of money unless her contract is subject to an equality clause by virtue of the Equal Pay Act 1970 (see Chapter 5), in which case it is discriminatory. To make an offer of employment to a woman on terms which are different from those offered to a man will be prima facie discriminatory. But if the employer can show that the variation was due to a genuine material difference between the two applicants which had nothing to do with their sex, it will not be unlawful. For example, if a woman is offered employment commencing at 9am because she has to take her children to school, a man must be offered the same facility if he is in a similar situation. A problem may arise if an offer is made which is more favourable than the terms enjoyed by existing employees, for the latter may well decide to make a subsequent complaint.

4.49 It is permissible to discriminate in the terms offered which relate to death or retirement (see para 4.75).

Refusing or deliberately omitting to offer employment because of a person's sex (s 6(1)(c))

4.50 In *Batisha v Say* a woman was turned down for a job as a cave guide because 'it is a man's job', and in *Munro v Allied Suppliers* a man was not taken on as a cook because women employees would not work with him. In both cases it was held that an act of discrimination had occurred. A more difficult situation arises it there is an act of discrimination, but in the final event no one is appointed to the post. Can it thus be argued that the person concerned has been treated less favourably? On this, there are tribunal decisions both ways; in *Roadburg v Lothian Regional Council*, the claimant was told that she was unsuitable because she was a woman. This was held to be unlawful discrimination even though no one was appointed to the post. In *Thorn v Meggitt Engineering*, the tribunal dismissed a claim of sex discrimination on its facts, but added that even if there had been discrimination, the claimant was treated no less favourably than a man, for no one was appointed to the job. It would appear that this decision is incorrect; once there has been a finding of unlawful discrimination, the remedy is a declaration, and an award may be made in respect of injury to feelings, even though no other pecuniary loss has been suffered (*Brennan v J H Dewhurst*, above).

To refuse to appoint a woman to a job, or to promote her, because she is married to a work colleague, could constitute indirect discrimination on grounds of sex, and direct and indirect discrimination on grounds of marital status (*Chief Constable of Bedfordshire Constabulary v Graham*).

4.51 An employer still retains his prerogative right to choose the person he believes will best do the job, and the fact that a rejected candidate has qualifications or experience which are better than the appointee will not be sufficient to found a claim of discrimination. As long as there is no evidence of discrimination on grounds of sex, the employer may select a candidate on the basis of any criteria he thinks fit. In refuting a claim, an employer may well point to the fact that women have been engaged in such positions before, and indicate that there were other reasons why the candidate was not offered employment. Thus in *Steere v Morris Bros* a woman applied for a job as a heavy goods vehicle driver. When she was rejected, she claimed she had been discriminated against. The employers were able to show that they had employed women drivers in the past, and the reason she was not appointed was because she lived too far away from the place of employment. The reasons for her non-appointment had nothing to do with her sex.

In relation to access to promotion, etc (s 6(2)(a))

Opportunity for promotion and training and benefits etc

4.52 To deny a woman an opportunity for promotion (eg by refusing to send her on a development course), or to restrict her training opportunities would be discriminatory, although it may be noted that a crash programme of single sexed training is permissible under ss 47–48 in order to alter an imbalance of the sexes in a job which has become apparent within the previous 12 months. The words 'benefits, facilities or services' are capable of covering almost any discriminatory practice in employment. For example, in *Peake v Automotive Products*, the terms and conditions of employment of men and women were the same. However, it was an established practice of the firm, going back some 30 years, that women and disabled persons were allowed to leave work at 4.25pm, whereas the men left at 4.30pm. This arrangement was made for safety reasons, in order to prevent women and handicapped employees from being jostled in the rush to the gate. The male claimant complained that this amounted to an act of unlawful discrimination on grounds of his sex. His claim was rejected by the employment tribunal, but on appeal, the EAT held that he had been refused access to a benefit (of leaving early) and had been subjected to a detriment (of not being allowed to leave at 4.25pm) on grounds of his sex. This decision was reversed by the Court of Appeal. Lord Denning held that the Act did not obliterate all the chivalry and courtesy which it was expected that men would give to women. Nor did the Act require that elemental differences of sex must be disregarded in the interpretation of an Act of Parliament. Arrangements which were made in the interests of safety or good administration were not infringements of the law. In the last analysis, Lord Denning was prepared to adopt the rule *de minimis non curat lex* (the law does not concern itself with trifling matters). This decision has been criticised on the ground that the interests of safety and good administration could be met without relying on a scheme which was fundamentally based on sex, and that some other equally efficacious manner of achieving these objects could be devised without perpetuating the myth of 'the weaker sex'. Indeed, the Court of Appeal subsequently held that the only sound reason for the decision in *Peake's* case is the *de minimis* rule, and in so far as the decision rested on chivalry and administrative convenience, it was no longer to be relied upon (*Jeremiah v Ministry of Defence*).

By dismissing a person, or subjecting her/him to any other detriment (s 6(2)(b))

4.53 The term 'dismissal' includes constructive dismissal (see para 17.24) and the non-renewal of a fixed-term contract (ERA, s 95).

4.54 A dismissal on grounds of sex is unlawful even though the employer acts under pressure from other employees. In *Munro v Allied Suppliers*, a man was offered a job as a cook. He was dismissed before he started work, as other women employees indicated that they would not work with him. This was held to violate the Act.

4.55 A 'detriment' can take many forms. Thus to dismiss a woman following a disciplinary hearing which she was unable to attend because of a pregnancy-related illness is to subject her to a detriment (*Abbey National plc v Formoso*). In *Day v T Pickles Farms Ltd* it was held that a failure to carry out a risk assessment when employing a woman of childbearing age, as required by reg 16 of the Management of Health and Safety at Work Regulations (see para 11.77) was to subject her to a detriment, as was a failure to investigate an allegation of sexual harassment in *Coyne v Home Office*.

4.56 A detriment may exist even though the employee is compensated for it. In *Jeremiah v Ministry of Defence*, it was the practice of the respondents not to require women to do certain dirty work, as they did not wish to take showers afterwards. When men did the work, they received extra pay. It was held that the fact that the employee was compensated for the dirty work by an additional payment did not mean that he was not subjected to a detriment. An employer cannot buy the right to discriminate.

Dismissal on grounds of sex and marital status

4.57 The employment tribunals have met with some difficulties in those cases where a woman has been dismissed, but sex, although relevant, has not been the primary consideration. In *Gubala v Crompton Parkinson*, the choice of a dismissal in a redundancy situation lay between a man and a woman. The woman had longer overall service, but the employers took into account the fact that the man was 58 years old, and had a family to support and a mortgage to keep up. The woman was young, married, with a husband who was working, and she was dismissed. It was held that this amounted to unlawful discrimination; the tribunal refused to accept the 'breadwinner' criterion as a basis of redundancy selection.

4.58 A somewhat different result was reached in *Goult v Reay Electrical*, where the claimant was dismissed when it was discovered that she had married a sales representative who was in the employ of a competitor. The employment tribunal held that she was not dismissed because of her sex, or her marital status, but because she had formed a relationship between an employee of her employer's principal competitor. The marriage was irrelevant except in so far as it indicated that there was a close relationship between her and her husband!

4.59 Further difficulties have been met in cases where a woman has been dismissed because she has announced an intention to get married. It will be recalled that discrimination on grounds of marital status is dealt with in s 3 of the Act. In *Bick v Royal West of England Residential School for the Deaf*, it was held that to dismiss a single woman who announced her intention to get married was not discrimination on grounds of her marital status, for she was not yet married! The tribunal did not appear to consider s 6(2)(b) (dismissal by way of discrimination) as there does not appear to have been any evidence that men were treated in a different manner if they made a similar announcement. On the other hand, in *McLean v Paris Travel Service*, it was contrary to the company's policy to employ married couples, and the claimant was dismissed when she announced her intention to marry the assistant manager. This was held to be contrary to s 6(2)(b), and she was awarded damages for injury to her feelings, as well as compensation for unfair dismissal.

4.60 A case which illustrates some of the difficulties arising from dismissal on grounds of sex and marital status is *Skyrail Oceanic Ltd v Coleman*, where the claimant was employed as a booking clerk in a travel agency. She then became engaged to a man who worked for a rival firm. The two employers discussed the matter, as it appeared that there would be a possibility of leakage of confidential information. It was agreed that the claimant's husband-to-be would be the breadwinner of the marriage. After the marriage had taken place, she was dismissed. An employment tribunal awarded her £666 compensation for unfair dismissal and £1,000 for injury to feelings under the Sex Discrimination Act. The EAT allowed the employer's appeal under the Sex Discrimination Act, but this was reversed by a majority of the Court of Appeal, who held than an assumption that men are more likely to be the breadwinner of the family than women was an assumption based on sex. Therefore, the dismissal of a woman based on that assumption amounted to sex discrimination.

Dismissal on grounds of pregnancy

4.61 To dismiss a woman because she is pregnant, or for a reason connected with her pregnancy, is automatically unfair under the provisions of the Employment Rights Act 1996 (see para 6.40). However, the question will sometimes be raised as to whether such dismissal is also an act of sex discrimination as well (this may be important because there is no limit to the level of compensation which may be awarded in sex discrimination cases (see *Ministry of Defence v Cannock*)).

4.62 There are two schools of thought on this question, The first school argues that since men cannot become pregnant, there is no question of treating a woman less favourably because of her sex. Therefore, a 'like with like' approach must be used, ie the treatment of a woman must be compared with the treatment of an analogous man in a similar situation. Thus, if a woman is off work because of pregnancy, the question would be, how would a man have been treated if he was off work for a similar period because of a sickness?

4.63 This approach was approved by the House of Lords in *Webb v Emo Cargo (UK) Ltd*, so far as UK domestic law is concerned. In this case, a female clerk informed her employer that she was pregnant, and would eventually be taking maternity leave of absence. The claimant was taken on as a temporary replacement, it being recognised that she would require several months' training in order to learn how to do the job. A few weeks after commencing her employment, she informed the employer that she too was pregnant. The employers dismissed her, and she therefore claimed that she had been unlawfully discriminated against on grounds of sex. Her claim failed. She was not dismissed because of her sex, or because of her pregnancy. A man who announced that he would be absent for a comparable period would, in the circumstances, have been treated in a like manner. The claimant's dismissal was therefore for a neutral reason.

4.64 The second school of thought stems from European law, and is based on an 'automatic approach' under the provisions of the Equal Treatment Directive (76/207/EEC). The approach here is to refuse to treat pregnancy as a pathological condition, and therefore the unavailability for work of a man, whether for medical or non-medical reasons, cannot be used for comparison purposes. Thus in *Dekker v Stichting Vormingscentrum voor Jong Volwassenen (VJV-Centrum) Plus*, the claimant applied for a job as a training instructor. In fact, all the applicants were women. The applicant told the selection committee that she was pregnant, but although she was the most suitable candidate, she was not offered the job. The reason was that the employers' insurers would not reimburse the employers for the sickness benefit they would have to pay her, because she was pregnant at the time of the application. Mrs Dekker claimed that the refusal to offer her employment was contrary to the Dutch equal treatment law, and also contrary to the Equal Treatment Directive EEC 76/207 (see para 1.72). The European Court upheld her claim. Whether a refusal to employ results in direct discrimination on grounds of sex depends on whether the reason for the refusal was a reason which applied without distinction to persons of both sexes, or whether it applied exclusively to one sex. Since she was refused employment because she was pregnant, and only women can be pregnant, the refusal was because of her sex. Further, the fact that there were no male applicants for the post was irrelevant, for if the reason for the refusal to employ her was a reason which exclusively applied to one sex, the reason is inherently discriminatory.

4.65 The House of Lords in *Webb v Emo Air Cargo Ltd* referred the appeal to the European Court of Justice for a ruling on these conflicting approaches. The ECJ confirmed the 'automatic' approach, and held that it was contrary to the Equal Treatment Directive to dismiss a woman who was employed for an unlimited term, and who was found to be pregnant shortly after her recruitment, notwithstanding that she was employed to replace a woman who was on maternity leave, and even though the employer would have dismissed a man who had been engaged in similar circumstances who required leave of absence for medical or other reasons. The ECJ seemed to think that if a woman risked dismissal because of pregnancy, there was a danger that she would be prompted voluntarily to terminate her pregnancy. Further, the Pregnant Workers Directive (92/85/EEC) prohibits the dismissal of a woman from the beginning of her pregnancy until the end of her maternity leave. Thus the protection offered by EC law during and after her pregnancy is not dependent on whether her presence at work is essential to the proper functioning of the undertaking in which she is employed.

4.66 But if a woman is dismissed for a reason other than pregnancy, even if that reason flows from the pregnancy, this is not an act of sex discrimination. In *Berrisford v Woodard Schools* the claimant was employed as a matron at a Church of England girls' boarding school. She informed the headmaster that she was pregnant. Initially, he congratulated her, and made certain proposals regarding married accommodation, but his attitude changed when the applicant informed him that she had no intention of marrying the father of the child. She was subsequently dismissed, and claimed she had been discriminated against on grounds of sex and family status, contrary to the Sex Discrimination Act and the Equal Treatment Directive. Evidence was given that the school governors expected somewhat high moral standards from their staff, and it was argued that the claimant was dismissed because her pregnancy manifested extra-marital sexual activity. The employment tribunal dismissed her complaint, holding that the reason for the dismissal was the adverse example to the pupils at the school conveyed by the pregnancy, coupled with the continuing unmarried status. The decision was upheld by the EAT. It was the example given to the pupils at the school which was the objectionable conduct, and a man who displayed continuing evidence of extra-marital sexual activity would have been treated in a similar fashion. *Dekker's* case was distinguished because it concerned a woman who was pregnant, and nothing more, whereas in the present case the dismissal was not because of pregnancy, but because of the adverse effect, by way of example, of the pregnancy on the pupils at the school.

As the school was not an organ of the state, the Equal Treatment Directive could not be enforced directly, but in any event, the EAT were not convinced that the Directive had been infringed, because no discrimination on grounds of sex had been shown.

4.67 A different approach was taken by the EAT in *O'Neill v Governors of St Thomas More School*. In this case, the claimant, who was unmarried, was employed to teach religious education and personal relationships at a Catholic school, it being expected that she would make the ideologies and ethos of the Catholic faith clear to her pupils. She then announced that she was pregnant, as a result of a relationship with a Roman Catholic priest who used to visit the school, and who was well known locally. She was invited to resign her post, on terms, but she refused to do so, and instead took maternity leave, and announced her intention to return to work. The school governors refused to permit her to return, and so she claimed that she had been discriminated against on grounds of her sex and/or pregnancy. An employment tribunal dismissed her complaint, holding that her dismissal was not because of her pregnancy, but because she was pregnant as a result of a relationship with a locally well-known Roman Catholic priest. The decision was reversed by the EAT. There is no distinction between pregnancy per se and pregnancy in the circumstances, because there are always circumstances which surround pregnancy, whether before, during or afterwards. The Sex Discrimination Act requires the employment tribunal to decide whether the treatment complained of was on the ground of sex, and the subjective motives of the discriminator were irrelevant.

4.68 A failure to carry out a risk assessment in respect of a pregnant woman, as required by the Management of Health and Safety at Work Regulations is sex discrimination. It is not necessary for the treatment of a pregnant woman to be compared with the employer's treatment of a comparable male employee, or a non-pregnant female employee. If the basis of the treatment is pregnancy, it is unlawful irrespective of the comparable treatment of men (*Hardman v Mallon (t/a Orchard Lodge Nursing Home*).

4.69 A dismissal on the ground of periodic absences from work due to an illness attributable to pregnancy or childbirth is not contrary to the Directive. In *Handelsog (acting on behalf of Larsson) v Dansk Handel & Service*, a woman took her statutory maternity leave following a pregnancy, but as she was still receiving treatment for an illness caused by her pregnancy, remained absent from work. She was dismissed because of her absence, and she claimed that her dismissal was contrary to the Directive, because her illness began during her pregnancy and continued afterwards. The ECJ dismissed her claim. Outside the period of maternity leave, laid down by national law, a woman has no more protection than a man would have in respect of absenteeism caused through illness.

Short-time working for women only

4.70 To put women only on short-time working is to subject them to a detriment, and hence is unlawful (*Morris v Scott*).

C. Discrimination in occupational pensions

4.71 Article 141 of the Treaty of Rome requires that men and women must receive equal pay for equal work. 'Pay' is defined as any basic wage or salary and '. . . any other consideration, whether in cash or kind, which the worker receives, directly or indirectly, in respect of his employment from his employer'. It will be recalled (see para 1.67) that the article has a direct effect, and can thus be enforced in national courts against both public and private employers.

ECJ perspective

4.72 In 1986 the European Court of Justice held that benefits paid under an occupational pension scheme are pay for the purpose of Art 141 (*Bilka-Kaufhaus GmbH v Weber von Hartz*). In a series of judgments the ECJ has given further rulings on how this complex topic should be treated in member states, which may be summarised as follows:

(a) The exclusion of part-time workers from access to an occupational pension scheme is in breach of Art 141 if the effect of that exclusion is to discriminate against one sex (ie women), because a greater number of women than men were excluded. However, because such discrimination is indirect, it may be objectively justified on grounds unrelated to sex discrimination, eg in order to discourage part-time work. However, it must be shown that there is a genuine need on the part of the business, the means are appropriate to that need, and are necessary.

(b) Dependants' benefits are also within the scope of Art 141, and thus subject to the principle of equality. Thus, if a scheme offers benefits for the worker's surviving spouse, this must apply to both sexes (*Ten Oever v Stichting* etc).

(c) It is not contrary to Art 141 for a pension scheme to award a bridging pension, to take into account the fact that the worker has not received a state pension. Since men and women historically receive a state pension at different ages, the bridging pension is designed to remedy an inequality, and is not therefore discriminatory (*Roberts v Birds Eye Walls Ltd*).

(d) The use of sex-based factors in calculating the actuarial value of pensions does not contravene Art 141. Thus, although the employer has a commitment at a given moment in time to pay a periodic pension, the employer's contribution to the scheme is concerned with funding arrangements to meet that commitment (*Neath v Hugh Steeper Ltd*).

(e) Trustees of an occupational pension fund, although not themselves party to the employment relationship, are bound to do everything in their power to ensure compliance with the principle of equal treatment under Art 141 (*Coloroll Pension Trustees Ltd v Russell*). Further, the rules of the pension scheme or the trust deed cannot be used as a means of avoiding the principle of equality, and, if necessary, the trustees would have to apply to the national courts for permission to amend these in order so to comply.

(f) Additional benefits which stem from additional voluntary contributions (AVCs) made by the employee are not covered by Art 141. If a worker transfers from one scheme to another consequent on a change in employment, the receiving scheme is bound to pay any increase in benefits in order to comply with Art 141 even though the transfer payment is not sufficient to meet this obligation (*Coloroll*).

(g) Social security schemes, which stem from national legislation, including retirement pensions, do not fall within Art 141, because these are determined by social policy, and do not arise out of the employment relationship (*Bestuur van het Algemeen v Beune*). But payments which flow from statutory provisions, such as statutory redundancy pay, are within Art 141 (*Barber v Guardian Royal Exchange Assurance Group*).

(h) Because of the potentially huge financial burden which would be imposed on pension funds if the decisions of the ECJ were to be applied retrospectively, it was ruled in *Barber* that Art 141 may not be relied upon to claim entitlement to a pension in respect of service prior to 17 May 1990 (the date of the decision) except in those cases where legal proceedings had commenced before that date. This also applies to dependants' benefits, which are only equalised in respect of a worker's service after that date (*Ten Oever v Stichting BGS*). However, access to pension schemes, ie the right to join, applies from 8 April 1976, the date when the ECJ held that Art 141 was directly enforceable (*Defrenne v Sabena*). This point may be of particular importance to part-time workers who have previously been excluded (although the employers may still argue that the exclusion was justified (*Fisscher v Voorhuis Hengelo*)), but they would be required to pay arrears of their own contributions. The time limits for asserting the right to join are to be determined by national law, which, in the case of the UK, are believed to be the same as those which apply to equal pay claims generally (see para 5.48). Existing employees may bring a claim at any time during their employment, but ex-employees must apply to an employment tribunal within six months from the date when the employment ceased.

The Pensions Act 1995

4.73 The Pensions Act 1995 (ss 62–66) provides that there shall be equal treatment in benefits in respect of pensionable service on or after 17 May 1990 (the date of the *Barber* decision), although it will be a defence if treatment is unequal due to actuarial factors. An equality clause on the lines of the Equal Pay Act is to be imported into all contracts of employment in relation to pension benefits. The legislation contains exceptions in relation to bridging pensions (due to the different ages at which men and women receive their state pension) and lists the circumstances in which sex-related actuarial factors may be taken into account.

Part-time employees

4.74 The major outstanding problems concern the right of part-time employees who had previously been excluded from pension schemes, whether domestic time-limits are to be applied when lodging claims, and how far back claims can be backdated. In *Magorrian v Eastern Health and Social Services Board* the ECJ ruled that the limitation in time laid down in *Barber* did not apply to the right to join an occupational pension scheme, because the right of access to such a scheme, as opposed to entitlement under the scheme, dates from the decision of the ECJ in *Defrenne v Sabena*, and not from *Barber v Guardian Royal Exchange*. Further, it was held that a national rule which limits the entitlement of a claimant to join an occupational scheme to a period which starts to run from two years prior to the date when proceedings were commenced is also prohibited. Such a rule would have amounted to the denial of an effective remedy under Community law. In *Preston v Wolverhampton Healthcare NHS Trust* the House of Lords referred two questions to the ECJ as to the compatibility of s 2(4) and s 2(5) of the Equal Pay Act with EC law, namely (a) the rule which requires a claim to be brought within six months from leaving employment, and (b) the rule which limits claims to a period not exceeding two years from the date of leaving employment. The court ruled that s 2(4) did not offend against the principle of effectiveness, and did not render it impossible or excessively difficult for a person to exercise rights conferred by EC law. However, the two-year time limit specified in s 2(5) was contrary to EC law, in so far as it prevented access to membership (*Levez v TH Jennings (Harlow Pools) Ltd*).

D. Exceptions to the Act

4.75 Provisions relating to death or retirement are excluded from the Sex Discrimination Act (s 6(4)), but this does not permit discrimination against a person in provisions relating to retirement in the field of promotion, training, transfer, demotion or dismissal. But it is permissible to discriminate in relation to retirement in the provision of benefits, facilities or services. Thus, if there is an age at which men retire, or beyond which they cannot be promoted, trained, etc, it is not permissible to have a lower age limit for women.

4.76 The age at which the state retirement pension is payable is also permitted to be discriminatory (EC Directive 79/7, Art 7).

E. Permissible discrimination

Health grounds (s 51(1))

4.77 Nothing in Pt II of the Act (which deals with discrimination in employment) shall render unlawful any act done by a person in relation to a woman if it is necessary to comply with any existing statutory provision concerning the protection of women, or a relevant statutory provision within the meaning of the Health and Safety at Work etc Act 1974, and the act was done for the purpose of the protection of women. Thus it is permissible to discriminate against women in order to protect them against definable health risks, which are specific to women, including risks associated with pregnancy and childbirth (see *Page v Freight Hire (Tank Haulage) Ltd*).

Genuine occupational qualification (s 7)

4.78 It is permissible to make arrangements which will lead to a person being offered a job, or to refuse another person that post, if the sex of the person is a genuine occupational qualification (GOQ) for the job, and it follows that an employer does not unlawfully discriminate if he does not employ, or if he denies an opportunity for promotion or transfer to, or training for, such employment to a person of the other sex.

4.79 The sex of a person is a genuine occupational qualification for the job in the following circumstances:

(a) The essential nature of the job calls for authentic male or female characteristics (excluding physical strength or stamina). Thus it is permissible to advertise for a man to play Hamlet, or for a woman to play Ophelia. It would be interesting to know if it is discriminatory to advertise for a man to play the role of a dame in a pantomime, or for a woman to take the role of principal boy! But if the job merely calls for an ability to haul around 25 kg parcels, it must be open to either sex.

(b) The job needs to be held by a person of one sex in order to preserve decency or privacy, because:
   (i) it is likely to involve physical contact with a person in circumstances where that person may reasonably object to it being carried out by a person of the opposite sex. For example, it may be presumed that women would object to men assisting them whilst trying on underwear. In *Etam plc v Rowan* a man applied for a job as a sales assistant in a shop which sold women's and girls' clothing. He was refused employment because the employers considered that a major part of the work involved personal contact with women when they were in a state of undress, and in response to a claim of sex discrimination, pleaded the defence of genuine occupational qualification. However, his claim was upheld by an employment tribunal and, on appeal, by the EAT. On the facts of the case, a man would have been able to carry out adequately the job of a sales assistant, and such functions as he could not perform could easily have been done by one of the other female sales assistants without causing any inconvenience or difficulty. Further, s 7(4) (see below), which negates the defence of genuine occupational qualification, was applied. In *Timex Corpn v Hodgson* the claimant was a supervisor who was dismissed for reason of redundancy. A female supervisor, who had less service, was retained. The

employers sought to justify this on the grounds that all other female supervisors were leaving and they needed to retain one woman supervisor (a) to
deal with the private problems of female shop-floor employees, (b) to take
women to the first aid room (a man would have to be accompanied), (c) to
ensure there was an adequate supply of sanitary towels and pills for period
pains kept in the ladies' lavatory, and (d) to take urine samples from women
engaged on work involving toxic materials. The EAT held that the male
employee had not been discriminated against on grounds of sex. The employers had discriminated by selecting the female supervisor to do a revised job.
They had failed to transfer a man to that job, and deliberately refused to offer a
man employment in that job. But the sex of the person who was to do the job
was relevant, and it amounted to a GOQ;

(ii)   persons of one sex might reasonably object to the presence of the opposite sex
because they are in a state of undress or using sanitary facilities. This might
cover, for example, lavatory attendants, or swimming pool attendants (see
Sisley v Britannia Security Systems Ltd);

(iii) the job is likely to involve the holder doing his work, or living, in a private
home, and needs to be held by a person of one sex because objection might
reasonably be taken to allowing a person of the other sex

(a) the degree of physical or social contact with a person living in the home,
or

(b) the knowledge of intimate details of such a person's life, which would be
allowed to, or available to, the holder of the job.

(c) The employee is required to live in premises provided by the employer, and those
which are available are not equipped with separate sleeping accommodation
and sanitary facilities, and it is not reasonable to expect the employer so to equip
those premises or to provide such facilities, or to provide other premises. Thus
employment on a remote site, or a lighthouse, could be single-sex.

(d) Where the job has to be done by a person in a hospital, prison, or other establishment for people who need special care, supervision or attention, and all the
inmates thereof are persons of one sex (disregarding the presence of persons of
the other sex whose presence is exceptional), and it is reasonable, having regard to
the essential characteristics of the establishment that the job should be held by a
person of a particular sex. This would cover, for example, a single-sex mental
institution.

(e) The holder of the job provides individuals with personal services promoting their
welfare or education, which can be most effectively provided by one sex. A tough
male youth club leader, for example, may be required for a boys' club.

(f) The job needs to be held by a man because it is likely to involve performance of
duties outside the United Kingdom in a country whose laws or customs are such
that such duties could not effectively be performed by someone of the opposite sex.
There could be difficulties, for example, in sending a woman to negotiate with an
eastern potentate! In *O'Conner v Kontiki Travel*, a woman was turned down as a
coach driver because, it was argued, she would have to drive through Muslim
countries, where women drivers are unacceptable. If true, this would have amounted
to a GOQ, but it was found that the only Muslim country to which the tour was

going was Turkey, and as no evidence had been produced that there would be such objections to women drivers in that country, this amounted to unlawful discrimination.

(g) The job is one of two held by a married couple.

4.80 It is not permissible to use the 'decency' defence when filling a vacancy if the employer already has employees of one sex capable of carrying out the above duties (except (g) above), whom it would be reasonable to employ on those duties and whose numbers are sufficient to meet the employers' likely requirements in respect of those duties without undue inconvenience (s 7(4)). But this has to be considered as at the time the alleged discrimination took place. Thus, if, at that time, the employer did not have sufficient female employees to carry out duties which would otherwise be reserved to them, then it would be permissible to refuse employment to a male applicant (*Lasertop Ltd v Webster*). Also, s 48 permits an employer to train members of one sex only for a job which has been previously performed exclusively, or nearly so, by members of the other sex during the preceding 12 months but the anti-discrimination provisions in selection and recruitment still apply. Thus positive action is encouraged, but not positive discrimination.

4.81 Supplementary genuine occupational qualifications apply when a person has had (or is proposing to have) a gender reassignment (see para 4.36). Thus, it will not be discriminatory if the employer can show that the treatment is reasonable, having regard to the following factors:

(a) the job involves doing work in, or living in a private home, and objection may be taken to allowing a person who has undergone gender reassignment from
   (i) having physical or social contact with a person living in the home, or
   (ii) gaining knowledge of intimate details of such person's life;

(b) reasonable objection could be taken to the holder of the job sharing accommodation or facilities in living premises provided by the employer whilst undergoing gender reassignment, and it is not reasonable to expect the employer to provide separate premises;

(c) the holder of the job provides vulnerable persons with personal services promoting their welfare (ss 7A–B).

It should be noted that post-operative transsexuals must now be formally recognised as being members of the sex to which they have reassigned (*Chief Constable of Yorkshire v A*);

F. Employment in Great Britain (s 10)

4.82 The Act only applies to employment at an establishment in Great Britain (*Deria v General Council of British Shipping*). Employment is to be regarded as being at an establishment in Great Britain if:

(a) the employee does his work wholly or partly in Great Britain, or

(b) the employee does his work wholly outside Great Britain, and
   (i) the employer has a place of business at an establishment in Great Britain,

(ii) the work is done for the purpose of the business carried on at that establishment, and

(iii) the employee is ordinarily resident in Great Britain at the time when he applies for or is offered employment, or at any time during the course of his employment.

G. Employment advertisements (s 38)

4.83 It is also unlawful to advertise in a manner which might be taken as indicating an intention to discriminate, and the use of job descriptions in advertisements with a sexual connotation, such as 'waiter', 'salesgirl', 'postman', 'stewardess' etc will be assumed to be discriminatory unless the advertisement contains an indication to the contrary. The EOC has issued a document called 'Guidance on Employment Advertising Practice' which contains some useful information and advice on this subject.

4.84 To determine whether an advertisement shows an intention to discriminate unlawfully, it must be read as a whole, according to what an ordinary reasonable person, without any special knowledge, would find to be the natural and ordinary meaning of the words used. In *Equal Opportunities Commission v Robertson*, the respondent placed an advertisement for 'a good bloke (or blokes to satisfy fool legislators)'. It was held that this might reasonably be understood to indicate that the job was not open to women, the word 'blokes' being inserted as a formality. On the other hand, an advertisement for a 'departmental manager' was not discriminatory, as in this context there was no sexist connotation.

The placing of a discriminatory advertisement does not, per se, give rise to an individual complaint (*Cardiff Women's Aid v Hartup*, see para 4.127).

H. Unlawful acts (ss 39–40, 42)

4.85 It is unlawful:

(a) for a person who has authority over another to instruct that other to do an unlawful act (s 39);

(b) to induce another to do an unlawful act by offering a benefit or threatening a detriment (s 40); and

(c) to aid another person to do an unlawful act (s 42) (see *A M v W C and SPV*). A person aids another if he helps or assists, whether or not the help is substantial or productive, provided it is not so insignificant as to be negligible (*Anyanwu v South Bank Students Union*).

4.86 It should be noted that ss 38, 39 and 40 may only be enforced by the Equal Opportunities Commission (see s 72).

I. Liability of employers (s 41)

4.87 Anything done by a person in the course of his employment shall be treated as done by his employer as well as by him, whether or not the act was done with the employer's knowledge or approval. At one time, the test to be applied was taken from the common law rules relating to vicarious liability (see para 10.92, and see *Irving v Post Office*), but this view is wrong. In *Jones v Tower Boot Co Ltd* an employee was racially harassed at work, by having to suffer physical and verbal abuse from his fellow employees. It was argued for the employers that the acts were not committed by their employees acting in the course of their employment, because it was no part of their work to do such acts, which were unauthorised and unconnected with anything the employees were employed to do. The Court of Appeal rejected the argument, and held that the employers were liable for racial discrimination. The words 'in the course of employment' were to be given a purposive construction, and were to be interpreted in the sense in which they are employed in everyday speech. The application of the phrase is a question of fact for each employment tribunal to resolve (see para 10.95).

4.88 If an act of sex discrimination (or sexual harassment) takes place at a social gathering of work colleagues, it is for the employment tribunal to consider, as an industrial jury, whether the circumstances are an extension of the employment. Factors to consider include (a) whether the person was still on duty, (b) whether the conduct took place on the employer's premises, (c) whether the social gathering was organised by or on behalf of the employer, and (d) whether the incidents took place immediately after work (*Chief Constable of Lincolnshire v Stubbs*).

4.89 But an employer will not be liable for such acts if he can show that he took such steps as were reasonably practicable to prevent the employee from doing that act, or doing in the course of his employment acts of that description (s 41(3)). Thus, if an employer can show that he had a system of proper supervision, had published an equal opportunities policy, and was unaware of the acts in question, it may be that he can successfully raise this defence. Thus in *Balgobin v Tower Hamlets* the EAT commented that it was difficult to see what steps could have been taken by the employers in practical terms to prevent harassment from occurring. If an employer seeks to reply on the defence set out in s 41(3), the employment tribunal must consider whether the employer took any steps at all to prevent an employee from committing an act of sex discrimination, and then consider what further steps could have been taken which were reasonably practicable (*Canniffe v East Riding of Yorkshire Council*).

J. Enforcement of the Act (s 63)

Remedies open to the tribunal

4.90 Any person may complain to the employment tribunal that another person has committed an act of discrimination. Initially, the conciliation officer will try to promote a settlement, but if this fails, the tribunal, if it finds the complaint well founded, may:

(a) make an order declaring the rights of the claimant;

(b) order the respondent to pay compensation, and may include an award for injured feelings, which is fundamental to a claim based on discrimination (*Murray v Powertech (Scotland) Ltd*). An award may also be made for psychiatric illness suffered as a result of sexual discrimination or harassment, and aggravated damages may also be awarded (*HM Prison Service v Salmon*). Since the Sex Discrimination and Equal Pay (Remedies) Regulations 1993, there is no limit on the amount of compensation which can be awarded, and the employment tribunal must assess the whole of the loss suffered (*Ministry of Defence v Cannock* and *Ministry of Defence v Wheeler*). Also, interest on the compensation element (but not on an award for injured feelings) may be awarded, both in respect of the period up to the date when the compensation is assessed and for the period following the promulgation of the award (but not if the full amount is paid within 14 days): see Employment Tribunals (Interest on Awards in Discrimination Cases) Regulations 1996 as amended; and/or

(c) make a recommendation that the respondent takes action to obviate or reduce the adverse effect on the claimant of any act of discrimination to which the complaint relates.

4.91 In the latter case, a failure to comply may lead to an increase in the amount of compensation awarded. However, the employment tribunal has no power to recommend that a certain wage shall be paid in the future, as this is covered by the provision which enables compensation for the loss suffered to be awarded (*Prestcold Ltd v Irvine*).

4.92 Damages may be awarded for unintentional indirect discrimination (ie falling within ss 1(1)(b) or 3(1)(b)) if the employment tribunal considers that it is just and equitable to make such an award and a declaration and/or a recommendation is insufficient (s 65(1B)). Aggravated damages are intended to deal with cases where the injury was inflicted by conduct which was high-handed, malicious, insulting or oppressive. Such damages should not be aggregated with or treated as part of damages for injury to feelings (*Scott v Commissioners of Inland Revenue*).

4.93 An employer's motive for discriminating is irrelevant to liability, but may be relevant to the award of compensation, which is made on just and equitable grounds (*Chief Constable of Manchester v Hope*).

Burden of proof (s 63A)

4.94 Once a complainant establishes a prima facie case of sex discrimination, the burden of proof will shift to the employer to show that there was a non-discriminatory reason for his actions, or a non-gender specific reason for the less favourable treatment. The decision in *King v Great Britain-China Centre* has thus been confirmed by the Sex Discrimination (Indirect Discrimination and Burden of Proof) Regulations 2001, which inserted s 63A into the SDA. In other words, a complainant need only show facts from which an inference can be drawn that he/she has been treated less favourably because of his/her sex; the burden of rebutting this will then fall on the employer. Thus in *ACAS v Taylor* a man claimed that he had been denied the opportunity to apply for promotion because his employers had operated a policy of positive discrimination in favour of women and, as the employers failed to rebut the allegation, his claim for unlawful discrimination succeeded (see *Igen Ltd v Wong*).

4.95 In *Barton v Investec Henderson Crosthwaite Securities* the EAT set out 12 principles which are intended to guide tribunals on the burden of proof in sex discrimination cases.

4.96 A complaint of discrimination in the field of employment must be laid before the employment tribunal within three months of the act complained of being done, unless it was not practicable to present it earlier (s 76). The 'act' of discrimination can be a single act, or a continuing one. In the latter case, the right to bring legal proceedings will continue until three months from the end of the period when the discrimination ceases. In *Calder v James Finlay Corpn Ltd*, the employers operated a mortgage subsidy scheme. In order to be eligible to join the scheme, employees had to be over the age of 25. Shortly after the claimant became 25, she applied for a mortgage subsidy, but this was refused, no reason being given. She continued in her employment for a further six months, she then left, and claimed that she had been discriminated against on grounds of sex. An employment tribunal concluded that the reason she was refused the mortgage subsidy was because of her sex, but also held that her application was out of time. On appeal, the EAT reversed the decision. Section 6(2)(a) of the Act makes it unlawful to refuse her access to benefits, facilities or services, and thus she was subjected to a continuing discrimination throughout her employment. Also, as long as the employment continued, she was being subjected to a detriment, contrary to s 6(2)(b). As her claim was brought within three months of her leaving her employment, she was entitled to succeed. Further, the EAT noted that s 76(6)(b) states that an act extending over a period shall be treated as done at the end of that period.

4.97 However, it is important to distinguish between an act of continuing discrimination and an act of discrimination which has continuing consequences. In the latter case, the time limit of three months will normally apply (see *Sougrin v Haringey Health Authority*, para 4.148). But if there is a deliberate omission to do something, time will run from the date when the discriminator is in a position to do that thing (*Swithland Motors plc v Clarke*).

4.98 The EOC may itself bring proceedings in respect of alleged violations of certain provisions in the Act (ie ss 38, 39 or 40, see above) within six months of the act complained of, and obtain an injunction from a county court or sheriff court to restrain a person from repeating the unlawful act at any time within five years of a non-discrimination notice (ss 71–72). The Commission may also bring a preliminary action in an employment tribunal on behalf of a person, even though that person has not made a complaint, and the employment tribunal can make an order of rights or a recommendation that appropriate action be taken to obviate or reduce the adverse effect of the discrimination (s 73).

4.99 The Commission may give help to persons who feel that they have been discriminated against, in order to assist them in obtaining the necessary information, and questionnaires have been approved which can be sent to the alleged discriminator. Assistance to an aggrieved person may also be given by means of advice, attempting to procure a settlement by conciliation, arranging for legal advice and assistance, and arranging and paying for legal representation. It may also undertake or assist in any research or other educational activities.

4.100 The Commission may carry out formal investigations, either on its own initiative or at the request of the Secretary of State, with specific terms of reference, and notice will be given to persons affected. Any person may be required to furnish information, or to attend a hearing and give oral information on specified matters, and to produce any relevant documents. If a person fails or refuses to comply, the Commission may apply to a county court (or sheriff's court) for an order requiring him to comply, and failure to do so may be punishable in like manner as neglecting a witness summons. To wilfully alter, suppress, conceal or destroy a document, or knowingly or recklessly to make a statement which is false in a material particular is an offence punishable on summary conviction by a fine not exceeding level 5 on the standard scale. In the light of their findings, the Commission may make recommendations with a view to promoting equality of opportunity between men and women (ss 57–61).

4.101 If, in the course of investigations, the Commission is satisfied that a person is committing an unlawful discriminatory act, or contravening an equality clause under the Equal Pay Act 1970, the Commission may issue a non-discriminatory notice. They must first inform the person of their intention, specifying the grounds, and give him an opportunity to make oral or written representations and take these into account. An appeal may be lodged to the employment tribunal within six weeks against any require-ment, and the tribunal may quash the requirement if it thinks it is unreasonable. A register of non-discrimination notices shall be kept, and if at any time within five years of the notice becoming final it appears to the Commission that the discriminatory act is likely to be repeated, the Commission may apply to a county court for an injunction restraining that person from doing so (ss 67–71).

4.102 The Act extends the anti-discrimination provisions to a number of other bodies and individuals, including office holders, partnerships, trade unions qualifying bodies, vocational training employment agencies, educational establishments, barristers, advo-cates, etc.

K. Application to the Crown

4.103 The Act applies to the Crown as it applies to a private person, including to service in the armed forces, although nothing is rendered unlawful if it was done for the purpose of ensuring combat effectiveness.

Racial discrimination

4.104 The Race Relations Act 1976 is intended to be a powerful influence in the fight to eliminate discrimination on racial grounds. The Act is modelled closely on the Sex Discrimination Act 1975, and an interpretive decision on one Act may be used when considering the meaning of the other.

4.105 There have been several amendments to the Act, in particular made by the Race Relations (Amendment) Act 2000 and the Race Relations Act 1976 (Amendment) Regulations 2003, the latter being in response to the requirements of EU Directive 2000/43/EC.

The employment provisions of the Act apply to persons in employment, which means employment under a contract of service or of apprenticeship, or a contract personally to execute any work or labour (s 78). Thus self-employed persons are covered, as well as employees, provided that the predominate purpose of the contract is the execution of personal work or labour (*Mingeley v Pennock and Ivory (t/a Amber Cars)*). Trainees on a government training programme are not within this definition, and are excluded from the Act's provisions (see *Daley v Allied Suppliers Ltd*, above, para 2.87). If the con-tract of employment is illegal, there may well be circumstances where the employee will nonetheless be able to pursue a claim (*Hall v Woolston Hall Leisure Centre Ltd*, see para 3.7). In *Adekeye v Post Office (No 2)* it was held that ex-employees were not persons who were employed under a contract of employment, but this case was reversed in *Rhys-Harper v Relaxion Group* (see para 4.26), provided that there is a connection between the discriminatory conduct and the employment relationship. Further, s 27A of the Act (inserted by the 2003 Regulations) makes it clear the post-employment discrimination or harassment which arises out of and is closely connected with the employment relationship is unlawful.

The Act generally applies to the Crown except in respect of the holders of a statutory office, and subject to any special rules and regulations applying to the Civil Service in respect of persons of particular birth, nationality, descent or residence (Race Relations (Prescribed Public Bodies) (No 2) Regulations 1994). Acts done by a constable in the course of performing his functions are to be treated as being done in the course of his deemed employment, with the chief constable being vicariously liable for any wrongful act.

A. Racial grounds (s 3)

4.106 The Act defines racial grounds as meaning colour, race, nationality or ethnic or national origins. Nationality and national origins are different concepts; the former refers to citizenship, whereas the latter term refers to a historical and/or geographical feature which would have revealed at some point in time the existence of a nation. Thus England and Scotland were once separate nations, and thus it is unlawful, for example, to discriminate against a person because of his national origin (*BBC Scotland v Souster*). An ability to speak a particular language is not, per se, an essential factor in the definition of a racial group, and a requirement of such an ability may be justified irrespective of racial or national origins. Thus in *Gwynedd County Council v Jones* it was accepted that Welshmen were a distinct ethnic group, but the EAT held that there was no distinction between Welsh-speaking Welshmen and English-speaking Welshmen. However, a requirement that applicants for a post should be able to speak Welsh was held, in the particular circumstances, to be justifiable.

4.107 The term 'ethnic' is appreciably wider than the term 'race'. In *Mandla v Dowell Lee* the House of Lords held that an ethnic group must regard itself as a distinct community by virtue of certain characteristics. These include:

   (a) a long shared history, of which the group is conscious as distinguishing it from other groups, the memory of which keeps it alive;

   (b) a cultural tradition, including social customs and manner.

4.108 In addition, some of the following factors may be relevant, ie:

   (a) a common geographical origin or descent from common ancestors;

   (b) a common language (but not necessarily peculiar to the group);

   (c) a common literature;

   (d) a common religion different from that of neighbouring groups;

   (e) being a minority or being an oppressed or a dominant group within a community.

4.109 Thus a Sikh born in the United Kingdom was held to have an ethnic origin (*Mandla v Dowell Lee*), as are Jews (*Seide v Gillette Industries Ltd*), and gypsies (*Dawkins v Department of the Environment*).

4.110 However, a comparison of the case of a person of a particular racial group with that of a person not of that group must be such that the relevant circumstances are the same or not materially different (s 3(4)). In *Wakeman v Quick Corpn*, Japanese managers, who were seconded from Japan to work in England, were paid more than locally recruited managers. It was held that the higher rate of pay was attributed to their status as secondees. As such, their circumstances were materially different from those of the claimant, who was English, so no proper comparison could be made as required by s 3(4) of the Act.

4.111 A number of cases have attempted to decide whether or not certain religious groups were racial groups within the meaning of the Act, but religion is now covered by the Employment Equality (Religion or Belief) Regulations 2003 (see para 4.196).

Direct discrimination (s 1(1)(a))

4.112 This occurs if on racial grounds a person treats another person less favourably than he would treat someone else. Thus if the grounds for the discrimination are racial, the race of the person discriminated against is irrelevant, for it is possible for A to discriminate against B on grounds of C's colour or race (*Race Relations Board v Applin*). In *Zarczynska v Levy* a barmaid alleged she was dismissed for refusing to obey an order not to serve coloured persons in a pub. The EAT held that even though she had not been personally discriminated against on grounds of her race, she had been treated less favourably on racial grounds, and was entitled to pursue a claim. (The case was remitted to the employment tribunal, which found that no such unlawful instruction had been given; see also *Showboat Entertainment Centre Ltd v Owens*.) In *Wilson v TB Steelworks* a white woman was on the point of being offered a job, but when she disclosed that her husband was black, the offer was withdrawn. It was held that this amounted to unlawful discrimination.

The fact that members of a racial group are treated differently does not, by itself, constitute unlawful discrimination. It must be shown that the treatment was less favourable on grounds of race (*Barclays Bank plc v Kapur* and *Weathersfield v Sargent*).

4.113 The Act specifically states (s 1(2)) that the segregation of a person on racial grounds is to be regarded as treating him less favourably, but this does not mean that congregation is unlawful. Thus to provide separate (but equal) toilet facilities for Asians and non-Asians would be discriminatory, and hence unlawful, but to allow an Asian night shift to develop in a factory because this is the wish of all concerned does not amount to unlawful conduct. The employer, however, would be acting unlawfully if he insisted that Asians went on the night shift (*Pel Ltd v Modgill*).

4.114 There can be unlawful discrimination under the Act even though it was done for a worthy motive. In *R v Commission for Racial Equality, ex p Westminster City Council*, a black person applied for a job as a refuse collector. He was given a temporary appointment, but this was later withdrawn, as it was feared that other workers would take industrial action. The High Court held that the CRE were entitled to issue a non-discrimination notice. For an employer to give in to such threats would frustrate the purpose of the Act.

Indirect discrimination (s I(I)(b) and (IA))

4.115 The meaning of indirect discrimination (the term is not used as such in the Act) is complicated because there are in fact two regimes to consider. The first occurs when:

(a) a person applies a requirement or condition which he applies equally to persons not of the same racial group;

(b) which is such that the proportion of persons from that same racial group who can comply is considerably smaller than persons who are not of that racial group;

(c) he cannot show that the requirement or condition is justified irrespective of the colour, race, nationality or ethnic or national origins of the person to whom it is applied; and

(d) it is to that person's detriment that he cannot comply.

4.116 The requirement or condition has to be one which the applicant 'must' comply with. If it is a factor which 'may' be taken into account, there is no indirect discrimination under s 1(1)(b). In *Meer v London Borough of Tower Hamlets*, the respondents advertised a vacancy for a head of their legal department. There were 23 applicants, 12 of whom were put on a 'long list'. The council applied 10 criteria for drawing up the 'long list', one of which was experience with Tower Hamlets. Of those on the 'long list' four had such experience. The claimant, who was not placed on the long list, complained that he had been indirectly discriminated against on ground of race, arguing that the proportion of this racial group who could comply with the requirement was smaller than other groups. His claim was dismissed. The requirement was not one with which the successful applicants 'must' comply; it was a factor which the local authority were entitled to take into account. A different view appears to have been taken in *Falkirk Council v Whyte*.

4.117 If a claim of indirect discrimination is made, it must be shown that the claimant has suffered a detriment. An unjustified sense of grievance does not constitute less favourable treatment, and an employee who, for sound reasons, is treated differently but no less generously than others in a different racial group cannot claim that he has suffered a detriment (*Barclays Bank plc v Kapur*).

4.118 Even though there is indirect discrimination, a complaint will not succeed if it can be shown that the requirement or condition is justified irrespective of race. In *Panesar v Nestlé & Co Ltd* a factory rule prohibited beards and long hair. This was indirect discrimination against the claimant, who was a Sikh, but the Court of Appeal held that the condition was justified in the interests of hygiene and safety.

4.119 To determine whether or not the requirement or condition was justified, the employment tribunal should consider (a) was the objective legitimate, (b) were the means used to achieve that objective reasonable in themselves, and (c) were those means justified when balanced on the principles of proportionality between the discriminatory effect upon the claimant's racial group and the reasonable needs of those applying the requirement or condition (*St Matthias Church of England School (Board of Governors) v Crizzle*).

4.120 The second definition of indirect discrimination was introduced by the 2003 Amendment regulations in order to comply with EU Directive 2000/43/ EC, and applies only to persons of racial, ethnic or national origins (not on grounds of colour or nationality). This occurs when:

(a) a person applies a provision, criterion or practice to another which he applies equally to persons not of the same race or ethnic or national origins, but

(b) which puts that other person at a particular disadvantage, and

(c) which he cannot show to be a proportionate means of achieving a legitimate aim.

4.121 It will be noted that the application of a 'provision, criterion or practice' is wider than a 'requirement or condition', and hence a case like *Meer v London Borough of Tower Hamlet* (above) would now probably be decided differently (assuming, of course, that the complaint was not based on colour or nationality!).

Victimisation (s 2)

4.122 It is unlawful to treat a person less favourably because he has:

(a) brought proceedings under the Act;

(b) given evidence or information connected with proceedings brought by another person;

(c) done anything under the Act in relation to the discriminator; or

(d) made allegations that a person has committed an unlawful act of racial discrimination.

However, it is not unlawful victimisation if a person is accorded less favourable treatment as a result of an allegation which is untrue and not made in good faith (*Aziz v Trinity Street Taxis*).

4.123 It is not necessary under s 2 to show that the alleged discriminator was consciously motivated because the person victimised had done one of the protected acts. Subconscious motivation will suffice to show victimisation. All the claimant has to show is that the reason (or principal reason) for the less favourable treatment was the fact that the person victimised had done the protected act (*Nagarajan v London Regional Transport*). Thus in *Chief Constable of West Yorkshire v Khan* a police officer made a complaint to an employment tribunal alleging that he had been the victim of racial discrimination, in that his application for promotion had not been supported. Before the claim was heard, he applied for promotion to another police authority, who wrote to his present employers seeking a reference. The latter's Chief Constable refused to provide a reference because he feared it would prejudice his own case before the impending employment tribunal hearing. It was held that the refusal was not 'by reason that' the claimant had brought proceedings, but because the Chief Constable needed to preserve his legal position in relation to them. The claim based on victimisation failed.

Harassment (s 3A)

4.124 A person subjects another to harassment where, on grounds of race or ethnic or national origins, he engages in unwanted conduct which has the purpose or effect of violating that other person's dignity, or creating an intimidating, hostile, degrading, humiliating or offensive environment for him. Conduct shall be regarded as having this effect if, having regard to the circumstances (including the perception of the person affected) it should reasonably be considered as having that effect. (Again, it should be noted that this definition does not apply to harassment on grounds of colour or nationality.)

4.125 The above definition was introduced by the 2003 Regulations. Earlier decisions (eg *Burton and Rhule v De Vere Hotels*) had treated racial insults as being harassment, by way of a detriment, for which an employer could be vicariously liable, but it is probable that cases which now come within the scope of s 3A should be considered afresh, particularly as *Burton and Rhule v De Vere Hotel* was overruled by the House of Lords in *MacDonald v Advocate General for Scotland*. It is now specifically unlawful for an employer to subject to harassment a person whom he employs or who has applied to him for employment (s 4(2A)). Whether an employer will be liable vicariously for the acts of his employees under s 32 (para 4.144) is another matter.

B. Racial discrimination in employment (s 4)

When is it unlawful to discriminate on racial grounds?

4.126 It is unlawful to discriminate against a person on racial grounds:

 (a) in the arrangements for determining who shall be offered employment;

 (b) in the terms on which employment is offered;

 (c) by refusing or deliberately omitting to offer him employment (s 4(1); *Johnson v Timber Tailors (Midlands) Ltd*).

4.127 Placing a discriminatory advertisement is not, by itself, part of the arrangements for determining who shall be employed. In *Cardiff Women's Aid v Hartup* a charity advertised for a black or Asian woman to fill the post of information centre worker. Mrs Hartup, who is white, did not apply for the job, but claimed that she had been discriminated against on grounds of race. It was held that the act of placing a discriminatory advertisement was not an act of discrimination within the meaning of s 4. It may have indicated an intention to discriminate, but this is actionable only at the instance of the CRE under s 29 of the Act (see para 4.139).

4.128 To adopt a screening policy, whereby members of a particular racial group are eliminated from consideration for employment, can amount to discrimination, even though the alleged discriminator is unaware of whether a particular job applicant is a member of that group (*Simon v Brimham Associates*). However, it is permissible to request, as part of the employment arrangements, that a job applicant produces evidence of his right to work in the UK (*Dhatt v MacDonalds Hamburgers Ltd*).

4.129 Once a person is employed, it is unlawful to discriminate against him on racial grounds:

 (a) in the terms of employment which are afforded to him;

 (b) in the way he is afforded access to opportunities for promotion, transfer or training, or any other benefit, facilities or services, or to refuse or omit to afford him access to them;

 (c) by dismissing him, or subjecting him to any other detriment (s 4(2)). In *De Souza v Automobile Association* it was held that a racial insult, by itself, was capable of constituting a detriment if the employee felt disadvantaged thereby. If an employee is given an instruction to carry out a policy which is racially discriminatory, and would clearly contravene the Act, and resigns his employment because he feels unable to carry out the policy, he has suffered a detriment, and consequently has been unlawfully discriminated against. It is not necessary for the discriminatory act to be because of that person's race (*Weathersfield Ltd v Sargent*). A dismissal for the purpose of this Act, includes a constructive dismissal (*Derby Specialist Fabrication Ltd v Burton*).

4.130 So far as persons employed in a private household are concerned, it is unlawful to discriminate on grounds of race, ethnic or national origins, although not apparently on grounds of colour and nationality! But the victimisation provisions do apply. This means that the previous private household exemption has virtually disappeared. Also s 75(5) allows discrimination on grounds of birth, nationality, descent or residence for Civil Service posts and employment with certain public bodies (see Race Relations (Prescribed Public Bodies) Regulations 1994).

Exception for genuine occupational requirement (s 4A)

4.131 There is an exception from some of the above provisions when the race, ethnic or national origins of a person is a genuine occupational requirement. Provided certain conditions are met, it is not unlawful to discriminate in such circumstances in the arrangements made for determining employment, refusing employment, affording access to opportunities for promotion, transfer, training or any other benefit, facilities or services, or dismissal or subjecting to a detriment. The conditions are where, having regard to the nature of the employment or the context in which it is carried out

(a) being of a particular race or particular ethnic or national origin is a genuine and determining occupational requirement

(b) it is proportionate to apply that requirement in the particular case, and

(c) either
   (i) the person to whom that requirement is applied does not meet it, or
   (ii) the employer is not satisfied, and in all the circumstances it is reasonable for him to be not satisfied, that the person meets it.

Exception for genuine occupational qualification (s 5)

4.132 Where the genuine occupational requirement provisions do not apply (eg because of colour or nationality), or the exception criteria are missing, the old law on genuine occupational qualification applies. Being of a particular racial group is a genuine occupational qualification for a job where:

(a) the job involves participation in a dramatic performance or other entertainment in a capacity for which a person of that racial group is required for reasons of authenticity;

(b) the job involves participation as an artist's or photographic model in the production of a work of art or of visual images, for which a person of that racial group is required for reasons of authenticity;

(c) the job involves working in a place where food and drink is provided to, and consumed by, members of the public in a particular setting (eg a Chinese restaurant), for which a person of that racial group is required for reasons of authenticity;

(d) the holder of the job provides persons of that racial group with personal services promoting their welfare, and those services can be most effectively provided by persons of that racial group.

4.133 In *Tottenham Green Under Fives' Centre v Marshall*, the EAT thought that the phrase 'promoting their welfare' was a wide expression, and the view was expressed that it was unnecessary to seek to limit the scope of the words. But in *Lambeth London Borough Council v Commission for Racial Equality*, the Court of Appeal refused to uphold the decision of a local authority to confine applications for vacant posts in their housing benefits department to applicants from Afro-Caribbean or Asian communities, because the jobs were essentially managerial in nature, and did not involve the provision of personal services promoting the welfare of a particular racial group.

4.134 The defence of genuine occupational qualification will be lost if the employer already has employees of the racial group in question who are capable of carrying out those duties, whom it would be reasonable to employ on those duties, and whose numbers are sufficient to meet the employer's likely requirements without undue inconvenience.

Contract workers (s 7)

4.135 As well as giving protection to job applicants and employees, the Act also covers contract workers, and thus pre-empts any attempt to circumvent the anti-discrimination provisions. It is unlawful for a principal to discriminate against a person, even though the latter is employed by a third party (eg an employment agency). It is also unlawful for the principal to discriminate against a contract worker:

(a) in the terms on which he is allowed to do the work;

(b) by not allowing him to do it;

(c) in the way he affords him access to benefits, facilities or services;

(d) by subjecting him to any other detriment.

4.136 Section 7 will also protect staff employed by one employer at premises controlled by another. Thus in *Harrods Ltd v Remick* the claimant was employed as a pen consultant for concessionaires who had a sales counter at Harrods store. Harrods withdrew her store approval because she failed to comply with their dress code. Consequently she was dismissed. It was held that she was entitled to pursue a claim for racial discrimination against Harrods, even though that firm was not her employer. The concessionaires were supplying employees to 'work for' Harrods within the meaning of s 7.

Employment in Great Britain (s 8)

4.137 The act only applies to employment at an establishment in Great Britain (*Deria v General Council of British Shipping*). Employment is to be regarded as being at an establishment in Great Britain if:

(a) the employee does his work wholly or partly in Great Britain, or

(b) the employee does his work wholly outside Great Britain, and
　　(i)　the employer has a place of business at an establishment in Great Britain,
　　(ii)　the work is done for the purpose of the business carried on at that establishment, and

(iii) the employee is ordinarily resident in Great Britain at the time when he applies for or is offered employment, or at any time during the course of his employment.

Post-termination discrimination (s 27A)

4.138 At one time it was thought that an act of discrimination which took place after the employment had ended could not be actionable, because the Act only applied to employees, not ex-employees (*Adekeye v Post Office*). This view, however, was disavowed in *Rhys-Harper v Relaxion Group plc*, where it was held that the legislation could apply to such discrimination, provided there was a substantive connection between the act of discrimination and the employment relationship. This has been confirmed by the new s 27A of the Act, which provides that that unlawful discrimination or harassment will be actionable when it arises out of and is closely connected with the employment relationship. Thus discrimination which takes place during an appeal against a dismissal (when technically the employee is no longer employed, see *J Sainsbury Ltd v Savage*), or in the giving of a reference (*D'Souza v London Borough of Lambeth*) would now be actionable.

C. Other unlawful acts

Discriminatory practices (s 28)

4.139 It is unlawful to apply a discriminatory practice, ie conduct which, while not amounting to discrimination, in fact is designed to produce unlawful discrimination. For example, if it is well known that blacks need not even bother to apply for a job at a certain factory, because they stand no chance of being appointed, this can amount to a discriminatory practice even though no one applies and is discriminated against.

Discriminatory advertisements (s 29)

4.140 Other than the permitted exceptions (ie where race is a GOQ) it is unlawful to publish an advertisement which indicates an intention by a person to do an act of discrimination (see *Cardiff Women's Aid v Hartup*, para 4.127).

Instructions to discriminate (s 30)

4.141 It is unlawful for a person who has authority over another to instruct him to do an unlawful act, or to procure the doing by him of an unlawful act (see *Commission for Racial Equality v Imperial Society for Teachers of Dancing*).

Pressure to discriminate (s 31)

4.142 It is unlawful to induce or attempt to induce a person to do any act which is unlawful. Thus to call (or threaten to call) a strike over the appointment of a black supervisor would be unlawful.

4.143 Proceedings in respect of the above four unlawful acts may only be brought by the Commission for Racial Equality, either by way of a non-discrimination notice or an application to the county court or employment tribunal, as appropriate.

Vicarious liability (s 32)

4.144 Anything done by a person in the course of his employment shall be treated as done by his employer, whether or not the act was done with the employer's knowledge of approval. However, the common law rules relating to vicarious liability, which used to be applied in such cases, are no longer applicable, and the phrase 'in the course of employment' is to be construed by a tribunal in a layman's sense, as a question of fact (see *Jones v Tower Boot Co Ltd*). It is a defence for an employer to show that he took such steps as were reasonably practicable to prevent an employee from doing the act in question, eg by proper supervision, having an equal opportunities policy, taking firm steps to bring to employees' notice that acts of discrimination or harassment will not be tolerated, etc. In *Martins v Marks & Spencer plc*, the Court of Appeal considered that, having regard to the arrangements made for interviewing the claimant, the firm's equal opportunities policy, their compliance with the CRE's Code of Practice on selection procedures, criteria and interviewing, and the selection of an interviewing panel to include a person with an interest in recruiting from ethnic minorities, the employers had made out a defence under s 32(3).

Aiding unlawful acts (s 33)

4.145 A person who knowingly aids another person to do an act which is unlawful shall be treated as himself doing the unlawful act. A person 'knowingly aids' if he helps or assists the other. The help must be substantial or productive, but not so insignificant as to be negligible (*Anyanwu v South Bank Students Union*). But a general attitude of helpfulness by the alleged aider is not enough to establish liability (*Hallam v Avery*).

D. Enforcement by individuals (s 54)

4.146 Any claim in respect of discrimination in employment must be submitted to an employment tribunal within three months from the date of the alleged act, unless it is just and equitable to extend the time limit. However, by virtue of s 68(7)(b), any act extending over the period shall be treated as having been done at the end of that period. Thus where there is a continuing act of discrimination, the three months time limit does not run until the discrimination ceases (*Barclays Bank plc v Kapur*). When submitting a complaint, there is a need to identify the alleged acts of discrimination, as amendments cannot be added at the tribunal stage (*Smith v Zeneca Ltd*).

4.147 In determining the time limits, a distinction has to be drawn between an act of continuing discrimination and an act of discrimination which has continuing consequences. In *Clarke v Hampshire Electro-Plating Co Ltd* the claimant, who was black, saw an advertisement for a supervisory job with his present employers. On 25 April he saw his employer about the vacancy, but was told that he would not be considered. On 4 September a white man was appointed to the job, and the claimant then submitted a complaint, alleging he had been discriminated against on grounds of race. The employment tribunal held that his complaint was out of time, because the discrimination (if this was so) dated from 25 April, but on appeal the decision was reversed by the EAT. Time will start to run from the date the cause of action crystallised, not from when the claimant feels he has been discriminated against. In this case, the claimant's cause of action had not crystallised when his application for promotion was rejected, but from the date a white man was appointed, because this provided the comparison which enabled him to believe that he had been discriminated against.

4.148 A somewhat different approach was taken by the Court of Appeal in *Sougrin v Haringey Health Authority*, where the claimant, a black nurse, appealed internally against her employer's decision to place her in a certain salary grade. Her appeal was unsuccessful, although an appeal by a white colleague succeeded. Six months later she submitted her application to an employment tribunal, arguing that she had been discriminated against on grounds of race, and that the discrimination was a continuing act. The employment tribunal held that the claim had not been submitted within the statutory time limits, a decision which was upheld by the EAT and the Court of Appeal. The regarding decision was a one-off act with the continuing consequence that she was being paid less than a white colleague. There was no suggestion that the employers had a policy to pay black nurses less than white nurses; had there been such a policy, it is arguable that there was a continuing act of discrimination (*Barclays Bank plc v Kapur*).

4.149 A copy of the complaint will be sent to a conciliation officer, but if he fails to promote a settlement, the matter will go to an employment tribunal for hearing. If it is decided that the complaint is well founded, the tribunal may make one of the following orders:

(a) a declaration of the rights of the claimant;

(b) an order that the respondent shall pay compensation, and there is no limit on the amount of compensation which can be awarded. If the act of discrimination has caused pecuniary loss, such as a refusal to offer employment, or dismissal from employment, the amount of damages is readily quantifiable. However, damages may also be awarded for injury to feelings, humiliation and insult. The award for these should not be minimal, but should be restrained. Injury to feelings will normally be of a relatively short duration, and the award should reflect this (*Sharifi v Strathclyde Regional Council*). Various attempts have been made to give guidelines on the principles to be adopted when tribunals make their awards of compensation (see *ICTS v Tchoula*). Generally, awards for injury to feelings fall into three categories, depending on the degree and frequency of the wrongful act, ie top (£15,000–£25,000), middle (£5,000–£15,000) and low (£500–£5,000) (see *Vento v Chief Constable of West Yorkshire Police (No 2)*);

(c) a recommendation that the respondent shall take, within a specified period, such action as appears to the tribunal to be practicable for the purpose of obviating or reducing the adverse effect on the claimant of any act complained of (*North West Thames Regional Health Authority v Noone*). If the respondent fails to comply with any such recommendation, the tribunal may increase the compensation award, or make such an award if they have not already done so.

4.150 An employment tribunal has jurisdiction to award compensation for personal injury caused by unlawful discrimination on grounds of race (and presumably, therefore, sex and disability), whether the injury is physical or psychiatric. It is not necessary to show that the injury is foreseeable; it is sufficient if the discrimination caused the injury. It follows that if a claim of this nature has been settled in the employment tribunal, no further action can be brought in the ordinary courts (*Sheriff v Klyne Tugs (Lowestoft) Ltd*).

4.151 Although there are a number of conflicting decisions on the point, it has recently been confirmed that, as a matter of principle, aggravated damages ought to be available in what are in effect statutory torts of race and sex discrimination, and an award made by an employment tribunal cannot be challenged unless it is manifestly excessive (*HM Prison Service v Johnson*).

4.152 A cause of action under the Act can be continued after the death of the claimant, by his personal representatives, under the provisions of the Law Reform (Miscellaneous Provisions) Act 1934 (*Lewisham and Guys Mental Health NHS Trust v Andrews*).

E. Burden of proof (s 54A)

4.153 If, in tribunal proceedings, a complainant proves facts from which the employment tribunal could conclude, in the absence of an adequate explanation, that the respondent has committed an act of discrimination or harassment, the tribunal shall uphold the complaint, unless the respondent proves that he did not commit the act in question. In other words, direct evidence of race discrimination is rarely forthcoming; it is more likely to consist of inferences raised from primary facts (*Igen Ltd v Wong*). If these lead to the provisional conclusion that there has been discrimination, the respondent will be required to give an explanation. If this is not forthcoming, or if it is unsatisfactory, the complaint will succeed. But the mere fact that an employer treats an employee unreasonably does not, by itself, lead to the conclusion that the employer has treated the employee less favourably on racial grounds (*Law Society v Bahl*).

4.154 The fact that the employer already employs people of different racial groups is not conclusive (*Johnson v Timber Tailors (Midlands) Ltd*), but it is a relevant consideration of evidential value (*Piperdy v UEM Parker Glass*). If an employer's replies to a questionnaire sent by the CRE are evasive, it could lead to an inference that discrimination took place (*Virdee v EEC Quarries Ltd*). Evidence of events which took place subsequent to the alleged act of discrimination is admissible where it is logically probative of a relevant fact (*Chattopadhyay v Headmaster of Holloway School*).

4.155 If discrimination takes place in circumstances which are consistent with the treatment being meted out because of a person's race, an employment tribunal should be prepared to draw the inference that it was unlawful discrimination, unless the alleged discriminator can satisfy them that there was some other innocent explanation (*Baker v Cornwall County Council*). Otherwise, the general burden of proving the case lies upon the claimant. If, after hearing all the evidence, the employment tribunal finds primary facts which, in the absence of explanation, point to unlawful discrimination, and no such acceptable explanation is offered, then the tribunal may find, by inference, that discrimination existed (*British Gas plc v Sharma*).

4.156 A claimant may be able to obtain the discovery of existing statistics, showing the number of persons from the different racial groups who have applied for posts, been engaged, or promoted, for such evidence may have some probative value, from which inferences may be drawn that the employer has adopted racially discriminatory practice or policies (*West Midlands Passenger Transport Executive v Singh*). But an employment tribunal has no power to order a respondent to produce details of the ethnic or racial composition of the workforce, where such evidence does not exist, for this is not 'discovery' of documents, and not 'particulars' of the grounds on which the respondents seek to rely. Nor is there power to order interrogatories (*Carrington v Helix Lighting Ltd*).

F. Enforcement by the Commission (s 58)

4.157 The Commission for Racial Equality has the power to carry out a formal investigation into any practice carried on by an individual or an organisation, either of its own volition or at the request of the Secretary of State, and has wide powers to obtain any necessary information. If the investigation is confined to the activities of named persons, an opportunity must be given for them to make oral or written representations (*Re Prestige Group plc*). A report may then be issued, with or without recommendations. If, in the course of such investigations, the Commission concludes that a person is committing an unlawful act, the Commission may serve a non-discriminatory notice on him requiring him not to commit any further such acts, to inform the Commission on what changes (if any) have been made in such practices, and to notify the other party concerned. Before issuing the notice, the Commission must inform the person, specifying the grounds, and offer him an opportunity of making oral or written representations.

4.158 If there is any repetition of the discriminatory act or practice within the five years following the issuing of a non-discriminatory notice, the Commission may obtain an injunction in the county court against that person, restraining him from committing further discriminatory practices. An appeal may be made against a non-discriminatory notice within six weeks to an employment tribunal, who may quash any requirement contained therein, or, if they so wish, substitute their own directions. On such an appeal, it is open to the person against whom the order has been made to challenge the findings of fact on which the order was made (*Commission for Racial Equality v Amari Plastics Ltd*). A public register will be maintained of all non-discriminatory notices.

G. Statutory immunity (s 41)

4.159 A discriminatory act shall not be unlawful if it is done in pursuance of any enactment, or any instrument made under any enactment, or in order to comply with any condition or requirement imposed by a Minister by virtue of any enactment. However, in *Hampson v Department of Education and Science*, the House of Lords gave a very restricted meaning to this immunity, holding that a decision given on a matter where the statute gives a discretion was not within the section.

Discrimination against disabled workers

A. The legislation

4.160 Following an extensive period of consultation, the Disability Discrimination Act 1995 was passed, with an avowed aim of eliminating discrimination against disabled persons. A code of practice has been issued and guidance notes are available. An employment tribunal should always make express reference to any relevant provision of the code or the guidance notes which has been taken into account when arriving at its decision (*Goodwin v Patent Office*). The Act has been substantially amended by the Disability

Discrimination Act 1995 (Amendment) Regulations 2003, and the Disability Discrimination Act 2005. In particular, the small employer exemption has been abolished, and the Act now applies to others who were formerly excluded from its provisions (police, fire-fighters etc). All employees are now covered (including persons on practical work experience), the only exclusion being members of the armed forces.

4.161 In many ways, the provisions of the Disability Discrimination Act are similar to those found in the Sex Discrimination Act and the Race Relations Act, but there are some important differences. There may be occasions when it is unwise to approach the Act on the basis of assumptions and concepts derived from the SDA and RRA, for there are certain significant differences in the wording of the respective Acts (*Rowden v Dutton Gregory*, and see *Liversidge v Chief Constable of Bedfordshire Police*). Thus, the Act contains no provision for indirect discrimination, because direct discrimination itself is capable of being justified (see s 3A(1)(b)), and regulations specify the circumstances in which discriminatory treatment is or is not justified. There are no like-for-like comparator principles, for the Act is dealing with how a disabled person is treated, not with the fact of his disability (*Clark v Novacold Ltd*).

4.162 There is nothing in the Act which prohibits an employer from requiring a job claimant to undergo a pre-recruitment medical examination and, indeed, if a person refuses such a request, there is no obligation to offer him employment (*X v EC Commission*).

B. Definition of 'disabled persons' (ss 1–2)

4.163 A person will be regarded as being disabled for the purposes of the Act if he has 'a physical or mental impairment which has a substantial and long-term adverse effect on his ability to carry out normal day-to-day activities'. There are thus three elements to consider.

Physical or mental impairment

4.164 The physical impairment must be real, and not the result of functional overlay (ie where the symptoms are imaginary manifestations of an individual's psychological state, see *Rugamer v Sony Music Entertainments UK Ltd*). But if there are physical symptoms, the existence or non-existence of a physical cause is irrelevant (*College of Ripon and York St John v Hobbs*), because an impairment may exist without any physical or mental causation. In other words, a claimant needs to show an impairment; but not why the impairment exists (ie, by reference to a particular physical or mental illness, see *Millar v Inland Revenue Commissioners*). A medical adviser can express an opinion about diagnosis, prognosis and observation of day-to-day activities, but it is for the employment tribunal to determine whether or not a person is disabled, and not for them merely to adopt the opinion of the medical adviser (*Abadeh v British Telecommunications plc*).

4.165 Addictions to alcohol, nicotine or other substances do not amount to an impairment for the purpose of the Act, although if there is a physical or mental impairment, the fact that it was caused by such addiction is not relevant (*Power v Panasonic UK Ltd*). What matters is the impairment, not how it is caused. A tendency to pyromania, kleptomania, physical or sexual abuse, exhibitionism or voyeurism are not impairments. Seasonal allergic rhinitis (hay fever) is excluded, but not if it aggravates another condition. Also excluded are tattoos or the piercing of the body by objects for decorative or non-medical purposes (Disability Discrimination (Meaning of Disability) Regulations 1996).

Substantial and long-term adverse effect

4.166 Any impairment must have lasted for at least 12 months, or be reasonably expected to last for that period, or reasonably be expected to last for life. It is no longer necessary for a mental impairment to arise from 'a clinically well-recognised illness', and thus physical and mental illnesses are to be treated alike from a diagnostic point of view. But vague expressions, such as 'depression', 'anxiety', 'stress' or 'nervous debility' will not, by themselves, lead to a conclusion that the person is disabled. Many instances of such illnesses do not last for a long period, and thus would fail to meet the requirement that the impairment must have a substantial and long-term adverse effect. However, any impairment, whether physical or mental, which ceases to have a substantial effect on a person's ability to carry out normal day-to-day activities is to be treated as continuing to have that effect if it is likely to recur (Sch 1, para 2(2)).

Persons who suffer from certain progressive illnesses, eg, HIV infection, cancer and multiple sclerosis, will be deemed to be disabled from the point in time of diagnosis, although certain types of minor cancers, which respond to quick and effective treatment, may be excluded by regulations. The Disability Discrimination (Blind and Partially Sighted Persons) Regulations 2003 provide that anyone certified or registered blind or partially sighted is deemed to be disabled for the purpose of the Act, and will no longer be required to establish that being blind or partially sighted has a substantial adverse effect on day-to-day activities. A severe disfigurement is to be treated as having a substantial effect on the ability of a person to carry out normal day-to-day activities.

4.167 Whether an impairment has a substantial effect on a person's ability to carry out normal day-to-day activities should not be judged by reference to whether he is able to carry out his job (*Goodwin v Patent Office*) but evidence as to how he carries out his duties at work can be relevant in assessing the employee's credibility, provided that the duties carried out can be regarded as being normal day-to-day activities (*Law Hospital NHS Trust v Rush*). If the effect of the impairment fluctuates, and is exacerbated by conditions at work, then an employee's ability to perform normal day-to-day activities both while at work and while not at work is to be taken into account when assessing whether the impairment has a substantial and long-term adverse effect (*Cruickshank v VAW Motorcast Ltd*).

4.168 To assess whether or not an impairment has a substantial adverse effect a tribunal should concentrate on what a claimant cannot do, or can only do with difficulty, and not on what he can do (*Leonard v Southern Derbyshire Chamber of Commerce*).

Normal day-to-day activities

4.169 An impairment is to be taken as affecting normal day-to-day activities if it affects a person with regard to mobility, manual dexterity, physical coordination, continence, ability to lift, carry or move everyday objects, speech, hearing, eyesight, memory or ability to concentrate, learn or understand, or perception of risks of physical danger (see Sch 1). The fact that a person is disabled within the meaning of other legislation (eg for the purpose of Disability Living Allowance) does not mean that he comes within the definition of disability within the meaning of the Act. The playing of games or sports does not constitute 'normal day-to-day activities', because such activities are only normal for a particular group of persons (*Coca-Cola Enterprises Ltd v Shergill*). But it is normal for a woman to put rollers in her hair and apply make-up to her face (*Ekpe v Metropolitan Police Comr*). The Guidance Notes give specific examples of normal day-to-day activities, and reference should be made to these Notes when reaching a decision in any particular case.

4.170 An impairment affects a person's ability to carry out normal day-to-day activities only if it affects one of the functions specified in Sch 1, para 4(1) to the Act. This includes 'memory or ability to concentrate, learn or understand'. In *Hewett v Motorola Ltd* it was held that an autistic employee's difficulty in understanding normal social interaction fell within para 4(1), and in *Dunham v Ashford Windows* an employee who had severe reading and writing difficulties was held to be suffering from a mental impairment.

C. Meaning of discrimination (s 3A)

There are three forms of discrimination to consider:

Unjustified, less favourable treatment (s 3A(1))

4.171 A person discriminates against a disabled person if, for a reason which relates to the disabled person's disability, he treats him less favourably than he treats or would treat others to whom that reason does not or would not apply, and he cannot show that the treatment in question is justified. Treatment is justified if the reason is both material to the circumstances of the particular case and substantial. Thus if the work output of a disabled person is less than that of an able-bodied person, it would be permissible to pay the former a lower wage (s 3A(1)).

4.172 The reason for the less favourable tre1atment must relate to the disability. If there is another (unconnected) reason, there is no breach of s 3A. Thus in *London Clubs Management Ltd v Hood* the employee was off sick because of a medical condition which amounted to a disability. He was refused sick pay, and claimed this amounted to less favourable treatment. His claim failed. The manager had decided not to pay sick pay to any of his staff because of the high absenteeism rate. Thus the reason why he was not paid sick pay was not because of his disability, but because of the employer's sick pay policy.

4.173 It is the task of a tribunal to investigate the facts and consider whether there was evidence on the basis of which it could conclude that the reason for the treatment was material in the circumstances and substantial. If the employer undertook a proper risk assessment, and formed an opinion based on appropriate medical or other evidence, it is not for the tribunal to reappraise that evidence and come to an opposite conclusion. If the decision taken by the employer is within the range of reasonable responses, and if the reason was material to the circumstances and substantial, the fact that the tribunal would have come to a different conclusion on that evidence is immaterial (*Jones v Post Office*).

Direct discrimination on grounds of less favourable treatment (s 3A(5))

4.174 A person directly discriminates against a disabled person (it will be recalled that there is no concept of indirect discrimination under the DDA) if, on the ground of the disabled person's disability, he treats the disabled person less favourably than he treats or would treat a person not having that particular disability whose relevant circumstances are the same or not materially different from those of the disabled person. Under this heading, justification is no defence (s 3A(5)–(6)).

4.175 The distinction between these two forms of direct discrimination requires an identification of the appropriate comparator. Under s 3A(1) (sometimes referred to as 'residual less favourable treatment') a comparison must be made with a person to whom the disability-related reason does not apply, ie s/he can be disabled or non-disabled, whereas under s 3A(5) an employer is making generalised assumptions about the disability or its effects. Under s 3A(1), justification may be a defence in appropriate circumstances, whereas under s 3A(5) a 'blanket ban' on disabled persons in general is incapable of being justified.

Failure to comply with duty to make reasonable adjustments

4.176 A person also discriminates against a disabled person if he fails to comply with a duty to make reasonable adjustments imposed on him in relation to the disabled person. Where a provision, criterion or practice applied by an employer, or any physical feature of premises occupied by him, places the disabled person at a substantial disadvantage in comparison with persons who are not disabled, it is the duty of the employer to take such steps as is reasonable for him to take in order to prevent the provision, criterion or practice, or feature, having that effect (s 4A). However, there is no such duty if the employer did not know, and could not reasonably be expected to know, that the disabled person is an applicant for employment or that the person has a disability and is likely to be affected by that provision, criterion, practice or feature (s 4A(3)).

4.177 It follows that if an employer fails to carry out a proper risk assessment of the disablement in order to prevent any arrangement by the employer, or any physical feature of the premises, from placing the disabled person at a substantial disadvantage, then he fails to comply with his duty to make a reasonable adjustment. Thus once a disability has been revealed, it will be necessary to obtain a proper assessment of the disabling condition, the prognosis, the effect of the disability on the employee's (or job applicant's) ability to perform his duties, the effect of the physical feature of the workplace, and the steps which might be taken to reduce or remove the disadvantages to which the disabled person would be subjected (*Mid-Staffordshire General Hospitals NHS Trust v Cambridge*).

4.178 The Act (s 18B) gives a list of examples which a person may take in order to comply with the duty to make reasonable adjustments. These include making adjustments to the premises, allocating some of the disabled person's duties to another person, transferring him to fill an existing vacancy, altering his working hours, assigning him to a different place of work, allowing him to be absent during working hours for rehabilitation, assessment or treatment, giving him training, acquiring or modifying equipment, modifying instructions or reference manuals, modifying procedures for assessment or testing, providing a reader or interpreter, and providing supervision or other support.

4.179 To determine whether it would be reasonable for an employer to take a particular step, regard shall be had to the extent the taking of the step would prevent the discriminatory effect, whether it would be practicable to take that step, the financial or other costs which would be incurred and the extent to which it would disrupt the employer's activities, the extent of the employer's financial or other resources, and the availability to the employer of financial or other assistance with respect to taking that step, the nature of his activities and the size of his undertaking, where steps would be taken in relation to a private household, the extent to which it would disrupt the household or disturb any person residing there.

4.180 Reasonable adjustments must be job related. It is not the duty of the employer to provide personal carers or special facilities (eg a disabled toilet must be provided, but not assistance in going to the toilet (*Kenny v Hampshire Constabulary*)).

4.181 Subject to the duty to make reasonable adjustments, the Act does not require a person to treat a disabled person more favourably than he treats others (s 18D) (but see *Archibold v Fife Council*).

D. Meaning of harassment (s 3B)

4.182 A person subjects a disabled person to harassment where, for a reason relating to the disabled person's disability, he engages in unwanted conduct which has the purpose or effect of violating the disabled person's dignity, or creating an intimidating, hostile, degrading, humiliating or offensive environment for him. Conduct shall be regarded as having this effect if, having regard to all the circumstances, including the perception of the disabled person, it should reasonably be considered as having that effect.

E. Victimisation (s 55)

4.183 It is unlawful to discriminate against a person (whether disabled or not) because that person has brought proceedings under the Act, or given evidence or information in connection with such proceedings, or alleged that some person has contravened the Act. However, this does not apply in respect of any allegations which are false and not made in good faith. The victimisation provisions apply equally to post-employment acts which arise out of and are closely connected to the relevant relationship (s 16A).

F. Discrimination in employment (s 4)

4.184 It is unlawful for an employer to discriminate against a disabled person:

(a) in the arrangements he makes for the purpose of determining to whom he should offer employment;

(b) in the terms on which he offers that person employment;

(c) by refusing to offer, or deliberately not offering, him employment.

It is also unlawful for an employer to discriminate against a disabled person whom he employs:

(a) in the terms of employment offered to him;

(b) in the opportunities which he affords him for promotion, transfer, training or receiving any other benefit;

(c) by refusing to afford him, or deliberately not affording him, any such opportunity;

(d) by dismissing him, or subjecting him to any other detriment;

(e) by subjecting him to any harassment.

4.185 A dismissal, for this purpose, includes the non-renewal of a fixed-term contract or a task contract (except if the employment is renewed), and a constructive dismissal (s 4(5)). However, s 4(6) states that s 4 only applies in relation to employment at an establishment in Great Britain, but there is some doubt as to the validity of this provision. A similar provision in the Race Relations Act was held by the EAT to the contrary to Art 48 of the Treaty of Rome, as being a fetter on the free movement of labour so far as workers in the European Economic Area are concerned. Since the Treaty of Rome overrides domestic law, employment tribunals may be expected to disapply s 4(6) (see *Bossa v Nordstress Ltd*).

The tests for unfair dismissal under the Employment Relations Act (see Chapter 17) are not necessarily applicable to the Disability Discrimination Act. Thus it is possible for a dismissal to be fair under the ERA, but it does not follow that it is non-discriminatory under the DDA (*Edwards v Mid-Suffolk District Council*).

If an employer gives an instruction to another that a discriminatory policy should be carried out, and that person resigns his employment because he feels unable to carry out that policy, he has suffered a detriment, contrary to s 4(2)(d). It is not necessary for the discriminatory act to be because of that person's disability (see *Weathersfield Ltd v Sargent*).

The 'purposive' approach

4.186 There is a danger of adopting a stereotype approach to disabled persons. Only a relatively small proportion of the disabled community are visibly disabled, ie in wheel-chairs, or carrying white sticks or other aids. The vast majority of disabled persons will have a physical or mental disability which may not be immediately obvious, and will only come to light when they fail to do that which a non-disabled person can do. Thus in deciding whether a claimant's impairment is substantial, a purposive approach should be taken by the employment tribunal, having regard to the guidance notes and the code of practice issued by the Secretary of State. The focus of the Act is on the activities which the claimant cannot do (or can only do with difficulty (see *Leonard v South Derbyshire Chamber of Commerce*)), rather than on the things he can do. 'Substantial' means 'more than minor or trivial' rather than 'very large' (*Goodwin v Patent Office*). But the list of examples in the guidance notes are illustrative, not exhaustive. In *Vicary v British Telecommunications*, the employers had relied largely on the opinion of their medical officer who was of the opinion that the claimant's disabilities were not substantial, and did not affect her normal day-to-day activities, a conclusion which the employment tribunal appeared to adopt. On appeal it was held that a medical expert is entitled to express an opinion based on observation and examination, but it was for the employment tribunal to make this finding of fact, based on their own assessment of the evidence.

4.187 It has been held that the failure to place a disabled person on a short list for interview did not, by itself, indicate that the employer had discriminated unlawfully, for frequently there are a large number of applicants for a particular job, and thus it is inevitable that only a limited number of applicants can be called for interview. In another case, an employee developed multiple sclerosis, and it was held that the employer acted unreasonably in dismissing him without taking heed of a report from a neurologist, who thought that the employee's prospect of working should be assessed on a 'try and see' basis. By and large, the employment tribunals appear to be applying the same tests under the new Act towards the dismissal of a disabled person as they did before the Act came into force, ie did the employer act reasonably in dismissing this employee for the reason put forward (see, eg, *Pascoe v Hallen and Medway*). Thus, a consideration of alternatives, proper consultation, a review of attendance and performance, providing additional support facilities, obtaining a full and up-to-date medical report, are all steps which a reasonable employer would take.

Discriminatory advertisements (s 16B)

4.188 It is unlawful to publish (or cause to publish) an advertisement which indicates that an application for employment may be determined by reference to the applicant not having a disability, or any reluctance of the person determining the application to comply with a duty to make reasonable adjustments.

Instructions and pressure to discriminate (s 16C)

4.189 It is unlawful for a person who has authority over another person to instruct him to do any act which is unlawful under the Act, or to procure the doing by him of such an act. It is also unlawful to induce any person to do an act which contravenes the provisions relating to employment services, by providing or offering to provide any benefit, or subjecting him to any detriment.

Liability of employers (s 58)

4.190 Anything done by a person in the course of his employment shall be treated as also done by his employer, whether or not it was done with the employer's knowledge or approval. However, in any proceedings brought under the Act, it will be a defence for the employer to prove that he took such steps as were reasonably practicable to prevent the employee from doing that act, or from doing acts of that description in the course of his employment.

Remedies

4.191 A complaint may be made to an employment tribunal that a person has been discriminated against because of his disability. If the complaint is well founded, the tribunal will make a declaration, and make an award of compensation, which may include an award for injured feelings. A recommendation may also be made that the employer takes action for the purpose of obviating or reducing the adverse effect on the claimant. If the employer fails to comply with the recommendation, the employment tribunal may increase the compensation award.

4.192 In respect of any such proceedings, the employment tribunal regulations make provision for a restricting reporting order to be made in cases where evidence of a personal nature is likely to be heard, as such evidence is likely to cause significant embarrassment to the claimant if reported. A similar power exists with regard to appeals before the EAT.

Disability Rights Commission

4.193 The Disability Rights Commission can carry out formal investigations, issue non-discrimination notices, give assistance in relation to proceedings, and prepare and issue Code of Practice and Guidance Notes. There is a questionnaire procedure, whereby individuals who believe they are victims of discrimination can put questions to the person whom they believe to be responsible.

4.194 It should be noted that only the Disability Rights Commission can bring proceedings in respect of a contravention of s 16B (discriminatory advertisements) or s 16C (instruction and pressure to discriminate). The DRC may present a complaint to an employment tribunal, which, if it finds that the complaint is well founded, shall make a declaration. If it appears to the DRC that the wrongdoer is likely to commit a further unlawful act, it may apply to the county court (in Scotland, a sheriff's court) for an injunction.

Annual reports

4.195 In respect of companies which employ (on average throughout the year) more than 250 employees, the annual directors' report must contain a statement describing such policy as the company has applied during the preceding year as to the employment, training, career development and promotion of disabled persons (Companies Act 1985, Sch 7 para 9).

Religion or belief

4.196 The Employment Equality (Religion or Belief) Regulations 2003 define religion or belief as meaning any religion, religious belief or similar philosophical belief. This simple definition is likely to cause problems. Although in most cases it will be fairly obvious whether a particular person has a religious belief (eg in respect of Jews, Catholics, Muslims etc), it is less clear whether persons with non-conventional faiths are covered, eg Druids, Rastafarians, Satanists, and others who follow various cults. For example, animal rights activists, pagans, etc have a 'belief' which would probably seek to bring themselves within the scope of the regulations, but would only succeed by arguing that they hold a 'similar philosophical belief' to a religion. Non-believers are not covered (except in respect of the victimisation and harassment provisions), although a professed atheist or humanist probably has a philosophical belief similar to that of religious belief. Political beliefs are not within the regulations, although there is sometimes a connection between a political party and religious organisations which may cause some difficulties in practice. In *Baggs v Fudge*, an employment tribunal held that a job applicant who was not interviewed for a post because he was a member of the British National Party could not succeed under the Religion or Belief Regulations because the BNP is a political party, and is not a religion or set of religious beliefs, or a set of similar philosophical beliefs.

4.197 Discrimination by way of victimisation is covered, as well as harassment, which has a definition identical to the new Race Relations Act provisions (see para 4.124). An exception to the employment provisions arises where the job has a genuine and determining occupational requirement for an individual to have a particular religion or belief, or where the employer has an ethos based on religion or belief, provided the requirement is proportionate. But the fact that a genuine occupational requirement exists will not justify discrimination in relation to terms of employment. There is also an exemption on grounds of national security. Selection for recruitment or for promotion must be on merit, irrespective of religious beliefs, but positive action to redress an imbalance of particular religions or beliefs is permitted (eg the placing of job advertisements in publications which reach specific religious groups).

4.198 The regulations mirror existing discrimination legislation in that they apply to job applicants, employees, workers, contract workers etc. Post-employment discrimination is covered if it arises out of or is closely connected with the employment. Anyone who works wholly or partly in Great Britain will be protected, as will a person who works wholly outside Great Britain if the employer has a place of business in Great Britain and the work is for the purposes of the business carried out there, and the employee is ordinarily resident in Great Britain.

A. Direct discrimination

4.199 Direct discrimination occurs when one person (A) treats another person (B) less favourably than he would treat other persons, and the reason is B's religion or belief. Indirect discrimination occurs if one person (A) applies a provision, criterion or practice, which he applies to other persons not of B's religion or belief, but which puts B at a disadvantage when compared with those others, and which cannot be shown to be a proportionate means of achieving a legitimate aim. Thus to dismiss a practising Christian employee for refusing to work on Sundays is indirectly discriminatory, in that it places a Christian at a particular disadvantage when compared with other persons. However, the employer will not be liable in such circumstances if he can show that the provision, criterion or practice is a proportionate means of achieving a legitimate aim (*Copsey v VWB Devon Clays Ltd*).

4.200 It will be unlawful to discriminate against a person on grounds of religion or belief in the arrangements the employer makes for determining who should be offered employment, omitting to offer employment, or in the terms on which employment is offered. Once employed, a person must not be discriminated against in relation to the terms of employment, opportunities for promotion, transfer, training or any other benefit, or in respect of dismissal or any other detriment.

4.201 However, there are two exceptions to the general rule on discrimination on grounds of religion or beliefs. The first applies where a particular religion or belief is a 'genuine and determining occupational requirement' for the job, having regard to the nature of the work, and it can be shown that it is proportionate to apply that requirement in the particular case. For example, a church is entitled to require that a minister of religion holds the requisite religious beliefs, although it is unlikely that the appointment of a cleaner would come within this exception. The second exception applies to employers who hold 'an ethos based on religion or belief' and it can be shown that a particular religion or belief is a genuine occupational requirement, which is a determining, though not decisive, requirement, and is proportionate. Thus, for example, if a family firm was owned and run exclusively by members of one particular faith, and its main dealings are with clients of that faith, this may amount to an ethos entitling recruitment from others of that faith.

B. Indirect discrimination

4.202 Indirect discrimination arises when a person applies a provision, criterion or practice which puts a person at a disadvantage when compared with a person not of the same religion or belief, and which cannot be shown to be a proportionate means of achieving a legitimate aim. Thus, in some circumstances a dress code could be indirectly discriminatory, if it affected a person of a particular religion or belief, unless there is a sound functional reason for it (eg compliance with health and safety requirements).

C. Harassment

4.203 Harassment on grounds of religion or belief arises if a person engages in unwanted conduct which has the purpose or effect of violating another person's dignity, or creating an intimidating, hostile, degrading, humiliating or offensive environment for that person. Conduct will have that effect only if having regard to all the circumstances, including the perception of the complainant, it should reasonably be considered as having that effect.

D. Victimisation

4.204 Victimisation arises when a person is treated less favourably because he has brought proceedings against the discriminator, given evidence in proceedings, done anything under the regulations, or alleged that the discriminator has committed an act which amounted to a contravention of the regulations.

E. Employer's liability for his employees

4.205 An employer will be liable for the acts of his employees, whether or not he approved of them. However, the employer will escape liability if he can show that he took reasonable steps to prevent those acts.

The Employment Equality (Religion and Belief) Regulations, reg 30(2)(a) provides that if an employer proves that the discriminatory provision, criterion or practice was not applied with the intention of treating the claimant unfavourably on grounds of religion or belief, compensation can only be awarded in limited circumstances. Otherwise, the usual remedies are available in the employment tribunal.

4.206 ACAS has issued guidance notes to accompany the regulations.

Age discrimination

4.207 The Employment Equality (Age) Regulations 2006 came into force on 1 October 2006, and this is the final piece of legislation to flow from the implementation of EC Directive 2000/78/EC (see para 1.88). The regulations follow the pattern of the sexual orientation and religion and belief anti-discrimination provisions, with appropriate modifications.

A. Discrimination on grounds of age (reg 3)

4.208 A person discriminates against another person if:

(a) on grounds of age, he treats that other person less favourably than he treats or would treat another person, or

(b) he applies a provision, criterion or practice which he applies to another person not of the same age group, but which puts the person to whom it is applied at a particular disadvantage when compared with that other, and which puts him at a disadvantage,

and he cannot show that the treatment, provision, criterion or practice is a proportionate means of achieving a legitimate aim.

Thus direct and indirect discrimination is permissible if there is objective justification for it.

B. Victimisation (reg 4)

4.209 It will amount to an act of victimisation if a person treats another less favourably because that person:

(a) brought proceedings against any person under the regulations;

(b) gave evidence or information in connection with those proceedings;

(c) has otherwise done anything by reference to the regulations; or

(d) alleged that any person has committed an act which would amount to a contravention of the regulations.

However, the protection against victimisation does not apply in respect of any allegation, evidence or information given by a person which is false and not made or given in good faith.

C. Instruction to discriminate (reg 5)

4.210 Discrimination occurs if a person gives another person instructions to discriminate and that other person either does so or complains to another about the instruction.

D. Harassment (reg 6)

4.211 A person subjects another to harassment where, on grounds of age, he engages in unwanted conduct which has the purpose or effect of:

(a) violating that other's dignity, or

(b) creating an intimidating, hostile, degrading, humiliating or offensive environment for that other person.

Conduct shall only amount to harassment if having regard to all the circumstances it should reasonably be considered to have that effect.

E. Discrimination in employment (reg 7(1))

4.212 It is unlawful for an employer to discriminate against a person on grounds of age:

(a) in the arrangements he makes for determining who shall be employed;

(b) in the terms he offers that person employment;

(c) by refusing or deliberately not offering him employment.

4.213 It is also unlawful to discriminate against that person:

(a) in the terms of employment offered to him;

(b) in the opportunities for promotion, transfer, training, or receiving any other benefit;

(c) by refusing to afford him any such opportunity; or

(d) by dismissing him, or subjecting him to any other detriment (reg 2).

4.214 However, reg 7(1)(a) (arrangements for employment) and reg 7(1)(c) (offers of employment) do not apply:

(a) in relation to a person whose age is greater than the employer's normal retirement age, or if the employer does not have a normal retirement age, has attained the age of 65, or who would within six months from the date of his application reach the employer's normal retirement age or the age of 65, as the case may be, and

(b) who, if recruited, would be an employee or a person in Crown employment. In other words, an employer can refuse to employ a prospective employee who is over the age of 65 (regs 7(5), 30).

Thus, the anti-discrimination provisions do not apply to employees (or Crown employees) who are either over the age of 65 or over the normal retirement age, or within six months of either, as the case may be.

F. Exception for genuine occupational requirement (reg 8)

4.215 Certain provisions do not apply where, having regard to the nature of the employment or the context in which it is carried out, possessing a characteristic related to age is a genuine and determining occupational requirement, it is proportionate to apply that requirement in the particular case, and either the person concerned does not meet that requirement, or the employer is not satisfied (and it is reasonable for him not to be so satisfied) that the person meets the requirement. The provisions in question are reg 7(1)(a) (arrangements for determining employment), 7(1)(c) (refusing to offer employment), 7(2)(b), (c) (opportunities for promotion, etc and refusing such opportunities), and 7(2)(d) (dismissal from any employment). For example, the age of a person may be a relevant factor in the acting profession, or in certain sports, etc.

G. Other provisions

4.216 There are further provisions in the regulations which relate specifically to contract workers, trustees and managers of occupational pension schemes, office holders, police, those in the serious organised crime agency, barristers, advocates, partnerships, trade organisations, qualification bodies, employment agencies, and so on.

4.217 There are also provisions which deal with the meaning of employment at an establishment in Great Britain, discrimination or harassment after the relationship has come to an end (which may have implications for the giving of references) (reg 24), the vicarious liability of employers and principals (reg 25), and aiding unlawful acts (reg 26). These provisions are identical to those contained in the Sexual Orientation and Religion and Belief Regulations (see paras 4.27 and 4.196 ff).

4.218 There are a number of exceptions to the above provisions. Thus, age discrimination is permitted on grounds of statutory authority (reg 27), safeguarding national security (reg 28), taking positive action (reg 29), a dismissal for reason of retirement of a person over the age of 65 (reg 30) and national minimum wage (reg 31). Further provisions relating to retirement are discussed at para 4.222.

H. Long service benefits (reg 32)

4.219 The general principle is that it is lawful to use length of service as a criterion for the provision of additional benefits. However, if an employee feels that he is at a disadvantage because the employer has used this criterion in relation to another employee, the former would need to have at least five years' service before he could make a complaint. The employer could then show that the reason the criterion was used was to fulfil a business need of the undertaking, eg, by encouraging loyalty or motivation, or rewarding the experience of some, or all of his workers. In other words, if an employee has been employed for five years, he is entitled to complain if he is not given a benefit based on long service whereas another employee has been given such a benefit. To resist such a complaint, the employer must show the 'business need' of encouraging loyalty, etc.

I. Enhanced redundancy payments (reg 33)

4.220 It is permissible for an employer to make an enhanced redundancy payment in which there is an in-built age factor, provided certain conditions are met. These are:

(a) the employee must be redundant (within the meaning of ERA, s 135). Employees who have less than two years' service may also be given an enhanced redundancy payment, as well as employees who volunteer to take redundancy;

(b) the method of calculation must be the same for all employees who are made redundant;

(c) the calculation is based on the statutory multiplier, ie one and a half week's pay for each year of employment in which the employee was not below the age of 41, one week's pay for a year of employment in which he was not below the age of 22, and half a week's pay for each year of employment below the age of 22;

(d) no more than 20 years' service is to count.

4.221 The employer may make an enhanced redundancy payment which is in excess of the statutory cap used for a week's pay purpose, and may increase the multiplier used to calculate the payment for each year's employment by more than one.

J. Retirement (Sch 6)

4.222 The rules relating to dismissal for reason of retirement are contained in Sch 6 and various amendments which are made to ERA, s 98. Transitional provisions dealing with terminations which take place before 1 April 2007 are contained in Sch 7.

4.223 Under Sch 6, the employer has three duties. These are:

(a) the employer must notify the employee of the date when the employee is due to retire;

(b) the employer must notify the employee of his right to request to work beyond the retirement date;

(c) the employer must consider any such request, and give a right of appeal against a refusal to allow the employee to work beyond the retirement date.

Notification of date

4.224 The employer must notify the employee of the date on which he intends the employee to retire. The notification must be in writing, and be given not more than one year nor less than six months before the dismissal. If he fails to so inform the employee, he has a continuing duty to notify the employee (in writing) until the 14th day before the dismissal. The employer must also notify the employee of the employee's right to make a request to continue in employment after the retirement date. The notifications must be given whether or not there is a term in the employee's contract which indicates when the retirement is expected to take place, or any other notification or information about the employee's date of retirement or right to request a continuation of his employment.

Employee's right to request to work beyond the retirement date

4.225 An employee has a statutory right to make a request to his employer not to retire on the intended retirement date. The request must propose that following the intended retirement date, the employment should continue either indefinitely, or for a stated period, or until a stated date. The request must be in writing, and state that it is being made under the provisions of the Employment Equality (Age) Regulations 2006, Sch 6, para 5(3). Only one such request may be made. If the employer has notified the employee not more than one year and not less than six months before the retirement date, the employee may make a request more than three months but not less than six months before the intended date of retirement, but if the employer has not complied with this provision, the request may be made before the intended retirement date, but not more than six months before that date.

4.226 The employer then has a duty to consider the request, and a duty not to retire the employee until it has been so considered. The employer shall hold a meeting with the employee within a reasonable period after receiving it, and give the employee notice of his decision as soon as is reasonably practicable. Obviously, if the employer accedes to the request there is no need to hold a meeting. And if it is not practicable to hold the meeting within a reasonable period, the employer may consider the request without holding the meeting, provided he considers any representations made by the employee. If the request is accepted, the employer will state that the employment shall continue indefinitely, or for a further specified period or date when the employment will end. If the decision is to refuse the request, the employer will confirm the date when the dismissal for reason of retirement will take place. If the request is refused, or is granted for a period which is shorter than that proposed by the employee, the employer will notify the employee of his right of appeal.

4.227 If the employer fails to notify the employee of the right to make a request, then, on a complaint to an employment tribunal, an award of up to eight weeks' pay (capped) may be made.

Right of appeal

4.228 The employee is entitled to appeal against the decision by the employer to refuse the request, within 14 days. The appeal shall be in writing, setting out the grounds for the appeal, be dated, and made as soon as is reasonably practicable after receiving the employer's decision. The employer must hold an appeal hearing within a reasonable period, although this would not be necessary if the employer decides to uphold the appeal. Both parties must take all reasonable steps to attend the meeting. If it is not practicable to hold the meeting within a reasonable period, the employer may consider the appeal without holding a meeting provided he considers any representations made by the employee. The employer must notify the employee of the decision as soon as is reasonably practicable. If the request is accepted, the decision will state that the employment will continue indefinitely or for a further specified period, or the date when the employment will end. If the appeal is refused, the employer will confirm that he wishes the employee to retire, and the date on which this will take place.

4.229 Where an appeal meeting is being held, the employee has the right to be accompanied by one companion, who may be a person chosen by the employee, or a worker employed by the same employer. The companion is permitted to address the meeting, but not to answer questions on behalf of the employee, although he may confer with him. The companion has the same protections as those which apply to employees who take time off work for trade union duties (TULR(C)A, ss 186–173).

4.230 If the employer fails to permit the employee to be accompanied at the appeal hearing, then, on a complaint to an employment tribunal, an award of two weeks' pay (capped) may be made. The employee and the companion have protection against a detriment because they exercised their rights under this provision, and any dismissal for this reason will be automatically unfair.

K. Dismissal for reason of retirement

No normal retirement age

4.231 If there is no normal retirement age, and the operative date of termination takes place before the employee reaches the age of 65, then any dismissal cannot be for reason of retirement (ERA, s 98ZA). This is so whether or not the employer has notified the employee of his right to make a request. If there is no normal retirement age, and the termination takes place after the date when the employee reaches the age of 65, and the employer has notified the employee of his right to make a request to continue in employment, any such retirement termination shall be taken as being the only reason for the dismissal, and any other reason shall be disregarded (ERA, s 98ZB).

Normal retirement age

4.232 If the employee has a normal retirement age, and the operative date of termination takes place before that date, such dismissal cannot be for reason of retirement (ERA, s 98ZC). If the normal retirement age is 65 or higher, and the employer has notified the employee of his right to make a request, any retirement after that date shall be treated as being the only reason for dismissal, and any other reason shall be disregarded. Any retirement before that date shall not be treated as a retirement termination (ERA, s 98ZD). The same principles apply if the normal retirement age is below the age of 65, ie if the employer has notified the employee of a right to make a request, and the termination takes place on the intended date of retirement, retirement shall be taken as being the only reason for the dismissal, whereas if the employment terminates before the intended date of retirement, the dismissal cannot be for reason of retirement (ERA, s 98ZE).

4.233 If the employer fails to notify the employee of his right to make a request in the above cases in the period of between six months and one year prior to the retirement date (see above, para 4.225) then, when determining the reason (or principal reason) for the dismissal, the employment tribunal shall pay particular regard to (a) whether the employer complied with the continuing duty to notify the employee up to the 14th day before the operative date of termination, (b) if he did subsequently comply with that duty, how long before the retirement date such notification was given, and (c) whether or not the employer held a meeting to consider the request (ERA, s 98ZF).

Fair/unfair dismissal for reason of retirement (ERA, s 98ZG).

4.234 A dismissal will be unfair if the employer fails to comply with any of the following statutory obligations:

    (a) the continuing duty to notify the employee of the employee's right to make a request, and the intended date of retirement;

    (b) the duty to consider the request and to hold a meeting with the employee;

    (c) the duty to consider an appeal against the decision to refuse the request.

4.235 As well as the usual compensation award, there will be a minimum basic award of (currently) £4,000.

4.236 The result of these changes is as follows.
A dismissal on grounds of retirement will be a fair dismissal if:

    (a) it is a genuine retirement dismissal;

    (b) it takes place on or after the planned retirement age of 65 (or lower age which has been set and can be objectively justified by the employer);

    (c) the 'duty to consider' procedure has been correctly followed.

4.237 A dismissal on grounds of retirement will be automatically unfair if:

    (a) prior to retiring the employee, the employer has not informed him of the right to request to continue working, nor informed him of the intended retirement date, or has so informed him less than two weeks before the retirement date;

(b) the dismissal takes place while the 'duty to consider' procedure has not been completed or not properly followed.

4.238 Obviously, a dismissal for some other reason than retirement, eg incompetence, theft, etc has to be determined by the usual principles of procedural and substantive fairness, and the age of the employee will be irrelevant.

4.239 However, before an employee can bring a claim for unfair dismissal under the regulations, the statutory grievance procedure (see para 12.39) must be followed.

4.240 Enforcement of the regulations are by way of a complaint to an employment tribunal within the usual three-month period, or further period if it would be just and equitable to accept a complaint outside the time limit. The burden of proof is the same as other anti-discrimination legislation (see para 4.94). On such a complaint, a tribunal may make a declaration, and make an award of compensation, which may be unlimited in amount. Interest on any award may be ordered. If the complaint is one of unintentional indirect discrimination, an award of compensation may only be made if the tribunal makes a declaration or recommendation (or both), and considers it just and equitable to award compensation. If a recommendation is not complied with, an award of compensation may be made, or an increase made to an award already made. There is a questionnaire procedure, and help and assistance may be provided by the Commission on Equality and Human Rights (see para 1.43) which formally comes into existence in 2007.

Other matters

4.241 (a) The upper and lower age limits on the right to receive redundancy payments have been abolished. The provision which permits the tapering down of the amount of redundancy payment for employees who are within a year of the upper age limit of 65 (or normal retirement age, if there is one) has also been abolished. The maximum number of years to count remains at 20. The age bands for the multiplier will remain, so that employees up to (and including) the age of 21 will receive half a week's pay for each year's employment, between the ages of 22 and 40 they will receive one week's pay for each year's employment, and over the age of 41 they will receive one and a half week's pay for each year's employment.

(b) There will be a consequential knock-on effect on contractual redundancy schemes which are generally more beneficial than the state scheme. These will have to be reconsidered in the light of the new regulations, and suitably amended to remove any semblance of age discrimination. The employer would need to show that long service 'fulfils a business need', etc.

(c) The age related factors which apply to the basic award in unfair dismissal cases will be removed, and entitlement will be in accordance with the above statutory redundancy provisions.

(d) The one year's qualifying length of service period will remain for unfair dismissal claims, as will the two-year qualifying period for redundancy payment claims.

(e) It is likely that selection for redundancy on the basis of 'last in first out' (LIFO see para 18.48) may now be regarded as being either direct or indirect discrimination on grounds of age, and hence some other non-discriminatory formula for redundancy selection will have to be used in the future, unless the discrimination can be justified.

(f) The Redundancy Payments Pensions Regulations 1965 (which permitted employers to offset certain pension or lump-sum payment against statutory redundancy payments) are revoked.

4.242 The Age Regulations have a number of implications for employment practices, which will have to be appropriately modified. Among these are the following:

(a) Employment advertisements which indicate an intention to discriminate (eg 'Young dynamic person required') are not per se unlawful, but may be used by an unsuccessful job applicant as evidence of discrimination if there is a refusal to offer employment. Further, a job specification advertisement which is potentially discriminatory ('Five years experience required') may be part of the arrangements for determining who should be offered employment.

(b) Job application forms which ask questions about age (date of birth, etc) are potentially discriminatory, as well as questions about a person's employment record since leaving school.

(c) Questions asked at interviews which are age related (eg 'Are you not a bit old for this job?') should also be avoided.

(d) Appointing a new older employee at a higher salary than an existing younger employee is potentially discriminatory, and not protected by the exception in reg 32 (which only applies to existing employees) unless there is objective justification.

(e) Objective justification will always be a defence to a claim of age discrimination, with factors such as health and safety, the need to facilitate employment planning, rewarding loyalty, training requirements, and ensuring a reasonable period of employment before retirement, etc, being some of the factors which may be taken into account.

ACAS have produced a Guidance document entitled 'Age and the Workplace' to which reference may be usefully made.

Rehabilitated persons

A. The Rehabilitation of Offenders Act 1974

4.243 The Rehabilitation of Offenders Act 1974 seeks to ensure that if a person has made a genuine effort to rehabilitate into society after conviction for a serious criminal offence, he may be spared the indignity and embarrassment of subsequently having to disclose his unsavoury past. Provided he does not commit a serious offence within the rehabilitation period, he may, at the end of that time, be regarded as a rehabilitated person, and his conviction will be treated as having been 'wiped off the slate'. The Act is somewhat complex, but the general rule is that the length of the rehabilitation period will depend on the age of the offender at the time of conviction, and the sentence given for the offence. Thus the period will vary from six months in the case when an absolute discharge was granted up to ten years in respect of a sentence of imprisonment of 30 months. A sentence of imprisonment of more than 30 months will never become 'spent'. Once a person has become 'rehabilitated' evidence of his previous conviction is not generally admissible, and he may not be asked about it or, if he is asked, he need not tell the truth, and may deny his previous conviction. The rehabilitation period runs from the date of the conviction, not from the expiry of the sentence.

4.244 So far as the law of employment is concerned, s 4(3)(b) of the Act provides that (subject to certain exceptions) a 'spent' conviction, or failure to disclose such, shall not be grounds for dismissing or excluding a person from any office, profession, occupation or employment, or for prejudicing him in any way in any occupation or employment. However, the limits of the section need to be noted. At common law, an employer has the right to please himself whether or not to employ someone and although to refuse to employ a rehabilitated person may be to 'exclude' him, the section provides no remedy for a person who may feel that he has been discriminated against. Equally, a refusal to promote a rehabilitated person may amount to prejudicing him in that employment, but again no remedy is provided. On the other hand, if an employee who was a rehabilitated person was dismissed, and the sole ground was the discovery of his past convictions, this would undoubtedly amount to an unfair dismissal if he was otherwise within the protection of the Employment Rights Act (see Chapter 17). In *Hendry v Scottish Liberal Club*, one of the reasons why the claimant was dismissed was connected with the discovery that he had been convicted many years ago of possessing cannabis. This conviction was 'spent' within the meaning of the Act, and hence it was not a statutory reason for dismissal.

4.245 In *Property Guards Ltd v Taylor and Kershaw* the two claimants were employed as security guards. On commencing their employment they signed a statement to the effect that they had never been guilty of a criminal offence. When the employers discovered that they had both been convicted of minor offences of dishonesty, they were dismissed. The EAT upheld the finding of the employment tribunal that the dismissals were unfair. In both cases the convictions were 'spent' within the meaning of the Act. They were entitled not to disclose their previous convictions.

4.246 If an employer subsequently discovers that the employee has had a previous conviction, he must make all necessary enquiries to ascertain whether or not the conviction is spent before he starts taking action. In *Brooks v Ladbroke Lucky Seven Entertainment*, the claimant was dismissed when it was discovered that he had had a prior conviction. It was argued on behalf of the employer that the dismissal was necessary in view of the nature of their business (as a gambling club), and as they did not know that the conviction was spent, they were not acting unreasonably. It was held that the employer should have sought further information about the nature of the offence and the penalty imposed, and a failure to do so rendered the dismissal unfair.

4.247 The main rehabilitation periods are as follows:

Sentence	Rehabilitation period
Imprisonment or youth custody of more than 6 months and up to 2½ years	10 years
Imprisonment or youth custody not exceeding 6 months	7 years
Fine or community punishment order or community rehabilitation order or detention and training order	5 years

Conditional discharge, bind over, care order, or supervision order	One year, or until the order expires, whichever is the longer
Absolute discharge 6 months	

4.248 Other sentences which come within the Act include orders for custody in a remand home, an approved school, an attendance order, and a hospital order. In respect of persons under the age of 18 at the time of conviction, the rehabilitation period is generally reduced by half. In the case of imprisonment, it is the period of sentence imposed by the court which counts (including a suspended sentence) not the actual time spent in prison. The rehabilitation period runs from the date of the conviction. A prison sentence (or youth custody sentence) of more than two and a half years is never 'spent'.

4.249 The Act does not apply to questions which are asked of a person in order to assess the suitability of a person for admission to the professions of medical practitioner, barrister, accountant, solicitor, dentist, dental hygienist or auxiliary, veterinary surgeon, nurse, midwife, ophthalmic or dispensing optician, pharmaceutical chemist, or a Scottish registered teacher. Such people must still tell the truth about their previous convictions. Nor can a person tell a lie if the questions are asked for the purpose of assessing his suitability for the following employments, namely, certain legal appointments and offices, certain employment connected with the punishment of offenders, constables, traffic wardens, probation officers, further education teachers, proprietors of independent schools, certain local government social workers, hospital workers, persons who work for building societies or who provide financial services, youth club leaders and employment with cadet forces. Certain other occupations are also excluded from the provisions of the Act (see the Rehabilitation of Offenders Act 1974 (Exceptions) Orders 1975 as amended), and see *Wood v Coverage Care Ltd*).

B. Access to criminal records

4.250 Employers who wish to know whether or not an applicant for employment has or has not got a criminal record may be able to use the new procedures set out in the Police Act 1997, which makes arrangements for access to criminal records for employment-related purposes. This Act enables a criminal record check to be made available by a new Criminal Records Agency from computerised national criminal records, in response to an application by a person who is the subject of the check. There are three types of certificates which are now available.

Criminal conviction certificate (s 112)

4.251 This certificate gives prescribed details of every conviction which is recorded in central police records. A 'conviction' for this purpose means a conviction within the meaning of the Rehabilitation of Offenders Act, other than a conviction which is spent. Alternatively, the certificate will record that there is no conviction. An employer cannot apply direct to the Criminal Records Agency for this certificate, but can request that the job applicant provides one as a prerequisite for employment.

Criminal record certificate (s 113)

4.252 This is a more detailed certificate, which will record every matter recorded in central police records, including a conviction which is spent under the Rehabilitation of Offenders Act. This certificate can be asked for by a person seeking employment in one of the occupations where a conviction under the Rehabilitation of Offenders Act must be disclosed, even though it would otherwise be spent. An application for this type of certificate will be made by the subject of the check, countersigned by a person who is listed in a register to be kept by the Secretary of State as being likely to employ persons in occupations which are excluded from that Act. It is likely that this certificate will be sought by persons who wish to be employed in a large number of occupations which are exempt from the 1974 Act, including the judiciary, police, Crown employment, probation officers, prison staff, professional groups generally, banking and financial services, carers/social workers, etc.

Enhanced criminal record certificate (s 115)

4.253 This certificate, as well as containing the information found in the criminal record certificate, may contain additional information provided by local police forces, including cautions and relevant non-conviction information. This certificate will be used when seeking employment caring for or being in sole charge of persons under the age of 18 or vulnerable adults, or being involved in training or supervising them. Again, the application will be made by the job-applicant, and countersigned by the registered person.

4.254 It is an offence for members and staff of any registered body to make an unauthorised disclosure of any information provided in a criminal records check or enhanced criminal records check.

4.255 A code of practice on the operation of the above provisions of the Police Act has been issued.

Unfair recruitment (TULR(C)A, s 137)

4.256 There are provisions in the Trade Union and Labour Relations (Consolidation) Act 1992 which protect a person from being refused employment on grounds of trade union membership or non-membership. These matters will be considered in Chapter 21.

A. Employment of women

4.257 Most of the statutory provisions passed for the protection of female employees have been repealed in so far as they enabled different treatment to be accorded to women. Thus women may now clean parts of machinery while in motion, they may work underground in mines, and perform a number of other tasks which were previously not open to them (see Employment Act 1989, s 9). This is in accordance with the Equal Treatment Directive (see para 1.72) and the desire of the Government to reduce the legislative and administrative burdens on industry.

4.258 However, a number of statutory provisions relating to the health and safety of women have been retained, particularly dealing with those risks associated with pregnancy, childbirth and other risks specifically affecting women (see para 6.8). Thus a woman may not work in a factory within four weeks of childbirth (Factories Act 1961, Sch 5, Public Health Act 1936, s 205), or in any employment within two weeks of childbirth (Maternity (Compulsory Leave) Regulations 1994). Women are prohibited from working in certain processes and activities involving lead products (including lead paint); there are limits on exposure to ionising radiations, and on working in an aircraft or at sea while pregnant (Employment Act 1989, s 4 and Sch 1). Indeed, it is lawful to discriminate against a woman in so far as it is necessary to comply with the above restrictions (see para 4.72).

4.259 Restrictions on hours of work (including overtime and night work) for women were abolished in the Sex Discrimination Act 1986 (s 7) but the position is now governed by the Employment Act 1989 (s 1) which effectively nullifies any statutory provision which produces a discrimination as regards access to employment and working conditions (see para 4.52).

B. Employment of young persons

4.260 Legislative provisions dealing with the health and safety of young persons (defined as persons over compulsory school leaving age) can be found in the Management of Health and Safety at Work Regulations 1999 (see para 11.77), and restrictions on the hours of work of young workers can be found in the Working Time Regulations 1998 (see para 7.47).

C. Adult workers

4.261 The sole remaining legislation imposing restrictions on the hours of work of adult workers are (1) Mines and Quarries Act 1954 (underground miners), (2) Hours of Employment (Conventions) Act 1936 (sheet glass workers), (3) Shops (Early Closing Days) Act 1965 (shop assistants), and (4) Transport Act 1968 (vehicle drivers) and the Working Time Regulations (see para 7.47).

Duty of local authorities

4.262 Section 71 of the Race Relations Act provides that it shall be the duty of every local authority to make appropriate arrangements with a view to securing that their various functions are carried out with due regard to the need:

(a) to eliminate unlawful discrimination, and

(b) to promote equality of opportunity and good relations between persons of different racial groups.

4.263 A local authority cannot use the powers conferred by this section to punish a person who has done no wrongful act (*Wheeler v Leicester City Council*).

A. Contract compliance

4.264 Section 17 of the Local Government Act 1988 provides that in exercising any function dealing with public supply or works contracts, a public authority must not take account of non-commercial considerations. These include such matters as a contractor's terms and conditions of employment, the composition of his workforce, arrangements for promotion, transfer or training of the workforce, or the country of origin of supplies to contractors, the location in any country of the business activities of contractors, etc.

4.265 Clearly, since race relations matters are non-commercial considerations, the 1988 Act imposes a limit on the operation of s 71 of the 1976 Act. However, s 18(2) of the 1988 Act permits a local authority to ask approved questions, in writing, seeking information or undertakings relating to workforce matters, and considering the responses to them, and may also include in draft contracts terms or provisions relating to workforce matters, if the information, the undertaking or the inclusion of the terms are reasonably necessary to secure compliance with s 71. A local authority may also request evidence in support of any answer given.

4.266 The Secretary of State will specify the approved questions and description of evidence which may be requested for the purpose of s 18(2).

4.267 Somewhat curiously, there are no corresponding statutory provisions relating to sex discrimination (*R v London Borough of Islington, ex p Building Employers' Confederation*).

Civil harassment

4.268 Civil liability for the statutory tort of harassment is contained in the Protection from Harassment Act 1997. Section 1(1) of the Act provides that a person must not pursue a course of conduct which he knows or ought to know amounts to harassment of another person. The test is whether a reasonable person in possession of the same information would think that the course of conduct in question amounts to the harassment of another person. To amount to harassment (a) the harassment must be intentional; (b) the alleged offender must have known or ought to have known that he was harassing another person if a reasonable person in possession of such information at the time of the alleged conduct would so regard it; (c) harassment includes alarming the person or causing distress; (d) there must be a course of conduct which involves harassment on at least two occasions; and (e) the same person has to be the victim on each occasion.

4.269 An employer may be vicariously liable for acts of harassment committed by an employee in the course of his employment. In *Majrowski v St Thomas's NHS Trust* an employee alleged that he was bullied, intimidated and harassed by his departmental manager. It was held that he was entitled to pursue his claim. An employer cannot escape vicarious liability for the acts of an employee by showing that those acts were criminal, or that the conduct was contrary to express instructions since vicarious liability is a loss distribution device based on social and economic policy (*Lister v Lesley Hall Ltd*). However, a different conclusion was reached by another division of the Court of Appeal in *Banks v Ablex Ltd*, which held that the tort of harassment was not complete unless the conduct of the alleged tortfeasor was intentional and was directed at another person on more than one occasion knowing that it would cause harassment to that person. In *Majrowski*, the House of Lords thought that the courts were well able to recognise the boundary between conduct which was unattractive, even unreasonable, and conduct which was oppressive and unacceptable. To cross the boundary from the regrettable to the unacceptable the gravity of the misconduct must be of an order which would sustain criminal liability under s 2.

4.270 There are several important differences between liability for harassment under the various discrimination statutes, and a claim under the Protection from Harassment Act. In an ordinary discrimination claim, the employer will be vicariously liable for an employee's act of harassment against another employee. However, there is a statutory defence available for the employer if he took such steps as were reasonably practicable to prevent the employee from doing the act in question. Thus the employer could show that he publicised and properly instituted an anti-harassment policy, with proper training, etc. This defence does not exist under the Protection from Harassment Act, where vicarious liability is established once it is found that there is a close connection between the employee's duties and the breach of the statutory duty. The only safeguard for the employer is for the court to decide whether in the circumstances it would be just and equitable to hold the employer vicariously liable. It should also be noted that employment tribunal proceedings in respect of a harassment claim cannot be brought unless the employee has raised a grievance with the employer, and allowed 28 days for a response (see para 12.49). No such obligation exists when bringing a claim for the statutory tort.

4.271 The Act also creates criminal liability for harassment, punishable on summary conviction by a term of imprisonment of up to six months, or a fine not exceeding level 5 on the standard scale, or both.

Criminal harassment

4.272 Section 4A of the Public Order Act 1986 (as inserted by s 154 of the Criminal Justice and Public Order Act 1994) also creates an offence of harassment. This is committed by a person if, with intent to cause another person alarm or distress,

(a) he uses threatening, abusive or insulting words or behaviour, or disorderly behaviour, or

(b) he displays any writing, sign, or other visible representation which is threatening, abusive or insulting,

thereby causing another person harassment, alarm or distress.

It appears that this offence may well be committed by an individual in an employment context, eg, by way of sexual harassment, using racial abuse, etc, and may even extend protection to classes of employees not currently protected in law, eg persons with disabilities or on grounds of sexual orientation. The new law may also be relevant to the law on picketing (see para 23.101). Any criminal liability will fall on the individual who committed the offence, not on his employer.

A person convicted of the offence of harassment faces a fine of up to £5,000, and/or a term of imprisonment of up to six months.

5

Equal Pay

5.1 The Sex Discrimination Act 1975 is concerned with the elimination of discrimination in the recruitment, training, promotion and other aspects of the employment relationship. The Equal Pay Act 1970 is concerned with the establishment, where necessary, of equal terms and conditions of employment. This Act, as amended, has now been examined by the EAT and higher courts on a number of occasions as well as by the European Court of Justice, and the broad principle has emerged that as it is essentially a reforming statute, it must be interpreted accordingly. The employment tribunals must therefore apply its provisions in accordance with the statutory objective of eliminating discrimination in terms and conditions of employment which exist solely because of a person's sex. For historical reasons, most of the claims made under equal pay legislation are made by women, but the law applies equally to men, where appropriate.

5.2 It must be stressed that the application of the Equal Pay Act and the various relevant regulations (as well as the decisions of the UK courts and tribunals), are subject to the overriding views of the European Court of Justice, applying Art 141 (formerly 119) of the Treaty, and the Equal Pay Directive. In the event of a conflict arising, or a disputed interpretation, it is European law which will be applied.

5.3 Article 141 provides that member states shall maintain the application of the principle that men and women should receive equal pay for equal work. As we have noted (see *Barber v Guardian Royal Exchange*, para 4.72), the term 'pay' is very wide, and means 'the ordinary basic or minimum wage or salary and any other consideration, whether in cash or kind, which a worker receives, directly or indirectly, in respect of his employment from his employer'. In *Worringham v Lloyd's Bank*, female clerical officers under the age of 25 were not required to contribute to a pension scheme. Male clerical officers under the age of 25 were required to contribute 5% of their salary to the scheme, but to compensate them for the difference the men were paid 5% more. The Equal Pay Act (s 6(1A)(b)) excluded terms relating to death or retirement or any provision made in relation to death or retirement. On a reference to the European Court of Justice it was held that Art 141 had a direct effect so as to confer an enforceable Community right on all individuals within the EEC. Thus the scheme operated by the bank was in violation of Art 141, which overrode s 6(1A)(b) of the Equal Pay Act (s 6(1A)(b) was subsequently repealed).

5.4 The Act can apply to self-employed persons as well as employees, for it covers 'employment under a contract of service or apprenticeship, or a contract personally to execute any work or labour'. In *Quinnen v Hovells*, the claimant was a self-employed salesman engaged by the respondent to demonstrate goods for sale in a department store. He complained that two female demonstrators were receiving a higher rate of pay, and the

EAT held that he was entitled to have his claim considered on its merits, for the definition of employment in the Act clearly covered self-employed persons.

5.5 Whereas under UK law, the burden of proof lies upon an applicant to show that, on the balance of probabilities, s/he is not receiving equal pay, the decision of the European Court in *Handels-og v Dansk Arbejdsgiverforening* (the '*Danfoss*' case) indicates that if a pay system manifestly produces inequalities of pay between the sexes, the burden lies upon the employer to show that the criteria used which produces those inequalities are not discriminatory. Since Art 141 (formerly Art 119) of the Treaty of Rome overrides domestic law, it follows that if there is a suspicion of discrimination in pay scales, the burden of proof shifts to the employer to justify pay differentials (*Enderby v Frenchay Health Authority*).

5.6 Men and women are entitled to equal pay if they are employed 'in the same employment'. This means that they must be employed at the same establishments at which common terms and conditions of employment are observed (s 1(6)), ie the same terms and conditions (*British Coal Corpn v Smith*). In *Leverton v Clwyd County Council*, a nursery nurse was employed by a local authority, and she sought equal pay with male clerical staff employed by the same authority in different establishments. She and her comparators were covered by the same national collective agreement, but they were on different pay scales, with different hours and holiday entitlements. The employers contended that there were no common terms and conditions, and hence that the Act did not apply, but this view was rejected by the House of Lords. The terms and conditions, as laid down in the collective agreement, were applied generally, even though there were differences when applied to individual employees (NB, the claim failed under the defence of 'genuine material factor' see para 5.30).

5.7 However, having a common employer is not the same thing as being 'in the same employment', or having pay and conditions attributed to a 'single source' (*Lawrence v Regent Office Care Ltd*). It is necessary to locate the single source with the body responsible for setting the relevant terms. The critical question is whether there is a single body responsible for the discriminatory pay differences of which the complaint is made. Thus, pay and conditions in the civil service are settled by each individual department, subject to overall budgetary control by the Treasury (*Robertson v Department for Environment, Food and Rural Affairs*).

5.8 The Act applies to associated employers (see para 2.4) but even if two employers are not associated in the legal sense, if there is sufficient connection between two employments in a loose and non-technical sense (eg where terms and conditions of employment and salary scales are determined by a joint negotiating body), an equal pay claim may be brought under Art 141 of the Treaty of Rome, which takes precedence over domestic legislation (*South Ayrshire Council v Morton*). But a cross-employer comparison can only be made where the differences in pay can be attributable to a single source (*Lawrence v Regent Office Care Ltd*).

5.9 The Act requires that the contract of employment of all women shall be deemed to include an equality clause. This will operate when a woman is employed either on:

(a) like work (ie work which is the same or broadly similar), or

(b) work which has been rated as being equivalent under a job evaluation scheme, or

(c) work which is of equal value to that performed by a man in the same employment.

If any of these three situations exist, then any term in a woman's contract which is less favourable than a man's contract shall be modified so as to be not less favourable, and any benefit in a man's contract shall be included in the woman's contract.

5.10 When considering an equality clause, the correct approach is to look at the situation term by term, so that a claimant can succeed in relation to any one particular element of the employment terms. The package approach, whereby more favourable terms can be set off against less favourable terms, is wrong (*Jørgensen v Foreningen AF Speciallaeger Sygeskringens Forhandlingsudvalg*).

5.11 If the same rules apply to men and women, and to both full-time and part-time workers, the fact that some workers are less well off in consequence is irrelevant. In *Barry v Midland Bank plc* a contractual redundancy scheme, which provided for severance pay to be based on final salary at the date of termination, did not breach the Act, even though part-time women workers received less under the scheme than full-time employees. Their final salary was less because they were working less, and they would have received severance pay on the same basis as male part-timers. A part-time employee cannot use a full-time colleague as a comparator in an equal pay claim, because it is the employment status, not gender, which creates the difference in treatment (*Lynn v Rokeby School Board of Governors*).

Like work (s 1(4))

5.12 To determine whether a woman is employed on like work, the Act states that the work must be the same or broadly similar, and any differences between the work done are not of practical importance. In *Capper Pass Ltd v Lawton*, a woman worked as a cook in a company directors' dining room, providing lunches for between 10 and 20 persons. She sought equal pay with two assistant chefs who worked in the factory canteen, and who prepared 350 meals each day. Other differences were that she worked 40 hours per week, and had no one supervising her, whereas the men worked 45 hours per week, and were under the supervision of a head chef. The EAT upheld a decision of the employment tribunal that she was entitled to equal pay. The work did not have to be the same; it was sufficient if it was broadly similar, and the differences were not of practical importance. It would have been wrong to take a too pedantic approach, or to find that there was no like work because of insubstantial differences.

5.13 If there are differences between the work done, the tribunals must ask if these are such that it is reasonable to expect to see them reflected in different wage settlements which contain no element of sex discrimination. Three such differences which may be of practical importance have been identified.

A. Different duties

5.14 In *Electrolux Ltd v Hutchinson* it was held that as well as there being a contractual obligation to perform different duties, those duties must be actually performed to an extent which was significant enough to warrant different pay treatment. In this case, men and women were performing broadly similar work, but the men were graded on a higher rate. The employers argued that the men had different contractual obligations, such as accepting transfer to different work, working compulsory overtime, and working nights. The EAT upheld a decision of the employment tribunal that the women were entitled to equal pay; the question had to be asked, what happens in practice? If and when the men performed these additional obligations, the situation could be dealt with by paying additional premiums. This, however, should not affect the basic grade which was applicable. In *Noble v David Gold & Son (Holdings) Ltd*, men worked in a warehouse loading and unloading, whereas women did lighter work such as sorting, packing and labelling. The Court of Appeal agreed with the finding of the employment tribunal that the women were not on like work. Nor was the work broadly similar, for the differences were of practical importance in relation to terms and conditions of employment.

5.15 Employees who have received different professional training, and thus could be called upon to perform different duties, are not employed in the same work (*Angestellten-betriebsrat der Wiener v Wiener*).

B. Different hours

5.16 In *Dugdale v Kraft Foods Ltd* men and women worked on broadly similar work, but the men had to work a compulsory night shift, and a voluntary shift on Sunday mornings. It would have been unlawful by virtue of the Factories Act 1961 for women to have worked on these occasions. It was held that the hours at which the work is performed is by itself no bar to equal pay at the basic rate. The men could be compensated for these extra burdens by a night shift payment or premium. The equality clause does not have to produce equal pay if in fact the men were paid for something which the women did not do, eg work nights.

5.17 But this reasoning only applies when the difference in hours applies only to men. If in fact *men and women* work different hours to other employees (men and/or women), then because the difference has nothing to do with the sex of the person who is working those different hours, the difference in hours is a genuine material difference other than sex, and hence basic rates can vary between the employees concerned (*Kerr v Lister & Co Ltd*, see para 5.32).

5.18 If a contract (or collective agreement) provides that full-time employees who work in excess of their normal contractual hours are entitled to an overtime supplement, but part-time workers do not get this supplement if they work above their normal contractual hours, this is not unequal treatment of the part-timers, the majority of whom are women. The overall pay is the same for the same number of hours worked. A part-time worker whose contractual working hours are 18, and who works for 19 hours, receives the same pay as a full-time worker who works 19 hours. If the part-time worker works more than the normal contractual hours of the full-time worker, the overtime supplement would be payable. Thus this arrangement is not discrimination against part-time workers, and not incompatible with Art 141 of the Treaty of Rome (*Stadt Lengerich v Helmig*).

C. Different responsibilities

5.19 In *Eaton Ltd v Nuttall*, a man and woman worked on like work, but the man received a higher rate of pay because his responsibilities were greater. He handled more expensive products, and consequently a mistake by him would have had far more serious financial consequences. The EAT held that it was proper to take into account the additional responsibilities which the job entailed.

Work rated as being equivalent (s 1(5))

5.20 A woman's work will be considered to have been rated equivalent to that of a man if it has been given equal value under a properly conducted job evaluation scheme, in terms of the different demands made upon an employee, eg effort, skill, decision, etc. In *Eaton Ltd v Nuttall* it was stated that such a scheme must be capable of satisfying the test of being thorough in analysis and impartial in application. Once it is established that it is a genuine scheme, it must be accepted by the parties and the employment tribunals, for the latter cannot act as an appeal court from a valid job evaluation scheme. In placing an employee in a particular grade, it is then proper to take into account such factors as merit, seniority, etc.

5.21 It is irrelevant that there is a difference between the actual points scored under the job evaluation scheme, if there is no difference in the allocation to a particular salary grade or scale at the end of the evaluation process. In *Springboard Sunderland Trust v Robson*, the claimant was awarded 400 points following a job evaluation, but on appeal this was increased to 410 points. She claimed equal pay with a male comparator who had been awarded 428 points. The relevant salary scales provided were Grade 3 for 360–409 points, and Grade 4 for 410–449 points. Thus, although her job was not rated as being equivalent to the comparator, her claim succeeded, because what mattered was the grade to be allocated to her following the evaluation, rather than the values assigned to her under the evaluation. However, if the job evaluation study produces a small, albeit significant difference between the claimant and her comparator, it cannot be said that the two jobs are rated as equivalent (*Home Office v Bailey*).

5.22 A job evaluation scheme has to be carried out with a view to evaluating jobs in terms of the demands made of a worker under various headings (eg effort, skill, decision, etc) so as to lead to a fair comparison with the comparator's job. This is the so-called 'analytical' approach, which is to be preferred to the 'felt fair' or 'whole job' approach (*Bromley v H & J Quick Ltd*).

Equal value: claims and procedure

5.23 In *EC Commission v United Kingdom*, the European Court held that the Equal Pay Act did not comply with Art 141 of the Treaty of Rome, for although the Act provided for equal pay when a job evaluation scheme was in existence, there was no way a woman could compel an employer to undertake such a scheme. Consequently, the Equal Pay (Amendment) Regulations 1983 were passed, which are designed to enable a woman to make a claim for equal pay on the ground that her work is of equal value to that of a man. To enable such a claim to be determined, a valid job evaluation study must be carried out.

5.24 The Equal Pay Act 1970 (Amendment) Regulations 2004 repealed the provision in the Equal Pay Act (s 2A(1)(b)) which enabled a tribunal to strike out an equal value complaint if it was satisfied that there were no reasonable grounds for determining that the work of the claimant and her comparator were of equal value. Nonetheless, tribunals have a general power to strike out any claim if it has no reasonable prospect of success. Also, under the new rules (s 2(A)(2), a tribunal can strike out an equal value claim if the claimant's work has been rated as unequal to that of the named comparator in a valid job evaluation study, unless the tribunal has reasonable grounds for suspecting that the job evaluation study is itself based on a system which discriminates on grounds of sex, or if it is otherwise unsuitable to be relied upon.

5.25 On an equal value claim, the tribunal has power to appoint its own independent expert to prepare such a study. Once an expert has been appointed the tribunal will not determine the case unless it has received his report. The tribunal can also withdraw any such instruction, for example, if the expert's report is taking an unreasonably long time to be produced. If no report is commissioned, the tribunal should not determine the matter without giving the parties an opportunity to adduce their own evidence (*Wood v William Ball Ltd*).

5.26 The Employment Tribunals (Equal Value) Rules of Procedure, contained in the Employment Tribunals (Constitution and Rules of Procedure) Regulations 2004, Sch 6, set out an improved procedure for dealing with equal value claims. Such cases form a small proportion of the cases which come before employment tribunals, but because of their complexity – sometimes involving a large number of claimants – they take up a disproportionate amount of time. Tribunals are given wide powers of case management, with timetables set out, depending on whether or not evidence is being given from an independent expert appointed by the tribunal. Standard directions will require an early exchange of information, with particular reference to identifying the areas of agreement and disagreement. There are also special rules which apply if the parties appoint their own experts, including requiring those experts to prepare a joint report of matters on which they agree and disagree. Annexed to the Employment Tribunals (Constitution and Rules of Procedure) Regulations 2004 is a timetable, in the form of a flow-chart, which indicates that an equal value claim which does not involve an independent expert should be heard within 25 weeks, and a claim which does involve an independent expert should take 37 weeks.

5.27 The first major case under the 1983 Regulations was *Hayward v Cammell Laird Shipbuilders Ltd*, where the claimant joined the company as a catering trainee. During the first three years of her employment, she was paid at the same rate as apprenticed painters, insulation engineers and joiners, but thereafter she was paid at a lower rate than these skilled workers. However, she enjoyed superior sickness benefits, paid meal breaks and extra holidays. Her claim for equal pay based on 'work of equal value' was referred to an independent expert, who evaluated the jobs under the headings of (a) physical demands, (b) environmental considerations, (c) skill and knowledge, (d) planning and decision making, and (e) responsibility. He concluded that the work of the claimant was of equal value with the three selected male comparators who were now earning higher rates. When the case came back to the employment tribunal, it was held that the terms and conditions of employment *as a whole* must be not less favourable, and not just the actual cash pay received by her. Thus her claim for equal pay was dismissed, and the decision was upheld by the EAT and the Court of Appeal. The argument was based on Art 141 of the Treaty of Rome, which provides that 'pay' means 'the ordinary basic or minimum wage or salary, and any other consideration, whether in cash or in kind, which a worker receives, directly or indirectly, in respect of his employment from his employer'. Thus it was thought that although her cash pay was less than her selected comparators, her other terms and conditions had to be taken into consideration.

However, on a further appeal, the House of Lords reversed the decision and upheld her claim. Lord MacKay, the Lord Chancellor thought that the word 'term' in s 1(2) of the Act meant a distinct provision or part of the contract, and, in this case, the basic salary of the appellant had to be compared with the basic salary in the men's contracts. Lord Goff stated that a simple question should be asked: is there, in each contract, a term of a similar kind, which makes comparable provision for the same subject matter? If so, then the term in the woman's contract and the men's contract can be compared, and if, on that comparison, the term in the woman's contract proves to be less favourable than the term in the men's, then the term in the woman's contract is to be treated as being modified so as to make it not less favourable. Their Lordships thought that the Equal Pay Act required the courts and employment tribunals to look at a particular term in a woman's contract which was less favourable, and did not require a holding that terms as a whole should not be less favourable.

If the 'term by term' approach is taken literally, it is not impossible for an equal pay claim to result in unequal pay, which would defeat the purpose of the Act. In *Degnan v Redcar Borough Council* the Court of Appeal avoided such a result by stating that the 'term' in question must be the same subject-matter. Thus the basic rate, bonus and attendance allowance were all part of one 'term' on remuneration, thus preventing a claimant from cherry-picking the most advantageous part of the remuneration packages of a number of male employees.

5.28 An equal value claim may be brought by a woman even though she works with men doing the same work and who are paid the same as she, as long as there is another man with whom she wishes to be compared earning a higher wage. In *Pickstone v Freemans plc* the claimant was a warehouse operative, who worked alongside other male warehouse operatives, and who all received the same pay. She brought an equal value claim, naming as her comparator a male checker warehouse operative who was paid at a higher rate. It was held that she was entitled to succeed under s 2(1)(c) of the Act. To hold otherwise would enable an unscrupulous employer to defeat equal value claims by ensuring that one man worked alongside women.

5.29 The principle of equal pay applies even if it is discovered that the claimant is in fact doing work which is of greater value than the comparator (*Murphy v Bord Telecom Eireann*), as long as she is paid less.

Genuine material factor (s 1(3))

5.30 Even though a woman can show that she is employed on like work, or work rated as equivalent, or work of equal value, the employer may still be able to resist an equal pay claim on the ground that the variation in pay 'is genuinely due to a material factor which is not the difference of sex'. However, at this stage an important distinction must be made. If the claim is based on like work or work rated as being equivalent under a job evaluation study, the employer has to show that the material factor which causes the difference in pay *must* be a material difference between the woman's case and the man's, whereas in a claim based on equal value, the material factor *may* be such a material difference. The distinction between these two cases is as follows. In a claim based on like work or work rated as the same, any variation in pay can only be based on non-sex factors (eg long service, red-circling, etc, see below). Market forces are not such a factor, for this was one of the reasons the Act was passed (*Clay Cross (Quarry Services) Ltd v Fletcher*, but see *Rainey v Greater Glasgow Health Board*, para 5.37). In equal value claims, however, there may be other forces at work which account for the difference in pay. For example, it may be necessary to pay the men more because their skills are in short supply, or because in that area it is necessary to pay the going rate for men in order to attract them, or because their work is more profitable and hence they demand higher pay. In other words, where equal value claims are concerned, since like is not being compared with like, there are a number of material factors at work which *may* (but not must) be a material difference.

5.31 The defence of 'genuine material factor' cannot apply to any difference in the actual work done, for this must be considered when it is decided whether or not there is like work or work rated as being equivalent. Thus if a man is employed lifting heavy weights, this is relevant to the question of whether a woman is employed on like work; it should also be given an appropriate weighting in any job evaluation scheme. Further, once like work or work rated equivalent has been established, there is a burden of proof on those who seek to show that there is a difference in treatment which is 'genuinely due to a material factor' which has nothing to do with the sex of the person concerned. Thus if the underlying reason for a difference in treatment is sex based, even though this is of historical origin, it cannot amount to a material difference. In *Snoxell v Vauxhall Motors Ltd* men and women were doing like work as inspectors. The men were in a 'red circle' group, ie their pay was higher because many years ago they were part of a separate male group who received higher wages, but as a result of a revision in pay structure, they were regraded. By being placed in the 'red circle' (so-called because of the practice of putting a circle in red around the names of the affected employees on the tables of wages) their higher wage rates were protected until the group was phased out. The red circle group was clearly an historical anomaly, but the EAT held that the women inspectors were entitled to equal pay with them, for s 1(3) could never provide a defence when past discrimination had contributed to the variation.

5.32 Non-sex-based factors which could amount to genuine material factors include additional responsibility allowances (*Waddington v Leicester Council for Voluntary Services*), extra pay for academic qualifications (*Murray v East Lothian Regional Council*), long service increments (*Honeywell Ltd v Scott*) a genuine mistake in putting an employee in the wrong salary grade (*Yorkshire Blood Transfusion Service v Plaskitt*) and differences in the place where the work is done (*NAAFI v Varley*). As noted above, a difference in hours which is not sex based could be a material difference. In *Kerr v Lister & Co Ltd* men and women doing the same work on the night shift were paid the same rate, but this was higher than that paid to the women who worked on the day shift. Thus the differences in the rate had nothing to do with sex; it was paid in order to attract workers (of either sex) to the night shift. Since the difference was between that of day and night work and not due to a difference of sex, there was a genuine material factor which justified the employers' contention that a woman worker was not entitled to equal pay.

5.33 Similarly, a red circle treatment whereby employees can have their wages protected for reasons other than sex could also amount to a genuine material factor. Thus if an employee on a higher grade is made redundant, and given employment on work which is graded at a lower rate, it is permissible to give him red circle treatment without attracting a successful claim for equal pay on the part of the other employees in the lower grade (*Charles Early and Marriott (Witney) Ltd v Smith*). This also applies if a man is demoted or downgraded, but is permitted to retain his former (higher) rate of pay (*Forex Neptune (Overseas) Ltd v Miller*). But if a man's wages are protected on a transfer, the employment tribunal must be satisfied that the reason was not just that he was a man, or that the job to which he was appointed was not one which has been exclusively reserved for men (*Methven v Cow Industrial Polymers Ltd*).

5.34 If the defence under s 1(3) is being raised, it is not sufficient to show that the difference in pay between the claimant and the comparator was due to a genuine material difference which was not the difference in sex. The employment tribunal must determine whether there is objective justification for the difference, subject to the test of proportionality (*Brunnhofer v Bank der Osterreichisschen Postparkasse*, applied in *Sharp v Caledonia Group Services Ltd*). Thus a grading scheme which operates according to skill, experience or ability can be an integral part of good management. As long as it is a genuine scheme, and operates irrespective of sex, it is not rendered inoperative by the Act (*National Vulcan Engineering Insurance Group Ltd v Wade*).

5.35 If a premium is paid, partly for working a rotating shift, and partly for working unsocial hours, it is not necessary to quantify precisely how the premium is made up. The employment tribunal should only be concerned with whether the scheme is genuine, not that it is fair (*Calder v Rowntree Mackintosh Confectionery Ltd*).

If the differences are due to length of service, the employer must show the terms and conditions relating to service increments, or at least show some evidence as to how the differences have come about. It is not sufficient merely to state the fact, without some attempt to justify any variation (*Honeywell Ltd v Scott*). Similarly, the mere attaching of a label, such as 'red circle' will not, without further evidence, constitute a defence (*Outlook Supplies Ltd v Parry*). However, it is permissible to take into account experience and training (*De Brito v Standard Chartered Bank*). But incremental pay scales, which are based on length of service, do not require to be justified (*Health and Safety Executive v Cadman*). As was stated in *Handels-og Kontorfuntionaererenes Forbund i Danmark v Dansk* (acting for *Danfoss*), 'Length of service goes hand in hand with experience, and since experience generally enables the employee to perform his duties better, the employer is free to reward him without having to establish the importance it has in the performance of specific tasks entrusted to the employee.'

5.36 The mere fact that a woman carried out the same duties as a man for a short period of time or as a deputy as a temporary measure does not entitle the woman to equal pay with that man, for basically their responsibilities are different (*Ford v R Weston (Chemists) Ltd*). Also, if a woman works substantially fewer hours than a man, eg as a part-timer, and men and women who work full-time are paid the same, the part-time nature of the employment is a relevant factor in concluding that the variation in her pay may be a genuine material factor (*Handley v H Mono Ltd*). However, in *Jenkins v Kingsgate (Clothing Productions) Ltd (No 2)* the EAT referred to the European Court the question as to whether a woman part-timer could claim the same hourly rate as a full-time man. The Court held that a difference in pay between full-time and part-time workers does not constitute discrimination prohibited by Art 141 of the Treaty of Rome unless it is in reality an indirect way of reducing the pay of part-time workers who were wholly or predominantly women. When the case returned to the EAT it was held that it was not sufficient for an employer to show that he had no intention of discriminating on grounds of sex. Any variation in the pay of part-time women and full-time men had to be justified by reference to some non-discriminatory objective. The case was thus remitted to the employment tribunal to determine whether the lower rates for part-time workers were reasonably necessary in order to reduce absenteeism and obtain the maximum utilisation of plant (but see now the Part-Time Workers (Prevention of Less Favourable Treatment) Regulations 2000, para 2.69.

5.37 In determining whether or not there is a genuine material factor between 'her case and his' in like work and work rated as equivalent claims the employment tribunal may have regard to the extrinsic forces which led to the man being paid more. In *Rainey v Greater Glasgow Health Board*, a health authority decided to set up its own prosthetic fitting service. The rates of pay for qualified prosthetists was to be on the same scale as medical physics technicians. However, in order to attract a sufficient number of qualified persons to get the service started, it was necessary to make a higher pay offer to those who came from the private sector. The claimant, who came into the service direct from her training, sought equal pay with a man on a higher salary who had come from the private sector. It was held that the difference in pay was due to a genuine material factor which had nothing to do with sex. The reason the man was paid more was because of the need to attract qualified persons (of either sex) from the private sector in order to form the nucleus of the new service. The House of Lords thought that the earlier decision of *Clay Cross (Quarry Services) v Fletcher* was unduly restrictive, because economic grounds, objectively justifiable, were capable of being a genuine material factor.

5.38 Thus, genuine economic considerations, such as a change in the volume of the work reflecting the profitability of the firm, may amount to a genuine material factor (*Albion Shipping Agency v Arnold*).

5.39 A disparity between other terms and conditions may constitute the defence of genuine material factor. In *Leverton v Clwyd County Council* (see para 5.6) the claimant was required to work 32½ hours per week and had holidays which were coterminous with school holidays, whereas the male comparators worked for 37 hours per week, and only had 20 days annual holidays. Thus the notional hourly rate (taken over the year) did not reveal any significant difference, and the inequality in pay was thus justified by the criteria of reasonable necessity and objective justifiability.

5.40 Also, as has already been noted, market forces may be raised as a genuine material factor which justifies unequal pay if the claim is based on equal value.

5.41 In *Enderby v Frenchay Health Authority*, the ECJ held that if statistical evidence discloses an appreciable difference in the pay of two jobs which are of equal value, one of which is carried out almost exclusively by women and the other predominantly by men, it is for the national courts to assess whether the statistics are significant. If a prima facie case of sex discrimination is revealed, the employer must show that the difference in pay is objectively justified on grounds other than sex. The state of the employment market, which leads an employer to increase the pay of a particular job in order to attract appropriately qualified workers may constitute such justification. But the use of separate collective bargaining arrangements which bring about a discriminatory effect is not an objective justification.

If the genuine material factor is due to the difference of sex, because the particular labour market is almost exclusively female, the defence in s 1(3) cannot apply. Thus in *Ratcliffe v North Yorkshire County Council* the claimant was employed as a dinner lady, her pay having been rated as equivalent to certain other manual jobs. Following the introduction of competitive tendering, the council set up a direct service organisation in order to compete with rival commercial firms who were bidding for school meals contracts. One contract was lost because the rival firm had lower labour costs, and so, in order to be able to compete for other contracts, the Council decided to reduce the pay of the dinner ladies. The claimant complained of a breach of the Equal Pay Act. It was held that although the need to reduce the pay of dinner ladies so as to compete in the open market was a material factor, the factor was due to the difference of sex, because the work was being done almost exclusively by women. The House of Lords stated that the Act must be interpreted without reference to 'direct or indirect discrimination'. As long as the work was rated as being equivalent to that done by male comparators, to reduce the pay of women amounted to a breach of the Act.

5.42 A point on which there has been some judicial observations, but no direct decision, concerns the 'anomalous' comparator. The question arises, must the woman compare herself with a representative man, or can she compare her position with any man, even though that man represents an anomaly? In *McPherson v Rathgael Centre for Children etc*, the claimant, a woman, worked alongside five men as an outdoor pursuits instructor. She, and all the men bar one, were on the same pay scale, which was appropriate to them as instructors without a teaching qualification. One man, however, was paid £1,500 more. This was because it had previously been assumed that certain qualifications he possessed entitled him to be paid as a qualified teacher. It was then discovered that this was not so, but it was decided to continue to pay him as a qualified teacher. The claimant brought a claim for equal pay with him. The employment tribunal dismissed her claim, holding that she was not being paid less than the norm, but rather the comparator was being paid more, due to an initial mistake which had never been rectified. There were men being paid the same rate as the applicant, and it was merely fortuitous that the person being paid more was a man. Thus it was held that the employers had established a defence under s 1(3). On appeal, the Northern Ireland Court of Appeal reversed the decision. It was not sufficient for the employer to show that he did not intend to discriminate on grounds of sex. There must be an objective justification for the variation which exists. An understandable error could not amount to the statutory defence.

However, the court queried whether the applicant was entitled to select the anomalous man as a comparator, rather than the other men who were paid at the same rate as she. Presumably, once the claimant succeeded in her claim, the other men would be entitled to claim equal pay with her, resulting in an escalation of all the salaries. Further, it cannot be right that the sex of the anomalous person gives a right to persons of the opposite sex, although not to a person of the same sex. However, as the matter had not been canvassed before the employment tribunal, the court reserved their opinion. Perhaps it should have been argued that the 'anomalous man' was analogous with a 'red circle' case.

Pay structures, etc

5.43 Any discrimination based on sex must be eliminated from an employer's pay structure, employment conditions, collective agreements, wage regulation orders, etc. Any term contained in a collective agreement, employers' rules, rules made by a trade union or an employers' association or professional or training body, which is discriminatory, is void. But this is without prejudice to the rights of the person discriminated against in respect of any lawful term of the contract (Sex Discrimination Act 1986, s 6).

5.44 An individual who considers that the terms of a collective agreement could affect him as being contrary to the principle of equal treatment may present a complaint to an employment tribunal. This applies to actual and potential employees. If the complaint is well founded, the tribunal will declare the term to be void (Sex Discrimination Act 1986, s 6(4A)). Also, a collective agreement which indirectly discriminates against part-time employees (the majority of whom are women) in contrary to Art 141 of the Treaty of Rome, unless the employers can objectively justify the discrimination (*Nimz v Freie und Hansestadt Hamburg*).

Remedies under the Act

5.45 A complaint by an aggrieved party of the contravention of the equality clause, including a claim for arrears of remuneration or damages, may be presented to an employment tribunal, and a dispute as to its effect may similarly be resolved on an application by the employer (s 2(1)). On such a complaint, the employment tribunal should first consider the contract of employment and draw its appropriate conclusions, but if there is no such guide, it is permissible for the tribunal to visit the premises and actually observe the woman at work and the man with whom she wishes to be compared (*Dorothy Perkins Ltd v Dance*). Moreover, the claimant may choose the man with whom she wishes to be compared, and the employment tribunal cannot substitute another man whom it thinks would be more appropriate for the purpose of comparison. Thus, if a woman is getting equal pay with some men, she can still seek equal pay with a man who is paid at a higher rate, if his work is the same or broadly similar, etc (*Ainsworth v Glass Tubes and Components*).

5.46 The claim can only be in respect of the salary the comparator was earning, ignoring any potential increments which could have been earned. In *Enderby v Frenchay Health Authority (No 2)* the claimant had worked for a health authority for six years. She successfully made an equal value claim, using as her comparator a man who had only been employed for one year. She argued that she was entitled to the pay her comparator would have received had he been employed as long as she, ie to include the potential increments he would have had. The Court of Appeal held that she was entitled to receive the same pay as her comparator was currently receiving (see also *Evesham v North Hertfordshire Health Authority*).

5.47 It is also possible to use a former employee as a comparator. In *Macarthys Ltd v Smith* a man was employed as a stockroom manager, and was paid £60 per week. He left the job, and four months later the woman claimant was appointed as stockroom manageress, and was paid £50 per week. She subsequently brought a claim for equal pay. This was upheld by the employment tribunal and EAT, but the Court of Appeal doubted that she could succeed under the Equal Pay Act. However, the matter was referred to the European Court to consider the effect of Art 141 of the Treaty of Rome. This Court held that the principle that men and women should receive equal pay for equal work applied also to the situation where a woman received less pay than a male predecessor, provided they were both doing the same or broadly similar work. Since, under the European Communities Act 1972, the provisions of EU law take precedence whenever there is a conflict with UK law, the interpretation of Art 141 had to be applied in UK courts, and the Court of Appeal subsequently upheld her claim. Indeed, an employee is entitled to bring an equal pay claim comparing herself with a predecessor who was employed over six years previously (*Kells v Pilkington plc*). While there may be evidential difficulties in pursuing such a claim, the matter is ultimately a question of fact.

5.48 A claim cannot be made to an employment tribunal if the claimant has not been employed in the employment within the six months preceding the date of the claim (s 2(4)). The six-month time limit runs from the date when the claimant left the employment, not from the time when she left the actual job on which her claim was based (*National Power plc v Young*). However, if an employer conceals information necessary for the bringing of proceedings, the six-month time limit will not start to run until the employee discovered (or could reasonably be expected to discover) the true facts. If the employee is a minor or suffering from a disability, the six-month time limit may also be extended (s 2ZA). If the employee has been employed under a series of employment contracts, the intervening periods will not count for the purpose of limiting the recovery of compensation. Nor will those periods count for the purpose of the calculation of the time limits.

5.49 Any award in respect of an equal pay claim made by an employment tribunal can be in respect of the period of six years from the date of the commencement of proceedings in England and Wales, and five years in Scotland (Equal Pay Act 1970 (Amendment) Regulations 2003). An award of interest may also be made, calculated in accordance with the provisions of the Sex Discrimination and Equal Pay (Remedies) Regulations 1993. No compensation for injury to feelings can be awarded. The claims brought under the various Discrimination Acts are based on statutory torts, whereas under the Equal Pay Act the claim is for a financial remedy based on a breach of contract (*Council of the City of Newcastle upon Tyne v Allen*).

Assistance with claims

5.50 With a view to helping a woman to decide whether to institute proceedings, s 7B of the Act enables her to use a prescribed questionnaire, and the employer has eight weeks in which to respond (Equal Pay (Questions and Replies) Order 2003). Such questions and answers will be admissible as evidence in any proceedings brought under s 2(1). If an employment tribunal finds that the employer has deliberately and without reasonable excuse omitted to reply, or the answer is evasive or equivocal, it may draw any conclusion which it considers it to be just and equitable to draw, including an inference that there is a contravention of the Act. The Secretary of State may also, on his own volition make a reference to an employment tribunal (s 2(2)), and may similarly use any such questionnaire.

6

Maternity, Paternity and Parental Rights

6.1 In this chapter we shall consider the various maternity, paternity and parental statutory rights, adopted as a result of the implementation of EU Directive 92/85/EEC on 'the introduction of measures to encourage improvements in the health and safety of pregnant workers who have recently given birth or are breastfeeding' and EU Directive 96/34/EEC on parental leave. Time off work in order to care for dependants will be considered in Chapter 7.

6.2 For the purposes of the Employment Rights Act 1996, childbirth is defined as the birth of a living child or the birth of a child whether living or dead after 24 weeks of pregnancy. Certain rights to be considered also apply on the adoption of a child.

Maternity rights

A. Time off work for antenatal care (ERA, ss 55–57)

6.3 An employee who is pregnant, and who, on the advice of a registered medical practitioner, registered midwife or registered health visitor, has made an appointment to attend any place for the purpose of receiving antenatal care, shall have the right not to be unreasonably refused time off work during her working hours to enable her to keep that appointment. This right arises from the moment the woman commences her employment, and is irrespective of the number of hours or days worked (but see below) or whether or not she is a permanent or temporary employee. The size of the employer's undertaking is also irrelevant. The only women who do not enjoy this right are those who are not employed under a contract of employment, or who are share fisherwomen, or women employed as members of any constabulary.

6.4 If requested to do so, she must produce a certificate stating that she is pregnant, and some documentary evidence of the appointment (but not the first appointment).

6.5 She is entitled to be paid for the period of her absence at the appropriate hourly rate (calculated in accordance with the provisions of s 56). If she is refused time off work, or if she is not paid for the time off taken, she may make a complaint to an employment tribunal (within three months of the date of the appointment in question, or within such further time as the employment tribunal considers to be reasonable) that her employer has unreasonably refused to permit her to have time off work, or has failed to pay her the whole or part of the amount to which she claims she was entitled. If the employment tribunal upholds her complaint, they will make a declaration to that effect, and also award her the amount of remuneration to which she is entitled (s 57).

6.6 It should be noted that the right is not to be unreasonably refused time off work. Thus it may be possible to argue that in particular circumstances it would be reasonable for the woman to make arrangements for antenatal care outside working hours (eg in the case of a woman who works part-time, or less than five days each week). Antenatal care is not defined in the Act, but undoubtedly includes antenatal relaxation classes and (possibly) classes in parentcraft, provided she attends on the advice of a medical practitioner etc (see *Gregory v Tudsbury Ltd*).

6.7 An employer cannot defeat a woman's statutory rights by rearranging her working hours or requiring her to work additional hours to make up for time lost (*Edgar v Giorgine Inns Ltd*). On the other hand, if a woman abuses the time off provisions, and takes additional time off work for activities which are not antenatal care, she will have no rights under the Act, and will be subject to the usual consequences which flow from disciplinary proceedings (*Gough v County Sports (Wales) Ltd*).

B. Risk assessment and suspension on maternity grounds

6.8 Under the Management of Health and Safety at Work Regulations 1999 (see Chapter 11) every employer is required to carry out a risk assessment, designed to ensure the health and safety at work of new or expectant mothers, defined as employees who are pregnant, who have given birth within the preceding six months, or who are breastfeeding.

6.9 The first requirement is that where the workforce includes women of childbearing age, *and* the work is of a kind which could involve risk to the health or safety (because of pregnancy or maternity) to a new or expectant mother, or to that of her baby, from any processes or working conditions, or from physical, biological or chemical agents (including those set out in Annexes I and II of Directive 92/85/EEC) the employer shall carry out a risk assessment; see reg 16. It should be noted that the provisions of the Management of Health and Safety at Work Regulations now confer a right of action in civil proceedings (see para 11.77). Thus in *Day v T Pickles Farm Ltd* the EAT thought that the failure to carry out a risk assessment on a woman of childbearing age could amount to sex discrimination.

6.10 The physical agents referred to are those which are likely to cause foetal lesions or disrupt placental attachment, eg shocks, movement, ionising or non-ionising radiation, extremes of heat or cold, travel, mental or physical fatigue, etc. The biological agents include those set out in Directive 90/679/EEC (the Biological Agents Directive) in so far as it is known that these agents can endanger the health of a woman or her unborn child. The chemical agents include dangerous substances set out in Directive 90/393/EEC (Carcinogens at Work Directive), Annex I. Also included are certain industrial processes, underground mining work, pressurised enclosures (eg underwater diving), work with certain viruses (unless immunised), lead and lead derivatives. Once the risk assessment has been carried out, the employer must provide all female workers of childbearing age with comprehensible and relevant information of the risks to their health identified by the assessment, and also with details of the preventative and protective measures which need to be taken to comply with the relevant statutory provisions (see Chapter 11).

6.11 The next requirement arises when the employer cannot take action under any relevant statutory provision (eg by providing protective clothing or equipment etc) which would avoid the risk; then, if it is reasonable to do so, and would avoid such risk, he must alter her working conditions or working hours. However, if it is not reasonable to do so, or if the alteration would not avoid the risk, then the employer must suspend her from work for as long as is necessary to avoid such risk (see para 6.16 below). It should be noted that an employer is not obliged to alter her working conditions or working hours, or to suspend her from work, unless she has informed him in writing that she is pregnant, or has given birth within the previous six months, or is breastfeeding.

6.12 Next, if a new or expectant mother works at night, and a certificate from a registered medical practitioner or registered midwife shows that it is necessary for her health or safety that she should not be at work for any period identified in the certificate, then the employer shall suspend her from work (subject to ERA, s 66 below). There is also a requirement under health and safety legislation for an employer to provide suitable rest facilities for a pregnant woman, or a woman who has given birth within the previous six months, or who is breastfeeding (Workplace (Health, Safety and Welfare) Regulations 1992, reg 25 (4)).

6.13 The maternity provisions stated above stem from ERA, s 66 because the Management of Health and Safety at Work Regulations are specified as being the 'relevant statutory provision' for the purpose of that section (see Suspension from Work (on Maternity Grounds) Order 1994). Additionally a woman is entitled to be suspended from work on maternity grounds due to any recommendation contained in an approved code of practice issued by the Health and Safety Commission under the Health and Safety at Work etc Act 1974, s 16 (see Chapter 11).

Flowing from her right to be suspended on maternity grounds, a woman will have two further rights.

Alternative work (ERA, s 67)

6.14 Before suspending a woman on maternity grounds, the employer, if he has available suitable alternative work, shall offer it to her. The alternative work must be of a kind which is suitable for her, and appropriate in the circumstances (see *Iske v P & O European Ferries (Dover) Ltd*). If the terms and conditions differ from her normal contract of employment, they must not be substantially less favourable (see *British Airways (European Operations at Gatwick) Ltd v Moore and Botterill*). A failure to make such an offer entitles the woman to bring a complaint to an employment tribunal; within the usual time limits, which may make an award of compensation as the employment tribunal considers to be just and equitable in all the circumstances.

However, she is not entitled to be paid if the employer offers her suitable alternative work which she unreasonably refuses to do.

6.15 The Pregnant Workers Directive (92/85/EEC) contains an absolute and express prohibition on exposure to the listed risks. However, the Management Regulations, reg 16 requires that risks to the health of a pregnant woman shall be avoided, which means that if the risk cannot be eliminated in its entirety, it must be reduced to its lowest acceptable level. Thus, if it is decided to remove a pregnant woman from her present job because of a perceived health or safety risk, this can be a pointless exercise if the new job offer contains equally perceived risks. To use a hypothetical risk as an excuse to demote a woman from her job (with a consequential reduction in salary) can amount to a detriment contrary to ERA, s 47C, and a failure to offer alternative employment on terms not substantially less favourable is contrary to ERA, s 67. It may be discrimination on grounds of sex, and could give rise to a potential constructive dismissal claim (*New Southern Railway Ltd v Quinn*).

Maternity suspension pay (ERA, s 68)

6.16 A woman who is suspended from work on maternity grounds is entitled to be paid a week's pay in respect of each week of suspension, reduced proportionately if the suspension is for less than a week. She is entitled to be paid her normal hourly rate of pay (ie the week's pay will be divided by the number of normal working hours). If her working hours vary from week to week they are to be averaged over the previous 12 working weeks. If she has not completed 12 weeks' service, an average shall be estimated from the agreed terms and conditions and from the work pattern of others in comparable jobs. A failure by the employer to pay the whole or any part of the remuneration due entitles the woman to bring a complaint to an employment tribunal, which, if it finds the complaint well founded, shall order the employer to pay the amount of remuneration due to her.

6.17 Finally, it should be noted that no period of continuous employment is required for a woman to have the above rights (in contrast to the general right to be suspended on medical grounds – see para 7.7, where continuous employment of one month is required).

C. Maternity leave (ERA, ss 71–74, Maternity and Parental Leave etc Regulations 1999 as amended)

6.18 There are three periods of maternity leave:

(a) Compulsory maternity leave. This prevents a woman from working for the period of two weeks immediately following the date of childbirth.

(b) Ordinary maternity leave (OML). All pregnant women are entitled to take 26 weeks OML irrespective of their length of service, provided they satisfy the relevant conditions.

(c) Additional maternity leave (AML). Employees who have at least 26 weeks' continuous employment are entitled to a further 26 weeks' AML at the end of their OML.

Compulsory maternity leave (ERA, s 72(1))

6.19 The taking of ordinary maternity leave or additional maternity leave is an option for women who are pregnant. It is not compulsory. It is not unknown for some women to want to return to work as soon as possible after the birth. To prevent this, ERA, s 72 provides that an employer shall not permit a woman to work within two weeks of childbirth. A contravention of this provision can lead to a fine of not exceeding Level 2 on the standard scale. Any prohibition arising under the Health and Safety at Work Act will also apply. Also it is an offence (punishable by a fine of up to Level 1 on the standard scale) to permit a woman to work in a factory within four weeks of childbirth (Public Health Act 1936, s 205; Factories Act 1961, Sch 5).

Ordinary maternity leave

6.20 An employee (not a worker) is entitled to 26 weeks OML irrespective of her length of service, her hours of work, whether or not she is a temporary or permanent employee or the number of persons employed by the employer. The only exclusions are in respect of members of the armed forces, share fisherwomen and members of the constabulary. In order to qualify for OML, the employee must notify her employer no later than the end of the 15th week before the expected week of confinement (EWC) of:

(a) her pregnancy;

(b) the expected week of confinement (the employer may request a medical certificate as evidence of this date); and

(c) the date on which she intends her OML to commence (this date cannot be earlier than the beginning of the 11th week before the EWC). If the employer so requests, she must specify this in writing. If she wishes to delay the start of her maternity leave, or wishes to bring the start date forward, she must give 28 days' notice.

6.21 If it is not reasonably practicable to give the appropriate 15 weeks' notice, she must do so as soon as is reasonably practicable. On receipt of the notice, the employer must notify the employee, within 28 days, of the date when her OML will end. If he fails to do so, he will not be able to complain if she returns to work too early or too late, and she may have a remedy under regs 19–20 in respect of any detriment or dismissal. Otherwise, if she wishes to return to work earlier than the notified date, she must give 28 days' notice of her intention.

6.22 OML will start on either (a) the date she has notified to her employer as the date she intends it to start, or (b) the day which follows the first day after the beginning of the fourth week before the EWC on which she is absent from work wholly or partly because of her pregnancy, or (c) the day which follows the day on which childbirth occurs. She can vary the date on which she intends to start her OML by giving her employer notice of the new date 28 days before the date originally specified, or 28 days before the date on which she intends her OML to start or, if that is not reasonably practicable, then as soon as is reasonably practicable. However, the revised date cannot be earlier than the beginning of the 11th week before the EWC, and the notification must be in writing if the employer so requests.

6.23 However, there are two exceptions to the notification requirements. These are:

(a) if the OML commences with the day which follows the first day after the beginning of the fourth week before the EWC on which she is absent from work wholly or partly because of pregnancy; or

(b) if her OML commences with the day which follows the day on which childbirth occurs.

6.24 In both cases she must notify the employer as soon as is reasonably practicable (in writing if he so requests) that she will be absent from work because of pregnancy or because she has given birth, and the date on which either event took place.

Terms and conditions during ordinary maternity leave

6.25 An employee who takes OML is entitled to the benefit of all the terms and conditions of employment which would have applied had she not been absent, whether or not they arise under her contract of employment. In other words, she is to be treated as if her contract of employment continues during her OML. The only exception is that she is not entitled to terms and conditions relating to remuneration. Thus contractual and non-contractual benefits, other than sums which would have been payable by way of wages or salary, must be continued, eg life and medical insurance, private use of a company car, mortgage subsidies, etc. Whether profit-related pay, bonuses and commissions which arises after the commencement of OML are payable will depend on the purpose for which and the terms under which these payments are to be made. The test is whether or not these can be defined as being 'wages or salary'.

6.26 A woman who takes maternity leave during a year when a bonus is payable must be paid the bonus for the periods when she is at work and for the fortnight of compulsory maternity leave. It is permissible to make a proportionate reduction to reflect the period of ordinary maternity leave and additional maternity leave (*Hoyland v Asda Stores Ltd*). The employee cannot take contractual annual leave during her OML, as this would come under the remuneration exclusion. She will be entitled to take paid annual leave during a period other than the period of her maternity leave, because maternity leave is not a holiday, and the time spent by a woman on maternity leave cannot count against her holiday entitlement. This means that her annual holiday entitlement must be taken either before the start of maternity leave or after its expiry (*Merino Gomez v Continental Industrias del Caucho*), although it is not certain if this rule applies if the current holiday year has expired.

6.27 Similarly, a woman who gives in her notice during her absence on OML (or who is given notice by her employer) is entitled to be paid for the statutory notice period (ERA, ss 88(1)(cc)), although this will not apply to notice given by either party if the period of notice to be given by the employer under the contract is at least one week longer than the statutory notice period (*Scotts Company (UK) Ltd v Budd*). However, she would not be entitled to contractual notice pay, as this would fall to be excluded under the definition of remuneration (ERA, s 71).

6.28 For her part, during the period of OML, the employee is bound by any obligations which arise under her terms and conditions of employment. Thus, she is still an employee, and must abide by relevant contractual obligations, such as confidentiality, etc (see Chapter 10). Obviously, she is not required to turn up for work, as this would be inconsistent with her statutory right.

Additional maternity leave (AML)

6.29 An employee who is entitled to OML (see above) and who has been continuously employed for a period of not less than 26 weeks at the beginning of the 14th week before the EWC is entitled to a further period of 26 weeks AML, which must commence immediately following the end of the period of OML.

Terms and conditions during AML (reg 17)

6.30 During the period of AML, the employee is entitled to the benefit of the employer's implied obligation of trust and confidence. She is also entitled to any terms and conditions relating to notice on termination by her employer, compensation in the event of redundancy, and the benefit of any disciplinary or grievance procedures. For her part, she is bound by any terms and conditions relating to the giving of notice by her, non-disclosure of confidential information, the acceptance of gifts or other benefits from third parties, and her participation in any other business. It will be noted that, in the absence of more favourable contractual terms, her statutory rights are fewer than those which pertain under her OML. However, statutory annual leave entitlement under the Working Time Regulations will continue to accrue, as will her right to statutory notice on dismissal (see s 88(1)(c) above).

6.31 The period of AML will count towards the period of continuous employment for the purpose of statutory employment rights, but not for the purpose of assessing contractual rights which depend on length of service, eg contractual leave provisions, annual increments, seniority rights, etc. Thus while AML will not count towards continuity, it will not break continuity (reg 18(5)(b)).

Right to return to work (reg 18–18A)

6.32 An employee who returns to work after her OML is entitled to return to the same job in which she was employed before her absence, on terms and conditions no less favourable than those which would have applied if she had not been absent. Since her service is deemed to be continuous, the period of OML will count towards any benefits which are dependent on length of service, eg seniority, pay increments etc. The 'job' to which she is entitled to return, means the nature of the work which she was employed to do in accordance with her contract, and the capacity and place which she is employed. Thus she need not return to the identical job. She must be permitted to return to the job she was doing under her contract before she took OML. Thus, if there have been changes during her absence, these will be irrelevant so long as the contractual obligations are the same (*Edgell v Lloyd's Register of Shipping*).

6.33 The position is similar (but not identical) when a woman returns from AML. She is entitled to return to her old job, on terms and conditions no less favourable than those which would have applied if she had not been absent. However, there are two exceptions to this rule. First, AML does not count towards contractual service-related benefits, eg seniority, pension rights, although it will count towards statutory continuity. Second, where it is not reasonably practicable for a reason other than redundancy for the employer to permit her to return to her old job, the employer must offer her another job which is suitable for her and appropriate for her to do in the circumstances.

6.34 There is no need for her to give notice to her employer of the date when she will be returning to work after OML or AML. It will be recalled (above, para 6.21) that once the employer has received notice that she intends to take OML or AML, he must write to her within 28 days confirming the date on which she is due to return to work. However, if she wishes to return earlier, she must give at least 28 days' notice of her intention to do so. If she returns to work without giving this notice, the employer is entitled to postpone her return to a date which will secure 28 days' notice (but not beyond the 26-week period of OML or the 52-week period of AML). If she actually returns to work without giving the notice, she is not entitled to be paid her contractual remuneration.

6.35 The general rule is that once OML or AML comes to an end, the employee has no right to postpone her return to work any longer. There are, however, three circumstances when she may do so. First, if the employer has failed to notify the employee of the date when her leave would end, and she reasonably believes that the period has not ended (regs 19(2)–20(3)). Second, if she is sick at the end of her maternity leave, she is entitled to be treated in the same way as any other employee who is off work sick. Thus she will have an entitlement to sick pay, and, if the absence is likely to last a length of time, the usual procedure for dealing with the long-term sick employee should be adopted (see para 17.87). Third, she may postpone her return to work by adding on another leave period, eg annual holidays, parental leave etc.

6.36 If the employee fails to return to work after her leave entitlement has come to an end, she should be treated as an unauthorised absentee, and dealt with under the appropriate disciplinary procedure. If she wishes to return to work, but the employer refuses to permit her to do so, this will amount to an automatically unfair dismissal if the reason was because she had given birth or exercised her rights to take OML or AML. But to this rule there are three exceptions. The first exception arises when there is a genuine redundancy situation; the other two exceptions apply when the refusal is based on a non-redundancy situation.

Redundancy dismissal (reg 10)

6.37 If it is not practicable, for reason of redundancy, for the employer to continue to employ her under her existing contract, she is entitled to be offered suitable alternative employment, where there is a suitable available vacancy, with the employer or an associated employer. The new contract must take effect immediately her existing contract comes to an end, the work to be done must be of a kind which is suitable and appropriate for her to do in the circumstances, with provisions as to capacity, place of employment, and other terms and conditions of employment which are not substantially less favourable than those which pertained under her previous contract (reg 10). It will be noted that this provision is mandatory; if there is suitable alternative employment, it must be offered to the woman who is on maternity leave in preference to men or other women who are not on maternity leave. If the employee unreasonably refuses the offer, the dismissal will not be unfair, and she will have no entitlement to redundancy pay (ERA, s 141). The duty to make the offer of suitable alternative employment starts when the redundancy situation arises, and continues up until the end of her maternity leave. A suitable vacancy is available even though the employer may not wish to fill it for economic reasons (*Community Task Force v Rimmer*). On the other hand, if there is no suitable alternative employment available, and her selection for redundancy has been fair under the normal rules (see para 18.37) she will have all the usual rights which apply to a redundancy dismissal (notice, redundancy payment, etc).

Not reasonably practicable (reg 20)

6.38 If it is not reasonably practicable for a reason other than redundancy to permit her to return to her original job, she must be offered a suitable alternative job, either with the employer or an associated employer. If she unreasonably refuses that offer, a dismissal will not be automatically unfair, but the fairness will fall to be determined by the normal rules on unfair dismissal. A failure to notify a woman who is on maternity leave that there is a vacancy for which she could have applied amounts to a fundamental breach of the implied term of trust and confidence entitling her to claim constructive dismissal (*Visa International Services Association v Paul*).

Small employer (reg 20)

6.39 Where a woman has taken AML (not OML), and it is not reasonably practicable for a reason other than redundancy for a small employer (ie one who employs five or fewer employees) to permit her to return to a suitable and appropriate job, or for an associated employer to offer a job of that nature (reg 20), the dismissal will not be automatically unfair. Again, the normal rules on unfair dismissal will apply. It is expected that this provision will be revoked in 2007.

D. Remedies

6.40 An employee is entitled not to be subjected to any detriment because she is pregnant, gave birth to a child, was suspended from work on maternity grounds, or took ordinary or additional maternity leave (ERA, s 47C). She will be deemed to have been unfairly dismissed if the reason for her dismissal was that she was pregnant, gave birth to a child, or took ordinary or additional maternity leave. It will also be unfair to select her for redundancy for any of these reasons (ERA, s 99, reg 20). According to the European Court of Justice it is not contrary to the Equal Treatment Directive to dismiss a woman after her maternity leave has come to an end because of absences due to a pregnancy-related illness, even though that illness first appeared during her pregnancy (*Handels-og v Dansk Handel*), although a different conclusion was reached by the Scottish EAT in *Caledonia Bureau Investment and Property v Caffrey*. It may well be that post maternity leave absences should be dealt with under the normal rules relating to sickness absences.

6.41 The dismissal of a pregnant woman who is unable to complete a fixed-term contract is sex discrimination under the Equal Treatment Directive and Pregnant Workers Directive, even though the woman knew she was pregnant when she was recruited, did not tell her employer, and her presence at work is essential for the proper functioning of the employer's business (*Tele-Danmark A/S v Handels (HK) per Brandt-Neilsen*). Equally, the non-renewal of a fixed-term contract on grounds of pregnancy is sex discrimination, although not if the reason for the non-renewal had nothing to do with the fact of pregnancy (*Jiminez Melgar v Ayuntamiento de los Barrios*).

6.42 Of course, if the employer did not know that she was pregnant, and dismisses her for a reason unconnected with her pregnancy, she will not be able to claim that her dismissal was contrary to s 99. An employer must know, or believe in the existence of an employee's pregnancy in order to be liable for automatically unfair dismissal (*Del Monte Foods v Mundon* approved in *Ramdoolar v Bycity Ltd*). Equally, if she is selected for redundancy, and the pregnancy or childbirth had nothing to do with her selection, then her right to a redundancy payment falls to be considered under s 135.

6.43 If an employer has engaged a temporary replacement to do the work of a woman who is absent because of pregnancy or childbirth, then, if he has informed him/her in writing that the employment will be terminated on the return to work of the latter, and the employer does in fact dismiss the temporary replacement in order to make room for the woman returning from maternity leave, the dismissal shall be regarded as being for some other substantial reason of a kind to justify the dismissal, but the employer must still show that he acted reasonably in treating that reason as a sufficient ground for dismissal (see Chapter 17). The same rule applies when a replacement is taken on when a woman is suspended on medical or maternity grounds (ERA, s 106).

6.44 An employee may exercise her contractual or statutory rights, whichever is the more favourable. Her remedy for a breach of her contractual rights (other than in respect of remuneration) is by way of a claim for breach of contract in the county court, or a breach of contract claim under the provisions of the Employment Tribunals Extension of Jurisdiction Order (see para 1.31) where the claim is outstanding on the termination of her employment. She may also claim that she has suffered a detriment contrary to reg 19, or claim unfair dismissal under reg 10 or reg 20. In those cases where the dismissal is not automatically unfair (see above, paras 6.37–6.39) she will need to have had the requisite period of continuous employment if she wishes to claim unfair dismissal, although this will not be necessary if she claims her dismissal was because of sex discrimination under the provisions of SDA (see Chapter 4).

6.45 Finally, a woman who is dismissed at any time while she is pregnant or after childbirth when the maternity leave period ends by reason of the dismissal is entitled to be given written reasons for her dismissal, without any request being made (see para 17.174). This rule will also apply if an employee is dismissed while absent from work during an ordinary or additional adoption leave period (see below). In both cases, no period of continuous employment is required (ERA, s 92 (4)(4A)).

E. Statutory Maternity Pay (SMP)

6.46 The Statutory Maternity Pay (General) Regulations 1986 (as amended) make provision for SMP to be paid by employers, and recouped by them from the national insurance contributions they pay to the Inland Revenue. SMP is payable for a period of 26 weeks to employees who satisfy the conditions of eligibility.

6.47 The first qualification for SMP is that the woman must be an 'employed earner', ie whose earnings attract a liability for employer's Class 1 national insurance contributions. This concept is slightly wider than the definition of 'employee' generally used in employment law, and refers to a woman over the age of 16 who is gainfully employed under a contract of service or an office holder whose earnings are chargeable to income tax under Schedule E. The result could well be that a woman may be regarded as self-employed for SMP purposes, and thus not entitled to this benefit (eg because no Class 1 contributions are being made) but an employee for the purpose of employment protection rights, and thus be able to benefit from the provisions relating to maternity leave and the right to return to work. A woman who is employed by a foreign organisation with no place of business in the United Kingdom will also not qualify for SMP, although women who work within the European Community are so entitled.

6.48 Second, she must have been continuously employed (not necessarily working) for a period of 26 weeks immediately before the 15th week before the expected week of confinement. There is no minimum number of hours qualification, she does not need to be actually working as long as the contract of employment is in existence, and there are a number of provisions which help her to retain continuity where it would otherwise be broken.

6.49 Third, she must satisfy the earnings rule, ie her average earnings (including overtime and bonuses) must be at or above the lower earnings limit at which national insurance contributions are payable. Average earnings are to be calculated over a period of eight weeks ending with the last pay day before the end of the qualifying week.

6.50 Fourth, she must produce a medical certificate stating the expected week of confinement, and give 28 days' notice to her employer of the date when she expects the liability for SMP to begin.

6.51 Finally, SMP is not payable for weeks when she is actually working, and there are additional exclusions in respect of women who are taken into legal custody or who go outside the European Economic Area, on the death of the employer, and if she changes her employer after her baby is born.

6.52 SMP is payable at two rates. For the first six weeks, SMP is earnings-related, ie 90% of the employee's normal weekly earnings. The remaining 20 weeks are paid at the prescribed rate, which currently is £108.85 per week or normal weekly earnings if lower than £108.85. SMP is subject to tax and NI contributions, and any other lawful deductions (eg pension contributions, trade union subscriptions etc). Any contractual remuneration (eg contractual sick pay or maternity pay) can be offset.

6.53 If a woman is entitled to a pay increase before the start of her maternity leave, or would have been awarded such an increase had she not been absent on statutory maternity leave, this must be taken into account when calculating her entitlement to SMP. If, during the period of maternity leave she becomes entitled to a pay increase, the employer must re-calculate her SMP entitlement accordingly (Statutory Maternity Pay (General) Regulations, reg 21(7)). If an existing employee feels that she has been denied such entitlement in the past, she has six years from the date of the ruling in *Alabaster v Woolwich Bank* to request a recalculation of her payment.

6.54 There are a number of provisions dealing with special situations which may arise, and which may affect entitlement to SMP. These include the dismissal of a woman because she is pregnant, when the employer becomes insolvent, if she is detained in legal custody, or working during the maternity pay period etc.

F. Maternity Allowance (Social Security Contributions and Benefits Act 1992)

6.55 A woman who does not qualify for statutory maternity pay may be entitled to maternity allowance (MA) paid to her direct by the Department of Work and Pensions. She must show that:

(a) she is pregnant, and has reached the start of the 11th week prior to the expected week of confinement;

(b) she has been employed as an employed earner or self-employed earner for at least 26 weeks in the 66 weeks preceding the EWC. These weeks to not have to be continuous, nor do they have to be with the same employer;

(c) her average weekly earnings are not less than the maternity allowance threshold (currently £30 per week). Earnings from more than one job will count if necessary.

6.56 Maternity allowance is paid for a period of 26 weeks, at a weekly rate of 90% of her average weekly earnings or the prescribed rate of MA (currently £108.85 per week). It is not payable to women who travel outside the European Economic Area, or who are in legal custody.

Paternity rights and adoption leave

A. Paternity leave (Paternity and Adoption Leave Regulations 2002, as amended)

6.57 In addition to taking 13 weeks' unpaid parental leave (see para 6.76) a father is entitled to take one or two weeks' paternity leave on the birth or adoption of a child, with pay at the statutory rate. Although 'paternity' is a peculiarly male concept, there are several circumstances when a woman may take paternity leave. Thus, if the partner of the birth mother or adoptive mother is a woman, then she will be entitled to paternity leave if she is a woman who has, or who expects to have, the main responsibility for raising the child. Also, if, when a couple adopt a child, the adoptive father takes adoption leave, the adoptive mother is entitled to take paternity leave. And if two people of the same sex living together adopt a child, one may take adoption leave and the other may take paternity leave.

6.58 The rules relating to paternity leave cater for paternity on the birth of a child and paternity arising from adoption. So far as the former is concerned, the right to paternity leave applies to employees (not workers) who have been continuously employed for at least 26 weeks ending with the week immediately preceding the 14th week before the expected week of birth. The employee must be the father of the child, or the mother's husband, or partner. Whether he is or is not the father of the child, he must have or expect to have the responsibility for the upbringing of the child. A 'partner' is a person who lives with the mother in an enduring family relationship, whether of the same or different sex, but must not be a relative of the mother.

6.59 So far as adoption is concerned, paternity leave may be taken in respect of a child who is under the age of 18 (there are special provisions relating to children who are adopted from overseas). Again, the employee must have been employed for at least 26 weeks ending with the week in which the child's adopter is notified of having been matched with the child. The employee must be married to, or the partner of the adopter, and have the main responsibility for the upbringing of the child. Again, a partner is a person (whether of the same or different sex) who lives with the adopter in an enduring family relationship.

6.60 An employee who wishes to take paternity leave can choose to take either one week or two weeks' leave. He cannot take odd days or non-consecutive weeks (a week, in this connection, is a period of seven days). The leave cannot be taken before the child is born (or the child is placed with the adopter) and must be taken within 56 days of the birth or placement. The employee must give his employer notice of the date from when he will take his leave, and the length of absence. If the employer so requests, the employee must provide a signed declaration stating (a) that the purpose of the absence from work is to take care of the child or support the child's mother (or adopter), (b) that he is the father of the child (or the mother's husband or partner) and that he expects to have responsibility for the upbringing of the child.

6.61 There are further provisions dealing with the effect of premature birth, stillbirth or the death of the child's mother, and multiple births, when only one period of paternity leave may be taken.

6.62 An employee who is absent from work on paternity leave is entitled to the benefit of all of the terms and conditions of employment that would have applied if he had not been absent (excluding terms and conditions concerning remuneration), and is bound by any obligation under those terms except in so far as they are inconsistent with his right to take paternity leave. He is entitled to return from his leave to the job in which he was employed before his absence, on terms and conditions not less favourable than those which would have applied had he not been absent. If, however, s/he has taken paternity leave as well as additional maternity leave or additional adoption leave, the right to return is limited to the considerations which apply in respect of those latter leave periods (see para 6.29, 6.70).

6.63 Otherwise, an employee is entitled not to be subjected to a detriment because s/he took paternity leave, and it will also be automatically unfair to dismiss a person because s/he took such leave.

B. Statutory paternity pay (SPP)

6.64 Statutory paternity pay (SPP) is payable to an employee who satisfies the conditions of eligibility. These are:

(a) he must have been employed for a continuous period of 26 weeks ending with the week immediately preceding the 14th week before the expected week of the child's birth, or the week in which the adopter was notified of the match being made;

(b) his normal weekly earnings in the 8 weeks ending with the relevant week are not less than the lower earnings limit for the payment of NI contributions;

(c) he gives at least 28 days' notice before the date from which he expects SPP or SAP to be paid (or, if that is not reasonably practicable, as soon as is reasonably practicable);

(d) he provides evidence of the child's birth, and provides a written declaration that he meets the conditions as to the relationship with the child's mother.

6.65 Currently, statutory paternity pay is payable at a weekly rate of either £108.85 from April 2006 or 90% of the employee's normal weekly earnings, whichever is the lesser sum.

C. Adoption leave (Paternity and Adoption Leave Regulations 2002, as amended)

6.66 These regulations also make provision for an employee who satisfies the prescribed conditions to be absent from work during an ordinary adoption leave period (OAL) of 26 weeks, with a further period of 26 weeks additional adoption leave (AAL). Both these leave periods mirror the maternity leave provisions, with appropriate modifications. There are exclusions in respect of members of the armed forces, share fisherwomen and members of the constabulary. The leave is in respect of a child who is under the age of 18 when placed with an adopter for adoption.

Ordinary adoption leave

6.67 To qualify for ordinary adoption leave, the employee:

(a) must have been employed for a period of not less than 26 weeks ending in the week in which s/he was notified that a match with the child to be adopted has been made;

(b) provide evidence of his/her entitlement; and

(c) inform the employer of the date when the child is expected to be placed for adoption and the date on which the employee has chosen for the leave period to begin.

6.68 The employer, for his part, must inform the employee of the date when the leave entitlement ends, taking into account any additional adoption leave to which the employee may be entitled. There are special provisions dealing with the situation arising from the interruption or termination of the child's placement.

6.69 An employee who takes ordinary adoption leave has the same rights as those enjoyed by a woman taking ordinary maternity leave. During the adoption leave period s/he is entitled to the benefit of terms and conditions of employment which would have applied if s/he had not been absent (excluding remuneration, unless there is a contractual right to this), and bound by any obligations arising from those terms and conditions. S/he is entitled to return to the work in the same job in which s/he was employed before his/her absence with seniority, pension and other rights and other terms and conditions which are not less favourable than if s/he had not been absent. No notice of return to work need be given, unless s/he intends to return to work before the end of the adoption leave period, in which case 28 days' notice of intention to return early must be given (see para 6.39).

Additional adoption leave

6.70 An employee who takes ordinary adoption leave is also entitled to additional adoption leave (AAL) for a period of 26 weeks beginning on the day after the last day of ordinary adoption leave. During this leave, the employee is entitled to the benefit of the employer's implied obligations of trust and confidence, and any terms and conditions relating to notice of termination, compensation in the event of redundancy, and disciplinary and grievance procedures. For his/her part, the employee is bound by the obligations of good faith, and terms and conditions relating to the giving of notice, disclosure of confidential information, accepting gifts, and taking other employment, etc.

6.71 At the end of the AAL period, the employee is entitled to return to work to the job in which s/he was employed before his/her absence, or, if that is not reasonably practicable, to another job which is both suitable and appropriate for him/her to do in the circumstance. Terms and conditions shall be no less favourable than those which would have been applicable had s/he not been absent, with seniority and pension rights etc as they would have been had the period of employment been continuous. In other words, the period of AAL does not count towards continuity, but does not break continuity. Notice of return need not be given (the employer should have informed the employee of the return date in response to the employee's notice of intention to take adoption leave), unless s/he intends to return before the expiry of AAL, in which case 28 days' notice of such intention must be given.

6.72 An employee has the right not to be subjected to any detriment because s/he has taken AAL, and it will generally be an unfair dismissal to dismiss him/her because s/he took AAL. However, there are three situations when the automatic unfair dismissal provisions will not apply.

(a) If it is not reasonably practicable by reason of redundancy for the employer to continue to employ the employee under his/her existing contract of employment, then, where there is a suitable vacancy, the employee is entitled to be offered alternative employment with the employer or the employer's successor or an associated employer. If the employee unreasonably refuses that offer, the reasonableness of the dismissal will be tested in the usual way under the provisions of ERA, s 94(4).

(b) If it is not reasonably practicable for a reason other than redundancy for the employer to permit him/her to return to a job which is suitable and appropriate in the circumstances, and an associated employer offers the employee a job of that kind, and the employee unreasonably refuses that offer, then again the reasonableness of a dismissal will be tested in the usual way under ERA, s 94(4).

(c) If immediately before the end of the AAL period the number of employees employed by the employer (added to the number employed by an associated employer) did not exceed five, and it was not reasonably practicable for the employer to permit the employee to return to a job which is both suitable and appropriate for him/her to do in the circumstances, or for an associated employer to offer a job of that kind. Again, the reasonableness of a dismissal must be tested under ERA, s 94(4).

D. Statutory adoption pay (SAP)

6.73 To qualify for statutory adoption pay, the adopter must:

(a) have been in employed earner's employment for a continuous period of at least 26 weeks;

(b) have normal weekly earnings in the eight weeks ending with the week in which the adopter is notified of the match which are not less than the lower earnings limit for the payment of national insurance contributions;

(c) elected to receive SAP (and not SPP).

6.74 The employee must give evidence of his/her entitlement to SAP, and there are provisions relating to disentitlement if the employee works for the employer or another employer during the SAP period, if the adopter is entitled to statutory sick pay, in legal custody, etc. SAP is payable for a continuous period of 26 weeks at a rate which is the lesser of £108.95 from April 2006 or 90% of the employee's normal weekly earnings. Contractual remuneration can be offset.

Recoupment by employer

6.75 An employer who pays SMP, SPP or SAP is entitled to recover 92% of the amount paid out by deducting the amount from PAYE tax and national insurance contributions which they make to the Inland Revenue every month. A 'small employer', ie one whose gross NI contributions payments (including employers and employees contributions) is £40,000 or less in the qualifying tax year is entitled to recover 100% of the payments made, and in addition can claim a compensation payment of 4.5% of the gross payments made.

Parental leave (Maternity and Parental Leave Regulations 1999–2001, regs 13–21)

6.76 An employee (man or woman) who has been continuously employed for one year, and has (or expects to have) responsibility for a child, is entitled to have parental leave for a period of up to 13 weeks (18 weeks if the child is disabled) in respect of each individual child, for the purpose of caring for that child. The right applies to all parents of children born or placed with them for adoption after December 1994.

6.77 A person has responsibility for a child if s/he has parental responsibility within the meaning of s 3 of the Children Act 1989 (as amended by the Adoption and Children Act 2002) or s 1(3) of the Children (Scotland) Act 1995. A mother automatically acquires parental responsibility; a father will do so if he is married to the child's mother or (in the case of an unmarried father) if he registers the birth jointly with the mother. Parental responsibility may also be acquired by a court order or by a formal agreement with the child's mother. Thus guardians and adoptive parents qualify for parental leave, but not step-parents or foster parents. However, the right does not apply to members of the armed forces, share fishermen and members of the constabulary.

6.78 The qualifying period of one year's employment will be measured backwards from the date when the leave is to start. There are more favourable rules in respect of parents of disabled children, who will be entitled, in certain circumstances, to count service with a previous employer (see reg 13(1A)).

6.79 Parental leave may be taken as soon as the child is born or adopted, and the right will last until the child reaches the age of five, or, in the case of an adopted child, until five years from the date of adoption or until the child reaches the age of 18, whichever is the sooner. If the child is in receipt of disability living allowance the right to parental leave is extended until the child reaches the age of 18.

6.80 Unlike paternity leave, maternity leave and adoption leave (see above) there is no requirement that parental leave shall be with pay, although other social security benefits may be available (income support, housing and council tax benefit etc) as appropriate.

6.81 An employee may only take up to four weeks' parental leave in any one year (Sch 2, para 8) in respect of any individual child. Leave may only be taken in weekly blocks; thus if an employee takes less than a week's leave it will count as one week out of his total 13-week entitlement (*South Central Trains Ltd v Rodway*). However, if the child is in receipt of disability living allowance, greater flexibility is allowed, and leave may be taken on a daily basis, so that up to 20 individual days' leave may be taken in any one year.

6.82 During parental leave, the employee's terms and conditions of employment are the same as those which are applicable during additional maternity leave. The employee is entitled to the benefit of the employer's obligation of trust and confidence, and any terms and conditions relating to notice of termination, compensation in the event of redundancy, and disciplinary and grievance procedures. For his or her part, the employee is bound by the obligation of good faith, and any terms and conditions relating to the giving of notice of termination, the disclosure of confidential information, the acceptance of gifts or other benefits, and participation in any other business. A period of leave will count as continuous service for the purpose of statutory employment protection rights.

6.83 If the employee has taken up to four weeks' parental leave (whether or not this was added on to paternity leave, ordinary maternity leave or ordinary adoption leave) s/he is entitled to return to the job he/she was doing before the absence. If parental leave followed a period of additional maternity leave or additional adoption leave or was more than four weeks, s/he is entitled to return to the job s/he was doing before the absence unless it is not reasonably practicable for the employer to permit the employee to return to the job, in which case the employer must offer a job which is suitable and appropriate for him/her to do in the circumstances. The terms and conditions must be no less favourable than those which would have applied if the employee had not been absent.

6.84 The regulations give power to employers and employees to enter into agreements which provide for a certain flexibility, by means of a collective agreement or a workforce agreement which must be incorporated into the individual contract of employment (see Sch 1 to the Regulations). In the absence of any such agreement, the default provisions of Sch 2 will apply. This states that the employee give at least 21 days' notice of the dates when leave is being taken, and the employer is entitled to request proof of entitlement. A father who wishes to take leave in respect of a child not yet born can give 21 days' notice of the expected week of confinement, and he may start his leave as soon as the baby is actually born, even if this is earlier or later than the anticipated date of birth. Adopted parents must also give 21 days' notice, although if this is not reasonably practicable, notice must be given as soon as is reasonably practicable. Except in relation to new fathers and adoptive parents, the employer may postpone the leave where he considers that the operation of the business would be unduly disrupted if the employee took the leave during the period in question, but the postponement cannot be for more than six months.

6.85 An employee may present a complaint to an employment tribunal that his employer has unreasonably postponed a period of parental leave, or has prevented him from taking such leave. If the employment tribunal find the complaint well founded, it shall make a declaration to that effect, and may award compensation to the employee, the amount being such as is considered to be just and equitable, having regard to the employer's behaviour and any loss suffered by the employee (ERA, s 80).

6.86 An employee has the right not to suffer a detriment because s/he took parental leave (ERA, s 47C) and it will be an automatically unfair dismissal to dismiss an employee because s/he took or sought to take parental leave (ERA, s 99).

7

Employment Protection

7.1 In this chapter we will consider a number of miscellaneous legal rights given to employees in the Employment Rights Act 1996 and other legislation. These are minimum standards which can be exceeded by agreement or negotiation, but they cannot be denied to an employee.

Guarantee payments (ERA, ss 28–35)

7.2 Provided an employee has been continuously employed for at least one month, the employer is bound to pay him a guarantee payment in respect of any whole day in which the employee is not provided with work because:

(a) there is a diminution in the requirements of the employer's business for work of the kind which the employee is employed to do, or

(b) any other occurrence affecting the normal working of the employer's business in relation to work of that kind.

In *North v Pavleigh Ltd* the owner of a company closed his factory for Jewish holidays. The employment tribunal held that no guarantee payment could be claimed. Section 28 only applies to a diminution of work, or an 'occurrence', such as a power failure or national disaster. It was not intended to cover the religious habits of the proprietor.

7.3 A guarantee payment is not payable if the workless day occurs in consequence of a trade dispute involving any employee of the employer or of any associated employer. In *Garvey v J & J Maybank (Oldham) Ltd* there was a national lorry drivers' strike, and pickets at the employer's entrance refused to let the firm's own lorries in or out. The employer ordered the firm's drivers (who were not involved in the strike) to cross picket lines, but they refused. As a result, there were insufficient supplies coming into the firm, and the claimant was laid off. It was held that he was not entitled to guarantee pay. The refusal of the drivers to cross the picket lines meant that the lay off occurred in consequence of a trade dispute. Nor is the employee entitled to the payment if the employer offers to provide alternative work which is suitable in all the circumstances (whether or not it is within the employee's contract) and he unreasonably refuses that offer (*Purdy v Willowbrook International Ltd*). The employee must also comply with reasonable requirements imposed by the employer with a view to ensuring that his services are available (*Meadows v Faithful Overalls Ltd*).

7.4 The employee is entitled to be paid at the guaranteed hourly rate (which is one week's pay divided by the number of normal working hours) for the number of normal working hours in respect of any whole day he is laid off. He is entitled to be paid for five working days in any period of three months, at a rate of a maximum of (currently) £18.90 per day (ERA, s 31). In other words, the present position is that an employee will be entitled to no more than £18.90 per day for a maximum of 20 days in each year. If the employee already has a contractual right to remuneration in respect of a workless day (eg by means of a collective agreement, etc) then any payment made under that agreement will go towards discharging the employer's liability to make the statutory guarantee payment, and equally, the latter will go towards discharging the contractual liability. If there is a guaranteed week agreement in existence, then the contractual remuneration shall be apportioned rateably between the workless days, and the statutory minimum will be used to 'top up' as appropriate. However, workless days when a contractual payment is made are taken into account when calculating the number of days guarantee pay is payable in any period of three months (*Cartwright v G Clancey Ltd*). It should be noted that if a contractual or statutory guarantee payment is being made, the employee is not entitled to apply for jobseekers' allowance.

7.5 If an employer fails or refuses to pay the whole or part of the guarantee payment, the employee may complain within three months to an employment tribunal. If they find the complaint well founded, they will order the employer to pay to the claimant the amount due to him.

7.6 If there is a collective agreement in force which already relates to guarantee payments, then all the parties thereto may apply to the appropriate Minister for an exemption order. This will be granted if he is satisfied that the statutory provisions should not apply to those employees, but the collective agreement must contain provisions for an aggrieved employee to take a dispute about non-payment of the guarantee payment either to arbitration (or other procedure) or to an employment tribunal. A number of such exemption orders have been granted.

Suspension on medical grounds (ERA, ss 64–65)

7.7 Provided an employee has been employed for not less than one month, he will be entitled to be paid remuneration if he is suspended from work in consequence of a requirement imposed by certain statutory provisions or a recommendation made in a code of practice issued or approved under s 16 of the Health and Safety at Work etc Act 1974 (see Chapter 11). The statutory provisions in question are (a) Control of Lead at Work Regulations 2002, (b) Ionising Radiations Regulations 1999, and (c) Control of Substances Hazardous to Health Regulations 2002. If a health risk occurs within the scope of these provisions, certain processes must be suspended, and the result now is that in these circumstances the affected employees will be entitled to be paid for a period of up to six months from the day when the suspension period begins. An employee is not entitled to be paid during the suspension period if he is incapable of work because of illness or injury, or if he unreasonably refuses alternative work offered to him by the employer (whether within the terms of his contract or not) or if he does not make himself available for work.

7.8 An employee who is thus suspended on medical grounds is entitled to a week's pay in respect of each week the suspension lasts, and though the contractual right to remuneration is unaffected, the contractual and statutory remuneration can be set off against each other as appropriate. If the employer fails to pay the whole or any part of the employee's remuneration, the latter may present a complaint to the employment tribunal within three months, and if it finds the complaint well founded, it shall order the employer to pay to the employee the amount due to him.

7.9 It must be stressed that a medical suspension payment can only be claimed if the employee is fit for work. In *Stallite Batteries Co Ltd v Appleton*, the claimant became ill after falling into a skip containing lead paste. In consequence, his blood lead level exceeded the limit laid down in the Control of Lead at Work Regulations 1998 but no medical suspension certificate was issued by the employment medical adviser. Nonetheless, the applicant's own doctor considered that he was not fit for work. The EAT held that he was not entitled to a medical suspension payment. He was not available for work due to sickness, and his claim was excluded by s 65(3) of the Act.

7.10 If an employee is dismissed for a reason which would otherwise amount to a medical suspension, he is only required to have been employed for one month (instead of one year) in order to present a claim for unfair dismissal (s 65(1)).

7.11 If the employer wishes to engage a temporary employee to take the place of the suspended employee, then, as long as he has informed the temporary employee in writing that the employment will be terminated when the suspension has ended, a dismissal of the temporary employee in order to allow the suspended employee to return to work will amount to 'some other substantial reason' for the dismissal (see Chapter 17), although the employer will still have to show that he acted reasonably.

7.12 For medical suspension from work on maternity grounds, see Chapter 6.

Time off work

A. For public duties (ERA, s 50)

7.13 An employer shall permit an employee of his who is a justice of the peace to take time off during his working hours for the purpose of performing any of the duties of his office (see *Riley-Williams v Argos Ltd*).

7.14 An employer shall also permit an employee who is a member of certain specified bodies to take time off work during his working hours for the purpose of attending at a meeting of the body or its committees or sub-committees, and to do any other thing approved by the body for the purpose of discharging its functions. The specified bodies are:

    (a) a local authority (including the Common Council of the City of London, a National Parks Authority and the Broads Authority);

    (b) a statutory tribunal;

    (c) a police authority or police member of the National Criminal Intelligence Service;

    (d) a board of prison visitors or prison visiting committee;

(e) a relevant health body (including a National Health Service trust, a health authority or health board;

(f) a relevant education body (managing or governing body of an educational establishment maintained by a local authority or (in Scotland) a school or college council or governing body of further education;

(g) the Environment Agency or the Scottish Environment Protection Agency;

(h) Service Authority for the National Criminal Intelligence Service or the National Crime Squad;

(i) a water and sewerage authority;

(j) General Teaching Council for England and for Wales.

7.15 There is no requirement that the employee be paid for taking time off work under s 50. The amount of time off permitted for these purposes, the occasions on which and the conditions subject to which time off may be taken are those that are reasonable in all the circumstances, having regard in particular to:

(a) how much time off is required for the performance of the duties;

(b) how much time off the employee has had already in respect of trade union duties and activities; and

(c) the circumstances of the employer's business and the effect of the employee's absence on the running of that business.

7.16 In *Walters v British Steel Corpn* the claimant was transferred to an essential job, and it was difficult to release him for certain public duties. When he took the job, he had agreed that his public duties would take second place. Consideration of safety required certain minimum manning levels, and his colleagues refused to cover for him. It was held that he was not entitled to time off work for public duties, as the circumstances of the employer's business had to be taken into account.

7.17 In considering the amount of time off to be given under s 50, the needs of the employee to perform his public duties adequately must be balanced carefully with the requirements of the employer to have the work done. In *Emmerson v IRC* the claimant was the leader of the opposition party on Portsmouth Council. He had been given 18 days' leave (paid) each year to perform his duties, but this was insufficient. His application for further unpaid leave of absence was refused by his employers, as it was argued that he could not be spared from his job. The employment tribunal thought that the problem could be overcome by appointing a deputy to give him some assistance, for in other areas there was more than one person doing the same job as the claimant, who should not be put at a disadvantage because he was extra-efficient. Since the claimant was prepared to use some of his own holidays for public duties, the tribunal thought that he should be given a further 12 days' leave of absence without pay. However, in *Corner v Buckinghamshire Country Council*, the EAT held that the employment tribunal has no power to make any recommendations of this nature, or to impose conditions.

7.18 Section 50 requires the employer to give time off work to the employee. Rearranging hours of work, and swapping duties so that the same number of hours are worked is not giving time off (*Ratcliffe v Dorset County Council*).

7.19 It has been noted that there is no legal requirement that the employee be paid for time off work under s 50. But if he is refused time off, he may present a complaint to an employment tribunal within the usual period of three months from the date of refusal. The employment tribunal must take account of all the relevant considerations (*Borders Regional Council v Maule*) including the employee's efforts to reorganise his commitments so as to produce a reasonable pattern of work, and if the complaint is upheld, the tribunal shall make a declaration, and may award compensation of such amount as it considers just and equitable, having regard to the employer's default and any loss sustained by the employee.

B. For occupational pension scheme trustees (ERA, s 58)

7.20 An employee who is a trustee of an occupational pension scheme is entitled to be given time off work, with pay during working hours for the purpose of:

(a) performing any of his duties as such a trustee; or

(b) undergoing training relevant to the performance of those duties.

7.21 The amount of time off which the employee is to be permitted to take, the purpose for which, the occasions on which and any conditions subject to which time off may be taken are those that are reasonable in all the circumstances, having regard to:

(a) how much time off is required for the performance of the duties as a trustee of the scheme and to undergo the relevant training; and

(b) the circumstances of the employer's business and the effect of the employee's absence on the running of that business.

7.22 The employee must be paid his normal remuneration, or his average hourly earnings, or a fair estimate of those earnings, for the time off work under these provisions. If the employer refuses to permit him to take time off work, or refuses to pay for time off work taken, a complaint may be made to an employment tribunal. If the complaint is upheld, the employment tribunal shall make a declaration to that effect, and make an award of compensation to the employee, as it thinks just and equitable.

C. For employee representatives (ERA, s 61)

7.23 An employee who is a representative of an independent trade union, or an elected employee representative (or candidate for election) has the right to be allowed reasonable time off work, with pay, for the purpose of performing his functions as such when the employer is required to consult on redundancies (see para 18.68) or on transfers of undertakings (see para 9.58). He is entitled to have access to the affected employees, and such accommodation and facilities as may be appropriate.

7.24 An employee representative has the right not to suffer a detriment because he performed any function or activity as such, and it will be an automatic unfair dismissal to dismiss him for the same reason.

D. To look for work (ERA, s 52)

7.25 An employee who is dismissed for reason of redundancy shall be entitled, before the expiration of his notice, to be given reasonable time off during his working hours to look for new employment or to make arrangements for retraining. This right, however, only applies to employees who have been continuously employed for more than two years. The redundant employee is entitled to be paid at his appropriate hourly rate, and if the employer unreasonably refuses to allow him to have the time off, or fails to pay him for it, a complaint may be presented to an employment tribunal within three months. An award of up to two-fifths of a week's pay may then be made.

7.26 It is not a prerequisite for time off that the employee should provide the employer with details of interviews or appointments he has made, as he is entitled to go to look for a job without having made any such arrangements. But if an employer thinks that the request for time off is not bona fide, it may be that he does not unreasonably refuse to permit it (*Dutton v Hawker Siddeley Aviation Ltd*).

E. To care for dependants (ERA, s 57A)

7.27 An employee is entitled to be permitted by his employer to take a reasonable amount of time off work during the employee's working hours in order to take action which is necessary:

(a) to provide assistance on an occasion when a dependant falls ill, gives birth, or is injured or assaulted;

(b) to make arrangements for the provision of care for a dependant who is ill or injured;

(c) in consequence of the death of a dependant;

(d) because of an unexpected disruption or termination of arrangements for the care of a dependant; or

(e) to deal with an incident which involves the child of the employee and which occurs unexpectedly in a period during which an educational establishment which the child attends is responsible for him.

Time off work under s 57A(1)(c) in order to take action which is necessary in consequence of the death of a dependent does not include the right to have time off work to deal with the emotional effect of a bereavement (*Forster v Cartwright Black*).

7.28 The employee must tell his employer the reason for the absence as soon as is reasonably practicable, and also inform him how long he expects to be absent.

7.29 A dependant is a spouse, child, parent, or person living in the same household as the employee, otherwise than by reason of his being an employee, tenant, lodger or boarder. Additionally, for the purpose of (a) and (b) above, a dependant can also be any person who reasonably relies on the employee for assistance on an occasion when he falls ill or is injured or assaulted, or to make arrangements for the provision of care in the event of illness or injury. For the purpose of (d) above, a dependant can also include any person who reasonably relies on the employee to make arrangements for the provision of care.

7.30 There is no service qualification for the enjoyment of the above rights, but equally there is no requirement on the employer to pay an employee who takes such time off work. Any such entitlement must depend on the terms of the contract of employment.

7.31 An employee may complain to an employment tribunal (within the usual time limits) that his employer has unreasonably refused to permit him to take time off work for any of the above purposes, and, if the complaint is well founded, the tribunal will make a declaration, and may award compensation as it considers to be just and equitable. Also, an employee has the right not to suffer a detriment because he took such time off work, and it will be automatically unfair to dismiss an employee for taking time off work for the above purposes. In *Qua v John Ford Morrison (Solicitors)* the EAT gave guidance on how time off work for dependants leave should be properly exercised, and the tests to be applied in determining whether there has been an automatically unfair dismissal under s 57A where the principle reason for the dismissal was that the employee had taken time off work to look after a dependant.

F. For young person for study or training (ERA, s 63A)

7.32 An employee who:

(a) is aged 16 or 17,

(b) is not in full time secondary or further education, and

(c) has not attained certain minimum standards or education as set out in the Right to Time Off Work for Study or Training Regulations 2001 (and/or the Right to Time Off Work for Study or Training (Scotland) Regulations 1999),

is entitled to be permitted by his employer to take time off during the employee's working hours in order to undertake study or training leading to the relevant qualification, which is an external qualification the attainment of which would contribute to the attainment of one of the prescribed standards set out in the above regulations, and would be likely to enhance the employee's employment prospects (whether with his employer or otherwise). If an employee is aged 18, but began such studies before attaining that age, he is entitled to continue until he ceases to be 18.

7.33 The amount of time off, the occasions on which, and any conditions subject to which time off may be taken are those that are reasonable in all the circumstances, having regard to:

(a) the requirements of the employee's study or training, and

(b) the circumstances of the employer's business and the effect of the employee's time off on the running of that business.

7.34 The employee is entitled to be paid whilst taking time off work for study or training purposes, at the appropriate hourly rate, calculated in accordance with the normal rules which define 'week's pay' and 'normal working hours' (see ERA, ss 220–229, 234, para 14.1). A complaint may be made to an employment tribunal, within the usual time limits, that the employer has unreasonably refused to permit the employee to have time off work as required by s 63A, or has failed to pay the whole or part of the remuneration due to him. If the complaint is upheld, the tribunal will make a declaration and award the remuneration due.

Statutory sick pay (SSP)

A. How the scheme works

7.35 Under the provisions of the Social Security Contributions and Benefits Act 1992, ss 151–163 and the Statutory Sick Pay (General) Regulations employers will be responsible for paying to their employees statutory sick pay in respect of the first 28 weeks of absence through sickness.

7.36 Originally, the whole amount of SSP paid out by employers could be recovered by means of deductions from national insurance contributions sent to the Inland Revenue, and there was also in existence a small employer's relief. However, these regimes have now been abolished and replaced by a percentage threshold scheme (PTS) designed to help all employers if they have a large number of employees off sick at the same time.

7.37 An employer can now recover SSP paid in a tax month where it exceeds 13 per cent of the employer's national insurance contributions liability in the same tax month. The excess amount of SSP paid can be deducted from the national insurance contributions due in that month (Statutory Sick Pay Percentage Threshold Order 1995).

7.38 To understand the scheme, certain expressions must be defined:

(a) *A day of incapacity for work*

This is any day when an employee is incapable, by reasons of some specific disease or mental or bodily disablement, of doing work of a kind he might reasonably be expected to do.

(b) *A period of incapacity for work*

This means any period of four or more consecutive days, each of which is a day of incapacity for work in relation to the employee's contract of employment.

(c) *A period of entitlement*

This period starts with the first day of incapacity for work, and ends when either
i.   the period of incapacity has ended, or
ii.   the entitlement to SSP has been used up, or
iii.   the contract of employment is terminated, or
iv.   a woman who is pregnant becomes disqualified under the provisions of the Act.

(d) *Qualifying days*

These are days on which the employee is required by his contract of employment to be available for work.

B. Qualifying conditions

7.39 To qualify for SSP, three conditions must be satisfied, namely:

(a) the employee's day of incapacity for work must form part of the period of incapacity for work (ie four or more consecutive days);

(b) the day must be within the period of entitlement;

(c) the day must be a qualifying day.

If there are two periods of incapacity (for the same or different reasons) separated by not more than two weeks, they will be treated as a single period of incapacity. This means that an employee will not have to requalify with another three 'waiting days'. Moreover, if an employee leaves his job and starts another one, his period of incapacity with his previous employer counts with his new one.

7.40 The entitlement to SSP is a flat-rate payment for a maximum period of 28 weeks in any one period of entitlement, or in any one tax year. Thereafter, the employee will be able to claim incapacity benefit. From April 1996 SSP is payable to all employees who meet the qualifying conditions and whose average weekly earnings are above the level at which national insurance contributions are payable.

7.41 The above provisions apply to part-time employees (provided they earn the requisite amounts) and there is no minimum service qualification. SSP will be deemed remuneration, and therefore subject to deductions in respect of tax and national insurance contributions. Married women and widows who pay reduced national insurance contributions will qualify for SSP even though they do not qualify for incapacity benefit.

C. Exclusions from entitlement

7.42 The following employees are excluded from entitlement:

(a) employees who are incapacitated from work for less than four days;

(b) employees who are over pensionable age (however, state incapacity benefit may be payable);

(c) employees who earn less than the current lower earnings limit;

(d) pregnant women whose first day of sickness is within the disqualifying period (ie 18 weeks beginning with the eleventh week prior to the expected week of confinement), or who are receiving SMP or MA;

(e) employees who would be workless on the day when the period of entitlement would begin because of a trade dispute, unless they can prove that they did not take part in the strike or did not have a direct interest in it;

(f) employees who are sick on the day they are due to start new employment (incapacity benefit may be payable);

(g) employees whose first day of sickness is within eight weeks of a claim in respect of one of the following state benefits – incapacity benefit, severe disablement allowance, invalidity pension, maternity allowance, or jobseekers' allowance if there has been a previous entitlement to incapacity benefit;

(h) employees who are in legal custody or who are outside the European Economic Area.

D. Leaver's statement

7.43 When an employee leaves his employment his employer must give him a 'leaver's statement' if the employee has a period of incapacity for work which is separated from the date the contract ends by 56 calendar days, and SSP was payable for one week or more. The new employer will take account of the weeks of SSP shown, which may reduce his maximum liability towards the new employee in his period of incapacity for work, by the amount shown on the statement.

E. Enforcement

7.44 If an employee has not been paid SSP, he may refer the matter to the local officer of the Inland Revenue, with an appeal to the local tax commissioners. A decision made in the employee's favour can be enforced in the county court, should this be necessary. Certain questions may be referred directly to the Secretary of State for Social Services for a decision, namely:

  (a) whether a person is, or was, the employee or employer of another person;

  (b) whether an employer is entitled to deduct SSP from his contribution payments;

  (c) whether two or more contracts of employment, or two or more employers, shall be treated as one for SSP purposes.

7.45 Any agreement which purports to exclude, limit or modify an employee's entitlement to SSP shall be void, but this does not prevent an employer from operating a sick pay scheme which is more favourable than the statutory scheme. Contractual sick pay may discharge the employer's liability for SSP, and any SSP payment will discharge contractual liability for the relevant days.

F. Self-certification of illness

7.46 Since June 1982, doctors are no longer required to issue sick notes until after seven days of absence from work (instead of three days). Employees now have to obtain incapacity benefit claims forms, which are widely distributed to trade unions, employers, doctors' surgeries, or are obtainable from the DSS. The form must be completed and signed by the employee, which amounts to a self-certification of absence through illness. If the illness lasts for a period longer than seven days, a continuation claim form can be obtained from the doctor (MED 3). The result will be that there will be a decline in some of the more dubious sick notes which hitherto have been difficult for an employer to challenge. It is generally felt that self-certification enables an employer to set up more efficient control procedures to monitor persistent absenteeism, and thus take effective action to deal with the problem.

Working Time Regulations 1998 (as amended)

A. The regulations

7.47 These regulations came into force in October 1998 and are designed to implement the provisions of the Working Time Directive (93/104/EC) and the Young Workers Directive (94/33/EC). They were amended in 1999 and more recently in 2003 to extend coverage to non-mobile transport workers in the sea, inland waterways and fishing sectors, all workers in the railway and offshore sectors, and all workers in the aviation industry who are not covered by the separate Aviation Directive (200/79/EC). The regulations also apply to junior doctors from August 2004, with the exception that the rules on weekly working time will be phased in, being progressively reduced to 56 hours per week by April 2007 and 48 hours per week by 2009. The DTI has issued Guidance Notes.

7.48 Generally, the regulations give a series of new rights to 'workers', a term which is wider than 'employees', and which also applies to a person working under a contract 'to do or perform personally any work or services for another party to the contract whose status is not by virtue of the contract that of a client or customer of any profession or business undertaking carried on by the individual' (reg 2(1)). This clearly covers casual, freelance and some self-employed workers, other than self-employed persons who are pursuing a professional or business activity on their own account. Thus in *Byrne Bros (Farmwork) Ltd v Baird* the claimant was a self-employed worker employed under a sub-contractor's agreement. He was taxed under Schedule D. The employer was not obliged to provide work, and the claimant was not obliged to do the work personally, although he was paid on a time basis. He claimed holiday pay for the Christmas and New Year closure under the Working Time Regulations. An employment tribunal upheld his claim, and the EAT confirmed the decision. As a 'labour-only sub-contractor' he undertook personally to provide work or services, and he did not work as part of 'any profession or business undertaking'. Thus he was a worker within the meaning of the regulations (see also *Cavil v Barratt Homes Ltd*). So too are bricklayers who work in gangs and who are paid by the employer directly to each gang member (*JNJ Bricklaying Ltd v Stacey*).

The main provisions of the Working Time Regulations 1998–2003 are as follows.

B. The main provisions

Regulation 4 (maximum weekly working time)

7.49 A worker's average working time for each seven-day period, including overtime, must not exceed 48 hours in any period of 17 weeks, although in certain circumstances (reg 21, special cases) the reference period can be 26 weeks, or 52 weeks if permitted by a collective agreement or workforce agreement (reg 23(b)). The regulation will not apply if the worker agrees in writing to working more than 48 hours each week (reg 5). The agreement may be for a specified or an indefinite period, but may be terminated by either side giving the appropriate notice of not less than seven days and not more than three months. For a worker to opt out of the 48-hour week, the consent must be expressly and freely given (*Pfeiffer v Deursches Rotes Kreuz*).

To calculate the average hours in any reference period, the formula to be applied is:

$$\frac{A+B}{C}$$

7.50 This requires some explanation. In any reference period, there will be days when the employee will not work, because of annual holidays, sick leave, maternity leave, etc. Clearly, to exclude those days from the calculation would distort the average hours worked. Therefore, those 'excluded days' must be added back in to the calculation. 'A' is the total number of hours worked during the reference period; 'B' is the total number of hours worked immediately after the reference period during the number of days equivalent to the number of excluded days. 'C' will be the number of weeks in the reference period. Thus the formula (A+B÷C) will give the average number of hours in the reference period, which will, in effect, be extended by the equivalent number of 'excluded' days.

7.51 If a relevant agreement is provided for successive 17-week reference periods, then each reference period will be self-contained, for the purpose of calculating average working hours. In the absence of any such agreement, the reference period will be a 'rolling' 17-week period, ie each week will be the start of a new 17-week reference period. Time spent on call is to be regarded as working time if the employee is required to be present and available at the workplace, but if he is merely contactable when on call, only time linked with actual work is to be regarded as working time (*Sindicato de Médicos de Asistencia Pública (SIMAP) v Conselleria de Sanidad y Consumo de la Generalidad Valenciana*).

Regulations 5A, 6A, 7 (young worker)

7.52 The working time of a young worker (ie who has attained the age of 15 but not the age of 18 and who is over compulsory school leaving age) shall not exceed 8 hours per day or 40 hours per week. A young worker shall not work during the restricted period, which is between 10pm and 6am or 11pm and 7am. An employer shall not assign a young worker to work during the restricted period unless the employer has ensured that the young worker will have the opportunity of a free assessment of his health and capacities before he takes up the assignment, and thereafter at such regular intervals as may be appropriate in his case.

Regulation 6 (length of night work)

7.53 The normal hours of work for a night worker (defined in reg 2) shall not exceed eight in any 24-hour period, again, the average being assessed over a 17-week period (which can be fixed successive 17-week periods, as set out in a relevant agreement, or, failing such agreement, a 'rolling' 17-week period). In *R v A-G for Northern Ireland, ex p Burns* the claimant worked a cycle of 15 shifts of eight hours' duration. During five of these, at least three hours of her working time fell between 11pm and 6am. It was held that she was a night worker within the meaning of reg 6. It was noted that the Directive defined a night worker as a person who works at night 'as a normal course', and this phrase was to be construed as meaning 'as a regular feature'.

7.54 An employer shall ensure that no night worker whose work involves special hazards or heavy physical or mental strain works for more than eight hours in any 24-hour period. The work shall be regarded as involving special hazards or physical or mental strain if it is identified as such in a collective agreement or a workforce agreement, or in a risk assessment carried out under the Management of Health and Safety at Work Regulations 1999. Further, a night worker will be entitled to a free health assessment before he takes up the assignment, with further such assessments at regular intervals. If a registered medical practitioner advises the employer that a worker employed by him is suffering from health problems connected with night work, then, if possible, the employer should transfer the worker to other work for which he is suited, and undertaken at times so that he ceases to be a night worker.

7.55 To calculate the average working hours of a night worker, the normal working hours during the reference period must be divided by the number of working days in that period. The formula is

$$A \div (B-C)$$

Again, an explanation is required.

7.56 From the number of 24-hour periods during the reference period ('B') must be deducted the number of hours (divided by 24 to equate days) which comprise or are included in the weekly rest periods, as provided for in reg 11 ('C'). The amount of the normal working hours during the reference period ('A') can thus be ascertained by dividing the normal working hours during the reference period by the number of working days in that period.

7.57 If a worker has worked for less than 17 weeks, the average will be calculated by reference to the period since the worker started to work for the employer.

Regulation 8 (pattern of work)

7.58 Where the pattern according to which the employer organises work is such as to put the health and safety of a worker employed by him at risk, in particular because the work is monotonous or the work-rate is predetermined, the employer shall ensure that the worker is given adequate rest breaks.

Regulation 9 (records)

7.59 An employer shall keep records of the maximum weekly working time, length of night working, and health assessments etc of night workers, in respect of each worker in relation to whom they apply, and keep such records for two years.

Regulation 10 (daily rest)

7.60 An adult worker is entitled to a rest period of not less than 11 consecutive hours in each 24-hour period during which he works for an employer, although a young worker is entitled to a rest period of 12 consecutive hours.

Regulation 11 (weekly rest periods)

7.61 A worker is entitled to an uninterrupted rest period of not less than 24 hours in each seven-day period during which he works for his employer, although this can be changed to two uninterrupted periods of 24 hours in each 14-day period, or one uninterrupted period of 48 hours in each 14-day period. A young worker is entitled to a rest period of not less than 48 hours in any seven-day period, although this can be altered in certain circumstances.

Regulation 12 (rest breaks)

7.62 Where a worker's daily working time is more than six hours, he is entitled to a rest break, which shall be for an uninterrupted period of 20 minutes (unless a collective agreement or workforce agreement specifies otherwise), to be spent away from the workstation. A young worker who works for more than four and a half hours shall be entitled to a rest break of at least 30 minutes, spent away from the workstation.

Regulation 13 (annual leave entitlement)

7.63 A worker is entitled to four weeks' annual holidays each year, and to receive his normal weekly pay during his holidays, calculated in accordance with ss 221–224 of ERA (reg 16). If the employment is terminated during the leave year, the worker will be entitled to proportionate pay in lieu. In the first year of employment the following calculation will apply. For each month (or part of a month) of service, a worker is entitled to $\frac{1}{12}$ of the annual leave entitlement. For example, a worker who works for three days a week has an annual entitlement of 12 days holiday each year. For workers who work five days a week, there is a rounding-up of accrued entitlement to half and full days. Thus if the amount of leave accrued is the fraction of a day other than half a day, it is rounded up to a half day; if the entitlement accrued is more than a half a day and less than a full day, entitlement is rounded up to the full day. Leave entitlement is only in respect of the holiday year in which it is due, and may not be replaced by a payment in lieu except on termination of the worker's employment.

7.64 To ascertain how much leave is owed on termination, the formula to use is (A×B)–C, where 'A' is the period of leave the worker is entitled to under the Regulations, 'B' is the portion of the leave year which has expired prior to the effective date of termination, and 'C' is the period of leave already taken by the worker. If a relevant agreement so permits, a worker who has already taken holiday entitlement in excess of his statutory entitlement can be required to compensate the employer, either by way of a payment, or doing additional work.

7.65 Where the contract of employment is terminated during the course of a leave year, and the employee has not taken his leave entitlement, reg 14(3) provides that he shall receive a payment in lieu, which shall be such sum as is provided for in a relevant agreement, or, if there are no such provisions, the formula (A × B)–C (above) will apply. In *Witley and District Men's Club v MacKay* the employee was dismissed for gross misconduct. A relevant collective agreement provided that in such circumstances accrued holiday pay would not be payable. When the employers refused to make any such payment, the employee claimed that there was a breach of the Working Time Regulations. His claim was upheld. The words 'such sum' in reg 14(3) did not mean 'no sum'. Thus an agreement which provided for no sum to be paid in respect of outstanding leave entitlement is void by virtue of reg 35(1), as an attempt to exclude or limit the operation of the regulations. This clearly leaves open the possibility of an agreement being upheld if it provides for a minimal or token sum to be paid.

7.66 It goes without saying that clauses sometimes found in existing employment contracts which specify that an employee dismissed for reason of gross misconduct shall not be entitled to accrued statutory holiday pay are no longer valid although this rule would not apply in respect of additional contractual entitlement.

7.67 The worker may give notice to the employer of the dates when he wishes to take his holidays, subject to the employer requiring the worker to take his holidays on particular dates. The worker must give twice the number of days' notice as days' leave he wishes to take. The employer can prevent the employee taking leave on a particular day by giving notice equivalent to the same number of days as the length of leave the employee wishes to take. However, the notice provisions are capable of being overridden by a relevant agreement, which may provide for longer (or shorter) periods of notice.

7.68 The commencement of the leave year should be specified in a relevant agreement, or, if there is no such agreement, it will run from the date the worker commenced employment.

7.69 There are conflicting decisions on whether holiday pay must be paid at the time when the worker is taking the holiday, or whether it can properly be paid along with basic pay but in *Robinson-Steele v RD Retail Services Ltd*, the ECJ held that in principle, rolled-up holiday pay is not permitted by the EC Directive. Workers who take statutory leave must be placed in the same financial position as they would be in if they were carrying on work. An arrangement whereby annual leave payments are staggered over the corresponding annual period of work is precluded by the Directive. In other words, the point in time when payment is made for annual leave must be so fixed as to ensure that the worker can take his holiday entitlement. However, if there are genuine rolled-up holiday payments, made transparently and comprehensibly, these may be offset against a worker's entitlement to payment when leave is finally taken. In other words, if the percentage of holiday pay allocated is clearly identified in the contract and/or on the payslip, and it is made clear that it is a true addition to the contractual rate of pay, credit for such payments may be given.

7.70 Accrued holiday pay is to be calculated on the basis of the number of working days in the year (ie 233 days per year), not on the basis of a calendar year of 365 days (*Leisure Leagues UK Ltd v Maconnachie*). If holiday pay is based on working hours, only contractual hours – not overtime hours – count for the purpose of computing the amount of the worker's holiday pay (*Bamsey v Albion Engineering Ltd*). A similar rule applies in respect of commissions payable (*Evans v Malley Organisation Ltd*). If the employee leaves his employment, having taken more than his annual leave entitlement, the employer can only recover the overpayment if there is a contractual provision to this effect, ie in the contract of employment, a workforce agreement or a collective agreement which has been incorporated into the individual contract (*Hill v Chapell*).

7.71 A worker is entitled to be paid his statutory holiday pay as long as there is a contract of employment in existence, at the appropriate rate, or on a pro rata basis. But a worker who has been absent for the whole of the leave year cannot claim holiday pay under reg 13. In *Commissioners for Inland Revenue v Ainsworth* a group of long-term sick employees claimed statutory holiday pay even though they had been on long periods of sick leave and had exhausted their entitlement to contractual and statutory sick pay. The Court of Appeal (reversing the EAT and overruling the decision in *Kigass Aero Components Ltd v Brown*) held that the purpose of the Working Time Regulations was to ensure minimum health and safety standards in relation to working time, so that workers can expect a minimum period of release from the pressures of work. To allow a worker who had been absent from work for a whole year to claim holiday pay in respect of that year would do nothing to further the interests of health and safety, and would amount to a windfall for a claimant.

7.72 The Court of Appeal also held that a claim for the non-payment of holiday pay must be brought under the provisions of the Working Time Regulations, not as an unlawful deduction under the provisions of ERA, s 23 (*List Design Group v Douglas* overruled).

The effect is that such a claim must be brought within three months of the initial breach of the right to annual leave, not three months from the last in a series of deductions.

C. Exclusions

7.73 There are a number of excluded sectors of employment and specified activities to which specific regulations do not apply, as follows.

Regulation 18

7.74 The regulations do not apply to certain seafarers, workers on sea-going fishing vessels, and workers on board certain ships and hovercrafts. Non-mobile workers in road, sea and inland waterways transport (eg clerical and administrative workers) are covered by the regulations, but mobile workers have limited exclusions. Doctors in training are now covered, with the 48-hour week being gradually phased in from August 2004. If a doctor is on call, but required to remain at a hospital, then periods of inactivity – even sleeping – can constitute working time. The fact that the doctor is required to be present at the place of work determined by the employer, and be available to provide services immediately in cases of need, means that such hours must be regarded as being within the ambit of the performance of his duties (*Landeshauptstadt Kiel v Jaeger*).

Regulation 19

7.75 Domestic servants in a private household are excluded from reg 4 (maximum weekly working time), reg 5A (young worker), reg 6 (length of night work), reg 6A (night work by young worker), reg 7 (health assessment for night workers), reg 8 (safe pattern of work).

Regulation 20

7.76 Workers who, on account of the specific characteristics of the activities engaged in, or where the duration of the working time cannot be measured or predetermined, or which can be determined by the worker himself. In particular:

   (a) managing executives or other persons with autonomous decision-making powers;

   (b) family workers;

   (c) workers officiating at religious ceremonies in churches and religious communities.

7.77 The above workers are excluded from reg 4 (maximum weekly working time), reg 6 (length of night work), reg 10 (daily rest), reg 11 (weekly rest period) and reg 12 (rest breaks).

7.78 It was formerly possible for this group of workers, who voluntarily work additional hours, to have these hours disregarded for the purpose of some parts of the regulations, but this has now been changed with the revocation of reg 20(2), the change being necessary to conform with the Working Time Directive.

Regulation 21

7.79 There is a limited exclusion for the following group of workers:

(a) workers whose activities are such that their place of work and place of residence are distant from one another, or whose different places of work are distant from one another;

(b) where a worker is engaged in security and surveillance activities requiring a permanent presence in order to protect property and persons, particularly security guards and caretakers or security firms;

(c) workers whose activities involve the need for continuity or service or production, particularly –
   (i) services relating to the reception, treatment or care provided by hospitals or similar establishments (including the activities of doctors in training), residential institutions and prisons,
   (ii) work at docks or airports,
   (iii) press, radio, television, cinematographic production, postal and telecommunications services and civil protection services,
   (iv) gas, water and electricity production, transmission and distribution, household refuse collection and incineration,
   (v) industries in which work cannot be interrupted on technical grounds,
   (vi) research and development activities,
   (vii) agriculture,
   (viii) the carriage of passengers on regular urban transport services;

(d) where there is a foreseeable surge of activity, particularly in –
   (i) agriculture,
   (ii) tourism, and
   (iii) postal services;

(e) where the worker's activities are affected by –
   (i) an occurrence due to unusual and unforeseeable circumstances, beyond the control of the worker's employer, or
   (ii) exceptional events, the consequences of which could not have been avoided despite the exercise of all due care, or
   (iii) an accident or the imminent risk of an accident;

(f) workers in railway transport whose activities are intermittent, who work on trains and whose activities are to ensure continuity and regularity of traffic.

7.80 In respect of the above group of workers, the following regulations do not apply, namely, reg 6 (length of night work), reg 10 (daily rest periods), reg 11 (weekly rest periods) and reg 12 (rest breaks). However, if a worker is required to work during what would normally be a rest period, the employer shall allow him to have a compensatory period of rest, or, if this is not possible, afford him appropriate protection (reg 24).

Regulation 23

7.81 This regulation provides that a collective agreement or a workforce agreement may modify or exclude the following regulations in relation to particular workers, namely reg 6 (length of night work), reg 10 (daily rest), reg 11 (weekly rest period) and reg 12 (rest breaks) (see *Prison Service v Bewley*). So far as reg 4 (maximum weekly working time) is concerned, such agreement can substitute a different period over which the average can be worked out, not exceeding 52 weeks (in place of 17 weeks).

7.82 There are also a number of other limited exclusions in respect of shift workers, offshore workers, workers in the armed forces, and young workers affected by *force majeure* or when no adult worker is available (regs 25–27A). There are also special rules for agricultural workers (Sch 2).

D. Enforcement

7.83 The Regulations can be enforced in three ways. First, inspectors from the Health and Safety Executive (or, in appropriate circumstances, enforcement officers of local authorities) are responsible for the enforcement of the following relevant requirements (see reg 28), namely:

(a) the duty of an employer to take all reasonable steps to ensure that the provisions relating to the 48-hour week have been complied with, and also to keep up-to-date records of workers who are subject to an opting out agreement;

(b) the duty of an employer to take all reasonable steps to ensure that a young worker's working time does not exceed 8 hours per day and 40 hours in any week;

(c) the duty of an employer to take all reasonable steps to ensure that a night worker's normal hours of work do not exceed an average of eight hours in each 24 hours;

(d) the duty of an employer to ensure that no night worker whose work involves special hazards or heavy physical or mental strain works for more than eight hours in any 24-hour period;

(e) the duty of an employer to ensure that a young worker does not work between 10pm and 6am (or 11pm and 7am);

(f) the duty of an employer to provide a free health assessment for a night worker and for a young worker who works at night, and for the health assessment to be repeated at regular intervals;

(g) the duty of the employer to provide adequate rest breaks when the work is monotonous;

(h) the duty of the employer to keep adequate records, and to retain them for two years;

(i) where a young worker is permitted under the regulations to work at night, the duty of the employer to ensure that he is supervised by an adult worker, and be allowed a compensatory period of rest;

(j) where the application of the regulations to special cases or shift workers is excluded, the duty of the employer to ensure an equivalent compensatory period of rest;

(k) where certain mobile workers are excluded from the regulations, the duty of the employer to ensure adequate rest.

7.84 It may be noted that although the above provisions are generally enforced by health and safety inspectors, it is the duty of the Civil Aviation Authority to enforce the provisions in respect of relevant civil aviation workers, and the duty of the Vehicle and

Operator Services Agency to enforce the provisions in respect of relevant road transport workers.

7.85 The powers of inspectors to enforce the regulations are identical to those possessed by inspectors under the Health and Safety at Work Act (see para 11.10), as are the offences which may be committed by a person who obstructs, inhibits, gives false information, etc, while the inspector is exercising his powers (see reg 29 and Sch 3).

7.86 In respect of the above matters, an employer may be prosecuted in the magistrates' courts, where a fine of up to £5,000 may be imposed, or an unlimited fine imposed in the Crown Court. Enforcement officers may also issue an Improvement Notice, requiring the employer to rectify matters specified therein, in order to ensure compliance with the statutory requirements, and a failure to comply with such notice can lead to a fine of up to £20,000, and/or six months' imprisonment in the magistrates' court, or an unlimited fine and/or up to two years' imprisonment in the Crown Court.

7.87 The second way in which the Regulations can be enforced is by way of a complaint by a worker to an employment tribunal, alleging that the employer has failed to comply with any of the following provisions:

(a) the daily rest periods for adult or young workers (reg 10);

(b) the weekly rest periods for adult or young workers (reg 11);

(c) rest break periods for adult or young workers (reg 12);

(d) entitlement to annual leave (reg 13);

(e) entitlement to equivalent compensatory rest, where the provisions of regs 10, 11 and 12 have been excluded or modified;

(f) entitlement to compensatory rest where the provisions of regs 10 and 11 have been excluded in respect of young workers serving in the armed forces, or where the *force majeure* exemption applies;

(g) the duty of the employer to pay a worker's statutory annual leave pay, or pay for leave outstanding on the termination of employment (regs 14, 16);

(h) mobile workers, where regs 10, 11 or 12 have been excluded;

(i) young workers who are not permitted to take compensatory rest periods.

7.88 A complaint to an employment tribunal must be brought within three months from the date on which it is alleged that the exercise of the right should have been permitted, or, in the case of holiday pay, from the date when the payment should have been made, although the employment tribunal may extend the period if it was not reasonably practicable to bring the complaint earlier. If the complaint is well founded, the employment tribunal may make a declaration, and may award compensation of such amount as the tribunal consider to be just and equitable, having regard to the employer's default in refusing to permit the worker to exercise the right in question, and any loss sustained by the worker attributable to that default. In the case of holiday pay, the amount due will be awarded.

7.89 A worker will also have the right (ERA, s 45A) not to be subjected to any detriment because:

(a) he refused to comply with a requirement that the employer imposed which would be in contravention of the regulations;

(b) he refused to forgo a right conferred by the regulations;

(c) he failed to sign a workforce agreement or an individual agreement opting out of the regulations;

(d) he performed any functions or activities as a workforce representative, or as a candidate in an election for workforce representatives;

(e) he brought proceedings against the employer to enforce a right conferred by the regulations;

(f) he alleged that the employer had infringed a right conferred by the regulations.

7.90 An employee (not a worker) also has the right not to be unfairly dismissed for any of the above reasons (ERA, s 101A), and also the right not to be unfairly selected for redundancy (ERA, s 105(4A)). Again, the complaint must be brought within three months from the date of the act complained of, with the usual extension of time if it was not reasonably practicable to bring the complaint earlier. If the complaint is upheld, the employment tribunal will make a declaration, and may make an award of compensation, on just and equitable principles. If the employee was unfairly dismissed, no qualifying period of employment is required, interim relief may be available (see para 17.175), and the minimum basic award, as well as an additional award (of between 26 and 52 weeks' pay), may be made as appropriate.

7.91 The third way of enforcing the regulations is to seek an appropriate remedy for breach of contract of employment. In *Barber v RJB Mining (UK) Ltd* pit deputies, although contractually obliged to work for 42 hours a week, regularly worked a considerable amount of overtime, in excess of 48 hours. They were asked to sign an agreement opting out of their rights under the regulations, but refused, and they sought from the court a declaration to the effect that they need not work at all until such time as their average working hours fell below the limit specified in reg 4(1). The High Court granted the declaration. It was held that it was clearly the intention of Parliament that their contract of employment should be read so as to provide that an employee should work no more than 48 hours a week during the relevant reference period. Thus reg 4(1) created a free-standing right which took effect as a contractual term in the contracts of employment of the pit deputies.

7.92 Similarly, in an action in tort for psychiatric illness caused by overwork and stress, it is proper to take into account the fact that the employer has breached the 48-hour week and daily rest provisions (*Hone v Six Continent Retail*, para 11.98) but working excessive hours, by itself, does not give rise to a claim for psychiatric injury (*Pakenham-Walsh v Connell Residential*).

Other employment rights

7.93 There are a number of further provisions giving employment protection rights which are contained in the Employment Rights Act and the Trade Union and Labour Relations (Consolidation) Act. These will be considered under the following headings:

(a) the right not to suffer a detriment or dismissal in health and safety cases (see Chapter 11);

(b) the right not to suffer a detriment or dismissal because of trade union membership or non-membership (see Chapter 21);

(c) the right to have time off work for trade union duties and activities (see Chapter 21);

(d) time off work for safety representatives (see Chapter 11);

(e) interim relief for dismissed trade unionists and non-unionists (see Chapter 21);

(f) interim relief in health and safety cases (see Chapter 11);

(g) the right not to be unfairly dismissed for asserting a statutory right (see Chapter 17);

(h) maternity, paternity and parental rights generally (see Chapter 6);

(i) time off work to act as a union learning representative (see Chapter 21);

(j) time off work for members of a European Works Council (see Chapter 23);

(k) right to request flexible working (see Chapter 2).

A. Sunday trading

7.94 The Sunday Trading Act 1994 was passed to reform the law relating to the circumstances when shops may be open on Sundays, and, at the same time, gave certain protections to employees who did not wish to work on Sundays. Identical provisions apply to betting workers, who work at a track for a bookmaker, or who work in a licensed betting shop. The relevant law is now set out in ERA, ss 36–43.

7.95 If an employee is a 'protected shop worker' or an 'opted out shopworker' he may refuse to work on Sundays. Any agreement or provision in the contract of employment will be unenforceable in so far as it requires him to work on Sundays. Further, a dismissal because an employee refuses to do Sunday work will be automatically unfair.

7.96 An employee will be a protected shop worker if:

- he was in employment as a shop worker on the day the Act came into force (26 August 1994);

- he was not employed to work only on Sunday;

- he has been continuously employed since the Act came into force and the date he complains of dismissal, detrimental treatment or attempts by the employer to require him to work on Sundays under his contract of employment; and

- he has been a shop worker throughout that period of continuous employment.

A person is also a protected shop worker if he cannot be required to work on Sundays under his contract of employment, whether this was entered into before or after the Act came into force.

7.97 An employee will be an opted-out shop worker if:

- under his contract he may be required to work on Sundays;

- but he is not employed to work only on Sundays; and
- he has given his employer an opting out notice stating that he objects to working on Sundays.

In these circumstances, the opted-out shop worker will obtain the statutory protections after three months from when the opting-out notice was served. However, an employer has a duty to provide any employee who could potentially be an opted-out shop worker with a statement in the prescribed form explaining his rights to become an opted-out shop worker (within two months from the commencement of the employment) and if the employer fails to do this, the three-month period referred to is reduced to one month.

7.98 A protected shop worker and an opted-out shop worker may decide to give his employer an 'opting-in notice' indicating that he wishes to work on Sundays or does not object to working on Sundays, in which case he will lose his status, provided he expressly agrees to work on Sundays or a particular Sunday. It would seem that any such agreement can be verbal or in writing.

7.99 It will be an automatic unfair dismissal:

(a) to dismiss an employee who is a protected or opted-out shop worker for refusing or threatening to refuse to work on Sundays;

(b) to dismiss an employee for giving or proposing to give an opting-out notice;

(c) to select a person for redundancy because he refused to work on Sundays, or because he is a protected or opted-out shopworker;

(d) to dismiss an employee because he has asserted his rights under the Act (ERA, s 101).

However, it should be noted that an opted-out shopworker has no protection until the expiry of the three-month notice period (above).

7.100 An employer cannot subject a person to a detriment because he is a protected or opted-out shop worker on the ground that he refuses to work on Sundays or because he has given an opting-out notice. However, an employer can offer financial or other inducements to such workers if they are prepared to work on Sundays, and those who are not so prepared are not thereby deemed to be suffering from a detriment (ERA, s 45).

7.101 An employee who has protected status will not lose that status by agreeing to work on a Sunday, provided he has not given an opting-in notice. However, an opted out employee will lose his status once he gives an opting-in notice, although presumably he can regain that status by giving a further notice.

7.102 Finally, it should be noted that there is no requirement of a period of continuous employment, or a minimum number of hours worked, for a worker to obtain rights under the Act.

B. Christmas shopping

7.103 The Christmas Day (Trading) Act 2004 prohibits a large shop from opening on Christmas Day for the serving of retail customers, but this does not apply to shops of a kind mentioned in the Sunday Trading Act 1994, Sch 1, para 3 (shops selling intoxicating liquor, motor or cycle supplies, pharmacies, petrol stations, etc). Also prohibited is the loading or unloading of goods except with the consent of local authorities. A large shop is one which has a relevant floor area exceeding 280 square metres.

C. Jury service (Juries Act 1974)

7.104 An employee who is summoned to attend for jury service must be given time off work for that purpose, unless he is within one of the excused categories, or unless he has been excused service on application to the appropriate authority or the court. Failure to attend without reasonable cause may result in a fine being imposed of up to £200. A juror is entitled to claim travel and subsistence allowances, and payment for financial loss at prescribed rates. An employee has the right not to be subjected to any detriment because he has been summoned for jury service (including a coroner's jury), but a failure to pay remuneration during such absence is not a detriment unless he is entitled to be paid under his contract of employment (ERA, s 43M). It will also be automatically unfair to dismiss an employee if the reason was his attendance at jury service, but this will not apply if the employer can show that the employee's absence was likely to cause substantial injury to the employer's undertaking, the employee knew of this, and the employee unreasonably refused to apply for an excusal form or deferral of the obligation to attend (ERA, s 98B).

D. Armed Forces Reserves

7.105 Reservists who are called up to serve in the armed forces (including those who volunteer for such service) have their civil employment rights protected by the Reserve Forces (Safeguard of Employment) Act 1985. When the military service comes to an end, an employer must re-employ the employee

(a) in the occupation in which he was last employed before the full-time service, on terms and conditions not less favourable than those which would have been applicable had he not undertaken full-time service, or

(b) if reinstatement is not reasonable and practicable, the employee must be offered the most favourable occupation, and on the most favourable terms and conditions which are reasonable and practicable in his case.

7.106 The employee must apply for reinstatement in writing, before the end of the third Monday after the full-time service has ceased, unless he was prevented from making it within that time by illness or other reasonable cause. The employer must be notified of a date (not more than three weeks) when the employee will be available for employment.

7.107 If the employer has already filled the vacancy, he cannot claim that it was not reasonably practicable to reinstate the reservist because he would have to dismiss that other person, and in practice it should be made clear to the replacement that the appointment may be for a temporary period.

7.108 A person who claims that his rights under the Act have been infringed may make an application to a reinstatement committee (see *Slaven v Thermo Engineers Ltd*). They may order the employer to reinstate the employee, or make an award of compensation of between 13 and 52 weeks' pay, depending on his length of service prior to being called up.

A further appeal will lie to an umpire. It is a criminal offence to fail to comply with an order of the reinstatement committee or the umpire.

7.109 If an employee is dismissed before the commencement of military service, and the reason is the call-up, then, in addition to a claim being made for unfair dismissal, the employer again faces the prospect of being prosecuted for a criminal offence.

7.110 Once the employee returns to his employment, his employment will be deemed to be continuous. The period of absence will not count towards continuity, but will not break it. However, if the employee received permission from the employer to go, he will be absent from work by arrangement or agreement, and the period of absence will count under the provisions of ERA, s 212(3) (see para 13.23).

7.111 The Reserve Forces Act 1996 makes provisions which would enable a reservist to be called out for a period of up to nine months, with the consent of his employer, and for employees to enter into employee agreements with registered employers specifying the maximum liability to service of the employee as a special member, events which will terminate that liability, and other terms relating to the obligations of a special member.

E. Access to medical reports

7.112 The Access to Medical Reports Act 1988 gives an employee the right to refuse permission to his employer who is seeking a medical report on the employee, the right to see any such report before it is supplied to the employer, and the right to correct any errors contained in the report.

7.113 A medical report is defined as being a report relating to the physical or mental health of an individual which has been prepared by the medical practitioner who is responsible for the clinical care of the individual. This would normally be the employee's own doctor or specialist consultant. Thus the Act does not apply to examinations and reports made by a company's own medical advisers, or a specialist report made on an ad hoc basis.

7.114 If an employer wishes to obtain a medical report from the employee's own doctor (or specialist), he must inform the employee, in writing, that he intends to make such an application, inform the employee of his rights under the Act, and obtain the employee's consent. If the employee refuses to give his consent, that is the end of the matter, and the employer may take any other steps he deems necessary, having regard to the refusal. Alternatively, the employee may agree to the application being made, but may insist on seeing the report before it is sent to the employer. He may then refuse consent to it being sent to the employer, or request the doctor to make amendments to the report which the employee considers to be incorrect or misleading. If the doctor refuses to do this, the employee may request the doctor to attach to the report a written statement from the employee, setting out his views in respect of any part of the report which the doctor declines to amend.

7.115 A doctor is not obliged to show to an employee any part of a medical report if he is of the opinion that the disclosure would cause serious harm to the employee's physical or mental health, or would indicate the doctor's intentions with regard to another person. Also, the doctor would not give access to any part of a medical report if this would reveal information about another person (unless that person consents).

7.116 An employee is entitled to access to a medical report which has been supplied for employment purposes any time within the preceding six months.

F. Rights in insolvency (Insolvency Act 1986, s 386, Sch 6)

7.117 If an employer becomes insolvent (through bankruptcy or liquidation) certain preferential debts are paid in priority to others. These include:

(a) up to four months' wages, up to £800 (Insolvency Act 1986, Sch 6);

(b) accrued holiday pay;

(c) any guarantee pay due under ERA, s 28;

(d) remuneration payable on medical suspension under ERA, s 64, or suspension on maternity grounds under ERA, s 66;

(e) any payment due for time off work for trade union duties (TULR(C)A, s 168), or time off to look for work (ERA, s 52) or time off for antenatal care (ERA, s 55);

(f) remuneration due under a protective award (TULR(C)A, s 189);

(g) holiday pay, contractual sick pay and statutory sick pay, and statutory maternity pay;

(h) employer contributions to occupational pensions schemes and state scheme premiums.

The maximum sum which can be treated as a preferential debt is £800.

G. Payments from the National Insurance Fund (ERA, ss 182–189)

7.118 Certain monies due to an employee as a result of the employer's insolvency may be paid by the Secretary of State out of the National Insurance Fund (see *Secretary of State for Employment v Forde*, para 2.15). He must be satisfied that the employer is insolvent (ie bankrupt, or, if a company, being wound up or in receivership, ERA, s 183), that the employee was entitled to be paid the whole or part of the monies due, that the employee has not received payment as a preferred creditor, and that the debt was incurred prior to the employer becoming insolvent. The debts are (see s 184):

(a) any arrears of pay for a period not exceeding eight weeks. This also includes any guarantee pay, remuneration or suspension on medical grounds and maternity grounds, payment for time off work for trade union duties, and the protective award (TULR(C)A, s 189);

(b) any minimum period of notice as computed by ERA, ss 86–90 (see Chapter 15). The rights of the employee to claim against the Secretary of State are no greater than those he has against the employer. In *Secretary of State for Employment v Wilson* the employee was dismissed without notice, but he obtained employment immediately. His former employers went into liquidation, and he claimed four weeks' notice from the Secretary of State. It was held that he was not entitled. He was under a duty as against his former employers to mitigate against his loss, and having done so, he would have had no claim against them. Consequently, he had no claim against the Minister. But the employee is not obliged to bring into account any social security benefits received (*Westwood v Secretary of State for Employment*);

(c) any holiday pay due in the preceding 12 months (but not exceeding six weeks' pay);

(d) any basic award compensation for unfair dismissal (but not a compensatory or higher award);

(e) any reasonable sum by way of reimbursement of the whole or part of a premium paid by an apprentice or articled clerk;

(f) any of the priority debts mentioned above (para 7.117) which have not been satisfied as preferential debts in bankruptcy or liquidation, for a period not exceeding in the aggregate eight weeks;

(g) statutory maternity pay (Statutory Maternity Pay (General) Regulations 1986).

It is important to note that not all debts owed by an employer to his employees are covered by the insolvency provisions of s 184, but only those which fall within the ambit of the statutory provision (*Benson v Secretary of State for Trade and Industry*).

Section 183 of ERA specifies the circumstances when a company can be regarded as being insolvent, namely (a) a winding up or administration order, (b) the appointment of a receiver or manager, or (c) a voluntary arrangement has been approved under the Insolvency Act. The burden is on the applicant to show that one of these events has taken place. The fact that a company has ceased trading, or that it is unable to pay its debts when due, or has been dissolved, does not necessarily mean that it is insolvent within the meaning of s 183 (*Secretary of State for Trade and Industry v Walden*).

There is a maximum liability on the National Insurance Fund of £290 per week in respect of any debt which is referable to a period of time (with a proportionate reduction for periods of less than a week). The Secretary of State is entitled to deduct tax and national insurance contributions (*Morris v Secretary of State for Employment*). The person who is in charge of the winding up must provide the Secretary of State with a statement of the amount of the debt which is owed to the employee, although this is not essential if more than six months have elapsed since an application by the employee was made, and there appears to be a further delay, in which case the Secretary of State has a discretion to make the payment. The Act also provides that the Secretary of State may make payment out of the Fund in respect of any unpaid contributions which an insolvent employer has failed to make to an occupational pension scheme.

7.119 By the Insolvency of Employer (Excluded Classes) Regulations 1983, the right to claim payments on insolvency is extended to employees who, under their contracts of employment, ordinarily work in a member state of the European Community.

7.120 If the Secretary of State fails to make any of these payments, a complaint may be made to an employment tribunal within three months from his refusal (or within such further time as is reasonable). If the tribunal thinks that the payment ought to be made, it shall make a declaration to that effect, and state the amounts which the Secretary of State ought to pay.

7.121 On making the payment, the Secretary of State becomes subrogated to the rights of the employee (or pension fund) as a preferential creditor in the insolvency.

7.122 For claiming unpaid redundancy payments from the National Insurance Fund, see para 18.63.

8

Protection of Wages

8.1 Under the provisions of the Truck Act 1831 the wages of manual workers had to be paid in current coin of the realm. That Act (together with a number of similar legislative provisions) was repealed by the Wages Act 1986, and cashless pay was made lawful for all employees. The actual mode of payment of wages is a matter for agreement between employer and employee.

8.2 A further object of the Wages Act was to prevent an employer from making a deduction from a worker's wages, or requiring the worker to make a payment to the employer (except in specifically defined circumstances), and to give added protection to workers employed in retail trade. In consequence, the provisions of the Truck Act 1896 relating to fines and deductions were also repealed.

8.3 The Wages Act itself was repealed and re-enacted in ss 13–27 of the Employment Rights Act 1996 (ERA) and it is to this Act that reference will be made. Some confusion sometimes arises because of the provisions of the Employment Tribunals Extension of Jurisdiction Order (ETEJO, see para 1.31) made under what is now s 3 of the Employment Tribunals Act 1996, which gives jurisdiction to employment tribunals to deal with breach of contract claims. However, there are several important differences which need to be noted, as follows:

(a) Claims under ETEJO can only be brought in respect of matters outstanding on the termination of employment, whereas ERA claims are made in respect of unlawful deductions and payments made during the existence of the contract of employment (*Capek v Lincolnshire County Council*).

(b) Claims under ETEJO can only be made by employees, whereas ERA claims can be made by 'workers', a category which is somewhat wider (see s 230 and para 2.16).

(c) Under ETEJO an employer can bring a counterclaim, but this not possible under ERA, and if an employer wishes to make some sort of 'set-off' claim, he must pursue it through the normal court machinery.

(d) A claim under ETEJO is essentially a common law claim for breach of contract, and is thus subject to the usual rules relating to mitigation of loss, whereas an ERA claim is a claim for a specific sum protected by statute, and the full sum must be awarded.

General restrictions on unauthorised deductions and payments (ERA, ss 13, 15)

8.4 An employer must not make any deductions from the wages of any worker employed by him, nor receive any payment from him, unless:

(a) the deduction or payment is required to be made or is authorised by a statutory provision; or

(b) the deduction or payment is authorised by a relevant provision in a worker's contract of employment. This can be a written term in the contract of which the employer has given a copy prior to the making of the deduction, or a term of the contract (express or implied, and if express, orally or in writing), the existence and effect of which the employer has notified to the worker in writing. Thus in *Kerr v Sweater Shop (Scotland) Ltd* it was held that the display of a notice by the employer, changing the company's rules so that a person dismissed for gross misconduct would not be paid accrued holiday pay, did not comply with the Act. The Act requires that the term must be 'notified to the worker'; this means that there must be a written notification given individually to each worker, eg by a statement inserted in the wage packet. The display of a notice was not sufficient to discharge the employer's obligation;

(c) the worker has signified in advance in writing his agreement to the deduction or payment.

These three categories need to be explored further.

A. Statutory deduction

8.5 The most usual type of deductions to be made under this heading will be income tax and national insurance contributions. Other examples include a deduction from earnings order made under the Child Support Act 1991 (whether or not the worker was correctly liable under that order: see *Reynolds v Cornwall County Council*), and an attachment of earnings order made by an appropriate court to secure payments of a maintenance order, judgment debts, fines, costs, compensation, forfeiture of recognisances, and legal aid contribution order, under the Attachment of Earnings Act 1971. But the statutory provision in question must specifically authorise the deduction or require it to be made (see *McCree v Tower Hamlets London Borough Council*); an employer cannot seek to rely on a statute which does not confer a power on an employer to do an act in consequence of which the alleged deduction is made (see *Morgan v West Glamorgan County Council*).

B. Contractual authorisation

8.6 The relevant provision in a worker's contract of employment must be contained in a written document, a copy of which has been given to the worker before the employer makes the deduction, or be a contractual term (whether express or implied, and, if express, whether oral or in writing) whose effect and existence has been notified to the employee in writing before the deduction is made.

8.7 It will be noted that the power to make the deduction need not be in the actual contract. It is sufficient if the employer has notified the worker in writing of the term. Thus an implied term, or an oral term, will suffice, provided that the notification is given to the worker individually. The mere display of a notice on a notice board will not suffice (see *Kerr v Sweater Shop (Scotland) Ltd* above).

C. Written consent

8.8 A deduction is permissible if the worker gives his written consent in advance. This provision is designed to cover those circumstances where there is no contractual term as such, but which are collateral to that contract. For example, an agreement to repay a loan made to purchase a season travel ticket, or the forfeiture of a week's pay from an employee who leaves without giving proper notice (see *Pename Ltd v Paterson*) will be valid, provided the appropriate prior written notification is given, and the worker consents to it, either expressly or impliedly, ie by continuing to work once the term has been validly brought to his attention (see *Kerr v Sweater Shop (Scotland) Ltd*, above). But the agreement must indicate with sufficient clarity the source from which the deductions are to be made, ie the worker's wages, and that the worker authorises the deduction from that source. Otherwise, all that may exist is an agreement to repay a loan, not an agreement which authorises a deduction from wages. Thus in *Potter v Hunt Contracts Ltd* the employer agreed to pay for the cost of an HGV driving course, on the understanding that the employee would repay some or all of the cost on leaving his employment. An agreement was drawn up requiring the employee to repay the fee incurred on a diminishing basis if he left the employment within two years. In fact, he left after one month, when most of the loan was still outstanding, and as this amount was more than the wages due to him on departure, he was not given any final wages. It was held that the deduction was unlawful. The loan agreement did not indicate that the repayment of the loan was to be made by way of deduction from wages.

8.9 It must further be noted that the worker's authority for the making of the deduction must not relate to anything that has happened before that authority was given. In other words, deductions must not have a retrospective effect, even if they are made with the worker's agreement. Thus a variation of a contract, or a worker's written consent, can only relate to future happenings (s 13(5), (6)). This is to prevent pressure being placed on a worker to agree or consent to deduction (*Discount Tobacco and Confectionery Ltd v Williamson*).

8.10 The contractual provisions or written agreement which authorise the deductions must be clear and unambiguous, for the mere fact that the worker owes the employer money does not entitle the latter to make a deduction. Employment tribunals can be very astute in striking down terms and agreements which contain ambiguities, the benefit of the doubt being given to the worker (see *Potter v Hunt Contracts Ltd* above). An employee's claim for part-payment of wages outstanding at the date of dismissal is not defeated by the fact that the dismissal was for reason of gross misconduct. The Apportionment Act 1870 applies when a contract of employment is terminated during the payment period, unless there is something in the contract of employment to the contrary (*Item Software (UK) Ltd v Fassihi*).

8.11 Even if the employer does have the right to make a deduction, he must still show that the deduction is in fact justified. Thus in *Fairfield Ltd v Skinner* a van driver was given a document indicating that the employer would charge the employee for private calls made from the van telephone, charge for private mileage, and that the employee would be liable for any excess insurance arising from damage caused to the vehicle. When the employee was dismissed, a sum of £305 was withheld from his final pay packet. The employee brought a claim under the Act, arguing that the deduction was unlawful. The employer responded by claiming that half of the amount deducted represented damage caused to the van whilst being used privately, and the remainder was a provisional deduction for private mileage and telephone calls made. An employment tribunal found that the employee had carried out repairs to the van at his own expense, and that there was no evidence as to how the deduction for private mileage and telephone calls had been calculated. Thus the deduction was unlawful. The decision was upheld by the EAT. The fact that an employer had the right to make a deduction did not mean that he can make a deduction, if in fact the deduction is not justified on the facts of the case, and, if there was a dispute on those facts, it was for the employment tribunal to resolve the matter.

What are 'wages'? (ERA, s 27(1))

8.12 The term 'wages' is defined as any sum payable to the worker by his employer in connection with his employment. These include:

(a) any fee, bonus, commission, holiday pay or other emolument referable to the employment, whether payable under his contract or otherwise;

(b) statutory sick pay, statutory maternity, paternity and adoption pay, guarantee pay, medical and maternity suspension pay, and payments for statutory time off work;

(c) payment made pursuant to a reinstatement or re-engagement order, interim relief order and protective award.

8.13 It will be noted that the definition is very wide. It includes overtime pay (*Bruce v Wiggins Teape (Stationery) Ltd*), shift payments (*Yemm v British Steel plc*) guaranteed monthly payments paid as a retainer (*Thompson v Tech Communications Ltd*), long service awards (*Clarke v Hays Distribution Services Ltd*), holiday pay (*Thames Water Utilities v Reynolds*) and accrued holiday pay (*Kerr v Sweater Shop (Scotland) Ltd*), commission not payable until after the employment has been terminated (*Robertson v Blackstone Franks Investment Management Ltd*) and so on. A service charge added to a customer's bill in a restaurant (see *Saavedra a v Aceground Ltd*), or a tip added to that bill when it is paid by cheque or credit card (see *Nerva v United Kingdom*) is part of an employee's wages, and while the actual distribution of these monies among different employees may be allocated by the employer on a specified or discretionary basis (in accordance with the contracts of employment of his staff) he cannot appropriate part of the charge to himself, for, in doing so, he is making an unlawful deduction within the meaning of the Act. In *Kent Management Services Ltd v Butterfield*, a discretionary bonus, expressed to be ex gratia, was held to be part of the employee's wages, although it was suggested obiter that if such payment was intended to be non-contractual and discretionary, and payable only on the employee achieving a satisfactory performance, words to that effect in the contract could well take the payment outside the Act.

8.14 Accrued holiday pay is 'wages' which an employee is entitled to receive unless there is an express term in the contract negating this right. For example, in *Greg May (Carpet Fitters and Contractors) Ltd v Dring*, the employee's contract stated that on the termination of his employment he would be entitled to accrued holiday pay. However, this would not be paid if he was dismissed through gross misconduct. The employers dismissed the employee for what they claimed to be gross misconduct, and refused to pay him the accrued holiday pay. The employee complained to an employment tribunal that the employers had made an unlawful deduction. It was held that whether or not the sum 'was properly payable' was for the employment tribunal to investigate. On the facts, the employee had not been guilty of 'gross misconduct', and hence the accrued holiday pay was properly payable.

8.15 However, a payment in lieu of notice is not 'wages' under the Act, because it constitutes 'damages' for breach of contract, and is paid not in connection with the employment but in connection with its termination. In *Delaney v Staples* the House of Lords held that payments made under a 'garden leave' dismissal (see para 19.6) constituted wages, but other situations where a payment in lieu of wages is made or promised were not within the Act, because the essential characteristic of wages was consideration for work done under a subsisting contract of employment. Thus a payment made in respect of a period after the contract has terminated cannot be wages. The matter now is perhaps academic, since the passing of the Employment Tribunals Extension of Jurisdiction Order (see para 1.31), except perhaps for a highly paid employee whose notice rights exceed the limits laid down in that Order.

What are not 'wages' (ERA, s 27(2))

8.16 The following payments are excluded from the provisions of the Act:

(a) a payment made by way of an advance under an agreement for a loan or by way of an advance of wages, although s 13 (above) will still apply to any deduction an employer may make from a worker's wages in order to recover that advance;

(b) any payment in respect of expenses incurred by the worker in carrying out his employment. It does not matter if there is an element of profit in those expenses, it is still excluded from the Act, for any such payment does not cease to be expenses merely because the employer is generous (*Southwark London Borough v O'Brien*);

(c) any payment by way of a pension, allowance or gratuity in connection with the worker's retirement or as compensation for loss of office. As noted above, a payment in lieu of notice is not within the Act (*Foster Wheeler (London) Ltd v Jackson*);

(d) any payment referable to a worker's redundancy, whether statutory or not;

(e) any payment made to a worker otherwise than in capacity as a worker;

(f) any benefits in kind are not wages, except a voucher, stamp or similar document which is capable of being exchanged for money, goods or services (whether on its own or together with any other such document). Thus luncheon vouchers are wages within the Act, but other benefits, such as free meals, accommodation, discounts, etc, are not.

What is a deduction? (ERA, s 13(3))

8.17 Where the total amount of wages paid on any occasion by an employer to a worker employed by him is less than the total amount of the wages properly payable (after lawful deductions), the amount of the deficiency shall be treated as a deduction made by the employer from the worker's wages on that occasion. Thus a reduction in wages amounts to a deduction. In *Bruce v Wiggins Teape* the employers agreed to pay enhanced overtime rates to employees who worked on a rolling night shift. It was subsequently decided (without the agreement of the employees or their trade union) to withdraw the enhanced payment. An employment tribunal held that the Act dealt with deductions from pay, not with reductions, but this was reversed by the EAT. The wages properly payable included the enhanced overtime rate, which the employers could not terminate unilaterally. Thus the deductions were unauthorised and therefore unlawful. If an employer reduced the hours of work of his employees without their consent, and pays them for the reduced working hours only, this can amount to an unlawful deduction from wages (*International Packaging Corpn (UK) Ltd v Balfour*). But if the employer has lawful contractual authority to transfer an employee from one shift to another, with a resultant loss of a shift premium allowance, there is no unauthorised deduction from wages within the meaning of s 13 (*Hussman Manufacturing Ltd v Weir*).

8.18 If a collective agreement, the terms of which are incorporated into the individual contracts of employment of employees, expressly provides for a reduction in rates of pay (eg when there is short-time working) such a deduction would not constitute a breach of the Act, although there would be a breach if the deduction could only be made with the approval of the employees and the trade union, and such approval was not obtained. It follows that if rates of pay are contained in a collective agreement which has been incorporated into the individual contracts of employment, these can only be changed in accordance with the terms of that agreement, not unilaterally by the employer (*Davies v Hotpoint Ltd*).

8.19 If there is no power in the contract of employment to demote an employee, then to do so and consequently reduce his salary would be an unlawful deduction under the Act (*Morgan v West Glamorgan County Council*). It will be recalled (see para 8.13) that in *Kent Management Services Ltd v Butterfield* the EAT held that even discretionary bonuses could constitute wages properly payable, if it was in the contemplation of the parties that outstanding commissions would be paid on termination of employment.

8.20 A failure to pay wages on time can amount to a deduction from wages (*Elizabeth Claire Care Management Ltd v Francis*). However, s 13(4) provides that a deficiency in wages, attributable to an error affecting the computation by an employer of the gross wages due to the employee, is not an unlawful deduction for the purpose of s 13(3). In other words, an arithmetical mistake is not an unlawful deduction, although a mistaken belief that certain monies ought not to be paid is a deduction (*Morgan v West Glamorgan County Council*, above).

8.21 Applications for holiday pay must be brought under the Working Time Regulations, not as a claim for unlawful deductions of wages under ERA (*Commissioners of Inland Revenue v Ainsworth, List Design Group Ltd v Douglas* overruled).

Excepted deductions and excepted payments (ERA, ss 14, 16)

8.22 The following deductions and payments, whether lawfully or unlawfully made, are not within the scope of the protection of wages provisions. The employee's remedy, if any, would be to sue for breach of contract in the county court (unless the employment tribunal has jurisdiction to deal with the case under the provisions of the Extension of Jurisdiction Order, see para 1.31).

(a) A deduction or payment for the purpose of reimbursing the employer in respect of an overpayment of wages (s 14(1)(a)), or an overpayment of expenses incurred by the worker in carrying out his employment (s 14(1)(b)), made to the employee for any reason. In *SIP Industrial Products Ltd v Swinn* an employer withheld part of an employee's wages as a reimbursement in respect of expenses which had been fraudulently claimed. An employment tribunal took the view that this deduction was not permitted by s 14(1)(b), because what the employee had done amounted to theft, and therefore had nothing to do with expenses incurred in the course of his employment. However, the EAT held that overpaid expenses made 'for any reason' were recoverable by the employer without being in breach of the Act.

If the worker disputes that there has been an overpayment, or claims that he is not required to repay the overpayment, this matter must be resolved in the ordinary courts, under the general law relating to mistake. It is now settled that there is no difference between a mistake of law and a mistake of fact (*Kleinwort Benson Ltd v Lincoln City Council*). All such overpayments are recoverable by the employer, except that he may not be able so to recover if

(i) he made a representation of fact which led the employee to believe that he was entitled to treat the money overpaid as his own, and

(ii) the employee, bone fide and without notice of the mistake, consequently changed his position (eg by spending the money), and

(iii) the overpayment was not caused by the fault of the employee.

The general principles to be applied in such circumstances stem from the law of restitution (see *Lipkin Gorman v Karpnale Ltd*).

(b) A deduction made in consequence of any disciplinary proceedings held by virtue of a statutory provision (s 14(2)). This provision probably refers to disciplinary proceedings held by the police or fire service (see *Chiltern House Ltd v Chambers*). Such proceedings, however, may be the subject of judicial review (*R v Leicestershire Fire Authority, ex p Thompson*).

(c) A deduction made in consequence of a requirement imposed on an employer by a statutory provision to pay the money over to a public body, if the deduction is made in accordance with the relevant determination of that body (s 14(3)). This is not quite the same as the lawful deductions which can be made under s 13 (above), and would cover a case where a public body (eg local authority) has power to require an employer to deduct a sum from the worker's wages and pay that sum to the authority in question.

(d) A deduction which is paid to a third party at the employee's request (s 14(4)). There must be a relevant provision in the contract, to which the employee has signified his consent in writing, or otherwise with the prior agreement or consent of the worker in writing. This exclusion would cover, for example, the check-off system, whereby an employer deducts trade union subscriptions from the worker's wages, and pays the money to the trade union (see Chapter 21).

(e) A deduction which is made by the employer because the worker has taken part in a strike or other industrial action (s 14(5), and see *Sim v Rotherham Metropolitan Borough Council*). Thus, if the employee is not performing any of his duties the employer may deduct an amount which represents a fair proportion of his salary (*Miles v Wakefield Metropolitan District Council*). If the employee alleges that the employer has deducted more than a fair proportion, his remedy is to bring an action in the county court, not in the employment tribunal. In *Sunderland Polytechnic v Evans* an employee took part in a half-day strike. The employer deducted a full day's salary from her monthly pay, and she complained that an unlawful deduction had been made from her wages. On her behalf, it was argued that s 14(5) only applied to a 'lawful' deduction, ie in respect of the half day she was on strike, and therefore the deduction of a full day's pay was not protected by s 14(5). The employment tribunal held that they had jurisdiction to determine if the deduction was indeed lawful, but this decision was reversed by the EAT. In an unusual move, the EAT decided to look at *Hansard*, and it was noted that in both the House of Commons and the House of Lords, Government ministers were quite clear in their views that if a worker believed that a deduction was not contractually authorised, the remedy would have to be an action in the county court, not in the employment tribunal. Thus, if the amount of the deduction is in dispute, the matter must be settled in the county court. A decision of the EAT to the contrary (*Home Office v Ayres*) was disapproved.

More difficult, perhaps, is the situation where the employee is taking part in 'other industrial action', eg by working his full contractual hours, but only performing part of his contractual duties during those hours (eg by way of protest). In such circumstances, the employer will be entitled to deduct part of the employee's wages, based on his assessment of the amount of time when the employee is not working properly (*Wiluszynski v London Borough of Tower Hamlets*).

(f) A deduction made with the prior agreement of the worker to satisfy an order made by a court or tribunal requiring the payment of any amount to the employer (s 14(6)).

Deductions and payments in retail employment (ERA, ss 17–18)

8.23 Special rules apply for the protection of persons who are engaged in retail employment, which is defined as:

(a) the carrying out of retail transactions, ie the sale or supply of goods or services (including financial services); or

(b) the collection by the worker of amounts payable in connection with retail transactions carried out by other persons, or other individuals in their personal
capacities.

8.24 The definition covers a wide range of activities, including shop assistants, bus
drivers, bank cashiers, insurance agents, petrol pump attendants, credit collectors etc.

8.25 The Act permits an employer to make deductions or require payments from the
wages of such retail workers in respect of cash shortages and/or stock deficiencies which
arise in the course of retail employment. These include shortages or deficiencies arising
from dishonest, negligent or other conduct by the employee, or any other event in
respect of which he has a contractual liability. Nor is it relevant that the amount of
the deduction or payment does not reflect the actual amount of the shortage or deficiency
(s 17(4)). But an employer cannot evade the provisions of the Act by defining wages
by reference to cash shortages or deficiencies, for in such circumstances the gross wages
are to be treated as being the amount they would have been but for the shortage or
deficiency (s 19).

8.26 Under ss 17–18 of the Act, it is permissible to make a deduction (or require a
payment) in respect of cash shortages or stock deficiencies subject to two conditions.
First, the requirements of s 13 (above) must be met, ie an appropriate contractual agreement enabling the deductions (or payments) to be made. This contractual arrangement
must have been agreed to before the happening of the event which was the cause of the
purported deduction, because, as we have seen (above, para 8.9) the Act is designed
to prevent pressure being put on the employee to agree to the deduction (*Discount
Tobacco and Confectionery v Williamson*). Second, the deduction (or demand for payment) must not exceed 10% of the gross wages payable on the day in question (see s 18).
If the shortage or deficiency is greater than the sum to be deducted or demanded the
employer may continue to deduct or demand the balance on subsequent pay days, provided that on each occasion the deduction or demand does not exceed 10% of the gross
wages payable.

8.27 If the employer wishes to make a demand for payment, he must do so in writing (on
one of the worker's pay days) and notify him (again in writing) of the total liability, prior
to receiving any payment (s 20).

8.28 Generally, the deduction or demand must be made within 12 months from the date
when the employer discovers the cash shortage or stock deficiency, except

(a) if the deduction is one of a series of deductions in respect of the same shortage or
deficiency in which case the 12-month period applied from the first deduction or
demand of the series, or

(b) if the employer ought reasonably to have discovered the cash shortage or stock
deficiency earlier, the 12-month period will run from the date when he ought to
have discovered it, not from when he actually did so.

8.29 However, once the employment comes to an end, there is no limit on the amount
which the employer may deduct or demand.

Excluded workers

8.30 The following workers are excluded from bringing a claim under the above provisions of ERA:

(a) members of the armed forces (s 192);

(b) employees who work under a crew agreement in a form approved by the Secretary of State (s 199(1)).

Complaints to an employment tribunal (ERA, s 23)

8.31 A worker may complain to an employment tribunal that his employer has:

(a) made a deduction or demanded a payment in contravention of ss 13–17;

(b) made a deduction which is outside the limit of 12 months as required by s 20(3);

(c) received a payment in respect of a cash shortage or stock deficiency without notifying the worker in writing of his total liability, or without making the demand in the prescribed manner as required by s 20(1);

(d) made a deduction or received a payment in excess of the limit of 10% of the gross pay on a particular day as permitted by s 21(1).

8.32 The complaint must be made within three months from the time when the deduction was made or the payment received by the employer, with the usual extension of time if the employment tribunal is satisfied that it was not reasonably practicable to present a claim earlier. The three-month period runs from the date when contractually the wages were due to be paid, not when they were actually paid (*Group 4 Nightspeed Ltd v Gilbert*). If the complaint is well founded, the employment tribunal shall make a declaration to that effect, and order the employer to reimburse the worker the amount of any unauthorised deductions made or payments received. It should be noted that there is no limit to the amount which the employment tribunal can order to be repaid. Further, if there is an unlawful deduction or payment, which the employment tribunal orders to be repaid, the employer will lose all rights to it, and may not seek to recover that which could lawfully be claimed from the employee by bringing an action at common law (*Potter v Hunt Contracts*).

National minimum wage

8.33 Under the provisions of the National Minimum Wage Act 1998 workers are entitled to be remunerated in any pay reference period at a rate which is not less than the national minimum wage (s 1). The actual hourly rate will be determined in regulations made by the Secretary of State after receiving a recommendation from the Low Pay Commission, but he may not differentiate between different areas of the country, different sectors of employment, undertakings of different sizes, persons of different ages (except, in certain circumstances those under the age of 26, see below) or persons of different occupations (s 2). There is no qualifying period of employment required, and no exclusion for small businesses.

8.34 The Department of Trade and Industry has produced a 'Guidance' booklet (running to 112 pages!) which, although not legally binding, gives guidance to employers and workers, and will doubtless be used by the enforcing authorities as a powerful aid to understanding and implementing the regulations.

8.35 The Act applies to all 'workers', as defined (which, it will be recalled, is a term wider than 'employee', see para 2.17), including agency workers and homeworkers, although there are a number of persons excluded by the Act, and a further number of persons excluded by the regulations made under the Act. So far as the Act is concerned, its provisions do not apply to share fishermen, voluntary workers, certain resident workers in religious communities, and prisoners, and serving members of the armed forces. Under the regulations, the following persons are excluded from the national minimum wage:

(a) apprentices below the age of 18, and apprentices between 19–26 in the first 12 months of their apprenticeship;

(b) certain workers in schemes funded by the European Social Fund, on government-funded training schemes, work experience or temporary work schemes or schemes to help the unemployed to find work (who are not employed by the employer for whom they work under the scheme);

(c) undergraduates on sandwich course placements, trainee teachers on placement;

(d) homeless persons taking part in certain schemes under which they are provided with shelter and other benefits in return for work;

(e) au pairs, nannies, and companions who are treated as a member of the employer's family;

(f) members of the employer's family who live at home and participate in running the family business.

8.36 It has been held that pupil barristers are not engaged under a contract of apprenticeship, and therefore do not qualify for the national minimum wage (*Edmunds v Lawson*). Agricultural workers covered by agriculture wages councils are entitled at least to the amount of the national minimum wage. Offshore workers are covered by the regulations.

8.37 The National Minimum Wage Regulations 1999 (as amended) deal with a number of substantive matters, including the relevant pay period, how pay is to be calculated, what is to be included and excluded if there is a non-monetary element in the pay received, and the method of calculating the hours (time work, salaried hours work, rated output work, fair piece rates and unmeasured work), extension to offshore employment, etc. Various items are included in the definition of pay, eg tips received via the employer (but not those obtained directly from the customer) and incentive payments (but these will only count in the pay period in which they are received). Other items, eg premium payments for overtime or shift work, benefits (company cars, health insurance etc) are to be excluded, but not the value of accommodation.

8.38 The hourly rate is payable for any period during which the worker is at the employer's disposal and carrying out his duties and activities (*British Nursing Association v Inland*

Revenue). It is payable for all times when a worker is required to be at the place of work and available for work, even though there may not be work available. But if a worker is permitted to use sleeping facilities at or near his place of work, only time when he is awake for the purpose of working will count (reg 15(1A)). In *Walton v Independent Living Organisation* a carer lived on her client's premises for 24 hours each day. She was responsible for the client's washing, ironing, shopping, preparation of meals and medication, but when not performing services for the client, she could do what she wanted. Her daily rate of pay was £31.40, and she claimed that this did not equate with the national minimum wage of (then) £3.60 per hour. Her claim failed. She was carrying out unmeasured work, not time work.

8.39 Every employer will be obliged to keep records (s 9), and if a worker believed that he is being remunerated at a rate which is less than the national minimum wage, he may require his employer to produce those records, and the worker may inspect and examine them, accompanied by any other person he thinks fit. The worker must first give notice to his employer (a 'production notice'), and the employer must produce the records at the worker's place of work or any other place at which it is reasonable for the worker to attend and inspect the relevant records (s 10). If an employer fails to produce the relevant records, or fails to allow the worker to inspect them, or fails to allow the worker to be accompanied by someone, the worker may make a complaint to an employment tribunal, who, if they find the complaint to be well founded, will make a declaration to that effect, and make an award to the worker of a sum equal to 80 times the hourly amount of the national minimum wage (s 11).

A. Enforcement by the worker

8.40 A worker who believes that he is being paid less than the national minimum wage may bring a claim in an employment tribunal or a county court, seeking the additional remuneration, either as a claim for unlawful deduction from wages under the Employment Rights Act (see para 8.4), or as a claim for breach of contract. On such a claim, the burden of proof is reversed, ie it will be presumed that the worker was not getting the national minimum wage until the contrary is proved by the employer (s 28). Further, employees have the right not to suffer a detriment or be dismissed (no qualifying period of employment being required) or victimised because they brought or became involved in proceedings relating to the enforcement of the national minimum wage (ss 23 and 25).

B. Enforcement by the state

8.41 The Secretary of State will appoint enforcement officers from the Inland Revenue who will have powers to require employers or an employment agency used by the employer or a worker who qualifies for the national minimum wage to produce any records, and be furnished with any explanation and any other additional information which might reasonably be needed in order to establish whether the Act is being complied with. The officer may disclose any relevant information to the worker. If the officer is of the opinion that a worker who qualifies for the national minimum wage is not being remunerated for any pay reference period at a rate at least equal to the national minimum wage, he may serve an enforcement notice on the employer, requiring him to remunerate the worker for the pay reference periods ending on or after the date of the notice at a rate at least equal to the national minimum wage. The enforcement notice may additionally require the employer to pay a sum due to the worker in respect of the employer's previous failure to pay that rate. In *IRC v Bebb Travel plc* it was held that the Inland Revenue had no power to serve enforcement notices in respect of workers who, although they were paid less than the prescribed amount in the past, had left the employment in question before the enforcement notices had been issued. However, this ruling was altered by the National Minimum Wage (Enforcement Notices) Act 2003 so as to enable enforcement officers to issue notices requiring employers to make good arrears of the national minimum wage to former workers who at any time within six years prior to the issue of the notice qualified for the minimum wage. The failure to comply with an enforcement notice is a criminal offence with daily financial penalties for failing to comply, and it is irrelevant that the employer is unable to comply with the notice because the worker in question has disappeared! The employer may appeal against the enforcement notice within four weeks to an employment tribunal. The employment tribunal will dismiss the appeal unless it is established that the facts were such that the officer had no reason to serve the notice, or that no sum was due to the worker, or that the amount specified as being due is incorrect.

8.42 If the amount specified in the enforcement notice is found to be incorrect, the employment tribunal has a duty to insert the correct figure. If the evidence is unsatisfactory, the tribunal must do the best it can on the material available (*IRC v St Hermans Estate Co Ltd*).

8.43 If the employer does not comply with the enforcement notice, the officer may present a complaint to an employment tribunal or commence civil proceedings in a county court, on behalf of the worker. The officer may also serve a penalty notice on the employer requiring him to pay a financial penalty to the Secretary of State. The penalty will be twice the hourly rate of the national minimum wage (as in force at the time of the notice) in respect of each worker for each day during which there has been a failure to comply. The employer may appeal against the penalty notice to an employment tribunal, who shall dismiss the appeal unless it is established that the facts are such that the officer had no reason to serve the notice, or that the penalty notice is incorrect in some of the particulars, or that the calculation is incorrect. If some of the particulars are incorrect, or if the amount is incorrect, the employment tribunal shall rectify the penalty notice, and it will take effect accordingly.

8.44 An officer may withdraw an enforcement notice, and/or replace it with another. He may also withdraw and/or replace a penalty notice if the facts are such that the officer concerned had no reason to serve the notice, or the calculation of the penalty was incorrect.

C. Offences (ERA, ss 31–33)

8.45 It is an offence to:

(a) refuse or wilfully neglect to remunerate a worker for any pay period at a rate which is at least equal to the national minimum wage;

(b) fail to keep or preserve records;

(c) make false entries in records;

(d) produce or furnish any record or information which he knows to be false;

(e) intentionally delay or obstruct an inspector, or refuse or neglect to answer any question or produce any document when required to do so.

8.46 If the offence committed by a body corporate is proved to have been committed with the consent or connivance of an officer of that body, or attributable to any neglect on his behalf, then he, as well as the body corporate, shall be guilty of an offence and liable to be proceeded against and punished accordingly.

8.47 A person guilty of an offence shall be liable on summary conviction to a fine not exceeding level 5 on the standard scale (currently £5,000).

8.48 From October 2006, there are three applicable rates of national minimum wage:

(a) adult workers (age 22 and over) are entitled to a minimum of £5.35 per hour;

(b) a development rate of £4.45 applies to 18–21 year olds (and workers aged 22 and over during the first six months in new employment, who are receiving accredited training);

(c) workers between the ages of 16–17 (excluding apprentices) are entitled to £3.00 per hour.

Apprentices under the age of 19, and apprentices aged 19–25 who are in the first 12 months of their apprenticeship are not entitled to national minimum wage.

9

Transfer of Undertakings

Background

9.1 At common law, a contract of employment was a personal contract between the employer and employee; when that relationship ceased, the contract of employment came to an end. Thus if a business was sold, the purchaser had the right to choose who he wished to employ, and the employee had the right to choose for whom he worked. Indeed, '. . . the right to choose for himself whom he would serve . . . constituted the main difference between a servant and a serf' (*Nokes v Doncaster Amalgamated Collieries*). Thus the sale or transfer of any business resulted in the termination of any existing contract of employment because at common law an employee's contract of employment cannot be transferred to another employer without his consent (*Bolwell v Redcliffe Homes Ltd*).

9.2 This position was altered by the Transfer of Undertaking (Protection of Employment) Regulations 1981 (familiarly referred to as 'TUPE'), designed to give effect to the Acquired Rights Directive (77/187/EEC). These regulations generally tried to put the transferee employer in the same position as the transferor, so that the rights and obligations contained in the contract of employment made between the transferor are passed to the transferee. Various changes to these regulations were made by the Collective Redundancies and Transfer of Undertakings (Protection of Employment) (Amendment) Regulations 1995–1999, the Pensions Act 2004, and the Transfer of Employment (Pensions Protection) Regulations 2005.

9.3 However, the application of the regulations gave rise to a number of legal and practical problems, and was not helped by a series of irreconcilable decisions from the European Court of Justice and UK courts. Difficult factual questions arose on such issues as what a transfer is, what an undertaking is, whether statutory as well as contractual rights were transferred, pension rights, and so on. The House of Lords gave its approval to the adoption of a 'purposive approach' to the regulations, which went far beyond the traditional strict and literal application of recognised canons of construction, in order that, as far as possible, the rights of employees could be safeguarded (*see Litster v Forth Dry Dock and Engineering Co Ltd*). Despite this novel approach, and the fact that the regulations were amended on several occasions, a number of outstanding issues remained unresolved.

9.4 After a lengthy consultation period, the Government introduced the Transfer of Undertakings (Protection of Employment) Regulations 2006. As well as seeking to clarify a number of small matters, the new regulations are designed to deal with the thorny issues raised by 'service provision changes', deal with certain matters arising from transfer-related dismissals and changes to terms and conditions of employment, require the transferor to notify the transferee of the identities of the employees to be transferred, as well as all rights and liabilities that will pass with the transfer, and provide for a certain amount of flexibility in cases where the transferor is insolvent and a 'rescue bid' is mounted. But the new regulations still retain the same convoluted jargon as their predecessor, and whether earlier legal decisions will survive is a matter for conjecture.

Who is covered by the regulations?

9.5 The regulations apply to an 'employee', defined as 'any individual who works for another person, whether under a contract of service or apprenticeship or otherwise' (reg 2(1)). This definition is somewhat wider than the one used in the Employment Rights Act, and may, for example, include agency supplied employees, casual employees, and so on. In *Mikkelson v Danmols Inventar A/S* the European Court of Justice held that the meaning of the term was for the national courts to decide. However, the definition does not include persons who work under a contract for services. In *Cowell v Quilter Goodison Co Ltd* the claimant was an equity partner in a firm of stockbrokers. The firm was then taken over by a limited company, which continued to employ the claimant as an employee. It was held that the claimant's service as an equity partner could not be counted for the purpose of establishing continuous employment, because he was not an 'employee' at the time of the transfer.

9.6 The regulations apply to a transfer of an undertaking, business or part of an undertaking or business situated immediately before the transfer in the United Kingdom to another employer, where there is a transfer of an economic entity which retains its identity (reg 3(1)(a)). An 'economic entity' is an organised grouping of resources which has the objective of pursuing an economic activity, whether or not that activity is central or ancillary (reg 3(2)). The transferee will not necessarily take over the contracts of employment of those employees who are only temporarily assigned to the organised grouping, and it will be a question of fact and degree whether an employee is or is not so assigned, depending on such factors as the length of time he has been in the group, the work he does in the group, whether or not he is reassigned to other work, and so on.

9.7 However, 'an organised grouping of employees' can, in some circumstances, constitute one person, eg, if the cleaning of business premises is carried out by a single person. Thus in *Schmidt v Spar-und Leihkasse der Fruheren* the claimant was the sole cleaner at a branch of a bank. The bank transferred cleaning duties to a contracting firm, who dismissed the claimant when she refused to accept new terms which she considered to be inferior to those previously enjoyed. The ECJ held that (1) the fact that there was no transfer of tangible assets was not decisive in determining whether there was a transfer for the purpose of EC Directive 77/187/EEC; (2) the decisive factor was whether the business retained its identity; (3) the fact that the activity was ancillary to the main activity carried on did not exclude the operation of the Directive; and (4) the fact that the activity was carried on by a single person also did not exclude the operation of the Directive.

A. Transfer of an undertaking or business

9.8 The European Court has held that it is for the national court to consider all the factual circumstances and assess whether they are characteristic of a transfer of an undertaking within the meaning of the Directive. Thus the undertaking or business transferred must be a stable economic entity, which retains identity after the transfer, but it need not be a profit-making entity (*Dr Sophie Redmond Stichting v Bartol*). The business or undertaking must be transferred 'as a going concern' (*Spijkers v Gebroeders Benedik Abattoir*), and thus the mere transfer of assets does not come under the regulations (*Premier Motors (Medway) Ltd v Total Oil Great Britain Ltd*). Thus the sale of equipment is not within the scope of the regulations, unless some other part of a business is transferred (*ECM (Vehicle Delivery Service) Ltd v Cox*). A building contract for a single project was not treated as an undertaking, because there has to be 'a stable economic entity' (*Rygaard v Stro Molle Akustik*), but this decision appears to rely heavily in the fact that it was an activity under a one-off short term contract (see *BSG Property Services v Tuck*).

9.9 There must be the transfer of an identifiable business (*Banking Insurance and Finance Union v Barclays Bank plc*) and the mere fact that staff are transferred from one status to another, eg by altering employees from direct staff to agency workers doing the same work is not a relevant transfer (*Wynnwith Engineering Co Ltd v Bennett*). The decisive factor appears to be whether the business retains an identity, but it is also necessary to take into account the nature of the undertaking concerned, whether tangible assets were transferred, the value of intangible assets at the time of the transfer, whether or not the majority of employees were taken on by the new owner, whether customers or goodwill were transferred, the degree of similarity between the activities carried on before and after the transfer, and the period, if any during which those activities were suspended (*Rask and Christensen v ISS Kantineservice A/S*). A useful test is whether the essential business activity is carried on by the new owner (*Kenny v South Manchester College*); conversely, if there is no transfer of goodwill a transfer may be outside the scope of the regulations (*Robert Seligman Corpn v Baker*).

9.10 Some confusion appears to stem from the decisions of the European Court in *Suzen v Zehnacker Gebaudereinigung GmbH* and *Oy Lukkene Ab v Liskojarvi*. In *Suzen* it was held that in the absence of a transfer of the workforce in a labour-intensive sector the EU Directive did not apply, and in *Oy Lukenne Ab* the same conclusion was reached in a case where there was an absence of an asset transfer in an asset-reliant sector. These decisions were discussed and distinguished in a series of cases (eg, *Betts v Brintal Helicopters, ECM (Vehicles Delivery Services) Ltd v Cox, OCS Cleaning Scotland Ltd v Rudden*, etc), decisions which generated more heat than light. The issue was then considered in *Scottish Coal Co Ltd v McCormack*, where a company took over mining operations without acquiring the outgoing company's plant or equipment. The Court of Session held that the two categories of 'labour intensive' and 'asset-reliant' were neither mutually exclusive nor exhaustively definitive. There is a range of intermediate possibilities, and the whole of the transaction, including the type of undertaking and the sector of activity in which it operates must be looked at to see whether any particular factor is decisive. It appears that no single factor should be isolated, but a multi-factorial approach should be taken (*P & O Trans European Ltd v Initial Transport Services Ltd*).

B. Transfer of part of a business

9.11 If part of a business is transferred, it is not necessary to show that it was a separate and self-contained business prior to the transfer. The part transferred has to be a recognisable and identifiable part of the business as a whole (*Green v Wavertree Heating and Plumbing Co Ltd*), which means that ancillary activities, such as cleaning, catering, etc are within the scope of the regulations (*Rask v ISS*). Problems sometime arise when an employee works for two or more companies in the same group, and one or more of those companies are transferred. In *Michael Peters Ltd v Farnfield*, the claimant was the chief executive of Michael Peters Group Ltd, a holding company for 25 subsidiary companies. The group experienced financial difficulties, and receivers were appointed. Four of the subsidiary companies were then sold to another company, but the parent company was not a party to the sale. An employment tribunal held that all the companies formed a single economic unit, that part of the parent company had therefore been transferred, and the claimant was unfairly dismissed when he was taken on by the transferee. However, the EAT reversed the decision. It was inappropriate to apply the concept of 'single economic unit' and impermissible to pierce the veil of corporate personality. The business of the subsidiaries was not the business of the parent company. By contrast, in *Sunley Turriff Holding Ltd v Thomson*, the claimant was the company secretary and chief accountant of Lilley Construction Ltd and of Lilley Construction (Scotland) Ltd. The contract of employment was with the former company, although part of his work involved the latter. Both firms went into receivership, and the Scottish company was sold by the receiver to Sunley Turriff Holdings Ltd. It was held that the claimant's contract of employment was automatically transferred to the transferee, because he was part of the undertaking transferred.

9.12 Whether an employee is 'assigned' to an organised group is a question of fact in each case (*Botzen v Rotterdamsche Droogdok Maatschappij*). Factors to be taken into account include the amount of time spent on a particular part of the business, the amount of value given to each part by the employee, the terms of the contract which detail the employee's duties, and how, if at all, the cost to the employer of the employee's services were allocated between the different parts of the employer's business (see *Duncan Web Offset (Maidstone) Ltd v Cooper*). Further, if an employee works at a particular job on a temporary basis, he has not been 'assigned' to the organised group in question, and thus will be outside the scope of the regulations (*Securiplan v Bademosi*).

9.13 What is his position if the employee performs services in part of the undertaking transferred, and also in part of the undertaking retained? The European Court of Justice in *Botzen v RDM* stated that the Directive protects those who are assigned to the transferred part, but this is not very helpful. Two theories are currently suggested by UK commentators. The first is to ascertain if the employee spends most of his activities in the department transferred, or for its benefit (the so-called 'location' theory). The second is to ascertain if the employee's post is part of the staffing structure of the department transferred (the so-called 'belonging' theory). The 'location' theory appears to have some support from the decision of the ECJ in *Botzen v RDM*, but the EAT in *Duncan Webb Offset (Maidstone) Ltd v Cooper* appears to have adopted the 'belonging' approach. The question as to whether or not the employee has been 'assigned' to the part transferred and the proportion of work he did for that part was to be determined on the facts by the employment tribunal. An employee does not have to work exclusively in the part of the undertaking transferred, and all the circumstances have to be taken into account (*Buchanan-Smith v Scheicher & Co International Ltd*).

C. Service provision change (reg 3(1)(b))

9.14 There has always been considerable uncertainty arising from 'outsourcing' or 'contracting out' of services, and the bringing back of services 'in house'. Typically, these will be labour intensive activities, such as cleaning services, catering, maintenance contracts, and so on. These situations are now covered by reg 3(1)(b), as follows.

A service provision change can arise in one of three ways:

(a) activities which cease to be carried out by a person (a client) on his own behalf, and are carried out instead by another person on the client's behalf (a contractor). Normally, this would be a group of employees being transferred, but a single employee employed by the employer can be so transferred to the contractor if that employee's activities are transferred (see *Schmidt v Spar*, etc, above);

(b) activities cease to be carried out by a contractor on a client's behalf, and are carried out instead by another person (a subsequent contractor). This would occur, for example, as a result of competitive tendering;

(c) activities cease to be carried out by a contractor or a subsequent contractor on a client's behalf, and are carried out instead by the client on his own behalf. In other words, they are brought back 'in house'.

Generally, in any of these circumstances, there will have been a transfer within the meaning of the regulations. However, there are three separate situations where the regulations will not apply even though there is a service provision change (see reg 3(3)).

Organised grouping

9.15 For a transfer to occur, there must be an organised grouping of employees which has as its principal purpose the carrying out of the activities concerned on behalf of the client. Thus if different employees are employed by a contractor to carry out an activity on behalf of a client, no transfer within the meaning of the regulations will take place if the client decides to use another contractor, because it would be unclear which employees should transfer. The group of employees is not an 'organised grouping'.

One-off business tasks

9.16 If the client intends that the activities will, following the service provision change, be carried out by the transferee in connection with a single specific event or task, or a task of short-term duration, then no transfer will occur. Thus if a client engages a contractor to perform a 'one-off' business task, or a task which will only last for a short time, the regulations will not apply if the client subsequently engages another contractor to perform the task. There may be an organised grouping of staff on the project, but the one-off buying in of services, or services of short-term duration, will not bring the regulations into operation.

Procurement/supply of goods for client's use

9.17 No transfer will occur if the activities consist wholly or mainly of the procurement or supply of goods for the client's use. Thus if a client engages a contractor to supply food to the client's canteen, a reallocation of that contract will not come within the regulations, because the main activity will be the procurement or supply of goods (it will of course, be a different matter if the client engages a contractor to operate the canteen).

D. Transfers within public administration (reg 3(5))

9.18 A reorganisation of public administration, or the transfer of administrative functions between public administration (eg from central to local government, etc) will not be a relevant transfer for the purpose of the regulations. However, such transfers will come within a Governmental Statement of Practice, 'Staff transfers in the Public Sector' which guarantees TUPE-equivalent protection for employees who are transferred from one public sector body to another. But transfers from the public sector to the private sector are within the scope of the regulations in the same way as transfers between private sector employers.

E. Employees who work outside Great Britain (reg 3(4))

9.19 In principle, the regulations apply to an undertaking situated in Great Britain immediately before the transfer, or, if there is a change in a service provision, where the organised grouping of employees is situated in Great Britain immediately before the transfer. But if the transfer of the business or service provision is governed by the law of an overseas country, and the employment of persons so employed in the business or service provision are governed by the laws of that country, the regulations will still apply if the employees concerned are an organised group of employees and the undertaking itself is situated in Great Britain.

The mechanics of the transfer

9.20 A relevant transfer may take place in a number of ways. It can be by the sale of a business (but not the sale solely of assets), a merger of two or more companies, a change of a licensee or franchisee, changing contractors or the contracting out of services, the sale of a sole trader's business or of a partnership, and so on. As long as there is a change in the identity of the employer it does not matter if a formal legal transfer has not taken place (*Landsorganisationen I Danmark v Ny Molle Kro*). Thus a transfer can take place on a grant, or the surrender and regranting of a lease (*Premier Motors (Medway) Ltd v Total Oil GB Ltd*), because what matters is that there has been a change in the identity of the employer, not necessarily a change in the ownership of the business. In *Young v Daniel Thwaites & Co Ltd* it was held that there was a relevant transfer when a change took place in the tenancy of a public house.

9.21 A transfer may be effected by two or more transactions, and the absence of a contractual link between the transferor and the transferee does not preclude the existence of a transfer. In other words, the business does not need to be transferred from the transferor to the transferee. In *Dines v Initial Healthcare Services Ltd* the claimant was employed by a firm of cleaners to clean at a hospital. The hospital then went to competitive tendering, and awarded the cleaning contract to another firm. The claimant was dismissed by her original employers and offered new but less favourable terms by the transferee. It was held that the transfer had taken place in two stages, ie the handing back of the cleaning contract to the hospital and the subsequent transfer of the cleaning contract to the new contractors. Hence there had been a transfer of the cleaning services, and the regulations operated.

9.22 It is also irrelevant whether or not property passes from the transferor to the transferee. Thus a concession, or a permit to operate a licence, comes within the regulations. The absence of a contractual link between the transferor and the transferee does not preclude the existence of a transfer, because this can result in two or more successive contracts which are part of the web of contractual relations, albeit that the end result (ie the transfer of assets and activities) is somewhat indirectly achieved (*Temco Service Industries SA v Imzilyen*).

9.23 There is no transfer if there is a take-over of shares, because the corporate personality of the company does not change (*Brookes v Borough Care Services*). Nor is there a transfer within the scope of the regulations if there is a transfer of administrative functions between public authorities (reg 3(5), *Henke v Gemeinde Schierke*, but see para 9.18 above).

9.24 The date when a transfer takes place is the date on which responsibility as employer for carrying on the business of the unit moves from the transferor to the transferee, and cannot be postponed to another date at the will of either party. Employment relationships existing at that date are deemed to be transferred on that date, subject only to the employee's objection to being transferred (*Celtec Ltd v Astley*).

The effect of the transfer

A. Contracts of employment (reg 4)

9.25 A relevant transfer shall not operate so as to terminate the contract of employment of any person employed by the transferor and assigned to the organised grouping of resources or employees that is subject to the relevant transfer, but any such contract shall have effect after the transfer as if originally made between the person so employed and the transferee. On completion of the relevant transfer, all the transferor's right, powers, duties and liabilities under or in connection with any such contract shall be transferred to the transferee, and any act or omission before the transfer is completed or in relation to the transferor in respect of that contract or person assigned to that organised grouping of resources or employees, shall be deemed to have been an act or omission of, or in relation to the transferee. Thus actual or potential claims which could be made against the transferor may be brought against the transferee, eg claims for discrimination (*DJM International Ltd v Nicholas*), breach of contract, unfair dismissal, redundancy payments, etc even though these occurred before the transfer took place. Liability for an industrial accident which occurred before the transfer is also transferred, although the transferee could claim the benefit of any insurance policy belonging to the transferor which covered the accident (*Bernadone v Pall Mall Services Group Ltd*). Clearly, it would make sense for the transferee to obtain an indemnity from the transferor against any such potential liabilities.

9.26 However, reg 4 does not transfer or otherwise affect the liability of any person to be prosecuted for, convicted of, or sentenced for, any offence (reg 4(6)).

9.27 This is the nub of the regulations, and constitutes a form of statutory novation of the contract of employment. The transferee 'steps into the shoes' of the transferor, and the contract of employment is continuous as from the date of the original contract of employment with the transferor. Rights and liabilities which existed under the original contract continue in favour of or against the transferee. For example, in *Morris Angel & Son Ltd v Hollande* the defendant was the managing director of a company called Altolight Ltd. His service agreement provided that he would not seek business from any person with whom the company had done business within one year of the end of his employment. The company was then sold to the claimants, who sought to enforce the restrictive covenant. It was held that the effect of TUPE was to put the claimants in the place of the transferor company, and the covenant operated in favour of the claimants, who were the transferees.

9.28 Regulation 4 operates to include matters which were done by the transferor before the transfer, in respect of the employee transferred, even though the transferee is unaware of those matters. In *DJM International Ltd v Nicholas* the claimant worked for a company for many years, but she was forced to retire when she reached the age of 60. Ten days later, she was re-engaged on a part-time basis, and two months after that, following a transfer of the undertaking, she commenced her employment with the respondent company. Five months later she was made redundant, and she brought a claim alleging that her previous employer (the transferor) had discriminated against her on grounds of sex when they terminated her employment at the age of 60 (although her claim was outside the normal three-month time limit, the employment tribunal exercised its discretion to extend the time limit). For the respondent it was argued that the contract of employment, in respect of which she was alleging sex discrimination, had been terminated before the transfer took place, and was not therefore transferred to the transferee. The EAT dismissed the argument, and upheld the claimant's right to pursue her claim. Regulation 5(2)(b) (now reg 4(2)(b)) is very wide, and applies not only to things done before the transfer in respect of the contract of employment, but also to anything done before the transfer in respect of a person's employment in that undertaking.

9.29 However, rights and liabilities are only transferred in respect of those employees who were 'employed immediately before the transfer'. In *Tsangacos v Amalgamated Chemicals Ltd* the claimant lodged a claim for unfair dismissal and race discrimination in March 1995. In July 1995 the employer ceased trading, and all the staff, etc were transferred to another company. The claimant sought to join the latter employers as respondents to his claim, but this was refused by an employment tribunal chairman, and the decision was upheld on appeal. The rights and obligations of the transferor are only transferred in respect of those employees who were employed immediately before the transfer, and this clearly did not include the claimant.

9.30 The meaning of the phrase 'employed immediately before the transfer' gave rise to a number of difficulties in the past, although the matter was resolved by the House of Lords in *Litster v Forth Dry Dock & Engineering Co Ltd*. The phrase includes not only those employees who were employed immediately before the transfer, but also those who would have been so employed had they not been unfairly dismissed because of the transfer, or a reason connected with the transfer that is not an economic, technical or organisational reason entailing a change in the workforce (reg 4(3)). In other words, dismissals unconnected with the transfer are to be ignored so far as the transferee is concerned, but obligations arising from dismissals which are connected with the transfer are transferred.

B. Statutory rights

9.31 It is clear that contractual rights are thus transferred. Also transferred are statutory rights, such as claims for equal pay, maternity rights, etc as well as liability for a protective award (*Alomo Group (Europe) Ltd v Tucker*). Restrictive covenants made by the employee with the transferor are also transferred, although these may need to be re-assessed in the light of the changed situation (*Morris Angel & Son Ltd v Hollande*, para 9.27). But a non-competition clause agreed by the transferred employee will not be enforced if it occurred by reason of the transfer (*Credit Suisse v Padiachy*) because an employee cannot waive rights under the contract which he had with the transferor (*Credit Suisse First Boston (Europe) Ltd v Lister*).

C. Other benefits

9.32 The question thus arises as to what other benefits are capable of being transferred, eg if the transferor employer has a permanent health insurance scheme or a profit sharing scheme which the transferee does not have. In *Mitie Managed Services Ltd v French* it was impossible for the transferee to offer the transferred employees a contractual benefit, but the EAT held that they were entitled to participate in a scheme of substantial equivalence. In *Bernadone v Pall Mall Service Group* the claimant suffered an accident at work in 1996. The following year the undertaking in which she was employed was transferred to a new employer. The claimant brought proceedings for damages against the transferor and the transferee. The transferor claimed that the liability had been transferred to the transferee, a claim which was upheld by the Court of Appeal. However, the Court went further and held that the transferor's right to an indemnity under their employer's liability insurance policy was also transferred by reason of TUPE.

9.33 Obligations under a share option scheme or profit sharing schemes are also transferred to the transferee (*Thompson v ASDA-MFI Group plc*) which can bring about the odd result that the transferee will have to pay profit-related pay based on the employee's performance with the transferor (*Unicorn Consultancy Services Ltd v Westbrook*).

9.34 Occupational pension schemes are not transferred under the regulations, either because they arise under legislation as opposed to contractual obligations, or because they were originally excluded from the Directive. That position remains basically unchanged (reg 10) and an employee whose contract of employment is so transferred is not entitled to bring a claim against the transferor for breach of contract or constructive dismissal arising out of a loss or reduction of his rights under such a scheme (reg 10(3)). However, under the Pensions Act 2004, s 257 if an employee is a member of an occupational pension scheme before the transfer, the transferee must ensure that the employee is eligible to become a member of a scheme operated by the transferee or a stakeholder arrangement. The specific requirements concerning the transferee's scheme are set out in the Transfer of Undertakings (Pension Protection) Regulations 2005. The minimum requirement is for the transferee to match the employee's contribution, up to 6% of salary, into a stakeholder pension, or offer an equivalent alternative. In the public sector, the Government will ensure the continuation of the policy set out in HM Treasury Note, 'A Fair Deal for Staff Pensions', which guarantees broadly comparable occupational entitlement when there is the transfer from the public to the private sector.

9.35 Early retirement benefits do not fall within the scope of the exclusion to be found in the Directive of terms relating to old age, invalidity or survivor's benefits, and therefore the transferee is obliged to offer early retirement benefits (including, where relevant, enhanced redundancy payments) which mirror those provided to the employees by the transferor (*Martin v South Bank University*).

9.36 If there is a transfer following the insolvency of the transferor, any relevant debts owed to the relevant employees (ie those transferred to the transferee and those who were unfairly dismissed by reason of the transfer or for a non-ETO reason (see below) connected with the transfer) are not transferred to the transferee, but will be met by the Secretary of State. This is in line with the existing provisions which are found in ERA, ss 166–170 and ss 182–190 (see para 7.118).

D. Variation of the contract of employment (reg 4(4))

9.37 Any purported variation of the contract of employment shall be void if the reason for the variation is the transfer itself, or a reason connected with the transfer that is not an economic, technical or organisational reason (ETO, see below) entailing changes in the workforce (reg 4(4)). But if there is a valid ETO reason, this new provision enables an employer and employee to agree to a change in the terms of the contract (reg 4(5)). In other words, an employer cannot unilaterally change the terms and conditions of employment of the employees transferred, but there are circumstances when the employer and employee can mutually agree to a variation of those terms, provided there is a genuine ETO reason.

9.38 Equally, a variation will be valid if it was for a reason unconnected with the transfer (reg 4(5)). In *Norris v Brown & Root Ealing Technical Services* employees were offered new terms of employment some two years after a transfer took place. The reason was because the employer was having cash flow difficulties. It was held that the contractual variations were not transfer-connected reasons, but because the employer was having cash flow difficulties. The unexpected loss of a major order could also be an example of circumstances which would permit a variation, as it would be unconnected with the transfer.

E. Permitted variations in insolvency proceedings (reg 9)

9.39 It is permissible to vary the contracts of employment of the transferee's employees when the transferor is subject to insolvency proceedings, if the objective is to safeguard employment opportunities by ensuring the survival of the undertaking which is the subject of the relevant transfer (this is to promote the 'rescue culture' in an attempt to facilitate employment prospects when an employer becomes insolvent). Two conditions must be present:

(i) The variation must be agreed between the transferee (or insolvency practitioner) and the appropriate representatives of the assigned employees. These will be either representatives of an independent trade union recognised by the employer, or, if there are no such representatives, employee representatives who have previously been appointed or elected who have authority to agree to the permitted variations on behalf of the employees, or employee representatives elected by assigned employees for the particular purpose.

(ii) If the representation is by non-union representatives, the agreement recording the permitted variation must be in writing, the employer must give the affected employees copies of the text of the agreement, and such guidance as they might reasonably require in order to fully understand it. The agreement must then be signed by each of the representatives.

The permitted variation shall then take effect as a term or condition of the assigned employee's contract of employment in place of any term of condition it varies.

Dismissal on transfers (reg 7)

9.40 Where, either before or after a relevant transfer, an employee of the transferor is dismissed, this will amount to an automatically unfair dismissal if the reason for the dismissal was the transfer, or a reason connected with it which is not an ETO reason. However, reg 7(2) provides that if the employee was dismissed for an economic, technical or organisational reason which entailed a change in the workforce of either the transferor or transferee, the reason for the dismissal will be treated as either being for redundancy (if that applies) or otherwise for a substantial reason of a kind such as to justify the dismissal of an employee holding that position (*Collins v John Ansell & Partners Ltd*). Thus slimming down an overstaffed workforce so as to enable the transferee to continue to operate successfully would be an ETO reason, and it is then for the employer to show that he acted reasonably in treating that reason as a sufficient reason for the dismissal. If the reason shown is redundancy (and redundancy is the commonest of the ETO reasons), the employee will be able to claim a redundancy payment.

A. ETO reason (regs 4, 7)

9.41 We have seen that it is permissible to vary the contracts of employment of trans-ferred employees (with their agreement) and to dismiss transferred employees, if there is an economic, technical or organisational (ETO) reason which entails a change in the workforce. This phrase is not defined in the regulations, and is therefore the subject of interpretation by the courts and tribunals. In a Guide to the Regulations published by the DTI, it is suggested that an economic reason would relate to the profitability or market performance of the transferee's business, a technical reason would relate to the nature of the equipment or production processes which the transferee operates, and an organisa-tional reason would relate to the management or organisational structure of the transferee's business.

9.42 Potentially, 'economic, technical or organisational reasons' is a wide concept, but it is generally given a restricted meaning. In *Wheeler v Patel,* the EAT held that an economic reason entailing a change in the workforce must relate to the conduct of the business concerned, so that the transferor's attempt to obtain a higher price for a sale by acceding to the demands of the transferee to dismiss the workforce does not constitute an economic reason. An earlier decision to the contrary (*Anderson v Dalkeith Engineering Ltd*) has been disapproved (see *Gateway Hotels Ltd v Stewart*). But a redundancy dismissal brought about solely to obtain a contract is an ETO reason, and is not analogous to a dismissal brought about solely to obtain a best price for the business *(Whitehouse v Charles Blatchford & Sons Ltd)*. If the transferee does not need the transferor's workforce, so that a redundancy situation is produced, this is within reg 7(2) (*Meikle v McPhail*). If, on the transfer of the business, employees are dismissed for reason of redundancy without the transferor being contractually required to do so, this will be evidence of the unfairness of the dismissals (*Litster v Forth Dry Dock and Engineering Co Ltd*). Even when there is an ETO reason which results in redundancies, the employer concerned must still act fairly in treating that reason as a sufficient reason for the dismissal (*Gibson v Ciro Cittero*). The standard way of dealing with redundancies must be followed, that is, fair selection procedures, search for alternatives, full consultation with the workforce and their representatives, etc.

9.43 The decision must be one made on the need to entail changes in the workforce. Generally, this could be a change in the number of employees employed, or a change in the functions of those employed. Thus if whole job contents have to be changed because of the transfer, this may constitute a change in the workforce (*Crawford v Swinton Insurance Brokers Ltd*). If something else is sought to be changed (eg the pay of the employees who are transferred) the resultant dismissal does not come within reg 7(2), and the dismissal will be unfair (*Berriman v Delabole Slate Ltd*). However, this does not prevent a mutually agreed variation for an ETO reason (see reg 4(5) above).

9.44 If the employee is unfairly dismissed in connection with the transfer, his rights lie against the transferee, not the transferor. This is so even if the dismissal took place before the transfer, if the reason was connected with the transfer. Thus in *Allen v Stirling District Council* the claimant was employed by the council's direct services department. Following competitive tendering, the work was awarded to an outside contractor. The claimant was dismissed by the council on 31 December, and the following day that outside contractor assumed responsibility for the service. The claimant brought a claim for unfair dismissal against the council, which failed. The Inner House of the Court of Session held that reg 4(2) was clear and unambiguous. All the transferor's duties and liabilities in connection with the contract of employment were transferred to the transferee. But a dismissed employee cannot compel the transferee to employ him, because the dismissal is not a legal nullity (*Wilson v St Helen's Borough Council*).

9.45 If a dismissal takes place at the time of the transfer, but is for a reason unconnected with the transfer, none of the above TUPE provisions apply, and the dismissal is to be tested under the usual provisions of ERA. For example, a dismissal which takes place following a disciplinary hearing would be unconnected with the transfer. So too would be the unexpected loss of a major order. A desire to harmonise terms and conditions of employment of the incoming employees with those of existing employees does not come within the ETO exception.

9.46 If an employee wishes to bring a complaint of unfair dismissal for a reason connected with the transfer under the provisions of TUPE, he is still required to meet the normal qualifying period of continuous employment of one year (reg 7(6)). If he wishes to claim a redundancy payment, he must be continuously employed for a period of two years.

Refusing a transfer (reg 4(7))

9.47 An employee is not bound to accept the transfer. He is free to choose for whom he will work, and cannot be compelled to work for an employer against his will. He can, at any time before the transfer, object to becoming an employee of the transferee. However, if he does so object, he will not be treated, for any purpose, as having been dismissed by the transferor (losing, for example, his right to a redundancy payment, see *Katsikas v Konstaninidis*). There is no particular form of refusal, but it must be clear and unequivocal, and can be made to either the transferor or transferee. A protest in advance of the transfer will not by itself amount to an objection unless it is followed by an actual refusal to consent to the transfer. Thus, it has been held that to express a preference for a redundancy payment as opposed to a transfer was not enough to constitute an objection to the transfer (*Senior Heat Treatment Ltd v Bell*). The employee has to specifically inform the transferor or transferee that he objects to the transfer.

9.48 There is no requirement that prior to the transfer the transferor must inform his employees of the identity of the transferee (*Secretary of State for Trade and Industry v Cook*), although the new requirements on consultation (see below) in practice will mean that the identity of the transferee will be known.

9.49 But an employee will be able to refuse to accept the transfer if it involves a substantial change in working conditions to his detriment. In these circumstances, reg 4(9) preserves the right of the employee to treat the contract of employment as having been terminated by the employer with notice (see *University of Oxford v Humphreys*). What amounts to a substantial change is a matter to be determined in each individual case. Thus the loss of status, a requirement to relocate which is unacceptable, or a sound medical objection to working in new premises, etc could amount to being a substantial change in working conditions. Further, the employee may resign his employment, and claim that he was constructively dismissed, although for a successful claim he would have to show that the change in working conditions amounted to a repudiatory breach of contract by the employer. In *Rossiter v Pendragon plc* the claimant was a car salesman. His employer operated a commission scheme which could be withdrawn or amended without notice. The business was then transferred to the respondent employer, who changed the commission scheme so that it was less beneficial to the claimant. Because of this, the claimant resigned and claimed he had been constructively dismissed. The Court of Appeal held that since there was no repudiation of the employment contract by the respondent employer, there was no liability for constructive dismissal.

9.50 Damages cannot be awarded against an employer in respect of his failure to pay wages to an employee in respect of a notice period which the employee has failed to work (reg 4(10)).

Employee liability information (regs 11–12)

9.51 The transferor shall notify the transferee of any employee liability information, ie information known to the transferor as to his rights, powers, duties and liabilities under or in connection with the contract of employment of any employee who is assigned to the organised grouping of resources that is the subject of the transfer. This will include:

(a) the identity and ages of employees to be transferred;

(b) the information contained in their statutory statement of particulars of employment;

(c) details or any formal disciplinary action or grievances raised in the previous two years (ie procedures to which the Employment Act (Dispute Resolution) Regulations 2004 apply);

(d) details of actual or potential legal action brought by the employees concerned in the previous two years or that the transferor has reasonable grounds to believe an employee may bring against the transferee arising out of the employee's employment with the transferor (ie, actual or potential claims); and

(e) information of any collective agreement which will have effect after the transfer in accordance with reg 5(a) above.

9.52 It must also include information about any employee who had been unfairly dismissed (in accordance with reg 7(1) above) because of the transfer. Employee liability information shall contain information as at a specified date not more than 14 days before the date on which the information is notified to the transferee. The notification shall be in writing (or made available in a readily accessible form) and given not less than 14 days before the relevant transfer or, if special circumstances make this not reasonably practicable, then as soon as is reasonably practicable thereafter. The notification may be given in instalments, and may come indirectly from a third party. If the specified information changes between the time when it has been provided and the time the transfer is completed, written notification must be given of those changes.

A. Remedy for failure to notify employee liability information (reg 12)

9.53 A transferee may present a claim to an employment tribunal that the transferor has failed to comply with the above provisions relating to employee liability information. The complaint must be made within three months of the relevant transfer (with an extension of time if it was not reasonably practicable to present the complaint within that period). If the employment tribunal finds the complaint to be well founded, it shall make a declaration to that effect, and may award compensation to the transferee to be paid by the transferor. The amount of compensation shall be such as the tribunal consider to be just and equitable, having regard to the loss suffered by the transferee, and the terms of the contract between the transferee and transferor under which the transferor may be liable to pay to the transferee in respect of any failure to notify the transferee of employee liability information.

9.54 The amount of compensation shall be not less than £500 per employee in respect of whom the transferor failed to comply with the provisions in reg 11, unless the tribunal considers it just and equitable to award a lesser sum. The transferee will be expected to take steps to mitigate against the loss suffered.

9.55 The purpose of regs 11–12 is to ensure that the transferee obtains full and accurate information about the rights and obligations which will be taken on, so that these can be honoured. At the same time, both the transferor and the transferee owe a duty of care to each other and to the affected employees not to negligently misrepresent the nature of various benefits which may or may not result from the transfer (*Hagen v ICI Chemicals plc*).

Other matters

A. Collective agreements (reg 5)

9.56 Where, at the time of the transfer, there exists a collective agreement made between the transferor with a recognised trade union in respect of employees to be transferred, then, in its application in relation to them, that agreement shall have effect as if made by or on behalf of the transferee with the trade union.

B. Trade union recognition (reg 6)

9.57 Where, before the transfer, an independent trade union is recognised by the transferor in respect of employees who are transferred, then, after the transfer, the union shall be deemed to have been recognised by the transferee to the same extent. However, this will only apply if, after the transfer, the transferred organised grouping of resources or employees maintains an identity distinct from the remainder of the transferee's undertaking. Any agreement for recognition may subsequently be varied or rescinded.

C. Consultation on transfers (reg 13)

9.58 On the transfer of an undertaking, it is clear that employees of the transferor and the transferee may be affected in some way. Regulation 13 provides that long enough before the relevant transfer to enable the employer of any affected employees to consult all persons who are appropriate representatives of any of the affected employees, the employer shall inform those representatives the fact that the relevant transfer is to take place, the date of the transfer, and the reasons for it, together with:

(i)   the legal, economic and social implications of the transfer for the affected employees;

(ii) the measures (if any) which he envisages he will take in relation to those employees; and

(iii) the measures (if any) which the transferor envisages the transferee will take in relation to the affected employees.

For this purpose, the transferee shall give to the transferor such information as will enable the transferor to perform his duty.

9.59 The information must be delivered to the appropriate representatives and, if either employer envisages that he will take measures in respect of any employees affected by the transfer, he shall consult with the appropriate representatives with a view to seeking their agreement to the measures to be taken. The employer will consider any representations made by the appropriate representatives, reply to them and, if he rejects them, state his reasons. If there are special circumstances which render it not reasonably practicable for the employer to consult as required, he will take such steps towards performing that duty as are reasonably practicable in the circumstances.

9.60 The appropriate representatives are the representatives of a recognised independent trade union, or, in any other case, representatives appointed or elected by them for some other purpose (who have authority to receive such information and be consulted about the transfer) or employees' representatives elected for this specific purpose. The employer shall allow the appropriate representatives access to the affected employees and shall afford them such accommodation and other facilities as may be appropriate.

9.61 If the employer has invited the affected employees to elect representatives, and the invitation was issued long enough before the time when the employer is required to give the information as required under reg 13 (above) to allow them to elect representatives by that time, the employer will have complied with the consultation provisions if he does consult as soon as is reasonably practicable after the election of the representatives. If the employees fail to elect representatives within a reasonable time after being invited to do so, the employer shall give the information to each of the affected employees. It should be noted that, unlike the provisions on consultation on redundancies (see TULR(C)A, s 188), there is no minimum number of employees who are affected before the duty to consult arises.

D. Election of employee representatives (reg 14)

9.62 If there is no independent trade union recognised by the employer, the affected employees are entitled to elect their representatives, and reg 14 lays down detailed requirements for such elections. These must be fair, the number of representatives must be sufficient to represent the interests of all the affected employees, the candidates for employee representatives must be affected employees, voting must be secret, no affected employee shall be unreasonably excluded from standing in the election, and so on. Employees' representatives have the right not to suffer a detriment because they performed any function or activity (including standing for election) and have the right to reasonable time off work with pay, access to the affected employees, and to be provided with appropriate accommodation and facilities. It will be an unfair dismissal to dismiss an employee because he was an employee representative or candidate, or proposed to perform any functions or activities as such.

E. Failure to inform or consult (reg 15)

9.63 A complaint may be made to an employment tribunal in respect of a number of potential failures by the employer, as follows:

(a) if there is a failure to arrange for the election of employee representatives, by any employees who are affected employees;

(b) if there is any other failure relating to employee representatives, by the relevant employee representative;

(c) if there is a failure relating to representatives of a trade union, by the trade union;

(d) in any other case, by any of the affected employees.

9.64 In respect of any such complaint, the employer may show that there were special circumstances which rendered it not reasonably practicable to perform the duty, and that he took all such steps towards its performance as were reasonably practicable in the circumstances.

9.65 If the complaint against the transferee is well founded, the employment tribunal shall make a declaration, and order appropriate compensation to be paid. If the complaint against the transferor is well founded, the employment tribunal shall make a declaration, and order the transferor to pay appropriate compensation. If the complaint is that the transferor failed to provide information about the measures which the transferee will take in connection with the transfer (and the transferor has given notice to the transferee that the latter will be made a party to the proceedings), the transferee may be ordered to pay appropriate compensation to the affected employees. The transferor and transferee shall be jointly and severally liable in respect of compensation payable. 'Appropriate compensation' means such sum not exceeding 13 weeks' pay, as the tribunal considers just and equitable having regard to the seriousness of the failure of the employer to comply with his duty. The maximum award of 13 weeks' pay should be made unless there are mitigating circumstances which would justify a reduction in the award (*Sweetin v Coral Racing*).

9.66 The complaint must be presented to the employment tribunal within three months of the date when the relevant transfer is completed, or three months from the tribunal's order that a payment shall be made. There is a discretion to extend the presentation date for such further period as the tribunal thinks reasonable. An appeal against all tribunal decisions made under the regulations will lie to the EAT on a point of law.

10

Performance of the Contract of Employment

Personal nature of the contract

10.1 A contract of employment is essentially one of personal service, which gives rise to duties and obligations on both sides, but the courts will not compel either side to carry out that contract by means of an order for specific performance or an injunction. In *Warner Bros Pictures Inc v Nelson* a film actress agreed to work for the claimants, and not to work for any other film company. It was held that an injunction would be granted restraining her from breaking the negative stipulation, for while she could not work for a rival film company, there were presumably other ways in which she could earn her living. However, the injunction would not be granted if its effect would be to compel the performance of the contract. In *Whitwood Chemical Co v Hardman* a manager agreed to devote the whole of his time to the company's business. He intended to work part-time for a rival company, and his employers sued for specific performance. It was held that the agreement was not enforceable, for while they could have obtained an injunction to restrain him from working for a competitor, the court would not compel him to work for the claimants.

10.2 By the same rule, the courts will not normally order an employer to continue to employ an employee (*Measham v AEEU*), though there are cases where this had been done (see para 10.5) and in recent years the courts have been more willing to do so than hitherto (see the cases cited in *Wadcock v London Borough of Brent*). There are also pressures on employers to offer reinstatement or re-engagement following employment tribunal proceedings (see Chapter 17) and a contract of employment may transfer from one employer to another when the Transfer of Undertakings (Protection of Employment) Regulations apply (see Chapter 9). But the rule generally remains. In *Chappell v Times Newspapers Ltd*, members of a trade union were carrying on a disruptive campaign in support of a wage demand. The employers' association sent a telegram to the union stating that unless the campaign was called off, the members would be regarded as having broken their contracts of employment and thereby terminated their engagements. Several employees brought an action for an injunction to restrain their employers from terminating their contracts. It was held that, even on the assumption that the employers were acting in breach of contract, an injunction would not be granted, for to do so would be to compel specific performance by the employers. In particular, an injunction will not be granted if damages would be an adequate remedy for the alleged breach of contract (*Alexander v Standard Telephones and Cables plc*).

10.3 An exceptional case was *Hill v CA Parsons & Co Ltd*, where, following the making of a closed shop agreement with a trade union, the employers wrote to the claimant giving him one month's notice of dismissal because of his failure to join the union. The court thought that the claimant, who was a senior engineer, was entitled to at least six months' notice, and granted an injunction restraining the employers from treating the notice as having terminated the contract. (The effect of this was to delay the dismissal until after the coming into effect of the Industrial Relations Act 1971, which would have protected the claimant from dismissal for non-membership of the union.) But the court conceded that there were special circumstances in the case which enabled them to grant the injunction. There was no loss of confidence between the employers and the claimant, for the employers were acting under union pressure, and therefore there was no difficulty in enforcing the continuance of the contract.

10.4 *Hill v CA Parsons & Co Ltd* was followed in *Irani v Southampton and South West Hampshire Health Authority*, where the claimant was employed by the defendants as a part-time ophthalmologist. The claimant quarrelled with the consultant in charge of the clinic, and he was thus dismissed, although the defendants failed to operate the disputes procedure laid down in the Whitley Council Conditions of Service. The claimant was granted an injunction preventing the defendants from implementing the decision without invoking the disputes procedure. The court advanced three reasons. First, there was no lack of confidence in the claimant, for his professional competence was not in issue. Second, the claimant was seeking the protection of the disputes procedure which was incorporated into his contract. Third, damages would not be an adequate remedy. The balance of convenience lay in the granting of the injunction.

10.5 Whether the employee retains the confidence of the employer must be judged on the circumstances of the case, including the nature of the work, the people with whom the work is to be done, and the effect on the employer's operations if the injunction is granted. In *Powell v London Borough of Brent*, the claimant was told that she had been selected for promotion. It was then thought that the selection may have been in breach of the council's equal opportunity code, and her promotion was rescinded and the post readvertised. The claimant brought an action for an injunction to restrain the council from treating her other than as being promoted. By the time the case came to court, she was able to show that she had worked in the senior post without any complaints about her work and there were no problems in her working relationships. It was held that the injunction would be granted. A bare assertion by her employers that there was a lack of confidence was not sufficient.

10.6 The normal remedy in such cases is for the employee who is being threatened with dismissal to seek an interlocutory injunction restraining the proposed dismissal until the trial of action. The court must then consider whether the balance of convenience requires such a course of action (see *American Cyanamid Co v Ethicon Ltd*), leaving the substantial merits of the case to be argued subsequently at a full hearing. However, in *Jones v Gwent County Council*, the court held that under the Rules of the Supreme Court a judge can give a final ruling on any question of law or construction of document without a full trial of action, and such ruling can finally determine the matter, subject to an appeal. In this case, the claimant had been subjected to two disciplinary hearings which ended in her favour. Nonetheless the council brought further disciplinary proceedings on the ground that her return to work would cause an irrevocable breakdown in relationships between management and staff. It was decided that she should be dismissed. It was held that a declaration could be made that her dismissal was not valid, and a permanent injunction was granted, restraining the council from dismissing her other than in accordance with the proper procedure as laid down in her terms of appointment, and unless proper grounds existed.

10.7 TULR(C)A, s 236 provides that no court shall compel an employee to work or attend at a place of work through the making of an order for specific performance, or an injunction. Thus an order cannot be granted, for example, to call off a strike.

Implied duties of the employer

10.8 We have seen (in Chapter 3) that there are a number of different ways by which the terms of a contract of employment may come into existence. We must now consider a number of duties and obligations which are imposed by law on both parties during the continuance of the performance of the contract. Some of these arise by virtue of the common law, but others arise out of the implications of legislative policy.

10.9 The distinction between those duties which are imposed by law and those which operate as an implied term of the contract is not at all clear. Prior to the massive explosion in employment law, which began in the 1960s, there were few legal authorities on the contractual nature of the employment relationship, and hence the courts were more ready to invent obligations as a necessary part of that relationship. In recent years there has been no dearth of legal authority arising from the contractual aspect, and hence rights have developed accordingly, whether as an express or implied term of the contract. But the more terms are expressly laid down, the less scope there is for implied terms to operate. Indeed, since an implied term cannot override an express term, and since express terms can exclude an implied term, the duties imposed by law begin to assume greater importance.

A. Implied duty of trust and confidence

10.10 Now that the age when management could 'hire and fire' at will has gone, it is possible to assert that the employer has a legal duty to treat his employees with due respect and consideration, mindful of their needs and problems, sympathetic to their difficulties. It is no longer possible to treat an employee as an expendable chattel, or as an object without feelings and emotions. This duty is implicit in a number of cases which will be considered in due course when dismissal or disciplinary policies are discussed, but it is particularly evident where the employer is alleged to have been carrying out provocative conduct. In *Donovan v Invicta Airways Ltd* the employee resigned after what he considered to be a number of incidents where he thought the employer was being unfair, and claimed damages for breach of contract. In the circumstances it was held that such conduct, though irritating, was not substantial enough to amount to a breach, but it was stated that there was an implied duty that each of the parties to a contract of employment should treat the other with such a degree of consideration and courtesy as would enable the contract to be carried on. Thus it is a breach of the implied term of trust and confidence to single out an employee on capricious grounds and to refuse to offer him the same terms as are offered to the rest of the workforce (*Transco plc v O'Brien*).

10.11 It will be recalled (see para 3.42) that in *Malik v BCCI SA* the House of Lords held that there was a duty on an employer to conduct his business so as not to damage an employee's future prospects in the labour market. While the *Malik* decision was probably decided on its own facts, it does raise a number of interesting possibilities, including, for example, the case of an employee who has been dismissed for misconduct alleging that his reputation has been damaged by a false accusation, and suing accordingly. In the words of Lord Nicholls: 'Employers must take care not to damage their employees' future employment prospects by harsh and oppressive behaviour or by any other form of conduct which is unacceptable today as falling below the standards set by the implied trust and confidence term.' But if the employer had reasonable and proper cause to act in the manner he did, then even though there are adverse consequences to the employee, there is no breach of the implied duty of trust and confidence (*Hilton v Shiner Ltd*).

10.12 Although to carry on a business in a corrupt and dishonest manner is an example of a breach of the implied term of trust and confidence, if a former employee wishes to claim damages as a result, he must produce credible evidence that prospective employers rejected his applications for employment on such grounds (*Bank of Credit and Commerce International SA v Ali*).

10.13 This duty arises at the outset of the employment, and continues during its performance right up to its termination. Employers will have to examine very closely their personnel and recruitment policies, for a mistake in selection or a failure to handle a problem in a proper manner could lead to an expensive action being brought in the future. For if an employer selects someone for a particular job, and that person does not have the necessary experience or capability for doing it, it is likely that the employer must accept some of the blame (*Bradley v Opperman Gears Ltd*). As a result, many employers are now commencing employees on the basis of a probationary period in order to assess properly their capabilities. The employer also has an obligation to ensure that the employee is provided with an adequate job description, with objectives clearly mapped out, is provided with adequate facilities and support staff, and is properly trained and supervised where necessary. A failure by the employer to attend to these and allied matters may well mean that any shortcomings on the employee's part may not be entirely his own fault, and it could well be unfair to dismiss him in these circumstances (*Burrows v Ace Caravan Co (Hull) Ltd*).

10.14 The frequent use of foul and abusive language by an employer can breach the implied duty of trust and confidence, entitling the employee to resign and claim constructive dismissal (*Horkulak v Cantor Fitzgerald International*).

10.15 However, there are limits to the duty of trust and confidence. For example, in *University of Nottingham v Eyett* it was held that the duty did not create a positive obligation on an employer to advise an employee that if he delayed taking retirement for another month, when he would have received a salary increase, his pension would have been correspondingly higher (see *Crossley v Faithful and Gould Holdings Ltd*, para 3.37).

B. Duty to provide work

10.16 The whole question of 'the right to work' is a confused one, principally because of the different meanings which may be given to the phrase. It may mean the right to work without a trade union membership card, as in *Hill v CA Parsons & Co Ltd*, or the right not to be unreasonably discriminated against, as in *Nagle v Feilden*, where the claimant argued that she had a right to obtain a licence to train horses despite the existence of an unwritten rule of the Jockey Club not to grant such licences to women. It can even mean the right to call on the state to provide jobs. In *Langston v AUEW* the claimant objected to being compelled to join a trade union. The other employees threatened a strike, and so Chrysler suspended him from work for an indefinite period. He claimed that he had been denied the right to work, and in the Court of Appeal it was suggested that the courts would protect a man's right to work in appropriate circumstances, particularly if he was being denied job satisfaction. However, when the case was remitted to the National Industrial Relations Court, it was held that such documents as the Universal Declaration of Human Rights, para 9 of the 1971 Code of Practice, and other poetic allusions were considerations of public policy, rather than statements of contractual rights, and it was the contract which is the determining factor.

10.17 As a general rule, the employer is not under an obligation to provide work for his employee. As Asquith J said in *Collier v Sunday Referee Publishing Co*: 'Provided I pay my cook her wages regularly, she cannot complain if I choose to take any or all of my meals out'. Indeed, there are many circumstances when the employer may find himself unable to provide work for his employees, for example, as a result of reorganisation, shortage of materials, lack of orders, due to a strike, etc, where the employer may prefer to keep his workforce together and pay them for doing nothing. However, there are certain special circumstances where the failure to provide work may result in the breach of a legal duty:

(a) If the failure to provide work can lead to a loss of reputation or publicity. In *Herbert Clayton and Jack Waller Ltd v Oliver*, an actor was given a leading role in a musical comedy. He was subsequently offered a lesser role, but at the same salary. It was held that the employer was in breach of contract, because the nature of the work was as important as the salary to be paid.

(b) If the failure to provide work leads to a reduction in the employee's actual or potential earnings. Thus an employee is entitled to be given an opportunity to earn his commission (*Turner v Goldsmith*) or to earn a reasonable sum if he is on piecework (*Devonald v Rosser & Sons*). In *Bauman v Hulton Press Ltd* it was held that the employers 'were bound to give the claimant a reasonable amount of work to enable him to earn that which the parties must be taken to have contemplated'. It was the lack of opportunity to earn premium payments for hours worked on night-shift and overtime which constituted the breach of contract by the employers in *Langston's* case (above).

(c) There are dicta in *Langston's* case which suggest that if an employee needs practice in order to maintain or develop his skills in employment, the employer is under a duty to provide a reasonable amount of work for this purpose. This view has received further support from the 'garden leave' cases (see *Provident Financial Group plc v Hayward*, para 19.7).

(d) Recent decisions seem to lean to the view that a failure to provide work may constitute a repudiation of the contract by the employer if it is possible to imply a term into the contract that the employer shall provide suitable work. This appears to be particularly true when the employee is appointed to a specific office. In *Breach v Epsylon Industries Ltd*, the EAT thought that some of the earlier decisions on this subject were somewhat out of date and perhaps old fashioned in their approach. Consequently, in modern cases there may be facts which more readily lead to the conclusion that there is an implied term to the effect that there is an obligation to provide work. In *William Hill Organisation Ltd v Tucker* it was stated in the Court of Appeal that times had moved on from the days when only musicians, actors etc were perceived as requiring regular exercise of their skills and public performances in order to keep up their reputation. All employees with specific skills are entitled to exercise those skills, even during notice periods, provided that there is work to be done (see para 19.8).

(e) If the contract of employment provides for suspension with pay pending the outcome of disciplinary enquiries, or criminal proceedings, there is no obligation on the employer to provide the employee with work or an opportunity to work overtime (*McClory v Post Office*).

C. Duty to pay wages or other remuneration when there is no work

10.18 The express terms of the contract will normally determine the amount of remuneration to be paid to the employee, but we must consider the situation where, because there is no work to do, the employee cannot earn his money. The question is, to what extent, if at all, does the employer undertake to pay the employee wages if the employer cannot provide work for the employee to do? To seek the answer, we must state the general rule, and then seek any modification which may exist by virtue of any express or implied terms of the contract of employment.

10.19 At common law an employee who is ready and willing to work is entitled to be paid wages, even though no work is available for him, unless there is a provision in the contract which enables the employer to withhold them (*Beveridge v KLM UK Ltd*). Clearly, this is the position in respect of salaried staff (who are paid weekly or monthly: see *Miller v Hamworthy Engineering Ltd*, para 3.94), and there is no legal distinction between them and hourly-paid workers or piece-workers. An hourly-paid worker is entitled to be paid for the number of hours he makes himself available for work, not the number of hours the employers permit him to work, and a piece-worker, though paid for the work actually done, is entitled to expect that the employer will give him an opportunity to earn his wages. Because of this general common law rule, it was a comparatively simple matter to imply into the contract of an employee a term that he would be paid if there was no work. In *Devonald v Rosser & Sons* the plaintiff was a piece-worker. His employers closed down the factory, and gave him one month's notice. It was held that there was an implied term in his contract that the employer would find him work to do, and he recovered damages based on his prior average earnings. An argument by the employers that there was a trade custom to the contrary was rejected by the court, because a custom has to be reasonable, certain and notorious. But if the failure to provide work was due to circumstances outside the control of the employer, different considerations could apply. In *Browning v Crumlin Valley Collieries* a colliery had to close down because it was in a dangerous condition, through no fault of the employers. It was held that there was an implied term that the employers were not obliged to pay wages in these circumstances.

10.20 The common law rule, however, can be varied by an express or implied term to the contrary and, of course, a statutory provision will always override the rule. Thus if the contract states that there shall be no payment during a lay-off or in respect of short-time working, the employers will incur no obligation to pay at common law. In *Hulme v Ferranti Ltd* the claimant was employed on terms that if there was no work, he would not be paid. He was laid off as a result of a strike involving other workers in the plant, and it was held that he was not entitled to be paid during that time. But the modern practice of concluding guarantee payment agreements lends greater credence to the view that the present law is that in respect of hourly or piece-workers, there is an implied term that they will not be paid during a lay-off or short-time working. For example, if an employer agrees to pay a minimum guarantee week to employees who have been employed by him for a certain period, those who do not qualify can scarcely be in a better position. The very existence of the guarantee payments rights in the Employment Rights Act 1996 (see Chapter 7) supports this view, for such rights would virtually be unnecessary if the common law rule was of general application. Nonetheless, a lay-off without pay is either a temporary suspension or a dismissal with the prospect of re-engagement, and the employer may only treat it as a suspension if there is an expressed or implied term in the contract giving him that right (*Jewell v Neptune Concrete Ltd*). In the absence of such a term the employee is entitled to treat the suspension as repudiatory conduct by the employer, and hence a dismissal. In appropriate circumstances (see Chapter 18) he may claim redundancy pay. Indeed, since there must be few contracts of employment which made provision for such eventuality, the Redundancy Payments Act 1965 was apparently based on the assumption that there was a general existence of an implied term that employees who are laid off or who are on short time are not entitled to be paid (see now ERA, s 147).

D. Payment of bonuses, etc

10.21 If a contract of employment contains an express term which provides for the payment of a bonus (or incentive scheme), problems may arise over interpretation, but not over entitlement. In the absence of any agreement, the courts will calculate or estimate what monies the employee would have received, and include that amount in the quantum of damages (*Addis v Gramophone Co Ltd*). However, difficulties frequently arise when the bonus scheme purports to be discretionary, because, in the absence of clear and precise wording (see, eg *Kent Management Services Ltd v Butterfield*), a legal obligation may nonetheless arise, as part of the implied duties of the employer. In *Mallone v BPB Industries plc* it was held that the directors of a company acted irrationally in cancelling mature share options, following the employee's dismissal for poor performance, even though the contract gave them an absolute discretion to reduce these by an appropriate fraction. Thus, despite the fact that discretion is expressed to be absolute or unfettered, the courts are willing to impose limits on such management prerogatives, by implying a term that a discretion cannot be exercised in a manner which no reasonable employer would have done.

10.22 As a general principle, a dismissed employee cannot claim compensation for the loss of a benefit to which he is not contractually entitled (*Lavarack v Woods of Colchester Ltd*), and if a bonus or other incentive scheme states that it is non-contractual the employer generally does not incur a legal binding obligation to make payments under the scheme (*Pendragon plc v Jackson (No 2)*). But if there is a discretionary bonus scheme the terms of which have been notified to the employee, he will become entitled to it until he has been notified that the scheme has been changed or withdrawn (*Chequepoint UK Ltd v Radwan*). Even after a dismissal, anticipated discretionary bonus payments can be claimed on the basis that, although there was no obligation on the employer to pay, the court will assume that the discretion would have been exercised in good faith (*Clark v BET plc*). Thus a refusal to make a non-contractual bonus payment will amount to a breach of contract if no reasonable employer would have exercised his discretion that way (*Clark v Nomura International*). There is an implied duty on the employer to exercise his discretion in good faith, and not capriciously (*Manor House Healthcare v Hayes*).

10.23 In an industry where there are high earnings and a competitive activity, a discretionary bonus scheme can be regarded as being part of the remuneration structure of the employers, and a contractual benefit to the employee, as opposed to being a mere declaration of the employer's right to pay a bonus if he so wishes. In such circumstances, the employee is entitled to a bona fide and rational exercise of the discretion by the employer in relation to the bonus scheme, and if the employer fails to do so, the employee is entitled to be compensated in respect of that failure (*Cantor Fitzgerald International v Horkulak*).

E. Duty of confidentiality

10.24 Just as there is a duty on employees not to disclose confidential information about the employer's business (see para 10.65) so there is a similar duty on an employer not to disclose to third persons confidential information about the employee. This duty does not depend on any express or implied term of the contract (*Lord Advocate v Scotsman Publications Ltd* per Lord Couldsfield). In *Dalgleish v Lothian and Borders Police Board*, the employers held the names and addresses of all their employees. They were asked to provide this information to a local authority, for the purpose of discovering the identity of persons who had not paid the poll tax. The claimants sought an interim injunction restraining the employers from disclosing this information, which was granted. The information was not in the public domain, and was given by the employees to the employers for the purpose of the employment relationship, and for no other purpose. Hence it retained a characteristic of being confidential information, which could not be disclosed without the consent of the employees.

10.25 The EC Data Protection Directive (95/46/EC) requires member states to enact laws designed to protect the rights to privacy with respect to the processing of personal data. The Data Protection Act 1998 defined 'data' as information which is being processed by means of equipment operating automatically in response to instructions given for that purpose, or is recorded as part of a relevant filing system, or forms part of an accessible record (including health records). An employer who records such data must comply with the eight data principles, set out in the schedules to the Act, and if he fails to do so, he may have to compensate employees who suffer as a result. Further, before processing computer records containing personal data and certain other types of data, this must be included in a notification to the Information Commissioner.

10.26 Under the Data Protection Act 1998 workers have a right to have a copy of any information that an organisation has on them, and may apply to the court to obtain an order requiring a data controller to correct inaccurate information thereon, and seek compensation where damage or distress has been caused. The Act created the post of Information Commissioner, who has produced an Employment Practices Data Protection Code which give guidance on how employment matters can be dealt with under the provisions of the Data Protection Act. The Code is in four parts, ie (a) Recruitment and Selection, (b) Employment Records, (c) Monitoring at Work, and (d) Information about Workers' Health. The Code itself is not legally binding, and any enforcement action has to be based on a breach of the Act. However, the relevant benchmarks would be cited by the Commissioner in such proceedings, and a disregard of those requirements is likely to mean that an employer does not comply with the Act.

10.27 Part 1 of the Code deals with advertising, applications and verifications, shortlisting and interviews of applications, pre-employment vetting, and retention of recruitment records.

10.28 Part 2 of the Code deals with procedures and penalties for storing personal data about employees and job applicants, as well as the processes for subject access requests.

10.29 Part 3 of the Code deals with monitoring at work. It covers the use of CCTV cameras, automatic checking software to monitor the use or misuse of emails, recording telephone calls, and videoing workers who are on sickness absence to ensure that they are not, in fact, malingering. Since a balance must be drawn between the worker's right to privacy and the employer's monitoring requirements, workers must be clearly informed of the purpose of those arrangements, and the employer must be satisfied that the particular arrangement is justified by the benefits which will ensure. The decision whether to monitor or not should be made by a senior member of staff, and it should be done with a minimum of intrusiveness, with spot checks and annual audits being preferred to continuous monitoring. All employees should, as far as possible, be treated equally.

10.30 Part 4 is entitled 'Information about workers' health' and covers such topics as occupational health schemes, medical examinations and testing, drug and alcohol testing, and genetic testing. Collecting and holding information about a worker's health may be intrusive, but may be done with a clear purpose and justified by real benefits.

F. Duty to indemnify

10.31 Any expenses reasonably incurred by the employee in the performance of his contract ought properly to be met by the employer. Normally, one would expect express agreement to this effect, for example, travelling or lodging allowances, but circumstances do arise when an employee spends his own money in pursuance of his employer's business, and it is submitted that he is entitled to be reimbursed. More difficult is the situation which arises when the employee commits a wrongful act. If this was done for the employer's business, and was authorised, or if the employee was acting under his employer's orders, then the employee is entitled to be indemnified for any personal loss he suffers.

10.32 For example, if an employer requires an employee to take out the firm's van, which has a defective tyre, and the employee is consequently fined, then it is reasonable to expect the employer to reimburse the amount, even though he may be prosecuted in addition. But if the work can be done in a lawful or unlawful manner, and the employee chose the latter option, the employer would not be required to reimburse such expenditure. For example, if the employee, in order to deliver some goods, parks illegally, then unless he was told to perform his work in this manner, he must bear any subsequent fine himself. In *Gregory v Ford*, the claimant was injured due to the negligent driving of the defendant, whose employer did not have a valid third-party insurance policy as required by the Road Traffic Act 1988. It was held that there was an implied term of the contract that the employer would not require the employee to do an unlawful act, and therefore the employer should indemnify the employee in respect of the damages which were awarded to the claimant. In *Re Famatina Development Corpn Ltd*, a consulting engineer employed by the company was asked to prepare a report on the conduct of the managing director. The latter brought an action for an alleged libel, which the engineer defended. It was held that he was entitled to be indemnified by the company for his costs in defending the action, for he had been requested by his directors to make the report, which was therefore in the course of his duties as an employee.

G. Duty to insure

10.33 In respect of work activities taking place within the United Kingdom, an employer is obliged to take out compulsory employers' liability insurance, for the benefit of his employees of at least £5 million (Employers' Liability (Compulsory Insurance) Regulations 1998). However, an employer owes no duty in tort to any employee who is working abroad to take out appropriate insurance cover against special risks, or to advise the employee to take out his own cover. In *Reid v Rush & Tompkins Group plc*, the claimant worked for the defendants in Ethiopia. He received severe injuries in a road accident, which was the fault of the other driver, for whom the defendants were not responsible. The claimant was unable to obtain compensation from the other driver, as there is no third-party insurance in Ethiopia, and so he claimed damages from his employers. His statement of claim was struck out. An employer does not owe a duty to inform or advise on the potential danger of suffering economic loss in the form of uncompensated injuries.

H. References

10.34 In the absence of any express contractual obligation, the general rule is that an employer is under no legal duty to provide an employee or an ex-employee with a reference (*Gallear v JF Watson & Son Ltd*) although in *Spring v Guardian Assurance plc* (see below) Lord Woolf suggested that there may be circumstances in which it is necessary to imply a term into a contract of employment that the employer would provide the employee with a reference, particularly in those areas of employment where it is normal practice to require a reference from a previous employer before employment is offered, eg in the financial services industry. An employer who does provide a reference about an existing employee who is seeking employment with another employer is under an obligation to ensure that it is fair and reasonable, and a failure to do so may amount to a breach of the implied duty of trust and confidence entitling the employee to resign and claim constructive dismissal. In *TSB Bank plc v Harris* the employers sent a reference to a prospective employer about the employee which was factually true, but potentially misleading. Thus it stated that there were a number of complaints against her which were outstanding, but these complaints had never been drawn to her attention, and she had never had an opportunity to comment on them or to give her explanation. Her claim for constructive dismissal was upheld, even though she was considering leaving in any case. There is a difference between leaving without a job to go to and leaving in order to go to another job.

10.35 But although the duty is to provide a reference which is in substance fair, true and accurate, it does not have to be full and comprehensive in every case. In *Bartholomew v London Borough of Hackney* the local authority commenced disciplinary proceedings against the claimant, in connection with alleged irregularities. Eventually, a settlement was reached whereby the claimant took voluntary severance, and the disciplinary action was terminated. Subsequently, in response to a request for a reference, the employers stated that at the time of leaving their employment, the claimant was under suspension, disciplinary action had been commenced, but this lapsed on the claimant's departure from the employment. The claimant claimed that the employers were in breach of their legal duty of care, because the reference, although factually correct, was unfair. The Court of Appeal dismissed his claim. Although the form of the reference might have been improved upon in some respects it was not unfair, inaccurate or false. The employers also owed a duty to the recipients of the reference not to be unfair or to mislead. The only duty on the employer is to take reasonable care not to give misleading information, not to make a selective provision of information, or make comments which could give rise to a false or misleading inference in the mind of the recipient (*Kidd v AXA Equity and Law Life Assurance Society plc*). The employer should not, in a reference, deal with matters which have not been put to the ex-employee, and which he has not had a fair opportunity of rebutting following a proper investigation (*Cox v Sun Alliance Life Ltd*).

10.36 While, as a general rule, there is no obligation on an employer to provide a reference for an ex-employee, the situation is different if the reason for the failure or refusal was an act of unlawful discrimination under the Sex Discrimination Act, Race Relations Act and the Disability Discrimination Act (see Chapter 4). All these Acts now provide that it is unlawful to discriminate against a person by subjecting him/her to a detriment, where the discrimination arises out of or is closely connected with the relevant relationship. Thus, if the reason for a failure to provide a reference was because a woman had brought a claim alleging unfair maternity dismissal, this would be an act of unlawful discrimination (*Coote v Granada Hospitality Ltd*). On the other hand if the refusal was based on other considerations, no victimisation has occurred (*Chief Constable of West Yorkshire v Khan*).

10.37 Several pitfalls can occur when providing a reference about an ex-employee to a prospective employer. First, a derogatory reference may expose the giver of the reference to an action for defamation. This may be defended on the ground that the statements made were true, or, if untrue, were made on an occasion when the law confers qualified privilege, and the statements were made without malice, in the sense of an improper motive. Next, the employer owes a duty of care to the ex-employee to ensure that the reference is not prepared carelessly or negligently, and will be consequently liable for damages in respect of any economic loss which flows from the negligent misstatement (*Spring v Guardian Assurance plc*). In this case, Lord Slynn suggested that the employers could avoid any liability by making it clear to the ex-employee that they will only provide a reference if he accepts that there will be a disclaimer of liability to him and to the recipient.

10.38 On the other hand, to give a commendatory reference about a prospective employee which is untrue, and which is relied upon by a subsequent employer to his detriment, may well lead to an action based on deceit or negligent misstatement, unless the reference is qualified by a disclaimer of responsibility (*Hedley Byrne & Co Ltd v Heller & Partners Ltd*).

10.39 A further problem associated with the provision of a reference can arise in dismissal cases. In *Castledine v Rothwell Engineering Ltd*, one of the reasons given by the employer for dismissing the firm's buyer was that he was incapable of performing his job adequately. The tribunal found this difficult to reconcile with the reference given by the employer, which stated that the employee 'had carried out his duties satisfactorily, often under difficult conditions'. Not surprisingly, the tribunal found that the employee had been unfairly dismissed! And in *Haspell v Restron and Johnson Ltd* the respondents gave a reference which was laudatory of the claimant. It was held that they were estopped from relying on criticisms of her performance as a reason for her dismissal.

I. The right to privacy

10.40 There are many occasions during the performance of the contract of employment when an employer will be monitoring the employee's performance, as a matter of routine. The problem arises when such actions become intrusive into an employee's private life. For example, an employer may wish to monitor the employee's telephone calls, in order to assess performance, ensure that quality standards are met, that customer satisfaction is achieved, and provide a valuable record in the event of a subsequent dispute with customers or suppliers, etc. But what happens when the employee's telephone call is of a personal nature? Does this amount to an unwarranted infringement of his right to privacy?

10.41 The routine use of e-mail and the internet by employees during working hours will exacerbate the problem. The temptation for employees to use these facilities for their own purposes is ever-increasing, whether it be for booking holidays, purchasing goods for private use, playing games, or downloading pornography! The questions must be thus posed: can the employer (a) implement surveillance, (b) listen in and/or record such activities and (c) take disciplinary action in the event of suspected misuse? Clearly, a balance must be drawn between the employee's right to privacy on the one hand, and the legitimate interests of the employer in ensuring that the employee is doing his work properly, and not abusing facilities provided.

10.42 So far as the law is concerned, Art 8 of the European Convention on Human Rights provides:

(a) Everyone has the right to respect for his private and family life, his home and his correspondence.

(b) There shall be no interference by a public authority with the exercise of this right except such as is in accordance with the law and is necessary in a democratic society in the interests of national security, public safety or the economic well-being of the country, for the prevention of disorder or crime, for the protection of health or morals, or for the protection of the rights and freedoms of others.

10.43 It will be recalled (see para 1.97) that the Human Rights Act 1998 is designed to give effect to the provisions of the European Convention, and although this only applies to public authorities, doubtless the courts and tribunals will use it as an aid in the decision-making process when dealing with the private employer.

10.44 The right to privacy was an issue in *Halford v United Kingdom*, where the claimant, who was a senior police officer, alleged that she had been turned down for promotion because of her sex, and brought a claim of sex discrimination. She also alleged that her telephone calls at work and at home were being intercepted for the purpose of obtaining information to be used against her in the tribunal proceedings. The sex discrimination case was settled, but she brought further proceedings in the European Court of Human Rights, claiming that the interception of her telephone calls was an infringement of her right to privacy. Her claim succeeded. The Court held that telephone calls made from business premises may be covered by the notion of private life and correspondence within the meaning of Art 8 of the Convention. The Court refused to accept the notion that an employer could, without prior knowledge of the employee, monitor calls made by the employee on telephones provided by the employer.

10.45 The Regulation of Investigatory Powers Act 2000 makes it a criminal offence, without lawful authority, to intercept a communication in the course of its transmission by post or by a public or private telecommunication system. However, interceptions may be lawful if the sender or intended recipient has consented to the interception, the interceptor has a warrant (or, in certain circumstances, without a warrant, eg to comply with an EU Convention on Mutual Assistance in Criminal Matters). Interception is also permitted when done by the postal or telecommunications service provider for purposes connected with the operations of the service.

10.46 There is no problem if the person making or receiving the communication consents to its interception, but the Regulation of Investigatory Powers Act 2000 enables employees to take legal action in tort against an employer whom they believe has unlawfully intercepted a telecommunication made to a third party on the employer's network. However, such an interception is permissible under the Telecommunications (Lawful Business Practice) (Interception of Communications) Regulations 2000, which were passed to give effect to the EU Telecoms Data Protection Directive (97/66/EC). By virtue of these regulations, employers may legitimately monitor or record all telecommunications transmitted over their systems, without the consent of the persons making those communications, for the following purposes, namely, to establish the existence of facts, to ensure compliance with regulatory or self-regulatory practices or procedures, for quality control purposes, for the purpose of detection or prevention of crime, to ensure the effectiveness of their telecommunications systems, or to check on whether the communications in question were relevant to the employer's business. The Information Commissioner has produced a Code of Practice on this topic (see Regulation of Investigatory Powers (Interception of Communications: Code of Practice) Order 2002).

J. Duty to ensure the employee's safety

10.47 The law on compensation for injuries at work will be considered in Chapter 11. Undoubtedly the most important aspect of the employer's duty which is implied by law is the duty to take reasonable care to ensure the safety of his employees.

Implied obligations of the employee

A. Duty of faithful service

10.48 Since the relationship between the employer and employee is one of trust and confidence the law implies into the contract of employment the term that every employee shall serve his employer faithfully. This is a fundamental obligation, and any serious or persistent course of conduct which is inconsistent with that obligation may well amount to a breach of contract. Examples which readily spring to mind include persistent lateness, incompetence, wilful neglect and theft of the employer's property. A strike, a go-slow, a work-to-rule, a sit-in, being contrary to the fundamental nature of the contract – which is to work in return for a reward – are also within this category, and an employee may be dismissed for them (see Chapter 21). The employee undertakes to perform his duties carefully and competently, with due regard for the interests of the employer. In *Secretary of State for Employment v Associated Society of Locomotive Engineers and Firemen* (see para 3.81) Roskill LJ thought that it was an implied term that each employee would not, in obeying lawful instructions, seek to carry them out in a manner which had the effect of disrupting the employer's business. Whether the 'implied term' theory can stand up to analysis is another matter; all members of the Court of Appeal were prepared to import some form of obligation of fidelity arising from the very nature of the contract of employment.

10.49 In *Sim v Rotherham Metropolitan Borough Council* (para 3.34) it was held that the contractual obligations of a person employed in a professional capacity were those defined by the nature of his profession and the obligations incumbent on those who follow that profession.

10.50 If an employee fails to perform part of his duties, but indicates that he is prepared to perform the remainder, the employer may make it clear that he is not prepared to accept such partial performance, and may lawfully refuse to pay the employee the whole of the remuneration due (*Wiluszynski v London Borough of Tower Hamlets*).

10.51 A wrongful act which does not necessarily benefit the employee may still be a breach of fidelity if it is harmful to the employer's business. In *Dalton v Burton's Gold Medal Biscuits Ltd* the employee was dismissed for falsifying the clock-card of a fellow employee, and this was held to be a fair dismissal. A more difficult situation arises if there is a conflict between the duty of fidelity on the one hand, and an obligation the employee owes by virtue of his membership of a professional organisation on the other. It is submitted that there is an implied term that the employer will not require an employee to act in a manner contrary to professional ethics, and that this would override the duty to the employer.

10.52 It is a breach of the employee's duty of faithful service to compete with the employer while he is still employed but it is not a breach if an employee indicates that he intends to take steps at some future date which will enable him to compete after the employment has ceased, in the absence of any restrictive covenant to that effect (see para 19.20). In other words, there is a distinction between an intention to set up in competition with the employer in the future, and competing with the employer while still employed. In

Adamson v B & L Cleaning Services Ltd, the employee was a foreman employed by a firm of cleaning contractors. The firm had a cleaning contract worth £60,000 per year. Tenders were invited for renewal, and the employee indicated that he had requested that his name be placed on the tender list. When the employers were informed of this, they asked him to sign an undertaking not to seek to obtain any contract for industrial cleaning while still in the firm's employment, but he refused to do so, and was dismissed. The dismissal was held to be fair. He was in breach of his duty of faithful service, which justified the termination of his employment. In *Ward Evans Financial Services Ltd v Fox* the employee's contract of employment provided that he would act at all times in the best interests of his employer. He purchased an 'off the shelf' company, which did not commence trading until after his employment had ended, and he also informed existing clients about the new company. It was held that he had acted in breach of his duty of fidelity.

10.53 An employee must not make a secret profit out of his position of trust for his own benefit, without the knowledge or informed consent of the employer, and to do so will amount to a breach of contract which will justify summary dismissal (*Neary v Dean of Westminster*). If the employee is in breach of a fiduciary obligation, then, if the normal remedies of damages or injunction are not sufficient, an action for an account of profits may be brought (*A-G v Blake*). It is probable that this rule also applies to overpayments of wages or expenses received by the employee (see para 8.22). Indeed, it is possible to argue that if an employee knows that he has been overpaid, and deliberately keeps the money, or spends it after he realises that he has been overpaid, then he has committed a criminal offence (*A-G's Reference (No 1 of 1983)*).

B. Duty to obey lawful and reasonable orders

10.54 The employee undertakes to obey all lawful and reasonable orders. In *United Kingdom Atomic Energy Authority v Claydon*, the employee's contract required him to work anywhere in the United Kingdom. He refused to transfer to another base, and was dismissed. The order was clearly lawful and reasonable, for it was within the express terms of the contract. In *Pepper v Webb*, a gardener used some choice expletives accompanied by words which indicated that he had no intention of obeying his employer's instructions, and it was this refusal, rather than the language which accompanied it, which was held to be the breach of contract.

10.55 But if the employee can show that the order was unlawful, he need not obey it. In *Morrish v Henlys (Folkestone) Ltd* the employee refused to falsify some records, and was dismissed. It was held that he was entitled to refuse to obey an unlawful order, and the dismissal was unfair. Whether an order is unreasonable may well be a question of fact in each case. In *Walmsley v UDEC Refrigeration Ltd* the claimant was dismissed after refusing to work in Wexford in Eire on the grounds that it was a hotbed of IRA activity. He could not substantiate these allegations, and it was held that he had refused to obey a reasonable order. Had he been told to go to Belfast, a refusal may well have been justified, for this might involve a serious risk which was not contemplated at the time of the formation of the contract (*Wicks v Charles A Smethurst Ltd*). An employee need not obey an order which would expose him to the risk of danger to life or liberty (*Ottoman Bank v Chakarian*).

10.56 To determine whether or not an order is reasonable, principles of good industrial relations may be taken into account. Thus in *Payne v Spook Erection Ltd*, a foreman was instructed to compile a merit table each week, listing the performance of 25 employees, and to send warning letters to those whose name appeared at the bottom of the list. As he did not see all the employees each week, he refused to operate the system, as he thought that it would be based largely on guesswork. He was told that unless he operated the system he would be dismissed, but he refused to comply. An employment tribunal, although they had little sympathy with the system, held the dismissal to be fair, but the decision was reversed by the EAT. In considering whether or not a decision of an employment tribunal was perverse, matters of good industrial relations could be considered. The weekly merit rating system was clearly unfair, and to dismiss the foreman for refusing to operate an unreasonable order was also unfair.

10.57 Difficulty is frequently caused by loose contractual expressions relating to overtime. If this is stated to be voluntary, then the employee is entitled to refuse. If it is stated to be worked by arrangement, then again, it becomes a matter for negotiation. But if it is clear that some overtime is to be worked, and the negotiations are merely about the details, the refusal may well be unreasonable, particularly if this is designed to bring improper pressure to bear on the employer (*Pengilly v North Devon Farmers Ltd*). As we have seen (in Chapter 3) a refusal to accept a demotion or a change in contractual terms is not necessarily unreasonable, but refusal to obey instructions which are within the contract may be unreasonable. In *Connor v Halfords Ltd* the employee was obliged to 'obey all orders and instructions received from the directors'. He was dismissed because he refused to go on a training course, and the dismissal was held to be fair.

10.58 An employee who refuses to obey a lawful and reasonable order, which was given in good faith and without any ulterior motive, is in repudiatory breach of contract, which the employer may accept by dismissing him without notice or pay in lieu of notice (*Macari v Celtic Football and Athletic Co Ltd*).

10.59 However, it does not follow that an employee who refuses to obey a lawful order may automatically be dismissed, any more than it can be said that an employee cannot be dismissed if he refuses to obey an order which is outside his contractual obligations, for the strict legal rights are only relevant in considering the 'lawfulness' of the dismissal, but not its fairness. Two employment tribunal decisions will illustrate this point. In *Wilson v IDR Construction Ltd* the claimant was contractually bound to move from site to site in accordance with management instructions. He was asked to move to a new site, but refused, as his wife was ill, and he was having difficulty with his car. Although his refusal to obey a lawful and reasonable order would have entitled the employers to dismiss him at common law, the tribunal held that this was not an invariable rule so far as unfair dismissal law was concerned. The employers should have given him a chance to explain his refusal, taken into account the genuineness of the reason, the fact that he had never refused to change sites before, and that his refusal related only to that one day. In the circumstances, the dismissal was held to be unfair. On the other hand, in *Robinson v Flitwick Frames Ltd* the claimant was dismissed following his refusal to work overtime, although he was not contractually bound to do so. All the other employees in his section worked the necessary overtime, and the claimant gave no satisfactory explanation for his refusal. The tribunal held that his dismissal was for 'some other substantial reason' and that the employers had acted reasonably in the circumstances, for it would have caused considerable problems if the claimant had to be employed on terms different from the other employees (see also *Farrant v Woodroffe School*).

10.60 If the employees are not prepared to give an undertaking that they will desist from future disruptive conduct, an employer may suspend them from work until they do so, and the employees, though willing to work, will not be entitled to remuneration for the period of suspension (*British Telecommunications plc v Ticehurst*).

C. Duty to use skill and care

10.61 The employee undertakes to perform his work competently, using reasonable skill and care. This, of course, must be combined with the employer's duty to provide all necessary assistance, etc (see above), but if the employer has done all he can, then a dismissal for incompetence will usually be fair. Also, the employee undertakes to take proper care of the employer's property. In *Superlux v Plaisted* the employee negligently allowed some of his employer's property to be stolen from a van, for which he was held responsible. On the other hand, a tribunal has held that an employee who negligently lost the company cat should receive some disciplinary action short of a dismissal! For a dismissal to be warranted, the act of negligence must be a serious one (*Comerford v Swel Foods Ltd*) or a series of minor acts of neglect (*Lowndes v Specialist Heavy Engineering Ltd*, para 17.80). It is an implied term of the contract of employment that an employee will exercise skill and care in the performance of his duties, and a breach of that term entitles the employer to claim damages in respect of the negligent performance of the contract. In *Janata Bank v Ahmed*, the employee worked as a bank manager. It was alleged that he had been negligent in the way he carried out his duties, and after his dismissal, the bank issued a writ claiming £34,640 damages. The Court of Appeal upheld the claim. He had failed to exercise proper skill and care, as implied by his contract. It is irrelevant that the cause of action arises in contract or in tort (see *Lister v Romford Ice and Cold Storage Co Ltd*).

D. Secret bribes and commissions

10.62 The employee undertakes not to accept any secret bribes or commissions or gifts, or any reward in respect of his work other than from his employer. This rule applies even though the employee is in no way influenced by the favours he has received, for there is always the possibility that there will be a suspicion that his conduct has been influenced, or that it might be affected in the future. Tips, however, are a recognised method of being paid, and do not constitute a bribe which must be disclosed. An employee can only serve one employer, and it will be inconsistent with his obligation of faithful service to accept anything from another person in respect of things done within the performance of his work. In *Boston Deep Sea Fishing and Ice Co v Ansell* the defendant was a managing director of the claimant company. He placed orders for supplies with other companies, from whom he received a commission. It was held that his dismissal was justified. It is a violation of the duty of honest and faithful service for an employee to have an interest in a firm which is transacting business with his employer without disclosing that interest, and on discovering the facts, the employer is entitled to dismiss the employee summarily (*Horcal Ltd v Gatland*).

10.63 The employer may also take steps to recover the amount of the bribe from the employee, and refuse to pay certain benefits which may be due (see *Tesco Stores Ltd v Pook*, para 10.89).

10.64 The rule is easy to state, but in practice it may be hard to apply, for there is no simple line between acts which are part of social or business intercourse and bribery. No one is going to quibble if a salesman offers a cigarette to the firm's buyer, or if two people go for a working lunch at a modest cafeteria. A hundred cigarettes or a slap-up lunch at an expensive restaurant may fall into a different category. Some firms may anticipate this problem by laying down the standards of conduct expected from those in a position of authority who may be affected by the rule. Employees may be warned not to accept gifts from suppliers, not to accept hospitality which might have a significant value, or to allow others to pay travel or hotel bills on their behalf.

E. Confidential information

10.65 There is a general rule that during the subsistence of the employment relationship, the employee must not disclose any confidential information about the employer's business to an unauthorised person. To do so will amount to a breach of contract, and a third party who induces an employee to break his contract of employment in this way may also be sued (see *Bents Brewery Co Ltd v Hogan*, para 23.37). To determine whether or not the information is indeed confidential, three requirements must be satisfied, namely:

   (a) the information must have the necessary quality of confidence;

   (b) the information must have been imparted to the employee in circumstances which import an obligation of confidence; and

   (c) there must have been an unauthorised use of the information to the detriment of the employer (*A-G v Guardian Newspapers (No 2)*).

10.66 The disclosure of information such as the profitability of the business, new models or designs, modes of operation, etc, could seriously harm the employer's business. Thus in *Foster v Scaffolding (GB) Ltd* the employee gave confidential information to a rival company which was to the disadvantage of his employer, and he was held to have been fairly dismissed. The unauthorised disclosure of trade secrets would also fall within this rule (*Lancashire Fires Ltd v S A Lyons & Co Ltd*), and indeed information may well be so highly confidential as to amount to a trade secret (*PSM International plc v Whitehouse*). But an employee's skill and knowledge are his own possessions, and are not subject to any such restrictions (*Printers and Finishers Ltd v Holloway*).

10.67 It has been held that the employee is not released from this obligation even when the information has been obtained or published by a third party (*Cranleigh Precision Engineering Ltd v Bryant*) although it seems likely that in such circumstances the quality of confidence has been lost (*A-G v Guardian Newspapers (No 2)*).

10.68 If an employer discovers that an unidentifiable employee is leaking information to the press, he may be able to obtain a court order which will lead him to identify the person concerned (generally known as a 'whistleblower'). Clearly, there is a conflict between the public interest which requires that the press shall protect the identity of its sources and the right of an employer to identify a disloyal employee, particularly when it is likely that that employee may disclose other sensitive information. In *Camelot Group plc v Centaur*

Communications Ltd the Court of Appeal set out certain principles which should be applied in such cases, but stressed that the resolution of such conflicts will very much depend on the facts of each case, ie the nature of the information disclosed, whether there is an allegation of wrongdoing, whether the information would eventually be in the public domain, etc. The law does not enable the press to protect the identity of a whistleblower in all circumstances.

10.69 However, there are some important exceptions to the rule against the non-disclosure of confidential information. Thus the rule will not apply if the employee is obliged by law to disclose the information. For example, an employee is under a legal duty to give any necessary information to an inspector carrying out an examination or investigation under the Health and Safety at Work etc Act 1974 (see Chapter 11) and to produce any necessary books or documents.

F. Public interest disclosures (ERA, ss 43A–43K)

10.70 Under the provisions of the Public Interest Disclosure Act 1998 (generally known as the 'Whistleblowers Act'), which inserted ss 43A–43L into the Employment Rights Act, protection is given to a worker (a definition which is wider than that of 'employee', and indeed is wider than the definition of 'worker' contained in s 230(3), see ERA, s 43K), who makes a protected disclosure to a specified individual in prescribed circumstances. The primary aim of the Act is to encourage the resolution of concerns through proper workplace procedures, and has a more limited application to a worker who decides to go outside those procedures.

10.71 There are three conditions to be satisfied for the Act to apply, namely (i) there must be a qualifying disclosure, (ii) the qualifying disclosure must be a protected disclosure, and (iii) the worker must have been dismissed or suffered a detriment in consequence of the disclosure.

10.72 (i) A qualifying disclosure must be one of the six categories of subject matter specified in ERA, s 43B, namely, any disclosure of information which, in the reasonable belief of the worker making it, tends to show one or more of the following:

(a) that a criminal offence has been committed, is being committed or is likely to be committed;

(b) that a person has failed, is failing or is likely to fail to comply with any legal obligation to which he is subject (*Parkins v Sodexho Ltd*);

(c) that a miscarriage of justice has occurred, is occurring or is likely to occur;

(d) that the health or safety of any individual has been, is being or is likely to be endangered;

(e) that the environment has been, is being or is likely to be damaged; or

(f) that information tending to show any matter falling within any one of the preceding paragraphs has been, is being or is likely to be deliberately concealed.

10.73 The standard to be used when considering the above categories is the subjective one, ie the worker does not have to prove the existence of any of the above state of affairs; he merely has to show that he had a reasonable belief that this was so. Clearly, if he fails to show that he had grounds for his belief, it may well be that a tribunal would find that his belief was not reasonable.

10.74 A disclosure will not be a qualifying disclosure if the worker commits an offence by making it (eg in breach of the Official Secrets Acts), or if the information is covered by legal professional privilege. However, the substance of the disclosure can relate to matters which take place anywhere in the world.

10.75 (ii) A qualifying disclosure will be a protected disclosure if it is made in one of the six ways set out in the Act. In other words, the disclosure must be made through the appropriate channels, set out in ss 43C–43H. Four of these categories are to named persons, while the further two categories are subject to more stringent conditions.

10.76 The disclosure must be made to one of the following persons:

(a) in good faith to his employer, or, where the worker reasonably believes that the relevant failure relates solely or mainly to the conduct of a person other than his employer, or any other matter for which a person other than the employer has legal responsibility, to that other person;

(b) in the course of obtaining legal advice (eg to a solicitor);

(c) where the worker's employer is an individual appointed under any enactment by a minister of the Crown, or a body any of whose members are so appointed, a disclosure made in good faith to a minister of the Crown;

(d) a disclosure in good faith to a prescribed person, and the worker reasonably believes that the relevant failure falls within the prescribed category, and the information disclosed, and any allegation made, is substantially true. The Public Interest Disclosure (Prescribed Persons) Order 1999 described the persons (and bodies) to which disclosure may be made for this purpose, and also described the matters in respect of which disclosure may be made. There are some 38 types of bodies so prescribed, including various regulatory bodies, local authorities, etc, and the matters which are the subject of a protected disclosure are generally those matters in which there is a serious public interest;

(e) in other cases, a disclosure must be made in good faith, the worker must reasonably believe that the information disclosed, and any allegation contained in it, are substantially true, the disclosure is not made for personal gain, in the circumstances it was reasonable for him to make the disclosure, and it meets one of the following conditions, namely:

(i) that at the time he makes the disclosure, the worker reasonably believed that he would be subject to a detriment if he made the disclosure to his employer or to the prescribed person, or

(ii) where there is no person prescribed, the worker reasonably believes that evidence relating to the relevant failure will be concealed or destroyed if he makes the disclosure to his employer, or

(iii) the worker has previously made a disclosure to his employer or to a prescribed person of substantially the same information.

10.77 To decide whether or not it was reasonable for the worker to make the disclosure, the Act states that regard should be had to the identity of the person to whom the disclosure is made, the seriousness of the relevant failure, whether the failure is continuing or likely to occur in the future, whether the disclosure is made in breach of any duty of confidentiality owed by the employer to any other person, any action which the employer has taken which might reasonably be expected to have been taken as a result of a previous disclosure, and whether in making the disclosure to the employer the worker has complied with any procedure whose use by him was authorised by the employer;

    (f) a disclosure will be protected if:
        (i)   it is made in good faith,
        (ii) the worker reasonably believes that the information disclosed, and any allegation made in it, are substantially true,
        (iii) the disclosure is not made for personal gain,
        (iv) the matter disclosed is of an exceptional serious nature, and
        (v) in all the circumstances, it was reasonable for the worker to make the disclosure.

10.78 For a whistleblower to obtain protection of the Act, it is not sufficient to show that he spoke the truth. His motives for making the disclosure are also relevant. Thus, if he makes a disclosure because of some personal antagonism, or other improper motive, this will be evidence of a lack of good faith, and he will lose the protection (*Street v Derbyshire Unemployed Workers' Centre*).

10.79 (iii) A worker who makes a protected disclosure has the right not to suffer a detriment as a result of the disclosure. If he is an employee, he has the right not to be dismissed (or be made redundant) in consequence of the disclosure. It will also be automatically unfair to dismiss an employee because he made a protected disclosure prior to the coming into force of the Public Interest Disclosure Act (*Miklaszewicz v Stolt Offshore Ltd*). The one-year qualifying period of employment does not apply, there is no upper age limit, and there is no ceiling on any compensation award. Interim relief is also available (ERA, s 128(1)(b)). If the worker is not an employee, he will have no right to complain of unfair dismissal, but if he is in fact dismissed, he can claim that this amounts to a detriment.

10.80 Any agreement between the worker and his employer (including one which purports to settle legal proceedings) is void in so far as it precludes the worker from making a protected disclosure (s 43J).

G. Patents, inventions and copyright

10.81 The law relating to inventions made and patents taken out by employees has been altered drastically as a result of the Patents Act 1977. According to s 39, an invention made by an employee shall belong to the employer if (a) it was made during the employee's normal duties, or if such duties were specifically assigned to him and in either case the circumstances were such that an invention might reasonably be expected to result from those duties, or (b) because of the employee's particular responsibilities, he has a special obligation to further the interests of the employer's undertaking. Any other invention made by an employee shall belong to him, notwithstanding any term to the contrary in the contract of employment (see *Reiss Engineering Co Ltd v Harris*). Even if the invention belongs to the employer, the employee may apply to the Comptroller General of Patents (or Patents Court) for an award of compensation, which may be awarded if the patent is of outstanding benefit to the employer (having regard to the size and nature of the employer's undertaking) and it is just that compensation should be awarded. The amount of compensation should be a fair share of the benefit which the employer has derived, taking into account a number of factors, including (a) the nature of the employee's duties, his remuneration, etc, (b) the effort and skill provided by others, including any advice and assistance received from other employees, (c) the contribution made by the employer, whether by way of assisting in the manufacture, marketing, or other contribution.

10.82 If the invention belongs to the employee, he is free to dispose of it as he wishes. If he assigns his interest to his employer (whether by way of an assignment in the right to a patent, or a licensing arrangement, etc), then he is still entitled to apply for an award of statutory compensation, if he can show that the financial return he has received is inadequate in relation to the benefit derived from the patent by the employer, and it is just that compensation should be paid in addition to the benefit received from the relevant contractual arrangement between the parties. Such compensation will amount to a fair share of the benefit which the employer has derived from the assignment or licence, taking into account, inter alia: (a) any condition granted in respect of the licence or the patent, (b) the extent to which the invention was made jointly by the employee and any other person, and (c) the contribution made by the employer in the making, developing, manufacturing and marketing of the invention.

10.83 However, an award of compensation cannot be made if there is in force a relevant collective agreement which provides for payment of compensation for inventions made by employees. The collective agreement is only relevant if it is made by a trade union to which the employee belongs and by the employer, or an employers' association to which the employer belongs, which is in force at the time of the making of the invention. Non-unionists, therefore, may apply for compensation under the Act.

10.84 By the Copyright, Designs and Patents Act 1988, if the maker of a written work is employed under a contract of employment, the employer becomes the first owner of the copyright (s 11). This rule extends to literary, dramatic, musical or artistic works, but it is subject to any agreement to the contrary. There are no provisions in this Act for employee compensation on the lines of the Patents Act 1977.

H. 'Moonlighting'

10.85 The employee is obliged not to act in any manner which is inconsistent with his duty of fidelity. In *Gibson v National Union of Dyers, Bleachers and Textile Workers* a full-time trade union official worked in a mill during his holidays. There was clearly a conflict of interests between his union position and his spare-time employment, and his dismissal was only held to be unfair because of the manner in which it was done. Indeed, the modern practice of 'moonlighting' whereby an employee undertakes spare-time work outside his employment hours can raise problems, particularly if the work is in competition with the employer's business. In *Gray v C & P Pembroke Ltd* the employee agreed not to be engaged in any other business without the written consent of his employer. Contrary to this agreement, he took a part-time job with a rival employer. As well as being in breach of an express term of his contract, it was also a breach of fidelity, and his dismissal was held to be fair. On the other hand in *Frame v McKean & Graham Ltd* the National Working

Agreement for the Building Industry provided that no operative should undertake any jobbing work on his own account. This had never been enforced or referred to by the employer, and there was no mention of it in his contract of employment. The tribunal held that his dismissal for doing some work for a former customer of the firm was unfair, but the decision seems to rely heavily on the fact that the employer had, in the past, condoned his employees doing spare-time work, and even allowed them to purchase materials for this purpose.

10.86 In the absence of any contractual term, it appears that the employee may not work for a competitor in his spare time. In *Hivac Ltd v Park Royal Scientific Instruments Ltd* an injunction was granted against the competitor restraining him from employing the claimant's employees who were making valves for him in their spare time. On the other hand, an employee cannot be restrained from working in a different business in his spare time which does not compete with his employer's business, provided, of course, that this does not interfere with his normal work.

10.87 An employee cannot undertake work for himself or for other persons during his working hours (*Wessex Dairies v Smith*) nor can he use his employer's materials or equipment for his own purposes (ignoring matters which come within the *de minimis* rule). Thus if he uses the employer's facilities or equipment, or profits from work done by other employees under his supervision, this would amount to a breach of the duty of fidelity, and the employer would be entitled to an account of those profits (*University of Nottingham v Fishel*).

I. Duty of disclosure

10.88 An employee is under no duty to disclose to his employer facts which are inimical to the employer (except in response to a direct question), nor to disclose his own misconduct (*Bell v Lever Bros Ltd*). However, if the employee acts fraudulently or dishonestly, particularly when acting on the employer's behalf in circumstances when trust and confidence is being reposed in him, then he is under a duty to disclose his own misconduct, and may be sued by the employer for any loss suffered as a direct result of that misconduct (*Item Software (UK) Ltd v Fassihi*). Also, he is under a duty to disclose the misconduct of his subordinates even if, by doing so, he incriminates himself. In *Sybron Corpn v Rochem Ltd*, a man called Roques was the European manager for Gamblem Chemical Co (UK) Ltd. During his employment, payments were made on his behalf by the company into a pension scheme, and on his retirement he received a lump sum payment. It was then discovered that Roques, together with several subordinates, had been conspiring to set up in direct competition with Gamblem, and the company sought restitution of the pension payments, claiming that under the rules of the pension scheme, Roques could have been dismissed for gross misconduct, and the payments would not have been made. The Court of Appeal held that the company was entitled to have the money repaid. As a senior executive, Roques was under a duty to report the continuing misconduct of his subordinates, and for this breach of duty he could have been dismissed summarily. The money was therefore paid under a mistake of fact, since, had Gamblem known about the breach, they could have invoked the rules of the pension fund.

10.89 An employee who takes a bribe or receives a secret commission is in breach of his duty of fidelity. The employer can recover the amount from the employee. Further, the employer would be entitled to refuse to pay certain benefits to the employee who is consequently dismissed because of taking a bribe, because there is an implied term in the contract of employment that such a breach would disentitle the employee to receive such benefits (eg share options) (*Tesco Stores Ltd v Pook*). The effect of this case and *Rochem*, is to weaken the principle established in *Bell v Lever*.

10.90 A major problem will arise if an employee discovered a fraud or criminal offence being perpetrated within his employer's organisation. Should he report it and, if so, to whom? The police? The employer's lawyers? Senior management? Is there a duty of confidentiality which prevents reporting the fraud to persons outside the organisation, and is reporting a breach of confidence? Would the fear of job prospects being damaged be sufficient to amount to a defence in civil and/or criminal proceedings? Some answers to these questions were given in *RGB Resources plc v Rastogi*, where a certified accountant was employed as a financial controller. The chief executive officer of the company and two other senior employees were implicated in the misappropriation of hundreds of millions of pounds of loan capital, and the company's liquidator took action against the directors and the financial controller for recovery of the money. For the liquidator, it was argued that as a senior executive, the defendant was under a duty to make enquiries about suspicious conduct of the other directors, and should have taken steps to prevent dishonest activities. Further, he should have disclosed these irregularities both internally and externally, but had failed to do so. It was held that the liquidator was entitled to recovery from the defendant. A senior employee is under a duty to investigate wrongdoings and, where appropriate, to make a full disclosure to internal auditors, the board of directors, or, if necessary, the police or financial watchdog. The precise course of action will have to vary in each case, but the more senior the employee, the more serious the conduct in question, and the more serious the adverse effect on the employer's business is likely to be, the greater will be the duty to report and make a full disclosure to the proper person or authority.

10.91 The obligations of an employee who leaves the employment, or who is about to leave, will be considered in Chapter 19.

Employer's vicarious liability

10.92 If an employee commits a wrongful (ie tortious) act in the course of his employment which causes injury or damage to a third party, the employee will, of course, be personally liable. In addition, however, the employer may be vicariously liable to compensate that third party. Two reasons are usually adduced for this principle. The first is that the employer, having initiated or created the situation where the employee has been in a position to cause the harm, should properly bear the loss; the second is the more practical reason that the employee will usually be unable to meet any substantial claim for damages, whereas the employer will normally have the financial resources to do so, or, at least, will be insured against such contingencies.

10.93 There are also a number of exceptional circumstances where an employer will be liable for the tortious acts of his independent contractors; for example, if he authorises the wrongful act, or where he has a responsibility to take care which cannot be delegated by employing someone else to do the work, eg if there is a hazardous task to be undertaken (see *Holliday v National Telephone Co*). It is also true that in recent years the courts appear to be gradually extending this principle of legal liability, and to that extent the distinction between an independent contractor and an employee (discussed in Chapter 2) is becoming possibly less important than before. But the general rule remains as stated.

10.94 The major problem is to determine which acts are committed by the employee 'in the course of his employment', and there are a number of marginal situations which cause difficulty. It is clear that if the employer expressly authorises the wrongful act, he will be liable. Equally the employer will be liable if he authorises the act, and the employee performs it in a wrongful manner, for this is the very essence of the legal principle under discussion. If the employer expressly forbids the act, he may still be vicariously liable if it can be shown that nonetheless the act was done in the scope of the employment, or for the purposes of the employer's business. In *Conway v George Wimpey & Co Ltd* the employers issued instructions to their drivers that no person other than a fellow employee was permitted to ride as a passenger in their lorries. In breach of these instructions, a driver gave a lift to a non-employee, and the passenger was injured as a result of an accident. It was held that the employers were not liable, for the express prohibition had taken the act (of giving lifts) outside the scope of the employment. But in *Rose v Plenty* the employers had made it clear that children were not allowed to travel on milk floats. In breach of this instruction, a milkman engaged a young boy to help him deliver and collect milk bottles, and as a result of negligent driving the boy was injured. The Court of Appeal held that the employers were nonetheless liable vicariously. The Court distinguished cases like *Conway v George Wimpey & Co Ltd* on the ground that in the latter case, employees who disregarded instructions by giving lifts to unauthorised persons were acting outside the scope of their employment, because what they did was not for the purpose of the employers' business. In *Rose v Plenty*, the act (of giving a lift to an unauthorised person), although prohibited, was done for the purpose of the employers' business and hence was within the scope of the employment.

10.95 The modern test is to concentrate on the closeness of the connection between the nature of the employment and the employee's wrongdoing (*Lister v Hesley Hall Ltd*). The idea of defining 'in the course of employment' by reference to an unauthorised or wrongful mode of doing an act authorised by the employer does not cope ideally with vicarious liability for intentional wrongdoing. Thus in *Fennelly v Connex South Eastern Ltd* a ticket inspector assaulted a railway passenger following an argument. It was held that the act was committed in the course of employment. The courts should look at the job in general terms, and not divide each step and task performed into categories and ask whether each was authorised.

10.96 If the employers permit the act, they cannot escape liability by prohibiting it from being done in a wrongful manner. In *Canadian Pacific Rly Co v Lockhart*, the employers issued instructions that staff should not drive uninsured cars while on company business. One of their employees disregarded this prohibition, and through negligent driving, injured the claimant. The employers were held to be vicariously liable. It was not the driving which was prohibited, and the prohibition merely limited the way in which the employee was to do his work. The same principle applies if the employee negligently performs his duties. In *Century Insurance Co Ltd v Northern Ireland Road Transport Board*, a driver of a petrol lorry, whilst transferring petrol from his lorry to an underground storage tank at a garage, struck a match in order to light a cigarette. He then threw the match on the floor, and an explosion ensued. It was held that the employers were liable. He was doing that which he was employed to do, namely, deliver petrol, although he was negligent in the manner in which he was performing his work.

10.97 The fact that the employee is seeking to obtain a personal gain will not necessarily take his acts outside the course of his employment. In *Lloyd v Grace, Smith & Co* a managing clerk of a firm of solicitors induced the claimant, a client of the firm, to sign some documents, which transferred the claimant's properties to him. The firm was held liable, even though they stood to obtain no personal gain from the wrongful act. The clerk was merely performing the class of duties for which he was employed. This principle was taken further in *Morris v CW Martin & Sons Ltd* where the claimant took a fur to a furrier for cleaning. This was stolen by an employee whose duty it was to do the work, and the employers were held liable.

10.98 For the purpose of vicarious liability, an employer may be a 'deemed temporary employer'. In *Hawley v Luminar Leisure Ltd* the claimant was visiting a nightclub when he was seriously injured by a doorman. The doorman was not employed by the nightclub, but by a security company to whom the nightclub had subcontracted its security. It was held that the nightclub exercised sufficient practical control over the doorman to make it the deemed temporary employer for the purpose of vicarious liability. The doorman was subject to the nightclub's code of conduct, was generally supervised by the nightclub manager, and given detailed instructions on where he should be stationed, who should be admitted, and what to do with troublesome customers.

11

Health and Safety at Work

Health and Safety at Work, etc Act 1974

A. Background to the legislation

11.1 As a result of the recommendations of the Robens Committee, the Health and Safety at Work etc Act 1974 was passed. In considering the then existing laws and practices relating to health and safety, the Committee came to a number of interesting conclusions. It found that in fact there was too much law, that much of it was unsatisfactory and unintelligible, and there was overlapping jurisdiction between those bodies whose task it was to enforce the law. The result of this was that there was a general feeling of apathy in the day-to-day implementation of safety rules, and little interest was shown in the subject. The new Act thus lays down the general legal obligations of all concerned in a single enactment, with the enforcement under the control of a unified administration. The old law (Factories Act 1961, Offices, Shops and Railway Premises Act 1963, etc) has been progressively repealed and replaced by regulations and approved codes of practice which are designed to maintain and improve the standards of health, safety and welfare.

11.2 Several fundamental changes were brought about by the new legislation. In the first place, the Act applies to people, not to premises. It covers all employed persons (with the exception of domestic workers), wherever they work, thus bringing within the orbit of safety legislation an additional 7,000,000 employees who were hitherto outside the protection of statutory rules. In addition, the Health and Safety (Training for Employment) Regulations 1990 apply the provisions of the Act to trainees on government sponsored training schemes as if they were employees. The Act also applies to people who are not employees, in so far as they may be affected by activities which are being carried on in places of work.

11.3 The Act applies to all employment situations, including (with appropriate modifications) to offshore installations and pipelines within UK territorial waters and areas designated under the Continental Shelf Act 1964, including construction work and diving activities. The Police (Health and Safety) Act 1997 applies the provisions of the Act to holders of the office of constable, even though they are not technically employees (Police (Health and Safety) Regulations 1999).

11.4 Next, it will be noted that obligations are placed on employers in their different capacities as manufacturers, suppliers, and importers of articles and substances to be used at work, to ensure that these can be used in safety and without risk to health. Health and safety has to be built into the design and manufacturing stages.

11.5 The emphasis of the Act is on criminal sanctions and enforcement of the law by new techniques, for the Act itself (unlike regulations made under the Act) does not give rise to questions of civil liability. The inspectorate appears to be using their powers of prosecution at the rate of 2,000 per year, which is small compared with the number of offences revealed by inspections, for the emphasis is on co-operation rather than compulsion. In addition, however, the new powers of issuing improvement and prohibition notices have been widely exercised, and these are proving to have very dramatic effects. Currently, about 12,000 such notices are issued each year.

11.6 Finally, there are a number of provisions designed to bring about a greater awareness by all concerned of the need to promote safety and health at work, and thus provide the impetus to the greater self-regulatory system which the Robens Committee thought to be desirable.

11.7 Some amendments to the Act have been made by the Consumer Protection Act 1987 (Sch 3). The Act now applies to fairground equipment and micro-organisms. Customs officers may detain articles and substances for the purpose of enabling enforcing officers to perform their duties, and s 6 of the Act (see para 11.49) was significantly improved.

11.8 We can examine the provisions of the Act under five headings.

B. Enforcement of the Act

11.9 The overall responsibility for supervising and administering the law on health and safety lies with the Health and Safety Commission (HSC), although the enforcement of the Act is the responsibility of the Health and Safety Executive (HSE) and enforcement officers (usually designated Environmental Health Officers) of local authorities, to whom there has been a transfer of authority in respect of certain specified types of premises (Health and Safety (Enforcing Authority) Regulations 1998). Neither the Secretary of State nor the HSC can instruct an enforcing authority to enforce any particular provision or institute proceedings in any particular case.

Powers of inspectors

11.10 All enforcing authorities will appoint inspectors, who will have the following powers, for the purpose of giving effect to the relevant statutory provisions:

(a) at any reasonable time, or, if there is a dangerous situation at any time, to enter premises;

(b) to take with him a constable if he has reasonable cause to apprehend any serious obstruction in the execution of his duty;

(c) to take with him any other authorised person and any equipment or materials required for any purpose for which the power of entry is being exercised;

(d) to make such examination and investigation as may be necessary;

(e) to direct that any premises shall be left undisturbed so long as is reasonably necessary for the purpose of examination or investigation;

(f) to take such measures and photographs and make such recordings as he considers necessary;

(g) to take samples of any articles or substances found in any premises and of the atmosphere in, or in the vicinity of, such premises. The Secretary of State may make regulations concerning the procedure to be adopted in such cases;

(h) in the case of any article or substance likely to cause danger to health or safety, to cause it to be dismantled or subjected to any process or test, but not to damage or destroy it unless it is for the purpose of exercising his powers. If the person who has responsibilities in relation to those premises is present, and so requests, the inspector shall exercise this power in that person's presence, unless he considers that it would be prejudicial to the safety of the state to do so. In any case, before exercising these powers, he must consult with appropriate persons for the purpose of ascertaining what dangers, if any, there may be in doing what he proposes to do;

(i) in the case of any article or substance likely to cause danger to health or safety, to take possession of it, and detain it for so long as is necessary in order to examine it, to ensure it is not tampered with before he has completed his examination, and to ensure that it is available for use as evidence in any proceedings for an offence, or in respect of matters arising out of the issuing of an improvement notice or a prohibition notice. He must leave a notice giving particulars of the article or substance, stating that he has taken possession of it, and, if practicable to do so, leave a sample with a responsible person;

(j) if conducting an examination or investigation under (d) above, to require any person whom he has reasonable cause to believe to be able to give any information to answer such questions as the inspector thinks fit to ask, and to sign a declaration of the truth of his answers;

(k) to require the production of, inspect, and take copies of any entry in, any books or documents which are required to be kept, and any other book or document which it is necessary for him to see for the purpose of any examination or investigation under (d), above;

(l) to require any person to afford him such facilities and assistance within that person's control or responsibilities, as are necessary for him to exercise his powers;

(m) any other power which is necessary for the purpose of exercising any of the above powers.

Improvement notices (s 21)

11.11 If an inspector is of the opinion that a person is contravening one or more relevant statutory provisions, or has done so and the contravention is likely to be continued or repeated, he may serve on him an improvement notice, stating that opinion, specifying the relevant statutory provision, giving reasons why he is of that opinion, and requiring that person to remedy the contravention within such period as may be specified in the notice, but not less than 21 days (ie the period in which an appeal may be made – see below).

Prohibition notices (s 22)

11.12 In respect of any activity covered by a relevant statutory provision, if the inspector thinks that those activities are carried on or are likely to be carried on so as to involve a risk of serious personal injury, the inspector may serve a prohibition notice. This will state his opinion, specify the provisions which give rise to that opinion, and direct that the activities to which the notice relates shall not be carried on by or under the control of that person on whom the notice was served unless the matters specified and any associated contravention are remedied. This direction takes effect at the end of the period specified in the notice or, if the notice so declares, immediately. Prohibition notices can be issued on persons, eg for a failure to wear protective eye shields. Activities are being carried on for the purpose of s 22 even though they are temporarily suspended (eg because of an accident). If there is a possibility that the activities may be resumed, the inspector is entitled to issue a prohibition notice requiring remedial action prior to the recommencement of those activities (*RailTrack plc v Smallwood*).

11.13 In the case of an improvement notice or a prohibition notice, the notice may (but need not) include directions as to the measure to be taken to remedy the contravention, which may be by reference to any approved code of practice or afford a choice between different ways of remedying the contravention. However, in respect of an improvement notice relating to a building, this cannot impose more onerous requirements than those imposed by the building regulations unless there is a statutory provision to the contrary. Also, if the notice relates to the means of escape in the event of fire, the inspector must engage in prior consultations with the fire authorities. Any improvement notice or a deferred prohibition notice may be withdrawn by the inspector before the expiry of 21 days, and may also be extended by the inspector at any time when an appeal is not pending.

Appeals against improvement or prohibition notices (s 24)

11.14 An appeal from the imposition of an improvement notice or a prohibition notice may be made to the employment tribunal, which can cancel or affirm it, or affirm it with such modifications as the tribunal thinks fit. For the purpose of hearing such appeals, the tribunal may include assessors specially appointed to sit with the regular members. Once an appeal has been lodged, this will suspend the operation of the improvement notice until such time as the appeal is disposed of or withdrawn; in the case of a prohibition notice, however, the lodging of an appeal will only suspend it if the tribunal so directs, and then only from the time it does so direct.

11.15 An appeal against an improvement notice or a prohibition notice can be made on a number of grounds.

11.16 First, it could be argued that there is no breach of a statutory duty. To determine this, a tribunal may refer to any relevant code of practice and guidance note. In *Sutton & Co Ltd v Davies* the employers were in breach of s 13 of the Factories Act 1961 in not guarding transmission machinery. They appealed against an improvement notice, arguing that they had operated for 27 years without an accident. The appeal was dismissed, for the requirements of the Act are absolute. But in *Brewer & Sons v Dunston* the inspector issued a prohibition notice on a machine. No accident had occurred in 18 years of use, and the tribunal held that there was no evidence to support the contention that there was risk of imminent danger. The distinction is that for an improvement notice, the sole issue is whether or not there has been a breach of a statutory provision, whereas a prohibition notice is concerned with whether there is a risk of serious personal injury.

11.17 Secondly, an appeal may be against the time limit imposed for remedying the defect, and there the tribunal may consider any serious embarrassment which may be caused to the company, and may take into account any history of recorded accidents at the firm. A company with a good record may well be given an extension of time so as to maintain production, so long as there is no immediate risk of danger or injury, and there is a willingness to make the appropriate modifications.

11.18 A third ground for appeal may be based on the absence of any risk or danger. In *South Surbiton Co-operative Society v Wilcox*, a cracked washbasin was made the subject of an improvement notice. It was argued that the breach was trivial, there was little risk to health, and that there must be many employers who are similarly in breach and who have not been served with improvement notices. Nonetheless, the notice was confirmed by the tribunal. The requirements of the Act were absolute.

11.19 But in *Associated Dairies Ltd v Hartley*, an improvement notice required the company to issue safety shoes free of charge to employees. In the previous year, one employee had been injured when the wheel of a truck ran over his foot. The company employed 1,000 employees, with a high turnover. Free footwear would have cost £20,000 in the first year. The tribunal held that the expense of providing protective footwear was disproportionate to the risk, and the notice was cancelled. In this case, the Act only required the employer to do that which was reasonably practicable.

11.20 A final ground for appeal may be based on the financial inability of the employer to comply with the order. Such an appeal is doomed from the start. In *TC Harrison (Newcastle-under-Lyme) Ltd v Ramsey*, the company appealed against an improvement notice which required them to paint and clean the walls of the factory, in accordance with s 1 of the Factories Act 1961. It was stated that their financial position was precarious due to difficult trading conditions, but the employment tribunal had no hesitation in confirming the notice. To do otherwise would be to allow a firm to keep its charges low so as to undercut competitors, thus obtaining an unfair advantage over those who complied with the legal requirements. An employer cannot be relieved of his statutory duties because of financial difficulties.

11.21 Unlike other proceedings before employment tribunals, appeals against improvement and prohibition notices may result in an order for costs being made against the unsuccessful party. Such an order is entirely at the discretion of the tribunal, who may take into account the conduct of the party in failing to remedy the breach, and the hopelessness or otherwise of the appeal (see Employment Tribunals (Constitution and Rules of Procedure) Regulations 2004, Sch 4). In *South Surbiton Co-operative Society v Wilcox* (above) no order for costs was made, as the tribunal considered that the breach was trivial.

11.22 A failure to observe the requirements of a prohibition or improvement notice is a criminal offence, and it is no defence in criminal proceedings to argue that the employer has done all that is reasonably practicable to comply. The proper forum in which to argue questions of practicability is the employment tribunal (*Deary v Mansion Hide Upholstery Ltd*).

11.23 An appeal against a decision of an employment tribunal relating to a prohibition or improvement notice must be made to the Divisional Court. The reason is that the failure to comply with such notices is a criminal offence and the EAT, which would normally hear appeals from employment tribunals, is only concerned with civil matters.

Crown notices

11.24 Because there is a rule of law that the Queen cannot be prosecuted in her own courts, it is not possible to enforce prohibition and improvement notices against Crown organisations, even though they employ large numbers of employees in various government departments. Consequently, the HSE devised the Crown Notice, which will be issued when a prohibition or improvement notice would be appropriate. Such notices have only a moral sanction, but are designed to draw attention to potential hazards, and, as copies are to be given to employees' representatives, will naturally attract publicity. About 40 such notices were issued annually. So far as the health service is concerned, a health authority is no longer to be regarded as a servant or agent of the Crown for the purpose of health and safety legislation (see National Health Service and Community Care Act 1990, s 60). Thus the normal prohibition and improvement notices can be served on these bodies, and they may also be prosecuted for offences.

Power to deal with imminent danger (s 25)

11.25 If the inspector finds on any premises any article or substance which he has reasonable cause to believe is a cause of imminent danger of serious personal injury, he may seize it and cause it to be rendered harmless whether by destruction or otherwise. Before doing so, if it is practicable for him to do so, he will give a sample with an identifiable mark to a responsible person. Thereafter, he will prepare and sign a report giving particulars of the circumstances, and give a copy to a responsible person at those premises, and also to the owner.

Enforcement powers of the court (s 42)

11.26 Where a person is convicted of an offence under any relevant statutory provision, the court may, in addition to, or instead of, imposing any punishment, order him to take such steps as may be specified in the order to remedy the matters specified, within such time as may be fixed. Failure to do so may amount to contempt of court, but an application may be made for an extension of the time limit. During the period given to remedy matters, the person cannot be liable for a failure to observe the provisions. After that time, if he continues with the contravention, he can be sentenced to six months' imprisonment and/or fined up to £20,000 in the magistrates' courts, or up to two years' imprisonment and/or an unlimited fine in the Crown Court.

11.27 If a person is charged with an offence in connection with the acquisition of explosives, the court may order the article or substance in question to be forfeited and either destroyed or dealt with as the court so orders. However, such order cannot be made unless the court gives the owner or any other interested party an opportunity to be heard.

Other matters

11.28 By s 26, if an inspector exceeds his statutory powers the enforcing authority may nonetheless indemnify him against the costs, damages, or expenses incurred if it is satisfied that the inspector acted in the honest belief that the act complained of was within his powers.

11.29 By s 28(8) an inspector is empowered to give information to employed persons (or their representatives) if it is necessary to do so for the purpose of keeping them adequately informed about matters affecting their health, safety or welfare. This may be factual information about the premises or anything going on, or information about action he has taken or is proposing to take. If he does this, he must also give the like information to the employer.

C. Statutory duties on health, safety and welfare

11.30 In general, there are three sets of guiding rules which will govern the operation of the law. The first of these is the general duties laid down in ss 2–9, and which must be observed by the specified persons. The second will be the regulations, which will supplement the law. The third will be the Codes of Practice, issued and approved from time to time. It must be borne in mind that a breach of the general duties laid down in ss 2–9 of the Act is a criminal offence, and does not give rise to civil proceedings (s 47), whereas a breach of the regulations will be actionable civilly unless the regulations themselves provide otherwise. However, by the Civil Evidence Act 1968, s 11 any conviction for a criminal offence is admissible in civil proceedings as evidence that the person so convicted committed the offence, and therefore, a claimant may point to the conviction as being relevant to the issue of civil liability.

11.31 Some of the general duties are absolute ones, which means that the person on whom the duty is placed must carry it out. Others are preceded by the words 'so far as is reasonably practicable'. This is a somewhat lesser standard. The employer must weigh, on the one hand, the time, trouble and expense, etc of meeting that duty against the risks involved and the nature of the obligation on the other hand. Also, the duty can only be performed against the background of current knowledge which the employer knows, or ought to know. However, in *Marshall v Gotham Co Ltd* it was suggested that a precaution which was practicable would not lightly be held to be unreasonable. In other words, a duty or obligation must be performed or carried out unless it would be unreasonable to do so. Further, s 40 of the Act states that in any proceedings for a failure to comply with a duty or requirement, it will be for the accused to prove that it was not reasonably practicable to do more than was in fact done.

Duties of the employer

Duties owed to his employees (s 2)

11.32 It shall be the duty of every employer to ensure, so far as is reasonably practicable, the health, safety and welfare at work of all his employees. In particular, the employer must:

(a) provide and maintain plant and systems of work that are, so far as is reasonably practicable, safe and without risks to health;

(b) make arrangements for ensuring, so far as is reasonably practicable, safety and absence of risks to health in connection with the use, handling, storage and transport of articles and substances (see *Page v Freight Hire (Tank Haulage) Ltd*);

(c) ensure the provision of such information, instruction, training and supervision as is necessary to ensure, so far as is reasonably practicable, the health, safety and welfare at work of his employees. If an employee has a limited command of the English language, there is need for a greater degree of training, instruction and supervision (*Tasci v Pekalp of London Ltd*). The employer must also give such information etc to his employees and to persons who are not his employees (eg to sub-contractors and their employees) if this is necessary to ensure the health and safety of the employees of the employer (*R v Swan Hunter Shipbuilders Ltd*);

(d) so far as is reasonably practicable as regards any place of work under his control, ensure the maintenance of it in a condition that is safe and without risks to health, and the maintenance of means of access and egress from it that are safe and without such risks;

(e) ensure the provision and maintenance of a working environment for his employees that is, so far as is reasonably practicable, safe, without risks to health, and adequate as regards facilities and arrangements for their welfare at work.

11.33 So far as the above duties are concerned, it will be noted that they bear a strong resemblance to the common law duties of care (see para 11.94), spelt out, perhaps, in greater detail. An employer is only responsible for premises over which he has actual control, but that does not absolve him from the duty of ensuring a safe system of work on the premises of another (*General Cleaning Contractors Ltd v Christmas*). The duty to provide a safe working environment would cover noise, fumes, heat, etc; welfare at work is not defined, but would presumably cover washing and toilet facilities, drinking water, and possibly eating arrangements.

Written safety policy (s 2(3))

11.34 Except for employers who employ less than five employees (see *Osborne v Bill Taylor of Huyton Ltd* and Employers' Health and Safety Policy Statements (Exception) Regulations 1975) it shall be the duty of every employer to prepare and revise as often as is appropriate a written statement of his general policy with respect to the health and safety at work of all his employees, and the organisation and arrangements for the time being in force for carrying out that policy, and to bring this statement to the notice of all his employees. The Act does not give any guidance on the contents of this written statement, for the object of the exercise is for each employer to sit down and think about his own safety problems and work out the necessary solutions. Clearly, this would prove to be without value if the employer merely copied out a draft scheme drawn up by someone else.

11.35 It is suggested, however, that the safety policy should at least deal with the responsibility of all employees, including the board of directors, all levels of management, supervisors and operatives, inspection procedures, arrangements for dealing with special hazards, emergency arrangements, including fire drill, the provision and use of safety precautions generally, supervision, training, research and consultative arrangements. In drawing up the safety policy, it may be sound procedure to seek advice from the Commission, the Executive, employers' associations, and to consult with trade union representatives, but it must be stressed that the statement is not a joint consultative document, but one for which the employer has ultimate responsibility. The Act requires the statement to be brought to the notice of all employees, but no guidance is given on how this is to be done. It would clearly not be sufficient to place the statement on the notice board, and hope that work people will read it as they go past, and so the more formal channels of written communication should be used. If it is known that a particular employee does not read English, presumably some other way must be found of bringing it to his notice. The employer is obliged to revise the written statement as often as may be appropriate; it is suggested that the statement should be looked at at least once a year, in the light of practical experience of operating the safety policy, and taking into account any suggestions which might be received.

Safety representatives and safety committee (s 2(4), (6), (7))

11.36 A trade union which is recognised by an employer may appoint safety representatives from among the employees in respect of whom the union is recognised (*Cleveland County Council v Springett*). The persons so appointed need not themselves be members of the union.

11.37 The legal requirements are contained in the Safety Representatives and Safety Committees Regulations 1977 (as amended) and a Code of Practice issued and approved by the Health and Safety Commission. An independent trade union shall notify the employer in writing of the name of the safety representative, who shall hold the appointment until the union terminates it, or he ceases to be employed at the workplace, or resigns. So far as is reasonably practicable, he shall have been employed by that employer for the preceding two years, or have had at least two years' experience in similar employment.

11.38 An employer has a duty to consult with safety representatives over a wide range of issues, with a view to making and maintaining arrangements which will enable him and his employees to co-operate effectively in promoting and developing measures to ensure the health and safety at work of employees, and checking the effectiveness of those measures (s 2(6)). In particular, there shall be consultation about the introduction of measures which may substantially affect the health and safety of employees, the arrangements for appointing or nominating the safety assistant, the provision of health and safety information, the planning and organisation of health and safety training, and the health and safety consequences of the introduction of new technologies (Management of Health and Safety at Work Regulations 1999).

Additionally, the safety representative has the following functions:

(a) to investigate the potential hazards and dangerous occurrences at the workplace, and to examine the causes of accidents;

(b) to investigate complaints by any employee he represents relating to that employee's health, safety, or welfare at work;

(c) to make representations to the employer about the above matters;

(d) to make representations to the employer on general matters affecting the health, safety and welfare at work of the employees at the workplace;

(e) to carry out inspections (see below);

(f) to represent employees in consultations with inspectors of the Health and Safety Executive;

(g) to receive information from the inspectors; and

(h) to attend meetings of safety committees in his capacity as safety representative.

11.39 In order to perform these functions adequately, the employer shall permit the safety representative to have time off work with pay during his working hours, and also for the purpose of undergoing training in aspects of those functions as may be reasonable in the circumstances (see *White v Pressed Steel Fisher*). To determine what is reasonable in the circumstances, regard must be had to HSC's Code of Practice. Factors to be taken into account include the contents of the course and how it relates to the particular health and safety function of the employee, and whether the training would assist him in performing those functions. The test is whether the training is reasonable in all the circumstances, not whether it was necessary (*Duthie v Bath & North East Somerset Council*). The safety representative is entitled to be paid his normal earnings or average hourly earnings. In *Davies v Neath Port Talbot County Borough Council* it was held that a part-time employee, who went on a full-time health and safety training course, was entitled to be paid on the same basis as a full-time male counterpart. The training course was 'work' within the meaning of Art 141 of the Treaty of Rome, and therefore she was entitled to equal pay.

11.40 Safety representatives are entitled to carry out an inspection of the workplace at least every three months (or more frequently with the employer's consent), and also further inspections if there has been some substantial change in the conditions of work (eg by the introduction of new working processes, or the coming to light of new information disclosing a potential hazard). Inspections may also be carried out after a notifiable accident has occurred or a notifiable disease contracted, for the purpose of determining the cause. The employer shall provide reasonable facilities and assistance, but he, or his representative, may be present during the inspection.

11.41 The employer shall establish a safety committee when at least two safety representatives make such a request. For this purpose, he shall consult with these representatives, and also those of any recognised trade unions. A notice must be posted stating the composition of the committee, which must be established within three months of the request being made.

11.42 A complaint may be made to an employment tribunal that the employer has failed to permit a safety representative to have time off work for these purposes, or has failed to pay for such time off. If the complaint is well founded, the tribunal shall make a declaration, and may make an award of compensation.

11.43 There was some doubt as to whether the Safety Representative and Safety Committee Regulations met the requirements of the 'Framework Directive' (89/391/EEC) because there was no means whereby employees in non-unionist firms could have a legal right to play their role in health and safety matters. Consequently, the Health and Safety (Consultation with Employees) Regulations 1996 were introduced. Under these regulations, an employer has two choices with respect to those employees who have no safety representative by virtue of the 1977 regulations. He can either consult with employees directly, or he can consult with one or more persons of any group of employees who were elected for the purposes of consultation, and who are referred to as 'representatives of employee safety'. There is no provision in the regulations as to how an employer shall organise any such elections, but apparently it is not necessary to have a statutory framework for this purpose (*R v Secretary of State for Trade and Industry, ex p UNISON*).

11.44 Under the 1996 regulations, employers must consult with their employees, or their elected representatives of employee safety, in good time, on matters concerning their health and safety at work, and, in particular, with regard to:

(a) the introduction of any measures at the workplace which will substantially affect the health and safety of those employees;

(b) the employer's arrangements for appointing or nominating a competent person to assist him, as required by reg 6(1) and 7(1)(b) of the Management Regulations;

(c) any health and safety information he is required to provide to the employees under any relevant statutory provision;

(d) the planning and organisation of any health and safety training he is required to provide by virtue of any statutory provision; and

(e) the health and safety consequences for the employees of the introduction of new technologies into the workplace (including the planning thereof).

11.45 In such consultations, representatives of employee safety have the following functions:

(a) to make representations to the employer on potential hazards and dangerous occurrences at the workplace, which affect the employees represented;

(b) make representations to the employer on general matters affecting the health and safety of employees, in particular, on matters referred to in paras (a)–(e) above;

(c) represent the group of workers he represents in consultations at the workplace with health and safety inspectors.

11.46 If the employer consults with employees directly, he must make available to them such information as is necessary to enable the employees to participate fully and effectively in the consultation process. If the employer consults with representatives of employee safety, he must make available such information as is necessary to enable them to carry out their functions. But the rights and functions of employee representatives under the 1996 regulations are more limited than those which apply under the 1977 regulations. In particular, they have no right to carry out workplace inspections, attend meetings of a safety committee, inspect statutory health and safety documents, or investigate employees' complaints and notifiable accidents or dangerous occurrences. However, such matters are provided for in the guidance notes which have been issued. An employee safety representative has the right to be paid when carrying out his functions as such, or is being trained.

Duty owed to non-employees (s 3)

11.47 It shall be the duty of every employer, and every self-employed person, to conduct his undertakings in such a way as to ensure, so far as is reasonably practicable, that persons who are not his employees who may be affected thereby are not exposed to risks to their health or safety. This duty applies not only to persons who are lawfully on the employer's premises, for example, students in an educational establishment, but also persons who are outside those premises, but who may be affected by the activities in question. Thus if there is a potential hazard on the employer's premises, he must provide information not only to his own employees, but to visitors and the employees of a sub-contractor who may be working there (*R v Swan Hunter Shipbuilders Ltd*). The employer also has a duty to specialist contractors who come on to the employer's site for the purpose of carrying on activities in respect of the employer's undertaking (*R v Associated Octel*).

Duties of controllers of premises (s 4)

11.48 Every person who has control of premises (not being domestic premises) must ensure, as far as it is reasonable for a person in his position to ensure, that so far as is reasonably practicable, all means of access thereto or egress therefrom, and plant and substance, in the premises, shall be safe and without risks to health in respect of persons who use those premises as a place of work (*Westminster City Council v Select Managements Ltd*). A person who has, by virtue of a contract of tenancy, the obligation to maintain or repair those premises, or be responsible for the safety or absence of risks therein, shall be the person to be regarded as being in control.

Duties of manufacturers, etc (s 6 as amended)

11.49 A duty is imposed on any person who designs, manufacturers, imports or supplies any article for use at work or any article of fairground equipment:

(a) to ensure, as far as reasonably practicable, that the article is so designed and constructed that it will be safe and without risks to health at all times when it is being set, used, cleaned or maintained by a person at work. However, s 6(8) provides that where a person designs, manufactures, imports or supplies an article for use at work or an article of fairground equipment and does so for or to another on the basis of a written undertaking by that other that he will take specified steps to ensure, so far as is reasonably practicable, that the article will be safe and without risks to health at all the above mentioned times, the undertaking will release the designer, manufacturer, importer or supplier (as the case may be) from this duty, to such an extent as is reasonable having regard to the terms of the undertaking. For example, if a person wishes to sell second-hand machinery, it might be advisable to extract a written undertaking from the purchaser to ensure its complete overhaul before putting it to use;

(b) to carry out or arrange for the carrying out of such testing and examination as may be necessary for the performance of the above duty. However, this does not require the repeating of any tests or examinations which may have been carried out by others, in so far as it is reasonable to rely on the results of those others' work;

(c) to take such steps as are necessary to secure that persons supplied by that person with the article are provided with adequate information about the use for which the article has been designed or has been tested, and about any conditions necessary to ensure that it will be safe and without risks to health at all times as are mentioned above, and also when it is being dismantled or disposed of;

(d) to take all such steps as are necessary to secure, so far as is reasonably practicable, that persons so supplied are provided with any revision of the above information by reason of it becoming known that anything gives rise to a serious risk to health or safety.

11.50 Similar obligations are placed upon persons who design, manufacture, import or supply articles of fairground equipment used for or in connection with the entertainment of members of the public.

11.51 There is also a duty on designers and manufacturers (but not importers or suppliers) to carry out or arrange for the carrying out of any necessary research with a view to the discovery and, so far as is reasonably practicable, the elimination or minimisation of any risks to health or safety to which the design or article may give rise, but again, this does not require the repeating of any research already carried out, if it was reasonable to rely on the results.

11.52 It is the duty of any person who erects or installs any article for use at work, or any article of fairground equipment, to ensure, so far as is reasonably practicable, that nothing about the way in which the article is erected, or installed makes it unsafe or a risk to health, when it is being set, used, cleaned or maintained by a person at work.

11.53 A duty is imposed on any person who manufactures, imports or supplies any substance:

(a) to ensure, so far as is reasonably practicable, that the substance will be safe and without risks to health at all times when it is being used, handled, processed, stored or transported by a person at work or in premises to which s 4 (above) applies;

(b) to carry out or arrange for the carrying out of such testing and examination as may be necessary for the performance of the above duty, but again this does not require the repeating of any tests or examinations which have been carried out by others, in so far as it is reasonable to rely on the results of those others' work;

(c) to take such steps as are necessary to secure that persons supplied by that person with the substance are provided with adequate information about any risks to health or safety to which the inherent properties of the substance may give rise, about the results of any relevant tests which have been carried out on or in connection with the substances, and about any conditions necessary to ensure that the substance will be safe and without risks to health at all such times as are mentioned above, and when it is being disposed of;

(d) to take such steps as are necessary to secure, so far as is reasonably practicable, that persons so supplied are provided with all such revisions of information as are necessary by reason of its becoming known that anything gives rise to a serious risk to health or safety.

11.54 A manufacturer of any substance is under a duty to carry out (or arrange for the carrying out of) any necessary research with a view to the discovery and, so far as is reasonably practicable, the elimination or minimisation of any risks to health or safety to which the substance may give rise, but he need not repeat any test, examination or research done by others in so far as it was reasonable for him to rely on the results thereof.

11.55 For the purposes of s 6, an absence of safety or a risk to health is to be disregarded in so far as it has arisen by an occurrence which could not be reasonably foreseen, and so far as the obligations placed on designers, manufacturers, importers and suppliers of articles and substances are concerned, regard may be had to any relevant information which has been provided by them to any person.

11.56 Section 6(7) provides that the above duties only extend to things done in the course of a trade, business or undertaking (whether for profit or not), and to matters within a person's control. The definition of 'article for use at work' (see s 53) is 'any plant designed for use or operation (whether exclusively or not) by persons at work, and any articles designed for use as a component in any such plant', a definition which may be somewhat restrictive. A substance is defined as being 'any natural or artificial substance (including micro-organisms) whether in a solid or liquid form or in the form of gas or vapour'.

11.57 An interesting point arises concerning the effect on civil contracts of the above provisions. Supposing, for example, an employer purchases a machine from a manufacturer, and this is delivered without safety instructions, or in an unguarded state. Could the employer reject the machine on the grounds that it was not fit for its purpose or not of satisfactory quality, contrary to the Sale of Goods Act 1979?

Duty not to charge (s 9)

11.58 An employer shall not charge any employee in respect of anything done or provided in pursuance of any relevant statutory provision (see Personal Protective Equipment at Work Regulations 1992, para 11.80).

Duties of employees

Duties at work (s 7)

11.59 Every employee is under a duty while at work:

  (a) to take reasonable care for the health and safety of himself and of others who may be affected by his acts or omissions at work; this could mean that an employee who failed or refused to wear or use safety precautions which are provided would be in breach of his legal duty;

  (b) as regards any duty imposed on his employer or any other person, to co-operate with him so far as is necessary to enable that duty to be performed or complied with.

Duty not to interfere with safety provisions (s 8)

11.60 No persons shall intentionally or recklessly interfere with or misuse anything provided in the interest of health, safety or welfare in pursuance of any relevant statutory provisions. This duty is wider than the old law, which was directed against 'wilful' conduct, defined as perverse or deliberate action. Intentional or reckless conduct does not need to be wilful.

Rights of employees

Right not to suffer a detriment in health and safety cases (ERA, s 44)

11.61 An employee is entitled not to be subjected to any detriment by an act or a failure to act by his employer on any of the following grounds:

  (a) having been designated by the employer to carry out activities in connection with preventing or reducing risks to health and safety at work, he carried out (or proposed to carry out) those activities;

(b) being a safety representative or member of a safety committee, he performed (or proposed to perform) any functions as such or took part in consultations or in an election as an employee safety representative;

(c) if there is no safety representative or safety committee where he is, or, if there are, it is not reasonably practicable to raise such matters, he brought the employer's attention (by reasonable means) to circumstances connected with his work which he reasonably believed were harmful or potentially harmful to health or safety;

(d) in circumstances of danger which he reasonably believed to be serious and imminent and which he could not reasonably be expected to avert, he left, or proposed to leave, or, while the danger persisted, he refused to return to, his place of work or any dangerous part of his place of work;

(e) in circumstances of danger which he reasonably believed to be serious and imminent, he took, or proposed to take, appropriate steps to protect himself or other persons from the danger. This is to be judged by reference to all the circumstances, including his knowledge, and the facilities and advice available to him at the time. However, he will not have been subjected to a detriment if he was so negligent in the steps he took that the employer treated him as a reasonable employer would have done in those circumstances.

11.62 An employee who believes that he has suffered a detriment contrary to s 44 may bring a complaint before an employment tribunal within the usual time limits. If the complaint is upheld, the tribunal shall make a declaration to that effect, and also award compensation to the complainant, the amount being such as the tribunal considers to be just and equitable in all the circumstances. This will include any expenses incurred and take account of any benefits lost. The employee is expected to mitigate against his loss, and the compensation award can be reduced on the ground of contributory conduct (see para 17.215).

11.63 But if a safety representative acts in respect of matters which are not within the area of the workplace for which he is a representative, or acts outside the laid down procedure, or acts in bad faith, then it may be that he is not pursuing a genuine health and safety matter, but is pursuing a personal agenda in order to embarrass the employer. In such circumstances, he may be disciplined as appropriate (*Shillito v Van Leer (UK) Ltd*).

Right not to be dismissed unfairly in certain circumstances involving health and safety cases (ERA, s 100)

11.64 It will be unfair to dismiss an employee because of any of the following circumstances arising out of health and safety matters:

(a) having been designated by the employer to carry out activities in connection with preventing or reducing risks to health and safety at work, he carried out (or proposed to carry out) those activities. In *Healey v Excel Logistics Ltd* a safety representative went to the site of another company in order to inspect an entry in that company's accident book concerning an accident which involved one of the employees he represented. His subsequent dismissal for doing so was held to be unfair, because his duties as a safety representative were not confined to incidents which took place on his employer's premises;

(b) being a safety representative or member of a safety committee he performed (or proposed to perform) any functions as such, or took part in consultations as an employee safety representative, or in an election of representatives of employee safety;

(c) if there is no safety representative or safety committee where he is, or, if there are, it is not reasonably practicable to raise such matters, he brought the employer's attention (by reasonable means) to circumstances connected with his work which he reasonably believed were harmful or potentially harmful to health or safety. In *Balfour Kilpatrick Ltd v Acheson* it was held that the taking of industrial action was not, in the circumstances, reasonable means whereby employees may bring health and safety concerns to the employer's attention;

(d) in circumstances of danger which he reasonably believed to be serious and imminent and which he could not reasonably be expected to avert, he left, or proposed to leave, or, while the danger persisted, he refused to return to, his place of work or any dangerous part of his place of work. In *Harvest Press Ltd v McCaffrey* an employee left work because he felt he was in danger of being injured due to the behaviour of another employee towards him, who had been abusive and aggressive. His dismissal for leaving work was held to be unfair, for s 100(1)(d) was not confined to circumstances of danger which arose from working methods or equipment;

(e) in circumstances of danger which he reasonably believed to be serious and imminent, he took, or proposed to take, appropriate steps to protect himself or other persons from the danger. This is to be judged by reference to all the circumstances, including his knowledge, and the facilities and advice available to him at the time. The term 'other persons' includes members of the public, as well as fellow employees, so that a chef who was dismissed because he refused to cook food which he believed to be unfit for human consumption succeeded in a claim for unfair dismissal under s 100 (*Masiak v City Restaurants (UK) Ltd*). However, his dismissal shall not be regarded as being unfair if he was so negligent in the steps he took that the employer treated him as a reasonable employer would have treated him in those circumstances.

11.65 It should be noted that if a dismissal is unfair by virtue of (a) or (b) above, and the employer refuses to reinstate or re-engage the employee following a tribunal order, an additional award (see para 17.227) can be made. The test to be applied is not only whether the employee genuinely feared for his safety, but whether that fear was based on reasonable grounds. This is a question of fact, to be determined not only by the nature of the potential danger, but the steps which the employee could have taken to follow any procedures laid down by the employer which would militate against the danger (*Kerr v Nathan's Wastesavers Ltd*). Otherwise, there is no limit on the amount of the compensation award if the dismissal (or selection for redundancy) was contrary to s 100.

11.66 However, when it comes to a dismissal on other grounds, the protection afforded to a safety representative is neutral. Like a shop steward, he has no specially privileged position, and thus may be selected for redundancy in accordance with the appropriate selection criteria (*Smiths Industries Aerospace and Defence Systems v Rawlings*).

Interim relief in health and safety cases (ERA, ss 128–130)

11.67 If an employee is dismissed for an inadmissible reason because he has been desig-nated to carry out health and safety activities, or is a safety representative or member of a safety committee (see para 11.64) and he proposed to carry out activities as such, he may apply for interim relief, within seven days following the effective date of termination of his employment. The procedure and remedies are similar to the interim relief provisions contained in TULR(C)A, ss 161–166 (see para 21.114).

D. Health and safety regulations (s 15 and Sch 3)

11.68 As has already been indicated, one of the main purposes of the Act was to replace the existing statutory provisions by regulations, and over a period of time, the 'old' law contained in the Factories Act 1961, Offices, Shops and Railway Premises Act 1963, and so forth (for a complete list, see column 3 in Sch 1 to the Act), has been phased out, and replaced with a system of regulations and Codes of Practice which, in combination with the other provisions of the Act, are designed to maintain and improve the standards of health, safety and welfare. Regulations are of three general types; first, there are those which lay down standards to be applied in most or all employment situations, second, there are those which are designed to control a particular hazard which may exist in a particular industry, and third, there are those which refer to particular hazards or risks but which may be found in a number of different industries. The view appears to be held that the use of regulations as a device for laying down legal standards is a superior method to legislation, for regulations are simpler and more flexible; they can be altered more readily in accordance with experience and technological progress, and will be more manageable to those who have to implement them.

11.69 Regulations are to be made by the Secretary of State either as a result of proposals made to him by the Commission, or on his own initiative, but in the latter case he must consult with the Commission and any other appropriate bodies. If the Commission makes the proposals, it, too, must consult with the appropriate government departments and other bodies (s 50). Regulations may:

(a) repeal or modify any existing statutory provision;

(b) exclude or modify in relation to any specific class of case any of the provisions of ss 2–9 (above) or any existing statutory provision;

(c) make a specific authority responsible for the enforcement of any relevant statutory provision;

(d) impose requirements by reference to the approval of the Commission or other specified body or person;

(e) provide that any reference in a regulation to a specific document shall include a reference to a revised version of that document;

(f) provide for exemptions from any requirement or prohibition;

(g) enable exemptions to be granted by a specified person or authority;

(h) specify the persons or class of persons who may be guilty of an offence;

(i) provide for specified defences either generally or in specified circumstances;

(j) exclude proceedings on indictment in relation to certain offences;

(k) restrict the punishment which may be imposed in respect of certain offences.

11.70 Additionally, the Deregulation and Contracting Out Act 1994 aimed at reducing burdens on industry imposed by regulatory measures, and improving the fairness, openness and transparency of enforcement procedures. This Act (now repealed and replaced by the Regulatory Reform Act 2001) empowered the Secretary of State to repeal or revoke pre-1974 legislation without going through the normal parliamentary procedures, a power which has already been exercised on about 50 occasions, thus eliminating a number of outdated health and safety measures. There is thus an ongoing scrutiny of legal provisions which has outlived their usefulness.

11.71 Schedule 3 to the Act contains detailed provisions about the content of regulations, wide enough to enable the Secretary of State and the Commission actively to pursue all avenues in the interests of health and safety. In particular, however, we may note two further important provisions. The first is the power to prohibit the carrying on of any specified activity or the doing of any specified thing without a licence granted for that purpose, which may be subject to conditions. The second is contained in the Companies Act 1985, s 235 so as to enable the Secretary of State to prescribe cases whereby directors' reports will contain such information about the arrangements in force for that year for securing the health, safety and welfare at work of the employees of that company (and any subsidiary company), and for protecting other persons against risks to health resulting from the activities at work of the employees. To date, no such regulations have been made.

11.72 A breach of duty imposed by regulations is, of course, punishable as a criminal offence. Additionally, a breach may give rise to civil liability, except in so far as the regulations provide otherwise.

11.73 A number of regulations have been passed since 1974 dealing with all aspects of health and safety law. Reference should be made to an established textbook on this topic.

E. The impact of European law

11.74 Article 137 of the Treaty of Rome provides that member states shall pay particular attention to encouraging improvements, especially to the working environment, as regards the health and safety of workers. Under this article, Directives may be adopted by the qualified majority voting system, and a considerable number of such Directives have been adopted, and others are currently under discussion. In particular, the 'Framework Directive' (98/391/EEC) and five 'Daughter Directives' have recently been given effect to by the so-called 'six-pack' regulations (see below). The general view taken by the HSC is that the European Directives do not involve any significant change in UK law, although they do require UK law to make explicit that which is generally regarded as being implicit. Legal standards on health and safety in the UK are very high, and it is not expected that the following of EU Directives will impose any onerous burdens on UK employers.

11.75 In particular, six regulations (the so-called 'six pack' regulations) came into force on 1 January 1993. These are (a) Management of Health and Safety at Work Regulations, (b) Personal Protective Equipment at Work Regulations, (c) Provision and Use of Work Equipment Regulations, (d) Workplace (Health, Safety and Welfare) Regulations,

(e) Manual Handling Operations Regulations, and (f) Health and Safety (Display Screen Equipment) Regulations. Many 'old' regulations have been revoked, and most of the existing protective legislation, found in the Factories Act 1961, Offices, Shops and Railway Premises Act 1963 etc, has now been repealed.

11.76 Fundamental to the new law is the need to take proactive steps to ensure health and safety at work of employees and others. These will include risk assessment in certain specified situations, provision of information to all those who may be at risk, health surveillance, the use of safety advisers, co-operation between employers, the provision of approved equipment and personal protection equipment and so on. Employees have a duty to use the equipment etc provided in a proper manner, to report shortcomings in the employer's protection arrangements or which represent a serious and immediate danger to health and safety.

Management of Health and Safety at Work Regulations 1999 (as amended)

11.77 These regulations set out the principles of prevention which should be applied, require employers to make risk assessments (in particular when women of child-bearing age are employed (see para 6.8) and in respect of young persons, see para 2.98), provide employees with appropriate health surveillance, appoint safety advisers, establish emergency procedures, provide training and information to employees, and cooperate with other employers where the workplace is shared. Employees are required to use all machinery, equipment substances etc in accordance with any relevant training and instructions, and to inform the employer of any dangerous work situation or shortcomings in the health and safety arrangements.

Workplace (Health, Safety and Welfare) Regulations 1992

11.78 Workplaces are to be maintained in an efficient state, repaired and cleaned. There must be sufficient fresh or purified air, reasonable temperature, and heating must not produce injurious fumes. Lighting must be suitable and sufficient, there must be sufficient floor area, suitable seats provided if the work can be done seated, floors and traffic routes must be suitable, and windows, skylights and ventilators must be safe. Doors, gates, traffic routes and escalators must be constructed with safety in mind. There must be suitable and sufficient sanitary conveniences, washing facilities, and drinking water, and accommodation for clothes not worn during working hours and for changing clothes where necessary. Rest facilities must be provided, with suitable arrangements to protect non-smokers from discomfort from tobacco smoke, and suitable facilities for eating meals.

Provision and Use of Work Equipment Regulations 1998

11.79 Work equipment must be suitable, efficiently maintained, kept in good repair and conform to any legislation which implements any relevant EC Directive. Employees must be given adequate health and safety information, written instructions where appropriate, and be properly trained. Effective measures must be taken to prevent access to any dangerous parts of machinery, and measures must be taken to prevent or adequately control certain specified hazards. Starting and stopping controls (including emergency stop controls) must be provided and clearly marked. Work equipment must be stable, capable of being isolated from all its sources of energy, maintenance operations must be carried out while work equipment is shut down, and warning devices clearly visible, unambiguous, easily perceived and understood.

Personal Protective Equipment at Work Regulations 1992

11.80 Personal protective equipment (PPE) is all equipment intended to be worn or held by a person at work which protects him from risks to health or safety. PPE is not suitable unless it conforms to applicable EC standards.

11.81 Employers must provide suitable PPE, which must be compatible with other such equipment worn. There must be an assessment of the suitability, and PPE must be maintained in an efficient state, kept in good repair, and cleaned or replaced as appropriate. Employers must provide employees with information, instruction and training about risks PPE will avoid or limit, and ensure that it is properly used. Employees must use PPE in accordance with instructions and training given, and report any defect or loss.

Manual Handling Operations Regulations 1992

11.82 Every employer must, so far as is reasonably practicable, avoid the need for his employees to undertake manual handling operations which involve the risk of injury. If such operations cannot be avoided, the employer must carry out an assessment of the operations, and take appropriate steps to reduce the risk of injury, and provide employees with indications of the risk and the weight of the load. Schedule 1 to the Regulations sets out a comprehensive list of questions to be asked and factors taken into account in order to avoid or minimise the risks from manual handling. Employees shall make proper use of any system of work provided.

Health and Safety (Display Screen Equipment) Regulations 1992

11.83 Employers are required to make an analysis of workstations for the purpose of assessing health and safety risks so as to reduce these to the lowest extent reasonably practicable. The activities of users must be planned, so as to ensure they have periodic breaks or changes in activities. If a user so requests, the employer must provide eye and eyesight testing, and provide special corrective appliances when needed. Adequate health and safety training must be given in the use of workstations, and information given about all aspects of health and safety relating to workstations.

Other regulations

11.84 There are a considerable number of other regulations on health and safety matters which have been passed since 1974. The most important of these (and the date of the most recent version) deal with the following topics; first aid (1981), electricity (1989), noise at work (2005), head protection (1989), construction design and management (2006), reporting of injuries, diseases and dangerous occurrences (1995), safety signs and signals (1996), construction (1996), confined spaces (1997), fire precautions (2005), employers' liability compulsory insurance (1998), major accident hazards (1999), ionising radiations (1999), protection of children (2000), asbestos (2006), lead (2002), hazardous substances (2002), work at height (2005) and so on. In addition, a number of regulations deal with specific industries and processes (railways, gas, transport, adventure activities, carriage of goods, offshore installations, compressed air, etc).

F. Codes of practice (s 16)

11.85 For the purpose of providing practical guidance with respect to the general duties imposed by ss 2–7 (above), or by any regulation or any existing statutory provisions, the Commission may approve and issue codes of practice which are suitable for that purpose. The Commission may also approve other such suitable codes which are drawn up by other persons or organisations, and thus there is no reason why a private firm or employers' organisation should not draw up its own code and submit it for approval, should this be thought desirable. One might also expect approval to be given to the existing British Standards Institution's own codes. The Commission cannot approve a code without the consent of the Secretary of State, and prior to obtaining this, must consult with government departments and other appropriate bodies. The codes may be revised from time to time, and the Commission may, if necessary, withdraw its approval from a particular code.

11.86 A failure on the part of any person to observe the provisions contained in an approved code of practice shall not of itself render that person liable to any civil or criminal proceedings, but in any such criminal proceedings, if a person is alleged to have committed an offence concerning a matter in respect of which an approved code is in force, the provisions of that code shall be admissible in evidence, and a failure to observe it shall constitute proof of the breach of duty, or contravention of the regulation or statutory provision, unless the accused can satisfy the court that he complied with the requirements of the law in some other equally efficacious manner. The codes, therefore, will be the guides to good safety practice, and if a person follows the provisions of the codes, he cannot be successfully prosecuted for an offence. If he fails to follow the relevant code, he may be guilty of an offence unless he can show that he observed the specific legal requirement some other way.

11.87 The Act contains no guidance on the use of the codes in civil proceedings, but it is likely that a failure to observe any such provision as is contained therein may well constitute prima facie evidence of negligence, which can be rebutted by evidence to the contrary.

G. Penalties (s 33)

11.88 Any person or body corporate (eg a company) may be charged with and convicted of an offence under the Act, and punished accordingly. In addition, if an offence committed by a body corporate is proved to have been committed with the consent of, connivance of, or attributable to any neglect on the part of, any director, manager, secretary or other similar officer, then he, as well as the body corporate may be guilty of an offence, and liable to be proceeded against and punished accordingly (s 37) (see *Huckerby v Elliott*).

11.89 In *Armour v Skeen*, a senior local government official was prosecuted for failing to prepare and carry out a safety policy, for this neglect of duty ultimately led to breaches of safety provisions which resulted in the death of an employee. It was held that the official was guilty of an offence under s 37. He was in a senior position in his organisation, and was therefore responsible for the general safety policy in his department. But in *R v Boal* the accused was an assistant manager in a bookshop. Following a visit by inspectors, he was prosecuted and convicted in respect of a number of offences. On appeal, it was held that criminal liability was to be imposed on persons in authority in the company who were the 'decision makers', with the power and responsibility to decide corporate policy. As the accused was an 'underling', his conviction was quashed.

11.90 Where the commission of an offence by a person is due to the default of another person, that other person may be proceeded against, whether or not proceedings are taken against the first mentioned person (s 36). No proceedings under the Act may be brought except by an inspector, or with the consent of the Director of Public Prosecutions (in Scotland, the Procurator Fiscal).

11.91 There is an anomaly, however, in that although Crown bodies (excluding health authorities) have the same obligations under the Act as other employers, they cannot be prosecuted, and it is not possible to issue improvement or prohibition notices against the Crown (see para 11.24). However, this rule does not prevent the prosecution of individual Crown employees.

11.92 If a person is found guilty of an offence on summary conviction in the magistrates' court, the maximum punishment is a fine of up to £5,000 or £20,000, depending on the nature of the offence, and/or six months' imprisonment. If proceedings are brought on indictment (ie in the Crown Court before a jury), there is the possibility of an unlimited fine, and in certain specified cases, up to two years' imprisonment. In *R v Howe & Son (Engineers) Ltd* the Court of Appeal gave guidance on how sentencing policies should be applied to convictions for health and safety offences.

H. Burden of proof

11.93 As a general rule, in criminal proceedings, it is for the prosecution to prove its case 'beyond reasonable doubt'. However, by the Health and Safety at Work Act, s 40, if the offence consists of a failure to comply with a duty or requirement to do something 'so far as is reasonably practicable', or to use 'the best practicable means', it shall be for the accused to prove that it was not reasonably practicable to do more than was in fact done, or that there were no better practicable means than were in fact used to satisfy the duty or requirement. When the burden of proof is thus placed on the accused, he may discharge that burden of proof on the balance of probabilities (*R v Carr-Briant*). In *Davies v Health and Safety Executive* it was held that this reversal of the burden of proof did not violate Art 6 of the Convention on Human Rights (see para 1.101).

Compensation for injuries at work

A. The extent of the duty owed

11.94 One of the prime duties of an employer is to ensure that his employees do not suffer an accident or injury while at work. There are a number of common law rules which determine the extent of that duty, and in addition there are certain statutory provisions designed to ensure the employee's safety which, if broken or not observed by the employer, may lead to an action for damages by an injured employee based on a breach of statutory duties. Frequently, the two actions are run together, so that an employee may succeed for breach of the common law duty and/or a breach of the statutory duty, though, of course, only one set of damages will be awarded. The purpose of the common law rules is to compensate for injuries incurred as a result of the employer's negligence; the object of the statute will be accident prevention enforced by criminal penalties, but with a potential liability for compensation as well. But as Goddard LJ said in *Hutchinson v London and North Eastern Rly Co*, 'The real incentive for the observance by employers of their statutory duties ... is not their liability to substantial fines, but the possibility of heavy claims for damages'. The whole question of compensation for injuries at work was reviewed by the Royal Commission on Civil Liability, but no significant changes were recommended in its report.

11.95 The duty owed by the employer is in respect of the employee's physical and mental health, including ill-health caused by overwork (*Johnstone v Bloomsbury Health Authority*), psychiatric illness (*Frost v Chief Constable of South Yorkshire Police*) and stress and anxiety caused thereby (*Walker v Northumberland County Council*). But if the employers do not know of the risk, or if, having knowledge, they take such steps as are reasonable in the circumstances to minimise the risk, or provide appropriate healthcare, no liability arises (*Petch v Customs and Excise Comrs*). A difficult case was *White v Chief Constable of South Yorkshire Police*, where it was held that a policeman was not entitled to recover damages for psychiatric illness suffered as a result of assisting in the aftermath of the Hillsborough disaster, either as an employee or a rescuer.

11.96 Liability for psychiatric injury caused by stress at work is no different in principle from liability for physical injury. The test is whether the injury is a foreseeable breach of the employer's duty of care. It does not follow that, because a claimant suffers from stress at work, and that the employer was in some way in breach of a duty to allow that to occur, that the claimant is able to establish a claim in negligence (*Hartman v South Essex Mental Health and Community Care NHS Trust*). As a result of a recent legal decision, the courts are likely to adopt a more cautious approach to claims for damages in respect of psychiatric injury caused by stress. In *Sutherland v Hatton*, the Court of Appeal heard appeals by employers in four unconnected cases against awards of damages to employees who had stopped work because of stress-induced psychiatric illness. Three of the appeals were allowed, while the fourth was dismissed 'not without some hesitation'. The Court laid down a number of practical propositions designed to help other courts deal with future claims. While conceding that it was the employer's duty to take reasonable steps to ensure the physical and mental health of his employees, it was held that in order for an employer to be liable, the stress-induced injury must be sufficiently foreseeable to be plain enough for any reasonable employer to realise that he should do something about it. The Court of Appeal stated that there were no occupations which are intrinsically dangerous to mental health, that employers are entitled to assume that employees can withstand the normal pressures of the job (unless they know of some particular problem or vulnerability), and that an employee who returns to work after being absent through sickness is implying that he is fit for work, and the employer is entitled to take that at its face value. To trigger a duty to take steps, the indications of impending harm to health arising from stress at work had to be plain enough for any reasonable employer to realise that he ought to do something about it, and the employer will only be liable if he fails to take reasonable steps, bearing in mind the magnitude of the risk, the gravity of the harm, the costs and practicability of preventing it, and the justification for running the risk. Thus it might be possible for the employer to suggest that the employee takes a sabbatical period of leave, or a transfer to other work, or a redistribution of the work, etc. Extra help may be provided, or a mentoring scheme introduced. But such assistance will depend very much on the employer's resources, and the interests of other employees at the workplace. An employer who offers a confidential advice service, with referral to appropriate counselling or treatment services, is unlikely to be found to be in breach of a duty to take care.

11.97 The court went on to point out that it is not enough that the occupational stress has caused the harm. It must be shown that it was the employer's breach of duty to take reasonable care for the health of his employees that has caused or materially contributed to the harm. An employer can only reasonably be expected to take steps which are likely to do some good, and if the only reasonable steps an employer could take in order to remove the employee from a job which is causing stress is to demote the employee or dismiss him, and the employer will not be in breach of his duty for allowing a willing employee to continue in his job. If there is no alternative solution, it is for the employee to decide whether or not to continue in the job, and risk a breakdown in his health, or whether to leave the employment and look for work elsewhere. Finally, the consequence of the breach of duty may be only one of many stressful events which affected an employee's state of health, and the employer should only pay for that proportion of the harm which is attributable to his wrongdoing.

11.98 But an employer should always be alert to the problems likely to be suffered by a stressed employee. In *Barber v Somerset County Council* the employee was the head of a department at a school. He had a very heavy workload, working between 60–70 hours per week. He was off work for three weeks suffering from 'overstressed/depression'. When he returned to work the school authorities were not very sympathetic towards him, and no steps were taken to improve the situation. The following term he found himself with the same or slightly heavier workload, and eventually left work altogether, suffering from moderate or severe depression. His claim for damages was upheld by the House of Lords. A prudent employer who knew that an employee had taken some time off work because of stress caused by work overload would have investigated the situation to see how the difficulties might be improved. If an employee works hours which are in excess of the 48-hour week, or in breach of the rest provisions, with the consequence that he suffers psychiatric injury caused by overwork, this can be taken into account when consideration is given to the foreseeability of the injury (*Hone v Six Continents Retail*). While every case will turn on its own facts, the principles laid down in *Stokes v Guest Keen Nettlefold* (see para 11.101) were approved, ie '. . . the overall test is still the conduct of a reasonable and prudent employer, taking positive thought for the safety of his workers in the light of what he knows or ought to know. . . .'.

11.99 The duty of the employer to take care is one aspect of the law of negligence which requires everyone to ensure that his activities do not cause injury or damage to another through an act of negligence. The standard of care which an employer must observe is, as Lord Oaksey pointed out in *Paris v Stepney Borough Council*, 'The care which an ordinary prudent employer would take in all the circumstances'. The employer does *not* guarantee that an employee will not be injured; he only undertakes to take reasonable care, and he will only be liable if there is some lack of care on his part in failing to prevent something which was reasonably foreseeable. The employee, on his part, must be prepared to look after himself, and not expect to be able to blame the employer for every incident which takes place. In *Vinnyey v Star Paper Mills*, the claimant was instructed by the foreman to clear and clean a floor area which had been made slippery by a viscous fluid. The foreman provided proper equipment and gave clear instructions. The claimant was injured when he slipped on the floor, and it was held that the employer was not liable, for there was no reasonably foreseeable risk in the performance of such a simple task. So too, in *Lazarus v Firestone Tyre and Rubber Co Ltd*, where the claimant was knocked down in the general rush to get to the canteen. The court held that this was not the sort of behaviour which grown persons could be protected against. Such cases are in line with a number of judicial statements made in recent years deprecating 'any tendency to treat the relationship between employer and skilled workman as equivalent to that of nurse and imbecile child' (per Lord Simmons in *Smith v Austin Lifts*), or that of 'schoolmaster and pupil' (per Devlin LJ in *Withers v Perry Chain Co Ltd*).

11.100 Equally, if an employer does not know of the danger, and could not be expected to know in the light of current knowledge, or did not foresee the danger and could not be expected to foresee it, he will not be liable. In *Down v Dudley, Coles Long Ltd* an employee was partially deafened by the noise from a cartridge-assisted hammer gun. At the then state of medical knowledge (ie in 1964), a reasonable employer would not have known of the potential danger of using this particular piece of equipment without providing safety precautions, and hence the employer was not liable for the injury. But once the danger is discovered, he must take all reasonable steps to protect his employees from the consequences of risks which have hitherto been unforeseeable. In *Wright v Dunlop Rubber Co*, the employers used an anti-oxidant known as Nonox S from 1940 onwards. The manufacturers then discovered that the substance was capable of causing bladder cancer, and informed the defendants that all employees who had been exposed to it should be screened and tested. This was not done for some time, and thus the employers, as well as the manufacturers, were held liable to the claimants.

11.101 The matter was summarised by Swanwick J in *Stokes v Guest, Keen and Nettlefold (Bolts and Nuts) Ltd*.

(a) The employer must take positive steps to ensure the safety of his employees in the light of the knowledge which he has or ought to have.

(b) The employer is entitled to follow current recognised practice unless in the light of common sense or new knowledge this is clearly unsound.

(c) Where there is developing knowledge, he must keep reasonably abreast with it, and not be too slow in applying it.

(d) If he has greater than average knowledge of the risk, he must take more than average precautions.

(e) He must weigh up the risk (in terms of the likelihood of injury and possible consequences) against the effectiveness of the precautions needed to meet the risk, and the cost and inconvenience.

11.102 Applying these tests, if the employer falls below the standards of a reasonable and prudent employer, he will be negligent. On the other hand, if the employer takes all such steps as are reasonably practicable, he will not be liable at common law (*Darby v GKN Screws and Fasteners Ltd*).

11.103 If, before his dismissal, an employee acquires a cause of action at common law (whether for breach of contract or breach of the duty to take reasonable care for the employee's health and safety) that cause of action remains unimpaired by the fact that the employee has brought a statutory unfair dismissal claim. Thus a claim for damages for psychiatric injury caused, for example, by a wrongful application of the contractual disciplinary procedure may succeed (*Eastwood v Magnox Electric plc*), even though there can be no award for psychiatric illness (or injury to feelings) caused by the manner of actual dismissal (*Dunnachie v Kingston upon Hull City Council*).

B. Duty to unborn children

11.104 Under the Congenital Disabilities (Civil Liability) Act 1976, an employer may be liable to a child of an employee who is born disabled as a result of any breach of legal duty, whether imposed by statute or by common law, to the child's parent. The child may thus sue in respect of a pre-natal injury suffered, whether or not the parent suffered any injury, and whether or not the employer knew of the existence of the foetus. The Act was intended to be a stop-gap measure until the passing of legislation consequent on the Pearson Report. The right of the child to sue is contingent on the existence of a right for the parent to sue; in other words, the claim is as good as, but no better than, the claim of the parent. Any contributory negligence on the part of the parent may reduce the child's damages.

C. Personal nature of the duty

11.105 The duty of the employer is a personal one, in the sense that he cannot absolve himself by delegating the duty to someone else. In *Wilsons & Clyde Coal Co Ltd v English*, the employer was compelled by law to employ a colliery agent who was responsible for mine safety; nonetheless, it was held that the employer was liable for an unsafe system of work in the mine. Thus it can never be a defence to argue that the employer has assigned the task of securing and maintaining safety precautions to a safety officer or other person.

11.106 Equally, the duty is owed to each employee as an individual, not to them all collectively. This means that one must take greater precautions when dealing, for example, with inexperienced employees, or with new and untrained employees or with young persons, etc, than one might do with more responsible staff. In *Paris v Stepney Borough Council* the claimant worked chipping away at rust and other superfluous rubbish which had accumulated underneath buses. Goggles were not provided for this work, for it was not customary to do so. The claimant only had one eye, and he was totally blinded when a splinter entered his good eye. It was held that the employers were liable. They should have foreseen that there was a risk of greater injury to the employee, and provided goggles for him, even though they may not have been under such a duty with respect to other employees.

11.107 Clearly, a higher standard of care must be shown to employees who lack a sufficient or adequate command of the English language, to ensure that they are properly trained and clearly instructed, so as not to cause injuries to themselves and to others. In *James v Hepworth and Grandage Ltd* the employers put up large notices informing employees that they should wear spats for their personal protection. Unknown to them, the claimant could not read, and when he was injured he claimed damages from his employers. His claim failed. He had observed other workmen wearing spats, and the court concluded that his failure to make enquiries meant that even if he had been informed about the notice, he would not have worn them. But with the growth of foreign labour in UK factories, the problem is likely to cause growing concern, particularly as such labour tends to concentrate in the initial stages in those industries which have serious safety hazards. The responsibility of the safety officer, as the 'agent' of the employer, to ensure that the work can be done in safety is likely to be very onerous in practice (see *Hawkins v Ian Ross (Castings) Ltd*).

11.108 An employer has a duty to warn an employee of risks to his health and safety where those risks are not common knowledge and cannot be guarded against by the taking of sensible precautions, and where that knowledge would affect the employee's decision to accept the work. But the employer does not guarantee absolutely the safety of the employee. In *White v Holbrook Precision Castings Ltd* the claimant was employed as a grinder. He developed Reynaud's Disease (vibration white finger) and sued for damages. His claim was dismissed. The claimant knew of the risk when he accepted the employment, and the employers were merely aware that the disease could cause minor discomfort. No precautions had ever been suggested or were viable. The claimant would still have taken the employment had he been specifically told of the risk. However, given the current state of medical and scientific knowledge, a different conclusion may well be reached nowadays (see *Shepherd v Firth Brown Ltd*).

11.109 It has long been held that, as a general rule, there is no onus on an employer to remove an employee from unsafe work, the onus being on the employee to decide for himself whether to continue to take on the work (*Withers v Perry Chain Co Ltd*, and *Henderson v Wakefield Shirt Co Ltd*). Still less is there an obligation on the employer to dismiss the employee, if that was the only alternative. Indeed, in *Sutherland v Hatton* it was stated that if the only reasonable and effective step would have been to dismiss or demote the employee, the employer would not be in breach of his duty in allowing a willing employee to continue in the job. It is for the employee to decide whether or not to carry on in the employment and take the risk of a breakdown in his health. But there may well be cases where, despite the employee's desire to remain at work notwithstanding the risk he ran, the employer would be under a duty in law to dismiss him for his own good so as to protect him from physical danger (see *Coxall v Goodyear GB Ltd*). In unfair dismissal proceedings, the employer would have to plead some other substantial reason, ie the common law duty. If disability discrimination proceedings were brought, the defence of reasonable adjustments would have to be raised.

11.110 Modern technologies and modern working methods inevitably bring about new and special problems, and legal decisions must be adapted from existing principles to meet the factual situations which arise. Thus claims have succeeded and failed in respect of repetitive strain injury or work related upper limb disorder (*Pickford v ICI plc; Alexander v Midland Bank plc*), vibration white finger (*Armstrong v British Coal Corpn*), work induced stress (*Petch v Customs and Excise Comrs; Walker v Northumberland County Council*), acts of violence (*Haughton v Hackney Borough Council*), breach of health and safety regulations (see para 11.68), and so on.

D. The threefold nature of the duty

11.111 Although recent cases have stressed that there is only one single duty to take care, it is convenient to examine the nature of that duty under three sub-headings.

Safe plant and appliances

11.112 This means that all the equipment, tools, machinery, plant, etc, where the employee works shall be reasonably safe for work. In *Bradford v Robinson Rentals Ltd*, a driver was required to drive an unheated van on a 400-mile journey during a bitterly cold spell of weather. It was held that the employer was liable when the driver suffered frostbite as a consequence. In *Close v Steel Co of Wales Ltd*, it was suggested by Lord Goddard that if an employer knows that a machine has a tendency to throw out flying parts so as to constitute a danger to the operative, this could well amount to common law negligence on the part of the employer if he fails to take reasonable precautions.

11.113 However, if an employer purchased tools or equipment from a reputable supplier, and has no knowledge of any defect in them, he will have performed his duty to take care, and will not be liable for negligence (see *Davie v New Merton Board Mills*). This would not be so if the equipment was bought second-hand from, say, a scrapyard. If a remedy existed in *Davie's* case, it would be for the injured employee to sue the person responsible for the defect under the general law of negligence as propounded in the leading case of *Donoghue v Stevenson*, but frequently this might prove to be difficult or impossible in practice. The employee might not be in a position to prove just who was negligent. It might be a firm of stevedores at the docks, a foreign manufacturer, and so on. In view of these problems, the law was changed with the passing of the Employers' Liability (Defective Equipment) Act 1969. This provides that if an employee suffers a personal injury in the course of his employment in consequence of a defect in equipment provided by his employers for the purpose of the employers' business, and the defect is attributable to the fault of a third party, the injury shall be deemed to be attributable to the negligence of the employer. Thus, should facts similar to *Davie's* case arise again, the employee would be able to sue his employer for the 'deemed' negligence, and the employer, for his part, would be able to recover the amount of damages paid from the third party whose fault it really was. At the same time, the Employers' Liability (Compulsory Insurance) Act 1969 was passed, to ensure that all employers had valid insurance cover to meet personal injuries claims from their employees.

11.114 If an employer is aware that there are defects in tools or equipment he has bought then he should withdraw them from circulation if he wishes to avoid liability. In *Taylor v Rover Co Ltd* a batch of chisels had been badly hardened by the manufacturers. One had, in fact, shattered, without causing any injury, but the batch was still in use when another chisel shattered, injuring the claimant in his eye. The employers were held liable.

Safe system of work

11.115 Here we must consider all the factors which concern the manner in which the work is to be done. The layout, the systems laid down, the training and supervision, the provision of warnings, protective clothing, special instructions, and so forth, are all relevant. In *Barcock v Brighton Corpn*, the claimant was employed at an electricity sub-station.

A certain method of testing was in operation, which was unsafe, and in consequence the claimant was injured. The employers were held liable. But if the employer gives proper instructions which the employee fails to observe, the employer will not be liable for a subsequent injury. In *Charlton v Forrest Printing Ink Co Ltd* a senior employee was required to collect the firm's wages of £1,500 each Friday from the bank. Because, several years earlier, there had been a wage snatch of the firm's payroll, the managing director had given instructions that the collection arrangements should be varied each week, for example, by using taxis instead of private cars, by going at different times and by different routes. Contrary to these instructions, in the course of time, a collecting pattern set in, and the employee suffered severe injuries when he was robbed in an attack. In the High Court, the judge found for the claimant arguing that the employers had been negligent in not employing a professional security firm, but this decision was reversed on appeal. The vast majority of firms of that size in that area made their own payroll collection, and hence the employers could not be said to be negligent in carrying on with that practice. Although there was a risk, they had taken reasonable steps to minimise or eliminate it. The Court of Appeal thought that the claimant's remedy would be through an application to the Criminal Injuries Compensation Board, which has funds for such contingencies.

11.116 If there are safety precautions laid down, the employee must be told what they are; if safety equipment is provided, it must be available for use. In *Finch v Telegraph Construction and Maintenance Co Ltd* the claimant was employed as a grinder. Goggles had been provided, but he was not told where they were. The employers were held to be liable when he was injured by a flying piece of metal whilst doing his work.

11.117 But if the employer, though not providing the safety precautions, can show that even if he had provided them the employee would not have used them, he may escape liability. In *Cummings (or McWilliam) v Sir William Arrol Ltd*, a steel erector fell from a scaffolding and was killed. The employer had provided safety belts in the past, but these had not been used, and they had been taken away to be used on another site. It was held that even though the employer was negligent in not providing the safety belts, it was unlikely that the employee would have used them had they been available. Accordingly, the employer's negligence was not the cause of the death, since this would have occurred anyway.

11.118 The more dangerous the process, the greater the need for safety precautions. On the other hand, the employer cannot be expected to be held liable in respect of accidents which occur in simple situations, as *Vinnyey's* case (para 11.99 above) illustrates. A situation which gives rise to some legal difficulties is where the employer provides the safety precautions, but the employees fail or refuse to use them. Is the duty of the employer a merely passive one, to provide and do no more? Or is it an active one, to exhort, propagandise, instruct or even compel their use? It is submitted that the answer to these questions can be given in four propositions.

  (a) If the risk is an obvious one, and the injury resulting from the failure to use the precautions is not likely to be serious, then the employer's duty is a passive one of merely providing the precautions, informing the employees and leaving it to them to decide for themselves whether or not to use them. In *Qualcast (Wolverhampton) Ltd v Haynes*, an experienced workman was splashed by molten metal on his legs. Spats were available, but the employers did nothing to ensure that they were worn.

The injury, though doubtless painful, was not of a serious nature, and the employers were held not liable.

(b) If the risk is that of a serious injury, then the duty of the employer is a higher one of doing all he can to ensure that the workmen will use the safety precautions which are provided. In *Nolan v Dental Manufacturing Co Ltd* a toolsetter was injured when a chip flew off a grinding wheel. Because of the seriousness of the injury should such occur, it was held that the employer should have insisted that protective goggles were worn.

(c) If the risk is an insidious one, or one the seriousness of which the employee would not readily appreciate, then again, it is the duty of the employer to do all he can by way of propaganda, contstant reminders, exhortations, etc, to try to get the employees to use the precautions. In *Berry v Stone Manganese and Marine Ltd*, the claimant was working in an environment where the noise levels were dangerously high. Ear muffs had been provided, but no effort was made to ensure their use. It was held that as the workmen would not readily appreciate the dangers of injury to their hearing if they did not use the ear muffs, the employers were liable, as they had failed to take steps to impress on them the need to use the protective equipment.

(d) When the employer has done all he can do, when he has not only provided the protection, but instructed on its use, advised on how to use it properly, pointed out the risks involved in a failure to use, and given constant reminders about its use, then he can do no more, and from that time he will be absolved from liability. Admittedly, this does not solve the problem, which is how to ensure that employees do their work safely. It is possible to make the use of safety equipment part of the contract of employment, or a provision in the works rules, and, it is submitted, a failure to observe these terms or instructions may, after due warning, enable the employer fairly to dismiss the employee. There appears to be no legal duty to do so in order to protect the employee from the physical consequences of his own folly.

Reasonably competent fellow employees

11.119 If an employer engages an incompetent person, whose actions injure another employee, the employer will be liable for failing to take reasonable care. In *Hudson v Ridge Manufacturing Co Ltd* an employee who was known to be prone to committing practical jokes, carried one of his pranks too far, and injured a fellow employee. The employer was liable. The answer in these circumstances, is, after due warning, to dispense firmly with the services of such a person, for he is a menace to himself and to others. On the other hand, in *Coddington v International Harvester Co of Great Britain Ltd*, for a joke, an employee, M, kicked a tin of burning thinners close to X, and another employee, Y, was scorched by the flames, and in the agony of the moment, kicked the tin away so that it enveloped the claimant in flames, causing him severe injuries. It was held that the defendants were not liable. There was nothing in M's previous conduct which suggested that he might endanger others, and his act was completely outside the scope of his employment. If a person is injured during horseplay, he would not be able to recover damages unless he could show that the injury was caused by a failure to take care which amounted to recklessness or a very high degree of carelessness, or that it was caused with intent to do harm (*Blake v Galloway*).

E. Breach of statutory duty

11.120 In *Groves v Lord Wimborne*, decided in 1898, it was held that a civil action would lie for injuries suffered by a workman because the factory owner had failed to fence dangerous machinery, as required by the Factory and Workshop Act 1878, even though the Act only specified criminal penalties for such failure. Thus the principle was established that if a statute requires the performance of a duty, and a person for whose benefit the duty is imposed is injured because of a failure by another to perform it, an action for damages will lie.

Four elements

11.121 So far as accidents and injuries at work are concerned, the general principle is that a civil action for breach of statutory duty will lie unless the Act (or regulation) expressly excludes such liability. Thus the Health and Safety at Work Act 1974 specifically excludes the right to bring a civil action in respect of a breach of ss 2–8, but further states that a breach of a duty imposed by health and safety regulations shall be so actionable except in so far as the regulations provide otherwise. For example, at one time the Management of Health and Safety at Work Regulations 1999 and the Fire Precautions (Workplace) Regulations provided that no civil action would lie for breach of duty imposed by those regulations (with certain exceptions), but this provision has now been revoked (Management of Health and Safety at Work and Fire Precautions (Workplace) (Amendment) Regulations 2003).

11.122 There are thus four elements of the tort of breach of statutory duty, namely, (a) that the defendant owed a duty to the claimant (*Hartley v Mayoh & Co*), (b) that there was a failure to carry out that duty (*Chipchase v British Titan Products Co Ltd*), (c) that the breach caused the damage (*McWilliams v Sir William Arrol & Co Ltd*), and (d) that the damage was the kind which the statute was designed to prevent (*Fytche v Wincanton Logistics plc*). Claimants will frequently bring such an action together with an action based on the tort of negligence, thus increasing the prospects of success, although, of course, only one amount of damages will be awarded. The main advantage in doing so is that, generally speaking, most statutory duties are absolute, ie a failure to perform the duty will inevitably mean that there has been a breach of that duty, whereas an action based on negligence is subject to various defences, eg reasonable foreseeability etc (see para 11.99).

The defendant must have owed a duty to the claimant

11.123 Whether a duty is owed to a particular claimant is a question of construction. Thus, if a statutory provision is made for the benefit of a particular class off persons, only those in that class can take advantage of the statutory protection (*Canadian Pacific Steamships Ltd v Bryers*). For example, the Management of Health and Safety at Work Regulations 1999 specify certain duties in relation generally to employees, and thus contract workers, agency workers, members of the public, etc are not so protected, and cannot sue for a breach of statutory duty by the employer. In *Ricketts v Torbay Council* the claimant tripped on an uneven surface in a council car park. She sued for damages, arguing that the car park was a workplace, and under reg 12 of the Workplace (Health, Safety and Welfare) Regulations there was a requirement that every floor in a workplace and the surface of every traffic route shall be suitable for the purpose, and that floors and surfaces must be free from anything that may cause any person to slip, trip or fall. She argued that 'any person' meant any person who was lawfully there. Her claim was dismissed by the Court of Appeal. The regulations were designed to protect persons at work in the workplace. Similarly, in *Reid v Galbraith's Stores* it was held that the provisions of the Offices, Shops and Railway Premises Act 1963 did not apply to a customer who was visiting the shop, as the Act was concerned with the protection of person who worked there.

There was a failure to carry out that duty

11.124 An employer will be in breach of the duty if he fails to observe the relevant statutory provision. Thus, when s 14 of the Factories Act 1961 (now repealed) stated that 'Every part of dangerous machinery shall be securely fenced' it imposed an absolute obligation to fence, and it was no defence for an employer to argue that it was impossible to fence the dangerous part and use the machine in question. The Act thus implicitly prohibited its use, and the factory occupier used the machine at his peril (*John Summers & Sons Ltd v Frost*). Similarly, reg 6 of the Provision and Use of Work Equipment Regulations 1998 provides that every employer shall ensure that work equipment is maintained in an efficient state, in efficient working order and in good repair, and an employer was held liable when an employee was injured because the front brake on his delivery bicycle broke, even though the employer had no knowledge of the defect (*Stark v Post Office*). The obligation imposed by the regulation was absolute.

11.125 On the other hand, if a statute or regulation imposed a duty to do something 'so far as is practicable' or 'to use the best practicable means', this is a high standard, but not an absolute one. Thus in *Richards v Highway Ironfounders (West Bromwich) Ltd* it was not known at the time that an invisible dust could cause silicosis, and thus the employer could not be held liable for failing to insist that employees should wear masks. A defendant cannot be held liable for failing to use a precaution which was not then invented, or failing to protect against a danger which medical science had not yet identified (*Adsett v K & L Steelfounders and Engineers Ltd*).

11.126 If a statutory provision requires that something should be done 'so far as is reasonably practicable' then again, different considerations apply. It is permissible to take into account on the one hand, the danger or hazard or risk of injury which may occur, and balance it against the cost, inconvenience time and trouble it would take to counter it. If the risk is insignificant in relation to the cost etc likely to be incurred, then it may not be reasonably practicable to take those steps (*Edwards v National Coal Board*). Thus in *Marshall v Gotham & Co* the roof of a mine collapsed due to a rare geological fault, injuring a workman. The court held that the danger was a very rare one. The roof had been tested in the usual way, and any further precautions taken would not have afforded complete protection against the danger. In the circumstances, the employers had done all that was reasonable. Similarly, a failure on the part of an employer to note a trivial risk would not give rise to liability (*Furness v Midland Bank plc*).

The breach caused the damage

11.127 The breach of the duty must have been a cause of the damage. This is the causation rule. Clearly if the damage caused is physical, there are generally few problems. When the damage caused is psychological, it is a matter of construction and evidence as to whether the damage was foreseeable. Thus in order to succeed in a claim for damages for psychiatric illness caused by stress at work, it must be established not only that it was reasonably foreseeable that overwork would lead to stress, but that the failure to carry out a risk assessment or health surveillance would lead to a breakdown in the stressed employees health (*Bonser v RJB Mining (UK) Ltd*). If there is a failure to carry out a risk assessment as required by the Management of Health at Work Regulations (or other regulations which impose this requirement) it is a likely conclusion that that breach was in some way responsible for the accident or injury (*Griffiths v Vauxhall Motors Ltd*).

11.128 But if the damage caused would have occurred even if the employer had complied with the statutory duty, there is no liability. In *McWilliams v Sir William Arrol & Co Ltd*, the employers provided safety belts on a site for the use of steel erectors, but as these were not being used by the employees, they were taken away to another site. A steel erector on the first site fell from scaffolding, and was killed. Although the employers were clearly in breach of their statutory duty to provide the safety belts, there was nothing to suggest that this employee, who had never used the belts before, would have worn them on the day he was killed. Thus the employers were held not liable for damages. The breach of the legal duty did not cause the damage, it would have occurred anyway.

The damage was the kind the statute was designed to prevent

11.129 The harm done must be of a type which the legislation is designed to prevent (*Gorris v Scott*). Thus in *Fytche v Wincanton Logistics plc* a driver was employed to collect milk from farms. He was provided with steel-capped safety boots, which were changed every six months. Water seeped through a tiny hole in one of his boots, and, because the weather was extremely cold, he contracted frostbite. He brought a claim under reg 7 of the Personal Protective Equipment Regulations, arguing that the boots were not in an efficient state or in good repair, as required by that regulation. His claim was dismissed by the House of Lords. The purpose of the safety boots was to protect against his feet being crushed by some heavy object while he was on the farms; it was not to prevent his feet from getting wet or cold. His only remedy would be an action for common law negligence, but as the judge found that there had been no breach of the duty of care (because the defect was not known to the employers, and could not have been discovered by reasonable care) his claim under this heading failed.

11.130 So far as the Management of Health and Safety at Work Regulations are concerned, there are some specific provisions which are likely to be relevant in civil litigation, including reg 3 (risk assessment), reg 6 (health surveillance), reg 8 (provisions for serious and imminent danger), reg 10 (information for employees), reg 14 (duties of employees) and reg 16 (risk assessment for new or expectant mothers). All other regulations have specific requirements, a breach of which may, in appropriate circumstances, give rise to civil liability.

F. Defences to an action for personal injuries

11.131 An employer (in reality his insurance company) may be able to raise a number of defences to an action based on negligence or breach of statutory duties, as appropriate.

Denial of negligence

11.132 The employer may deny that he failed to take reasonable care, or claim that he did all that a reasonable employer would have done in the circumstances. In *Latimer v AEC Ltd* a factory floor was made slippery owing to the interaction of water from an unprecedented rainfall with the oily surface of the floor. The management ordered sand and sawdust to be spread around, but there was not enough to cover the whole factory. The employee slipped on an untreated part and was injured. It was held that the employer had done all that a reasonable employer could have done, having regard to the nature of the risk. The only other alternative would have been to close down the factory, which would have been unreasonable in the circumstances. In *Brown v Rolls-Royce (1971) Ltd* the claimant contracted dermatitis owing to the use of an industrial oil. The employers did not provide a barrier cream on the advice of their chief medical officer, who doubted its efficacy. It was again held that the employers were not liable, for they were entitled to rely on the skilled judgment of a competent adviser, and no more could be expected. Indeed, the medical officer had instituted his own preventative methods, as a result of which the incidence of dermatitis in the factory had decreased.

11.133 The duty of the non-specialist employer in these circumstances is somewhat different. After all, not every firm can be expected to employ their own medical officer. Nonetheless, they must pay attention to the current literature which is available to them, either through their employers' associations or other sources. In *Graham v Co-operative Wholesale Society Ltd* the claimant worked in a furniture workshop where an electric sanding machine gave off a quantity of fine wood dust. This settled on his skin and caused dermatitis. No general precautions were taken against this, although the manager had received all the information which was commonly circulated in the trade. It was held that the employers had not been negligent. They did not know of the danger, nor ought they to have known. They had fulfilled their duty to take resonable steps to keep their knowledge up to date.

The injury was the sole fault of the employee

11.134 If it can be shown that the accident or injury was solely due to the fault of the employee, the employer will not be liable. In *Jones v Lionite Specialities Ltd* a foreman was addicted to a chemical vapour from a tank. One weekend he was found dead, having fallen into the tank. The employers were not liable. In *Brophy v Bradfield & Co Ltd* a lorry driver was found dead inside a boiler house, having been overcome by the fumes. He had no reason to be there, and his employers had no reason to suspect his presence. Again, the employers were not liable. And in *Horne v Lec Refrigeration Ltd*, a tool-setter had been trained to operate a machine, but was killed because of his failure to operate a safety drill. The employers were not liable, even though they were in breach of their statutory duty to ensure secure fencing.

11.135 It used to be inferred that this defence was one of *volenti non fit injuria*, ie that a person consents to the risk of being injured. But the doctrine of consent rarely succeeds in employment cases. The fact that an employee knows that he runs the risk of being injured does not mean that he consents to that risk because of the employer's negligence (*Smith v Baker & Sons*). The payment of 'danger money' to specialised employees (eg stunt artistes) may indicate that there is a special risk which cannot be guarded against, and to that extent consent may be raised; but even so, the real question to be asked is: was the employer negligent in the circumstances?

11.136 Moreover, the Unfair Contract Terms Act 1977 applies to those employment situations where the employer seeks to exclude his liability for injury to the employee by means of a prominently displayed notice or even a contract term. Section 2 of the Act states that a person cannot by reference to a contract term or to a notice exclude or restrict his liability for death or personal injury resulting from negligence. Thus an employer cannot escape his legal responsibility if he has been negligent.

Contributory negligence

11.137 This defence is based on the Law Reform (Contributory Negligence) Act 1945, which provides that if a person is injured, partly because of his own fault and partly due to the fault of another, damages shall be reduced to the extent the court thinks fit, having regard to the claimant's share in the responsibility for the damage. The defence is successfully raised in a number of cases. The employer will argue that even though he was negligent, so too was the injured employee, and a reduction in the amount of damages awarded will be the result. The actual percentage reduction made is scarcely based on scientific principles, and appeal courts may take a different view of the share of the blame to be apportioned.

11.138 Although in *Jayes v IMI (Kynoch) Ltd* the court of Appeal had held that there was no principle in law that rules out a finding of 100% contributory negligence, the case was disapproved by a more recent decision of the court in *Anderson v Newham College of Further Education*. There is a distinction between arguing that a claimant is 100% contributorily negligent and arguing that an accident was entirely due to the fault of the claimant. Thus, if there has been a breach of a statutory duty by an employer it must be shown not only that the worker's breach of the same statutory duty was as great as that of the employer, but also that the employer did all he could to ensure compliance by the worker. If there is no breach of statutory duty by the employer, no question of contributory negligence arises (*Anderson v Newham College of Further Education*).

New intervening act

11.139 An employer will not be liable if the injury is caused by a new intervening act, ie by a person or event over which or whom the employer has no control. In *Horton v Taplin Contracts Ltd* the claimant was standing on the platform of a scaffolding tower. A fellow worker, with whom he had previously had an altercation, deliberately pushed the tower over, and the claimant suffered serious injuries. He claimed damages from his employer, alleging a breach of the Provision and Use of Work Equipment Regulations, reg 5 and reg 20 (work equipment must be suitable for the purpose, and work equipment must be stabilised) as well as reg 5 of the Construction (Health Safety and Welfare) Regulations (employers must keep the workplace safe for any person at work there). The claim failed. Under reg 5 of PUWER the suitability of work equipment was to be measured by taking into account those hazards which were reasonably foreseeable. The obligation to stabilise the equipment under reg 20 only arose when this was necessary for the purpose of health and safety, which introduced considerations of foreseeability. Finally, the scaffolding tower was a safe place of work; it only became unsafe as the result of the deliberate, violent and unpredictable act of a third party.

11.140 Similarly, in *Yorkshire Traction Co Ltd v Searby*, a bus driver, while sitting in his driver's seat, was assaulted by a passenger. A county court judge held that the employers had been negligent in not inserting a screen to separate the driver from passengers, and thus there was a failure to provide work equipment which was 'suitable'. The decision was reversed by the Court of Appeal. In the first place, his trade union had strongly objected to the insertion of such screens, as these were considered to be a safety hazard. Indeed, some drivers had taken action to have the screens removed from their buses. It was further found that the risk of injury to bus drivers was very low. Thus the measure of the risk, the perceived disadvantages, and the attitude of the workforce was such that the failure by the employers to fit screens did not amount to negligence at common law. So far as a breach of statutory duty is concerned, the regulations do not require complete and absolute protection. In assessing the suitability of work equipment the test for liability involved a consideration of the degree of risk. Since the incidence of injury to drivers from passengers had been very low, it could not be said that the work equipment (ie the bus) was unsuitable.

G. Limitation of actions (Limitation Act 1980)

11.141 Any action in respect of negligence, nuisance or breach of statutory duty which has resulted in personal injury must be brought within three years from the date when the cause of action accrued, or from the date when the claimant had knowledge of the injury. 'Knowledge' in this connection, means when the injured person had knowledge that:

(a) the injury was significant;

(b) the injury was attributable wholly or partly to the act or omission which gave rise to the legal liability;

(c) the defendant was responsible;

(d) any other fact supporting the bringing of an action against the defendant.

A person's knowledge includes knowledge which he might reasonably be expected to acquire from facts which are observable by him, or from facts ascertainable by him with the help of medical or other expert advice which it is reasonable for him to seek. The Act does not apply in Scotland, where the Prescription and Limitations (Scotland) Act applies.

12

Disciplinary, Dismissal and Grievance Procedures

12.1 During the performance of the employment contract the employer may find it necessary, through the appropriate manager, foreman or supervisor who is charged with the necessary responsibility, to exercise some form of disciplinary authority over the employee. This may take one of a number of forms, ranging from counselling, informal warnings, etc, through to final warning or dismissal. The prime objective must be corrective, not punishment. Disciplinary procedures and powers must be exercised in a manner that will enable the employee to retain his position as a valued member of the staff, and not used purely as a matter of form of mechanical exercise. Thus adherence to a well-drafted disciplinary procedure is an essential part of any decision-making process. Equally, there will be occasions when the employee will wish to pursue a grievance over the way he is treated, and a suitable grievance procedure is the obvious channel to be used.

Disciplinary procedures

A. Procedures in operation

12.2 From the employer's point of view, there are likely to be three categories of 'hearings', and it is important to establish from the outset the distinctions. First, there is an informal interview or counselling session, at which matters can be discussed. So long as this session does not result in any form of disciplinary sanction, the worker does not have the right to be accompanied (see below) and matters are best resolved by the parties concerned. Second, there is the investigatory type of hearing, which is designed to ascertain facts and collate evidence. Again, the employee has no right to be accompanied even though the meeting could lead to disciplinary proceedings (*Skiggs v South West Trains Ltd*). Finally there is the disciplinary hearing itself, which can be of the statutory or non-statutory nature, and where certain fundamental principles will apply. The important thing is that employers should not allow the informal interview or investigatory hearing to turn into a disciplinary hearing and, if there is a possibility that this is going to happen, those hearings should be terminated and a formal disciplinary hearing convened.

Investigations by the employer

12.3 Clearly, no disciplinary action should be taken in advance of proper investigation by the employer. As Megarry VC stated in *John v Rees* (see para 12.22) the paths of the law are strewn with examples of unanswerable charges which were eventually answered. But there are certain limits on the extent to which an employer may properly make enquiries into an incident, particularly if the charge is a serious one, such as theft, for there may well be an improper interference with the processes of justice (*Tesco (Holdings) Ltd v Hill*). On the other hand, when an allegation is made against an employee, which is disputed, a most careful and conscientious investigation must be carried out, and the investigator must focus no less on evidence which may exculpate the employee, or at least point to his innocence. This is particularly so when the employee is suspended, and has thus been denied an opportunity of being able to contact potentially relevant witnesses (*A v B*).

12.4 Whether an employer should carry out his own investigations after being informed that criminal charges are to be brought against an employee in respect of matters arising out of his employment is a question of circumstances. On the one hand, it is incumbent on an employer to embark on some form of investigation involving at least an interview with the employee, to give him an opportunity to state his position. On the other hand, if the circumstances are so blatant and sufficient to warrant a belief as to the employee's guilt, no further investigation is necessary. Within this spectrum there are many situations where a further consideration of the position, including an interview with the employee, should be considered before disciplinary action is taken (*Lovie Ltd v Anderson*).

12.5 The employer is not obliged to hold a full-scale trial, but there must be a careful examination of all the relevant matters. An investigation should not be conducted with such haste that important evidence is overlooked (*Johnson Matthey Metals v Harding*), neither should it be delayed so long that issues become stale and hazy in the minds of witnesses (*Marley Homecare v Dutton*). There is no particular form of procedure to be adopted, as long as the employee is given a fair hearing (*Bentley Engineering Co v Mistry*). If it is necessary to consider an investigation in advance of criminal proceedings, it is still possible to discuss the matter without prejudicing a fair trial (*Harris (Ipswich) Ltd v Harrison*), and a decision may be made on the basis of known facts, even though the employee has been advised to remain silent. If the evidence produced is sufficiently indicative of guilt (in the absence of any explanation) the employer is entitled to take some action. If, however, there are doubts, fairness may require the employer to wait until the criminal proceedings have been concluded (*Harris and Shepherd v Courage (Eastern) Ltd*). The object in holding a full investigation is to confirm suspicions or clear up doubts as to whether or not a particular act of misconduct has occurred (see *British Home Stores v Burchell*). If an employee admits the offence, there is no need for a full investigation, unless some useful information could come to light (*Royal Society for the Protection of Birds v Croucher*).

12.6 When an allegation of an employee's misconduct has been made by an informant, a balance must be maintained between the need to protect the informant and respect his anonymity, and providing a fair hearing to the accused employee. In *Linfood Cash and Carry Ltd v Thomson*, the EAT laid down the following guidelines which could usefully be followed:

(a) the information should be reduced into writing, although it may be necessary to 'doctor' the statement in order to prevent identification;

(b) the statement should contain all the relevant facts, including dates, times, places, etc, the opportunity of the informant to observe clearly and with accuracy, circumstantial evidence, and whether the informant had any reason to fabricate the evidence, whether from a personal grudge or any other reason;

(c) further investigation should then take place to confirm, corroborate or challenge the information;

(d) tactful enquiries should be made about the background of the informant, and to find any other information which would add to or detract from the value of the information given;

(e) if the informant is not prepared to attend the disciplinary hearing, a decision will have to be taken on whether to continue or not;

(f) if it is decided to continue, the person responsible for conducting the hearing should interview the informant, and assess the weight to be given to the information;

(g) the written statement of the informant should be made available to the employee and his representatives;

(h) if there are matters to be put to the informant, the person conducting the hearing should adjourn to make further enquiries;

(i) full and careful notes of the disciplinary hearing should be taken;

(j) evidence from the investigation officer should be prepared in a written form.

12.7 However, such tactics may not always result in the protection of the anonymity of the informant, as an employee who has been dismissed in consequence of information provided in this manner may be able to obtain from the High Court an order compelling his former employer to disclose the identity of the informant, so as to pursue an appropriate remedy, eg defamation and/or malicious falsehood (*P v T Ltd*).

12.8 A distinction must be drawn between the investigatory function and the disciplinary function. If the same person undertakes both, there is usually no problem, but when they are separate and distinct, there is an obligation to give an employee a hearing at both stages. In *Budgen & Co v Thomas*, an employee was dismissed after she had signed a written confession that she had stolen a small sum of money. The matter had been investigated by the security officer, and on the basis of his report, which was sent to the company's head office, the decision to dismiss was taken. This was held to be unfair. She was an 18-year-old girl, diabetic, and subsequently claimed that she was confused at the time she signed the confession, and that it was not true. It could not be said that in view of her personal circumstances the management would have dismissed her had she been given the opportunity to present her case; the person who took the decision to dismiss should at least have given her a hearing.

12.9 A person who is a witness in investigatory proceedings should not act as a judge in disciplinary proceedings, otherwise this could be regarded as a breach of the principles of natural justice. However, there may be occasions when the person who has to take the decision to dismiss is also the person who witnessed the incident, and while this can be acceptable (and indeed inevitable) it is preferable for this dual role to be avoided (*Moyes v Hylton Castle Working Men's Social Club*). Also, a person who is involved in the investigatory stage should not, if possible, be involved in the appeal stage, as this would put him in a situation of being a judge in his own cause, and justice would not be done, as well as not appearing to be done (*Byrne v BOC Ltd*). However, in the case of small employers, this counsel of perfection may not be possible.

12.10 In those cases where witnesses are not part of the employer's organisation, it is not necessary for the employer to carry out a quasi-judicial hearing, with a confrontation and cross-examination of those witnesses (*Ulsterbus Ltd v Henderson*). In *Sainsbury's Supermarket Ltd v Hitt*, the Court of Appeal confirmed that the band of reasonableness approach applies to the conduct of investigations as much as to other procedural and substantive decisions to dismiss a person from his employment for conduct. Thus provided an employer carries out an appropriate investigation, gives the employee a fair opportunity to explain his conduct, etc, it would be wrong for an employment tribunal to suggest that further investigations should have been carried out for, by doing so, they are substituting their own standards of what was an adequate investigation for the standard that could be objectively expected from a reasonable employer.

B. Types of disciplinary and grievance procedures

12.11 There are three sets of rules which must be followed. First, there is the ACAS Code of Practice Disciplinary and Grievance Procedures in Employment, which should be studied in detail by all levels of management. A failure to follow the Code of Practice will not mean automatically that any action taken will inevitably be unfair (*Lewis Shops Group v Wiggins*) but employers ignore it at their peril. Employment tribunals should always consider the Code of Practice as a guide when assessing the reasonableness of any action taken, and any relevant provisions should be taken into account when determining the issues before them (*Lock v Cardiff Railway*).

12.12 Next, there are the new statutory dismissal, disciplinary and grievance procedures, introduced by the Employment Act 2002, with which an employer is required to comply, though not as contractual terms. These new statutory procedures are the minimum standards which are to be met by every employer and (where appropriate) every employee. A failure by either side to comply with them may result in the application of sanctions by an employment tribunal (see para 12.64). Any term or agreement to oust the operation of the statutory procedures will have no effect. It is hoped that by encouraging employers to follow these minimum statutory procedures and employees to utilise the grievance procedures, the number of disputes which end up in employment tribunals will be reduced.

12.13 Finally, there will be the normal contractual or non-contractual disciplinary and grievance procedures (many of which will have already been in existence for some time), which are still valid and should still function, provided they meet at least the standards set down by the statutory procedures. They can, however, be more expansive. A failure to follow contractual procedures may constitute a breach of contract by the employer. This may result in (a) the employee seeking an injunction to restrain the employer from taking disciplinary action in breach of the procedure (*Peace v City of Edinburgh Council*) (b) the employee resigning and claiming that he was constructively dismissed (see Chapter 17) or (c) the employee seeking damages at common law, based on the length of time he would have been employed had the appropriate procedure been followed (*Gunton v London Borough of Richmond upon Thames*). But a failure to follow a procedure in relation to a dismissal will not render that dismissal unfair if the employer can show that the dismissal would have taken place if the procedure had been followed, and the statutory procedure was followed (see para 12.18).

C. Drawing up procedures

12.14 The responsibility for drawing up disciplinary and grievance procedures is on the employer. Clearly, if he can obtain the co-operation and assistance of any relevant trade union, or of his employees, so much the better, but in the absence of any such co-operation, the employer must act unilaterally. There are practical advantages in having trade union involvement in drawing up procedures, and challenges alleging unfairness are less likely to succeed if agreed procedures are followed.

12.15 The important thing is that the employer does not have to prove that an offence took place, or even satisfy himself beyond all reasonable doubt that the employee committed the act in question. The function of the employer is to act reasonably in coming to a decision. Thus in *Ferodo Ltd v Barnes*, an employee was dismissed for vandalism. The employment tribunal was not satisfied that the employee was guilty, and therefore held that the dismissal was unfair. This finding was reversed by the EAT. The question was not whether or not the employment tribunal was satisfied that the employee was guilty, but whether they were satisfied that the employer had reasonable grounds for believing that the employee had committed the offence, and had acted reasonably in dismissing for that offence. The employer is not concerned to apply standards of proof which may be relevant in a criminal court. In *Docherty v Reddy*, the employee was dismissed for stealing 50p from the till. The employers took into account that they had suspected him of stealing similar sums on previous occasions, and it was held that they were entitled to have regard to their past suspicions. Clearly, a suspicion of previous theft is hardly evidence which would be admitted in a criminal court, but the issues are different. The employer is having to decide whether or not he wishes to retain the employee, not whether or not he was guilty of a particular offence. Thus the test is, what would a reasonable employer have done on the facts which he knew, taking into account the Code of Practice and current industrial relations practice (*Parkers Bakeries Ltd v Palmer*). The employment tribunal must not act as a court of appeal, nor retry a case, and the fact that in subsequent criminal proceedings an employee is acquitted of a charge against him is irrelevant to the issue of whether or not the employer has acted reasonably (*Davies v GKN Birwelco (Uskside) Ltd*).

12.16 Evidence which is not admissible in criminal proceedings may fairly be considered by an employer in disciplinary proceedings (*Dhaliwal v British Airways Board*) and a confession which would be inadmissible in a criminal court is also properly admissible before a disciplinary board (*Morley's of Brixton Ltd v Minott*).

12.17 If an employee pleaded guilty to a criminal offence in a court of law, or has been found guilty by the court, it is reasonable for an employer to believe that the offence has been committed by the employee. Any other conclusion 'would be ridiculous' (*P v Nottinghamshire County Council*). The fact of conviction might well form an adequate basis for dismissal, although the nature of the offence would be a relevant factor. Thus to dismiss for a trivial offence would not be reasonable (*Secretary of State for Scotland v Campbell*).

12.18 If the employer fails to follow his own disciplinary and dismissal procedures, but follows the statutory procedures, such failure will not by itself be regarded as making the employer's action unreasonable, if it can be shown that the employer would have dismissed the employee had the correct procedure been followed (ERA, s 98A(2)) (see *Polkey v A E Dayton Services Ltd*).

D. Composition of procedural bodies

12.19 The composition of any disciplinary body will doubtless be determined by each employer in accordance with the size of the firm and the circumstances of each case. The procedure will lay down who can exercise authority, the extent of the authority, and the circumstances when it is exercised. For example, informal warnings may be given at a certain level by supervisors, formal warnings should be given in writing, and signed by someone who has power to issue and act on them, and so on. If an appeal may be made to a disciplinary board, its composition should be specified, with due regard to providing substitutes as appropriate. Otherwise a failure to do this may result in a dismissal being rendered unfair when it may have been fair. Thus in *Westminster City Council v Cabaj*, the employee was dismissed. He was entitled to appeal to an appeal tribunal consisting of three council members. At the actual hearing, only two council members turned up, and they proceeded to hear the appeal, and dismissed it. The employee was not asked if he agreed to the appeal being heard by two members. The Court of Appeal held that where there is a failure to comply with a contractually enforceable disciplinary procedure, it was for the employment tribunal to determine whether a consequent dismissal is fair or unfair, and there is no automatic assumption of unfairness. The employment tribunal must decide the issue in accordance with the matters set out in ERA, s 98. But where public institutions are concerned, the persons sitting on the appeal body must have been validly appointed, and there is no power to ratify an invalid appointment (*R v Secretary of State for Education, ex p Prior*).

12.20 In *Clark v Civil Aviation Authority*, the EAT gave some broad guidance on how disciplinary proceedings should be conducted. The purpose of the meeting should be explained, those present identified, representation should be arranged, the employee should be informed of the allegations being made, the evidence should be presented in statement form or through witnesses, the employee or his representative should be permitted to ask questions, the employee should be permitted to call witnesses, he or his representative will then explain or argue his case, both sides can then argue on the allegations and any possible consequences, including mitigation, and the employee will finally be asked if there is any further evidence or enquiry which will help his case. The decision will then be reduced to writing (whether or not an earlier oral decision has been given).

12.21 Particular care should be taken when it is proposed to take disciplinary action against shop stewards, and the Code of Practice recommends that it is advisable to discuss the circumstances of the case with a full-time official of the union concerned. However, being a shop steward is not a passport to disciplinary immunity (*Fowler v Cammell Laird (Shipbuilders) Ltd*).

12.22 A disciplinary hearing must be conducted fairly. To achieve this, a number of rules should be observed.

(a) The employee is entitled to know the nature of the charge against him, in sufficient detail to enable him to prepare his case (*Hutchins v British Railways Board*). It is no bad thing to put this in writing, particularly if the employee's command of English is weak, so that he can get someone else to explain to him the nature of the allegations he has to meet (*Sharma v West Yorkshire Passenger Transport Executive*). Witness statements should be shown to him (*Louies v Coventry Hood and Seating Co Ltd*) although it is acknowledged that there may be occasions when it is necessary to preserve anonymity (*Linfood Cash and Carry Ltd v Thomson*, see para 12.6). But in *Fuller v Lloyds Bank plc* an employee of the respondents was in a public house on Christmas Eve, and received severe facial injuries from a glass which the claimant held in his hand. The employers took statements from a number of witnesses, but these were not disclosed to the claimant, as a matter of policy. Following a disciplinary hearing, he was dismissed, and claimed his dismissal was unfair. An employment tribunal dismissed his claim, arguing that the claimant knew the nature of the allegations. An appeal to the EAT failed. The procedure adopted was not so defective as to make the overall result unfair. Thus there is no universal requirement of natural justice or general principles of law that in all cases a witness statement must be shown to an employee who has been accused of misconduct. It is only a failure of natural justice if the essence of the case against the employee is contained in the statements, and he has not been otherwise informed of the nature of the case against him (*Hussain v Elonex plc*). There is no rule of law which requires an employer to permit an employee to cross-examine, during a disciplinary hearing, colleagues who have made allegations of misconduct by the employee. The employer must carry out a reasonable investigation into the alleged wrongdoing, not carry out a forensic or quasi-judicial investigation (*Santemera v Express Cargo Forwarding*).

(b) An employee should always be given an opportunity to state his case (*Tesco (Holdings) Ltd v Hill*) no matter what the circumstances are. He is entitled to plead that he did not do the alleged act, or that he did not intend the construction which has been put on it, or that mitigating circumstances relating to his case should be taken into consideration (*Budgen & Co v Thomas*, below). To dismiss a woman who, because of a pregnancy-related illness, is unable to attend a disciplinary hearing is to cause her to suffer a detriment on grounds of pregnancy, and is therefore direct sex discrimination (*Abbey National plc v Formoso*). However, it is not essential that he should be present in person throughout the hearing, when all the evidence is being given, if his representative is there (*Pirelli General Cable Works v Murray*). The opportunity given to an employee to 'state his case' cannot be underestimated or undervalued. The reason is perhaps obvious; as Sir Robert Megarry said in *John v Rees*: '. . . the path of the law is strewn with examples of open and shut cases which, somehow, were not; of unanswerable charges which, in the event, were completely answered; of inexplicable conduct which was fully explained; of fixed and unalterable determinations that, by discussion, suffered a change. Nor are those with any knowledge of human nature who pause to think for a moment likely to underestimate the feelings of resentment of those who find that a decision against them has been made without their being afforded any opportunity to influence the course of events.'

However, in rare cases, where there is no possibility of any explanation of the conduct alleged, or where misconduct is admitted by the employee, it is legally permissible (although possibly in practice undesirable) to dispense with disciplinary formalities (*Clarke v Trimoco Motor Group Ltd*). Thus in *Sutherland v Sonat Offshore (UK) Inc* the employers had a strict rule forbidding alcohol or drugs while employees were on a drilling unit. The appellant was given a routine drug test, which showed the presence of cannabis in his urine, and the result was confirmed in further tests. He was dismissed without being given a proper chance to state his case, but the EAT upheld a finding of an employment tribunal that his dismissal was nonetheless fair. The requirement for investigation was met by the testing procedures, there was no possibility of an error and there was no way the substance could have been ingested by some other means, eg 'passive smoking'. Thus the employers were entitled to act on the evidence before them without involving the full disciplinary procedure.

(c) He should be permitted the right to be represented or accompanied in accordance with the procedure (*Rank Xerox (UK) Ltd v Goodchild*). There is now a statutory right to be accompanied (see below).

(d) He should be informed of his right to appeal to a higher level of management, who have not previously been involved in the decision (*S C Brown Communications Ltd v Walker*), or to an independent arbitrator. If he fails or refuses to exercise that right, then he does not contribute to the unfair dismissal, nor does he fail to mitigate his loss (*William Muir (Bond 9) Ltd v Lamb*). As a matter of principle, a person who takes the decision to dismiss should not take any part in the appeal process (*R v Chief Constable of Merseyside Police*), although it has to be conceded that this counsel of perfection cannot be applied to small firms.

E. Right to be accompanied: Employment Relations Act 1999, ss 10–15

12.23 Section 10 of the Employment Relations Act 1999 creates a new right for a worker, when invited by his employer to attend a disciplinary or grievance hearing, to make a reasonable request to be accompanied by a single companion, who can be either:

(a) an official of an independent trade union (not necessarily one recognised by the employer); or

(b) a trade union official who has been certified by the trade union as having had experience or having received training in acting as a worker's companion in such hearings (eg a shop steward); or

(c) another of the employer's workers.

12.24 The right to be accompanied is triggered by any hearing which has the characteristic of a disciplinary sanction, however it is described. An investigatory meeting or one which could only result in a genuine informal warning, will not attract the statutory right to be accompanied. But a requirement to undergo retraining, coaching or counselling is not a disciplinary sanction since it does not contain an element of penalty or punishment (*London Underground Ltd v Ferenc-Batchelor*).

12.25 The companion is entitled to address the hearing in order to put the worker's case, sum up that case, respond to any views expressed at the hearing, and to confer with the worker during the hearing. He is not entitled to answer questions on behalf of the worker, or address the hearing if the worker does not wish him to do so. Nor can he prevent the worker from explaining his case or prevent any other person from making a contribution to the hearing. However, there is no obligation on any person, whether or not he is a trade union official, to take on the role of companion.

12.26 The statutory right does not include a right to be accompanied by a lawyer or any other person, although the employer is free to permit such person to attend the hearing, either in accordance with an express term in the procedure or on an 'ad hoc' basis.

12.27 If the worker makes a request to be accompanied, but the chosen companion is not available at the time proposed for the hearing, the employer must postpone the hearing to a time proposed by the worker. The alternative time must be reasonable, and within five working days after the date proposed by the employer.

12.28 The employer shall permit a worker to have time off work for the purpose of accompanying another worker, and, when acting in the capacity of a trade union official, this will count as trade union duties for the purpose of TULR(C)A, ss 168–173 and thus the time off work will be with pay.

12.29 The right to be accompanied applies to workers as defined, including agency workers, homeworkers, persons in Crown employment and members of the staff of the House of Lords and House of Commons (s 13). However, persons employed by the Security Services, Secret Intelligence Service and Government Communications Headquarters are excluded from the above provisions (s 15).

12.30 A complaint may be made to an employment tribunal (within the usual time limits) that the employer has failed to permit the worker to exercise his rights under s 10, which, if it finds the complaint to be well founded, shall make a compensation award of up to two weeks' pay (s 11).

12.31 A worker has the right not to suffer a detriment because he sought to be accompanied or to accompany another, and any dismissal because of the exercise of the above rights will be automatically unfair. The qualifying periods of employment and the age limits do not apply, and interim relief will be available, as appropriate (s 12).

F. Appeal procedures

12.32 If the initial procedure is flawed in some way a refusal by the employer to permit an employee to exercise the right of appeal to which he is contractually entitled will render a dismissal unfair (*West Midland Co-operative Society v Tipton*). If an employer's decision to dismiss would be fair at the time when the appeal machinery is exhausted, that decision does not become unfair because further information comes to light after the appeal has been dismissed (*Greenall Whitley plc v Carr*).

12.33 Whether an appeal hearing should be a rehearing of all the evidence *de novo*, or a review of all the evidence with an opportunity to make further representations, is a matter of style. However, if there is a substantial unfairness at the original hearing, this is unlikely to be corrected on review, and the appeal should then be a rehearing, when the unfairness can be rectified (*Whitbread & Co plc v Mills* and *Sartor v P & O European Ferries (Felixstowe) Ltd*). Thus if an initial decision to dismiss was unfair, the defect can be cured by a rehearing of the case by way of appeal (*Adwihalli v Export Guarantee Department*) provided there is a complete rehearing of all the evidence, and not merely a review of the original decision (*Lloyd v Taylor Woodrow Construction Ltd*).

12.34 However, it is very important that internal appeals procedures operated by commercial concerns should not be cramped by legal requirements which impose impossible burdens on the way they conduct their affairs. In *Rowe v Radio Rentals* the claimant was alleged to have been guilty of gross misconduct, and was dismissed by the area manager. An appeal was made to the regional manager and at the hearing the area manager outlined the facts of the case and remained present throughout the hearing. It was held that the appeals procedure was perfectly fair, even though it may appear to have offended against the rules of natural justice. It was inevitable that those who take the original decision to dismiss must be in daily contact with their superiors who would be hearing the appeal. Rules about lack of contact cannot be applied in the majority of cases. The EAT quoted with approval Lord Denning in *Ward v Bradford Corpn*: 'We must not force these disciplinary bodies to become entrammelled in the nets of legal procedure. So long as they act fairly and justly, their decision should be supported'.

12.35 If an employee is dismissed, but is given a right to make an appeal in accordance with the company's disciplinary procedure, what is his legal position up to the time the appeal is heard? There are two possibilities.

12.36 First, if he is dismissed (with or without notice) the dismissal takes effect from the effective date of termination, and the fact that an appeal is pending does not alter that date. In *J Sainsbury Ltd v Savage* the applicant was dismissed for gross misconduct. On the effective date of termination he did not have the requisite period of continuous employment (26 weeks, as the law then was), but by the time the appeal was heard, more than 28 weeks had elapsed since the commencement of his employment. It was held that he could not pursue a claim for unfair dismissal. Thus using domestic appeal machinery merely suspends the dismissal; if the appeal is rejected, the original decision is confirmed (*Natt v Hillingdon Area Health Authority*).

12.37 Second, if he is dismissed, and placed on full pay pending an internal appeal, there is a suspension which does not terminate the contract, and hence he is still an employee up to the time of the appeal hearing (*Duffy v Northampton Area Health Authority*).

12.38 On the other hand, if a person is dismissed, and then his appeal against dismissal is allowed, his period of employment is to be regarded as being continuous, for it is implicit in the contract that the period between the dismissal and appeal is one of suspension, and the result of the ultimate decision of the appeal process relates back to the date of the purported dismissal (*Howgate v Fane Acoustics*).

Statutory dispute resolution procedures (Employment Act 2002, s 30 and Sch 2)

12.39 Every contract of employment shall have effect to require the employer and employee to comply with the requirements of statutory disputes resolution procedures, notwithstanding any agreement to the contrary. However, private disciplinary dismissal and grievance procedures will still apply as long as they are not inconsistent with the statutory procedures. A failure by an employer or an employee to comply with the minimum statutory procedures will have certain adverse legal consequences.

The statutory procedures for dealing with dismissal, disciplinary and grievance matters is as follows.

A. Statutory dismissal and disciplinary procedure (SDDP)

12.40 The standard procedure for dealing with dismissal or disciplinary matters is as follows:

(a) *Step 1* The employer must set out in writing the employee's alleged misconduct or characteristics or other circumstances which leads him to contemplate dismissing or taking disciplinary action against the employee. A copy of this statement must be sent to the employee, together with an invitation to attend a meeting to discuss the matter. Further, the employer must inform the employee what the basis was for including in the above written statement the ground or grounds given in it, and the employee must be given a reasonable opportunity to consider his response to that information.

(b) *Step 2* The meeting must take place before the employer can take any action, except precautionary suspension (see para 12.100). The employee must take all reasonable steps to attend the meeting. After the meeting, the employer must inform the employee of his decision, and notify him of his right of appeal if he is not satisfied.

(c) *Step 3* If the employee wishes to appeal, he must inform the employer of his decision. The employer must then invite the employee to attend a further meeting and, again, the employee must make all reasonable efforts to attend. However, the employer may put any dismissal or disciplinary action into effect before the appeal hearing takes place. After the appeal hearing, the employer must inform the employee of the final decision.

B. Modified procedure in cases of summary dismissal for gross misconduct

12.41 Where an employee is dismissed summarily for gross misconduct (see para 16.8), a modified procedure must be put into effect.

(a) *Step 1* The employer must set out in writing the nature of the employee's gross misconduct which led to the dismissal, specifying what the basis was for thinking at the time of the dismissal that the employee was guilty of the alleged misconduct.

A copy must be sent to the employee, together with notification of a right to appeal against the decision.

(b) *Step 2* If the employee wishes to appeal, he must inform the employer accordingly. The employer must then invite the employee to a meeting, to which the employee must take all reasonable steps to attend. After the appeal hearing, the employer must inform the employee of the final decision.

C. General requirements

12.42 In respect of the above statutory procedures, the following general requirements will apply, so far as applicable.

(1) Each step and action under procedure will take place without unreasonable delay.

(2) The timings and location of meetings must be reasonable.

(3) Meetings must be conducted in a manner that enables both employer and employee to explain their cases.

(4) In the case of appeal hearings, the employer should, so far as is reasonably practicable, be represented by a more senior manager than the one who attended earlier hearings (obviously, this counsel of perfection cannot be applied to small employers, where there is unlikely to be anyone in a higher position than the person who took the initial decision).

It should be noted that the employee has the right to be accompanied at any of the above meetings, in accordance with the provisions of the Employment Relations Act 1999, ss 10–15 (see para 12.23).

D. Applying/disapplying statutory procedures

12.43 The Employment Act 2002 (Dispute Resolution) Regulations 2004 state (1) the circumstances in which the standard dismissal, disciplinary and grievance procedures, including the modified procedures, will apply, (2) the circumstances when they will not apply, and (3) the circumstances in which the parties are treated as having complied with the procedures.

The standard dismissal and disciplinary procedures apply

12.44 The standard dismissal and disciplinary procedures will apply when an employer contemplates dismissing or taking relevant disciplinary action against an employee. 'Relevant disciplinary action' means action, short of dismissal, which the employer asserts to be based wholly or mainly on the employee's conduct or capability, other than suspension on full pay or the issue of warnings (whether oral or written).

12.45 The modified dismissal procedure applies when the employer dismisses the employee without notice by reason of his conduct, the dismissal occurred at the time when the employer became aware of the conduct (or immediately thereafter), the employer was entitled to dismiss the employee without notice or a payment in lieu of notice by reason of that conduct, and it was reasonable for the employer to dismiss the employee before enquiring into the circumstances in which the conduct took place. However, the modified dismissal and disciplinary procedures do not apply to such a dismissal if the employee presents a claim to an employment tribunal relating to the dismissal at a time when the employer has failed to send a statement to the employee setting out the alleged misconduct, the basis for the employer's belief, and the employee's right of appeal.

The standard dismissal and disciplinary procedures do not apply

12.46 Neither the standard nor the modified dismissal and disciplinary procedures will apply in the following circumstances:

(a) if all the employees dismissed are of the same description or category, and the employer offers to re-engage all who were dismissed;

(b) when 20 or more employees are dismissed as being redundant;

(c) if at the time of the dismissal the employee is taking part in an unofficial strike or unofficial industrial action, or the employer engaged in a lock-out, and the employee was not offered re-engagement within three months but others who were so affected were offered re-engagement (ie there was selective re-engagement);

(d) if the reason for the dismissal was that the employee took protected industrial action which would be unfair because it took place within the eight-week protected period (see TULR(C)A, s 238A(2));

(e) if the employer's business suddenly ceases to function because of some unforeseen event;

(f) if the dismissal was because the employee could not continue to work in the position he held without contravening a statute;

(g) if the employee is covered by a dismissal procedures agreement under ERA, s 110 (no such agreements are currently in force).

The standard dismissal and disciplinary procedures will be treated as having been complied with

12.47 The standard dismissal and disciplinary procedure will be treated as having been complied with if the employee has submitted an application to an employment tribunal for interim relief, and while the employer has set out the grounds for the action in writing, and held a meeting, the employee has not exercised his right to appeal.

12.48 The standard dismissal and disciplinary procedure will also be treated as being complied with if the employee has appealed under a procedure which operates by virtue of a collective agreement made between two or more employers and an independent trade union.

E. Statutory grievance procedure

12.49 The statutory grievance procedure to be followed by employees is as follows.

(a) *Step 1* The employee must set out the grievance in writing and send a copy to the employer.

(b) *Step 2* The employer must invite the employee to at least one meeting to discuss the grievance, but the meeting must not take place unless the employee has informed the employer what the basis was for the grievance, and the employer has had a reasonable opportunity to consider his response to that information. The employee must take all reasonable steps to attend. After the meeting, the employer must inform the employee of his decision in response to the grievance, and notify the employee of his right to appeal against that decision if he is not satisfied with it.

(c) *Step 3* The employee must inform the employer if he wishes to appeal against the decision. The employer must then invite the employee to a further meeting, and the employee must take all reasonable steps to attend. After the appeal hearing, the employer must inform the employee of his final decision.

The standard grievance procedure will apply

12.50 The standard grievance procedure will apply in relation to any action by an employer which could form the basis of a complaint under a jurisdiction listed in Sch 3 or 4 to the Employment Act 2002 (see below). A grievance is defined as a complaint by an employee about action which his employer has taken or is contemplating taking in relation to him.

Modified procedure for ex-employees

12.51 Where the person raising the grievance is a former employee, a modified procedure will apply.

(a) *Step 1* The ex-employee must set out the grievance in writing, and the basis for it, and send a copy to the employer.

(b) *Step 2* The employer must set out his response in writing and send a copy to the ex-employee.

12.52 The modified grievance procedure will apply where:

(a) the employee has ceased to be employed by the employer;

(b) the employer was unaware of the grievance before the employment ceased, or was so aware, but the standard grievance procedure was not commenced or was not completed before the last day of employment and the parties have agreed in writing that the modified procedure should apply.

The standard or modified grievance procedure will not apply

12.53 Neither the standard nor the modified grievance procedures apply where:

(a) the employee has ceased to be employed by the employer;

(b) neither procedure has been commenced;

(c) since the employee ceased to be employed it has ceased to be reasonably practicable for him to set out the grievance in writing and send a copy to the employer;

(d) the employer has dismissed or is contemplating dismissing the employee;

(e) the employer is contemplating taking action short of dismissal against the employee, based on his conduct or capability (but not if the action was suspension on full pay or the issue of a written or oral warning). However, the procedures will so apply if the grievance is that the employer is taking (or contemplating taking) disciplinary action which could amount to unlawful discrimination (see below).

12.54 Further, it should be noted that the statutory grievance procedure does not apply where the employee is making a protected disclosure within the meaning of ERA, ss 43A–43J (see para 10.70) unless the employee intends that the making of the disclosure itself constitutes the raising of a grievance.

The standard or modified grievance procedure will be treated as being complied with

12.55 The parties will be treated as complying with the standard or modified grievance procedures in the following circumstances:

(a) where the employer took or is taking disciplinary action against the employee, and one of the reasons for the grievance is that that action would amount to unlawful discrimination under the Equal Pay Act, Sex Discrimination Act, Race Relations Act, Disability Discrimination Act, Employment Equality (Religion or Belief) Regulations, or Employment Equality (Sexual Orientation) Regulations.

(b) The grounds on which the employer took or is taking disciplinary action are unrelated to the grounds he originally asserted.

12.56 In the above circumstances, the parties will be treated as having complied with the standard or modified grievance procedure if the employee has set out his grievance in a written statement sent to the employer, before there has been an appeal under the disciplinary and dismissal procedures or, if the procedures have not been followed, before presenting a complaint arising out of that grievance to an employment tribunal.

(c) If the employee has ceased to be employed by the employer, but he has set out his grievance in writing and sent it to the employer, but since the end of the employment it has ceased to be reasonably practicable to hold a meeting or an appeal hearing, the parties will be treated as having complied with the standard or modified grievance procedure.

(d) If an appropriate representative (ie official of an independent trade union or employee representative with authority to represent employees under an established procedure) of the employee having a grievance has written to the employer setting out the grievance (specifying the names of at least two employees, of whom one is the employee having the grievance), the parties will be treated as having complied with the requirements of the standard or modified grievance procedure.

(e) Where there is a collective agreement made between two or more employers and an independent trade union which provides for a grievance procedure, which the employee uses, the parties shall be treated as having complied with the statutory or modified grievance procedure.

Grievance letters

12.57 There is no particular formality for a grievance letter. All the employee needs to do is to set out his/her grievance in writing. Thus in *Shergold v Fieldway Medical Centre* the claimant wrote a three-page letter setting out her reasons for resigning her employment.

She did not state that the letter was intended to raise a grievance, but her employer invited her to a meeting to discuss the matter before accepting her resignation. It was held that the fact that the written grievance was contained in a letter of resignation was irrelevant. Nor was it necessary to make it clear that the letter was intended to invoke the grievance procedure, or that every detail of the complaint be set out.

12.58 A grievance letter does not have to expressly state that it is intended as such. Any document which raises a grievance can be treated as having complied with the statutory procedure (*Mark Warner Ltd v Aspland*). Thus a letter sent by a representative of the employee (eg, a solicitor or other adviser) can amount to the raising of a grievance within the Act (*Stewart v Barnetts Motor Group Ltd*). Any contractual grievance procedure which is more elaborate than the statutory grievance procedure cannot undermine the latter. If a claimant has complied with the statutory procedure for making an application for flexible working, he does not have to comply with the statutory grievance procedure before submitting a claim for unfair constructive dismissal (*Commotion Ltd v Rutty*).

12.59 The nature of the grievance must be substantially the same as the subsequent complaint. Thus a letter complaining about non-payment of holiday pay cannot be held to be compliance with the grievance procedure in a subsequent complaint about some form of discrimination.

12.60 However, it is important to distinguish between the standard and modified grievance procedures. In the standard grievance procedure, the employee must set out the grievance in writing. If the modified procedure applies, the employee must state the basis for the grievance, ie, the grounds of the grievance as well as an outline of the grievance itself. A failure to do so may mean that the technical requirements of a grievance letter are not complied with (*Thorpe & Solell Investments v Poat and Lake*).

12.61 There is no requirement on the employee to have the grievance dealt with by the employer under the statutory procedure before submitting a resignation (*Galaxy Showers Ltd v Wilson*) and a failure to follow the employer's contractual grievance procedure will also not debar the employee from making a claim of constructive dismissal (*Thorpe & Soleil Investments v Poat and Lake*). There is some force in the view that to permit a claim to proceed to a tribunal hearing when the employee has presented a grievance letter which is coupled with an immediate resignation, is a violation of the spirit, if not the letter, of the changes made by the 2002 Act. A grievance letter coupled with the giving of notice of termination at least allows for the employer to seek a resolution of the problem.

12.62 There are also three important general exceptions to the use of the procedures, when the statutory procedures do not apply. These are:

(a) if a party believes that using the relevant procedure would result in a significant threat to himself, or any other person or property;

(b) the party has been the subject of harassment or continuing the relevant procedure would result in further harassment; or

(c) it is not practicable for the party to commence or continue the procedure within a reasonable time.

12.63 However, if the statutory procedure has been commenced, and any of the above situations arise, the parties will be treated as having complied with the procedure.

F. Failure to comply with the statutory procedures

12.64 If either party fails to comply with a requirement of the standard or modified dismissal, disciplinary or grievance procedures, the non-completion shall be attributable to that party, and neither party shall be under any obligation to comply with any further requirement. However, this does not apply if the parties are to be treated as complying with the procedure (above). If an employer or employee fail to attend a meeting organised in accordance with the statutory procedure for a reason which was not foreseeable, this will not be treated as having failed to comply with the requirements of the procedure.

12.65 (1) If the employer or the employee fails to complete the statutory disciplinary, dismissal procedures (Employment Act 2002, s 31), then in respect of certain specific complaints which are set out in Sch 3 of the Employment Act 2002, various financial penalties can be incurred by the employer or employee, as appropriate (Employment Act 2002, s 31).

12.66 (2) If the employee (a) fails to put his grievance in writing to his employer, or (b) less than 28 days has passed since he did so, or (c) the day on which he did so was more than one month after the end of the original time limit for making a complaint, then in respect of certain specified complaints which are set out in Sch 4 to the Act, he shall not be entitled to present a complaint to an employment tribunal (Employment Act 2002, s 32).

12.67 (3) If the employer fails to comply with his duty to provide written particulars of the contract of employment (Employment Act 2002, s 38), then in respect of certain claims specified in Sch 5 to the Employment Act 2002, various financial penalties shall be incurred by the employer (Employment Act 2002, s 38).

12.68 The specified complaints are listed in Sch 3 (non-completion of statutory procedures, s 31), Sch 4 (complaints about grievances, s 32) and Sch 5 (failure to give written particulars, s 38). At the present time, the complaints to which Schs 3, 4 and 5 apply are identical (the Secretary of State may add to them by regulation), except that the Employment Tribunals Extension of Jurisdiction Order 1994 and its Scottish equivalent have been excluded from Sch 4. The reason is that s 32 (complaints about grievances) applies to employees, whereas complaints under the Order can only be brought by ex-employees, because the claim must arise or be outstanding 'on the termination of the employee's employment'. Hence the inclusion of the order in Sch 4 was unnecessary.

12.69 Otherwise, the complaints to which Schs 3, 4 and 5 apply are as follows:

Equal Pay Act 1970 (equality clauses)

Sex Discrimination Act 1975, s 63 (discrimination in employment field)

Race Relations Act 1976 (discrimination in employment field)

Trade Union and Labour Relations (Consolidation) Act 1992, s 146 (detriment in relation to trade union members and activities

Trade Union and Labour Relations (Consolidation) Act 1992, Sch A1 para 156 (detriment in relation to union recognition rights)

Disability Discrimination Act 1995, s 8 (discrimination in employment field)

Employment Rights Act 1996, s 23 (unathorised deductions or payments

Employment Rights Act 1996, s 48 (detriment in employment)

Employment Rights Act 1996, s 111 (unfair dismissal)

Employment Rights Act 1996, s 163 (redundancy payments)

National Minimum Wage Act 1998, s 24 (detriment in relation to national minimum wage)

Employment Tribunals Extension of Jurisdiction (England and Wales) Order 1994 (breach of employment contract and termination)

Employment Tribunals Extension of Jurisdiction (Scotland) Order 1994 (corresponding provision for Scotland)

Working Time Regulations 1998, reg 30 (breach of the regulations)

Transnational Information and Consultation of Employees Regulations 1999, reg 32 (detriment in relation to Works Councils)

Employment Equality (Sexual Orientation) Regulations 2003 (discrimination in employment field)

Employment Equality (Religion or Belief) Regulations 2003 (discrimination in employment field).

Employment Equality (Age) Regulations 2006

G. Extension of time limits

12.70 Under the normal rules, an employee generally has three months from the date of any cause of action to present a claim to an employment tribunal (see Chapter 20). However, the regulations specify the circumstances when an extension of time for a further period of three months is permitted, as follows.

12.71 (1) If the statutory dismissal and disciplinary procedure applies, and the employee presents a complaint to an employment tribunal after the normal time limit, but had reasonable grounds for believing that when the time limit expired, that a dismissal or disciplinary procedure, whether statutory or otherwise, was being followed (including an appeal procedure). Thus if the matter in question is still being dealt with under the statutory dismissal, disciplinary procedure, or under a procedure set out in a collective agreement made between two or more employers and an independent trade union, the period will be extended for a further three months (see Chapter 20).

12.72 (2) If the statutory grievance procedure applies, including the modified procedure, and

(a) the employee presents a complaint to the employment tribunal within the normal time limits but he is not permitted to do so because he has failed to set out his grievance in writing in accordance with s 32(2)(3) of the Employment Act 2002, or

(b) he presents a complaint to the employment tribunal after the expiry of the normal time limit but he has set out his grievance in writing as required within the normal time limit.

H. Adjustment of awards

12.73 If the relevant statutory dismissal and disciplinary procedure has not been followed by the employer, and the failure to do so is wholly or mainly attributable to the fault of the employer, with the consequence that the employee is dismissed, then the employee will be treated as having been unfairly dismissed. This will be so even though the employer could show that the employee would have been fairly dismissed had the procedure been followed. If an order for reinstatement or re-engagement is made, the tribunal also must make a minimum award of four weeks' pay, unless it considers that such an award would result in injustice to the employer (ERA, s 98A).

12.74 Where the non-completion of the statutory dismissal and disciplinary procedure was attributable wholly or mainly to a failure by the employer to comply with a requirement of the procedure, and the dismissal is ultimately found to be unfair, the tribunal must increase any award by between 10% and 50%, although there is a discretion to use a lesser percentage as it considers just and equitable in all the circumstances. If the non-completion of the statutory procedure is wholly or mainly attributable to the failure of an employee to comply with a requirement of the procedure, or fails to exercise his right of appeal under it or bring an unfair dismissal claim before the employer's appeal procedure has been exhausted and the dismissal is held to be unfair, the tribunal may reduce any award made by between 10% and 50%, although again there is a discretion to make no reduction or a lesser reduction as it considers to be just and equitable in all the circumstances (Employment Act 2002, s 31).

12.75 If an employee brings a complaint under any of the jurisdictions listed in Sch 5, and the tribunal finds in his favour, but makes no award in respect of the claim, and the employer had failed to provide the written statement as required by ERA, s 1 or s 4 (see para 3.102), it must make an award of between two and four weeks' pay. The same rule applies if an award is made in respect of the particular complaint (Employment Act 2002, s 38).

Disciplinary rules

12.76 The actual rules which an employee is expected to observe can be found either in the disciplinary procedure itself, or in the works or staff rules (see Chapter 3) or even a combination of both. At one time it was customary to write them on a prominently displayed notice posted somewhere in the works, but this is not particularly satisfactory nowadays. The important thing is that they must be brought to the employee's attention, whether on an induction course, or in a specially prepared handbook or other suitable method. In *Pitts v Revertex* the employer posted a notice near the canteen on a notice board stating that any employee who absented himself without authority would be guilty of gross misconduct. The applicant was found to be absent, and was dismissed. It was held that if a rule was so important, posting a notice was not sufficient. It should have been communicated individually to each employee. The need to communicate the relevant rules to the employees concerned was stressed once again in *Brooks (W) & Son v Skinner*, where the employers agreed with a trade union that employees who over-indulged themselves at a Christmas party so that they were unable to attend work would be instantly dismissed. This agreement was not communicated to the employees. The applicant was dismissed for failing to turn up for work on the nightshift after a Christmas party, and his dismissal was held to be unfair. He would not have realised that this conduct would attract instant dismissal, and his lack of knowledge of the rule meant that the employers had acted unreasonably.

12.77 The rules should be clear and readily understandable by all affected employers, and should not be confused with extraneous matters. In *Rigden-Murphy v Securicor Ltd*, the claimant was dismissed after being seen to be breaking a company rule concerning the transfer of money from a bank to his vehicle. The rule in question was contained in a manual, which had 'Ten golden rules'. At the end, there was a statement that a failure to comply may lead to instant dismissal. Some of the 'rules' were in fact mere exhortations, such as 'Beware of complacency. Build up the habit of self-discipline'. Other rules had in the past been dealt with by a warning. It was held that the dismissal was unfair. The rules were somewhat ambiguous, in that they contained matters which were unconnected with discipline, and there was no clear line between those rules which attracted dismissal as a punishment, and those which were dealt with (if at all) with lesser severity.

12.78 Employment tribunals had, in the past, been most inconsistent in dealing with rules which contain automatic as opposed to discretionary sanctions. For example, in *Jones v London Co-operative Society* the staff code in a departmental store stated that an incorrect recording of a customer's purchase was a serious offence, 'and the employee *will be* summarily dismissed'. It was held that such a rule was too rigid, for it failed to distinguish between a genuine error and a calculated act. On the other hand, in *Lindsay v Fife Forge*, the works rules stated that employees who left the premises without permission '*may be* subject to instant dismissal' and the employment tribunal held that this did not amount to a clear and specific warning!

12.79 The problems caused by such sophistry can be illustrated by comparing *Dalton v Burton's Gold Medal Biscuits Ltd* and *Meridian Ltd v Gomersall*. In the former case, a man of 22 years' service was dismissed for a clocking offence, the works rules stating that such action 'will result in instant dismissal'. The National Industrial Relations Court held the dismissal to be fair. In the latter case, it was stated in the works rules that anyone guilty of a clocking offence 'will render themselves liable to instant dismissal'. The EAT upheld a tribunal decision that a dismissal was unfair, because the employee might take the view that to be caught once, even suspected of doing it previously, would not necessarily lead to an instant dismissal!

12.80 The question, in reality, is not the mandatory nature of the sanction, but whether the employer acts reasonably in imposing that sanction, or whether some other equally efficacious sanction could be imposed. It must be wrong to dismiss an employee for minor misconduct no matter how strongly worded is the rule, for the mandatory nature of a disciplinary rule does not exclude the jurisdiction of the employment tribunal to decide whether or not the employer has acted reasonably (*Ladbroke Racing Ltd v Arnott*). On the other hand, automatic penalties fail to permit an employer to take account of mitigating circumstances, the employee's record, general conduct and so forth. The employer should be able to tailor the punishment to the offence, and then to the offender. He should be consistent in his procedures, but can be flexible in his punishments. In *Elliott Bros Ltd v Colverd* the EAT resolved doubts by stating that there is no legal requirement that a rule must indicate that a breach would inevitably lead to a dismissal, and a rule book did not need to indicate a distinction between the possibility and inevitability of dismissal. However the rule is worded, the employer is entitled to look at all the circumstances.

12.81 An employer must be prepared to justify any alleged disparity of treatment between different employees. In *Hadjioannou v Coral Casinos Ltd* the claimant was dismissed for breaking a rule which forbade socialising with members or guests at a gambling club. He argued that in the past other employees had broken the rule and had not been dismissed. In upholding a decision of the employment tribunal that the dismissal was fair, the EAT commented that action taken by the employers in previous cases was only relevant in three circumstances (a) to show that there may be certain categories of misconduct which may be overlooked (or at least not dealt with by the sanction of dismissal), (b) if it leads to the conclusion that the purported reason for the dismissal was not the real or genuine reason, and (c) to show that some lesser penalty would have been more appropriate. The EAT went on to comment that it was of the highest importance that flexibility should be retained, and employers should not be encouraged to think that there was a 'tariff' approach to industrial misconduct (see *Paul v East Surrey District Health Authority*, para 17.123).

12.82 Disparity of treatment is acceptable if culpability is not the same. In *Securicor Ltd v Smith*, the claimant and another employee were security guards, collecting and delivering cash. The employers had strict rules about the way they did their work. Following an incident when the rules were breached, the employers held a disciplinary hearing, and both employees were dismissed. An appeal was made to the area manager, who affirmed the dismissals. Both employees then lodged a further appeal to a special panel set up by the company, and at this level it was decided that as the other employee was less blameworthy, he would not be dismissed, but the dismissal of the claimant was confirmed. An employment tribunal held that his dismissal was unfair. They held that the original decision to dismiss both men was reasonable, but the final appeal body acted unreasonably in dismissing one employee but not the other on the ground that the other employee was less blameworthy. The decision was confirmed by the EAT. However, the Court of Appeal reversed the decision. The real question was whether the final appeal panel's decision was so unreasonable that no reasonable employer would have accepted it. Indeed, had the employers refused to accept the decision of the appeal panel not to dismiss the other employee, he would have had an unanswerable case for unfair dismissal in an employment tribunal. The appeal panel, having thoroughly investigated the matter, had distinguished the culpability of the two employees, and their decision was not unreasonable.

12.83 Similarly, disparity of treatment is permitted if disciplinary records are not the same. In *Harrow London Borough v Cunningham*, the claimant and a fellow worker were found to be doing unauthorised work in circumstances which amounted to gross misconduct. The claimant was dismissed, but his fellow worker was given a final warning. The reason for this was that the claimant had already been in receipt of a final warning, whereas his fellow worker had a clean disciplinary record. An employment tribunal held that the dismissal of the claimant was unfair, on the ground that both of them should have been treated equally, but the decision was reversed by the EAT. An employer is entitled to take into account aggravating factors, including an employee's previously poor disciplinary record as compared with the other employee concerned, as well as mitigating circumstances which affect one employee when compared with the other.

12.84 Once an employer lays down a particular rule, a failure to enforce it consistently may weaken any subsequent attempt to do so. In *Frame v McKean & Graham Ltd*, the claimant was dismissed for doing work on his own account contrary to the working rules for the industry. His dismissal was held to be unfair. The rule had never been enforced in the past, and indeed, such conduct had been condoned. Moreover, he had not taken any work away from the employer, for the customer for whom he worked had severed the relationship with the employer.

12.85 Rules may be of a general nature, eg defining conduct which, by the generality of the law of employment, cannot be tolerated; they may be specific, defining the sort of conduct which *this* employer will not tolerate, and they may be special, dealing with instant circumstances which have not arisen hitherto.

A. General rules

12.86 These are rules which govern conduct which is such that by common consent, disciplinary sanctions will be imposed. Examples which readily spring to mind include theft of the employer's property, theft from fellow employees, serious neglect, wilful damage, dangerous practices, and so on. It is not generally advisable to list all the matters which come under the heading of gross misconduct, for this could mean that an employee would be saved from dismissal who committed an act which was so outrageous that no-one thought it would ever happen (*Gardiner v Newport County Borough Council*). In *Clarkson v Brown, Muff & Co Ltd*, 'gross misconduct' was defined as being 'dishonesty, arson, violence, obscenity, neglect and insubordination'. It was held that this definition did not cover an employee who had been telling lies. Some firms make it clear that the definitions of gross misconduct contained in their rules are examples only, and any list of misdeeds is not intended to be exhaustive!

B. Specific rules

12.87 These rules cover the sort of misconduct which *this employer* will not tolerate under any circumstances. Thus each employer must judge for himself the standards which are to apply, based on his own circumstances. Thus fighting, swearing, lateness, absenteeism, drunkenness, trading, betting, and so forth, may all amount to industrial misconduct which, in the individual case, attracts disciplinary sanctions. Such rules must be fair and reasonable. In *Turner v Pleasurama Casinos Ltd*, the claimant was an inspector who was employed to observe gaming tables, to ensure that there was no dishonesty by croupiers. He was dismissed for 'neglect of duty' after a complaint that a croupier and a member of the public had been cheating under his nose. The allegation was denied by him, but after a full and proper investigation, the employer found against him. It was held that the dismissal was fair; the gaming world is a hard world, and even the smallest of mistakes could not be tolerated.

12.88 Provided such rules meet the standards of reasonableness, they can generally be enforced. In *Higham v International Stores*, the claimant was given to wearing sandals and clogs, and other casual clothes. He was told that he must comply with the company's requirement to wear proper shoes and socks, and to wear a tie and overall when serving customers. After failing to heed due warnings, he was dismissed for not complying with the rules. It was held that an employer is entitled to insist on a reasonable standard of dress. What was reasonable is always a question of fact, to be determined in each case by all the circumstances. Different standards apply in Bond Street and in Petticoat Lane. In this case, the shop had a middle class clientele in a conventional town, and the dismissal was thus fair.

C. Special rules

12.89 Since the rules cannot conceivably cover every possible situation, an employer must be free to lay down a rule specifically to deal with a matter which has not hitherto arisen. In *Spiller v Wallis Ltd* a company rule stated that employees should not have deep emotional relationships with other members of the staff which might impair their marital status. This rule had been promulgated after an incident where the spouse of an employee had come on to the premises and created an unpleasant scene. The claimant was in fact having a love affair with a senior employee, and she refused to discontinue the relationship. Her dismissal was held to be fair. She was told of the rule, but chose not to comply. NB: Whether such a rule contravenes Art 8 of the European Convention on Human Rights (see para 1.101) is a matter upon which no doubt the tribunals will shortly adjudicate!)

12.90 Finally, the interpretation of the rules, and their reasonableness, is a matter for the employment tribunal to determine. In *Palmer v Vauxhall Motors Ltd*, the claimant was dismissed for spending 15 minutes in the club bar after her lunch break. It was alleged that this constituted gross misconduct in accordance with the works rules. It was held that even though the rules were somewhat ambiguous, the employment tribunal was entitled to find that the dismissal was fair. The EAT would only reverse that finding if it could be said that no person instructed in the relevant law could have come to that decision.

Disciplinary powers

12.91 The exercise of disciplinary powers is a corrective function, not punitive. The object is to improve an employee's performance, so that he can remain a valued and useful employee, not to give vent to management frustrations. The choice of the disciplinary sanction must therefore reflect this objective, and should, so far as is possible, be tailored to the individual case, bearing in mind the need to show some form of consistency in like cases. The Code of Practice should be borne in mind at all times.

A. Fines and deductions

12.92 It is possible to impose a fine or make a deduction for bad or negligent work, but the new principles laid down to prevent unlawful deductions (see para 8.4) must be observed. There must be a specific contractual power, and in respect of persons employed in retail employment the restrictions in ERA, s 18 must be observed. Deductions or payments made in consequence of disciplinary proceedings held under a statutory provision are excluded from the Act (eg police and fire service).

12.93 The Act specifically states that the only remedy for a breach is by way of a complaint to an employment tribunal under s 23, but it is submitted that an unauthorised deduction or payment may still give rise to a complaint of constructive dismissal. Thus, in *Lethaby v Horsman Andrew and Knill Ltd* the employer made a deduction from the employee's wages to cover the loss of the firm's property. This was done in the absence of any contractual authority to make such a deduction, and the employee, who refused to agree to it, resigned. It was held that this constituted repudiatory conduct by the employer of the contract, and as such constituted a dismissal (see Chapter 17).

12.94 The employer's power to fine or make deductions must be contained in the express terms of the contract, and it is now no longer possible to rely on an implied term, or (more likely) a customary term to this effect. This makes a number of current employment practices of dubious validity. For example, some firms make a practice of deducting 15 minutes from the pay of an hourly worker when he is a few minutes late (known as quartering); it is doubtful if the unilateral imposition of such a practice would be upheld in law.

B. Suspension without pay for misconduct

12.95 If there is an express term in the contract which permits the employer to suspend an employee for a specific reason, such as misconduct, the courts will uphold such a term provided the suspension is carried out in strict conformity with the laid down procedure. Sometimes the grounds for suspension, and the procedure to be adopted, will be laid down in the works rules, and the extent to which those rules will form part of the individual contract of employment will be a question of fact in each case. Even so, if an employee is, or ought to be, aware of the practice of a firm, or if there is a custom in the trade or industry or locality, then he will be bound by it. In *Bird v British Celanese Ltd* an employee was suspended for two days in accordance with the firm's practice, and this was held to be a valid exercise of disciplinary power by the employer.

12.96 Alternatively, the grounds for suspension and procedure to be adopted may be contained in a collective agreement, in which case there may be an express or implied incorporation of those terms into the individual contract of employment. In *Tomlinson v London, Midland and Scottish Rly Co* a trade union negotiated with the defendant company an agreement which, inter alia, laid down the procedure for dealing with breaches of discipline, and this was held to have been incorporated into an employee's contract of employment.

12.97 It is clear that the right of suspensory lay-off must be based on a contractual power, which will be either expressed, or implied, or based on custom and practice. The courts and tribunals are quite willing to discover such a power when minor disciplinary matters are concerned, though they appear to require strict proof if there is a major disciplinary matter which can lead to a dismissal. Recently, the EAT held that it may not be difficult to draw an inference that a contract contains an implied power to suspend as a disciplinary matter, or to enable an investigation to take place (*Pirie and Hunter v Crawford*). But in the total absence of such a power, it is clear that the employer may not purport to exercise it, for this would virtually enable him to assess unilaterally the damages for an employee's misconduct. It further follows that if an employee is wrongfully suspended without pay, he may recover any lost pay by way of damages. In *Hanley v Pease & Partners*, an employee was suspended for one day without pay, and it was held that he was entitled to the money which had been withheld.

12.98 If an employer lawfully suspends an employee, the legal position at common law appears to be that the employment has been temporarily put in abeyance, with a right for the employee to apply for reinstatement at the end of the suspension period (*Marshall v English Electric Co Ltd*). Presumably there is no break in continuity of employment in these circumstances. If the suspension is wrongful, the employee will be entitled to treat this breach as repudiatory conduct by the employer, and he will be entitled to resign and sue for wrongful or unfair dismissal. In *Davies v Anglo Great Lakes Corpn* an employee was suspended without pay after allowing his trade union membership to lapse, and this was held to be repudiatory conduct by the employer.

12.99 But if an employee decides to resign as a result of wrongful suspension he may find the tribunal somewhat unsympathetic, for he would have to argue that he was entitled to resign by reason of the employer's (wrongful) conduct, which the tribunal may not accept as a valid reason, particularly if the employer had reasonable cause to suspend, and the employee's conduct would otherwise have to be dealt with by a dismissal which would have been fair. It can hardly be right for an employer to be saddled with the burden of compensation if he exercises a lesser disciplinary power than he might have done. Another view which may be taken is that the employee's conduct was such that it 'contributed' to the repudiation by the employer, and hence reduced compensation may be awarded. Thus if the employee's conduct is such as to warrant a dismissal, but the employer suspends him without having the contractual power to do so, an action for unfair dismissal would probably fail because the constructive dismissal would be justified because of the misconduct, while an action for wrongful dismissal is unlikely to meet with any greater success. There have been a number of cases where the tribunals have held that an employee should not have been dismissed for misconduct, but the offence warranted some lesser disciplinary measure, such as suspension, even though the employer had no contractual right to do so. Thus in *Unkles v Milanda Bread Co Ltd* an employee was dismissed for smoking in breach of the company's rules. The tribunal thought that an appropriate penalty might have been a suspension for one month without pay, but there is no evidence in the report to suggest that the employer had the power to do this by virtue of the contract of employment. In seeking to encourage employers to exercise this lesser power, it would be inconsistent for the tribunals to penalise them for doing so.

C. Precautionary suspension

12.100 If an employee is suspended as a precautionary measure, and not for disciplinary purposes, the position is somewhat different. In *Jones v British Rail Hovercraft Ltd* the employee was suspended from duty without pay pending the outcome of investigations and proceedings against him which were brought by the police. He claimed that this amounted to a dismissal, but this argument was rejected. The rule book, which was part of his employment conditions, mentioned the distinction between precautionary and punitive suspension, and it was reasonable for the employer to take precautionary steps to protect his interest and his property. That the suspension was without pay could be dealt with by making up his back pay if the proceedings ended in his favour.

12.101 The Code of Practice states that precautionary suspension pending investigation should be with full pay, and this is probably correct in the absence of any contrary term in the contract. This could give rise to difficulties if the investigation is outside the control of management, for this could possibly go on for weeks or months. It is submitted therefore that precautionary suspension should be with pay if there is to be an internal investigation, but this may not be the rule in the case of external investigations. If this were not so, then the only alternatives available to the employer would be to retain an employee on full pay, or to dismiss him, and it is submitted that suspension without pay may turn out to be a better practice in some cases. In *Conway v Matthew, Wright & Nephew*, the claimant was a nightwatchman, and he was charged by the police with maliciously causing damage to the company's property. The company investigated the matter, and dismissed him. Subsequently, all criminal charges against him were dropped. It was argued that the company should have suspended him pending the outcome of criminal proceedings, but it was held that there was no legal obligation to do so, as it could have been many months before such charges were disposed of. The employers were under no obligation to refrain from dismissing him until the guilty conduct was established beyond reasonable doubt in a criminal court.

12.102 However, an employer should beware of using suspension as a knee-jerk reaction to a problem, for there may well be circumstances where such action is in fact not warranted. In *Gogay v Hertfordshire County Council* the claimant was a residential care worker at a children's home. A child made some vague allegations of sexual abuse, which caused the employers to suspend the claimant while investigations were carried out. These concluded that there was no truth whatsoever in the allegations and the claimant was offered reinstatement. However, she was unable to return to work because she was suffering from clinical depression brought on by the suspension, and she subsequently brought a claim for loss of earnings and damages for personal injury. It was held that her claim would succeed. The employers should have undertaken further enquiries before deciding to suspend the claimant pending an investigation into an allegation of sexual abuse. Further, the claimant could have been transferred for a short time, while the enquiries proceeded, or given a short period of leave. In the circumstances, the employers were in breach of the implied term of trust and confidence.

12.103 If there is an express contractual right to suspend with or without pay pending an investigation, this is subject to an implied term that the imposition of the suspension and its continuance would be on reasonable grounds. In *McClory v Post Office* three postmen were involved in a fight with employees from another office, and they were arrested and charged by the police with various offences. The Post Office suspended them on full pay, but without any payment for overtime which they would otherwise have worked. After making various enquiries, they were permitted to return to work some seven months later, and subsequently were acquitted of all the criminal charges. They brought an action for a declaration that their suspension had been in breach of their contracts of employment and they also sought damages for loss of overtime pay which they would have earned but for the suspension.

It was held that there was no breach of the employment contract. There was no duty on an employer to give reasons for the suspension or to give the employee an opportunity to be heard before it was imposed. The court refused to import the rules of natural justice into what is essentially a contractual arrangement between employer and employee. There was an implied term that the employer would exercise the express contractual right to suspend and to continue to suspend, only on reasonable grounds. To hold otherwise would enable an employer to suspend indefinitely. On the facts of the case, the employer had acted reasonably, and that aspect of the claim was dismissed.

The court also dismissed the claim for loss of overtime pay. The employees could not show that they had a right to overtime pay, only an obligation to work overtime when required. There was no duty on the employer to provide overtime on a regular basis, and thus the loss of a chance to work extra hours could not constitute the basis of a legal claim.

12.104 There is no legal requirement to suspend an employee prior to the undertaking of a full investigation, and a failure to do so does not weaken an allegation of gross misconduct. As a general rule, it is unwise to draw any conclusion from the act of or absence of suspension (*East Berkshire Health Authority v Matadeen*). If an employee is absent from work because he is suspended, there is no obligation for him to return to work until the suspension is lifted (*Hassan v Odeon Cinemas*).

D. Warnings

12.105 An employer does not need contractual power to issue warnings, but frequently this will be the subject of a disciplinary code or part of the works rules. These may state the procedural steps (for example, first oral warning, first written warning, final written warning), before further disciplinary action is taken. Strict adherence to these steps is necessary and a failure by the employer to observe them may lead to difficulties in unfair dismissal proceedings. Thus a failure to give a warning in writing as required by the agreed procedure resulted in a dismissal being held to be unfair in *Raymond v Sir Lindsay Parkinson Ltd.*

12.106 Nonetheless, the warning system must be operated sensibly, not merely as a form of mechanical procedure. It is possible to give an employee a final warning for a serious misdemeanour without having first to go through the processes of informal warning, first written warning, etc; equally, the fact that an employee has received a final warning does not mean that the next occasion on which he commits an 'offence' will be visited with an automatic sanction. Either course could lead to ludicrous results. There is no substitute for a full and fair investigation of all the facts. In *Newalls Insulation Co Ltd v Blakeman*, the claimant was dismissed for being absent on two occasions within 14 days, following a final warning for absenteeism. Prior to this, he had had two verbal warnings. The EAT held that the employment tribunal should look at all the circumstances of the case, and not simply whether it was reasonable to dismiss for two days' absence after the final warning. The issues were, what happened before the final warning was given, how many absences were there, why was he absent, and how did the absences fit in as part of the general picture?

12.107 A warning can deal with specific conduct which is the subject of complaint, and it should also deal with general matters, so that the totality of the employee's conduct can eventually be taken into account. This solves the problem, sometimes raised by management, as to whether or not, having given three warnings for one type of misconduct, it is necessary to give a further three warnings in respect of a different series of offences! Thus in *Donald Cook v Carter*, the claimant received a number of warnings; one for using bad language, and a year later, another one for the same offence. Two months later he was given a final warning for inefficiency, with a threat to demote or dismiss. Three months later he was given another final warning for leaving work before the normal finishing time and he was suspended for five days. He was then guilty of inefficiency, and was dismissed. The employment tribunal held that the dismissal was unfair, in that he should have been given a further final warning, but this was reversed by the EAT. As long as the matter leading to the dismissal was properly investigated and the proper procedure followed, it was not open to the employment tribunal to find that fairness required a further warning being given, or that the employers should have suspended the employee, as they had done so previously.

12.108 This approach was confirmed by the EAT in *Auguste Noel Ltd v Curtis*, where an employee was dismissed for mishandling company property. He had previously received two final written warnings for different offences. An employment tribunal held that the previous warnings were not relevant, but the decision was reversed on appeal. The existence of previous warnings, the dates, numbers, and substance of the complaints were all relevant matters which an employer was entitled to take into account.

12.109 It is for the employer to determine the nature of the disciplinary sanction, and, generally speaking, an employment tribunal should not attempt to assess whether or not a final warning should or should not have been given. However, if there is something to suggest that a final warning was 'manifestly inappropriate' or given without prima facie grounds, then the employment tribunal will scrutinise carefully the employer's decision. In *Co-operative Retail Services Ltd v Lucas*, the employee was given a final warning for failing to carry out certain instructions. She did not appeal against this within the internal procedure. Two months later she was dismissed following three further incidents. It was accepted by the employer that the three incidents which led to the dismissal were of a minor nature, and did not warrant dismissal by themselves. An employment tribunal decided that the events which led to the final warning being given did not justify such a serious disciplinary sanction, and thus decided to ignore it. Since the other incidents did not warrant dismissal, her dismissal was unfair. On appeal, the EAT confirmed the decision. The employment tribunal was entitled to look at the background against which the final warning was given, and consider whether it was a reasonable response of a reasonable employer. This was a judgment of fact which the employment tribunal was entitled to make.

12.110 A final warning is a severe penalty which just stops short of a dismissal. It is frequently imposed when a dismissal is a permissible and obvious sanction but, for reasons relating to the particular employee, is not imposed. To issue a final warning in respect of a relatively minor incident of misconduct can be a disproportionate response to the employee's conduct, and may enable the employee to resign and claim constructive dismissal (*Stanley Cole (Wainfleet) Ltd v Sheridan*).

12.111 If a warning is stated to last for a certain length of time, then clearly it will lapse at the end of that time. In *Bevan Ashford v Malin* a letter was handed to the employee on 29 January 1992, stating that a final written warning would remain on his personal file for a period of 12 months from the date of the letter. He was dismissed following his involvement in an incident at work on 29 January 1993. The employment tribunal held that the final written warning had expired at midnight on 28 January 1993, and ought not to have been taken into account when considering the disciplinary action to be taken following the incident which occurred the following day, and the decision was confirmed by the EAT. The general rule is that penal documents should be construed strictly, and also any ambiguity has to be construed against the maker. Thus the final warning had expired the day before the conduct which led to the dismissal occurred, and could not be relied upon as a ground for dismissal.

12.112 The warning should refer to the past conduct which is the subject of complaint, and to future conduct. It should, where possible, state the remedial action to be taken, and should specify the period of time in which such action should be taken. Frequently, a disciplinary procedure will specify the length of time the warning will last, but perhaps a better approach is for the warning itself to state the operative period, for mechanical and automatic approaches to disciplinary problems are not sound policy. A warning can also be suspensive, when it will stay on the employee's record until such time as it is removed, or can be ignored, or resolutive, which will lapse on compliance. The latter can therefore be ignored when its objective has been achieved. In *Duncan v GEC Telecommunications Ltd* an employee failed to send in a medical certificate as required by the company's rules. After being warned, she sent in an appropriate certificate. A few months later she again failed to send in a medical certificate. It was held that the earlier warning had lapsed on her compliance, and therefore her dismissal was unfair.

12.113 A warning may lapse after a certain period of time, but an employer is not to be criticised because he is over-generous and extends the warning period, instead of acting on it. Being over-generous is not the same as being unreasonable (*Kraft Foods Ltd v Fox*). Further, a warning which is itself the subject of a pending appeal may be taken into account by an employer when considering dismissal for subsequent misconduct (*Tower Hamlets Health Authority v Anthony*).

12.114 Tribunals have frequently stressed the need to issue warnings before the power of dismissal is exercised. The warnings should be given by a person in authority, should be clear, incisive and firm. They should make clear the nature of the conduct which will not be tolerated, and spell out in no uncertain terms that the consequence of a failure to heed the warning will be a dismissal. Formal warnings should be given in writing and this is of particular importance when there are language or communication problems.

12.115 Failure to follow these rules may lead to the tribunal making a finding adverse to the employer. In *Wells v West Ltd* the employers gave a warning to an employee that his 'employment might be in jeopardy'. In holding that this was not a sufficient warning, the tribunal held that those who use circumlocutions will have to bear the burden which they subsequently impose. In *Bendall v Paine and Betteridge* the employee was given a verbal warning that smoking would not be tolerated on the premises. It was held that a failure to give a written, final warning meant that the dismissal was unfair. And in *Rosenthal v Louis Butler Ltd* the employee used some offensive language to her manager. It was held that she ought to have been warned about future conduct, and been given an opportunity to apologise before dismissal was warranted.

12.116 It must be stressed that there is no rule of law which requires warnings to be given in all cases; it is merely a rule of good industrial relations practice. Warnings are matters of substance, not procedure (*James v Waltham Holy Cross UDC*). Whether a warning should have been given will depend on all the circumstances of the case, including its effectiveness, and the alternative course which may have been available or adopted. If a tribunal considers that had a clear warning been given, a dismissal would not have been necessary, then it will conclude that a dismissal without such a warning will be unfair (*Jones v GEC Elliott Automation Ltd*). Conversely, if a warning would have had no effect, then a failure to give one will not by itself render a dismissal unfair (*AJ Dunning & Sons (Shopfitters) Ltd v Jacomb*). There should be no need to give a warning to a highly paid and qualified employee that he will be dismissed if there is dissatisfaction with his work, for he should know this. Nor is there a need to give an educated person in a responsible position a warning that he must co-operate with his head of department (*Farnborough v Governors of Edinburgh College of Art*). Each case must be determined on its own merits.

12.117 If an employee is given a final warning against which he has appealed, there is no rule of law which requires the employer to await the outcome of the appeal before dismissing for another disciplinary offence (*Stein v Associated Dairies*).

E. Reprimand

12.118 The same is probably true about a reprimand, which is a mark of displeasure about past conduct and a warning about the future. Tribunals have held that misconduct which is not 'gross' should in some circumstances be punished by a reprimand rather than a dismissal, though to what extent a reprimand constitutes a punishment is somewhat difficult to see. Further, employers could be forgiven for thinking that this area of tribunal law is full of hazardous speculation, for when 'misconduct' becomes 'gross' is a somewhat subjective concept. In *King v Motorway Tyres and Accessories Ltd* a manager told his superior to 'fuck off' in the course of an argument. It was held that this did not amount to gross misconduct sufficient to warrant dismissal, and that in view of his long service and satisfactory record, he should have been 'severely' reprimanded! The precise distinction between a reprimand and a severe reprimand, and whether the latter is equivalent to a final warning, has yet to be decided. It is submitted that a reprimand is an appropriate sanction to be used when taking disciplinary action against management, or staff employees.

F. Demotion

12.119 An employee whose conduct is such that the employer has lost all confidence in his ability to do the job in question may be demoted, with or without review, and at a lower earning rate if this is appropriate. If there is an express power to do this in the contract or rules, then provided the sanction has been fairly exercised, there should not be any legal problem. In the absence of such a power, a demotion imposed following a disciplinary hearing is not a breach of contract when it is a lesser penalty than the dismissal which could otherwise have been imposed (*MacKay Decorators (Perth) Ltd v Millar*). If the employee refuses to accept the demotion, he can either resign and claim constructive dismissal, or leave it to the employer to dismiss him. If the employer has acted fairly, and with the interests of the employee at heart, such dismissal will be fair. In *Hall v Lodge*, the claimant was promoted from a supervisory post to manage a shop. Following serious stock deficiencies, her appointment was terminated, and she was offered re-engagement as a supervisor at another branch, at a lower salary. This offer was refused, so she was dismissed. It was held that her dismissal was fair. The company had made a mistake in promoting her too soon to a job which was too big for her. Having realised this, they then acted fairly by considering the alternatives which were available, by offering her a post which was within her competence. However, there is no legal requirement that an employer should demote a person who is incompetent (*Bevan Harris Ltd v Gair*).

12.120 But if a demotion on disciplinary grounds is out of all proportion to the offence, the employee may regard the employer as having repudiated the contract, and claim constructive dismissal. In *BBC v Beckett*, the claimant was employed for 14 years as a scenic carpenter. He was negligent in his work on one occasion, and was demoted to the position of building maintenance carpenter, at a lower salary. He resigned and claimed constructive dismissal, a claim which was upheld by the employment tribunal and by the EAT. The punishment was out of all proportion to the offence, given his long period of satisfactory service.

G. Transfer

12.121 Similar considerations apply to the transfer of an employee from one department to another, or one job to another. This power, however, would be used in different circumstances. Merely to transfer an incompetent employee from one department to another is to export one's problems from one manager to another. Transfer is best used as a means of overcoming personality clashes, so as to minimise the likelihood of future problems arising, or to place an employee in a job which he can do, rather than leaving him doing work which is beyond his competence. In *High v British Railways Board*, it was held that a disciplinary transfer which resulted in the employee suffering a drop in his earnings did not give rise to a claim for constructive dismissal.

H. Alternative employment

12.122 In appropriate cases, it may be unfair to dismiss an employee without considering whether there was any alternative work he could do, notwithstanding that he cannot be permitted to continue in his old job. However, there is no requirement that this should be investigated before the decision to dismiss is taken, as opposed to after the decision has been taken but before the expiry of any period of notice which may be given. To hold otherwise would mean that an employee would be unfairly dismissed notwithstanding that during his notice period alternative employment was found for him and the notice never took effect (*P v Nottinghamshire County Council*).

I. Other sanctions

12.123 There are a number of other disciplinary powers which may be used on appropriate occasions, and provided these are exercised in accordance with the relevant rules and procedures, these should cause few problems. For example, it may be possible to withdraw privileges for a certain period of time so as to deny to an employee certain non-contractual benefits, or to provide for the loss of so many years' seniority for certain purposes (but this does not affect the operation of the legal rules relating to continuity of employment). An employee who is persistently late in starting work may have flexi-time withdrawn, as an alternative to, or a precondition of, the implementation of other disciplinary action.

J. Non-employment situations

12.124 The above instances of disciplinary powers can only apply to acts of employees committed in the course of employment. An employer has no inherent power to discipline for acts which have occurred outside the employment, though if such acts adversely affect the employer's business, he may be justified in dismissing the employee (see Chapter 17). But if an employee is convicted of an offence outside his employment which may have an effect on his job, the employer should consider the employee's long and blameless record, and consider, for example, if some other means of dealing with the situation can be found. In *Jones v R M Douglas Construction Ltd* the employee, who was a plant engineer, was dismissed after being convicted of handling a stolen engine. The tribunal thought that the employer should have given some consideration to demoting him to his original trade of mechanic/fitter. Clearly, such a power cannot be found in the contract of employment, and amounts to a unilateral assessment by the employer of the necessary steps to be taken to protect his interests. A demotion is, as we have seen, equivalent to a dismissal, and one can only assume that if such steps are taken in serious disciplinary cases, the exercise of a lesser disciplinary power short of dismissal will, in cases of grave misconduct outside the employment, also be looked upon more favourably by the tribunals.

12.125 If the employee is convicted of an offence in connection with matters outside his employment, he is still entitled to present his side of the story to his employers, and the latter should not treat the fact of conviction per se as being conclusive without at least giving a chance to the employee to state his version (*Parsons v LCC*).

13

Continuous Employment

Continuity of employment

13.1 In order to obtain certain statutory rights, it is necessary to show that an employee has been continuously employed for a certain length of time, depending on the right in question. The statutory provisions which provide for continuity of employment are contained in ss 210–219 of the Employment Rights Act 1996, which provide 'a complete definition of what is meant by "continuously employed" ' (*Wood v York City Council*), and the Employment Protection (Continuity of Employment) Regulations 1996. Continuity of employment is a statutory concept (*Colinson v BBC*), generally used for two statutory purposes, namely (a) to determine whether an employee has been employed for a particular length of time so as to qualify for a specific statutory right, and (b) to ascertain the employee's length of employment for the purpose of obtaining certain financial benefits (ie a basic award (see para 17.186) and a redundancy payment (see para 18.62). However, for some statutory rights, no period of continuous employment is required.

13.2 There is nothing to prevent an employer from so arranging employment contracts so as to prevent continuity, and thus avoiding liability for unfair dismissal and redundancy payments. If there are legitimate breaks in employment, and re-employment does not become an arrangement by virtue of s 212(3)(c) (see below), continuity can be defeated (*Booth v USA*).

13.3 Continuity of employment is a concept which is only of importance in a statutory context. Thus, if an employer and employee make a private agreement to treat a particular period of employment as being continuous, this may create a private right, but cannot be used to enforce any statutory right, unless the statutory rules are also met. In *Secretary of State for Employment v Globe Elastic Thread Co Ltd*, an employee worked for a company for 22 years. He was then transferred to another company, after receiving assurances that his employment would be treated as being continuous. Five years later, he was made redundant, and he sought a redundancy payment based on the combined service. The House of Lords held that he was only entitled to a statutory redundancy pay in respect of the latter five years' employment. The private agreement may have given him a contractual right against the employers, but could not be used for the purpose of enforcing a statutory right. Similarly, in *Hanson v Fashion Industries (Hartlepool) Ltd*, an employee went on strike. Nine weeks later, she was re-engaged under a contract which stated that her continuous employment was to start afresh. In subsequent litigation to enforce a claim for maternity pay, it was held that her continuous employment had not been broken by the strike, for the statutory provisions (see below) came into play which preserved her continuity, and a private agreement cannot override those provisions.

Counting and computing continuity (ERA, ss 210–219)

13.4 The counting of a period of continuous employment is done in weeks, but the computation is done in months and years (s 210(3)). This requires some explanation. The rule is that to determine if an employee's employment, whether continuous or successive or broken, can be counted as being continuous is done on a week-by-week basis, because there is a general rule that continuity is broken by a complete week which does not count towards continuity (s 210(4)), unless continuity is preserved by one of the special rules (see below). A week will count, for the purpose of establishing continuity, if it is governed by a contract of employment, irrespective of the number of hours or days worked during the week. But a 'week', for the purpose of determining whether there has been a break in employment, means a complete week from Sunday ending with a Saturday (*Jennings v Salford Community Service Agency*).

13.5 Continuity is not broken unless there is a complete week in which there is no contract of employment. If there is one day in any week which is governed by a contract of employment, it matters not how or why a gap occurred, or what the employee did during that gap. Thus if an employee leaves one employer to work for another employer, but returns within a week of so leaving, continuity is preserved (*Sweeney v J S Henderson (Concessionaires) Ltd*).

13.6 However, the computation of the length of continuous employment is done in months and years. Thus, if an employee commences work on (say) 21 January 2004, he will complete two years' employment on 20 January 2006, assuming there is no break in his employment of a whole week. Similarly, if he commences employment on (say) 19 August 2006, he will have been continuously employed for three months on 18 November 2006. The terms 'years' and 'months' are to be treated as calendar years and months respectively.

13.7 Thus, in order to establish a period of continuous employment, it is necessary to ascertain the day when the employment commenced, the day when it ceased, whether there were any weeks which break continuity, and whether there were any weeks which do not break continuity, but which do not count towards continuity. Formerly, there were special rules to be observed in respect of part-time workers, who worked less than 16 hours per week, but these restrictions were abolished in 1995, and now part-time workers are to be treated in the same way as full-time workers, irrespective of the number of hours worked each week. Indeed, service prior to the change in 1995 is to be counted (ERA, Sch 2, para 14(1)).

13.8 The first rule to note is that there is a presumption that continuity of employment exists. Thus, once an employee can show the date on which he commenced work, his employment will be presumed to be continuous until the effective date of termination (s 210(5), and see *Nicoll v Nocorrode Ltd*). Thus an employee can change his place of work, his terms of employment, or even his contract of employment, without his continuity being affected, provided he remains employed by the same employer (*Wood v York City Council*) or an associated employer. An agency worker who is supplied to an employer on a temporary basis, and who is then taken on as a full-time employee, has continuity of employment from the date he commenced his temporary work (*RNLI v Bushaway*).

13.9 Continuity begins on the day the employee starts work under the contract of employment, although if the starting day is in fact a non-working day (eg a holiday or a Sunday) the employment will be continuous from that date, even though he does not actually commence working until a day or two later (*Salvation Army v Dewsbury*). If there are periods which do not count towards continuity, but do not break continuity (see below) the commencement of the period of employment is advanced by the period in question (s 211(3)). If a written statement of terms and conditions of employment given under ERA, s 1 contains a starting date, that will not be conclusive, if in fact the true starting date was different (*System Floors (UK) Ltd v Daniel*).

13.10 When a period of continuous employment ends will depend on the statutory right which is being claimed by the employee. For employment rights generally, and unfair dismissal claims in particular, it will be 'the effective date of termination' (see para 20.22). If the claim is for a statutory redundancy payment, the period will end on 'the relevant date', which will normally be the effective date of termination, although there are some variations on this (ERA, ss 136(3), 145(3)(b), 145(5), 145(7), 153). There are also provisions dealing with the termination of employment on the death of the employer and employee (ERA, ss 133(1), 174 and 176(1)).

13.11 The employment must be legal for it to be continuous. Thus any period when the employment is illegal cannot count towards continuity, and will break continuity. Thus, if a person has no legal right to work in the UK (see para 2.102) any time spent so working cannot count towards continuity. If a legal contract becomes tainted with illegality (see para 3.8), continuity will be broken, and will have to start again from when it becomes legal. In *Hyland v J H Barker (North West) Ltd*, the employee was employed from 1967. For four weeks in 1982 he arranged with his employer that he would receive a tax-free lodging allowance, whereas in fact he returned home every night. Clearly, this arrangement was illegal, being an attempt to defraud the Inland Revenue. Thus, when he was dismissed a year later, it was held that the four-week period had broken the continuity, and that therefore he lacked the necessary qualifying period of employment to bring a claim for unfair dismissal.

13.12 Continuity of employment exists if an employee commences work for a subsidiary or associated employer of the original employer, or if there is a takeover of the business (not just its assets) or on the transfer of an undertaking. Nor is it relevant that the employee's job changed. In *Lord Advocate v De Rosa* the employee was employed by Isaac Barrie (Transport) Ltd for 17 years, when the business was transferred to Isaac Barrie (Contractors) Ltd. There was no interruption in his employment, but he changed his job from transport manager to docks manager. It was held that his redundancy payment was to be calculated by reference to both periods of employment, and the fact that there had been a change in his employer and in his terms and conditions of employment was irrelevant.

Preserving continuity (s 212)

13.13 There is a general principle that if an employee is dismissed, or resigns, or his contract of employment comes to an end in some other lawful manner (frustration, project termination etc), then, if he is subsequently re-engaged, continuity will have been broken if there is a gap of more than one week between the two employments, and he will have to start again so far as computation is concerned. However, there are a number of rules which enable an employee to preserve continuity, despite the existence of a break between the two periods. Sometimes, the weeks in question may be added into the counting of continuity, although sometimes they are not to be counted, even though they do not break continuity.

13.14 Any week during the whole or part of which an employee's relations with his employer are governed by a contract of employment will count when computing the employee's period of employment (s 212(1)). Thus, if an employee is off work sick, away on a holiday, or otherwise absent with permission, the weeks in question will still count, as long as the contract of employment is still in existence. The whole of the period when a person is on ordinary maternity, paternity or adoption leave will count towards continuity.

13.15 Continuity will also be preserved in the following three circumstances (s 212(2) below), provided two conditions are met. First, there must be no contract of employment subsisting (because otherwise there would be no need to rely on these provisions to preserve continuity). Second, the employee must be re-employed during the relevant period. In other words, s 212(2) does not guarantee continuity; it merely preserves it in circumstances when it would otherwise be lost.

A. Incapable of work because of sickness or injury (s 212(3)(a))

13.16 For this rule to apply, the contract of employment must have been terminated (whether by dismissal or frustration or resignation etc). If so, then if the employee is re-employed within 26 weeks, his employment will be deemed to be continuous. In other words, he is entitled to be absent from work for up to 26 weeks after his contract of employment has ended without suffering a break in continuity should he be re-employed. He must, however, have been incapable of work, not merely absent from work (*Scarlett v Godfrey Abbott Group Ltd*). In *Donnelly v Kelvin International Services* the employee resigned from his employment with the respondent because his doctor advised him to obtain lighter work. He obtained employment with another employer, but five weeks later resumed his employment with the respondent. He was subsequently dismissed, and his claim for unfair dismissal could only proceed if he could link the two periods of employment in order to establish the necessary continuity. An employment tribunal dismissed his claim, holding that although he had resigned his employment because of sickness, he was not incapable of work because of that sickness, because he had demonstrated his fitness for work by obtaining other employment. The EAT allowed the employee's appeal, and remitted the claim for reconsideration by another tribunal. The phrase 'incapable of work' did not mean incapable of work of any kind. It referred to the work which the employee was doing prior to the period which interrupted the continuity of employment, and the fact that the employee had taken up other work during the period of interruption did not mean that he had ceased to be capable of the work he was doing by reason of sickness, within the meaning of s 212(3)(a). The proper approach was to look at what happened in the intervening period between the two employments in question. If, for example, the employee took employment of light work, in the hope that he may be able to return to his previous employment in time, this may not interrupt the period of continuity. But if the intervening employment was undertaken as full-time permanent employment, then it was possible to conclude that his absence from the first employment was not because of incapacity for work.

13.17 A different result was reached in *Pearson v Kent County Council*, where the employee decided to resign his employment on 31 May on health grounds. He was offered, and accepted, a less demanding job with his employers, and commenced his new position on 11 June. Four years later he was made redundant, and sought to link the two periods of employment for the purpose of enhancing his claim for statutory redundancy pay. His claim failed. There was no medical reason why he could not have commenced his new job immediately after he left his former position. Thus, he was not incapable of work because of sickness or injury, and because there was a break of more than one week, the two periods of employment could not be linked to form one period of continuous employment.

B. Absent from work on account of a temporary cessation of work (s 212(3)(b))

13.18 Weeks will count when an employee is absent from work (again, without a contract of employment) on account of a temporary cessation of work. This provision was probably designed to deal with those industries where there may be lay-offs, eg the construction industry, but the practical effect has been much wider (see *Fitzgerald v Hall, Russell & Co Ltd*). In particular, it should be noted that a lay-off and a temporary cessation of work are the same thing (*Murray v Murray (t/a Newholme Decorators)*).

13.19 The term 'cessation of work' means that the work which the employee was employed to do must have ceased (*Fitzgerald v Hall Russell & Co Ltd*) or the quantum of work no longer exists. If an employee is 'laid off' because existing work has been redistributed, there has been no cessation of work (*Byrne v Birmingham City Council*). Further, the work which has ceased must be paid work, not voluntary work (*University of Aston in Birmingham v Malik*). Nor is the reason for the cessation relevant; it may be due to shortage of orders, shortage of supplies, cash flow problems etc (*Hunter v Smith's Dock Co Ltd*). There must be an interruption in the availability of work which, but for that interruption, would have been performed by the employee.

13.20 The absence from work must be 'temporary'. This is a question of fact, to be looked at with hindsight, not foresight. Although there is dicta in *Ford v Warwickshire County Council* (see below) to suggest that 'temporary' means 'lasting only for a relatively short time', this guidance has not always been followed (eg see *Bentley Engineering Co Ltd v Crown*, where a period of absence of two years was held to be temporary!). The whole of the employment history must be examined, and evidence may be adduced as to the expectations of the parties. In *Ford v Warwickshire County Council* the claimant was a teacher who was employed on a sessional basis. Each year she taught for three terms, and when the July term ended, her contract came to an end. Each year she was re-employed in September. This arrangement continued for eight years, and when she was not re-engaged at the commencement of a new session, she sought compensation for unfair dismissal and redundancy. The House of Lords held that the word 'temporary' was used in the sense of being 'transient' so that the absence was for a relatively short time. This was a question of fact to the determined by the employment tribunal. Thus, successive periods of employment with the same employer will be continuous under s 212(3)(b) if the length of time between those periods is short compared with the length of time the employment has lasted. In such circumstances, the intervals in between can truly be regarded as being temporary.

13.21 There have been a number of cases where employees have been employed on 'intermittent' contracts, each of varying lengths, and being separated by varying periods of non-employment. The correct approach in such cases is to consider all the relevant circumstances, and in particular to consider the lengths of the periods of absence from work in the context of the employment as a whole (*Sillars v Charrington Fuels Ltd*). Sometimes employment tribunals try to circumvent this enquiry by finding that 'a global contract' exists (see para 2.158), but with mixed success. So far as seasonal workers are concerned, if a greater time is spent out of employment than in, the period of non-employment cannot be regarded as being an absence because of a temporary cessation of work (*Berwick Salmon Fisheries Co Ltd v Rutherford*).

13.22 It will be clear that if an employee resigns, or is dismissed, and subsequently re-employed by the employer (or an associated employer, see para 2.7) he cannot be regarded as being absent from work because of a temporary cessation (*Wessex National Ltd v Long*). If, during the period of absence, the employee takes what he regards as being other permanent employment, then the absence ceases to be because of the temporary cessation of work. But if he takes temporary employment, making it clear that he was seeking to be re-employed by his former employers, continuity will be preserved (*Thompson v Bristol Channel Ship Repairer and Engineers Ltd*).

C. Absent by arrangement or custom (s 212(3)(c))

13.23 Continuity is preserved if the employee's absence from work is such that, by arrangement or custom, he is regarded as continuing in the employment of his employer for any purpose. Clearly, if an employee's contract enables such absence, eg sabbatical leave, s 212(3)(c) has no relevance. The section only applies if the contract does not exist, and would cover, for example, an employee who has been seconded from one employer to another, or someone who has been given leave of absence for personal reasons. Indeed, the 'arrangement' need not have been made between the employer and the employee, but can arise from an agreement between the employer and a trade union (*Taylor v Triumph Motors Ltd*). Keeping an employee 'on the books' can be an arrangement for the purpose of continuity within s 212(3)(c), especially if the contract of employment has previously been frustrated (*G F Sharp & Co Ltd v McMillan*).

13.24 The arrangement must have been to preserve continuity for any purpose. In *Lloyds Bank Ltd v Secretary of State for Employment* an employee worked one week on and one week off for five years. She became pregnant, the employers paid her statutory maternity pay, and sought to recover the amount from the Maternity Fund. It was held that her employment was continuous for five years, her absence was by arrangement, and, having rightfully paid her the money, they were entitled to a rebate from the Fund. But in *Letheby & Christopher Ltd v Bond* a casual barmaid took leave over a Christmas period. Although this was by arrangement, there was no arrangement that the absence would preserve continuity, for she worked under a number of separate contracts, and it was not possible to say that any contract of employment would have continued after the cessation of the previous contract. Thus the absence broke her continuity.

13.25 However, the arrangement must have been made before the period of absence ceases (*Murphy v A Birrell & Sons Ltd*). One made after the absence has ceased may give rise to private contractual rights, but cannot affect the statutory position. Thus in *Morris v Walsh Western Electric UK Ltd* the appellant was summarily dismissed. Two months later he was re-employed, and was told by the company's general manager that the intervening period would be treated as being a period of unpaid leave. He subsequently terminated his own employment, and claimed that the two combined periods of employment gave him sufficient continuity to bring a case of constructive dismissal. His claim was dismissed by an employment tribunal and the EAT. The statutory provisions envisage that the arrangement exists when the employee is absent from work, not when he returns to work. A contrary view, expressed in *Ingram v Foxon*, that a retrospective arrangement could preserve continuity, was disapproved.

13.26 The 'arrangement' for the purpose of s 212(3)(c) must be such that there was a mutual recognition by the parties that the employee, although absent from work, nevertheless continues in the employment of the employer. Whether such mutual recognition in fact exists will depend on the circumstances and, in particular, any correspondence between the parties, and what the employee was told before taking the period of absence (*Curr v Marks & Spencer plc*).

13.27 There are few cases dealing with 'custom' in modern employment law generally, let alone with reference to s 212(3)(c). Industry-wide customs (of the kind which would be upheld at law) rarely exist nowadays, as the greater formalisation of contracts of employment and collective agreements takes place. Older cases (eg *Sagar v Ridehalgh*) are no longer particularly relevant. But in *Gray v Burntisland Shipbuilding Co* a recognised custom in the shipbuilding industry whereby workers laid off when work ran out were recalled when more work became available, was used to establish continuity under the statutory provision. In *Ford v Warwickshire County Council* (above) the EAT commented that detailed evidence about customs in certain industries could be usefully given, and, if there was an appropriate custom in the teaching profession, it should be brought to the attention of the employment tribunal for consideration.

Re-employment after unfair dismissal (s 219)

13.28 The Employment Protection (Continuity of Employment) Regulations 1996 (as amended) (made under ERA, s 219) deal with the situation where a person is reinstated or re-engaged in consequence of any of the following events, namely:

(a) a claim made under an approved dismissal agreement (s 110: see para 17.4 ff);

(b) the presentation by the employee of a complaint of dismissal, ie under ERA, or in respect of sex, race or disability discrimination;

(c) action taken by a conciliation officer of ACAS under the Employment Tribunals Act 1996, s 18 (see para 20.37);

(d) the making of a compromise agreement authorised by ERA, s 203(3);

(e) as a result of an arbitration award made under an approved ACAS arbitration
     scheme (see para 1.12).

13.29 In any of these circumstances, the employee's continuity of employment is deemed
to be preserved, and the period beginning with the date on which the dismissal took effect,
and the date when the re-engagement or reinstatement took place, will count in the
computation of the employee's period of continuous employment.

13.30 The re-engagement or reinstatement must be 'in consequence of' any of the above
actions. The mere fact of re-engagement or reinstatement, by itself, for some other reason,
will not ensure continuity (*Gardener v National Coal Board*), unless the provisions of
ERA, s 212(3)(c) apply, it being recalled that this cannot apply to an arrangement which
purports to be retrospective (*Morris v Walsh Western UK Ltd*).

Weeks which do not count towards continuity (ss 215–217)

13.31 There are certain circumstances when weeks of absence do not count towards
continuity, but do not break continuity. The non-counting weeks are used to advance the
starting date of the employment, by seven days for each non-counting week (s 215(2))
(except weeks spent abroad in redundancy cases: see below). The non-counting weeks
arise in the following circumstances.

A. Periods spent working abroad (s 215(1))

13.32 A person who works outside Great Britain is generally excluded from employment
rights and weeks of employment abroad will not normally count. However, there are
circumstances when a period of employment spent outside Great Britain will count in
computing continuous employment as if it were employment in Great Britain. Thus, if an
employee works outside Great Britain, and his contract is then varied so that he works
inside Great Britain, the whole of his period of employment will be continuous for the
purpose of establishing a qualifying period of employment rights generally. However, for
the purpose of calculating statutory redundancy pay, a week of employment abroad will
not count towards continuity (but will not break continuity) if the employee spent the
whole or part of the week working abroad, and he was not an employed earner for the
purpose of national insurance contributions.

B. Strikes and lock-outs (s 216)

13.33 Any week during which, or during part of which, an employee takes part in a strike
will not count towards continuity, but will not break continuity. This rule applies whether
the strike is official or unofficial. However, the strike must be connected with terms and
conditions of employment, and not, for example, a 'political' strike. If an employee is
dismissed while on strike, and subsequently re-engaged, the weeks on strike will be
deducted from his continuous employment, but continuity is preserved (*Hanson v Fashion
Industries (Hartlepool) Ltd*). The total number of days deducted will be the actual number

of days (not the number of working days) falling in the period between the last day when the employee worked and the day when he resumed work (s 216(2)). Thus, non-working days, eg Saturday and Sunday, can be deducted. If, during a strike, an employee takes another job, and is subsequently re-engaged then, if that job was a temporary one, his continuity will be preserved; but if it was a permanent job (eg there is evidence that he so regarded it) he will be treated as if he left his original employment, and continuity will be broken (*Bloomfield v Springfield Hosiery Finishing Co Ltd*).

13.34 Issues sometimes arise as to whether or not the employee is 'taking part' in a strike, or is absent from work during an industrial dispute for some other reason (see *Coates v Modern Methods and Material Ltd*). It is not relevant that the employer 'knows' that the employee took part in the strike, for the test is an objective one (see *Manifold Industries Ltd v Sim*). Indeed, off-duty employees, and employees who are away from work sick may be regarded as taking part in strike action in appropriate circumstances (see *Bolton Roadways Ltd v Edwards*).

13.35 Similarly, continuity of employment is not lost if the employee is absent from work because of a lock-out (s 216(3)), but there does appear to be a difference, in that if the contract of employment still subsists, s 212(1) (above) applies, and days when an employee is locked out will still count towards continuity. This is because s 216(1) only refers to strikes, not to lock-outs. It is only when there is no contract of employment in existence that s 216(3) provides that the number of days falling within the period between the employee's last working day and the day he resumes work are to be deducted from the start of the employee's period of continuous employment.

C. Military service (s 217)

13.36 An employee who is obliged to serve as an armed forces reservist may apply under the Reserve Forces (Safeguard of Employment) Act 1985 to be reinstated in his former employment within six months of the termination of the period for which he was called up. Weeks when the employee was called up will not count towards continuity, but continuity will not be broken.

Change of employer

13.37 As has been noted, if there has been a transfer of an undertaking within the meaning of the TUPE regulations (see Chapter 9) there is an automatic transfer of the contract of employment from the transferor to the transferee. Curiously enough, the regulations make no mention of continuity of employment being preserved in such circumstances, although there can be little doubt that this will happen, for otherwise the UK would be in serious breach of its obligations to transpose the Acquired Rights Directive into domestic law. It would seem that the provisions of ERA, s 218 are sufficient for this purpose, even though many of the legal decisions on this section were decided prior to the introduction of TUPE.

13.38 There are a number of circumstances to consider.

(a) There is a transfer to which TUPE applies. Regulation 5(1) states that the contract shall have effect as if originally made between the person so employed and the transferee. This clearly preserves the continuity of the employee so transferred (*Royal Ordnance plc v Pilkington*).

(b) There is a transfer to which ERA, s 218(2) applies. This section provides for continuity to be preserved when there is a transfer of a trade, business or undertaking from one employer to another. There must be a recognised and identifiable part of the business transferred, not merely a collection of assets (*Melon v Hector Powe Ltd*).

(c) Statutory change of employer: here ERA, s 218(3) applies when an Act of Parliament substitutes one employer for another (see *Gale v Northern General Hospital NHS Trust*, where the rule was held not to apply).

(d) Although at common law the death of an employer would normally terminate the contract, ERA, s 218(4) provides that if the employee is kept on by the personal representative or trustee of the deceased employer, continuity will not be broken.

(e) If an employee is employed by two partners, and one of them leaves the partnership (for whatever reason) there is no break in the continuity of employment. Section 218(5) ensures continuity when two partners are succeeded by one of them as sole principal (*Stevens v Bower*).

(f) If an employee is transferred from an employer to an associated employer, the transfer does not break continuity (s 218(6)). However, the two employers must be 'associated' in the legal sense, in accordance with the definition contained in ERA, s 231 (see para 2.7).

(g) If an employee transfers from employment by the governors of a school maintained by a local education authority to employment by that authority, continuity is preserved (ERA, s 218(7)). Employees who transfer from one hospital to another, or from an NHS hospital to one with trust status, will generally have continuity preserved by ERA, s 218(8) (see also National Health Service and Community Care Act 1990, s 6), and certain senior hospital appointees whilst undergoing training, which involves being successively employed by different health authorities, have continuity for a number of employment protection rights specified in ERA (Employment Protection (Continuity of Employment of National Health Service Employees) (Modification) Order 1996). For redundancy payment purposes, if an employee transfers from one local authority to another, or to or from certain specified bodies, continuity is preserved (Redundancy Payments (Continuity of Employment in Local Government etc) (Modification) Order 1999). But a transfer to or from a body not included in Sch 1 to the Order will not give rise to continuity (*Liversidge v London Residuary Body*). Similarly, continuity is preserved on a transfer from one NHS body to another (Redundancy Payments (National Health Service) (Modification) Order 1993).

13.39 In particular, it should be noted that artificial breaks in employment consequent on a transfer are not generally favoured, and s 218, combined with TUPE, are to be given a broad interpretation so as to preserve continuity where possible (*Macer v Abafast Ltd*).

The effect of the continuity rules

13.40 The purpose of establishing continuity of employment is to enable an employee to qualify, by virtue of the length of his employment, for certain statutory rights. In particular, however, additional years of employment which can be saved by the continuity rules are of great value to an employee whose employment ultimately comes to an end for reason of redundancy, for he can then obtain a larger redundancy payment (or an increased basic award if he was unfairly dismissed). Thus, when there is a transfer of a business from one employer to another, if there is no continuity, he can apply for his redundancy payment, and then start again with his new employer; on the other hand, if there is continuity, the new employer takes over the obligations to make a redundancy payment should this prove necessary in the future. In principle, if the employer makes a redundancy payment to the employee, whose contract is then renewed by the same or another employer (eg by virtue of the TUPE Regulations, see Chapter 9), continuity of employment is broken for redundancy payment purposes (ERA, s 214). There must be a full payment of redundancy money due, the payment must be in pursuance of a statutory obligation to pay (*Rowan v Machinery Installations (South Wales) Ltd*), not a voluntary payment (*Ross v Delrosa Caterers Ltd*) and must not have been paid by virtue of an employment tribunal decision (*Richards v S and H E Fielding Ltd*). Continuity will also be broken if a redundancy payment has been made by the Secretary of State under the provisions of ERA, ss 166–167 (see para 18.64), provided he is satisfied that the requisite conditions for the payment have been met (*Secretary of State for Trade and Industry v Lassman*).

13.41 However, if the employee is re-engaged on condition that the redundancy payment is repaid, and he does so, continuity of employment is not broken (Employment Protection (Continuity of Employment) Regulations 1996, reg 4).

14

Normal Working Hours and a Week's Pay

Normal working hours

A. Employment Rights Act, ss 221–229

14.1 In order to quantify part of the amount of money payable to an employee in respect of the violation of certain specific statutory rights, it is necessary to ascertain the employee's weekly pay, which is done by reference to the employee's 'normal working hours'. The Employment Rights Act sets out precise formulae for determining how a week's pay is thus to be calculated and, in certain specific cases, puts a cap on that amount.

B. Contractual provisions

14.2 The Act envisages that there are a number of different possibilities when trying to assess an employee's 'normal working hours', and it is therefore necessary to choose the one which is most appropriate in the circumstances, so as to calculate the week's pay. To do this, one must start with a consideration of the contract of employment. Thus, if the contract specifies normal working hours, that will generally be conclusive, and it is immaterial that the employee works more or less than those hours, unless it can be shown that there has been a variation (express or implied) of the contract (*ITT Components (Europe) v Kolah*). If the contract is silent on this matter, the employment tribunal must infer the relevant term from what happens in practice (*Larkin v Cambos Enterprises (Stretford) Ltd*). Thus in *Armstrong Whitworth Rolls Ltd v Mustard* the contract of employment required the employee to work 40 hours per week. He was then asked to work for 60 hours per week, in order to ensure 24-hour coverage of the plant. He did this for seven years and, when made redundant, it was held that his contract of employment had been varied, so that he was entitled to a redundancy payment on the basis of a 60-hour week.

14.3 Overtime is generally excluded from normal working hours, unless it is included in the minimum number of hours fixed by the contract. In other words, it must be guaranteed by the employer and obligatory for the employee (*Tarmac Roadstone Holdings Ltd v Peacock*). If the employer is entitled, but not obliged, to call for overtime working, such hours as are worked will not count towards normal working hours, even though the employee is bound to work overtime under the terms of his contract (*Lotus Cars Ltd v Sutcliffe*). In *Bamsey v Albion Engineering and Manufacturing plc* the employee worked under a contract that entitled him to a basic working week of 39 hours. In fact, he regularly worked a shift pattern which averaged 60 hours per week. He was paid for his period of annual leave on the basis of a 39-hour week, and he claimed that he should have been paid at the same rate as averaged, with overtime, while at work. His claim failed. The Working Time Regulations incorporated the definition of working hours contained in ERA, s 234 and overtime could only be included in a week's pay if it was obligatory on both sides as contractual obligations.

14.4 It is then necessary to establish how much the employee was paid for those hours. Remuneration, for this purpose, can be quite wide. Clearly, wages or salaries will be included, but also contractual bonuses paid on a regular basis, eg per shift, or per site, or for undertaking additional duties (*A & B Marcusfield v Melhuish*). Commission payments are also included, although a commission paid annually has to be apportioned over the period when the employee actually worked (*J & S Bickley Ltd v Washer*), and consequently averaged over a period of 12 weeks (see below). Expenses do not count as remuneration if they are a reimbursement of an employee's expenditure, but will count if they represent a profit in the employee's hands (*S and U Stores Ltd v Wilkes*). However, expenses which represent a profit must have been declared to the Inland Revenue, otherwise there is a danger that the contract may be illegal (*Tomlinson v Dick Evans U Drive Ltd*). Payments in kind (car, accommodation, food etc) will not count (*Skillen v Eastwoods Froy Ltd*), although it should be noted that such benefits may be taken into account when determining any relevant compensation award. Tips and gratuities do not count if they are paid by the customer, not the employer (*Palmanor Ltd v Cedron*), but a service charge which is distributed among employees in a fixed proportion will count as part of a week's pay (*Tsoukka v Potomac Restaurants Ltd*). A lodging allowance is not part of a week's pay, although a deduction from pay in respect of lodging clearly would be. Overtime premiums also do not count (*British Coal Corpn v Cheesbrough*).

14.5 When calculating 'a week's pay' for statutory purposes, it is the gross pay which counts, not net pay (*Secretary of State for Employment v John Woodrow & Sons (Builders) Ltd*). Moreover, the amount must be calculated on the basis that the employer is complying with his legal obligations. Thus, in *Cooner v P S Doal & Sons*, an employee was paid less than that to which he was entitled under a Wages Council order, and it was held that it was pay under the order which counted, not the lower wage actually paid. Although the Wages Councils orders have now ceased to exist, the principle applies to the new minimum wage legislation (*Paggetti v Cobb*).

A week's pay

A. Quantifying a week's pay

14.6 Having ascertained an employee's normal weekly hours, and how much he is paid for those hours, we can now work out his week's pay for statutory purposes. The following four circumstances should cover all situations.

Remuneration does not vary (ERA, s 221 (2))

14.7 If an employee's remuneration does not vary in normal working hours (whether he be an hourly or weekly paid employee, or is paid for any other period) then the amount of a week's pay is the amount which is payable under the contract of employment. If the employee is paid by the hour, then the week's pay is to be determined as if he worked his full contractual hours in that week.

Remuneration varies with the amount of work (ERA, s 221(3))

14.8 If the amount of remuneration does vary with the amount of work done in the period (eg piece workers) the week's pay is ascertained by finding the average hourly remuneration payable in the 12 weeks ending with the calculation date. If, in any of those 12 weeks, no remuneration was payable for hours when the employee was actually at work, earlier weeks can be taken into account, so as to bring the number up to 12 (s 223). Only weeks when the employee actually works will count (*Adams v John Wright & Sons (Blackwall) Ltd*). Thus if an employee is paid for work actually done in a week, even if those earnings were abnormally low, the week will count. If an employee is a recent recruit, so that he does not have 12 weeks' employment to take into account, an employment tribunal can determine an amount which fairly represents a week's pay, taking into account the amount already received, the remuneration offered in the contract, the remuneration of comparable employees of the same employer, and remuneration received by comparable employees of other employers (ERA, s 228). Weeks with a previous employer which count towards continuity (see Chapter 13) may be taken into account (ERA, s 229).

Remuneration varies according to the time of work (ERA, s 222)

14.9 If an employee is a shift worker, or works on a rota, so that the hours when he is required to work differ according to the time of the day or the day of the week, with the consequence that his remuneration will correspondingly be different, the week's pay will be the average hourly rate multiplied by the average weekly hours in the period of 12 weeks prior to the calculation date. Again, earlier weeks can be counted, if necessary (see above).

No normal working hours (ERA, s 224)

14.10 If the employee had no normal working hours, the week's pay is determined by taking the employee's average weekly earnings for the period of 12 weeks prior to the calculation date. If the employee was not paid during any of those weeks, earlier weeks can be included, if necessary, to make up the 12-week period, even if the employee agreed to waive an entitlement to be paid, which otherwise was legally required to be paid (*Secretary of State for Employment v Crane*).

B. Capping a week's pay (ERA, s 227)

14.11 In respect of the following claims, there is a limit to the amount of a week's pay which can be calculated, which currently is £290 per week. These claims are:

(a) basic award for unfair dismissal;

(b) additional award of compensation for unfair dismissal;

(c) statutory redundancy pay;

(d) arrears of pay (up to eight weeks), statutory notice, and holiday pay (up to six weeks) and a basic award, payable on an employer's insolvency (ERA, s 186);

(e) right not to be unjustifiably disciplined by a trade union (TULR(C)A, s 67);

(f) unreasonable exclusion from a trade union (TULR(C)A, s 176);

(g) failure to give employment particulars (Employment Act 2002: see para 3.112);

(h) failure to comply with the Flexible Working (Procedural Requirements) Regulations, see para 2.134);

(i) failure to consult under the Transfer of Undertakings (Protection of Employment) Regulations.

14.12 It will be noted that guarantee pay (see para 7.2) is limited to £18.90 per day (ERA, s 31) with a maximum of £94.50 in any period of three months. Pay for time off work to look for another job (see para 7.25) is limited to two-fifths of a week's pay, not capped (ERA, s 54). In all other instances where a week's pay is used for calculation purposes, it is the actual gross pay which has to be taken into account.

C. The calculation date (ERA, ss 225–226)

14.13 The date on which the above calculations are to be made will differ, depending on the nature of the employee's claim. Each statutory right has its own formula. For guarantee pay (s 30), it will generally be the day on which the guarantee payment is payable (unless a new contract or variation has been entered into, in which case it will be the last day when the old contract was in force). The calculation date in respect of a claim for remuneration for time off with pay to look for work (s 52) is the day the employer gave notice of termination for reason of redundancy. For time off work for antenatal care (s 55) the calculation date is the date of the appointment, and for time off work for employee representatives (s 62) and time off work for study or training (s 63A) the calculation date is the date on which time off was taken or should have been permitted. For suspension on medical grounds (s 64) or maternity suspension (s 66), the calculation date is generally the day before the suspension begins. If a request is made for contract variation (s 80F) the calculation date is the date on which the application was made.

14.14 For redundancy payment claims, if contractual notice was given which was greater than the statutory notice which could have been given, the calculation date will be the day on which, counting backwards from the effective date of termination, the statutory notice could have been given. If less than statutory notice was given, the calculation date will be the date that notice expires, and if no notice is given, the date the contract terminated. For payments due to an employee on the employer's insolvency, the calculation date becomes the 'appropriate date', ie the date on which the employer became insolvent (for holiday pay and arrears of pay). For the basic award, it will be the later of the dates when the employer became insolvent, or the employment was terminated, or the basic award was made, as the case may be. For other payments (ie statutory notice, statutory redundancy pay), the calculation date will be the later of the dates when the employer became insolvent or the employment was terminated (ERA, s 186).

15

Rights in Notice

15.1 One of the features which distinguishes a contract of employment from other contractual situations is that a contract of employment is one of continuous obligation, with, generally speaking, no specified time for its ending. Thus, apart from certain exceptions (eg fixed-term contracts, summary dismissal, retirement age, project termination) if either the employer or employee wishes to terminate the contract, notice of such termination must be given. Whether or not there is a termination is a factual and legal question (see para 17.10), but to be operative, the notice must give a clear indication of the actual date of termination (*Morton Sundour Fabrics Ltd v Shaw*, para 18.8). This chapter will explore the rights and duties of the parties to give and receive lawful notice in the event of a termination, ie if there is a dismissal or resignation.

Notice to be given by the employer

15.2 The period of notice to be given by the employer will first be determined by having regard to the contract of employment, as required by ERA, s 1(4)(e). In theory, this is a matter of negotiation between the employer and employee, although in practice it is the employer who will usually dictate the terms, depending on factors such as the need to harmonise terms with those of other employees in similar positions, the nature of the employment, the seniority of the employee's position, and so on.

15.3 If the contract of employment is silent on this matter, at common law, reasonable notice must be given. Again, what is reasonable will depend on the employee's position, the industry, nature of the work, etc. For example, in *Hill v C A Parsons & Co Ltd*, the Court of Appeal expressed the view that a senior engineer would have been entitled to between six months' to one year's notice, and there are a number of decisions (dating from the nineteenth century and the earlier part of the twentieth century) which deal with what would be reasonable notice for employees such as head gardeners, domestic servants, journalists, commercial travellers, chorus girls, hairdressers' assistants, and so on. The more senior the status, the more notice an employee is entitled to receive (*Clark v Fahrenheit 451 (Communications) Ltd*).

15.4 However, irrespective of the contractual terms, by statute, certain minimum periods of notice must be given (see ERA, s 86(1)). These periods are to be determined by the length of the employee's period of employment. Thus, after one month's employment, the employee is entitled to one week's notice, and this will apply until he has been employed for two years. Thereafter, he will be entitled to a week's notice in respect of each year's continual employment, ie two weeks' notice after two year's employment, up to a statutory maximum of 12 weeks' notice in respect of employment which has lasted for 12 years or more. But if contractual notice is for a period which is longer than that to be given by statute, the contractual notice will prevail.

15.5 If a contract of employment comes to an end because of the operation of the doctrine of frustration (see para 17.55) no statutory or contractual notice can be or need be given (*G F Sharp & Co Ltd v McMillan*).

15.6 Notice to terminate a contract of employment may be given at any time, even before the employment has commenced. Thus in *Sarker v South Tees Acute Hospitals NHS Trust*, the claimant was offered a post in July, and was due to start work in October. However, the offer was withdrawn in September. The claimant brought a claim for her contractual notice, under the provisions of the Employment Tribunals Extension of Jurisdiction Order (see para 1.31). The EAT held that her contract had been terminated, and she was entitled to her contractual notice.

A. Giving notice

15.7 Notice may be given by either side either orally or in writing. In either case, apart from summary dismissal, it will run from the day after it is given (*West v Kneels Ltd*), unless a later date is specified, but it cannot operate unless the recipient has had an opportunity to know of it. Thus, if a letter giving notice to an employee is not received on a particular day (because the employee is not at home, or because of a postal strike etc), it will only operate when the employee has had a reasonable opportunity to read it (see *Brown v Southall and Knight*, para 17.8). If there is a collateral contract (see para 3.15) to the main contract, notice must be given in respect of both of them.

15.8 The general common law rule is that once notice has been given, it cannot be unilaterally withdrawn either by the employer (*Riordan v War Office*) or the employee (*Brennan v C Lindley & Co Ltd*) although it can be withdrawn by mutual agreement between the parties (*Harris and Russell Ltd v Slingsby*). The notice period may also be extended by mutual agreement (*Mowlem Northern Ltd v Watson*). However, modern cases draw a distinction between the deliberate giving of notice (by either party) and a resignation or dismissal given 'in the heat of the moment.' In such circumstances (usually following some form of argument) it is incumbent on the recipient to ascertain whether the other party really meant what he said (*Kwik-Fit (GB) Ltd v Lineham*, and see para 17.47).

15.9 If the employer gives notice to terminate the contract of employment, and during the period of that notice the employee gives a counter-notice that he intends to leave at an earlier date, the employee has still been dismissed for the reason for which the employer's notice was given (ERA, s 95(2); see *Ready Case Ltd v Jackson*). However, if the employee resigns during the notice period, rather than giving a counter-notice, he will be regarded as not having been dismissed but as having resigned (*Walker v Cotswold Chine Home School*), unless the employer agrees to him leaving, before the expiry of their notice, in which case it is treated as being a variation of the employer's notice of dismissal (*McAlwane v Boughton Estates*). There are special provisions dealing with the counter-notice to be given by an employee when he is dismissed for reason of redundancy (see para 18.32). Further, it should be noted that during the notice period, an employee retains those statutory rights relating to time off work (see ERA, ss 50–63 and TULR(C)A, ss 186–190, and see below, para 15.16).

B. Taxation of payments

15.10 The taxation of payments on the termination of employment is now covered by the Income Tax (Earnings and Pensions) Act 2003. The position is somewhat complicated because some such payments are taxable in full, some only partly so, and some not at all. The general principle is that if the payment constitutes 'earnings', such as salary to the date of termination, accrued holiday pay, benefits in kind, etc, full income tax and national insurance contributions must be deducted. Money paid as an inducement to enter into a restrictive covenant is taxable (even if it becomes unenforceable), but not the affirmation of an existing covenant. On the other hand, money paid by way of compensation for breach of contract is generally free of tax up to £30,000.

C. Pay in lieu of notice

15.11 In *Delaney v Staples*, Lord Browne-Wilkinson listed four circumstances when a payment in lieu of notice may be made, with different consequences in each case. These are:

(a) the employer gives the appropriate notice of termination to the employee, but does not require him to work during the notice period. In effect, the employee is on 'garden leave'. Generally, there is no breach of contract in not requiring the employee to work until the termination date (but see para 19.6). Tax and national insurance contributions must be deducted, and restrictive covenants will normally be enforceable;

(b) the contract provides that the employer may terminate the contract, either with notice or summarily on the payment of a sum of money in lieu of notice. Here, two alternative ways are set out whereby the contract may be lawfully terminated. If the employer fails to make the payment, the employee can sue for the money as a debt. If the employer makes the payment, income tax should be deducted;

(c) the employer and employee mutually agree to bring the contract of employment to an end, for an agreed payment. Technically, there is no breach of contract, but even though the payment is not strictly 'earnings', it is taxable in full;

(d) the employer summarily dismisses the employee and makes a payment of money in lieu of notice. This is the most common category of payment in lieu of notice. Since the employer is seeking to extinguish a claim for damages (for breach of contract) the payment is free from tax up to £30,000.

15.12 It follows that if there is no payment at all made in lieu of notice (or if the payment made is in respect of a lesser period than the full notice period), any subsequent payment must be regarded as damages for breach of contract, the first £30,000 of which will not be liable to income tax.

15.13 Either party may waive his right to receive contractual or statutory notice (ERA, s 86(3)) and, in particular, an employer may decide to give a payment in lieu of the employee working during the notice period. Indeed, if the contract of employment gives the employer an option to make a payment in lieu of notice, the employee has no right to work out his notice, or to be compensated for non-contractual benefits he would have obtained had he worked his notice (*Marshall (Cambridge) Ltd v Hamblin*). But an employer cannot use the device of making a payment in lieu of notice to prevent an employee from achieving his contractual earnings, eg commissions, etc. An employee who is on piecework must be given enough work to enable him to earn his usual earnings, and this rule applies equally during the notice period (*Devonald v Rosser & Sons*).

15.14 Additionally, as well as his salary, the employee is entitled to be compensated for the loss of other contractual benefits (car, health insurance, accrued holiday pay etc) for the period had the notice been worked out. Further, it was held by the Court of Appeal in *Abrahams v Performing Right Society* that if a contract states that there is a contractual entitlement to pay in lieu of notice, the full amount due is payable and there is no duty to mitigate against any loss. The duty only arises if the employer is not contractually bound to make the payment in lieu. Thus in *Cerberus Software Ltd v Rowley* the contract of employment provided that the employer could either give six months' notice of termination or make a payment on termination in lieu of notice. The claimant was dismissed without notice and without a payment in lieu. After five weeks, he obtained employment at a higher salary, but nonetheless he claimed damages for wrongful dismissal. The Court of Appeal held that a provision in a contract which enabled the employer to make a payment in lieu of notice gives the employer a choice, and is inconsistent with the employee having a right to insist on such payment being made. Consequently, the employee's remedy was for damages for breach of contract, and the measure of such damages was the amount the employee would have received had the employment continued, subject to the ordinary rules relating to mitigation of damages. *Abraham v Performing Right Society* was distinguished because in that case there was a contractual entitlement to pay in lieu, which was not subject to the duty to mitigate, whereas in *Cerberus* the employer had a choice whether or not to make a payment in lieu. In other words, there is a difference between a claim for contractual entitlement and a claim for liquidated damages. In the latter event, where the claim is for damages for breach of contract, the mitigation rules apply.

D. Rights during the notice period (ERA, ss 88–91)

15.15 During the period of notice, the employee will still have certain statutory rights, contained in ERA, ss 88–91. If the employer gives notice, the employee must have been employed for one month or more to obtain the statutory rights, but he will not have any of these rights if the notice to be given by the employer must be at least one week more than the statutory notice laid down in ERA, s 86(1). Thus in *The Scotts Co (UK) Ltd v Budd* the claimant was employed for 17 years, and thus entitled to statutory notice of 12 weeks. He was off work sick for two years, and the employers terminated his employment, giving him the 13 weeks' notice to which he was entitled under his contract. He claimed that he was entitled to be paid for the weeks of his notice period. His claim was dismissed by the EAT. Section 87(4) of ERA makes it quite clear that the entitlement to be paid during the notice period does not apply if the notice to terminate must be at least one week longer than the statutory period of notice. If an employee has been employed for five years, and is given four weeks' contractual notice, or five weeks' statutory notice, the provisions of ss 88–91 apply. However, if the employee gives notice (after being employed for one month or more) he will be able to enjoy these statutory rights only for the statutory notice period required of an employee, ie one week (s 86(1)), even though he gives a longer period of notice.

15.16 The statutory rights in question are as follows:

(a) Where the employee has normal working hours, he is entitled to be paid for those hours when he is ready and willing to work, but

    (i)   the employer does not provide work (s 88(1)(a)), or

    (ii) he is incapable of work because of sickness or injury (s 88(1)(b)), or

    (iii) the employee is absent from work because of pregnancy or childbirth or parental leave, adoption leave or paternity leave (s 88(1)(c)), or

    (iv) he is absent from work in accordance with the terms of the contract relating to holidays (s 88(1)(d)).

    S/he is entitled to be paid at the average hourly rate, produced by dividing a week's pay by the number of normal working hours. It should be noted that, for the purpose of ss 88–91, a 'week's pay' is not subject to the statutory limit which is applied in unfair dismissal and redundancy claims. Any payment made by the employer by way of sick pay, statutory sick pay, statutory maternity pay, paternity pay, statutory paternity pay, adoption pay, statutory adoption pay, holiday pay etc, can be offset.

(b) If the employee does not have normal working hours, the employer shall pay a week's pay (or average weekly remuneration – calculated over a period of 12 weeks), for each week of the notice period, provided the employee is ready and willing to do work of a reasonable nature and amount in order to earn a week's pay (s 89(1), (2)). S/he is also entitled to be paid for periods when s/he is off work because of sickness or injury, absent through pregnancy or childbirth, or parental leave, adoption leave, parental leave or paternity leave, or absent because of contractual holidays (s 89(3)). Any payments made by the employer can be offset (see above).

(c) ERA, s 91 provides that an employer is not required to make payments under ss 88–89 in respect of any period during which the employee is absent from work with leave from the employer granted at the request of the employee, including any period of time off work taken for the purpose of public duties, looking for work or making arrangements for retraining, antenatal care, acting as an occupational pension scheme trustee, or taking part in trade union duties and activities. At first sight this would appear to be strange, but in fact there is no problem. ERA, ss 50–63 and TULR(C)A, ss 168–170 contain their own remedies for such absences from work, and thus the employee must pursue them under the appropriate section, without reference to ERA, ss 89–90.

15.17 Section 91 further provides that no payment is due to an employee under ss 88–89 in the following circumstances:

(a) if the employee gives notice, and then takes part in a strike;

(b) if the employer gives notice, and the employee then takes part in a strike (because he cannot be said to be ready and willing to perform some work);

(c) if, during the notice period, the employee commits an act which amounts to a breach of contract, eg something which amounts to gross misconduct, and the employer dismisses the employee forthwith (s 91).

15.18 The above rights contained in ss 88–90 apply when either the employer or employee give notice of termination of the contract. If the employer terminates the contract without notice, then the rights conferred by ss 88–90 shall be taken into account when assessing his liability for breach of contract.

Time off to look for work (ERA, s 52)

15.19 An employee whose employment has been terminated because of redundancy has the right to have time off work (with pay) to look for work or make arrangements for retraining during his notice period. This topic has been dealt with in Chapter 7.

E. Contractual rights during notice

15.20 It is always open to an employer to give lawful notice to terminate the contract, and to require the employee to work during the notice period. If the employee fails or refuses to do so, he will not be entitled to his pay under s 88 (above), because he is not able or willing to work. As an alternative, the employer may give lawful notice, but not require the employee to work during the notice period. During this period, the employee will be entitled to all the contractual benefits. For his part, the employee may be restrained from working for a competitor during the notice period, if by doing so the employer would suffer serious harm (*Evening Standard Co Ltd v Henderson*), but, on the other hand, the fact that the employee takes another job during the notice period is not repudiatory conduct by him, in the absence of a garden leave clause (see para 19.6). Further, since the notice money is contractually due to the employee, there is no requirement to mitigate against his loss (*Hutchings v Coinseed Ltd*).

15.21 If, during the notice period, there is a wage increase (eg as a result of negotiations with a trade union) the employee is entitled to be paid that increase. However, if, subsequent to leaving the employment, a wage increase is negotiated which is backdated to a period when the employee was working, it would appear that he has no legal entitlement to that increase (*Leyland Vehicles Ltd v Reston*). In legal reasoning, the employee has not given 'consideration' for the increase, because he has already worked under his contract, and 'past consideration is no consideration'.

F. Dispensing with notice

15.22 If a contract provides that an employee may be dismissed with immediate effect, he is still entitled to contractual notice or to a payment in lieu of notice (*T & K Home Improvements Ltd v Skilton*). But if an employee is dismissed without notice or without a payment in lieu of notice, he is under a duty to mitigate against his loss, and must give credit in respect of any earnings from his new employment (*Gregory v Wallace*).

15.23 If an employee commits a 'fundamental breach of contract' which warrants summary dismissal (see para 16.8), the employer need not give notice of termination. If the employer commits a fundamental breach of contract entitling the employee to resign and

claim constructive dismissal (see para 17.24) the employee need not give notice of termination. Nor need an employer give notice if the contract had already been frustrated, and
the fact that the employer keeps an employee 'on the books' when he is unlikely to return
to work may be the sort of arrangement contemplated by ERA, s 213(3)(c) (see para
13.23), but no contract of employment will be in existence (*GF Sharp & Co Ltd v McMillan*).
If an employee is on a fixed-term contract (ie one with a fixed date of expiry) no notice of
termination need be given, and a letter sent to the employee confirming that the contract
will expire on a certain date is not a letter of dismissal (*London Underground Ltd v
Fitzgerald*). However, notice will be required if the employer wishes to terminate the
contract prior to the expiry of the fixed term (*Dixon & Constanti v BBC*), or if the
employee wishes to resign before the end of that term, particularly if there is a restrictive
covenant in force (*Thomas Marshall (Exports) Ltd v Guinle*).

15.24 If an employee is on a probationary period for a certain length of time, the successful completion of which will result in him being confirmed in his position, this is not a
fixed-term contract, and he may be given lawful notice prior to the expiry of the probationary period. The employer is not obliged to employ the employee for the whole of the
probationary period (*Dalgleish v Kew House Farm Ltd*). A training contract may or may
not be a fixed-term contract, depending on how it is worded. If it is, it cannot be brought
to an end until the period of training has expired, except for gross misconduct.

15.25 A project contract will expire when the project has been completed, and thus no
notice need be given (*Ironmonger v Movefield Ltd*, see para 2.120). If an employee's contract comes to an end by virtue of a contractual provision relating to retirement age, again,
no notice of termination need be given.

G. Notice and time limits

15.26 Once notice (by either side) is given, the effective date of termination, for unfair
dismissal and redundancy pay purposes, is the date the notice expires, and the time for
bringing a complaint before an employment tribunal will run from that date. However, an
employer cannot 'short notice' an employee (ie give less notice than the statute requires)
so as to prevent the employee from satisfying the qualifying period of employment. Thus
if an employee has been employed for 51 weeks, and is dismissed without notice, his
effective date of termination is the day he leaves, and, not having a requisite period of one
year's continuous employment, he would appear to be unable to lodge a claim for unfair
dismissal. However, ERA, s 97(2) provides that the effective date of termination is the date
on which his statutory notice would have expired. In other words, he is entitled to add to
the period of employment the week's notice to which is entitled by statute. On the other
hand, the dismissal will only operate for computation purposes from the date when the
statutory notice expires, not from the date when his contractual notice (had it have been
given) would have expired. Thus, if the employee has been employed for 50 weeks, and is
entitled to four weeks' notice, but is dismissed immediately with pay in lieu of notice, his
period of continuous employment is two weeks short of the qualifying period. He is only
entitled to add on the period of statutory notice, not his potential contractual notice (see
Fox Maintenance Ltd v Jackson, para 17.4(c)). This provision also applies to constructive
dismissal claims (ERA, s 97(4)). However, s 97(2)–(4) only applies for the purpose of
determining the qualifying period of employment (s 108(1)), the calculation of the basic

award (s 19(1)), and the calculation of a week's pay where this has been increased by the Secretary of State during the statutory notice period (s 227(3)). A similar extension of the period of continuous employment is contained in s 92(7), with respect to written reasons for dismissal.

15.27 The continuous period of employment is not extended for the purpose of extending the time limit within which a claim for unfair dismissal may be brought. In other words, an unfair dismissal claim must be brought within three months of the effective date of termination, not from when the statutory notice period would have expired. The effective date of termination is the date on which the employment relationship ends, and that date cannot be varied by any subsequent agreement between the parties. However, the notice that determines the effective date of termination can be varied, so that there can be a subsequent agreement that the effective date of termination can be brought forward or pushed backward, and time will start to run from the new date (*Palfrey v Transco plc*). Finally, it may be noted that an employee who has been given notice may commence proceedings for unfair dismissal without waiting for the notice period to expire, or within three months from the effective date of termination (ERA, s 111(3)).

H. Notice pay on insolvency (ERA, ss 182–186)

15.28 If an employer becomes insolvent (eg bankrupt or wound up; see s 183), so that the contract of employment is no longer capable of being performed, then clearly that contract has terminated. In such circumstances, the employee may make an application for his statutory notice to be paid from the National Insurance Fund. If the Secretary of State is satisfied that the employee is so entitled, he will pay out of that Fund the amount of statutory notice set out in s 86 (above) (as well as certain other payments, see para 7.118), although the 'week's pay' for the purpose of this provision, is limited to the statutory maximum as laid down (currently £290 per week). Other contractual benefits cannot be recovered from the Fund. The employee will be under a duty to mitigate against his loss (*Westwood v Secretary of State for Employment*), and an employee who obtains fresh employment immediately or during what would have been his notice period can only recover in respect of the period of loss, if any (*Secretary of State for Employment v Wilson*). Any award made by the Secretary of State from the Fund will be based on pay net of income tax.

Notice to be given by the employee

15.29 An employee is required to give due notice of termination, as laid down in his contract of employment. If there is no such term, then, in theory, he should give reasonable notice, depending on his position, the industry, etc. There does not appear to be any legal authority on this point. We are therefore left with the statutory notice period, set out in ERA, s 86(2), which provides that an employee who has been continuously employed for one month or more has to give at least one week's notice.

Employer's remedies

15.30 If the employee fails to give the required notice of termination of his contract, technically the employer has two remedies. The first arises where there is a restrictive covenant prohibiting the employee from working for a competitor etc (see Chapter 19). The employer may be able to obtain an injunction to prevent a breach of this term. However, he will not be able to obtain an order for specific performance of the contract (TULR(C)A, s 236).

15.31 Second, in theory, the employer may sue for damages for breach of contract, although such actions are virtually unknown this century, and the most an employee stands to lose if he fails to give the requisite notice is his reputation, if any, as a responsible employee. But if, for example, in anticipation of an employee commencing work, the employer incurs considerable expenses (eg purchases equipment or machinery, or hires premises, or enters into an abortive advertising campaign), an action for damages against an employee who fails to meet his contractual obligations could well succeed (*Batty v Melillo*).

15.32 An employer may attempt to pre-empt this problem by providing, in the contract of employment, that he may withhold arrears of wages and/or accrued holiday pay if an employee fails to give proper notice or work out that notice in accordance with the contract.

15.33 So far as the withholding of wages is concerned, this would appear to be perfectly legal, but only in so far as the amount withheld is a genuine pre-estimate of the loss, and not a penalty clause (*Dunlop Pneumatic Tyre Co Ltd v New Garage & Motor Co*). Such deduction would not contravene ERA, s 13(1) (see para 8.4) because the deduction would have been authorised by the employee's contract of employment. For example, in *Giraud UK Ltd v Smith* the employee's contract of employment required him to give four weeks' notice of termination. If he failed to give such notice, the employer would be entitled to deduct from his final payment an amount equivalent to the number of days short. When he left his employment without notice, the employers refused to pay him payments due to him, claiming that under the contract they were entitled to deduct a payment equivalent of four weeks' pay. It was held that the clause was not a lawful liquidated damage clause, because it did not represent a genuine pre-estimate of the loss or damage suffered. Essentially, it was a penalty clause, and was unenforceable.

15.34 So far as accrued holiday pay is concerned, the provisions of reg 13 of the Working Time Regulations must be borne in mind (see para 7.63), and any such deduction would not be lawful.

Employee's remedies

15.35 If an employer fails to give notice to the employee, or gives notice which is less than the contractual or statutory notice (whichever is the longer) the employee's remedy is to bring an action either in the ordinary courts or in the employment tribunal, under the Employment Tribunals Extension of Jurisdiction Order (see para 1.31). A court action would be appropriate if the amount claimed by way of damages is in excess of £25,000, because that is the maximum sum which could be awarded by an employment tribunal. Further, an action for breach of contract may be brought in the ordinary courts any time within six years from the breach, whereas a claim in an employment tribunal must be brought within three months beginning with the effective date of termination, or, if there was no such date, within three months from when the employee last worked, or, if it was not reasonably practicable to present the claim in either of those periods, within such further period as the employment tribunal thinks reasonable.

15.36 The claim by the employee is one for breach of contract, the measure of damages being the monies he would have earned had he been given proper notice. If there was an element of discretion in certain payments (eg annual salary increases, bonuses) it must be assumed that the employer would have exercised that discretion in good faith, and thus they form part of the loss suffered (*Clark v BET plc*). The claim is subject to the common law rule that the innocent party to a breach of contract must take reasonable steps to mitigate against his loss. Thus, if the employee is dismissed without notice, and the following day he obtained fresh employment on equivalent or improved terms and conditions, then, since he has lost nothing, he is not entitled to anything (*Secretary of State for Employment v Wilson*). In *Hardy v Polk (Leeds) Ltd* the claimant was entitled to eight weeks' contractual notice. She was unfairly dismissed without notice, but started a new job after four weeks. It was held that as she had partially mitigated against her loss she was only entitled to compensation for four weeks. Further, credit must be given by the employee for any payment received by way of jobseekers' allowance (*Westwood v Secretary of State for Employment*). In order words, the object of the exercise is to place the employee in the same position financially as he would have been had lawful notice been given.

15.37 In certain special circumstances, an employee may be able to obtain an injunction to restrain an employer from terminating the contract of employment without proper notice. Generally speaking, it has to be shown that the trust and confidence which should exist between employer and employee remains (*Hill v C A Parsons Ltd*), but an injunction may also be obtained where it can be shown that the employer has failed to operate a contractual disciplinary procedure, particularly where damages would not be an adequate remedy for the manner in which a dismissal without notice was carried out. The modern test to be applied is 'the workability' of the situation (*Robb v London Borough of Hammersmith and Fulham*).

15.38 It should be noted that there is no implied term that an employee will not be unfairly dismissed (eg without going through proper procedures), and thus the only damages which can be awarded are those which relate to contractual notice (*Fosca Services (UK) Ltd v Birkett*).

16

Wrongful Dismissal

Background

16.1 Under the law which existed prior to 1971 an employer was entitled to dismiss an employee for any reason or no reason at all; the only issues which arose related to whether or not the employee was entitled to a certain period of notice, or whether his conduct was such as to warrant instant (summary) dismissal without notice. There were certain special cases where the right not to be dismissed was enshrined into an employee's contract by virtue of a special 'status' (see para 2.65), and there were other cases where when a dismissal could not be carried out unless the rules of 'natural justice' were observed (see *Ridge v Baldwin*), or because the approval of some other person or body had to be obtained (eg *Cory Lighterage v Transport and General Workers' Union*). These matters are now largely of historical interest.

16.2 In 1971 the Industrial Relations Act created the right for many employees not to be unfairly dismissed, and though that Act was repealed, the relevant provisions were substantially re-enacted (with some minor amendments) in the Trade Union and Labour Relations Act 1974, and further changes were made by the Employment Protection Act 1975. All the relevant law was brought together in the Employment Protection (Consolidation) Act 1978, and further amendments were made in subsequent legislation. The Employment Rights Act 1996 (as amended) contains most of the relevant statutory provisions currently in force.

16.3 But although the new legal right has largely subsumed the old common law learning, it is still necessary to examine the old law relating to wrongful and summary dismissal, because there may be situations when the common law remedy is more advantageous, or indeed, the only remedy available. In particular, we may note the following circumstances:

(a) the maximum compensation award for unfair dismissal is currently £58,400 plus an appropriate basic award. A highly paid employee who is entitled to a long period of notice may be able to obtain substantially higher damages at common law (see *O'Laoire v Jackel International Ltd*, para 16.25);

(b) an employee who lacks the relevant period of continuous employment to qualify for unfair dismissal rights may nonetheless sue for wrongful dismissal either at common law or in the employment tribunal under the provisions of ETEJO (see para 1.31). However, if the employee is summarily dismissed, or given less than the contractual notice, with the result that he lacks the necessary qualifying period of continuous employment to pursue a claim for unfair dismissal, he cannot claim damages for the loss of the opportunity to claim unfair dismissal. The EAT has held that in the light of *Johnson v Unisys Ltd* (see para 3.43) the decision in *Raspin v United News Shops Ltd* to the contrary is no longer good law (*Virgin Net Ltd v Harper*);

(c) an employee who is past the normal retiring age, or who is over the age of 65, or who worked abroad, may be able to bring a claim for breach of contract based on wrongful dismissal (*Age Concern Scotland v Hines*);

(d) a fair dismissal may nonetheless be a wrongful dismissal if proper notice has not been given (*Treganowan v Robert Knee & Co Ltd*);

(e) an application for unfair dismissal is likely to be time barred if it is not brought within three months from the effective date of termination, whereas a common law action for wrongful dismissal may be brought within six years of the breach;

(f) the rules relating to damages are different. In particular, a common law action does not permit a reduction for contributory conduct, and the mitigation rules are not the same;

(g) the dispute may contain a public law element, and not be concerned with strict contractual rights (*R v Secretary of State for the Home Department, ex p Benwell*);

(h) a dismissal which is in breach of a contractual or statutory dismissal procedure may enable an employee to bring a common law action for breach of contract (*Shook v London Borough of Ealing*) or to seek an injunction to restrain the breach (*Irani v Southampton and South West Hampshire Health Authority*), or seek a declaration as to his legal rights. But the employee's remedies in such circumstances may be limited to damages for the period up to which he would have been employed had the correct procedure been followed (*Gunton v London Borough of Richmond*). There is no implied term in a contract that an employee has the right not to be unfairly dismissed (*Fosca Services (UK) Ltd v Birkett*).

16.4 Since the jurisdiction of the employment tribunals is concurrent in many respects with that possessed by the ordinary courts, an employee will thus opt for whichever cause of action will produce the most advantageous results (see para 1.31).

16.5 If, before his dismissal, an employee acquires a cause of action at common law (whether for breach of contract or breach of the duty to take reasonable care for the employee's health and safety) that cause of action remains unimpaired by the fact that the employee has brought a statutory unfair dismissal claim. Thus a claim for damages for psychiatric injury caused, for example, by a wrongful application for the contractual disciplinary procedure may succeed (*Eastwood v Magnox Electric plc*), even though there can be no award for psychiatric illness (or injury to feelings) caused by the manner of actual dismissal (*Dunnachie v Kingston upon Hull City Council*). Damages for injury to feelings, aggravated and exemplary damages may be awarded in detriment cases, as well as race, sex and disability cases, but not in unfair dismissal cases.

Wrongful dismissal

16.6 There are a number of ways in which wrongful dismissal may occur:

(a) the employer terminates the employment without notice, or with less notice than the employee is entitled to receive under the terms of his contract or the statutory provisions (see Chapter 15);

(b) a fixed-term contract is terminated by the employer before the date it was due to expire;

(c) a contract for the completion of a specific task is terminated by the employer before the task has ended;

(d) the employer terminates the employment without carrying out the disciplinary procedure which has been incorporated into the employee's contract (*Gunton v London Borough of Richmond*);

(e) the employee is selected for redundancy in breach of a selection procedure which has been incorporated into his contract (*Alexander v Standard Telephones and Cables plc*);

(f) the employer wrongfully repudiates the contract, his actions indicating that he no longer intends to be bound by the contract (*General Billposting Co Ltd v Atkinson*). The employee 'accepts' the repudiation by resigning, or, if appropriate, keeps the contract alive and sues for whatever remedy is available (*Rigby v Ferodo*, see para 3.94). For example, if the employer has unilaterally reduced the employee's wages, a claim may be made under the appropriate provisions of the Employment Rights Act (see Chapter 8). On the other hand, if the employee delays action, he may be taken to have affirmed the contract, unless the employer has given him time to make a decision (*Bliss v South East Thames Regional Health Authority*). Whether the employer has in fact repudiated the contract is a matter to be determined in the particular circumstances of the case (*General Billposting Co Ltd v Atkinson*). Thus, if the employer fails or refuses to provide work for the employee (see para 10.17) or makes it impossible for the employee to do his work (*Collier v Sunday Referee Publishing Co Ltd*), or unilaterally attempts to vary the contract of employment, such actions can amount to a breach of contract by the employer which enables the employee to accept by resigning, and claiming wrongful dismissal. This is the common law counterpart of the statutory concept of 'constructive' dismissal, which will be dealt with in Chapter 17;

(g) the contract specifies that a dismissal may only take place in certain specified circumstances, or on specified grounds, and the employer dismisses for some other reason not stated in the contract (*McClelland v Northern Ireland General Health Services Board*).

16.7 However, if the contract expressly permits the employer to terminate the employment without notice on the payment of a sum of money in lieu of notice, and the employer summarily dismisses the employee, the dismissal is not wrongful, whether or not the employer pays the money in lieu of notice, because he is acting within the strict terms of the contract. In such circumstances, the employee may sue for the sum due under the contract, as liquidated damages, and the employee is under no duty to mitigate against his loss (*Abrahams v Performing Right Society*, and see below).

Summary dismissal

16.8 In *Jupiter General Insurance Co v Shroff* the Privy Council stated that summary dismissal was a strong measure, to be justified only in the most exceptional circumstances. Nonetheless, there are a number of well-recognised grounds on which an employer may dismiss an employee summarily; these include gross misconduct, wilful refusal to obey a lawful and reasonable order, gross neglect, dishonesty, and so forth (see, eg *Blyth v Scottish Liberal Club*). Whether the conduct in question is serious enough to warrant dismissal is always a question of fact in each case, and the standards to be applied are those of the current *mores*, not those which may have become somewhat outdated. In *Wilson v Racher*, Edmund-Davies LJ said 'Many of the decisions which are customarily cited in these cases date from the last century and may be wholly out of accord with current social conditions. What would today be regarded as almost an attitude of Czar–serf, which is to be found in some of the older cases where a dismissed employee failed to recover damages, would, I venture to think, be decided differently today. We have by now come to realise that a contract of service imposes upon the parties a duty of mutual respect'. It is thus clear that many of the older decisions on this subject lack authority today, and must be treated with reserve, if not disdain.

16.9 But certain principles remain constant. In *Sinclair v Neighbour* a manager took £15 from a till and left an IOU in its place. He intended to replace the money a few days later. His conduct was regarded as being dishonest and his summary dismissal was upheld. In *Ross v Aquascutum Ltd* the employee was a nightwatchman. He was observed to be absent from the building he was guarding for two hours of each night, and it was held that his conduct constituted a breach of contract so serious as to justify summary dismissal. When considering conduct which results from the interaction of human personalities, it is necessary to apply the standards of ordinary people, not those of the angels. In *Pepper v Webb* a gardener was asked to do certain work, but he refused to do so in language which was somewhat vulgar. His summary dismissal was held to be justified, for by refusing to obey a lawful and reasonable order he had broken his contract. Indeed, his conduct had been such as to give rise to a history of complaints for insolence, and the incident which gave rise to his dismissal was merely the last straw. On the other hand, in *Wilson v Racher* a gardener swore at his employer using some even choicer obscenities. Although this could have amounted to gross misconduct, the court held that '... it requires very special circumstances to entitle a servant who expresses his feelings in such a grossly improper way to succeed in an action for wrongful dismissal'. On the facts of the case, the special circumstance existed, and these lay in the employer's own conduct which had provoked the outburst.

16.10 The breach of an express term of the contract or of a provision in the works rules may justify summary dismissal, provided it has been brought expressly to the attention of the employee that there is certain conduct which the employer will on no account tolerate. Certain airlines, for example, have a rule that any pilot who takes drugs (other than on medical prescription) or is discovered drunk whether on or off duty will be instantly dismissed. Other employers may specify other conduct which is detrimental to the business and which may warrant summary dismissal. For example, smoking in prohibited areas, unhygienic practices in food premises, breach of safety rules which may lead to hazards or risk of injury to others, all constitute conduct which may, in the special circumstances, warrant dismissal. The importance of having a consistent and well-defined policy on this subject will be stressed when the cases dealing with unfair dismissal are discussed.

16.11 An employee is not in breach of his contract of employment merely because he indicates his intention to open a business in competition with his employer. In *Laughton and Hawley v Bapp Industrial Supplies Ltd* the two claimants, who were employed by the respondents, wrote to the company's suppliers stating that they intended to commence trading in the near future, and asked for product lists, prices and terms. When the employers discovered this, the employees were dismissed instantly without notice. The dismissals were held to be unfair. There was no abuse of their positions as employees, no breach of any covenant in restraint of trade, and no disclosures of trade secrets or confidential information. The employees had not failed to devote their efforts to their employer's business during working hours, and thus their activities did not constitute gross misconduct. But where a managing director formed a new business entity, sought to persuade his employer's major client to transfer business to it, and induced two senior employees to join him in the new venture which was in direct competition with the employer, it was held that this amounted to gross misconduct warranting summary dismissal (*Marshall v Industrial Systems and Control Ltd*). An employee has a duty to his employer to act in good faith and in the employer's best interests. Thus, if he seeks to divert to himself a contract which his employer is seeking to obtain with a third party, this will amount to dishonest conduct which would warrant summary dismissal (*Item Software (UK) Ltd v Fassihi*).

16.12 A more difficult problem arises if conduct of the employee is in the nature of neglect, which causes damage to the employer. Should one consider the act itself, which may be of a minor or major nature, or should one consider the consequences, which may be insignificant or serious? In *Savage v British India Steam Navigation Co* it was stated that it was the nature of the act, not the consequences, which was relevant. A failure to observe instructions which resulted in damage was held to be of sufficient seriousness to warrant summary dismissal in *Howe v Gloucester and Severnside Co-operative Society*, but excessive zeal which caused damage did not warrant such drastic measures in *Newlands v Howard & Co Ltd*. Neglect by senior employees who hold responsible positions appears to amount to a greater dereliction of duty than junior staff, and hence more likely to attract instant dismissal. As a general rule, for an employee to be summarily dismissed on the grounds of neglect, the neglect should be something approaching habitual conduct, but a single act of neglect could justify instant dismissal if its consequences are likely to be serious enough (*Taylor v Alidair Ltd*).

16.13 A strike is a breach of contract by the employee, and is thus an act of such a nature as to justify summary dismissal. So too is any other conduct designed to disrupt the employer's business, such as go-slow tactics, work-to-rule, etc. Persistent lateness, drunkenness, fighting, swearing, immorality, skylarking, are all examples of conduct which could attract summary dismissal in particular circumstances. But it must be stressed that although dismissal would not be wrongful at common law, in most cases, the test of 'fairness' will have to be considered additionally, and this will be explored later in Chapter 17.

16.14 A summary dismissal takes effect immediately. Any rights an employee may have, eg for pay in lieu of notice, expenses, etc may be claimed by an action for damages for breach of contract in the ordinary courts (*Octavius Atkinson & Sons Ltd v Morris*) or the employment tribunal (see para 1.31).

Remedies for wrongful dismissal

16.15 It must be stressed that an action for wrongful dismissal is different from a claim for unfair dismissal, although there may well be some overlap in certain instances. But, in particular, it should be noted that the sole issue in a wrongful dismissal action is whether or not the employer has broken the contract of employment. The 'reasonableness' of the employer's conduct is not in issue, nor does 'contributory conduct' by the employee come into the equation. Also, care must be taken to distinguish between payments made by the employer, and awards against an employer made by a court or tribunal. It is with the latter that this chapter is concerned.

16.16 The normal remedy for wrongful dismissal is for the innocent party to bring an action for damages, although sometimes an application for an injunction or a declaration will be made. Also, if the breach of contract consists not in a dismissal, but an alteration in the terms of the contract which is not permitted by the contract, the employee can, at his option, either accept the breach and resign (claiming wrongful constructive dismissal) or refuse to accept the breach, and sue on the contract as it stands, thus seeking to insist that the employer performs the contract (see *Dietman v London Borough of Brent*). The majority of wrongful dismissal claims are brought in the county court or the High Court, although, with the new concurrent jurisdiction conferred on employment tribunals by the Extension of Jurisdiction Order, more and more claims are now being brought under a procedure which is cheaper and comparatively expeditious.

16.17 In rare cases, an employee may seek a public law remedy, by way of judicial review, generally when a private law remedy either does not exist, or would be inadequate in the circumstances (*R v Chief Constable of Merseyside Police, ex p Calveley*).

A. Damages

16.18 The general principle in contract law (and it must be remembered that employment law is basically concerned with a contract of employment) is that the purpose of damages is to put the innocent party in the position in which he would have been had the contractual obligations been performed, insofar as it is possible to do this by a monetary award. Thus, since an employer may always give notice to terminate the contract, then this will become the starting point for any claim. If the employer terminates the contract without notice, or gives less notice than the contract or the statutory provisions require, then damages will be initially limited to the period of notice that should have been given (*Fosca Services (UK) Ltd v Birkett*, and see Chapter 15). Similarly, if the contract was for a fixed term, and is prematurely terminated, damages will be the loss suffered by the employee as the result of the employer's action. However, if a fixed-term contract gives the employer the right to terminate before the end of that term, then damages will be limited to the notice period (*British Guiana Credit Corpn v Da Silva*). If the employer is in breach because he has failed to follow a disciplinary procedure which has been incorporated into the contract, damages will be limited to the period of time it would have taken the employer to put the contractual procedure into effect (*Dietman v Brent London Borough Council*). An apprentice who has been wrongfully dismissed may recover damages for the loss of training and work experience he would have gained had the contract not been broken or the diminution of his future prospects (*Dunk v George Waller & Son Ltd*). Artistes may be able to recover for loss of publicity (*Withers v General Theatre Corpn*), or the loss of enhancing their reputation (*Herbert Clayton & Jack Waller Ltd v Oliver*, see para 10.17).

16.19 Because there may be certain complications arising out of income tax liability and national insurance contributions, the actual computation of the financial loss may present problems. In principle, an employee is entitled to the net loss suffered (ie after the deduction of tax and national insurance), and whether one should start with the gross salary, less deductions, or the net figure grossed up, will frequently depend on the amounts at stake. It would appear that the latter course is more advantageous if the amount is comparatively large, whereas the former method appears to be appropriate when the length of the notice period is relatively short (*Shove v Downs Surgical plc*).

16.20 Also to be taken into account are commissions, bonuses, gratuities etc, which were contractually due to the employee (*Addis v Gramophone Co Ltd*), including an enhanced contractual redundancy payment (*Basnett v J & A Jackson Ltd*) but not discretionary payments (*Lavarack v Woods of Colchester Ltd*). Damages for breach of contract can also include accrued pension rights, because there is no difference between a lost pension and lost pay (*Silvey v Pendragon plc*). Fringe benefits, eg company car (in so far as it was permitted for private use), subsidised mortgages, free lunches, the loss of the right to obtain share options (if there was a contractual right) or options already granted (*Chapman v Aberdeen Construction Group Ltd*), private medical insurance, rent-free accommodation etc, can be quantified and their value claimed. Expenses are not normally allowable, as they represent a reimbursement for expenditure incurred by the employee on behalf of the employer. Indeed, if it can be shown that the expenses were in fact a device to boost the employee's income, and were not genuinely incurred, it may be argued that this was an attempt to avoid paying income tax on the employee's salary, and, as such, the contract was illegal, and did not give rise at all to any cause of action (see para 3.8).

16.21 Also included in the compensation which may be awarded will be the loss of other actual or potential benefits, such as pension rights and/or the employer's potential pension contributions, profit sharing schemes, the lost value of share options (*Micklefield v SAC Technology*), outstanding holiday pay, loss of statutory protection rights (*Stapp v Shaftesbury Society*), loss of the opportunity to claim a redundancy payment (*Basnett v J & A Jackson Ltd*), and so on. An employee's claim for part-payment of wages outstanding at the date of dismissal is not defeated by the fact that the dismissal was for reason of gross misconduct. The Apportionment Act 1870 applies when a contract of employment is terminated during the payment period, unless there is something in the contract of employment to the contrary (*Item Software (UK) Ltd v Fassihi*).

16.22 At common law, no damages may be awarded for the manner of dismissal (*Addis v Gramophone Co Ltd*), whether by way of injured feelings, psychiatric illness, loss of reputation or difficulty in finding fresh employment (*Boardman v Copeland Borough Council*).

The decision of the House of Lords in *Malik v BCCI* (see para 3.42) is concerned with a complaint relating to a breach of trust and confidence owed by the employer to his employees during the period they were employed, and is not concerned with the actual manner of dismissal (*Johnson v Unisys Ltd*). There can be no claim at common law for damages for psychiatric illness if an employer conducts a campaign designed to deprive an employee of his job by fabricating evidence for the purpose of conducting disciplinary proceedings. *Johnson v Unisys* established that unfairness in the manner of dismissal does not give rise to a common law action, whether it is founded on contract or tort. Such matters must be the subject of employment tribunal proceedings (*Eastwood v Magnox Electrical plc*). But in *McCabe v Cornwall County Council*, the Court of Appeal appear to have taken a somewhat different view, and permitted a claim to proceed on the basis that there is no automatic bar to such an action just because a dismissal results from the alleged breach of trust and respect.

16.23 Damages for breach of contract at common law are always subject to the rule that the innocent party must take reasonable steps to mitigate against his loss, which, in this context, involves looking for other suitable employment. Any earnings from such employment (or from self-employment) can be deducted from the loss suffered (*Shove v Downs Surgical plc*). Thus if an employee is dismissed without notice, and obtains other employment, he must give credit for any earning from his new employment in respect of any payment for the period of notice he should have received (*Gregory v Wallace*). The problem here, however, is that the burden of proof is on the employer to show that the employee has failed to take reasonable steps to mitigate his loss (*London and South of England Building Society v Stone*). This he may be able to do, either by reference to matters known to him, or by obtaining some form of discovery from the employee concerning his attempts to seek alternative employment. Whether an employee has taken reasonable steps to mitigate against his loss is a question of fact to be determined by the court, bearing in mind all the circumstances, including the employee's age, mobility, personal commitments, qualifications, experience, and so on. For example, in *Brace v Calder*, the claimant was dismissed from a partnership as a result of a change in the partners, but offered his old job back by the new partners. He refused this offer, and it was held that he had failed to mitigate his loss, and was therefore only entitled to nominal damages. On the other hand, in *Yetton v Eastwoods Froy Ltd*, a managing director was dismissed from his post, but was offered the job of assistant managing director. It was held that his refusal of this job, which was a significant step down, was not unreasonable.

16.24 It is not unusual for a contract of employment of a senior executive to contain a provision that in the event of a wrongful dismissal the employer will make a lump sum payment by way of liquidated damages, which may in fact be in excess of any amount which would be recoverable at common law (sometimes referred to as 'golden parachutes'). In principle, such damages may be unenforceable, since they may amount to being a penalty clause as they fail to taken into account the duty of the employee to mitigate against his loss by seeking alternative employment. In *Murray v Leisureplay plc* the contract provided that in the event of a dismissal, a chief executive would be entitled to one year's gross salary plus certain benefits. The High Court held that this provision was a penalty clause, rather than liquidated damages, and that consequently it was unenforceable. However, the decision was reversed by the Court of Appeal. The clause would only be a penalty if the party seeking to avoid the terms could show that it was 'extravagant and unconscionable' in amount. The clause may have been generous, but it was not unconscionable.

16.25 It is unusual, but not impossible, to bring a claim for unfair dismissal as well as an action for wrongful dismissal, although either the court or tribunal can stay one action, pending the outcome of the other (*Carter v Credit Change Ltd*). If one claim does not fully resolve the whole matter, the second action may then be resorted to. One would expect there to be a general rule that any award made in one jurisdiction would be deducted from an award stemming from the second claim. Thus, an award made by an employment tribunal will normally identify the various headings of loss in respect of which compensation is to be awarded, and double recovery of any particular loss would not be permitted in subsequent High Court proceedings. However, where the loss is in excess of the statutory compensation award, it may not always be possible to identify the particular heading awarded by the employment tribunal, and therefore there may not be an element of double recovery. Thus, in *O'Laoire v Jackel International*, an employment tribunal held that the claimant had been unfairly dismissed, and assessed his loss at £100,000. However, they could only award compensation of £8,000, which was the maximum compensation award at that time. The claimant then brought an action in the High Court, and the judge held that the sum of £8,000 had to be deducted from the damages of £100,000. However, the Court of Appeal held that this was wrong. It was clearly not possible for the employment tribunal to assess the maximum compensation award with reference to any particular head of loss, and thus the rule against double recovery did not apply.

16.26 The general principle relating to any award of damages by a court is that they should be paid net of tax (*British Transport Commission v Gourley*). However, the Income Tax (Earnings and Pensions) Act 2003, ss 401–404 provide that damages for wrongful dismissal are not taxable in the hands of the recipient unless they exceed £30,000. Thereafter, tax must be deducted at the employee's highest marginal rate. Thus a court must award a gross sum which, after tax, would leave the employee with a net sum which represents his loss.

B. Injunction and/or declaration

16.27 An employee who feels that he has been wrongfully dismissed may be able to bring an action for an injunction to restrain a breach of contract, or seek a declaration as to what are his rights under the contract. These are equitable remedies, and therefore will only be granted at the court's discretion. If an application is made for an interlocutory injunction pending the trial of the action, the principles laid down in *American Cyanamid Co v Ethicon* will apply, ie (a) has the claimant shown that there is a triable issue, and (b) does the balance of convenience favour the granting of the injunction? In particular, as we have seen (para 10.1), the courts will rarely grant an injunction if the effect is to compel specific performance of the contract. Exceptionally the court will do so in perhaps two circumstances, ie (a) if there is no loss of trust and confidence in the employee (*Powell v London Borough of Brent*) or (b) where the dismissal was in breach of natural justice or of a contractual disciplinary procedure (*Gunton v London Borough of Richmond*). It must be shown that damages would not be an adequate remedy (*Wadcock v London Borough of Brent*). A person seeking an injunction must first of all have pursued all internal remedies in so far as they are available (*R v BBC, ex p Lavelle*).

16.28 Similarly, an employee may seek a declaration as to his contractual rights. This remedy will usually be sought when an employee refuses to accept a decision by an employer which is outside the terms of the contract. For example, in *Stevenson v United Road Transport Union* an employee was dismissed without being given reasons (in breach of the contractual procedure), and a declaration was granted that the dismissal, in breach of natural justice, was void. A declaration may be sought if an employer unilaterally reduces an employee's wages, or otherwise purports to act in breach of the contract (*Rigby v Ferodo Ltd*). As with all equitable remedies, the employee must act expeditiously, (*Dietman v London Borough of Brent*).

C. Suing for breach of contract

16.29 An employee is not bound to accept a breach of contract which falls short of a wrongful constructive dismissal, and may, instead of suffering the breach in silence, sue for the loss suffered, while not accepting the alleged employer repudiation. Thus in *Rigby v Ferodo Ltd*, the employee recovered damages for loss of wages when the employer unilaterally reduced his earnings; in *Miller v Hamworthy Engineering Ltd* an employee recovered lost pay when put on short-time working without contractual authority; and in *Keir and Williams v Hereford and Worcester County Council*, damages were awarded to employees when an employer withdrew their car allowance. The correct procedure in such cases is for the employer to give lawful termination of the contract (ie by giving the requisite period of notice) and then to offer the employees new contracts with new terms before the notice period expires. A unilateral variation of the contract, by itself, is not a termination and offer of re-engagement under a new contract (*Burdett-Coutts v Hertfordshire County Council*). Thus by lawfully terminating the contract, the employer avoids any liability for wrongful dismissal, although it must be borne in mind that an employee's rights to claim unfair dismissal will be unaffected. Whether the dismissal is in fact fair or unfair will depend on all the circumstances of the case (see Chapter 17).

D. Public law remedies

16.30 The circumstances in which public law remedies (by way of judicial review) can be used to resolve private employment disputes, and the grounds on which decisions of public bodies can be challenged, have already been discussed (see para 2.162). But despite the attempt by Woolf LJ in *McLaren v Home Office* to lay down the principles which should be adopted when dealing with such applications, no coherent set of rules has ever been finally laid down, and the courts have developed the law on this subject on a case by case basis (*R v Derbyshire County Council, ex p Noble*). The actions brought generally seek an injunction and/or a declaration.

17

Unfair Dismissal

17.1 The statutory provisions relating to unfair dismissal are to be found in ss 94–107 of the Employment Rights Act 1996. The interpretation of those provisions by the courts and tribunals has led to thousands of reported decisions which have laid down guidelines varying from legal ingenuity, through sound common sense, and ending up, on occasions, with cabalistic mystery! But many decisions can only be explained on their own special facts and on a consideration of the actual evidence presented to the tribunal, and it must be borne in mind that employment tribunal decisions are not, in themselves, binding precedents. Sometimes the successful claimant will be awarded a reduced compensation because of his own contributory conduct, and there have been cases where a dismissal though unfair, has resulted in a nil award.

17.2 Nonetheless, the decisions of the reported cases repay detailed study. In the first place, they give guidance to a generalised stream of thought which is rapidly becoming dominant thinking in employment law; guidance on how an employer should act so as to be regarded as being reasonable and fair, guidance on how disciplinary procedures should be operated, and on when an employer may adopt standards which are less than those expected by a perfectionist. Secondly, the decided cases point out the pitfalls into which other employers have fallen, and thus enable a conscientious personnel manager so to direct his policies as to avoid those very traps. Finally, they provide interpretation of the legislative provisions which have a persuasive effect until a higher court has had an opportunity to pronounce on their validity.

17.3 Every employee to whom the Act applies has the right not to be unfairly dismissed, and the remedy for the infringement of that right is by way of a complaint to the employment tribunal, and not otherwise (ERA, s 94). This means that unfair dismissal cases must go to the employment tribunals, whereas a person who wishes to sue in respect of *wrongful dismissal* must bring the action in the ordinary courts in the normal way, or in the employment tribunal as appropriate (see para 16.3).

Exclusions

17.4 The following categories of employees are not protected by the unfair dismissal provisions of ERA:

(a) any employment as a master or member of the crew of a fishing vessel where the employee is remunerated by a share of the profits;

(b) merchant seamen may pursue claims for unfair dismissal provided they are employed to work on ships registered in Great Britain (ie excluding Northern Ireland, the Isle of Man and the Channel Islands) unless their employment is wholly outside Great Britain, or they are not ordinarily resident in Great Britain (ERA, s 199(7), (8)). In *Wood v Cunard Line Ltd*, the claimant was engaged in Southampton, and then joined a ship which cruised around the Caribbean. It was held that his employment was wholly outside Great Britain.

Under the Employment Protection (Offshore Employment) Order 1976, employees who work in oil rigs and offshore installations in UK territorial waters or areas designated under the Continental Shelf Act 1964 are not excluded from the provisions of the Employment Rights Act 1996;

(c) apart from specific statutory provisions (see para 17.5) any employment where the employee has been continuously employed for less than one year. The period of continuous employment begins with the day on which he is due to start work under the contract not from the date on which he actually commences work (*Salvation Army v Dewsbury*). If notice of termination is given, the day on which the notice is given must be disregarded (*West v Kneels Ltd*). As has been noted (see para 15.26), an employee who had been employed for one week less than the qualifying period of one year, and is dismissed, is entitled to add to his computation the week's statutory notice to which he is entitled (s 97(2)), but not his contractual notice (see *Fox Maintenance Ltd v Jackson*, para 15.26). But if he is dismissed without notice for gross misconduct, he cannot rely on s 97(2) 'To pull him past the post' (*Ahmed v National Car Parks Ltd*)!

The fact that the reason for the dismissal is designated as 'gross misconduct' does not preclude the operation of s 97(2), for the employment tribunal can enquire into the facts on their merits, and decide whether in the circumstances the employer was entitled to terminate the contract without notice. If they decide that the employer was not so entitled, s 97(2) comes into operation (*Lanton Leisure Ltd v White and Gibson*).

For the general rules relating to continuous employment, see Chapter 13;

(d) under the provisions of the Employment Equality (Age) Regulations (see para 4.207), a dismissal on the grounds of retirement will be a fair dismissal if:
   (i) it is a genuine retirement dismissal (and not, eg, on some other grounds, such as incompetence, etc),
   (ii) it takes place on or after the default retirement age of 65 or lower age which has been set and which can be objectively justified by the employer, and
   (iii) the 'duty to consider' procedure has been correctly followed (see para 4.225).

(e) any employment covered by a dismissals procedure agreement which has been designated and approved by the Secretary of State. This enables an employer and an independent trade union to create their own dismissals procedure which, provided it conforms with the laid down criteria, may be approved by the Minister, and those employees covered by it are excluded from the provisions of the Act. There are no such agreements currently in force;

(f) an agreement to submit the dispute to arbitration under a scheme prepared by ACAS (see TULR(C)A, s 212A inserted by s 7 of the Employment Rights (Dispute Resolution) Act 1998) (see para 1.12);

(g) employees who work for foreign governments and other international organisations which enjoy diplomatic immunity (eg see *Gadhok v Commonwealth Secretariat*) can only bring appropriate claims if that diplomatic immunity is waived; otherwise the employment tribunals have no jurisdiction (*Mukoro v European Bank for Reconstruction and Development*). However, by the State Immunity Act 1978, a state is not immune in respect of proceedings relating to a contract of employment if (a) the contract was made in the United Kingdom, or (b) the work is to be wholly or partly performed in the United Kingdom. The Act does not apply if at the time of the claim the applicant was a national of the state concerned, or at the time when the contract was made he was neither a national of the United Kingdom nor habitually resident here, or if the parties have agreed to exclude the provisions of the Act;

(h) persons who serve as a member of a constabulary maintained by virtue of an enactment, or who have the powers or privileges of a constable (ERA, s 200). This includes members of the British Transport Police (*Spence v British Railways Board*) but not prison officers (Criminal Justice and Public Order Act 1994, s 126);

(i) originally, ERA, s 196 excluded the right to claim unfair dismissal for employees who, under their contracts of employment, ordinarily worked outside Great Britain. However, that section was repealed in 1999 (in order to comply with the Posted Worker Directive), and was not replaced. It therefore fell to the judiciary to determine if there was jurisdiction to apply unfair dismissal law to cases concerning employees who worked abroad, but whose employment had some connection (albeit a tenuous one) with this country. There were particular problems concerning expatriate employees, such as airline pilots, employees who worked in military bases abroad, overseas representatives of British firms, foreign newspaper correspondents, and so on. The result was a series of conflicting and irreconcilable decisions. However, in *Lawson v Serco Ltd* (which involved three joint appeals) the House of Lords gave some guidance on how such cases should be decided.

Giving the leading judgment, Lord Hoffman identified three factors which would determine whether the employment tribunal had jurisdiction in such cases.

(i) Standard cases. The test normally to be applied is whether the employee was working in Great Britain at the time of his dismissal. The terms of the contract may be relevant, but the ultimate test was where the employee was actually working at the time.

(ii) Peripatetic employees. Here, the 'base test' (originally propounded by Lord Denning in *Todd v British Midlands Airways Ltd*) was the best solution. The base will be the place where the employee ordinarily worked, even though he may spend considerable periods of time elsewhere.

(iii) Expatriate employees. An employee who was working and based abroad will not normally come within the protection of the UK legislation, unless there are strong factors which would lead to a contrary conclusion. Generally, he would be so covered if he was working within an extra-territorial enclave of a foreign country. Thus, in the *Lawson* case, the claimant was employed by a UK-based firm to work as a security officer in Ascension Island, a volcanic island in the South Atlantic. Under this test it was held that he could pursue a claim of constructive dismissal in this country.

However, there are bound to be difficult decisions to be made regarding an employee who works abroad for a British employer for the purpose of a business carried on in the UK (eg, a sales representative, or an employee who works abroad for the purpose of a business which belongs to a British owner (eg, a newspaper correspondent whose dispatches are sent to different countries, see *Financial Times v Bishop*), etc.

(For the principles applicable in claims for race, sexual orientation and religion or belief discrimination claims, see paras 4.82 and 4.137).

17.5 No qualifying period of employment is required in respect of a dismissal alleged to be unfair if the reason was:

(a) connected with pregnancy or childbirth, or the employee took ordinary or additional maternity leave, ordinary or additional adoption leave, paternity leave, or parental leave, or time off to look after dependants, declined to sign a workforce agreement for maternity and parental leave purposes, or performed functions as a workforce representative (ERA, s 99 and Maternity and Parental Leave Regulations 1999, reg 20);

(b) to do with health and safety (ERA, s 100, see para 11.64);

(c) because a shop or betting worker refused to work Sundays (ERA, s 101, see para 7.99);

(d) the exercise of a right under the Working Time Regulations (ERA, s 101A, see para 7.90;

(e) the performance of functions as a trustee of occupational pensions scheme (ERA, s 102);

(f) the performance of a function as an employee representative (ERA, s 103, see para, 18.69);

(g) the employee made a protected disclosure (ERA, s 103A, see para 10.79);

(h) the assertion of a statutory right (ERA, s 104, see para 17.157);

(i) the exercise of a right under the National Minimum Wage Act (ERA, s 104A);

(j) the taking of action in connection with a tax credit (ERA, s 104B);

(k) membership or non-membership of a trade union (TULR(C)A, s 154, see para 21.78);

(l) the employee took protected industrial action (TULR(C)A, s 238A, see para 21.104);

(m) the employee did a wide range of actions in connection with the statutory procedure for recognition or derecognition (TULR(C)A, Sch A1; see para 21.53);

(n) he did acts in connection with his rights under the Part-time Workers (Prevention of Less Favourable Treatment) Regulations 2000;

(o) he did acts in connection with his rights under the Transnational Information and Consultation of Employees Regulations 1999 (see para 23.134);

(p) he took action in connection with his rights under the Fixed-Term Employees (Prevention of Less Favourable Treatment) Regulations 2002;

(q) he undertook jury service (ERA, s 98B; see para 7.104);

(r) selection for redundancy for any of the above reasons (ERA, s 105).

17.6 If a person is over the normal retiring age, or over the age of 65, he is not excluded from bringing a claim for unfair dismissal if the reason for the dismissal was for any of the above reasons.

17.7 If a person is dismissed as a result of being suspended from work on medical grounds, s/he is only required to have one month's continuous employment (see ERA, s 64(2), para 7.7). To obtain protection because of making an application for flexible working, s/he needs to be employed for 26 weeks (see para 2.136).

What is a dismissal? (ERA, s 95)

17.8 As a general rule, a dismissal will not operate until it has been received by the employee (*Widdicombe v Longcombe Software Ltd*). Thus if it is sent by post, it will be effective from the time when the employee has actually read the letter, or had a reasonable opportunity to do so. In *Brown v Southall and Knight* the employers sent a letter of dismissal to the claimant who, at that date, did not have the requisite period of continuous employment. He was away on holiday when the letter arrived, and thus did not read it until he returned a week later, by which time he had the necessary qualifying period. It was held that he was entitled to pursue his claim for unfair dismissal. Of course, if he deliberately did not open the letter, or went away in order to avoid reading it, he would have been debarred from saying that the notification of the dismissal was not given to him (see also *McMaster v Manchester Airport plc*).

17.9 There are four ways in which a dismissal may take place.

A. Employer termination

17.10 Where the contract of employment is terminated by the employer, with or without notice. It follows that (subject to the doctrine of constructive dismissal, discussed below) if an employee resigns of his own volition, there is no dismissal. In *Elliott v Waldair (Construction) Ltd* the claimant was engaged as a driver, and mainly drove a heavy lorry. It was decided that this work was too hard for him, and he was instructed to drive a smaller van. This he refused to do because it would reduce his opportunity of overtime earnings, and he resigned. It was held that the order to drive a different vehicle at the same hourly rate but with less opportunity to earn overtime could not be said to constitute a dismissal by the employer.

17.11 Equally, a mutually agreed termination does not amount to a dismissal. In *Harvey v Yankee Traveller Restaurant*, the claimant became pregnant, and although her employer made various arrangements to accommodate her, these were not satisfactory. After a discussion with her employer, she agreed to resign. It was held that this could not amount to a dismissal. A warning that a dismissal is being contemplated in the future (eg for reason of impending redundancy etc) is not a dismissal (*Doble v Firestone Tyre and Rubber Co Ltd*).

17.12 The fact that the employer invited the employee to resign may, however, constitute a dismissal, for the alternative may be expressed or implicit in the request. In *Robertson v Securicor Transport Ltd* the claimant had broken a company rule by signing for a container which had not been received. When this was discovered, he was given the alternative of resigning or being dismissed, and he chose the respectable course. It was held that he had been dismissed nonetheless. But although a resignation under duress may be a dismissal (*East Sussex County Council v Walker*), an invitation to resign as an alternative to facing a disciplinary hearing which may result in a dismissal is not, by itself, a dismissal (*Martin v Glynwed Distribution Ltd*). If the choice is put to the employee 'perform your contract or resign' this is not a dismissal, for the employee is making a decision not to carry out the terms of the contract which the employer is legally entitled to expect.

17.13 To falsely inveigle an employee to resign may also amount to a dismissal (*Caledonian Mining Co Ltd v Bassett and Steel*).

17.14 A dismissal can take place even though the employee invites this course of action. In *Thomas v General Industrial Cleaners Ltd* the claimant was in poor health, but did not wish to resign because of fears that he might lose certain benefits. He left the decision to the employers, who accepted the initiative and terminated his employment. The tribunal held that there was a dismissal by the employers.

17.15 A dismissal takes place if an employer unilaterally imposes radically different terms of employment, which are so substantially different as to have the effect of destroying the basis of the old contract. In *Alcan Extrusions v Yates* the employers unilaterally made changes in working hours, shift systems, weekend and bank holiday workings, shift premiums etc. The employees agreed to work the new system under protest, reserving their rights to claim unfair dismissal and/or redundancy payments, which they subsequently did. An employment tribunal chairman held that they had been dismissed, and the decision was upheld by the EAT. It was not correct to argue that the imposition of contractual changes can only be characterised as a potentially repudiatory breach, giving the employee an option to resign and claim constructive dismissal. Substantial departures from the original contract constitutes a dismissal in its own right.

17.16 A warning of a possible dismissal in the future is not a dismissal. In *Rai v Somerfield Stores Ltd*, the claimant was away from work. He was informed that if he did not return to work by 9 April he would be dismissed. He did not turn up at work on that date, but three days earlier, on 6 April, he presented a claim to an employment tribunal of unfair dismissal. It was held that the tribunal had no jurisdiction to hear the complaint. It had been presented three days before the termination of his employment, and was therefore premature. An employee may bring a complaint once notice has been given, even though it has not expired (ERA, s 111(3)), but in this case, he had not been dismissed with or without notice. He had merely been informed of the consequences which may follow if he failed to turn up for work, but dismissal was not inevitable, for the employer could still have unilaterally withdrawn the threat.

17.17 Traditionally, the words used by the employer to denote that a dismissal has taken place are usually quite clear and explicit, but the niceties of social intercourse are not always observed in real life. In *Kendrick v Aerduct Productions*, the employer told an employee to 'fuck off'! Could this be construed as being equivalent to 'you're fired'? Or was it an expression of abuse with no other ulterior implication? If the words used are ambiguous, the employment tribunal must ask themselves, what would a reasonable man understand by the expression in the context of the industry and the surrounding circumstances? In *Futty v D and D Brekkes Ltd* the employee was a fish filleter. During an altercation with the foreman he was told 'if you do not like the job, you can fuck off'. He took this as a dismissal, found another job and claimed compensation. It was held that in the context of the particular trade, the words meant no more than 'if you do not like the work you are doing, you can clock off'. Indeed, had the applicant not received a promise of another job, he would have gone back to work the following day, and hence he had resigned, and had not been dismissed. But there is little doubt that there can be circumstances where telling an employee to 'fuck off' will amount to a dismissal (*a fortiori*, telling him to 'fuck off and piss off', see *King v Webb's Poultry Products (Bradford) Ltd*).

17.18 Equally, if the words used are unambiguous, the employment tribunal must give them their natural and ordinary meaning (*Sothern v Franks Charlesly & Co*).

17.19 A further refinement on this theme was pursued in *Davy v Collins (Builders) Ltd*. During an argument, the employer said to the employee 'if you are not satisfied, you can fuck off'. The employee left and brought a claim for unfair dismissal, which failed. With dialectic ingenuity the tribunal drew a distinction between an employer saying 'I am not satisfied, so you can fuck off', and 'if you are not satisfied, you can fuck off'. In the former case there is likely to be a dismissal; in the latter case, the employer is saying to the employee, 'If you don't like it, you can lump it' and the claimant, not liking it, lumped it!

17.20 It is thus not the actual words which are used which are significant, but the intention behind them, and this must be ascertained from all the surrounding circumstances and the accompanying words as well as the industry, the relationships between the parties, and so on (*J & J Stern v Simpson*). If an employer or his manager, speaking in anger, behaves in a way which he might not do ordinarily, and utters abusive words, the employment tribunal should consider very carefully whether the words amount to a dismissal, or whether they were little more than abuse (*Chesham Shipping Ltd v Rowe*). Events which followed the utterance of the offensive words and preceding the departure of the employee may be taken into account in so far as they throw light on the employer's intentions (*Tanner v DT Kean Ltd*).

17.21 Once a dismissal (or resignation) has taken place, it cannot be withdrawn unilaterally (*Harris and Russell Ltd v Slingsby*), but words used in the heat of the moment, and withdrawn almost immediately may be ignored, for it is vital to good industrial relations that either the employer or the employee should be given the opportunity to recant (*Martin v Yeoman Aggregates Ltd*).

B. Fixed-term contract expires

17.22 Where the employee is employed under a limited-term contract, a dismissal takes place if that term expires without being renewed under the same contract. But a dismissal which takes place in this manner must still be tested for fairness in terms of the reasonableness of the employer's action in not renewing the contract. Thus if there is a genuine need for an employee to have a fixed-term contract (eg of a temporary nature, or for a specific purpose, etc) then it may be reasonable not to renew this after expiry. It is important that employees should not be deprived of their statutory rights by dressing up an ordinary job as a fixed-term contract (*Terry v East Sussex County Council*). Further, when a fixed-term contract expires, an employer may be acting unreasonably if he fails genuinely to consider the employee for employment in some other suitable post (*Labour Party v Oakley*) (see now the Fixed-Term Employees (Prevention of Less Favourable Treatement) Regulations 2002, para 2.119).

C. Completion of a limited-term contract

17.23 A limited-term contract is a contract which is not intended to be permanent and which will end either on the expiry of a fixed term, or on the performance of a specific task, or the occurrence of a specific event (or on the failure of an event to occur). If an employee is employed under such a contract which terminates by virtue of the limiting event without being renewed, this will amount to a dismissal under ERA. The effective date of termination is the date on which the termination takes effect.

D. Constructive dismissal

What amounts to constructive dismissal?

17.24 Where the employee himself terminates the contract, with or without notice, in circumstances where he is entitled to terminate it without notice by reason of the employer's conduct: this is known as 'constructive dismissal', for although the employee resigns, it is the employer's conduct which constitutes a repudiation of the contract, and the employee accepts that repudiation by resigning. The employee must clearly indicate that he is treating the contract as having been repudiated by the employer (*Logabax Ltd v Titherley*), and if he fails to do so, by word or by conduct, he is not entitled to claim that he has been constructively dismissed (*Holland v Glendale Industries Ltd*).

17.25 The doctrine of constructive dismissal has had a somewhat chequered history. The real problem was to determine the nature of the conduct of the employer which entitles the employee to resign. Did such conduct have to amount to an actual breach of contract by the employer, or could any unreasonable conduct by the employer be sufficient to entitle an employee to resign? For a long time the latter theory held sway, leading to some of the most bizarre and eccentric decisions in the whole of employment law. This view was firmly disposed of by the Court of Appeal in *Western Excavating (ECC) Ltd v Sharp*, and all previous decisions must be read subject to this case. The facts were that the employee was dismissed for taking unauthorised time off work. He appealed to the internal disciplinary board, which substituted a penalty of five days' suspension without pay. This he accepted, but being short of money, he asked his employers if he could have an advance on his accrued holiday pay. This was refused. He then asked if he could have a loan of £40, but this too was refused. Consequently he resigned (in order to get his holiday pay) and brought a claim for unfair dismissal, alleging that he was forced to resign by virtue of the employer's conduct. His claim was upheld by the employment tribunal; the conduct of the employers was so unreasonable that the employee could not fairly be expected to put up with it, and justified him leaving. On appeal, the EAT was not sure that they would have come to the same decision had they heard the case, but held that the employment tribunal were entitled to come to that decision. This was reversed by the Court of Appeal. The test for constructive dismissal was to be determined by the contract test, ie did the employer's conduct amount to a breach of contract which entitled the employee to resign. The 'unreasonable conduct' theory was dismissed as leading to a finding of constructive dismissal on the most whimsical grounds. Since there had been no breach of contract by the employers in *Sharp's* case (for the employers were under no contractual obligation to make the payments which were requested) there was no dismissal, constructive or otherwise.

17.26 It follows, therefore, that only those cases where the employer's conduct amounts to a significant breach, going to the root of the contract, can now be regarded as being authoritative. There must be a breach of contract by the employer, not merely a failure to act reasonably (*Wadham Stringer Commercials (London) Ltd v Brown*). Thus, if the employer tries to impose a unilateral change in employment terms, such as a change in the job, a significant change in hours (*Simmonds v Dowty Seals Ltd*), a lowering in earnings (*RF Hill Ltd v Mooney*), a significant change in the location of employment (*Courtaulds Northern Spinning Ltd v Sibson*), a demotion, then provided there is no contractual right to do so, such conduct will entitle an employee to resign. But a failure to pay salary on the due date was held not to have been so serious a breach in *Adams v Charles Zub Associates Ltd*. The employer's action did not show an intention not to be bound by the contract.

17.27 It must be borne in mind that although a constructive dismissal may amount to a dismissal in law, whether the dismissal is fair or unfair has still to be determined by the facts of the case, and whether or not the employer has acted reasonably (*Industrial Rubber Products v Gillon*).

Genuine dispute over contract

17.28 If there is a genuine dispute concerning the nature of the parties' contractual obligations, this does not indicate an intention on the part of the employer to break the contract, and hence this will not be grounds for claiming constructive dismissal. In *Frank Wright & Co Ltd v Punch* the claimant claimed that he was entitled to receive cost of living increases in his salary. The employers disputed that they were contractually obliged to pay, and so he resigned, claiming constructive dismissal. The EAT held that where there was a genuine dispute as to the construction of a contract, or a genuine mistake as to fact or law, the courts would be unwilling to hold that an expression of intent by a party to carry out the contract in accordance with his (possibly erroneous) interpretation amounts to a repudiation of that contract. In *Bridgen v Lancashire County Council* the Master of the Rolls (Sir John Donaldson) expressed the view that the mere fact that a party to the contract takes a view of construction which is ultimately shown to be wrong does not, of itself, constitute repudiatory conduct. It has to be shown that he did not intend to be bound by the contract as properly construed. If the reasoning in these two decisions is correct, a number of previous decisions on constructive dismissal must be regarded as being of doubtful authority.

Employer's breach of an implied term

17.29 More difficult are those cases where the employee claims he is entitled to resign because the employer has broken an implied term of the contract (see para 3.35) because the nature of these terms may sometimes be a matter for speculation and conjecture. In *British Aircraft Corpn v Austin* a failure to investigate a complaint about the inadequacy of protective spectacles was held to be a breach of the employer's implied duty to take reasonable care for the employee's safety, and in *Graham Oxley Tool Steels Ltd v Firth* it was held that there was an implied term that the employer will provide a proper working environment. If no reasonable employer would have expected the employee to work in those conditions, then there is a fundamental breach of the contract of employment (*Dutton & Clark Ltd v Daly*). It will be recalled that there is an implied duty of mutual respect, and therefore any action by or on behalf of the employer which runs contrary to that duty may amount to constructive dismissal. This could be the use of foul and abusive language (*Palmanor Ltd v Cedron*), making unjustifiable complaints or giving unjustified warnings (*Walker v Josiah Wedgwood*), making statements which destroy or seriously damage the relationship of trust and confidence which must exist between the parties (*Courtaulds Northern Textiles Ltd v Andrew*), such as ill-founded allegations of theft (*Robinson v Crompton Parkinson Ltd*), offensive and insensitive conduct by a supervisor (*Hilton International Hotels (UK) Ltd v Protopapa*), and so on.

17.30 There is no implied term in a contract which entitles an employee to facilities for smoking, and if an employer introduces a general rule which has the effect of banning smoking on the premises, this does not operate so as to frustrate the employee's attempt to perform the contract because he cannot comply with the rule. Such a rule has a legitimate purpose, and the fact that it bears hard on a particular individual does not warrant an inference that the employer had repudiated the contract so as to enable the employee to claim he has been constructively dismissed (*Dryden v Greater Glasgow Health Board*, see para 3.81). Indeed, it is more likely that there is an implied term that the employer will provide a safe working environment, and a non-smoker who is forced to work in areas where he would be affected by the smoking habits of other employees can claim constructive dismissal for a breach of that term (*Waltons & Morse v Dorrington*).

17.31 Even if there is an express term in the contract enabling an employer to transfer the employee to another location, there is an implied term that the employer will give reasonable notice of the transfer and, where appropriate, relocation and other allowances will be made, so as to make it feasible for the employee to comply with the contractual obligation to transfer (*United Bank Ltd v Akhtar*).

17.32 A further problem arises when the employer makes life as difficult or as uncomfortable as possible, in the hope (or expectation) that the hint will be taken, and the employee will resign. No doubt a great deal will depend on the extent of the evidence which shows whether or not the employer is in breach of an express or implied term of the contract. Situations do occur when the parties wish to part company, but the employer is scared to take the initiative for fear of having a claim being brought against him, and the employee is reluctant to resign without at least having an opportunity to collect some financial reward which is available under modern legislative provisions. It is here that the vagaries of the doctrine of constructive dismissal present the greatest menace, for the uncertainties are enormous.

17.33 In *Haseltine Lake & Co v Dowler* the claimant was told that there was no future with the firm for him and that he should seek another job elsewhere. Eventually he found another job, resigned his employment and claimed he had been constructively dismissed. The EAT rejected his claim. No date had been fixed by the employers for his resignation, and before a contract of employment can terminate, there must be an ascertainable date on which it came to an end. This was not a case of 'resign or you will be dismissed', and therefore there was no repudiation of the contract by the employers.

17.34 Although the 'implied term' theory has effectively replaced the unreasonable conduct test, it can be just as capricious and whimsical in its results. In *FC Gardner Ltd v Beresford* an employee resigned because she had not had a pay increase for two years, whereas other employees had. It was held that although there was no express term of the contract relating to pay increases, in most cases it was possible to imply a term that an employer would not treat an employee capriciously, arbitrarily or inequitably in matters of remuneration. The EAT remitted the case to the employment tribunal to ascertain whether or not in fact the employer had thus treated the employee, and if so, there would be a good claim for constructive dismissal under the new test in *Western Excavating (ECC) Ltd v Sharp.*

17.35 But this does not mean that a failure to give an annual pay rise to an employee is a breach of contract, for it is impossible to say that there is an implied term to that effect. The test is whether such failure is arbitrary and capricious. Thus, if the employer can show a good reason, such as inadequate performance by the employee, there is no breach of the duty of mutual trust and confidence (*Murco Petroleum Ltd v Forge*).

17.36 Occasionally, the 'unreasonable conduct' test makes a reappearance in a new disguise. It will be recalled that in constructive dismissal cases, one must look for the breach of contract. There is generally no difficulty in ascertaining the express terms, but legal authorities are clear that the implied terms are discovered by looking at what was 'obvious', so obvious in fact that the parties omitted to insert them (para 3.35). However, in *Pepper and Hope v Daish* the EAT took the view that it was possible to imply a term into a contract if it was 'reasonable' to do so! In this case the applicant negotiated a personal hourly wage rate for himself in December 1978. In January 1979 there was a general increase for all hourly workers of 5%, but this was not given to the claimant. He resigned and claimed constructive dismissal. It was held that he could succeed, on the basis that it was reasonable to imply a term into his contract that he would also be given general wage increases. It will be noted that the reasoning in this case is inconsistent with the later decision in *Frank Wright & Co (Holdings) Ltd v Punch* (para 17.28) for there appeared to be a genuine dispute as to the interpretation of the contract.

17.37 The EAT returned to orthodoxy in *White v Reflecting Roadstuds Ltd.* Here, the employee was working in the employer's despatch department but, at his own request, he was transferred to the mixing department, which involved higher pay, but also harder work. After about a year, he requested a move to lighter work, which was not then possible. From then on, his attendance deteriorated, and, after being given a formal warning, he was transferred to the pressing department, which involved a considerable drop in his pay. He then resigned, claiming that the decision to move him to another department constituted a fundamental breach of his contract of employment. In their defence, the company pointed to a flexibility clause in the contract which gave them the right to transfer employees to alternative work if the requirements of operational efficiency so dictate, and also that a willingness of employees to do so was a condition of the contract. An employment tribunal held that the express right to transfer from one department to another was subject to two implied terms, namely (a) that it would be exercised in a reasonable manner, and (b) that the transfer would not result in a unilateral reduction in the employee's pay. On appeal, the EAT reversed the decision on both grounds. On the first point, the EAT stated that to imply a term that a flexibility or mobility clause should be handled reasonably would be to introduce the 'reasonableness' test into constructive dismissal cases by the back door and would fly in the face of the authority of *Western Excavating (ECC) Ltd v Sharp*. Although a 'capricious' decision would not create any difficulty (*United Bank Ltd v Akhtar*), if there are reasonable and sufficient grounds for operating the clause, the employers are entitled to reach such decisions. On the second point, it was held that if an employer acts within the contract, the fact that the change results in a unilateral reduction in the employee's pay does not constitute a fundamental breach of the contract (see *Spafax Ltd v Harrison*).

17.38 Also, if the employer is in breach, but the employee does not resign, and subsequently alleges a further breach, the employment tribunal should take into account the whole of the employer's conduct, and not merely the latest incident which led to the resignation (*Lewis v Motorworld Garages Ltd*).

17.39 Lawful conduct by an employer is not capable of constituting a repudiation (*Spafax Ltd v Harrison*). Thus a disciplinary transfer, carried out in accordance with a proper procedure, which results in an employee suffering a drop in his earnings, is not a constructive dismissal (*High v British Railways Board*). Nor can an employee claim constructive dismissal merely because he is moved away from that part of his job which he enjoys the most on to less interesting work, if he is contractually obliged to do that work (*Peter Carnie & Son Ltd v Paton*). However, a disciplinary sanction which is disproportionate to the offence, even though carried out in accordance with the terms of the contract, can be a constructive dismissal (*BBC v Beckett*, para 12.120).

17.40 If an employer gives lawful notice, this is not a breach of trust and confidence so as to enable an employee to claim constructive dismissal. In *Kerry Foods Ltd v Lynch* the employer wanted an employee to change from five days a week to six days, but the employee refused to do so. His employer then stated that he would be given lawful notice to terminate the contract, and then be re-engaged immediately on the new terms. Before the notice expired, the employee resigned and claimed constructive dismissal. His claim failed. There was no breach of contract by the employer.

17.41 Since the employee is claiming that the employer has broken the contract, he must resign as a result of that breach (*Holland v Glendale Industries*). If he continues to report to work, he may be deemed to have waived the breach, and can hardly bring a claim subsequently based on the employer's repudiation, for 'the law does not allow him to have his cake and eat it' (*Hunt v British Railways Board*). But if he protests about the breach, but stays on until he finds himself another job, he may not necessarily be deemed to have accepted the employer's breach (*Miller v Shanks & McEwan*) provided that he acts reasonably expeditiously (*WE Cox Toner (International) Ltd v Crook*). But a distinction must be drawn between the waiver of a breach and the non-waiver of a continuing breach.

17.42 If there is a series of breaches which lead the employee to look for another job before handing in his notice, the employment tribunal must consider whether those breaches were the effective cause of a resignation. They do not have to be the sole cause. If the taking of other employment was the consequence of the breaches, then the employee can claim he has been constructively dismissed (*Jones v Sirl & Son (Furnishers) Ltd*). Constructive dismissal may occur in a 'last straw' situation. In *Lewis v Motorworld Garages Ltd* it was stated that the breach of the implied obligation of trust and confidence may consist of a series of actions on the part of the employer which cumulatively amount to a breach of the term, even though each individual incident may not do so. The 'last straw' need not itself be a breach of contract by the employer, but it must contribute, however slightly, to the sustained breach of the implied term of trust and respect. An entirely innocent act by the employer cannot be the 'last straw', even if the employee mistakenly interprets it in that light (*Omilaju v Waltham Forest London Borough Council*).

17.43 If the employer announces an intention to break the contract at a future date, and the employee does not accept the breach, it is open to the employer to inform the employee that the contract will be performed. The employee will thus lose the right to claim constructive dismissal (*Norwest Holst Group Administration Ltd v Harrison*). On the other hand, if the employee accepts the constructive dismissal, and gives notice to terminate the contract, conduct between the resignation and termination can be taken into account when assessing compensation (*Peterborough Regional College v Gidney*).

Constructive dismissal *may* be fair dismissal

17.44 It must be stressed that the fact that there is constructive dismissal does not necessarily mean that the dismissal is unfair (*Ford v Milthorn Toleman Ltd*), and there have been a number of cases where a constructive dismissal has been held to be a fair dismissal (eg *Savoia v Chiltern Herb Farms Ltd*). Thus if an employer demotes an employee, without contractual authority, this will amount to a constructive dismissal, but if the demotion was brought about by a well-founded suspicion of dishonesty, the dismissal may be fair (*Hilton v Shiner Ltd*). Even if it is unfair, compensation may still be reduced for contributory conduct. An employer faced with a constructive dismissal claim should be prepared to fight it on two fronts: (a) he may argue that there was no dismissal, and (b) in the alternative, if there was a dismissal, it was fair because . . . etc. A failure to adopt this course may result in a finding that there was a (constructive) dismissal, and, if no reason for the dismissal is advanced, it must automatically be unfair (*Derby City Council v Marshall*). Whether an employer's conduct amounts to a constructive dismissal is a question of fact for the employment tribunal to determine (*Woods v W M Car Services (Peterborough) Ltd*).

A failure to follow a grievance procedure is not, by itself, relevant in a constructive dismissal claim, because it is the conduct of the employer which is in issue (*Tolson v Mixenden Community School*). But certain claims for constructive dismissal will not be entertained by an employment tribunal unless the employee has followed the appropriate statutory procedure (see para 12.66).

Termination of the contract

17.45 There are a number of ways in which a contract may come to an end, but which do not amount to a dismissal in law.

A. Resignation

17.46 If an employee resigns, then (unless it is a constructive dismissal) he has not been dismissed. If the words used by the employee are clear and unambiguous (eg 'I am leaving, I want my cards') then there are no grounds for the employment tribunal to find that the words have a significance other than their plain meaning (*BG Gale Ltd v Gilbert*). If the words are ambiguous, then the test is, what would a reasonable employer have understood by those words in that context (*Tanner v Kean Ltd*)? If an employee is threatened that if he does not resign he will be dismissed, a consequent resignation will amount to a dismissal, but if his resignation is brought about by other factors, such as an offer of a financial inducement, this is not a dismissal (*Sheffield v Oxford Controls Co Ltd*).

17.47 Words spoken or action taken by an employee in the heat of the moment or under extreme pressure should not necessarily be taken at face value. The employer should allow a reasonable time to elapse before accepting such an apparent resignation to see whether this was what was really intended. If the employer fails to make a proper investigation, he runs the risk that an employment tribunal may hold that there are special circumstances where the apparent resignation was not really intended by the employee (*Kwik-Fit (GB) Ltd v Lineham*).

17.48 For a resignation to be effective to terminate the contract there must be an ascertainable date (express or implied) on which it will take effect. To say 'I am resigning at some future point in time' is a statement of intention, not a resignation, but to say 'I am resigning' is not ambiguous, for it indicates a present intention (*Sothern v Franks Charlesly & Co*). An employment tribunal is entitled to conclude on the evidence that the words of apparent resignation used by the employee 'in the heat of the moment' should not be accepted at their face value (*Sovereign House Security Services Ltd v Savage*).

17.49 If the employee indicates an intention to resign, but in terms which are somewhat equivocal, so that the position is mistakenly construed by the employer as a resignation, although the employee has not in fact resigned, this can be relied upon by the employer for the purpose of supplying an employment tribunal a potentially fair reason for the dismissal (for some other substantial reason, see below) even though, in error, the employer is seeking to hold the employee to the alleged resignation. What matters are the facts which led to the dismissal/resignation, not the precise label put on it by the employer (*Ely v YKK Fasteners (UK) Ltd*).

17.50 If an employee resigns, giving lawful notice, the employer may bring the employment to an end at an earlier date than that on which the employee's notice expires, provided he is entitled to exercise the option of making a payment in lieu of notice. If the employer does this, he does not dismiss the employee, for the resignation is still effective (*Marshall (Cambridge) Ltd v Hamblin*).

17.51 Whether an employee has resigned or was dismissed is a question of fact for the employment tribunal to determine, and their findings cannot be challenged unless their conclusions were such that no reasonable employment tribunal could have reached them (*Martin v Glynwed Distribution Ltd*).

B. Constructive resignation

17.52 If a breach of contract by the employer entitles the employee to resign and claim constructive dismissal, then why should not a breach of contract by the employee entitle the employer to claim that the contract has been terminated by 'constructive resignation'? This view was supported by a number of decisions by the EAT and employment tribunals, but must be discounted in the light of the decision of the Court of Appeal in *London Transport Executive v Clarke*, and all earlier decisions must be read in the light of this case. The facts were that Clarke wanted to go to Jamaica on extended unpaid leave, but permission was refused by the employers as he had already exhausted his entitlement under the rules. When he asked what would happen if he went without permission he was told that his name would be removed from the books. Nonetheless he went to Jamaica, stayed for seven weeks, and on his return he submitted a medical note, which the employment tribunal viewed 'with some surprise'. While he was away, the employers wrote to his home address, stating that if no reply was received within 14 days, it would be assumed that he did not wish to continue his employment, and eventually his name was removed from the books. When he returned from Jamaica, he applied for his job back, and when this was refused, he claimed he had been unfairly dismissed. For the employers, it was argued that the applicant had 'resigned' but this view was rejected. It is trite law that if a person breaks a contract, the other party has two options; he can either accept the breach, and treat the contract as being at an end, or refuse to do so, and treat the contract as still subsisting. If he accepts the breach, he terminates the contract. Thus Clarke had been dismissed, and had not resigned. However, the Court of Appeal then went on to find that the dismissal, in the circumstances, was fair.

17.53 There is no doubt that this analysis is correct. The reason for the doctrine of constructive dismissal is because there is a statutory provision for it (ERA, s 95(1)(c)). There is no statutory doctrine of constructive resignation. Thus if an employee walks out of his job, or commits any other breach of contract, but nonetheless claims that he is entitled to resume his work, the employer must expressly or impliedly accept the repudiation, and this will constitute a dismissal. He must then satisfy the employment tribunal that in the circumstances, having regard to the equity and substantial merits of the case, he acted reasonably in treating the repudiatory conduct as sufficient reason for dismissing the employee.

C. Implied resignation

17.54 However, it is submitted that there may be circumstances of implied resignation or resignation by conduct. Thus, if an employee disappears, and does not respond to the employer's communications, or if it is discovered that the employee is working for another employer, it may not be difficult to infer that he has resigned his employment. The point was made by Sir John Donaldson in *Harrison v George Wimpey & Co Ltd*. 'Where an employee so conducts himself as to lead a reasonable employer to believe that the employee has terminated the contract, the contract is then terminated.'

D. Frustration of the contract

17.55 If the performance of the contract of employment is rendered impossible by some intervening event, then it will be terminated by frustration, not by dismissal. In *Anyanwu v*

South Bank Student Union the claimant was a salaried officer of the student union. He was expelled from the university and excluded from its premises, whereupon the student union treated his contract of employment as being at an end. A claim for unlawful discrimination was dismissed by an employment tribunal, and the decision was upheld on appeal. Impossibility of performance meant that the contract ended by frustration. Frustration can only arise where there is no fault by either party, eg where accident or illness prevents the employee (or employer) from performing the contract. Where there is fault by one party, this is repudiatory conduct, not frustration. It is thus up to the other party to accept the repudiation and terminate the contract, or keep the contract open, as he chooses (*London Transport Executive v Clarke*, above). Clearly, if the repudiatory conduct was serious (eg being sent to prison) it would be rare for the dismissal to be categorised as being unfair (*Norris v Southampton City Council*).

17.56 There are two situations which commonly occur, and which may give rise to the doctrine of frustration. The first is long-term absence through accident or illness (*Notcutt v Universal Equipment Co (London) Ltd*), the second is imprisonment (*FC Shepherd & Co Ltd v Jerrom*).

17.57 To decide whether or not a contract will terminate by frustration, regard must be had to the length of time the employee is likely to be away from his work, and thus be unable to perform his contract, the need for the employer to obtain a replacement, the length of time he has been employed, his position, and so forth. In cases where the employee is absent for a long time through sickness, all these factors are relevant, and in addition the employer must consider the nature of the illness (or injury), how long it has continued and the prospects for recovery, as well as the terms of the contract, including the provision of sick pay (see *Marshall v Harland and Wolff Ltd*). The mere absence from work, even for a long time, will not automatically constitute frustration. Thus in *Maxwell v Walter Howard Designs Ltd* the claimant was away sick for nearly two years, during which time he sent in regular sick notes. His job, as a cabinet maker, was one which did not need to be filled by a permanent replacement, and so, despite the passage of time, it was held that the contract had not been frustrated.

17.58 But if it is clear that on the medical evidence, the employee is unlikely to return to work for a considerable time, then there must come a point at which the employer is entitled to decide that the employee will not be returning to work, and consequently treat the contract as being frustrated. The problem is, when, exactly, does that point in time come about, and to this question there is no easy answer (see *Scarr v FW Goodyear & Sons Ltd*). In employment cases, the courts and tribunals must guard against too easy an application of the doctrine of frustration, especially when redundancy occurs, or where the true reason for the dismissal is disability (*Williams v Watsons Luxury Coaches Ltd*).

17.59 In *Egg Stores (Stamford Hill) Ltd v Leibovici*, the EAT stated that there may be a long process before it can be said that illness has brought about a frustration of the contract. But if the time arrives when one can say that matters have gone on for so long, and the prospects for future employment are so poor, that it is no longer practical to consider the contract as still subsisting, then frustration will occur. Among the matters to be taken into account to reach this conclusion are (1) the length of the employment, (2) how long it would have been expected to continue, (3) the nature of the job, (4) the nature, length and effect of the illness, (5) the need to appoint a permanent replacement, (6) the risk to the employer of acquiring further obligations in respect of redundancy payments or unfair dismissals, (7) whether wages are still being paid, (8) the acts and statements of the employer in relation to the employee, including his failure to dismiss, and (9) whether in all the circumstances a reasonable employer could be expected to wait for the employee any longer. To this we may add (a) the terms of the contract as to sick pay, and (b) a consideration of the prospects of recovery (*Williams v Watsons Luxury Coaches Ltd*).

17.60 That none of these tests, by themselves, can be conclusive can be seen from the decision in *Hart v AR Marshall & Sons (Bulwell) Ltd* where the claimant became sick in April 1974. In August of that year, the employers engaged a permanent replacement but the claimant continued to send in sick notes. In January 1976 he presented himself for work, but was told there was no job for him, and he was given his cards. He claimed that this constituted unfair dismissal, but the EAT upheld a tribunal finding that the contract had been frustrated. The failure by the employers to act on the absence by dismissing the claimant was not, by itself, evidence that they will continue to regard him as an employee. Otherwise an employer would be in a difficult situation with regard to a sick employee; if he dismissed him prematurely, this might be unfair, if he engaged a temporary replacement, he might have to pay compensation at the end of that contract in order to permit the sick employee to return to work. Nor was the fact that the employee continued to send in sick notes indicative of anything other than that the employee was keeping in touch in case there was a prospect of future employment. The crucial factor appears to be the finding that the claimant occupied a key position, which had to be filled, and thus the contract was frustrated.

17.61 If it is clear that the employee is permanently unfit to do his job, the contract will be frustrated. The fact that the employer keeps the employee 'on the books' may be an arrangement which falls short of a contract of employment, of the sort expressly recognised in ERA, s 212(3)(c) (see para 13.23) as being relevant to the question of continuity of employment when no contract is actually in existence. But if the contract is frustrated the statutory or contractual rights to notice on termination do not apply (*G F Sharp & Co Ltd v McMillan*).

17.62 Imprisonment, though self-induced, is not strictly speaking repudiatory conduct, for it does not amount to a breach of the contract of employment. But there is an inherent contradiction, because the doctrine of frustration arises when an event occurs without the fault of either party, and a person who had been given a custodial sentence will invariably be at fault. The answer appears to be that the person asserting the frustration (ie the employer) must show that there was no fault on his part, and the person against whom frustration is being asserted (ie the employee) cannot rely on his own misconduct by way of an answer (*FC Shepherd & Co Ltd v Jerrom*).

17.63 Frustration arises by operation of law, not a conscious decision by the parties, and whilst it is not necessary to be able to point to the exact moment in time when the relationship between the parties is dissolved, the burden of proving that the contract has been frustrated lies on the employer. Thus, if an employee is sent to prison, this can be an instantaneously frustrating event or a potentially frustrating event. Accordingly, regard has to be paid to:

(a) when it was commercially necessary for the employer to make a decision about the employee's future;

(b) what a reasonable employer would consider to be the likely length of the employee's absence; and

(c) whether it was reasonable to engage a permanent rather than a temporary replacement (*Chakki v United Yeast Co Ltd*).

E. Consensual termination

17.64 A consensual termination arises when the employment is terminated by mutual agreement, and the reason for that agreement is generally irrelevant (*Birch v Liverpool University*). Since there is no dismissal, no statutory rights ensue. If a person is given the option of working part-time or being made redundant, and chooses the latter option, there is a dismissal for reason of redundancy, and it is not a consensual termination (*Lassman v De Vere University Arms Hotel*). Also, a person who volunteers for redundancy has volunteered to be dismissed, and is entitled to a redundancy payment (*Burton Allton and Johnson Ltd v Peck*).

17.65 A mutual agreement whereby the employment will come to an end on the happening of a future event is not a consensual termination. In *Igbo v Johnson Matthey Chemicals Ltd* the claimant wished to take extended leave. She signed a document which stated that she agreed to return to work by a certain date, and that if she failed to do so the contract of employment would automatically terminate. She failed to return to work on the due date, and her employers treated the contract as being at an end. She claimed that she had been unfairly dismissed. The Court of Appeal applied ERA, s 203 which stipulates that any provision in an agreement shall be void in so far as it purports to limit the operation of any provision in the Act. The document she signed purported to take away her right to claim that she was unfairly dismissed, and it was therefore void. The Court of Appeal overruled earlier authorities on this topic (including the case of *British Leyland (UK) Ltd v Ashraf*) and remitted the case to the employment tribunal to determine whether her dismissal was fair or unfair.

17.66 However, a mutual agreement to bring a contract of employment to an end, made for good consideration, after the employee had received proper advice, and made without duress, is effective. In *Logan Salton v Durham County Council*, the claimant was due to attend a disciplinary hearing which was to consider a recommendation that he be dismissed. An agreement was then reached whereby, on terms, his employment would come to an end by mutual agreement. He subsequently claimed he had been unfairly dismissed, but his claim failed. The agreement was not void by virtue of ERA, s 203 because it was not a contract of employment, or the variation of a contract of employment. The EAT distinguished this type of situation from that which occurred in *Igbo v Johnson Matthey Chemicals* (above).

17.67 The distinction between a resignation and a termination by mutual agreement is that the former is a unilateral act by the employee, whereas the latter requires the consent of both parties, because otherwise there may be a breach of contract by one party. Thus if an employee gives notice, he resigns. If the employer and employee agree that the employee may leave without giving notice, it is a mutual termination (*L Lipton Ltd v Marlborough*).

Fair and unfair dismissal (ERA, s 98)

A. Is it fair?

17.68 Once it has been established that a dismissal has taken place, it must then be determined whether or not the dismissal was unfair. Section 98 of the Employment Rights Act 1996 lays down six grounds on which a dismissal is capable of being fair, as follows:

> (a) a reason relating to the capability or qualifications of the employee for performing the work of the kind which he was employed by the employer to do. 'Capability' includes any assessment by reference to skill, aptitude, health or other physical or mental quality, and 'qualifications' means any degree, diploma or other academic, technical or professional qualification relevant to the position which the employee holds;
>
> (b) a reason which relates to the conduct of the employee;
>
> (c) the retirement of the employee;
>
> (d) the redundancy of the employee;
>
> (e) because the employee could not continue to work in the position which he held without contravention (either on his part or on the part of the employer) of a restriction or a duty imposed by or under a statute;
>
> (f) some other substantial reason such as to justify the dismissal of an employee holding the position which he held.

17.69 Whether a particular dismissal based on one or more of these reasons will be fair or unfair will depend on whether in the circumstances of the case (including the size and administrative resources of the employer's undertaking) the employer acted reasonably or unreasonably in treating the reason as a sufficient reason for dismissing the employee, and the question will be determined in accordance with equity and the substantial merits of the case (ERA, s 98(4)). Further, whereas it is for the employee to prove that he was dismissed, it is for the employer to show the reason for the dismissal, and that it was one of the above reasons. It will then be for the employment tribunal to find, on the basis of the evidence presented, whether or not the employer had acted reasonably in treating that reason as a sufficient ground for dismissal. Thus if he fails to show the reason, or fails to show a reason which is one of the above, the dismissal is automatically unfair. In *Raynor v Remploy Ltd* a group general manager was dismissed for alleged lack of business judgment and general inefficiency. He had been employed for five years, and the tribunal rejected the company's allegations as spurious. Since there was no evidence of incapability, the dismissal was unfair. In *Castledine v Rothwell Engineering Ltd* (see para 10.39) the tribunal refused to accept the general allegations of incompetence, pointing to the favourable reference given to an employee subsequent to his dismissal. The employer cannot expect to win his case if he fails to give or call evidence on which the tribunal can reach its conclusion on the reason for the dismissal or its reasonableness, and general allegations without such evidence will normally be insufficient. In *Whitaker v Milk Marketing Board*, an artificial inseminator was dismissed for incompetence and misconduct. Although the Board mentioned various farmers who were supposed to be dissatisfied with the service they had received, none was called to give evidence, and the dismissal was held unfair.

Two-stage procedure

17.70 Broadly speaking, there are two stages in the process of determining whether or not a dismissal was fair. The first is the means whereby the decision is reached. This involves going through proper procedures (see Chapter 12) bearing in mind especially the provisions of the Code of Practice (*Lock v Cardiff Railway Co Ltd*), and, where relevant, the statutory dismissal and disciplinary procedures, so that there is a full investigation, a proper hearing, a right to appeal, etc. The second stage is the actual decision taken, bearing in mind the reason for the dismissal, the need to consider mitigating circumstances, consistency and/or flexibility as appropriate, the terms of the contract, the size and nature of the employer's undertaking, and so on. No single factor, by itself, can be conclusive, and each case will turn on its own peculiar facts.

Has the employer acted reasonably?

17.71 Further, the test is 'did the employer act reasonably?' not 'did the employment tribunal agree with what the employer did?' (*Grundy (Teddington) Ltd v Willis*). An employment tribunal is not entitled to substitute its own views for those of the employer (*Foley v Post Office*). A decision on whether the employer acted reasonably is a question of fact for the employment tribunal to decide (*Iceland Frozen Foods Ltd v Jones*), which can only be challenged if the decision was perverse or based on an incorrect perception of the law.

17.72 In *Anandarajah v Lord Chancellor's Department*, the President of the EAT, Waite J, made a major policy statement about the use of precedents in employment tribunal hearings. Although these are of great practical assistance, they must not be relied upon as being of binding authority, but rather treated as guidelines. He continued:

> Sometimes the judgment in a particular case will be found to express, in helpful and concise language, some concept which is regularly found in this field of enquiry and it becomes of great illustrative value. But reference to such a case can never be a substitute for taking the explicit directions of the statute as a guiding principle.

17.73 To determine whether or not the employer has acted reasonably in dismissing the employee, the current test is 'What would a reasonable employer have done'? There is a band of reasonableness within which one employer might decide to dismiss, whilst another might decide not to do so. If the circumstances of the case are such that a reasonable employer might dismiss, the dismissal will be fair even though not all the employers would take that view (*British Leyland (UK) Ltd v Swift*). The 'band of reasonableness' test was challenged (somewhat belatedly) by the EAT in *Haddon v Van Den Bergh Foods Ltd*, but in *HSBC v Madden* the Court of Appeal disagreed, and reaffirmed the correctness of the 'range of reasonable responses' test as laid down in *Iceland Frozen Foods Ltd v Jones*. Further, the *Burchell* test (para 17.118) applied to the assessment of the fairness of the dismissal under s 98(4), not to establishing the reason for the dismissal under s 98(1)–(3).

17.74 In *Kent County Council v Gilham* the Court of Appeal stressed once again that whether or not an employer acts reasonably is a question of fact for the employment tribunal. That two employment tribunals, considering the same broad issues, had reached opposite conclusions did not indicate that either had misdirected themselves in law. It is endemic in the system that different answers will be given to broadly similar situations, and the decision cannot be challenged just for that reason. But on rare occasions higher courts will interfere if the decision of the employment tribunal is thought to be perverse (*British Railways Board v Jackson*).

17.75 The point in time at which the reasonableness of the employer's decision to dismiss is to be tested is when the employment comes to an end, not when the decision is taken, nor when the notice to terminate is given (*Stacey v Babcock Power Ltd*). Thus if an initial decision to dismiss was unfair because of a defect in the disciplinary proceedings, it may be cured if an appeal hearing is properly conducted (see *Clark v Civil Aviation Authority*, para 12.20). The reason for the dismissal is to be assessed both at the time notice of termination was given right through to the actual date of the termination of the contract (*West Kent College v Richardson*). Matters which come to light after the employment has ended are generally irrelevant (*Greenall Whitley plc v Carr*).

Automatically unfair dismissals

17.76 Certain dismissals are automatically unfair, and no question arises as to whether or not the employer has acted reasonably. These are dismissals connected with:

(a) pregnancy or childbirth, the taking of ordinary or additional or compulsory maternity leave, ordinary or additional adoption leave, parental leave or paternity leave, or time off to look after dependants, declining to sign a workforce agreement for maternity or parental leave purposes, the performance of functions as a workforce representative (ERA, s 99, and Maternity and Parental Leave Regulations 1999);

(b) a health and safety case (ERA, s 100);

(c) a shop or betting worker who refuses to work on Sundays (ERA, s 101);

(d) the exercise of a right under the Working Time Regulations (ERA, s 101A);

(e) performing a function as trustee of an occupational pension fund (ERA, s 102);

(f) performing a function of an employee representative (ERA, s 103);

(g) the making of a protected disclosure (ERA, s 103A);

(h) the assertion of a statutory right (ERA, s 104);

(i) the exercise of a right under the National Minimum Wage Act (ERA, s 104A);

(j) taking action with regard to a tax credit (ERA, s 104B);

(k) membership or non-membership of a trade union (TULR(C)A, s 154);

(l) the taking of protected industrial action (TULR(C)A, s 238A);

(m) doing a wide range of actions in connection with the statutory procedure for recognition or derecognition (TULR(C)A, Sch A1, see para 21.53);

(n) doing acts in connection with rights under the Transnational Information and Consultation of Employees Regulations 1999 (see para 23.134);

(o) doing acts in connection with an employee's rights under the Part-time Workers (Prevention of Less Favourable Treatment) Regulations 2000 (see para 2.69);

(p) a failure by the employer to comply with the relevant statutory disciplinary and dismissal procedure (ERA, s 98A, and see para 12.39);

(q) the exercise of rights in connection with an application for flexible working (ERA, s 104C) (see para 2.139);

(r) taken action under the Fixed-Term Employees (Prevention of Less Favourable Treatment) Regulations 2002: see reg 6);

(s) selection for redundancy for any of the above reasons (ERA, s 105);

(t) a dismissal on the ground of retirement if prior to retiring the employee, the employer has not informed him of his right to request to continue working, nor informed him of the intended retirement date, or has so informed him less than two weeks before the retirement date, or the dismissal takes place while the 'duty to consider' procedure has not been completed or not properly followed (Employment Equality (Age) Regulations 2006, see para 4.234).

B. Reasons for the dismissal

17.77 Although the Act lays down potentially fair reasons for dismissal, it will be convenient to make further sub-divisions, so that in practice a number of potential reasons for fair dismissal appear. This enables a more practical analysis to be made. Bearing this in mind, we can examine the general approach of the courts and tribunals to the problems of dismissals.

Inherent inability

17.78 To dismiss an employee who is not capable of performing his job properly will be fair provided the employer acts reasonably in the circumstances. Thus, faced with the problem of an incompetent worker, what does the reasonable employer do? He enquires into the matter, to find out why the employee cannot do the job adequately. Has he been trained properly, so that he knows how the job should be done? Has he been properly supervised, been given an adequate job description? Does he have proper equipment, sufficient support staff and facilities? In other words, the employer's first task is to find out the reason for the alleged incompetence, and so far as it is possible, do something about it from the employer's point of view.

17.79 For example, in *Davison v Kent Meters Ltd* the claimant was dismissed for assembling nearly 500 components in the wrong sequence. She claimed that she had followed the pattern of work in accordance with the instructions received from her chargehand, but the latter denied having shown her how to assemble the parts, and maintained that she was entirely to blame for the errors. The employment tribunal thought that if the chargehand had not shown her what to do, he should have done so, and the mistakes were therefore hardly her fault! Further, he should have checked on her performance, and supervised her properly. Not surprisingly, the dismissal was held to be unfair.

17.80 A warning should not be given merely for the sake of conforming with a laid down procedure, for this is to treat it as a mechanical system with no real significance. A warning is designed to do a job of work; it should have as its purpose the object of bringing an employee away from the brink of dismissal. It follows, therefore, that if the employee is suffering from an irredeemable incompetence, no amount of warnings will make any difference, and therefore there cannot be a need to issue them (*Sutton and Gates Ltd v*

Boxall). In *Littlewoods Organisation Ltd v Egenti* the EAT pointed out that there is a distinction between disciplinary procedures and capability procedures. The former should be applied strictly, whereas this does not need to be so with regard to the latter. To give a warning in capability cases is not a matter of procedure; it is a matter of substance (*AJ Dunning & Sons (Shopfitters) Ltd v Jacomb*). In other words, the question is, would a warning have done any good? Would it have rendered this dismissal unnecessary? If the answer is yes, then the warning should have been given. If the answer is no, then, since no amount of warnings would make any difference, there is no need to give them. Thus in *Lowndes v Specialist Heavy Engineering Ltd* the claimant was dismissed after five serious and costly errors. No written warnings were given, and he was not allowed an opportunity to state his case. The dismissal was held to be fair; it would have made no difference had a different procedure been adopted. Nowadays, however, procedural fairness is essential (see para 12.39).

17.81 Finally, the reasonable employer will consider alternatives before he dismisses the employee. Is there some other work which can be offered within the level of competence of the employee? Would he accept it if it was offered? Would he make a success of it? Clearly, much will depend on the circumstances of the case. In *Bevan Harris Ltd v Gair*, the claimant, who had been employed as a foreman, was dismissed after 11 years' service for poor performance, about which he had been warned on four occasions. The employment tribunal held the dismissal to be unfair, because a reasonable employer would have demoted him rather than resort to dismissal. The decision was reversed by the EAT. The employer had given serious consideration to offering the claimant another job, but had decided against it. The small scale of the business, and the loss of confidence in the employee's abilities, meant that the decision to dismiss fell within the band of reasonableness and, in the circumstances, the dismissal was fair.

Neglectful incompetence

17.82 Here we must consider the employee who could do the job, but is not achieving his potential. The object of the exercise is to bring him up to the standards which he is capable of reaching, and for this purpose, the disciplinary procedure should be invoked, in accordance with the gravity of the matter.

17.83 If an employee is not working as well as he could, then a warning is appropriate; if he is refusing to obey instructions or is being generally uncooperative, then he should be told, firmly and by someone in authority, of the consequences which are likely to ensue. If the tribunal considers that had a clear warning been given a dismissal would not have been necessary (*Winterhalter Gastronom Ltd v Webb*), then it will conclude that a dismissal without such warning been given will be unfair (*Jones v GEC Elliott Automation Ltd*). An employee with long service is entitled to more consideration, if only because the employers can hardly be heard to say that it took them many years to discover his incompetence, but the fact that the employer has tolerated poor performance in the past is not conclusive, if the employee fails to respond to proper warnings (*Gozdzik v Chlidema Carpet Co*). A newly appointed employee should be given a chance to prove himself, and not be judged on short-term results. Senior staff should have a greater appreciation of what is expected from them, whereas employees not in the managerial range should have greater attention paid to their requirements. If possible, the employer may consider giving the employee further training, should suitable facilities be available, assuming, that is, that the employee would be likely to benefit from such training. If the employee refuses to take advantage of this offer, at least the employer has acted in a reasonable manner, and a consequent dismissal may well be fair (*Coward v John Menzies (Holdings) Ltd*).

17.84 If there is a minor act of neglect, a warning is appropriate, to be followed, as necessary, with a further or final warning. A serious act of neglect might lead to an immediate final warning. But there are some acts of neglect which dare not be repeated, and hence dismissal is not inappropriate. In *Taylor v Alidair Ltd*, an airline pilot landed his aeroplane in a manner which caused some concern among the passengers and crew. After a proper investigation, it was decided that he had been negligent, and was dismissed. This was held to be fair: there are some activities where the degree of skill required is so high, or where the potential consequences of a departure from the highest standards are so serious, that one failure is sufficient to justify dismissal. A warning in such cases is totally inappropriate.

17.85 The law which prevents unfair dismissal must not be used to impede the efficient management of business by compelling employers to retain incompetent employees (*Cook v Thomas Linnell & Sons Ltd*), and once an employer has lost confidence in the employee's ability to do the job, then it is reasonable to dismiss and offer other employment should this be available. But the employer is not bound to create a vacancy if none exists; he should at least consider the possibility, and consider if the employee would make a success of it (*Brush Electrical Machines v Guest*).

17.86 If an employee is dismissed because of his incapability, the correct test to apply is whether the employer honestly and reasonably held the belief that the employee was not competent, and whether there are reasonable grounds for that belief. It is not necessary for the employer to *prove* that the employee was incompetent (*Alidair Ltd v Taylor*). In other words, the test under s 98(4) is a subjective one. The employment tribunal must consider the employer's state of mind as well as his reasons. But it is sufficient if the employer honestly believes on reasonable grounds that the employee is incompetent.

Long-term sickness

17.87 An employee who is absent from work for a long time because of sickness or ill-health is entitled to sympathetic consideration by the employer, but the employer can only be expected to act within sensible limits. The questions to be asked are (a) how long has the employment lasted, (b) how long had it been expected the employment would continue, (c) what is the nature of the job, (d) what was the nature, effect and length of the illness, (e) what is the need of the employer for the work to be done, and to engage a replacement to do it, (f) are wages continuing to be paid, (g) why had the employer dismissed (or failed to do so), and (h) in all the circumstances, could a reasonable employer have been expected to wait any longer (*Egg Stores (Stamford-Hill) Ltd v Leibovici*)? In other words, the employer is entitled to consider his business needs, as well as the employee's situation. An important point to consider is 'has the time arrived when the employer can no longer reasonably be expected to keep the absent employee's post open for him?' (*Hart v AR Marshall & Sons (Bulwell) Ltd*). Thus if an employee is away for a long time, the employer should not dismiss as an automatic matter, but consider whether it is necessary to dismiss. The employer should make all necessary enquiries, from the employee, from his doctor, and if possible obtain an opinion from the firm's medical advisers (*East Lindsey District Council v Daubney*).

17.88 In all cases where dismissal on the grounds of ill-health is being considered, there is a need for enquiry, consultation, warnings, a search for alternatives etc, before the decision is taken (*A Links & Co Ltd v Rose*). The purpose of consulting with the employee about his health is to weigh up the situation, balancing the need of the employer to get the work done against the employee's need for time in order to recover his health. Without such consultation, the employer may act precipitously, with unfair consequences. But consultation is not demanded by law; if it is clear that the consultation would not have made any difference to the result, a failure to consult does not make a dismissal unfair (*Taylorplan Catering (Scotland) Ltd v McInally*).

17.89 Earlier cases had stated that an employer should warn an employee that unless he returns to work he will be dismissed, but this view is erroneous, for an employee cannot be warned that he has got to be in good health. However, the employer should make all proper and necessary enquiries from the employee, and not act in a precipitous manner. Perhaps the best way to express the employer's obligation is to say that he should treat the employee with sympathetic consideration, and that he should hold the job open for as long as is possible. In *Coulson v Felixstowe Dock & Rly Co Ltd* the claimant was away from work due to ill-health for considerable periods of time. He could no longer perform his duties, and was put on light clerical work. He was told that if he could not return to his old job, he would be regraded, and was given six months in which to prove his fitness. However, he fell ill again and was dismissed. It was held that the employer had treated the employee with every consideration, but there must come a time when the employer cannot be expected to keep someone on who is not doing his work. The tribunal had to consider fairness to the business as well as to the employee.

17.90 On the other hand, in *Converform (Darwen) Ltd v Bell*, the claimant was a works director who was off work because of a heart attack. He recovered, but the employers refused to permit him to return to work, as they thought there was the risk of another attack. His subsequent dismissal was held to be unfair. A risk of future illness cannot be used as a ground for fair dismissal unless the nature of the employment is such that the risk made it unsafe for the employee to continue in the job.

17.91 A good employer will try to fix a date by which time he must know when the employee expects to be able to give information about the likely date of return to work (*Marder v ITT Distributors Ltd*), but once having explained and discussed the situation with the employee, the employer is entitled to make a decision in the light of the information available (*Spencer v Paragon Wallpapers Ltd*).

17.92 In *Merseyside and North Wales Electricity Board v Taylor* the Divisional Court held that there is no rule of law which requires the employer to create a special job for an employee who is off sick. Nor is there a rule that an employer is obliged to find alternative employment for an employee plagued by ill-health. Each case must be judged on its own facts in the light of the employer's circumstances. It may be that the employer has some light work available of the kind which is within the employee's capacity to do, and the employee should be encouraged to take such a post, even at reduced rates of pay, before dismissal is considered.

17.93 In larger firms it may be possible for the company to place a sick employee in some form of holding department, so that he can recommence employment when fit, but there are certain legal problems about such a course which require further consideration. In *Burton v Boneham & Turner Ltd*, the management placed an employee in such a holding department after several spells of absence through illness. It was held that such conduct amounted in law to a dismissal, although in the circumstances, it was held to be fair. On the other hand, in *Parker v Westland Helicopters Ltd* a sick employee was transferred from the department concerned with sick employees to a holding department, where she had to wait for a suitable vacancy before being employed again. As this was done with her agreement, on the facts it was held that no dismissal had taken place.

17.94 The legal significance of placing employees in a holding department has yet to be fully explored. In *Marshall v Harland & Wolff Ltd* the NIRC held that such a transfer meant that the employee ceased to be employed in a legal sense, but the employers merely undertook some obligation to provide work if and when possible. If this is so, then the act of placing in the holding department could well be as the result of a frustrating event, and should not amount to a dismissal (*G F Sharp Ltd v McMillan*). On the other hand, it has been suggested (*O'Reilly v Hotpoint Ltd*) that such transfer suspends the contract of employment. If this view is correct, then continuity will doubtless be preserved for redundancy and other purposes for 26 weeks (ERA, s 212(3)(a)), and presumably there is a legal (as opposed to moral) obligation to find an employee work when he recovers. It is clear that the matter should be subject to a defined policy which can be stated in the works/staff rules, so that the legal situation will be determined by the contractual obligations which can be laid down by the parties in accordance with the objective which they seek.

17.95 If an employee is retired (or dismissed) on ill-health grounds, the employment tribunal should not be concerned with whether or not the illness was caused or contributed to by the employer, but should consider whether the employer acted reasonably in dismissing the employee for that illness (*London Fire and Civil Defence Authority v Betty*, doubted in *Edwards v Governors of Hanson School*).

17.96 Employers cannot be expected to go to unreasonable lengths in seeking to accommodate a sick employee, and what is reasonable is largely a question of fact and degree in each case (*Garricks (Caterers) Ltd v Nolan*). There is no absolute rule that an employer must consult with the employee's general practitioner (and indeed, since this could result in a breach of professional confidence, it may not be a profitable exercise), although it may be desirable to do so if the employee gives his consent (see *Tower Hamlets London Borough v Bull*). In the last analysis, the employer must act within the range of reasonable responses, depending on the circumstances (*Rolls Royce Ltd v Walpole*).

17.97 The Disability Discrimination Act 1995 (see para 4.160) makes significant changes to the law relating to the dismissal of long-term sick employees, for many sickness/ill health absences may well come within the definition of a disability within the Act. Thus dismissals on health-related grounds will be affected by the requirements for employers to make reasonable adjustments to cater for employees who are disabled within the meaning of the Act, and dismissal on the ground of long-term sickness will only be justified if no such adjustments are possible, or if the employee rejects them. In particular, a failure to consult with a disabled person prior to taking a decision to dismiss can amount to a failure to make a reasonable adjustment (*Rothwell v Pelikan Hardcopy Scotland Ltd*). Further, the employment tribunals are likely to take a more robust approach to claims that the contract of employment has been frustrated on grounds of long-term sickness, possibly by restricting the doctrine to those employees whose illness makes them virtually totally incapable of working.

17.98 An employee who is away from work through illness etc is still within the pool of selection for redundancy, but the usual criteria of consultation etc must be applied (*Hill v General Accident Fire and Life Insurance Co*).

Persistent absenteeism

17.99 The employee who is persistently away from work (whether because of illness or other reasons) for short periods at a time presents a different problem. This employee can be cautioned about his absences; he can be confronted with his record, told that it must improve, and be given a period of time in which an improvement can be monitored. Indeed, the employer should not ignore the powerful medicinal effect of a final warning, and a failure to give one may mean that the employee is unaware that the situation is causing the employer great concern. The effect of such a warning might be to stimulate the employee into seeking proper medical advice in case there is an underlying cause of the continuous minor ailments, it may deter the employee from taking time off when not truly warranted, and it may even lead the employee to look for other work where such absences could be tolerated (*Smith v Royal Alfred Merchant Seamen's Society*).

17.100 The employer should approach the situation with 'sympathy, understanding and compassion'. Factors to be taken into account include: (a) the nature of the illness, (b) the likelihood of it recurring, (c) the length of the various absences and the spells of good health in between, (d) the need of the employer to have that work done by that employee, (e) the impact of the absences on other employees, (f) the adoption and carrying out of the policy, (g) a personal assessment of the ultimate decision, and (h) the fact that the employee is fully aware that his employment will be terminated unless there is an improvement (*Lynock v Cereal Packaging Ltd*).

17.101 At the same time, the employer can hold out a helping hand; he can enquire from the employee the nature of all these minor ailments, offer such medical help as the firm can provide, provide counselling, etc, in those cases where the employment is itself a major contributing factor to the illness, and so on.

17.102 In practice, it is essential to establish the reason for the absences, as this may well determine the appropriate procedural steps to be taken. For example, the employer may have issued a policy statement on alcohol or drug abuse, which may override standard procedures. In most cases, it will be necessary to interview the employee on his return to work, which will assist in establishing the reasons for the absence, assess the likelihood of recurrence, and determine whether the appropriate 'trigger' has been reached under any attendance procedure. If an underlying medical condition is suspected, advice may be given on the need to seek further treatment. Alternative employment may be considered, or flexibility introduced into attendance improvement schemes. In other words, a great

deal can be done to resolve the problem, rather than merely consider dismissal as a solution (*Kerrigan v Rover Group Ltd*).

17.103 In *International Sports Ltd v Thomson* the claimant was away from work for about 25% of the time, with a variety of complaints (all of which were covered by medical certificates) including dizzy spells, anxiety and nerves, bronchitis, virus infection, cystitis, althrugia of the left knee, dyspepsia and flatulence. She was given a series of warnings, including a final warning, and before deciding to dismiss her, the company consulted their medical adviser. He saw no useful purpose in examining her, as none of the previous illnesses could be verified, there was no common link between them and she was not suffering from any chronic illness. She was then dismissed, and the EAT held that the dismissal was fair. The company had undertaken a fair review of her attendance record, she had been duly warned and given the opportunity to make representations. A further medical investigation would have produced no worthwhile results. There must come a point in time when a reasonable employer is entitled to say 'Enough is enough'.

17.104 It is normal for many firms to have contractual entitlement to a certain amount of sick leave, some of which may be regarded as 'certified' or covered by sick notes. Certainly, an employee should keep his employer informed by the proper means, and a failure to do so may mean that the employee contributes to his own dismissal and receives reduced compensation. But sick notes, by themselves, can never be conclusive, for there are serious doubts about their factual validity. Thus, if an employer believes that a sick note is phoney, or may not be accurate, then he is entitled to disregard it (*Hutchinson v Enfield Rolling Mills Ltd*).

17.105 In *Wilkes v Fortes (Sussex) Ltd* the EAT placed particular emphasis on a consideration of the size of the firm in determining whether or not it would be fair to dismiss an employee who is off work intermittently for sickness reasons. In a large firm, the disruption caused by such illnesses may be minimal; it is easy to have a float of overmanning to cover for absent employees. But in a small business, such absences may be extremely serious or even disastrous.

17.106 If a person's health is such that continued employment may well constitute a hazard, either to himself, to other employees, or is likely to cause damage to property, then provided the employer undertakes full consultation with the employee, and obtains expert medical opinion, this is capable of being a fair dismissal (*Spalding v Port of London Authority*), and it is not necessary for the employer to wait until an accident occurs before taking steps to dismiss (*Parsons v Fisons Ltd*). In *Finch v Betabake (Anglia) Ltd* the claimant was an apprentice motor mechanic. The employers received a report from an ophthalmic surgeon that the boy could not continue to work without undue danger to himself and to others. He was therefore dismissed. It was held that the circumstances in which an apprentice could be dismissed were limited, but in the circumstances, the dismissal was fair.

17.107 If the persistent absenteeism is due to factors other than ill-health, then warnings, as appropriate, should be given. It has been suggested that a dismissal because of an unacceptable level of short-term persistent absenteeism should properly be considered under the heading of 'some other substantial reason' rather than capability or conduct (*Post Office v Wilson*).

17.108 The ACAS Advisory Handbook gave some guidance to employers on how to handle persistent short-term absenteeism. It was stated that:

(a) absences should be investigated promptly, and the employee asked for an explanation;

(b) if there is no medical evidence to support frequent self-certified absences, the employee should be asked to consult with a doctor to establish whether medical treatment is advisable, and/or whether the underlying reason for the absence is work-related;

(c) if, following a full and careful investigation, there appears to be no valid reason (medical or otherwise) for the absences, the matter should be dealt with under the appropriate disciplinary procedure;

(d) if the absences are due to domestic problems, the employer should consider whether an improvement in attendance is likely;

(e) the employee should be told what improvement in attendance is expected, and warned of the likely consequences if this does not happen;

(f) if there is no improvement, the employee's age, length of service, performance, should be considered, as well as the availability of alternative work. These factors must be balanced against the effect of past and future absences on the business.

17.109 Finally, an employer would need to consider whether persistent absenteeism is due to a long-term illness of the kind covered by the Disability Discrimination Act (see para 4.160), and hence appropriate consideration should be given to the need to make reasonable adjustments, where possible.

Lack of qualifications

17.110 There have been very few cases concerning the lack of qualifications for the job as a reason for dismissal. In *Blackman v Post Office* a telegraph officer was required to pass an aptitude test, but he failed after a maximum number of attempts. It was held that his dismissal was fair on the ground of lack of qualifications. But there must be a contractual obligation (express or implied) to hold the relevant qualification. In *Litster v M Thom & Sons Ltd* the applicant was employed as a foreman fitter/driver. Government regulations required that special driving licences had to be obtained for drivers of heavy goods vehicles, and the claimant failed the necessary test. Nonetheless he was continued in employment as a fitter. His contract of employment contained no reference to the necessity of having an HGV licence. Following a dispute, he was told that unless he obtained such a licence, he would be dismissed. It was held that since his contract did not require him to hold that particular licence, a dismissal based on his lack of qualifications would be unfair.

17.111 However, it may be permissible to go outside the formal requirements of the contract. In *Tayside Regional Council v McIntosh*, the employers advertised for a vehicle mechanic, an essential requirement being that the successful applicant should have a driving licence. The claimant was appointed to the job, but his contract of employment made no mention of the need to hold a driving licence. He was subsequently disqualified from driving, and as there was no other suitable employment for him, he was dismissed.

The EAT held that he had been fairly dismissed. The nature of the job clearly required the holding of a valid driving licence.

17.112 But even though it can be shown that the employee lacks the necessary qualification for the job, the employer must still act reasonably in treating that reason as a sufficient ground for dismissal. Thus in *Sutcliffe & Eaton Ltd v Pinney* the claimant was dismissed from his job as a trainee hearing aid dispenser after he failed to pass the necessary examinations. It was held that the employers should have applied for an extension of his training period so that he could take the examination again. In other words, as always, the reasonable employer will look around for alternatives to dismissal.

Conduct inside the employment

17.113 Under this heading we can consider all those acts of the employee which occur during the performance of the contract, and which are alleged to have an adverse effect on that contract. Such acts may be sub-divided in accordance with their gravity, ie acts of trivial nature (minor misconduct), serious matters (major misconduct) and extremely serious matters (gross misconduct). The importance of such a classification lies in the methods which are required to be adopted to solve the problem in question. For acts of minor misconduct, these can usually be dealt with by a warning (informal, then perhaps formal), but it would be wrong to utilise the full weight of a disciplinary sanction in order to deal with a trivial matter. Thus to give an employee a final warning 'if you come in late again you will be dismissed' is bound to lead to trouble at some later stage, for the sanction is out of all proportion to the offence. Such a person could be dealt with, for example, by a short period of suspension. Further, for some acts a single repetition would suffice to warrant dismissal (eg theft) and hence the warning would spell this out. But other acts may have to be monitored over a period of time, (eg lateness, absenteeism), and hence the warning will indicate the period, spell out the improvement required, and state the ultimate sanction. An act of major misconduct could be handled by an immediate final warning, without the need to go through stages in a procedure (ie informal warning, first written warning, etc), for the seriousness of the matter is sufficient to leap over other stages. And acts of gross misconduct, once proven, can lead to instant dismissal without notice, for this amounts to a breach by the employee which in effect repudiates the contract.

17.114 For all acts of misconduct, the employer must show that he gave the matter a prompt and thorough investigation, that he gave the employee an opportunity to state his case, interviewed witnesses and collected evidence so far as it was possible to do so, but there are limits to the power of an employer to investigate, and indeed, it may well be improper for him to do so on occasions. This is particularly true when the matter is to the subject of criminal charges or investigation by the police. Thus in *Carr v Alexander Russell Ltd*, the claimant was dismissed when it was learned that the police had found some company property in his possession, and that he was to be charged with theft. It was held that the employers had no duty to carry out any detailed form of enquiry, for it would have been improper of them to do so, and a subsequent trial might have been seriously prejudiced.

17.115 There is no absolute prescription that an employee must be given an opportunity to explain his conduct before he is dismissed, though this course is clearly desirable. In

Parker v Clifford Dunn Ltd the employers received information from the police that the claimant had admitted stealing from the company. He was therefore dismissed in accordance with the works rules. He did not appeal through the procedure, and made no protestation of innocence. His dismissal was held to be fair; it was reasonable for the employers to rely on the police investigations rather than carry out their own. But the mere fact that the police intend to charge an employee with theft is not conclusive, as they may decide not to proceed with the charge, or the evidence may be too weak to secure a conviction, and so on. Some enquiry may therefore be necessary (*Scottish Special Housing Association v Cooke*).

17.116 The acts which can constitute misconduct inside the employment are too numerous to categorise. Fighting, swearing, trading, drunkenness, betting, horseplay, incompetence, theft, neglect, dangerous or obstructive conduct, clocking offences, breach of safety rules, immorality, refusal to obey orders, breach of hygiene rules, insubordination, unauthorised absenteeism, disloyalty, breach of confidence, taking unlawful drugs, sleeping while on duty, computer hacking or seeking unauthorised access to a computer program, telling lies, unsuitable clothing, dishonesty, taking property without authorisation and lateness, have all, in their turn, been the subject of employment tribunal proceedings. To deal with such conduct, the employer must consider the gravity of the offence, its effect on the employment generally, and the previous history of the employee. In other words, the employer, it is submitted, must take into account the offence, and the offender.

17.117 It is not the function of the employment tribunal to substitute its views and opinions for those of management, but merely to decide if management has acted reasonably. For example, if an employee has committed an act of theft, it is for management to decide what should be done in the circumstances of the case, and provided a fair procedure is adopted, the eventual decision is that of management. In *Trusthouse Forte Hotels Ltd v Murphy*, the claimant was a night porter. He kept a small supply of liquor for hotel guests, but when his stock was checked, there was a deficiency of £10. He admitted taking some of this for his own use, and was dismissed. The employment tribunal found this to be unfair, but the decision was reversed on appeal by the EAT. It would place an unreasonable burden on employers if they could not fairly dismiss employees who had stolen property which had been entrusted to their care. Although management might have been influenced by compassionate grounds, and might have decided not to dismiss an employee who had stolen a small amount of property, a reasonable management may have taken either view. Hence it was not possible to argue that this employer had acted unreasonably.

17.118 Nor need the employers prove that an offence has been committed beyond reasonable doubt, for this would impose on them a higher commitment than would ever be possible to fulfil, and impose a duty which rightfully belongs to a court of trial. The employers must genuinely believe that the employee has been guilty of the misconduct in question, they must have reasonable grounds for that belief, and they must have carried out such investigation into the matter as is reasonable in the circumstances (*British Home Stores v Burchell*). In *Laurie v Fairburn* the claimant was dismissed because the employers believed that she was stealing from them. The employment tribunal was not convinced that this was so, and held the dismissal to be unfair. This was reversed on appeal; the question is not whether or not the employee was guilty, or would have been found guilty if tried, but whether it was reasonable for the employers to dismiss her, taking into account all the circumstances and facts known to the employers at the time of the dismissal.

17.119 If an employee makes a confession, this is a fact which the employer is entitled to take into consideration when forming his views, and the rules about the non-admissibility of confessions made involuntarily (the Judge's Rules) have no application in such circumstances (*Morley's of Brixton Ltd v Minott*).

17.120 Where an employee has pleaded guilty to a criminal offence, or been found guilty by the decision of a court or the verdict of a jury, it is reasonable for an employer to believe that the employee committed the offence. Any other conclusion would be ridiculous (*P v Nottinghamshire County Council*). This is so even if the employee alleges that he pleaded guilty on the advice of his lawyers, in order to avoid a prison sentence (*British Gas plc v McCarrick*).

17.121 The fact that an employee faces criminal charges subsequently, and is acquitted on those charges, is also irrelevant to the issue of the fairness of the dismissal. In *Da Costa v Optolis* the claimant was dismissed from his job as a book-keeper for not keeping proper accounts, and he subsequently faced criminal charges, though these ended in his favour. It was held that the fact the Crown Court had acquitted him did not preclude a finding by the employment tribunal that the dismissal was fair. The issues involved were different. In the Crown Court, it had to be decided whether he was guilty of the charge beyond reasonable doubt, whereas in the employment tribunal, it had to be shown whether the employer had reasonable grounds for dismissing him.

17.122 It must surely be sound policy for the employer to be consistent in his procedure, flexible in his decisions. Thus an employer may take into account the fact that the employee has had a long record of exemplary conduct (*City of Edinburgh District Council v Stephen*), but the importance of such mitigating factors is a matter for the employer's discretion (*AEI Cables Ltd v McLay*). In *Taylor v Parsons Peebles Ltd* the claimant, who had been employed for 20 years without complaint, was dismissed for fighting. The EAT held the dismissal to be unfair. The company's policy had to be considered in the light of a reasonable employer's reaction to the incident. Given that the applicant had 20 years' good conduct, a reasonable employer would not have applied a rigid sanction of automatic dismissal. In failing to take account of mitigating circumstances, the employers had acted unreasonably. In *Hadjioannou v Coral Casinos Ltd* (see para 12.81) it will be recalled that the EAT stressed the need for flexibility in dealing with industrial misconduct, saying that a tariff approach was not correct.

17.123 An employee who admits that his conduct is unacceptable, and accepts advice and help to avoid any repetition may be treated differently from an employee who refuses to accept responsibility for his actions, argues with management, or makes unfounded allegations that his colleagues have conspired to make false accusations against him (*Paul v East Surrey District Health Authority*).

17.124 If the conduct in question amounts to gross misconduct, then this should be acted upon immediately by management, for a delay may lead the employment tribunal to conclude that the conduct was not so wrongful as to warrant the drastic punishment of instant dismissal, although in rare cases it is proper to dismiss summarily a long time after the event (*Refund Rentals Ltd v McDermott*). Normally, it would be reasonable to suspend pending an investigation, but again, this counsel of perfection cannot always be followed (*Conway v Matthew Wright & Nephew Ltd*).

17.125 If the conduct falls under the heading of breach of works rules (eg smoking in prohibited areas, fighting, failing to observe safety precautions, etc) then provided the rule is a reasonable one, has been duly promulgated and brought to the attention of the employees, then the tribunals will usually uphold management action (*Richards v Bulpitt & Sons Ltd*), particularly if there has been an act of dishonesty (*British Railways Board v Jackson*). But a minor breach should not be treated as an excuse for dismissal, no matter how strongly worded the rule may be (*Ladbroke Racing Ltd v Arnott*).

17.126 Before dismissing for gross misconduct, the employer should consider any alternative course of action, for it is not inconsistent with a finding of gross misconduct to offer the employee alternative employment in a different capacity (*Hamilton v Argyll and Clyde Health Board*). Each case must be considered on its merits, taking into account the special facts and mitigating circumstances. If, in the past, an employee has not been dismissed for a similar offence, management should enquire into those circumstances. The dangers of a tariff or consistent approach in cases where there is no true comparability should be avoided (*Procter v British Gypsum Ltd*).

17.127 Equally difficult is conduct by the employee which is strictly within his contractual rights, but which is obstructive in nature. In *Pengilly v North Devon Farmers Ltd* it was held that a refusal to work overtime, even though not compulsory within the terms of the employee's contract, warranted a dismissal, as the refusal was contrary to the normal practice, and the employee was trying to put improper pressure on the employer. But in *Burns v Ideal Timber Products* it was held that a refusal to work overtime in order to get the employer to improve working conditions did not amount to improper pressure.

17.128 The conduct of the employee must in some way reflect on the employment relationship. In *Thomson v Alloa Motor Co Ltd*, the applicant was employed as a petrol pump attendant. One day she finished work, and drove off in her car, but collided with a petrol pump, causing substantial damage. She was summarily dismissed, because of the seriousness of the damage and the fact that her employers would have to sue her for compensation. The dismissal was held to be unfair. The accident had no bearing on her ability to do her work, it was an incident unlikely to be repeated, and her employers were undoubtedly covered by insurance.

17.129 While it may not generally be possible to dismiss an employee who is acting within the terms of the contract, it should be possible to call for a variation of that contract, or to terminate it and offer a new one (see Chapter 3). Provided the proper procedure is adopted, a subsequent dismissal may well be for 'some other substantial reason' (see below).

17.130 Other types of conduct which have been held to warrant dismissal include a refusal to wear the appropriate clothing required for the job (*Atkin v Enfield Hospital Management Committee*), wearing provocative badges contrary to instructions and warnings (*Boychuk v Symons Holdings Ltd*), carrying on sexual relations during business hours (*Newman v Alarmco*), passing on information to a former employee of the firm who is working for a competitor (*Smith v Du Pont (UK) Ltd*), refusing to cut exceptionally long hair after being warned of a safety hazard (*Marsh v Judge International*), breach of works rules (*Palmer v Vauxhall Motors Ltd*), suspected dishonesty (*Parkers Bakeries Ltd v Palmer*), breach of safety instructions (*Wilcox v HGS*), fighting (*Parsons & Co Ltd v McLoughlin*), being a drug addict (*Walton v TAC Construction Materials Ltd*), taking drugs contrary to a zero tolerance drugs policy (*O'Flynn v Airlinks the Airport Coach Co Ltd*), refusal to go on a training course (*Minter v Wellingborough Foundries Ltd*), unauthorised access to a computer (*Denco Ltd v Joinson*), misusing the office computer to access hardcore pornography (*Hillingdon London Borough Council v Thomas*) and so on.

17.131 Every employer is strongly urged to observe the provisions of the Code of Practice on Disciplinary and Grievance Procedures, and although a breach of the Code will not automatically make a dismissal unfair (*Lewis Shops Group v Wiggins*), in practice it can be said that the provisions of the Code matter most when the decision to dismiss is at its weakest. Thus it is still possible to dismiss summarily for gross misconduct (*Retarded Children's Aid Society v Day*), but procedural fairness should always be observed, and a failure to follow the Code's recommendations may lead to a finding that the dismissal was unfair, even though the compensation may be reduced because of the employee's contributory conduct.

Conduct outside the employment

17.132 The problem which arises here is, what has it got to do with the employer what an employee does outside his working hours? The answer will depend on a number of factors, including the nature of the employment, the position held by the employee, the nature of the incident and its effect on the employer, on customers, on fellow employees, and so on. If it can be said that the conduct in question has an adverse effect on the employer's business; then a dismissal may be fair. For example, the conduct may be a conviction by a court of law for a criminal offence unconnected with the employment. In *Richardson v City of Bradford Metropolitan Council* the claimant was a senior meat inspector, who was convicted of theft of money from his local rugby club on several occasions. When his employers were informed, he was suspended, but as there were no other suitable vacancies which could be offered to him, he was dismissed. This was held to be fair. The integrity of a public servant who was in a position of trust was of prime importance. In *Bradshaw v Rugby Portland Cement Co Ltd* the claimant was dismissed following a conviction for incest with his own daughter, for which he was placed on probation by the Crown Court. The dismissal was held to be unfair. The offence had no bearing on his work as a quarryman, the firm's customers would not have objected to his continued employment, and his relationship with his fellow-employees had not deteriorated to the extent that they objected to working with him. There must have been strong mitigating circumstances for the court to deal with the matter so leniently, and the tribunal did not see any reason to impose a further punishment. Clearly, different considerations would have applied had the applicant been (say) a schoolmaster. In *Gardiner v Newport County Borough Council* the claimant was a lecturer at an art college, in charge of a foundation course on which were pupils who were between the ages of 16–18. He was convicted of gross indecency with another man in a public lavatory, and his dismissal by the college was held to be fair. The tribunal held that *Bradshaw*'s case was no authority for saying that a person who receives a moderate punishment from the court is immune from dismissal, for the courts are frequently being reminded in mitigation that whatever punishment they impose is only part of the misfortune which will befall the accused. The employers could not be expected to waive the consequences which the courts had anticipated and possibly allowed for in fixing the penalty. Nor is it relevant that the employer never told the employee of the kind of conduct outside his employment which would warrant dismissal, for an employer cannot possibly specify or anticipate all the possible circumstances which may lead to a dismissal. To hold otherwise would mean that an employee would be safest from dismissal if he committed some act which was more outrageous than anyone ever envisaged.

17.133 If the employee is charged with a criminal offence, then clearly the employer will need to make a decision about whether the employment can continue, in advance of a hearing in the criminal courts. The employee should be interviewed (strictly, this is not part of the disciplinary procedure, because no breach of internal discipline has occurred), and invited to explain the position. If he intends to plead guilty, the employer can then make a decision, depending on the circumstances, nature of employment, position held etc. If the employer considers that valuable customers would be lost if the employment continued, he should first attempt to ascertain the views of those customers, and not just make bland assumptions. If the employee states that he intends to plead not guilty, then ideally he should be suspended until the outcome of the criminal proceedings. Whether this suspension should be with pay or without pay is a matter of style and agreement, taking into account the length of time it will be before the hearing takes place, the circumstances of the employer's business, the seriousness or otherwise of the offence, and so on. If there is a collective agreement or a disciplinary procedure which provides that suspension on full pay will be appropriate where investigations cannot be completed, then that agreement or procedure must be followed (*Securicor Guarding Ltd v R*).

17.134 Thus an employer is entitled to make a judgment based on the criminal conduct of the employee, as to whether or not the conviction has impaired the employee's ability to do the job, and whether there has been a loss of confidence in the employee (*Robson v Brian Mills*). In *Moore v C & A Modes* the claimant was a section leader in a store, where she had been employed for 20 years. It was alleged that she had been caught shoplifting at another store. Her consequent dismissal was held to be fair. No-one should be more alive to the damage caused by shoplifters than such an employee, and it was unreal to expect an employer in the retail trade not to dismiss an employee whom he believed to be stealing from another store. In *Mathewson v R B Wilson Dental Laboratory Ltd*, the claimant was arrested during his lunch break for purchasing a small amount of cannabis. His subsequent dismissal was held to be within the range of reasonable responses which a reasonable employer might take.

17.135 'Moonlighting', ie the taking of additional employment outside normal working hours, may be grounds for dismissal if this has an adverse effect on the employer's business. It will be recalled (para 10.86) that in *Hivac Ltd v Park Royal Scientific Instruments Ltd* the employees were in breach of their contracts for which they could have been dismissed, although this was prevented at the time by the operation of the Essential Works Order. The court stated that it would be reluctant to impose on the employees a restriction which would hamper their ability to increase their earnings in their spare time, but on the facts they were inflicting great harm on the employer's business. In *Gray v C & P Pembroke Ltd* the claimant agreed to not engage in any other business without the written consent of the employer. Contrary to this agreement he took a part-time job with a rival company, and this was held to be a breach of faith for which he could be fairly dismissed. However, in *Nova Plastics Ltd v Froggatt* the claimant was employed as an odd-job man. He was dismissed when it was discovered that he was working for a rival firm. The dismissal was held to be unfair. Having regard to the nature of his work as an odd-job man, he could hardly be contributing very seriously to the competition from the rival firm, and in the circumstances there was no breach of duty towards his own employer merely because he worked for a competitor in his spare time.

17.136 In some circumstances, it may be relevant to consider whether or not the outside activity is compatible with the dignity of the employee holding a particular post; in other circumstances an employer may be entitled to forbid an employee engaging in certain leisure pursuits or additional employment if the result is that the employee is too exhausted to follow his normal occupation. If an employee wishes to stand at a parliamentary or local election, this is of concern to the employer only if the activity spills over into the employment scene. For example, supposing a supervisor, who controls a labour force made up largely of coloured immigrant workers, announces his intention of standing for election as a National Front candidate. It could be argued that the potential disruption likely to be caused to a contented workforce may well justify an employer dismissing the employee concerned. An employment tribunal has held that the holding of political beliefs is not 'a religion, religious belief or similar philosophical belief' within the meaning of the Employment Equality (Religion or Belief) Regulations 2003 (see para 4.196). In *Pay v Lancashire Probation Service*, the claimant was dismissed from his job as a probation officer when it was discovered that in his spare time he was performing shows at various hedonist and fetish clubs, and also acted as a director of a company which sold bondage and sado-masochistic products. It was held that his dismissal was fair, because his activities were incompatible with his position, and there would be potential damage to the reputation of the employer if those activities became public knowledge. An argument that his rights under the Human Rights Act 1998, Art 8 (right to privacy) and Art 10 (freedom of expression) had been violated was not upheld, because of the justification defences provided by the Convention (see para 1.101).

17.137 The conduct in question must be such as to cause a loss of confidence in the employee. Thus in *Whitlow v Alkanet Construction Ltd* the claimant was asked by the company's executive to do some work on the latter's house. There he met the executive's wife, and love play took place between them in the house, and they had sexual intercourse elsewhere. Although the tribunal recognised that the claimant had been subjected to a temptation which few men would have resisted, his dismissal was held to be fair.

Redundancy

17.138 The commonest ground for a dismissal is for reason of redundancy. This will be considered in Chapter 18.

Statutory restriction

17.139 An employer cannot be expected to continue to employ an employee if such employment would be contrary to the law. For example, if an employee is employed as a driver, and it is a term (express or implied) of his contract that he should hold a valid driving licence, then clearly, if he loses that licence, the employee is barred from pursuing that occupation by statute (Road Traffic Act 1974, s 84). Additionally, the employer may be guilty of an offence if he permits a disqualified driver to drive. But this does not mean that a dismissal will always be fair in such circumstances. The test is, as always, the reasonableness of the employer's action (*Sutcliffe and Eaton Ltd v Pinney*). He must consider the length of the disqualification, the needs of the business, whether the employee can do his job without driving a motor vehicle, whether alternative arrangements can be made, whether the employee could be given some other work to do until his licence is restored, and so on. In *Mathieson v WJ Noble* the claimant was a salesman who was disqualified from driving. He made arrangements to engage a chauffeuse at his own expense to drive him around during the period of disqualification, but his employers decided to dismiss him. It was held that the employers had acted unreasonably in not giving him a chance to see if the new arrangements were satisfactory. This may be contrasted with *Appleyard v FM Smith (Hull) Ltd* where it was an essential requirement for the mechanics that they should hold valid driving licences so that they could test vehicles which they had repaired. When the claimant lost his licence, the company had given some thought to placing him elsewhere in the business, but this was not practicable in such a small firm, and his dismissal was held to be fair.

17.140 There are a number of other legal restrictions on the employment of certain employees in special circumstances. In *Gills v Wall's Meat Co Ltd* the claimant, who was a Sikh, was involved with dealing with open meat. When he commenced employment he was clean shaven, and did not observe his religion by growing a beard, but after a while he was 'converted back to the paths of righteousness' and grew a beard. To have continued to employ him in this capacity would have involved a breach of the Food Regulations 1970, and so the employers, after offering him alternative employment which he refused, dismissed him. This was held to be fair. (It may be noted that a refusal by a Sikh to wear a safety helmet on a construction site as required by regulations made under the Health and Safety at Work etc Act does not entitle an employer to dismiss him as long as he is wearing his turban, see Employment Act 1989, s 11.)

Some other substantial reason

17.141 It was never intended that the above reasons for fair dismissal could constitute an exhaustive catalogue of the circumstances in which the employer would be justified in terminating the services of an employee, and there have been a number of cases where 'some other substantial reason' for the dismissal has been held to be fair. In *Wilson v Underhill House School Ltd* the claimant was a schoolteacher in a school which was in financial difficulties, and which could not pay in full a pay award. All the other teachers except her agreed to take less, but she refused and was dismissed. Her dismissal was held to be fair for some other substantial reason. In *Foot v Eastern Counties Timber Co Ltd* the claimant, who was a valued employee, was dismissed when it was discovered that her husband had started a business which was in competition with the employers. It was held that the company had acted reasonably in dismissing an employee who had access to confidential information at a time when her husband was running a rival business. In *Farr v Hoveringham Gravels Ltd* the company had a rule that employees must live within reasonable travelling distance of the firm, and they dismissed a manager who had moved to live 44 miles away. A person in his position may have to be called out in an emergency, and this would prove to be difficult in view of the distance involved. Hence the dismissal was fair.

17.142 It has to be recognised that frequently the legitimate interests of the employer in making a change in employment terms are irreconcilable with the equally legitimate interests of the employee. Thus a sound good business reason for a particular reorganisation has to be looked at in that context (*St John of God (Care Services) Ltd v Brooks*).

17.143 An employer need not wait until a problem arises before he takes action to protect his commercial interests. In *O'Brien v Prudential Assurance Co*, the claimant applied for a job as a district insurance inspector, but deliberately concealed that he had a history of mental illness. When this came to light, the company obtained further medical reports, on the basis of which he was dismissed. Again, this was to be for some other substantial reason, and in the circumstances fair. As an inspector, he would have to go into people's homes, and the company could not risk the possibility that an unsavoury incident might occur.

17.144 Although an employee is not legally obliged to accept a variation in the terms of his contract, a refusal to do so may amount to a substantial reason for dismissal if it is in the commercial interests of the firm that a variation should be made, and it is a reasonable request to make in the circumstances. In *Muggridge and Slade v East Anglia Plastics Ltd* the employers found it necessary to change the working hours, and fairly dismissed two ladies who refused to accept the change, and in *RS Components v Irwin* (see para 19.20) the company fairly dismissed a salesman who refused to sign a restrictive covenant. But if an employee refuses to sign a restrictive covenant which is unreasonably wide, this will not be a potentially fair reason for dismissal. Nor is it necessary for the employee to make a counter-proposal; if the employer wants the benefit of a restraint clause, he must make sure that the proposal is a reasonable one (*Forshaw v Archcraft Ltd*). However, a dismissal for refusing new contractual terms may be unfair if there is no immediate need for the variation (*Evans v Elemeta Holdings Ltd*).

17.145 A change in employment terms may well be necessary even though these are to the detriment of the employee, if commercial necessity so dictates, for a contract of employment cannot remain static throughout the whole of its existence. In *Sycamore v H Myer & Co Ltd* the claimant refused to accept a new payment system which would have resulted in his wages being reduced from £130 per week to about £90 per week. The new system was negotiated with the trade union because the old method of payment was clearly defective. All the other employees accepted the change, and it was held that the claimant's dismissal was for some other substantial reason, and fair in the circumstances. The new terms were not ungenerous, and had been negotiated with the trade union concerned. In *Storey v Allied Brewery*, the respondents introduced a rota system of working due to the changing pattern of their trade. The claimant refused to work on Sundays, as she wished to go to church. Her dismissal was held to be fair. The change was necessary in the interests of economy, and to balance and share the workload with all the relevant employees. In *Oliver v Sperry Vickers*, the claimant was dismissed for refusing to accept a change in his job title and job content following a reorganisation of the supervisory structure. He was the only one of 22 employees affected who refused. Although this involved minor additions in his duties, he would have received a higher rate of pay. The dismissal was held to be for some substantial reason, and in the circumstances, fair, for he had no reasonable objection to the change.

17.146 A change in working hours does not give rise to a redundancy, but a dismissal due to a refusal to accept such a change consequent on a reorganisation may be for some other substantial reason (*Barnes v Gilmartin Associates*).

17.147 The test in these cases is whether the offer of new terms is within the range of offers which a reasonable employer would make in the circumstances. The task of weighing the advantages to the employer against the disadvantages to the employee is merely one factor to be taken into account (*Richmond Precision Engineering Ltd v Pearce*). Whether or not other employees have accepted the proposed changes, and whether a trade union have recommended acceptance of the changes are relevant factors to be taken into account. The imposition of the new terms and conditions does not have to be solely on the ground that the changes are vital for the survival of the business, and other valid reasons may be equally acceptable (*Catamaran Cruisers Ltd v Williams*).

17.148 If an employee is dismissed because he refuses to carry out an order which is not within his contractual obligations, this may be a factor in deciding whether or not he has been unfairly dismissed, but it is not determinative of the issue. There may be sound organisational reasons for the employer seeking to change working conditions or altering the terms of the contract. If the employee has been given ample warnings of the changes, and ample time to discuss his concerns a dismissal for refusing to accept the changes could well be fair (*Farrant v Woodroffe School*).

17.149 A difficult situation arises when an employer knows that a disciplinary offence (eg theft) has been committed, but is unable to identify the actual person responsible. Can he then dismiss all the suspects? In *Parr v Whitbread & Co plc* the claimant was a branch manager of an off-licence. There were three other employees working in the shop. It was discovered that the sum of £4,600 was missing, but the circumstances were such that each of the four employees had an equal opportunity of committing the theft. After carrying out a thorough investigation, all four were dismissed. An employment tribunal held that the dismissal was for some other substantial reason, and fair in the circumstances, and the decision was upheld by the EAT. The following guidance was offered: (1) the act must be one which would justify dismissal if committed by an individual; (2) the employer must carry out a reasonable and thorough investigation; (3) as a result of the investigation, the employer must reasonably believe that one of the employees committed the act; (4) the employers must have acted reasonably in identifying the group of employees one of whom could have committed the act; and (5) as between the members of that group, the employer could not reasonably have identified the actual perpetrator.

17.150 But the employer does not have to dismiss all of the group, if he can show solid and sensible grounds for differentiating between members of the group. In *Frames Snooker Centre v Boyce*, three managers had access to a safe in the employers' premises. After several burglaries had occurred, the police formed the view that each burglary was an inside job. There was no evidence against any of the managers, but the employer decided to dismiss two of them. He did not dismiss the third, because she was his daughter, and he had faith in her honesty and integrity. An employment tribunal held that the dismissal of the two managers was unfair because of the failure to dismiss all the suspects, but the decision was reversed on appeal. There is no 'all or none' principle in dismissing a group when it is not possible to identify the culprit.

17.151 A breakdown in confidence between an employer and a senior executive, for which the latter was responsible because of an inappropriate style of management, is capable of being some other substantial reason for the dismissal. But if a dismissal is procedurally unfair, it is still open to an employment tribunal to find that there was a 100% chance that a fair procedure would have reached the same result, and compensation may be reduced by that percentage (*Perkin v St George's Healthcare NHS Trust*).

17.152 To dismiss one of two incompatible employees in order to restore harmony among the workforce (*Gorfin v Distressed Gentlefolk's Aid Association*) may be fair provided that steps are taken to investigate the conflict and attempts are made to see whether or not an improvement in the relationship can be effected (*Turner v Vesteric Ltd*). Equally, to dismiss an employee who is unable to obtain a fidelity bond (*Moody v Telefusion Ltd*), can be a substantial reason for dismissal. If an appointment is expressed to be of a temporary nature, pending the return to work of an absent employee, this could also constitute grounds which a tribunal may feel justified a dismissal. In particular, the Employment Rights Act 1996, s 106 provides that in two specific instances the dismissal of a temporary employee will be regarded as a substantial reason. These are where a temporary replacement is taken in because there has been a suspension on medical grounds, or a temporary appointment has been made to replace a woman who is absent on the grounds of pregnancy, childbirth, maternity or adoption. In these cases the replacement must be informed in writing of the temporary nature of the appointment, and that he/she may be dismissed when the absent employee returns to work. However, although such dismissal amounts to a substantial reason, it will be without prejudice to the application of the rule that the tribunal must find that the employer has acted reasonably in treating the reason as sufficient ground for dismissal.

17.153 If an employee indicates that he intends to resign his employment, with the result that the employer engages a replacement in anticipation, the employer is entitled to refuse to accept a late notification that the employee has changed his mind, and his dismissal may be fair for some other substantial reason (*Ely v YKK Fasteners Ltd*).

17.154 An employment tribunal will not accept any reason advanced by the employer as coming within the definition of another substantial reason. In *Hedger v Davy & Co Ltd* the employer received a request from an employment agency for a reference in respect of the applicant. This was held not to be another substantial reason for the dismissal. And in *Wadley v Eager Electrical Ltd* the claimant was a valued worker who had been employed for 17 years. His wife, who worked at the same firm, was summarily dismissed for theft, and the employers felt that they had lost confidence and trust in the applicant. They also felt that his continued employment would have an adverse effect on customers. His dismissal was held not to be for some other substantial reason. It was unfair to dismiss an employee because some other person in the household was fairly dismissed. But a dismissal because of third party pressure may amount to some other substantial reason (*Davenport v Taptonholme for the Elderly*).

17.155 It must be remembered that even though a reason is capable of being another substantial reason for the dismissal, the employer must still act reasonably in treating that reason as a sufficient reason for dismissal. To do this, he should have a full investigation of the problem, and explore any alternatives which may be available (*Scott Packing and Warehousing Co v Paterson*). There is no absolute requirement that consultation with the employee should take place, but this is one of the factors to be taken into account in determining if the employer has acted reasonably (*Hollister v National Farmers' Union*). In *Johnson v Tesco Stores Ltd* the claimant made a false statement on his job application form. He was subsequently employed for 18 months before the falsity came to light, during which time he was perfectly satisfactory. Nonetheless he was dismissed, and this was held to be unfair. In *Debaughn v Star Cinemas (London) Ltd* it was contrary to the company's policy to employ people who had had previous criminal convictions, particularly for violence, and they dismissed a doorman who had been employed satisfactorily for 12 months when it was discovered that he had failed to disclose a previous conviction for assault. This was held to be fair. The distinction between these cases lies in the fact that in the former case, there was no real need to act on the information which had come to light, whereas in the latter case the firm's policy could not admit of exceptions for very sound reasons.

17.156 It is frequently useful for an employer to plead or argue 'some other substantial reason' in addition to another reason advanced, for this enables him to have two bites at the cherry! Thus, to dismiss an employee who has been sent to prison may be regarded as conduct or frustration or some other substantial reason. But whatever the 'label', the employer must always be prepared to show that he had acted reasonably in treating the reason as a sufficient reason for dismissing the employee (*Bouchaala v Trusthouse Forte Hotels Ltd*).

C. Dismissal for asserting a statutory right (ERA, s 104)

17.157 It will be unfair to dismiss an employee because:

(a) he has brought proceedings against an employer to enforce a relevant statutory right; or

(b) he has alleged that the employer has infringed a right of his which is a relevant statutory right.

17.158 The relevant statutory rights for the purposes of s 104 are as follows:

(a) all the rights contained in ERA for which the remedy for infringement is to make a complaint or reference to an employment tribunal;

(b) the following rights made under TULR(C)A – the right not to have the deduction of unauthorised or excessive trade union subscriptions, or unauthorised payment to the union's political fund, right not to have action taken short of dismissal on the ground of union membership or non-membership, right to have time off work for trade union duties or activities, or as a learning representative.

Identical rights are conferred by the Working Time Regulations, Part-time Workers (Prevention of Less Favourable Treatment) Regulations 2000, Fixed-term Employees (Prevention of Less Favourable Treatment) Regulations 2002, Transnational Information and Consultation of Employees Regulations 1999, and Transfer of Undertakings (Protection of Employment) Regulations 2006.

17.159 It will also be unfair to select a person for redundancy on any of the above grounds (see para 18.57).

17.160 The right will apply irrespective of the employee's length of service, because no qualifying period of continuous employment is required. Nor does the upper age limit apply.

17.161 It is immaterial whether or not the employee in fact has the right, or whether or not it has been infringed, as long as the employee makes the claim in good faith. Nor need the employee specify the right, as long as it is made reasonably clear to the employer what the right claimed to have been infringed was. Thus, for example, if an employee were to bring a claim before an employment tribunal alleging that he is entitled to a right contained in the Working Time Regulations, and he is dismissed in consequence, the dismissal would be in breach of s 104, irrespective of whether his claim was justified. Thus if an employee genuinely but mistakenly believes that he has the statutory right in question, or genuinely believes that an infringement of his statutory rights has occurred, a consequent dismissal would be unfair (*Philip Hodges & Co v Crush*). The employee cannot be expected to know the precise legal terminology of the right, or the section number of the statutory provision alleged to have been infringed, and it is sufficient if the employee makes it reasonably clear to the employer what right he is relying on (*Jiminez v Nelabrook Ltd*). It would appear that a mere proposal by the employer that a statutory right may be infringed (eg a proposal to reduce wages in circumstances which would amount to an unlawful deduction contrary to ERA, s 13) is not sufficient (*Mennell v Newell & Wright (Transport Contractors) Ltd*, below).

17.162 But the employee must be able to identify the right alleged to have been infringed by the employer, and if he cannot show that he ever made an allegation that the employer had been in breach of a statutory duty, then the allegation could not be the cause of his dismissal (*Mennell v Newell & Wright (Transport Contractors) Ltd*).

17.163 The interesting thing about this new right is that the 'dismissal' referred to in s 104 must inevitably include a constructive dismissal. Hence, if an employee feels that he is being deprived of his statutory rights, he can resign and make a claim accordingly.

D. Other dismissals

17.164 For dismissals on grounds of trade union membership or non-membership, in closed shop situations, lockouts, strikes, and industrial pressure, see Chapter 21. Dismissal on grounds of sex, race, disability or age are dealt with in Chapter 4, maternity dismissals in Chapter 6, and dismissals in health and safety cases in Chapter 11.

E. National security

17.165 As already noted, there is a special procedure to be adopted by employment tribunals when dealing with complaints made by members of the security service which involve issues of national security (see para 2.159).

Written reasons for dismissal (ERA, s 92)

17.166 When an employee is dismissed, either with or without notice, or where a limited-term contract terminates without being renewed, he is entitled to receive, on request, and within 14 days, a written statement of the reasons for his dismissal. This statement is admissible in any proceedings before a tribunal or a court. He will not be so entitled unless he has been continuously employed for one year (except for maternity or adoption reasons, see below).

A. Adequacy of the statement

17.167 To be adequate under s 92, the written statement must be such that anyone reading it can know the essential reasons for the dismissal. No particular technicalities are involved, and no particular form required (*Horsley Smith and Sherry Ltd v Dutton*). The employment tribunal must consider three issues, namely (a) was there a failure to provide written reasons, (b) was the failure unreasonable, and (c) are the particulars of reasons given inadequate or untrue?

17.168 The first issue will be largely a question of fact. The reasons must be contained in a document sent for the purpose of complying with the request. Filling in Form ET3 (respondent's reply to an application to an employment tribunal) is not sufficient compliance (*Rowan v Machinery Installations (South Wales) Ltd*). Nor is it sufficient compliance to refer to other documents, although the sending of documents which contain those reasons is sufficient compliance with s 92 (*Kent County Council v Gilham*).

17.169 On the second issue, the test of reasonableness is an objective one, ie the standard of behaviour to be expected from a reasonable employer. Thus in *Daynecourt Insurance Brokers Ltd v Iles* the employers ignored a request for written reasons for dismissal following an instruction from the police not to answer any correspondence or deal with the matter which was the subject of an investigation, and it was held that the failure to comply was reasonable in the circumstances. Equally, if the employer genuinely and reasonably believes that no dismissal had taken place then a failure to provide written reasons would be reasonable (*Broomsgrove v Eagle Alexander Ltd*). The fact that the employee knows of the reason does not render the failure to comply with the request reasonable.

17.170 Finally, the reason given by the employer must be the true reason for the dismissal, but it does not have to be a reason adequate enough to justify the dismissal. That is a matter for subsequent investigation should the employee pursue his claim for unfair dismissal (*Harvard Securities plc v Younghusband*).

17.171 But s 92 has to be strictly construed. In *Keen v Dymo Ltd* the employers sent the written reasons by second class post, so that these arrived a day outside the 14-day period. This was held to be an unreasonable refusal to supply written reasons.

17.172 If the employee does not make a request for written reasons, he cannot complain that the reasons which were given were untrue, and an employment tribunal has no power to make an award under s 92 in the absence of any such request (*Catherine Haigh Harlequin Hair Design v Seed*).

17.173 A complaint may be presented to an employment tribunal that the employer has unreasonably failed to provide a written statement, or that the statement which has been given is inadequate or untrue. If the tribunal finds the complaint well founded, it may make a declaration as to what it finds to be the employer's reasons for the dismissal, and must make an award of two weeks' pay (ERA, s 93). This award is not subject to the statutory maximum of £290 per week. The complaint can only be considered by an employment tribunal if it is presented together with a claim for unfair dismissal (ERA, s 93(3)).

B. Written reasons for dismissal on grounds of maternity or adoption (ERA, s 92(4), (4A))

17.174 A woman is entitled to written reasons for her dismissal if she is dismissed at any time while she is pregnant, or after her childbirth in circumstances in which her ordinary or additional maternity leave period ends by reason of her dismissal. She does not need to have the requisite period of continuous employment, and she must be given the written reasons irrespective of whether or not she makes a request for it. The same rule applies if an employee is dismissed while absent from work during an ordinary or additional adoption leave period.

Interim relief (ERA, ss 128–132)

17.175 If an employee complains that the reason for his dismissal was because he was exercising his rights under s 100(1)(a)–(b) (health and safety), s 101A(1)(d) (representative of the workforce for the purpose of the Working Time Regulations), s 102(1) (trustee of occupational pension schemes), s 103 (employee representative under TULR(C)A or Transfer of Undertakings Regulations), or s 103A (protected disclosure) he may make an application for interim relief. A similar application may be made under the provisions of TULR(C)A, ss 161–166 (dismissal for trade union membership and activities, etc) and TULR(C)A, Sch A1, para 161 (playing a role in proposing or opposing trade union recognition). The procedure and remedies are similar to those outlined at para 21.114.

Remedies for unfair dismissal

A. Reinstatement and re-engagement orders (ERA, s 113)

17.176 If an employment tribunal finds that the employee has been unfairly dismissed, it shall explain to him that it has the power to make an order that he be reinstated or re-engaged, and shall ask him if he wishes the tribunal to make such an order. If he expresses such a wish, the tribunal may make the necessary order.

17.177 The requirement for the employment tribunal to explain its powers to award reinstatement or re-engagement is mandatory. However, if there is a failure to do so (and in practice many tribunals do so fail) this will not render any other award made a nullity. The order made without compliance with s 113 will only be set aside if the employee has been prejudiced, or if he has suffered an injustice, in consequence of the failure (*Cowley v Manson Timber Ltd*).

17.178 If the order is for reinstatement, the employer shall treat the employee in all respects as if he had not been dismissed, and the tribunal may specify the amount of arrears in pay payable to the employee, and rights and privileges, including seniority and pension rights, which must be restored to him, and the date by which the order must be complied with. If the employee would have benefited from an improvement in his terms and conditions of employment had he not been dismissed, the order shall require him to have those improvements. If the tribunal orders re-engagement, this is an order that the employee be re-engaged by the employer or by his successor, or an associated employer, in employment comparable to that from which he was dismissed, or other suitable employment. The tribunal will specify the terms on which the re-engagement will take place, stating the identity of the employer, the nature of the employment, the remuneration, any arrears of pay, any rights or privileges which must be restored to him (including seniority and pension rights) and the date by which the order must be complied with. If in either case the tribunal makes an order in respect of arrears of pay it will take into account (for the purpose of reducing the employer's liability) any sums received by the applicant between the date of dismissal and the date of reinstatement or re-engagement, by way of wages in lieu of notice, *ex gratia* payments, remuneration received from another employer, social security benefits, and any other benefits as the tribunal thinks appropriate.

17.179 It must be stressed that the tribunal has a discretion in making either of these orders. It must first consider whether to make an order for reinstatement, and in doing so, it must take into account three considerations:

(a) whether the claimant wishes to be reinstated;

(b) whether it is practicable for the employer to comply with an order for reinstatement;

(c) where the claimant caused or contributed to some extent to the dismissal, whether it would be just to order his reinstatement.

If the tribunal decides not to make an order, it shall then consider whether to make an order for re-engagement, and if so, on what terms. Again, there are three considerations to take into account:

(a) any wish expressed by the claimant as to the nature of the order;

(b) whether it is practicable for the employer or his successor or an associated employer to comply with the order;

(c) where the claimant has caused or contributed to some extent to the dismissal, whether it would be just to order his re-engagement, and if so, on what terms (see *Boots Co plc v Lees-Collier*).

If a re-engagement order is made, it shall, so far as is reasonably practicable, be on terms which are as favourable as an order for reinstatement, unless the tribunal takes into account the contributory fault of the claimant.

17.180 The main restriction on making reinstatement or re-engagement orders appears to be the practicability of doing so. If a permanent replacement has been engaged in place of the dismissed employee, the tribunal shall not take this into account for the purpose of deciding whether it was practicable for the employer to comply with the order unless the employer shows:

(a) that it was not practicable for him to arrange for the dismissed employee's work to be done without engaging a permanent replacement; or

(b) that he engaged the replacement after the lapse of a reasonable time without having heard from the dismissed employee that he wished to be reinstated or re-engaged, and that when the employer engaged the replacement, it was no longer reasonable for him to arrange for the dismissed employee's work to be done except by a permanent replacement.

17.181 It is also submitted that earlier tribunal decisions on the impracticability of making reinstatement or re-engagement recommendations are still valid. For it should be noted that 'practicable' does not mean 'possible'. Thus the orders are unlikely to be made:

(a) if the dismissal was in a redundancy situation, or if reinstatement would result in redundancies (*Cold Drawn Tubes Ltd v Middleton*);

(b) the claimant is unfit for work (see *Rao v Civil Aviation Authority*); or

(c) if there is some friction or personal animosity either with the employer or with fellow-employees (*Coleman v Magnet Joinery Ltd*); or

(d) if the employer is a small firm, with few staff, reinstatement or re-engagement should only be ordered in exceptional circumstances, as there is a close personal relationship between the parties which may make such an order impracticable (*Enessy Co SA v Minoprio*); or

(e) if there is mistrust between the parties (*Nothman v London Borough of Barnet*); or

(f) if the order is likely to be ineffective (*ILEA v Gravett*); or

(g) if there has been a breakdown in trust or confidence between the employer and employee, eg if the dismissal was for alleged misconduct (*Wood Group Heavy Industrial Turbines Ltd v Crossan*); or

(h) if the employee's job has disappeared following a reorganisation (*Thamesdown Borough Council v Turrell*).

17.182 In other words, the practicability of ordering reinstatement or re-engagement must be looked at in a subjective and pragmatic sense, bearing in mind the particular circumstances of the case. The employer is entitled to give a logical and reasonable explanation why there are no vacancies, and to make a commercial judgment about the best interests of the business. An employment tribunal is not entitled to substitute its own views for those of management, provided the decision not to re-engage is in the bracket of reasonableness, for the test is whether it is practicable, not whether it is possible (*Port of London v Payne*). In practice, very few reinstatement or re-engagement orders are made, as very few applicants request this remedy.

17.183 If an employee is reinstated or re-engaged following an order to that effect from the employment tribunal, his continuity of employment is preserved, and the period between his dismissal and reinstatement or re-engagement counts towards his continuity (Employment Protection (Continuity of Employment) Regulations 1996). This also applies if reinstatement or re-engagement follows a compromise agreement, or action taken by a conciliation officer, or a claim based on a designated dismissal procedure or following an ACAS sponsored arbitration award.

B. Compensatory awards (ss 117–127A)

17.184 If the order for reinstatement or re-engagement is made, but its terms are not fully complied with, the tribunal may make an award of compensation of such amount as it thinks fit, having regard to the loss sustained by the claimant in consequence of the employer's failure to comply with those terms. There shall be deducted from any such award the amount of any award made because the dismissal is unfair due to a failure to follow the statutory dismissal procedure (ERA, s 117(2A)).

17.185 If an order is made, but the claimant is not reinstatement or re-engaged at all, then the tribunal will make an award of compensation. This will be under three headings:

(a) basic award

(b) compensatory award

(c) additional award.

Again, there shall be deducted from the compensatory award any award made because the dismissal was unfair due to a failure by the employer to follow the statutory dismissal procedure (ERA, s 123(8)).

17.186 If no order for reinstatement or re-engagement is made, the tribunal will make an award which will consist of:

(a) basic award

(b) compensatory award.

17.187 *Basic award (i).* In two instances this will amount to two weeks' pay, with a minimum of (currently) £290 per week. These are:

(a) Where an employee's contract is renewed, or he is re-engaged under a new contract, he is not regarded as having been dismissed under his old contract (s 138). If the terms and conditions of the new contract (including capacity and place in which he is employed) differs from the previous contract, and during the trial period the employer or employee terminate the contract for a reason connected with the difference, the employee will be treated as having been dismissed on the date on which his previous contract ended. If the reason for that dismissal was redundancy, he will be entitled to a minimum basic award of two weeks' pay (s 121(a)).

(b) Where there is an offer to renew the contract, or an offer of re-engagement under a new contract, and the provisions of the contract as to capacity and place of employment, and other terms and conditions would not differ from the old contract, or, if they do differ, but the offer constitutes an offer of suitable alternative employment, the employee is not entitled to a redundancy payment if he unreasonably refuses that offer (see para 18.28). This also applies if the employee unreasonably terminates the contract during the trial period. Nonetheless, he is entitled to a basic award of two weeks' pay (s 121(b)).

17.188 *Basic award (ii).* Where a dismissal has been held to be unfair because the employee was selected for dismissal because of trade union membership or activities (TULR(C)A, s 152), or because he was designated to carry out health and safety activities or was a health and safety representative (ERA, s 100(1)(a)–(b)), or because he was a workforce representative under the Working Time Regulations (ERA, s 101A(d)), or was a trustee of an occupational pension scheme (ERA, s 102(1)), or an employee representative for consultation purposes (ERA, s 103), or was selected for redundancy for any of these reasons, the minimum basic award shall be (currently) £4,000.

17.189 *Basic award (iii).* If the employee has been unfairly dismissed, and there has been a failure to carry out the statutory dismissal procedure (see para 12.39), and the basic award would otherwise be less than four weeks' pay, the employment tribunal shall increase the award to four weeks' pay, although it need not do so if it considers that the increase would result in an injustice to the employer (ERA, s 120(1A)).

17.190 *Basic award (iv).* The Employment Equality (Age) Regulations 2006 have altered the formula for the basic award, so as to eliminate all age related factors. The basic award will depend on the number of years the employee has been employed (with a maximum of 20 years' service to count) and his normal week's pay (capped). There is no lower or upper age limit, and the tapering provision which used to apply to employees over the age of 64 has been abolished. There will be a multiplier of one half of a week's pay for each year's service below the age of 21, one week's pay for each year's service between the ages of 22 and 40, and one and a half week's pay for each year's service over the age of 41.

17.191 The amount of the basic award can be reduced in three circumstances (ERA, s 122).

(a) If the employer has made an offer to reinstate the employee, so that in all respects he would be treated as if he had not been dismissed, and the employee unreasonably refuses that offer, the employment tribunal may reduce the basic award by an amount it thinks to be just and equitable. (Note that if the offer is made with different terms and conditions, an unreasonable refusal will not justify reducing the basic award, although it may be relevant to reduce the compensation award, because the employee has failed to mitigate his loss.)

(b) If the employee's conduct prior to the dismissal (or, where notice was given, before notice of dismissal) was such that it would be just and equitable to reduce (or further reduce) the basic award, the employment tribunal may do so. Normally, the conduct in question would have caused or contributed towards the dismissal, but this is not essential so far as the employment tribunal's powers under this section are concerned. Indeed, conduct which only comes to light after the dismissal (which occurred before the dismissal) may be grounds for reducing the basic award, eg if it is subsequently discovered that the employee had set up a rival business during his employment, or had been stealing from his employer. But misconduct during the notice period is not a ground for reducing the basic award, even though it would not be just and equitable to make that award, although it may be grounds for reducing the compensation award.

It is not permissible to make a reduction of the basic award on grounds of contributory conduct if the reason for the dismissal was redundancy, except in those cases where the dismissal was for an inadmissible reason (trade union membership or activities (TULR(C)A, s 157), designated safety representatives (s 100), occupational pension scheme trustee (s 102), and employee representative (ss 101A and 103)), when the minimum basic award of (currently) £4,000 applies (s 120). In such cases, if the employee caused or contributed to the dismissal, there may be a reduction in the amount by which the minimum basic award exceeds the normal basic award (s 122(3)). Thus, assume that the employee was dismissed for one of the inadmissible reasons, and his contribution towards the dismissal is assessed at 50%. Assume also that his normal basic award would have been £1,080 (based on four years' service). Since he is entitled to £4,000 by virtue of s 120, we deduct the former sum from the latter, leaving, £2,920; 50% of this sum is £1,460 which is deducted from £4,000, making a total basic award of £2,540. But if the conduct led to a selection for redundancy for trade union reasons (membership, non membership or activities) no reduction can be made for contributory conduct (TULR(C)A, s 155), eg if an employee was selected for redundancy because he refused to join a particular trade union.

(c) If an employee was dismissed for reason of redundancy, and was given a redundancy payment, the amount paid by the employer or awarded by a tribunal is to be deducted from the basic award. Normally, this would extinguish the basic award altogether. But the fact that a redundancy payment was made will not extinguish the basic award if the real reason for the dismissal was not in fact redundancy (*Boorman v Allmakes Ltd*).

17.192 The entitlement to a basic award is automatic once a dismissal is held to be unfair, and cannot be reduced on the ground that there has been no financial loss to the claimant (*Cadbury Ltd v Doddington*). It is payable even if no compensation award is made (*British United Shoe Machinery Co Ltd v Clarke*). It cannot be reduced on the ground that the claimant has failed to mitigate against his loss, because there is no provision to this effect (*Lock v Connell Estate Agents*). And it cannot be reduced when an *ex gratia* payment or a severance payment is made, unless it is made clear that the payment is in respect of all compensation an employee is entitled to should the employee subsequently bring a claim in an employment tribunal (*Chelsea Football Club and Athletic Co Ltd v Heath*). There is no requirement to make the same reduction in the basic and compensatory awards on the grounds of contributory conduct (*Optikinetics Ltd v Whooley*).

17.193 When assessing a week's pay for the purpose of the basic and compensation awards, the employment tribunal must not disregard the employer's obligation to pay the national minimum wage, and must base the award on what the employee should have received under the National Minimum Wage Act (see Chapter 8), rather than on what he actually received (*Paggetti v Cobb*).

C. Compensatory award (ERA, s 123)

17.194 This award will be such amount as the employment tribunal considers just and equitable in all the circumstances, having regard to the loss sustained by the claimant in consequence of the dismissal, in so far as that loss is attributable to action taken by the employer, including any expenses reasonably incurred by him, and the loss of any benefits which he might reasonably have expected to have had (ERA, s 123(1)). Once an employment tribunal finds blameworthy conduct on the part of the employee which brought about his dismissal, it must reduce the compensation award by some proportion, under the just and equitable rule (*Optikinetics Ltd v Whooley*).

17.195 Under the 'just and equitable rule' the employment tribunal has a wide discretion, even so far as awarding nil compensation in appropriate cases (*W Devis & Sons Ltd v Atkins*). For example, in *Courage Take Home Trade Ltd v Keys*, the claimant accepted a sum in settlement of his claim, but then continued with proceedings for unfair dismissal, because, as the settlement did not involve ACAS, it was not binding. The employment tribunal did not think it was just and equitable to make a compensatory award, and declined to do so. If, after the dismissal, it is discovered that the employee had been guilty of conduct before the dismissal which would have merited dismissal, then it may not be just and equitable to award full or any compensation (*W Devis & Sons Ltd v Atkins*), but post-termination conduct should not be taken into account (*Soros v Davison*). If a redundancy dismissal is unfair because of the lack of consultation, the employment tribunal should assess the likelihood of there being a fair dismissal had there been proper consultation, and make an appropriate award on that basis (*Mining Supplies (Longwall) Ltd v Baker*).

17.196 There is no limit on the amount of a week's pay for the purpose of calculating the financial loss, although there is a statutory maximum limit on the compensatory award of (currently) £58,400 (which can be exceeded if an additional award is made: see below). If the reason for the dismissal was because the employee acted as a health and safety representative (ERA, s 100) or because he made a protected disclosure (ERA, s 103A), or if he was selected for redundancy for either of those reasons, there is no limit on the amount of the compensatory award (s 124(1A)). The employment tribunal must assess the compensatory award judicially, and specify how it is made up, but they can, and do, use a 'broad brush' approach (*Norton Tool Co Ltd v Tewson*). Only financial loss may be taken into account, for the object is to compensate the claimant, not to punish the employer for his wrong behaviour. The manner of dismissal cannot be the subject of a compensatory award, unless there is evidence that this has caused financial loss, eg if it affected the claimant's reputation, making him less attractive to future employers. Thus, unlike awards made in discrimination cases, no award can be made for injured feelings. It follows that if the claimant has lost nothing, eg if he has obtained other employment immediately, no award under this head can be made other than awards made because of a failure to follow statutory procedures (see para 12.65). The assessment of past losses should not be too difficult, but, when assessing future losses, the employment tribunal must inevitably indulge in a form of speculation. The burden of proof is on the employee to show the past and/or future loss, but this should not prove to be an onerous task in practice (*Adda International Ltd v Curcio*).

17.197 Generally speaking, there are six headings to consider.

Immediate loss of earnings

17.198 The immediate loss is the loss incurred between the date the employment was terminated and the date when the employment tribunal assess the loss. In some cases, a considerable time may have elapsed between these two dates, while issues of procedure and/or liability are being argued. Nonetheless, if the employment tribunal feel that the claimant has taken reasonable steps to mitigate his loss, the length of time which may have elapsed is irrelevant (*Gilham v Kent County Council (No 3)*). The claimant's loss is assessed by reference to the net pay he would have received, although bonuses, overtime pay and pay increases can be taken into account, had these been likely (*Mullet v Brush Electrical Machines Ltd*). Tips which form part of normal remuneration (*Palmanor Ltd v Cedron*), expenses, to the extent they represent a profit in the hands of the employee (*S & U Stores v Wilkes*), and the loss of the opportunity to obtain an enhanced redundancy payment (*Lee v IPC Business Press Ltd*) are all part of the loss suffered. The loss of private use of a company car can be valued either by using the annual tables produced by the AA or RAC, or using the Inland Revenue calculations. Free or subsidised accommodation, private medical insurance, subsidised mortgage schemes (*UBAF Bank Ltd v Davis*) and luncheon vouchers are all benefits, the value of which can be calculated.

17.199 If, at the time when the employment tribunal assess the loss, the employee has obtained fresh employment with the same or a lower earnings, those earnings can be offset when assessing the net loss, but compensation does not end merely because an employee has found fresh employment (*Dench v Flynn & Partners*). A problem may arise if the employee obtains employment which is better paid, because then compensation will be based on his loss during the period of unemployment, but the excess between his old and new salary also falls to be deducted (*Ging v Ellward Lancs Ltd*). However, because this can lead to an unfair result on occasions, the employment tribunal may fall back on the 'just and equitable' principle, and ignore this rule, particularly when there has been a long period of time between the dismissal and the date when compensation is assessed (*Fentiman v Fluid Engineering Products Ltd*). The principles to be adopted in these circumstances were set out by the EAT in *Whelan v Richardson*, where it was held that loss of earnings should be calculated from the date of dismissal up to the date when the applicant obtains higher paid permanent employment. Similarly, credit must be given in respect of earnings from self-employment (*Justfern Ltd v D'Ingerthorpe*).

17.200 Income support and/or jobseekers' allowance is not deducted at this stage, but are subject to the recoupment provisions (see para 17.232). There are conflicting authorities on how invalidity benefit received should be treated (compare *Rubenstein v McGloughlin* and *Puglia v C James & Sons*), but the better view appears to be that it is correct to deduct the amount of invalidity benefit received from the compensation award (*Chan v London Borough of Hackney*). The same rule applies to incapacity benefit (*Morgans v Alpha Plus Security Ltd*). Housing benefit is differently treated, and should not be deducted (*Savage v Saxena*). Money received under an early retirement scheme or ill-health retirement scheme is not to be deducted (*Smoker v London Fire and Civil Defence Authority*).

17.201 If an employee is dismissed without notice and without pay in lieu of notice, but nonetheless finds work within what would have been the statutory notice period, he is still entitled to receive compensation for that period, because that is a legal entitlement, not to be deducted from the compensatory award (*TBA Industrial Products Ltd v Locke*). But if the employee's notice period would have been particularly long (eg on the premature termination of a fixed-term contract), the additional notice period will not be added to the compensatory award, on the ground that the employee should have mitigated against his loss (*Vaughan v Weighpack Ltd*). If the employee is dismissed without notice but given his proper entitlement in lieu of notice, credit for this sum must be given (*Addison v Babcock FATA Ltd*), although the EAT in Scotland appear to have come to a different conclusion on this point (*Finnie v Top Hat Frozen Foods*).

17.202 *Ex gratia* payments should always be offset, to the extent that these exceed the basic award (*Horizon Holidays Ltd v Grassi*), as should severance payments (*Darr v LRC Products Ltd*). Income tax rebates received by the employee during his period of unemployment should be ignored unless there are substantial sums involved (*MBS Ltd v Calo*).

Future loss

17.203 The employment tribunal must estimate the likely future loss, inevitably by indulging in speculation. They can take into account all the relevant circumstances, eg the age of the applicant and his general employability, his personal circumstances, his health (*Fougère v Phoenix Motors*), local employment conditions, the scarcity of jobs in a particular trade, industry, the current economic climate (*MacNeilgae v Arthur Roye Ltd*) and so on. They must form a judgment as to how long it will be before the claimant obtains comparable employment (*Courtaulds Northern Spinning Ltd v Moosa*). There is no objection, in theory, to consider making an award for the rest of the claimant's working life (see *Morganite Electrical Carbon Ltd v Donne*) although the existence of a maximum award of £58,400 will inevitably come into play at some point. If a claimant has become self-employed, future loss can be estimated to a point when he establishes an income comparable with that he has lost. As a general rule, the more senior the employee, the longer it may take him to obtain fresh employment, but the whole exercise is speculative. Of course, when assessing future loss, the employment tribunal will already have at its disposal much of the information needed on past losses, and will merely be projecting those losses forward for a period of time. Thus if the employee obtained new employment after the date of dismissal at a higher rate of pay, the employment tribunal should calculate the compensatory award from the date of the dismissal up to the date when the new employment commenced, and not up to the date when the tribunal makes the award (*Whelan v Richardson*, but see *Dench v Flynn & Partners*, below).

17.204 If the employment tribunal has evidence which would lead to the conclusion that the claimant would have lost his job anyway at some point in time, eg because of the redundancy situation, then that is a factor which should be taken into account when assessing the past and future loss of earnings (*Young's of Gosport Ltd v Kendell*). Equally, a supervening event, eg illness, which arises after the dismissal, and which causes the claimant to be out of work for a long time, is not a loss which is attributable to the action taken by the employer. But if the illness was brought on to some extent by the employer's action, that is a matter which an employment tribunal can take into account, for a certain period of time, at least (*Devine v Designer Flowers Wholesale Florist Sundries Ltd*).

17.205 Since the employment tribunal is projecting the claimant's loss into the future, there is authority for the proposition that the employer should receive a discount of around 2–5% for accelerated payment, although there may be a premium of a similar amount in respect of a delayed payment (*Melia v Magna Kansei Ltd*). It has been suggested that this brings into the calculations a complication which should not be introduced (*Les Ambassadeurs Club v Bainda*). Losses which are too remote from the employer's actions should also be excluded. For example, if the claimant obtained permanent employment, that is a fact which will normally break the chain of causation, so that if he has lost that employment at the time when the employment tribunal is assessing compensation, the subsequent period of unemployment is not a future loss which could have been contemplated (*Courtaulds Northern Spinning Ltd v Moosa*). But this rule is not one of universal application, for the ultimate duty of the employment tribunal is to make an award which is just and equitable (see *Dench v Flynn & Partners*, para 17.221). There is also an overlap between the question of remoteness and the claimant's duty to mitigate against his loss, which can usually be resolved by the application of the 'just and equitable' principle (*Simrad Ltd v Scott*).

In *Norton Tools Co Ltd v Tewson*, decided in 1972, it was held that only quantifiable pecuniary loss could be compensated for, and non-economic loss was not recoverable. In *Dunnachie v Kingston upon Hull City Council*, the Court of Appeal threw doubt on the correctness of that decision, holding that the provision in the Act which provided for compensation to be 'just and equitable in all the circumstances' could include a sum in respect of injury to feelings, pride and self-respect. However, on appeal, the decision in the *Dunnachie* case was reversed by the House of Lords, who held that no award for non-economic loss of that nature may be made under the statutory provisions.

Expenses

17.206 The employment tribunal may award to the claimant any expenses reasonably incurred by him in consequence of the unfair dismissal. This could include money spent seeking fresh employment, eg on travelling to interviews, on buying-selling a home in order to obtain employment in a different area, or on setting up a new business (*Gardiner-Hill v Roland Berger Technics Ltd*). However, legal expenses incurred in the bringing of the employment tribunal proceedings cannot be awarded under this heading, although there is a residue power for the employment tribunal to make an award of costs in appropriate cases (see para 20.102).

Loss of statutory rights

17.207 Since it will take some time before a claimant is employed in a new job long enough to obtain the benefit of a number of statutory rights, (in particular, he will have to wait for a further year before he is protected against a future unfair dismissal), the employment tribunals will usually award a modest sum of £200 by way of compensation for this loss (*S H Muffett Ltd v Head*). Also, in the case of a claimant who had a long period of service with his former employer, it is possible to make an award in respect of the loss of the right to have a long period of statutory notice (*Arthur Guinness Son & Co (Great Britain) Ltd v Green*).

Loss of pension rights

17.208 The loss suffered by a claimant under this heading will sometimes depend on the type of pension scheme, ie final salary scheme or money purchase scheme. The former scheme does not depend on contributions to the fund by the employer and/or employee, whereas the latter schemes are so dependent. So far as the compensatory award is concerned, a claimant may have lost (a) pension rights accruing to him since the dismissal, (b) future pension rights, and (c) the loss of enhancement of accrued pension rights. To assist in resolving and quantifying the loss, reference may be made to the Government's Actuary's Guidelines *Industrial Tribunals–Compensation for loss of pension rights*; see also *Clancy v Cannock Chase Technical College*.

Additional award of four weeks' pay

17.209 If an employee is regarded as being unfairly dismissed because of a failure by the employer to complete the statutory dismissal procedure (see para 12.74) (whether or not the dismissal is unfair for any other reason), and an order is made for reinstatement or re-engagement, the employment tribunal shall also make an award of four weeks' pay, although this need not be done if it considers that such an award would result in an injustice to the employer (ERA, s 112 (5)(6)).

Increased compensation

17.210 If an award for unfair dismissal falls to be increased because of a failure by the employer to complete the statutory dismissal procedure (see para 12.74) the compensation award may be increased by between 10% and, if the tribunal consider it to be just and equitable to do so, up to 50%, unless there are exceptional circumstances which would make the increase unjust or inequitable (Employment Act 2002, s 31).

D. Reducing the compensatory award (ERA, s 123(4), (6))

Mitigation of loss

17.211 A dismissed employee is under a duty to mitigate against his loss so far as possible (*Scottish and Newcastle Breweries plc v Halliday*). This means that he should take reasonable steps to obtain other employment, taking into account his skills, personal circumstances, health, etc (*Fourgère v Phoenix Motor Co Ltd*). Whether a claimant has taken such reasonable steps is a question of fact in each case (*Gardiner-Hill v Rolands Berger Technics Ltd*). Thus, if an employer changes his mind about a dismissal, or recognises that it is unfair, and offers reinstatement or re-engagement on suitable terms which the employee unreasonably refuses, this may indicate that he has not taken reasonable steps to mitigate against his loss, and compensation may be reduced accordingly (*Hepworths Ltd v Comerford*). A failure by an employee to invoke an internal appeals machinery is not a failure to mitigate against the loss (*William Muir (Bond 9) Ltd v Lamb*), for the rules relating to mitigation apply to conduct after the dismissal (*McAndrew v Prestwick Circuits Ltd*). However, that failure may now fall to be considered under the provisions contained in the Employment Act 2002, s 31 (see para 17.224).

17.212 If, after being dismissed, the claimant decides to have a complete change of career, which involves retraining, the employment tribunal may find that such action was reasonable, and the loss of income during the training period may be the subject of compensation. A failure to seek alternative employment in such circumstances is not a failure to mitigate against the loss (*Orthet Ltd v Vince-Cain*).

17.213 The burden of proof lies on the employer to show that the claimant has failed to mitigate against his loss (*Fyfe v Scientific Furnishing Ltd*). An employment tribunal is not bound to consider this heading unless it is raised by the employer, along with some supporting evidence. The employment tribunal should identify the steps taken to mitigate the loss, find the date by which such steps would have produced an alternative income, and then reduce the amount of compensation by the amount of income which would have been earned (*Savage v Saxena* and see *Hardy v Polk (Leeds) Ltd*).

17.214 So far as mitigation is concerned, the following principles were laid down by the Court of Appeal in *Wilding v British Telecommunications plc*:

(a) it is the duty of the employee to act as a reasonable person unaffected by the prospect of compensation from his former employer;

(b) the onus is on the former employer as the wrongdoer to show that the employee has failed in his duty to mitigate his loss by unreasonably refusing an offer of re-employment;

(c) the test of reasonableness is an objective one based on the totality of the evidence;

(d) in applying that test, the circumstances in which the offer was made or refused, the attitude of the former employer, and all the surrounding circumstances, including the employee's state of mind, should be taken into account;

(e) the court or tribunal should not be too stringent in its expectations of the injured party.

Contributory conduct

17.215 Where an employment tribunal finds that the dismissal was to any extent caused or contributed to by any action of the claimant, it shall reduce the amount of the compensatory award by such proportion as it thinks just and equitable, having regard to that finding (ERA, s 123(6)). In *Nelson v BBC (No 2)*, the Court of Appeal stated that there are three matters which must be taken into account under this heading. First, the action of the employee must be culpable or blameworthy; second, that action must have caused or contributed towards the dismissal; and, third, it must be just and equitable to reduce the compensatory award by the specified proportion. For example, in *Scottish Co-operative Wholesale Society Ltd v Lloyd* a dismissal was held to be unfair because no specific warnings had been given to the claimant. But he had failed to reply to complaints which had been made against him, failed to obey certain instructions, and failed to achieve a modest sales target. All these factors were held to be conduct which contributed towards the dismissal and were therefore grounds for reducing the compensatory award. A failure to follow works rules, using company property for private purposes, unco-operative conduct, failure to apologise for wrongful acts (eg swearing at a manager), failure to explain unauthorised absences, a refusal to give an explanation for certain conduct, failing to return to work on time after holidays, and so on, have all been held to be grounds for reducing the compensatory award.

17.216 Since the conduct must in some way be blameworthy or culpable, matters which are beyond the employee's control, eg ill health (*Slaughter v C Brewer & Sons Ltd*) ought not to be taken into account. Similarly, an employee who is incompetent or incapable does not contribute to his dismissal, provided he is trying his best (*Kraft Food Ltd v Fox*), although if an employee is lazy, indolent, or does not make an effort to improve or avoid errors, he does so contribute. Further, the conduct in question does not have to be the main reason for the dismissal; it is sufficient (for the purpose of reducing the compensatory award) for it to have played a material part in the dismissal (*Robert Whiting Designs Ltd v Lamb*). A senior employee who is dismissed for serious misconduct must expect to have his compensatory award reduced substantially, for a higher standard of conduct is expected from him (*McPhail v Gibson*).

17.217 It is unlikely that the employment tribunal would reduce the compensatory award in cases of constructive dismissal, but there is no reason in principle why this cannot be done, because the employee's conduct may have played a material part in the events which led to his resignation (*Morrison v Amalgamated Transport and General Workers' Union*). For example, in *Polentarutti v Autokraft Ltd*, the employee machined a number of defective hubcaps. Subsequently, the employer refused to pay him for working overtime, and he resigned, claiming constructive dismissal. Although his dismissal was held to be unfair, the employment tribunal reduced the compensatory award by two-thirds on the ground that his poor workmanship contributed to the dismissal. The EAT dismissed an appeal by the employee, holding that there was a sufficient link between the events in question which justified a reduction in the award.

17.218 If a claimant was dismissed on the ground of his non-membership of a trade union, no reduction can be made in the compensatory award because he refused to join a trade union (see *Transport and General Worker's Union v Howard*). Nor can a reduction be made if the dismissal was because of his trade union membership or activities (TULR(C)A, s 155). If an employee is dismissed because he took part in a strike, and it is subsequently held that that dismissal was unfair on ground of selective re-engagement (see para 21.83), a reduction for contributory conduct should not be made merely because he took part in the strike. It is only where there was some individual blameworthy conduct additional to or separate from the participation in industrial action that the employment tribunal should consider reducing the compensatory award (*Crosville Wales Ltd v Tracey*).

17.219 Contributory conduct has resulted in some cases with a reduction as high as 80–90%, and for some time there was doubt as to whether it was a proper reduction to make, because there appears to be a logical inconsistency in saying that an employee was treated unfairly, and yet contributed to that extent towards his dismissal. However, in *Maris v Rotherham Corpn* the House of Lords thought that there was no particular problem in finding a dismissal unfair, yet reducing the compensatory award by 100%. Compensation should only be awarded when it is just and equitable to do so, and it cannot be just to award compensation when the employee was totally responsible for his dismissal. Nor is there an inconsistency in finding a dismissal unfair yet not awarding compensation.

17.220 The assessment of the percentage reduction to be taken into account because of contributory conduct is essentially a question of fact, to be determined by the employment tribunal (*Hollier v Plysu Ltd*).

Remoteness of loss

17.221 The tribunal must compensate the employee for the loss caused by the employer's wrongful conduct. That loss does not cease when the employee finds new alternative employment, because it is quite possible for the loss to continue. Thus, if the new employment is at a lower rate of pay, or is of a temporary nature, or entails additional expense by way of travel, relocation etc, these factors can be taken into account when assessing the compensation. In *Dench v Flynn & Partners*, the claimant was unfairly dismissed. She obtained employment with another firm but this only lasted for two months. The Court of Appeal held that the tribunal was wrong to limit the compensation award up to the time when she had obtained the new employment. The question was whether her losses were attributable to her unfair dismissal.

17.222 If an employee decides not to seek other employment, but to make a career change by going on a training course a tribunal may take the view that this is a reasonable course to take, having regard to the employee's age, the state of the employment market, the level of remuneration, the viability of the course, etc. However, there may well come a point in time when the loss suffered by the employee is too remote from the employer's wrongful action. Thus in *Simrad Ltd v Scott* an electronics technician was unfairly dismissed. She decided to change career and took a course in nursing. Although the tribunal thought that she had acted reasonably in taking up a new career, the EAT held that compensation was not payable from the time she commenced the nursing course, because this was too remote to be attributed to the actions of the employer. However, a contrary conclusion appears to have been reached in *Orthet Ltd v Vince-Cain*, see para 17.212).

17.223 In some cases, it may well be reasonable for the employee to become self-employed, and this should not be held against him, when weighed against his employment prospects generally. In *Gardiner-Hill v Roland Berger Technics* a 55-year-old managing director acted reasonably in setting up his own specialised business. Clearly, his initial loss was greater than if he had attempted to obtain immediate employment, but the loss was not too remote, although it could not be expected to go on indefinitely! Expenses reasonably incurred in setting up a new business are not too remote, but again, a sensible limit should be imposed.

Failure to complete statutory procedure

17.224 If an employee fails to complete the statutory disciplinary and dismissal procedure (see para 12.74) the employment tribunal can reduce any award by 10% and, if it thinks it just and equitable to do so, by up to 50%, unless there are exceptional circumstances which would make the reduction unjust or inequitable (Employment Act 2002, s 31).

E. Order of adjustments to compensation awards

17.225 The tribunal must first ascertain the employee's loss in consequence of the dismissal, insofar as that loss is attributable to the action of the employer. The following adjustments to that amount may be made in the following order, where applicable:

(a) a deduction of any payment made to the employee as compensation for the dismissal (eg a payment in lieu of notice, or an *ex gratia* payment, but not an enhanced redundancy payment) (*Digital Equipment Co Ltd v Clements*);

(b) a deduction of any sum earned by the employee by way of mitigation of the loss, or to reflect the failure by the employee to mitigate against the loss (ERA, s 123(4));

(c) a percentage reduction under the *Polkey* principle, reflecting the fact that the employer would have a fair reason for the dismissal had the relevant contractual disciplinary procedure been followed (*Rao v Civil Aviation Authority*);

(d) an increase in the compensation because the employer has failed to follow the statutory dismissal/disciplinary procedure or a decrease in compensation because the employee has failed to comply with the statutory procedure (eg by failing to comply with a requirement of the procedure, or to exercise a right of appeal (Employment Act 2002, s 31);

(e) an increase because the employer has failed to provide written particulars of employment (Employment Act 2002, s 38);

(f) a percentage reduction because the employee has contributed to the dismissal (ERA, s 123(6));

(g) the deduction of any enhanced redundancy payment to the extent that it exceeds the basic award (ERA, s 123(7));

(h) a deduction under the recoupment provisions.

17.226 After all these adjustments have been made, the statutory cap of £58,400 is applied.

F. Additional award (ERA, s 117)

17.227 It will be recalled that if an employer totally ignores a tribunal order to reinstate or re-engage the employee, an additional award can be made. This order should not be made if the employer satisfied the tribunal that it was not practicable to comply with the order, but since the tribunal will have already considered this point when making the order (see above) it will presumably be open to the employer to adduce new evidence as to why it is not practicable to do so. Otherwise, if re-engagement or reinstatement is ordered and not complied with, and the reason for the dismissal was because of race, sex or disability discrimination, or victimisation for trade union membership, employee representation, pension scheme trustee, breach of working time provisions, or health and safety reasons, there will be an additional award of between 26 and 52 weeks' pay. A week's pay for the purpose of the additional award shall not exceed £290.

17.228 However, in the case of a highly paid employee, or where proceedings have been considerably delayed, the total of the maximum of the basic, compensatory and additional awards may not be adequate to meet the loss actually suffered and it may be cheaper not to comply with the reinstatement order. In such cases, ERA, s 124(3) enables an employment tribunal to make a compensation award which is at least equal to the amount of pay lost between the date of dismissal and what should have been the date of reinstatement or reengagement, to show their disapproval of the employer's decision (see *Selfridges Ltd v Malik*), at the same time taking into account the employee's conduct and failure to mitigate against his loss (*Mabirizi v National Hospital for Nervous Diseases*).

17.229 Severence payments made may be deducted from the additional award to the extent that the basic and compensatory awards are exceeded (*Darr v LRC Products Ltd*).

G. Interest on awards

17.230 By the Employment Tribunals (Interest) Order 1990, interest is payable on all tribunal awards (but not the recoupment element) after 42 days from the date the decision is recorded and sent to the parties. Interest is also payable on awards made by the EAT. Any award by way of costs or expenses is excluded. If on a review or appeal the award is varied, interest accrues on the amount as varied. However, by the Employment Tribunals (Interest on Awards in Discrimination Cases) Regulations 1996, interest on awards made in respect of injury to feelings may be made from the date of the act of discrimination to which the complaint relates.

17.231 The rate of interest is the rate currently prescribed under the Court Funds Rules 1987 and the Act of Sederunt (Interest in Sheriff Court Decrees or Extracts) 1975.

H. Recoupment of unemployment benefit

17.232 Under the heading of the compensation award, a sum of money is ascertained as the loss suffered, and the tribunal will then deduct from that sum the amount of jobseekers' allowance which the claimant has received. In fact, this amounts to the Government providing a subsidy to the employers, and thus regulations have been passed enabling the Government to recoup this money from the employer (see Employment Protection (Recoupment of Jobseekers' Allowance and Income Support) Regulations 1996). The consequence is that the tribunal must ascertain the prescribed element (which is the gross loss of earnings from the date of dismissal until the date of the hearing), and this may be withheld from the claimant until the Secretary of State has served a notice on the respondent to pay the whole or part of the prescribed element to the Department. When this has been received, the Secretary of State will pay to the claimant the sum due less the jobseekers' allowance he has received. Recoupment only applies in respect of the period for which compensation is assessed (*Hosnan v Al Baca Ltd*).

17.233 Recoupment does not apply when a settlement is reached without a tribunal hearing, because private settlements (with or without the assistance of the conciliation officer) are not within the scope of the regulations.

18

Redundancy

18.1 The basic purpose of the Redundancy Payments Act 1965 was to compensate a long-serving employee for the loss of a right which he has in a job. There may be other benefits or advantages, such as the need to encourage mobility of labour, redistribute economic skills, and assist in the process of rationalisation of resources, but whether such objects are being achieved must be a matter for the economist rather than the lawyer. The compensation paid is in respect of the loss suffered, and is not intended as a benefit to tide the redundant employee over a period of difficulty. Thus if a person is made redundant, he is entitled to his payment even if he obtains employment elsewhere immediately; similarly, he is entitled to jobseekers' allowance in addition to his redundancy money.

18.2 The Act has been repealed and replaced by corresponding provisions in the Employment Rights Act 1996, and in this chapter appropriate references will be made to the latter Act. The provisions relating to collective redundancies are to be found in the Trade Union and Labour Relations (Consolidation) Act 1992 as amended.

Provisions of the Employment Rights Act 1996

A. Persons covered by the Act

18.3 The Act applies to 'employees', ie persons who have entered into a contract of service or apprenticeship. In order to qualify generally, the employee must have at least two years' continuous employment with that employer (but see Redundancy Payments (Continuity of Employment in Local Government, etc) (Modification) Order 1999, and Redundancy Payments (National Health Service) (Modification) Order 1993, which make provisions for continuity of employment for certain local government and health service employees who move from one employer to another).

18.4 The usual problem arises with the definition of the term 'employee', illustrated, perhaps, by *Challinor v Taylor* (see para 2.26), which shows one of the disadvantages of being self-employed. A partner is not an employee for redundancy purposes (*Burgess v O'Brien*), nor is a clergyman working at a Mission (*Parker v Orr*). A managing director or director of a company who has executive responsibilities may claim if he has a service contract, but in *Buchan v Secretary of State for Employment* it was held that a person who is a controlling shareholder of a company is always able to block his dismissal, and therefore he cannot be an employee for redundancy payment purposes. However, the decision has been doubted (see *Sellars Arenascene Ltd v Connolly*, para 2.12). Nor does the appointment of a receiver alter the position, because if he was not an employee before that appointment, he cannot be one by reason of the appointment. It follows that the Secretary of State was not obliged to make a redundancy payment out of the National Insurance Fund to the controlling director of a company which went into receivership. The EAT further suggested that *Lee v Lee's Air Farming Ltd* (see para 2.11) could not be relied on in the context of employment protection legislation to support the view that a controlling shareholder of a company could also be an employee of that company. A person may pay a self-employed insurance stamp, and yet be regarded as an employee, for, as we have already seen, this fact is not conclusive evidence as to the true status. The matter is one to be decided in each case on its own special facts.

B. What is dismissal? (s 136)

18.5 A dismissal takes place if:

(a) the employer terminates the contract (with or without notice);

(b) a fixed-term contract expires without being renewed;

(c) the employee is employed under a limited-term contract and the contract terminated automatically on the completion of a particular task or upon the occurrence or non-occurrence of a specific event, without the employment being renewed (whether under the same contract or otherwise);

(d) the employee terminates the contract with or without notice in circumstances which are such that he is entitled to do so by reason of the employer's conduct (*Millbrook Furnishing Industries Ltd v McIntosh*); and

(e) the employment is terminated by the death, dissolution, liquidation of the employer, or the appointment of a receiver.

18.6 We have seen in Chapter 3 that a variation of a contract may amount to a new agreement. If the variation is accepted by both sides, then there is no dismissal, and continuity of employment is preserved. But a variation unilaterally imposed by the employer may amount to a dismissal. In *Marriott v Oxford and District Co-operative Society (No 2)*, a foreman was told that he would be employed at a lower status and at a reduced rate of pay. This was held to be a dismissal. If the employee accepts the changed situation for a short time under protest there will still be a dismissal, though clearly there will come a point when he will be deemed to have accepted the change if he continues in employment. If the express or implied terms of the contract permit a variation, then no dismissal takes place if the employer exercises his rights thereunder. In *McCaffrey v EE Jeavons & Co Ltd* an express term of the contract stated that the employee should work anywhere in the United Kingdom. He was asked to move from Bristol to Reading, but he refused. His subsequent resignation was held not to amount to a dismissal.

18.7 If the employer and employee mutually agree to 'part company' this will not be a dismissal, unless there is a clear intention to this effect. But the fact that a contract specifically states that it can only be determined by mutual consent or with appropriate notice does not mean that if appropriate notice has not been given it must have been determined by mutual consent (*Hellyer Bros v Atkinson*). For example, some employers may call for 'volunteers' to be made redundant, and they will qualify for payments despite their willingness to be dismissed (*Burton, Allton and Johnson Ltd v Peck*) but a mutual agreement whereby the employee accepts terms for early retirement does not constitute a dismissal (*Birch and Humber v University of Liverpool*). If an employee is given the option of being transferred to part-time working, or being made redundant, and he chooses the latter option, there is a dismissal for reason of redundancy, and it is not a consensual termination (*Lassman v De Vere University Arms Hotel*).

18.8 If an employee is told that there may be possible redundancies in the future, he may be penalised if he acts precipitously. In *Morton Sundour Fabrics Ltd v Shaw* a foreman was warned of impending redundancies, and he left the firm to take other employment. His initiative went unrewarded, for it was held that as he had not been dismissed, he was not entitled to a redundancy payment (see also *International Computers v Kennedy*).

18.9 As long as the employee is on the books of the firm, he is still employed, even though he is not working or not being paid. In *Marshall v Harland & Wolff Ltd* the employee was absent from work for 18 months because of illness. The company then decided to close down the works, and gave him four weeks' notice of dismissal. It was held that he was nonetheless entitled to a redundancy payment, for the employers had not discharged the burden of showing that the contract had come to an end by virtue of frustration through illness.

18.10 An employer may dismiss an employee with appropriate notice. If, during the period of that notice, the employee gives a written counter-notice, stating that he intends to leave before the notice expires, the employee is still regarded as having been dismissed. However, the employer is not bound to accept the counter-notice, and may (again in writing) inform the employee before the end of the counter-notice that he does not accept it, and require him to work until the expiry of the original period of notice. The sanction is that the employer may contest the redundancy payment, and the tribunal has power to reduce it either in whole or in part, as it thinks just and equitable. On the other hand, if there is a mutual agreement that the employee may leave early, this constitutes a variation of the employer's notice, not a consensual termination of the contract (see para 17.64). The employee, therefore, will still be regarded as having been dismissed (*McAlwane v Boughton Estates Ltd*).

C. Dismissal for reason of redundancy (s 139)

18.11 For a claim to be made, the employee must be dismissed for reason of redundancy. In *Sanders v Ernest A Neale Ltd* employees went on a work-to-rule campaign in protest against management actions. The employers sacked them, and eventually the factory closed down. It was held that they were not entitled to redundancy payments. They were dismissed because they would not give an undertaking to work normally, and the dismissals caused the redundancy, rather than the redundancy bringing about the dismissals (see *Baxter v Limb Group of Companies*, para 21.95). There is a statutory presumption (s 163(2)) that if an employee is dismissed, it is presumed to have been for the reason of redundancy unless the contrary is proved. The burden of proof is on the employer to show the reason, and if none is forthcoming, or if the tribunal does not accept the reason as a genuine one, the statutory presumption will arise. However, if the employer does show a reason other than redundancy, the question may arise as to whether the dismissal was fair or unfair, but there will be no liability to redundancy payments.

18.12 A dismissal shall be for reason of redundancy if it is wholly or mainly attributable to:

(a) the fact that the employer has ceased, or intends to cease, to carry on that business for the purposes for which the employee was employed; or

(b) the employer has ceased or intends to cease to carry on that business in the place where the employee was employed; or

(c) the fact that the requirements of that business for employees to carry out work of a particular kind, or for them to carry out that work in the place where they were so employed, have ceased or diminished or are expected to cease or diminish.

Cessation of business

18.13 This is a recognisable situation which produces a few legal problems. In *Gemmell v Darngavil Brickworks Ltd* the firm closed down temporarily for a period of 13 weeks so that repairs could be carried out, and the dismissed employees were held to be redundant, as a temporary cessation is within the meaning of the Act. If the part of the business where the employee works is closed down, but the rest of the business (in its corporate sense) carries on, there is still a cessation of the business.

The employer moving his place of business

18.14 Section 139(1)(a)(ii) provides that a dismissal shall be for reason of redundancy if it is due to the fact that the employer has ceased to carry on business in the place where the employee was employed. According to a recent decision of the EAT, this is a factual matter, not a contractual one. In other words, the test to be applied is where, in fact, the employee worked, not where, under his contract, he was required to work. Thus in *Bass Leisure Ltd v Thomas*, the employee worked from the company's depot in Coventry. It was then decided to close the depot, and transfer it to a suburb of Birmingham, some 20 miles away. Her contract stated that the employer reserved the right to transfer her to any other alternative place of work in order to meet the needs of the business. After working from the new depot for a short while, she found that it involved too much travelling, and she resigned, claiming a redundancy payment. The EAT held that the place where she was employed was at Coventry, and that her contractual terms were evidential in defining the place of her employment. However, it was not permissible to take into account those terms which permitted a variation of the place of employment. The EAT also held that earlier decisions, which take into account mobility clauses (eg *United Kingdom Atomic Energy Authority v Claydon*) were not to be followed. This view has been given the approval of the Court of Appeal in *High Table Ltd v Horst*, where it was stated that the true test is a factual one, to be determined by the circumstances, and the fact that there was a mobility clause in the contract did not mean that 'the place where the employee was employed' extended to every place where he could be employed. If an employee only worked at one location for the purpose of his employer's business, the place where he was employed cannot be extended merely because there was a mobility clause. However, if an employee worked in different places, the contract would be helpful in determining the extent of the place where he was employed.

However, the test of the suitability of alternative work (see below) would still need to be met.

18.15 If the employer moves his place of work, whether the move is sufficient to constitute a redundancy situation will be a question of fact, depending on the distance between the old and the new premises, and the resultant inconvenience caused to the employees affected. In *Managers (Holborn) Ltd v Hohne*, the claimant was the manageress of premises in Holborn. The company decided to move its premises to Regent Street, a short distance away. It was held that it could not be said that there was an implied term in her contract that she would only work in Holborn. Both premises were in Central London, and easily accessible. To hold that the employers had broken the contract would mean that it would have been a breach had the employers moved just around the corner, even though the claimant's work or her travel had been completely unaffected.

Surplus labour

18.16 In this situation the employer requires fewer employees for existing work (*Carry All Motors Ltd v Pennington*), or there is less work for existing employees (*Chapman v Goonvean and Rostowrack China Clay Co*), and consequently some are redundant. The redundancy can arise because the work has been reorganised, thus requiring fewer employees to do the same work, or because of the introduction of labour-saving devices, or a change in the work pattern which requires the same number of employees but a different kind of skill, or one to whom different terms and conditions of employment will apply. But the time of day in which the work is to be performed does not make it 'work of a particular kind' so that if there is a reduction in the need for night workers, who are thus transferred to day working, this does not amount to a redundancy. In *Johnson v Nottinghamshire Combined Police Authority*, clerks were employed from 9.30am to 5.30pm. It was decided to introduce a shift system whereby they would work from 8.00am to 3.00pm and from 1.00pm to 8.00pm in alternate weeks. The clerks refused to do the shift work, and were dismissed. It was held that the change in the hours was to promote greater efficiency, and they were not entitled to redundancy payments (see also *Barnes v Gilmartin Associates*).

18.17 This reasoning was confirmed by the Court of Appeal in *Lesney Products & Co Ltd v Nolan*, where the company reorganised its working hours so that instead of the employees working one long day shift plus overtime, they were required to work two day shifts. Employees were offered work on the double day shift, and those who refused were dismissed. It was held that they were not entitled to redundancy payments. A redundancy only arises if there is a change in the terms and conditions of employment due to the fact that the employer's need for work of a particular kind is ceasing or diminishing. A reorganisation of work which results in reduced earning does not produce a redundancy situation if there is still the need for the same number of employees doing the same overall work, and the only change is that they earn less wages. The law should not inhibit the ability of the employer to reorganise the workforce so as to improve efficiency. The fact that overtime is reduced does not create a redundancy, if the employer's requirements for the work to be done, and the employees to do the work, are the same as before. But if an employee is on a temporary contract, which is not renewed, this can be a redundancy, even though it is known at the time of his appointment that there would be no work for him at the end of the period. ERA, s 136(1)(b) clearly provides that a failure to renew a fixed-term contract is a dismissal for redundancy purposes, and this would be unnecessary if there was no entitlement to a redundancy payment on the expiry of such a contract (*Lee v Nottinghamshire County Council*).

18.18 In *Hindle v Percival Boats Ltd* the claimant was engaged in repairing wooden boats. The amount of work was declining because of the introduction of fibreglass, and it was uneconomical to retain his services, so he was dismissed because 'he was too good and too slow'. Although he was not replaced (a fact which is sometimes used to determine whether or not a redundancy exists) his work was carried out by other employees working overtime. A majority of the Court of Appeal thought that the employers had rebutted the presumption of redundancy. In another leading case (*North Riding Garages Ltd v Butterwick*) the employee was the manager of a repair workshop. New employers took over the business, and introduced new working methods to which the employee could not adapt. He was dismissed for incompetence and inefficiency, and applied for a redundancy payment. It was held that if the new methods had so altered the nature of the work that there was a lessening of the work of a kind he was formerly employed to do, this would amount to redundancy. On the facts, however, the overall requirements of the firm had not changed. It was the inability of the employee to change and adapt to new methods which brought about his dismissal.

18.19 In considering the definition of redundancy, earlier cases appear to have concentrated on the work which the employee actually did (the function test) and the work which the employee was obliged to do under his contract (the contract test); but in the recent case of *Safeways Stores plc v Burrell* it was stated that both these approaches were wrong, and that it is the statutory definition which must be considered. The true test requires employment tribunals to consider whether there was a diminution or cessation in the employer's requirement for *employees* to carry out work of a particular kind, and not to focus on the work of the individual employee.

18.20 The issue was finally resolved by the House of Lords in *Murray v Foyle Meats Ltd* where it was held that the key word on which tribunals should concentrate is 'attributable'. Thus if a dismissal of an employee was 'attributable' to a diminution of the employer's need for employees, then it is irrelevant to consider either the contractual obligations or the functions which the employee performed.

D. Transferred redundancy

18.21 If an employee is redundant, but, in accordance with a redundancy procedure he is retained in another post because he has seniority, and the holder of that other post is consequently dismissed, can the latter claim that he was redundant? Such transferred or 'bumping redundancy' has been considered in a number of cases, the prevalent view being that such a claim is valid and statutorily correct. Thus in *Elliott Turbomachinery v Bates*, a redundant employee was transferred to the claimant's department, 'bumping' the applicant out of a job. It was held that he was redundant. This line of cases was supported by the EAT in *Safeway Stores Ltd v Burrell*, but more recently another division of the EAT has expressed disagreement (*Church v West Lancashire NHS Trust*), where it was stated that a bumped employee was not dismissed for reason of redundancy, but rather because of the application of a procedure which required the dismissal of that employee to complete a reorganisation.

18.22 However, in *Murray v Foyle Meats Ltd* (above) the House of Lords approved *Safeway Stores Ltd v Burrell*, and thus a transferred redundancy is still a redundancy under the Act.

E. Presumption of redundancy

18.23 Section 163(2) of ERA provides that if there is a dismissal, it is presumed to be by reason of redundancy, unless the contrary is proved. Thus if two employees are dismissed, although only one is redundant, they are both entitled to rely on the statutory presumption (*Willcox v Hastings*) in the absence of evidence to the contrary.

F. Renewal or re-engagement (ERA, s 138)

18.24 If the employee's contract of employment is actually renewed, or he is re-engaged under a new contract made before the end of his previous contract, and the renewal or re-engagement takes place immediately on the end of that employment, or within four weeks thereof, he will not be regarded as having been dismissed under the old contract. This does not apply if the new contract differs, as to capacity, place of employment, or other terms and conditions of employment.

18.25 The employee is entitled to have a trial period of four weeks, or such longer period as may be agreed between the parties for the purpose of retraining the employee under that new contract. In the latter case the new agreement must be made before the employee starts to work under the new contract. It must be in writing, specifying the length of the trial period, and the terms and conditions of employment which will apply after the trial period. If before or during the trial period the employee terminates the contract, or the employer does so for a reason connected with the new contract, the employee shall be treated as being dismissed on the date on which his previous contract ended, and for the reason he was dismissed under that contract (*McKindley v William Hill (Scotland) Ltd*). However, in *Hempell v W H Smith & Sons Ltd* the EAT stated that this did not preclude an enquiry under s 98(4) to ascertain whether the dismissal during the trial period was fair or unfair. In other words, even if the employee accepts the job after a trial period, s 138(3) only provides that he has not been dismissed for reason of redundancy; he may (or may not) have been unfairly dismissed from his old job, and he is entitled to have that issue resolved by an employment tribunal (*Jones v Burdett Coutts School*). If before or during the trial period the employee unreasonably terminates the contract, he shall not be entitled to a redundancy payment by reason of his dismissal from the previous contract.

18.26 The statutory right to a trial period applies to those employees who are dismissed by the employer, or whose fixed-term contract has expired. However, on several occasions the EAT have decided that an employee who is constructively dismissed has a reasonable period within which to decide whether or not to accept the repudiation by the employer or to carry on with the new contract offered. The statutory trial period of four weeks does not commence until after the expiry of that reasonable period (*Turvey v CW Cheyney & Son Ltd*). In *Air Canada v Lee* the applicant worked as a telephonist. The employers moved their premises and she was asked to work in a basement office, with no natural light. She objected, but worked there for three months, when she left. It was held that she had been made redundant when she was asked to move: it was reasonable that she should try the new premises for three months, even though the statutory period had expired.

18.27 Since an employee has a statutory right to a trial period, a refusal to offer him one may lead to a finding that his dismissal was unfair (*Elliot v Richard Stump Ltd*). The statutory trial period of four weeks is four calendar weeks, not four working weeks (*Benton v Sanderson Kayser Ltd*).

G. Offer of suitable alternative employment (s 141)

18.28 If the employer makes an offer (whether in writing or not) to the employee to renew the contract of employment, or to re-engage him under a new contract, which is to take effect on the expiry of the old contract or within four weeks thereafter, then:

(a) if the provisions of that new contract as to capacity, place at which employed, and other terms and conditions of employment would not differ from the corresponding terms of the previous contract; or

(b) these terms and conditions do differ, but the offer constitutes an offer of suitable employment,

and in either case the employee unreasonably refuses that offer, then he will not be entitled to a redundancy payment.

18.29 When making an offer of alternative employment to an employee who is potentially redundant, the employer should provide the employee with as much information as is necessary to enable the employee to make an informed choice. In particular, the employee is entitled to know about the financial prospects in the alternative position (*Fisher v Hoopoe Finance Ltd*). It is a question of fact and degree in each case. In *Sheppard v National Coal Board* a redundant carpenter was offered a similar job which would have involved more travelling, less overtime, and the loss of certain fringe benefits. It was held that the additional travel was not excessive, and the loss of overtime did not, by itself, render the employment less suitable. The loss of the fringe benefits was more important, and it was held that the offer was not of suitable employment.

18.30 The suitability of the offer of alternative work must be assessed objectively, whereas to assess whether or not the employee's refusal is unreasonable (whether in relation to the offer to renew the old contract on the same terms or the offer of suitable alternative employment) it is permissible to take into account subjective considerations (*Cambridge & District Co-operative Society Ltd v Ruse*). Thus the employee's own personal problems which may arise through taking up the offer are relevant factors. Domestic difficulties, inadequate or inconvenient travel facilities, lack of suitable educational facilities for children, loss of friends, have all been matters which have been held to constitute reasonable grounds for refusal of the offer (*Paton Calvert & Co Ltd v Westerside*). The test is whether the employee made a reasonable decision on the basis of the facts that appeared before him, or ought reasonably to have appeared at the time. There is no room for the test of the range of reasonable responses of a reasonable employee (*Hudson v George Harrison Ltd*). An employee does not act unreasonably in refusing to accept alternative employment if he feels he cannot achieve a satisfactory standard in the new post (*Spencer v Gloucestershire County Council*).

18.31 But a personal whim or fad cannot constitute a reasonable refusal. In *Fuller v Stephanie Bowman (Sales) Ltd* the claimant was a secretary working in Mayfair. The employers decided to move the office to Soho. The claimant rejected the offer of employment at the new premises, for these were above a sex shop, and as she was opposed to 'money for sex' activities, she found the move too distasteful. Her application for a redundancy payment failed. The tribunal pointed out that the commercial exploitation of sex was no less in Mayfair than in Soho (except, perhaps a little more discreet), and if this was the basis of her reasoning, she should move away from London altogether. Her dislike of working near a sex shop was based on a personal fad, and thus it was held that she had unreasonably refused alternative employment.

H. Laying off and short-time working (s 147)

18.32 An employer may find himself in a difficult economic situation which may be envisaged to be of a temporary nature, and he may decide, instead of dismissing his employees, to lay them off temporarily, or to put them on short-time. A lay-off is where there is no work for the employees and no remuneration provided; short-time working is defined as being where less than half the normal week's pay is earned. If the lay-off or short-time has lasted for more than four consecutive weeks, or more than six weeks in any 13, then the employee may give written notice (not more than four weeks after the lay-off or short-time has finished) that he intends to claim a redundancy payment. He must then give the requisite notice to terminate his contract, and will be entitled to be considered redundant. The employer may agree to meet the claim, or refuse to do so and serve a counter-notice within seven days on the ground that he reasonably expects to be able to provide at least 13 weeks' continuous employment without further resort to lay-offs or short-time working. If the claim or counter-notice is not withdrawn, the matter will be determined by the employment tribunal, which will consider whether or not there was a reasonable prospect of full employment for 13 weeks. If the counter-notice is withdrawn by the employer, or the 13 weeks' continuous employment fails to materialise, the employee is entitled to be paid redundancy money.

18.33 If the employer offers work, but the employee refuses the offer because the rate of pay is too low, the employer has still offered to provide the work, and if, had he accepted the work the employee would have earned more than half a week's pay, there is no short-time working (*Spinpress Ltd v Turner*).

18.34 But an employer has no inherent right to lay off workers as he chooses. In the absence of an express right to do so in the contract, such unilateral action can be regarded as a repudiation of the contract, and hence a dismissal. Thus (in theory) at least one week's notice should be given of such intended lay-off (*Johnson v Cross*). But if the employer reserves the right to resort to a lay-off in the contract, the employee cannot treat this as a termination.

18.35 If the employer has a contractual right to lay off for an indefinite period (eg in the building industry) the employee's remedy is under s 148, and he cannot claim that the lay-off was for such an unreasonable length of time as to constitute a constructive dismissal (*Kenneth MacRae & Co Ltd v Dawson*).

18.36 It should be noted that the introduction of short-time working, without any contractual authority to do so, could result in a claim being made for unauthorised deductions from wages, under ERA, s 13 (*International Packaging Corpn (UK) Ltd v Balfour*).

Fair/unfair redundancy dismissals

A. Guidelines for good industrial relations practice

18.37 Although a redundancy situation may be grounds for dismissal, in respect of which the employee may be able to obtain a redundancy payment (see para 18.61), it does not follow that such a dismissal will automatically be fair, or that the employer acts reasonably in treating that reason as a sufficient ground for dismissal. In *Williams v Compair Maxam Ltd* the EAT laid down five principles for good current industrial relations practice which should be adopted in appropriate circumstances:

(a) the employer will give as much warning as possible of impending redundancies so as to enable trade unions and employees to consider alternative solutions and seek alternative employment:

(b) the employer will consult with the unions as to the best means by which the desired object can be achieved with as little hardship as possible. In particular, the criterion for selection should be agreed, and the actual selection should be made in accordance with that criterion;

(c) the criterion for selection should not depend solely on the opinion of the person making the selection, but should be one which can be objectively checked;

(d) the employer must ensure that the selection is made in accordance with that criterion, and will consider any representations made;

(e) the employer will ascertain whether there is any alternative employment which can be offered.

18.38 However, the principles laid down in *Williams v Compair Maxam Ltd* are guidelines, not rules of law. They refer primarily to the situation found in large companies when a significant number of redundancies are being contemplated. They should be applied with caution in small firms (*Meikle v McPhail*) or where there is no trade union involved. The principles should not be regarded as a shopping list with a finding of unfairness if one or more points have not been followed (*A Simpson & Son (Motors) v Reid*).

B. Handling redundancies

18.39 The fact that the employer has a redundancy policy is not, by itself, conclusive of anything. The employer must be prepared to justify that policy, and show, in particular, that it is fair and non-discriminatory (*Whiffen v Milham Ford Girls' School*). Whatever method of selection is used for redundancy purposes, it must be fair in general terms and reasonably applied in relation to the employee(s) concerned (*British Aerospace plc v Green*). Bearing this in mind, there are three ways in which redundancies should be handled.

Consideration of alternatives

18.40 Faced with a redundancy situation, the reasonable employer considers whether it is necessary to act on it, or whether there is some other way of dealing with the problem. For example, it may be possible to restrict recruitment, cut down on overtime, introduce work-sharing, introduce short-time working. In *Allwood v William Hill Ltd* the employers closed down 12 betting shops and declared the managers redundant. No warning was given and no alternative employment within the company was offered. It was held that merely because a redundancy situation existed, it did not follow that the employees had to be made redundant. There was a high wastage in the industry, and more effort should have been made to transfer them to other establishments, even on a temporary basis. The employers should also have considered retraining the employees until vacancies arose through wastage or expansion. It may be possible to offer a redundant employee another job which amounts to a demotion, and leave it to him to decide whether or not to accept (*Avonmouth Construction Co Ltd v Shipway*).

18.41 The reasonable employer also takes steps to see if the employee can be absorbed elsewhere in the concern, or with associated companies (*Vokes Ltd v Bear*), but the employer need only take such reasonable steps as are available for this purpose, and though an employment tribunal must scrutinise critically a complaint of unfair redundancy, it should also guard against adopting a standard which is unrealistic, and it should not find a dismissal unfair merely as a means of topping up an inadequate redundancy payment (*British United Shoe Machinery Co Ltd v Clarke*). If an employer merely states that he decided not to offer a redundant employee alternative work, without advancing any reasons for the decision, he does not discharge the burden of showing that he has acted reasonably (*Thomas and Betts Manufacturing Ltd v Harding*). If the employer has failed to act reasonably in searching round for alternative employment, the employment tribunal must consider whether in fact any loss has accrued to the employee as a result of that failure, or whether in fact it made no difference. In the latter case, there could be a finding that the dismissal was consequently not unfair, or that even if it was unfair, no loss was suffered by the employee, and therefore he is not entitled to any compensation.

Lack of consultation

18.42 To dismiss without warning or proper consultations, or without considering the recommendations of the Code of Practice relating to redundancies, may also result in a finding that a dismissal is unfair. But a failure to consult with the unions as provided by TULR(C)A, s 188 (see Chapter 18) does not by itself mean that a dismissal is unfair (*Forman Construction Ltd v Kelly*). At the same time, consultation with trade unions does not preclude consultation with individuals (*Walls Meat Co Ltd v Selby*). If the employer fails to consult with the affected individuals, he must supply a cogent reason why it was not possible to do so (*Holden v Bradville Ltd*).

18.43 The fact that the employer has established a policy not to consult in the event of redundancies being imminent, based on previous experience and the wishes of the workforce in the past, is not, per se, sufficient reason not to consult (*Ferguson v Prestwick Circuits Ltd*), particularly when the criteria for selection is vague and subjective (*Graham v ABF Ltd*). Even a small company is expected to act reasonably. Thus, if redundancy is being proposed, the size of the undertaking may affect the nature or formality of the consultation process, but it does not excuse the lack of consultation (*De Grasse v Stockwell Tools Ltd*).

18.44 In *Mugford v Midland Bank plc* the EAT suggested three propositions for the guidance of employment tribunals. (1) If there is no consultation with trade unions or individuals when redundancies are contemplated, a dismissal will normally be unfair, unless a reasonable employer would have concluded that consultation would be an utterly futile exercise. (2) Consultation with a trade union does not of itself release the employer from an obligation to consult with individuals concerned. (3) It will be a question of fact and degree for the employment tribunal to consider whether such consultations as had taken place were so inadequate as to render a dismissal unfair. The lack of consultation by itself does not automatically lead to a finding of unfairness.

18.45 A warning that redundancies are being contemplated, coupled with an indication of the selection procedure, does not satisfy the requirements of a fair procedure. Consultation must be fair and genuine. An opportunity must be given to the affected employees to express their views (*Rowell v Hubbard Group Services*). Thus in *Heron v Citilink-Nottingham* the employers found it necessary to make significant economies, and dismissed the claimant without any warning. The EAT held that his dismissal was unfair. For there to be exceptional circumstances which obviates the need for consultation, it had to be shown that it was necessary to dismiss the applicant when they did, and at no later date. It may well be that had he been consulted, he may have been able to make suggestions as to how the situation could be ameliorated. He may have agreed to accept a more junior post, or work for a lower salary. Unless the employer consults the employee in such circumstances, the latter will have no opportunity to put forward any suggestions.

18.46 It had been suggested that a redundancy dismissal without consultation can only be fair if the employer took a deliberate decision not to consult (see *Robertson v Magnet Ltd (Retail Division)*) but this view was rejected by the Court of Appeal in *Duffy v Yeomans and Partners Ltd*. What matters is whether consultation would have been useless, taking into account the circumstances known to the employer at the time.

18.47 If a dismissal is unfair because of a failure to consult, the employment tribunal must consider whether consultation would have made any difference, or whether the employee would have had a chance of being retained in his employment. If the answer is uncertain, then a percentage assessment should be made to reflect the probability that he would have been retained (*Dunlop Ltd v Farrell*), because the claimant must still show that a loss has resulted from the unfairness, and the employment tribunal must not speculate, guess, or indulge in conjecture. The claimant must show a sensible and coherent suggestion as to what was the result of the failure to consult or warn, and what would have happened had there been no such failure. The employer must then refute such suggestions (*Barley v Amey Roadstone Corpn Ltd*). The employment tribunal may then decide that the failure made little or no difference, and reduce compensation to an amount they deem appropriate, to reflect the additional period of time by which the employee's employment would have been extended had consultations taken place (*Mining Supplies (Longwall) Ltd v Baker*).

Proper selection procedures

18.48 It is the duty of the employment tribunal to examine the employer's procedures for selecting redundancies to ensure that these are fair. Even a selection system which is based on custom and practice in the industry can be challenged if it is unreasonable (*Watling & Co v Richardson*). The tribunal is entitled to know (a) who made the decision to select, (b) what information was taken into account, and (c) upon what criteria the information was assessed (*Bristol Channel Ship Repairers Ltd v O'Keefe*). Otherwise unfair selection for redundancy may also amount to an unfair dismissal. Faced with the decision of choosing which employee(s) shall be made redundant, the employer must engage in a genuine exercise in reaching his choice. If there is an established procedure in existence, he should follow it; in the absence of such pre-arranged procedure, the general rule in industry for redundancy selection used to be based on the principle of 'Last In First Out' (LIFO), although this appears to be falling out of favour in recent times, being replaced by a more sophisticated system based on skills, flexibility, etc. Also, if too much weight is given to long service, this may prove to be potentially discriminatory of younger employees, and possibly in breach of the provisions of the Employment Equality (Age) Regulations 2006 (see para 4.241). However, long service should always be considered as an important feature of any redundancy agreement (*Brook v London Borough of Haringey*). LIFO is always subject to any reasonable and proper modification, particularly if this has been considered by shop stewards and management acting in concert (*Crump v Chubb & Sons Lock and Safe Co Ltd*). In *International Paint Co Ltd v Cameron* it was held that the customary arrangements of LIFO, without further specification, had to be based on continuous service, not cumulative service, so that an employee with longer continuous service ought to be retained in preference to an employee with a longer overall service, but less continuous service.

18.49 If there is no agreed procedure or customary arrangement, the employer may take into account long services, superior abilities and experience, and the respective hardship caused. In *Selby and Tesse v Plessey Co Ltd*, it was held that a selection based on an effective evaluation system, which was customary in the company, was fair. Adherence to a redundancy agreement made with a trade union is generally sufficient evidence to rebut unfairness (*Taylor v Conveyancer Ltd*) though a failure to consult that union as provided by the agreement may be unfair. However, if the decision has to be made in a hurry for sound reasons, and consultations with the union or employees would result in serious delay, the employer does not act unfairly in failing to consult (*Guy v Delanair (Car Heater) Ltd*). Selection for redundancy will also be unfair if it is discriminatory on grounds of sex, sexual orientation, race, disability, part-time worker, fixed term employee, religion or belief, age etc (see Chapter 4).

18.50 Although the actual selection criteria is for management to determine, it is sound practice to agree this in advance with trade unions. The more vague and subjective the criteria, the greater is the need to consult with affected employees (*Graham v ABF Ltd*). It is the employer's responsibility to set up a fair system of selection, and to administer it fairly. If selection for redundancy is based on proper assessments, it is not for the employment tribunal to engage in a re-assessment exercise (*Eaton Ltd v King*).

18.51 In *Clyde Pipeworks v Foster*, selection for redundancy was based on a points system, which took into account bad time-keeping, workmanship, absenteeism, and merit on conduct. This procedure had been agreed with the unions, but they were not consulted about its implementation. It was held that there was no need to involve the unions in the detailed arrangements for selection for redundancy, provided the method was fair in general terms. But if management were to take into account improper factors (such as a disciplinary warning which should have been expunged from his record) there could be an unfair selection (*Pyle v Cleeson Civil Engineering Ltd*). If jobs are interchangeable between departments, then the basis for selection is between employees of the same description within the whole concern, not on a departmental basis (*Wailes Dove Bitumastic v Woolcocks*).

18.52 If a dismissal for redundancy is generally fair in terms of the procedure adopted and the selection criteria, it does not become unfair because of a failure by the employer to give the affected employees a right of appeal against their dismissal, even though an employee dismissed for gross misconduct would have that right. There is no suggestion in the Code of Practice that there should be a right of appeal against a dismissal for redundancy (*Robinson v Ulster Carpet Mills Ltd*). The advantage of having an appeal machinery is that an original decision to dismiss for redundancy which is unfair can be cured if there is a complete rehearing on appeal (*Lloyd v Taylor Woodrow plc*).

18.53 But if there is an appeal procedure, it must be operated fairly, and not be a mere sham. Thus, if selection for redundancy is based on a points system which had been agreed with union representatives, an employee is still entitled to know how his own marks had been calculated, otherwise he will have no material with which to present his case on appeal (*John Brown Engineering Ltd v Brown*).

18.54 To select a woman for dismissal because she is pregnant, or on maternity leave of absence, would be unfair under s 99 (see para 6.37), but if a woman is made redundant because of the operation of a fair selection procedure then the fact that she is or was pregnant is coincidental, and has nothing to do with her selection. Her dismissal would be fair in accordance with the usual criteria (*Brown v Stockton-on-Tees Borough Council*). Equally, a long-term sick employee may still be selected for redundancy, even though this terminates his entitlement to sickness pay under the employer's scheme (*Hill v General Accident Fire and Life Assurance Corpn plc*).

18.55 In the last analysis, the test is not whether the employment tribunal agrees with the actual selection made by the employer, but whether the employer acted reasonably. Thus it is not the duty of the employment tribunal to decide who they would have made redundant had they had to make the choice, but to ensure that management acts from genuine motives. In *Grundy (Teddington) Ltd v Willis*, the choice for making an employee redundant lay between two persons. Management chose one, but the employment tribunal held that this was unfair, in that the other should have been chosen. The EAT reversed this finding; the ultimate decision must remain with management, provided it acts fairly.

18.56 If an employee is given notice of dismissal, for reason of redundancy, and during that notice period new work becomes available, it may be unfair not to rescind the notice and offer further employment to him (*Stacey v Babcock Power Ltd*). However, if the alternative employment becomes available after the employee's contract of employment has ended, an employer does not act unreasonably in failing to offer that employment to him (*Octavius Atkinson & Sons Ltd v Morris*).

C. Unfair selection for redundancy (ERA, s 105)

18.57 It is unfair to dismiss a person for redundancy if the reason for his/her selection for dismissal was (a) health and safety reason (s 100), (b) protected or opted-out shop worker (s 101), (c) refusal to comply with a requirement in contravention of the Working Time Regulations (s 101A), (d) acting as a trustee of an occupational pension fund (s 102), (e) acting as an employee representative (s 103), (f) making a protected disclosure (s 103A), (g) asserting a statutory right (s 104), (h) asserting a right under the National Minimum Wage Act (s 104A), (i) taking action to obtain a tax credit (s 104B), (j) taking action under the Transnational Information and Consultation of Employees Regulations 1999, (k) taking action under the Part-time Workers (Prevention of Less Favourable Treatment) Regulation 2000, or the Fixed-Term Employees (Prevention of Less Favourable Treatment) Regulations 2002. Unfair selection for trade union membership and activities etc is covered by TULR(C)A, s 153. Unfair selection for redundancy by reason of pregnancy, maternity leave, parental leave, time off to care for dependants, and workforce agreement cases is dealt with in the Maternity and Parental Leave etc Regulations 1999 (see Chapter 6) and there is similar protection for persons who take paternity and adoption leave. Such dismissals will be automatically unfair, and no continuous period of continuous employment is required, and there are now no age limits.

D. Dismissal during the period of notice (s 140)

18.58 If an employee has been given due notice that he will be dismissed for reason of redundancy, and whilst he is working out that notice, he commits an act of misconduct which is sufficiently serious to warrant his instant dismissal without notice, and he is summarily dismissed, the question will arise as to whether or not he is entitled to his redundancy payment. On the assumption that the dismissal was justified (eg because the employee refused to obey a lawful order (*Cairns v Burnside Shoe Repairs Ltd*), or because the employee stole from the employer (*Jarmain v E Pollard & Co Ltd*)), then the employment tribunal shall determine whether it is just and equitable that the employee should receive the whole or part of the redundancy payment, as it thinks fit. In *Lignacite Products Ltd v Krollman* the claimant was given notice of redundancy. He was then found stealing from his employers and summarily dismissed. The employment tribunal reduced his redundancy pay by 40%, and the EAT upheld the decision. It is difficult to reconcile this decision with the more recent case of *Bonner v H Gilbert Ltd*.

18.59 If an employee is given notice of dismissal by reason of redundancy, and during his notice period he takes part in a strike, then although this is conduct which entitles the employer to terminate the contract without notice, the employee is not barred from getting the whole of his redundancy payment (s 143). However, if an employee is on strike, and then is dismissed for reasons of redundancy, his claim will fail. The reason is that s 140 of the Act provides that the employee will not be entitled to a redundancy payment if the employer, being entitled to terminate the contract of employment, terminates it, with or without notice. Since an employee who is on strike is in breach of his contract, the employer is entitled to terminate it. In other words, s 143 deals with the situation when an employee is dismissed for reason of redundancy, and then goes on strike. In *Simmons v Hoover Ltd* employees who were actually on strike were dismissed for reason of redundancy, and it was held that s 140 operated, and s 143 did not operate to save their claim.

Excluded classes of employees

18.60 The following employees are not eligible for, or will not be entitled to, a redundancy payment:

(a) a person employed under a fixed-term contract for two years or more, if before that term expires, he agrees in writing to exclude his rights to make a claim (s 197(3)). This is one of the very few circumstances when an employee can forgo his legal rights (see para 20.41). However, this exclusion only applies to agreements made before 10 July 2002;

(b) a miscellaneous class of employees, ie share fishermen, and men and women over the age of 65 or normal retiring age. Domestic servants employed in a private household *are* within the scope of the Act, unless the servant is a close relative of the employer (s 161);

(c) an agreement made between an employers' organisation and a trade union may provide exemption from the Act by a ministerial order on an application by both parties thereto, provided the conditions in s 157 are satisfied.

Claims for redundancy payments

18.61 A claim must be made to the employment tribunal within six months from the relevant date, which is the date of the expiry of the notice to terminate the employment, or the date when the contract expires, or the date on which a fixed-term contract comes to an end. The tribunal has a discretion to admit a claim which is outside the time limit if it thinks it would be just and equitable to do so, but no claim can be entertained after 12 months have elapsed. The claim, if admitted or successful, must be met by the employer. The amount of the claim will be determined by the length of time the employee has been employed, his normal week's pay, and his age.

18.62 The calculation of the amount of the redundancy payment will be determined in accordance with the rules on continuous employment (see Chapter 13) normal working hours and a week's pay (see Chapter 14) and age. For each year's continuous employment below the age of 22 (with no lower age limit) an employee is entitled to one half a week's pay; for each year's employment between the ages of 22 and 40, he will be entitled to one week's pay; for each year's employment over (and including) the age of 41, he will be entitled to one and a half weeks' pay. There is no longer an upper or lower age limit, and the tapering provision which used to apply to employees over the age of 64 has been abolished. However, an employee will still have to have been employed for two years or more, and no more than 20 years' employment may be counted when calculating the payment. The maximum week's pay to count is (currently) £290. When making the payment, the employer shall give to the employee a written statement showing how the amount of the payment is calculated, and it is an offence, punishable on summary conviction by a fine not exceeding level 1 on the standard scale, not to do so (s 165). If an employer gives a lump sum to a redundant employee without indicating how it is made up, this may be regarded as an *ex gratia* payment, not intended to be by way of a redundancy payment (*Galloway v Export Packing Services Ltd*).

Payments by the Secretary of State (ERA, ss 166–170)

18.63 If an employee claims that, despite taking all reasonable steps, the employer has failed or refused to make him a redundancy payment, or claims that the employer is insolvent, he may apply to the Secretary of State for a redundancy payment, to be paid out of the National Insurance Fund. An employer will be insolvent if:

(a) he is an individual, and he has been adjudged bankrupt or made a composition or arrangement with creditors, or he has died and his estate falls to be administered under the Insolvency Act 1986 (there are comparable provisions for Scotland); or

(b) if a company, there has been a winding-up order or an administration order made, or a resolution for a voluntary winding up has been passed or a receiver or manager appointed.

18.64 Once the Secretary of State has made the payment due to an employer's insolvency, this will break continuity of employment for those employees who are re-engaged by virtue of the Transfer of Undertakings (Protection of Employment) Regulations 2006 (*Lassman v Secretary of State for Trade and Industry*, and see Chapter 9).

Consultation on redundancies (TULR(C)A, ss 188–192)

A. EC Directive on Collective Redundancies

18.65 Article 2 of the EC Directive on Collective Redundancies (75/129/EEC) lays down the principle that when an employer is contemplating collective redundancies, he shall consult with employee representatives. Although a Directive is generally enforceable against a state body (see *Foster v British Gas*, para 1.68) this Directive is not so unconditional or sufficiently precise as to be capable of direct enforcement (*Griffin v South West Water Services Ltd*). Requirements for such consultations were provided for in the Employment Protection Act 1975, s 99, and repeated in the Trade Union and Labour Relations (Consolidation) Act 1992, s 188 (as amended by the Trade Union Reform and Employment Rights Act 1993). However, in *EC Commission v United Kingdom* infringement proceedings were brought alleging that neither the Transfer of Undertakings Regulations 1981 (see Chapter 9) nor the provisions of TULR(C)A correctly transposed the Directive, because there were no provisions which would require an employer to consult with employee representatives when the employer did not recognise a trade union. The UK Government argued that employee representation was traditionally based on the voluntary recognition by employers of trade unions, and therefore if an employer did not recognise a trade union, there were no 'employee representatives' with whom to consult. Nonetheless, the European Court held that the UK Government was in breach of the Directive. Legislation had to ensure that there was a mechanism whereby employee representatives were designated so as to enable employers to consult with them.

18.66 Section 188 of TULR(C)A was thus amended by the Collective Redundancies and Transfer of Undertakings (Protection of Employment) (Amendment) Regulations 1995, although it was not certain whether these regulations fully implemented the Directive, because although there arose a duty to consult with either trade unions or employee representatives, there was no mechanism by which those representatives could be elected. Thus the Collective Redundancies and Transfer of Undertakings (Protection of Employment) (Amendment) Regulations 1999 were passed to regularise the position. These latter Regulations make provision for the election of employee representatives (by inserting s 188A into TULR(C)A), and other changes).

18.67 However, there is still some doubt as to whether UK law adequately transposes the EC Directive. Section 188 requires consultation to take place when an employer is 'proposing' redundancies, whereas the Directive requires consultation when the employer is 'contemplating' redundancies (see *MSF v Refuge Assurance plc*).

B. Who, and when to consult

18.68 Where an employer is proposing to dismiss as redundant 20 or more employees at one establishment within a period of 90 days or less, he shall consult with the appropriate representatives of any of the employees affected by the proposed dismissals (and not just those whom the employer proposes to make redundant), or may be affected by the measures taken in connection with those dismissals. The appropriate representatives are:

(a) if the employees are of a description in respect of which an independent trade union is recognised (whether or not the affected employees are members of the trade union concerned, see *Northern Ireland Hotel and Catering College v National Association of Teachers in Further and Higher Education*), representatives of that union. Whether a trade union is recognised for the purpose of the consultation provisions is a question of fact (see Chapter 23). In any other case,

(b) either employee representatives who have been appointed or elected by the affected employees for some other purpose, who have authority to receive information or be consulted about proposed dismissals, or employee representatives who have been elected by the affected employees for consultation purposes, in an election which satisfies the requirements set out in s 188A.

If there is no recognised trade union, the employer must consult with either existing representatives or representatives elected for TUPE consultation purposes. If there are no trade union or elected representatives, the employer must invite the employees to elect representatives. If they fail to do so within a reasonable time, the employer must give each affected employee the information he would otherwise have given to the representatives (*Howard v Millrise Ltd*).

18.69 The employer shall allow the appropriate representatives access to the employees affected, and shall afford those representatives such accommodation and facilities as may be appropriate, and time off work for training (ERA, s 61). An employee who is an employee representative, or a candidate for election as such, has the right not to suffer a detriment on the ground that he has performed any function or activity as such, the right to have time off with pay to perform his functions, and the right not to be unfairly dismissed because he performed any function or activity as such.

18.70 The consultation shall begin in good time, and, in any event, if the employer is proposing to dismiss 100 or more within 90 days or less, consultation shall begin at least 90 days before the dismissals take effect. If less than 100 (but 20 or more) are to be dismissed within the 90-day period, consultation must begin at least 30 days before the dismissals take effect (see *Junk v Wolfgang Kuhnell*).

What is an establishment?

18.71 The term 'establishment' is not defined in the Act, and has thus been the subject of interpretation by the tribunals. In *Clarks of Hove Ltd v Bakers' Union* it was held that separate premises can amount to one establishment, if there is no separate accounting, management or trading. In *Barratt Developments (Bradford) Ltd v UCATT* the company, which had its headquarters in Bradford, operated 14 building sites in Lancashire. On each site there was a temporary shed, with a telephone link to the headquarters. It was decided to reduce the labour force, and 24 employees were made redundant, being selected from eight different sites. It was held that all 14 sites were part of one establishment, and as there had been a failure to consult with the trade union, a protective award would be made.

18.72 However, in *Rockfon A/S v Specialarbejderforbundet i Danmark* the European Court of Justice noted that member states used different terms to describe an 'establishment', including undertaking, work centre, local unit, place of work, and so on. Since the term is one of European law, a uniform interpretation must be given. The ECJ held that the term 'establishment' must be understood as meaning the unit to which the workers who are made redundant are assigned to carry out their duties (see para 9.12). It is not necessary for the unit in question to have its own management structure which can carry out a redundancy programme independently. The irony is that in an attempt to extend the coverage of the Directive so as to protect as many employees as possible, this definition is probably a narrow one, for UK law triggers the consultation provisions only when more than 20 from one establishment are to be dismissed.

The consultation provisions

18.73 An employer is 'proposing to dismiss' employees as redundant (thus triggering the consultation provisions of the Act) when, 'following a diagnosis of the problem, specific proposals are formulated, with redundancies as one of the available options' (*Hough v Leyland DAF Ltd*). 'Proposing to dismiss' means 'proposing to give notice of dismissal'. A proposal means something less than an actual decision that dismissals are to be made, and something more than a possibility that they may occur (*Leicestershire County Council v Unison*). Thus where directors of a company were considering the options of either selling the business as a going concern or selling it as a development site, this amounted to a proposal to dismiss the workforce, even though no final decision had been reached on which option they would adopt (*Scotch Premier Meat Ltd v Burns*).

18.74 The actual notice of dismissals can be issued during the consultation period, provided that the dismissals do not take effect until after the consultation period has elapsed. But if an employer issues dismissal notices the day after consultations begin, it may be thought that he does not intend meaningful consultations to take place (*National Union of Teachers v Avon County Council*). Similarly, if the employer does not give the appropriate representatives sufficient time to consider the proposals before they are implemented, meaningful consultation is being denied (*Transport and General Workers' Union v Ledbury Preserves (1928) Ltd*).

18.75 The purpose of consultation is to consult about ways of:

(a) avoiding the dismissals;

(b) reducing the numbers of employees to be dismissed; and

(c) mitigating the consequences of the redundancies (TULR(C)A, s 188(2)).

18.76 Consultation with employee representatives does not mean reaching an agreement, but should be undertaken by the employer with a view to reaching agreement. Thus, the consultation process must be genuine. If a redundancy situation is presented as a *fait accompli*, subsequent consultations may not be a genuine and open-minded review of the decision (*GMB and AEEU v Campbell's UK Ltd*). In *Middlesbrough Borough Council v TGWU* it was held that the consultations on avoiding redundancies had been a sham, because the decision on numbers had already been taken.

18.77 True consultation involves:

(a) consulting with employee representatives when the proposals are still at a formulative stage;

(b) giving adequate information to which those representatives can respond;

(c) giving adequate time for the response; and

(d) a conscientious consideration by the employer of the response (*Rowell v Hubbard Group Services Ltd*).

18.78 But consultation does not imply agreement with those representatives, nor the adoption of any proposals made by them (*R v British Coal Corpn, ex p Price*).

A. Disclosures required by the employer

18.79 In such consultations, the employer must disclose (in writing to the appropriate representative):

(a) the reasons for his proposals;

(b) the numbers and descriptions of employees whom it is proposed to dismiss as being redundant;

(c) the total number of employees of that description employed by the employer at that establishment;

(d) the proposed method of selecting the employees who are to be dismissed;

(e) the proposed method of carrying out the dismissals, with due regard to agreed procedure, including the period over which dismissals are to take effect; and

(f) the proposed method for calculating any redundancy payments to be made, other than statutory redundancy pay (s 188(4)).

18.80 Having provided the above information, the employer must consider any representations made by the appropriate representatives and reply to them. If he rejects any of those representations, he must state his reasons. It must be stressed that the employer's duty is to consult with the representatives. He does not have to reach any agreement, and the final decision is his. In *Perez v Mercury Display Ltd* the employer consulted with a trade union about a redundancy. The employer wanted selection to take place on the basis of LIFO, but the union wanted volunteers to be selected. The employer gave to the union his reasons for rejecting the representations, and dismissed the employees on the basis of LIFO. It was held that the employer had complied with his statutory obligations.

B. Special circumstances

18.81 If there are special circumstances which render it not reasonably practicable for the employer to comply with any of the above provisions relating to consulation or considering representations, he shall take all such steps as are reasonably practicable in the circumstances. Special circumstances may exist if a company becomes insolvent but insolvency per se is not a special circumstance, for reasonable and prudent management may well foresee such a possibility (*Clarks of Hove Ltd v Bakers' Union*). The sudden appointment of a receiver would be a special circumstance (*FTATU v Lawrence Cabinet*). The loss of a key order (*AUEW v Cooper Plastics*) and the unexpected failure to obtain a renewal of an important contract (*National Union of Public Employees v General Cleaning Contractors*) have also come within this defence. But the fact that the employer genuinely believes that he has not recognised a trade union for the purpose of collective bargaining does not constitute a special circumstance which would render it not reasonably practicable to comply with the obligation to consult (*Joshua Wilson & Bros Ltd v Union of Shop, Distributive and Allied Workers*). Special circumstances may also be said to exist if delicate negotations are taking place which may be prejudiced if consultations are carried on with the union (*Association of Pattern Makers and Allied Craftsmen v Kirvin Ltd*). A circumstance is likely to be special if it is sudden, as opposed to being gradual or foreseeable with reasonable prudence (*Union of Shop, Distributive and Allied Workers v Leancut Bacon Ltd*).

18.82 The dismissal of employees in order to make the sale of a business more attractive to buyers, or the absence of orders, are not special circumstances within the meaning of the Act (*GMB v Rankin and Harrison*). A failure on the part of a person who controls the employer (eg a multinational corporation in control of a subsidiary) to provide information to the employer also does not constitute a special circumstance (s 193(7)).

18.83 An employer does not fail to consult if he deals only with an accredited shop steward, for there is no requirement that the information should be conveyed to a full-time union official (*General and Municipal Workers' Union v Wailes Dove Bitumastic*).

C. Protective award (TULR(C)A, s 189)

18.84 If the employer fails to consult as required by s 186, a trade union or an employee representative or an employee who has been or may be dismissed as redundant may present a complaint to an industrial tribunal (s 189). It further appears that an employee who has been dismissed for reason of redundancy may be able to bring a complaint that the employer has failed to invite potentially redundant employees to elect appropriate employee representatives as required by s 188. If the employer wishes to plead that it was not reasonably practicable for him to comply with these provisions, he must show that this was so, and that he took all reasonably practicable steps in the circumstances. Otherwise, if the tribunal finds the complaint to be well founded, it will make a declaration to that effect, and may also make a protective award, which is remuneration for a protected period for those employees who were dismissed (or whose dismissal was being proposed) and in respect of whom the employer has failed to comply with the legal requirements. The protected period is such time as the tribunal considers to be just and equitable, having regard to the seriousness of the employer's default, but shall not exceed 90 days.

18.85 If a protective award is made, every employee to whom it relates shall be entitled to one week's pay for each week of the protected period, with proportionate reductions in respect of a period which is less than one week. There is no maximum week's pay for the purpose of the protective award, because the statutory cap in ERA, s 227 does not include a protective award. If the employer has already made any payment to the employee in respect of any period falling within the protected period, or by way of damages for breach of contract, this will not reduce the employer's liability to pay remuneration under the protective award, and conversely, any payment made under a protective award will not reduce any liability to pay any sum due in respect of a breach of contract by the employer for that period.

18.86 If an employment tribunal finds that the employer is in default of the consultation provisions, then the making of a declaration to that effect is mandatory, but the amount of the protective award is discretionary. The purpose of the protective award is to provide for a sanction against an employer for being in breach of the statutory consultation provisions, rather than to compensate employees for the loss which they have suffered in consequence of the breach. The maximum period of 90 days' protective award should only be reduced if there were mitigating circumstances justifying a reduction to the extent which the tribunal considers appropriate (*Susie Radin Ltd v GMB*; decisions to the contrary in *Talke Fashion Ltd v Amalgamated Society of Textile Workers and Kindred Trades*, and *Spillers-French Ltd v Union of Shop, Distributive and Allied Workers* were disagreed with).

18.87 An award for a failure to consult on redundancies is determined by the seriousness of the employer's default, not his ability to pay. Thus if the employer fails to consult and has become insolvent, a maximum award may still be made, the point being that it will be the Secretary of State who will have to pay (*Smith v Cherry Lewis Ltd*). The protective award is essentially punitive in nature, and the employment tribunal should use the 90-day award as a starting point. However, mitigating factors can be taken into account so as to reduce the award, such as if the employer had taken some genuine steps to provide information or has attempted some form of consultation (*Amicus v GBS Tooling Ltd*).

18.88 As a result of consultations with the appropriate employee representatives, there may well be an agreement that employees will leave the firm before the appropriate period of 90 or 30 days has expired. Whether the agreement has been reached with the employee representatives or employees on an individual basis, it is probably void by virtue of TULR(C)A, s 288, which prevents the contracting out of the various statutory rights. It is clear therefore that the dismissals will take effect before the end of the consultation period, and there will be a breach of the Act. However, on a complaint that the employer has failed to consult within the statutory period, the employment tribunal will make the mandatory declaration, but not a protective award (*Association of Scientific, Technical and Managerial Staffs v Hawker Siddeley Aviation*).

18.89 If, during the protected period, the employee is fairly dismissed for some reason other than redundancy, or if he unreasonably resigns, then his entitlement to the protective award shall cease from the time his contract is terminated. If the employer makes an offer to renew the contract, or to re-engage under a new contract, so that the renewal or re-engagement would take effect before or during the protected period, or the offer constitutes an offer of suitable employment, and the employee unreasonably refuses that offer, then he shall not be entitled to any payment under the protective award in respect of any period during which but for the refusal he would have been employed.

18.90 Once a protective award has been granted, then any individual employee may present a complaint to a tribunal that the employer has failed, in whole or in part, to pay him the remuneration under that award. If the complaint is well founded, the tribunal shall order the employer to make that payment (*Howlett Marine Services Ltd v Bowlam*).

18.91 The fact that the employer has failed to consult in accordance with the above provisions is irrelevant to the issue as to whether a particular employee's redundancy is fair or unfair (*Forman Construction Ltd v Kelly*).

18.92 It should be noted that, for the purpose of the consultation provisions only, the definition of redundancy is not the same as the one laid down in ERA, s 139. Under TULR(C)A, s 195, when considering the consultation provisions, references to dismissals for reason of redundancy are references to a dismissal not related to the individual concerned (or for a number of reasons not so related). This wider definition throws out some interesting possibilities. For example, suppose an employer decides to give lawful notice to all his employees, coupled with an offer to re-engage them all on changed terms of employment. Since this 'dismissal' is not related to an individual, it is submitted that prior consultations with employee representatives are required under TULR(C)A, s 195 (*GMB v Man Truck and Bus UK Ltd*).

Notification of mass redundancies to the minister (TULR(C)A, s 193)

18.93 If an employer is proposing to make redundant 100 or more employees at one establishment within 90 days, or 20 or more employees within 30 days, he must notify the Secretary of State of his proposals within 90 or 30 days respectively before any notice of redundancy has been issued. He must also give a copy of this notification to the representatives of any recognised independent trade union and/or to any elected representatives. If there are special circumstances which make compliance not reasonably practicable, he shall take all such steps as are reasonably practicable. But a failure on the part of a person who controls the employer to provide information to the employer does not constitute a special circumstance (s 193(7)).

18.94 An employer who fails to give the required notification to the Secretary of State may be prosecuted in the magistrates' court, and is liable on conviction to a fine not exceeding level 5 on the standard scale (TULR(C)A, s 194(1)).

19

Duties of Ex-employees

19.1 We have seen (Chapter 10) that during the subsistence of a contract of employment, the relationship between an employer and employee is one of trust, confidence and faith, and any course of conduct which is inconsistent with those obligations may well amount to a breach of contract. In this chapter we shall consider the more limited obligations which apply to an employee who is about to leave his employment (whether voluntarily or otherwise), or who has actually left that employment. The law must strike a delicate balance. On the one hand, an employee has a right to earn his living, and knowledge and skills obtained in his former employment will doubtless enable him to continue to do so; on the other hand, an employer is entitled to limited protection against an employee who may well be seeking to compete. An employer is not entitled to have protection from competition per se; he is entitled to have some limited protection in respect of confidential information, trade secrets, and so on.

Employees who are about to leave their employment

19.2 The mere fact that the employee is seeking employment with a competitor is not, by itself, a breach of the duty of fidelity, in the absence of any evidence that the employee is wrongfully seeking to disclose confidential information or trade secrets (*Harris & Russell Ltd v Slingsby*). But an employee who is about to leave his employment may attempt to make preparatory steps, either during his working hours, or in his own time, to prepare himself for future employment. He may attempt to solicit customers or suppliers, poach staff, or use information which has been imparted to him in confidence. His status and position as an employee, the nature of the work he is seeking to do, the custom and practice of the industry, etc, may well be relevant factors to be taken into account when determining the rights of his employer.

19.3 If the employee engages in such activities during his working hours, or uses his employer's premises or equipment to do so, then doubtless he will be in breach of his duty of fidelity. Thus in *Roger Bullivant Ltd v Ellis* a managing director left his employment in order to set up a rival business. He took with him copies of a card index, which listed the names and addresses of all the company's customers. This was held to be a breach of the implied duty of fidelity, and an injunction was granted to restrain him from entering into or fulfilling any contract made with or through any person whose name appeared on the card index. However, this does not necessarily apply if the employee pursues such activities in his own time and uses his own premises or equipment (*Balston Ltd v Headline Filters Ltd*).

19.4 There appears to be a somewhat subtle distinction between a definite intention to compete with the employer and mere preparatory activities. Thus to tender for work already being undertaken by the employer (*Adamson v B & L Cleaning Services Ltd*) or to rent and equip premises for his own business (*Lancashire Fires Ltd v SA Lyons & Co Ltd*) or to approach customers with a view to doing business with them (*Wessex Dairies v Smith*) or to copy out a list of the employer's clients with a view to approaching them after the employment has ceased (*Robb v Green*) are clearly competing activities which will amount to a breach of the duty of faithful service. But an employee who merely indicates, whether by word or deeds, that he intends to compete with his employer at some future point in time is not acting in breach of his implied duty of fidelity (see *Laughton and Hawley v Bapp Industrial Supplies Ltd*, para 16.11).

19.5 If, while still employed, an employee seeks to entice away existing fellow employees, this can amount to a breach of the duty of fidelity, especially if the activities of the employee have gone beyond the mere preparatory stages. But the law on this point is not absolutely clear, and the position of the employee is very relevant. A managing director who seeks to entice away senior staff (*Marshall v Industrial Systems and Control Ltd*) is more likely to be in breach of his duty of fidelity than a more junior member of staff (*Tithebarn Ltd v Hubbard*).

Garden leave

19.6 Because of legal uncertainties which surround the enforcement of post-termination restrictive covenants, some employers seek to obtain some protection from their employees' future competition by inserting a 'garden leave' clause into their contracts. This clause operates when lawful notice of termination is given, either by the employee or employer. During the notice period, the employee is not required to work, but is entitled to his full contractual terms and conditions. For his part, the employee remains bound by the implied duty of fidelity, and cannot work for a competitor, nor disclose trade secrets or confidential information, etc.

19.7 There must be an express contractual term which permits the employer to put the employee on garden leave, and this should set out the rights and obligations of both parties. The garden leave requirement can only be enforced if it is reasonable in terms of the length of time it operates, and if it is intended to protect the employer's genuine interests. During the garden leave period the employer is entitled to have a limited protection against the employee going to work for a competitor, or disclosing confidential information (*Provident Financial Group plc v Hayward*), and if the employee acts in a manner contrary to the agreement the employer's remedy is for an injunction and/or damages, as appropriate. However, it must be stressed that such remedies are discretionary. And if, contrary to the terms of the garden leave, the employee works for a non-competitor, or discloses information which is not confidential, this will not amount to a breach of the garden leave clause, but he may be in breach of his contract of employment, and the employer may terminate the contract and/or sue for damages.

19.8 But garden leave clauses, like restrictive covenants, are inherently contracts in restraint of trade, and hence will only be enforced by the courts if they are reasonable, ie justified by reference to the legitimate business interests of the employer. Whether or not a court will uphold such a clause is a matter of discretion, to be determined on the facts of each case. On the one hand, there may be little damage to the employee if he is held to the agreement, for he will still be receiving his pay and other contractual entitlements; on the other hand there could well be considerable potential damage to the employer if the employee goes to work immediately for a rival firm (*Euro Brokers Ltd v Rabey*). The employer's legitimate interests have to be balanced against the employee's right to work, especially when it is necessary to practise and exercise his skills and talents (*William Hill Organisation Ltd v Tucker*). After all, it is to be expected that senior employees will seek employment in the same line of business, and will not take kindly to enforced idleness, even if they are being paid. And employers will sometimes have exaggerated fears as to the damage likely to be caused to their business if the employee takes employment with another firm (*JA Mont (UK) Ltd v Mills*).

19.9 A garden leave clause does have one advantage over a post-termination restrictive covenant. If the latter is drafted too widely, it will be void and unenforceable. The covenant must stand or fall on its own terms (but see para 19.42), unless the court can use the 'blue pencil' rule to give it limited validity. However, when considering a garden leave clause which is too wide in its operation, the courts appear to be quite willing to interpret it and, if necessary, modify it, so as to give effect to its intentions. Thus in *Symbian Ltd v Christensen* the employee's contract, which was terminable on six months' notice, contained a clause which prohibited him from working for anyone during the notice period. The employers learned that he was about to work for a competitor, and applied for an injunction to restrain him from doing so. Clearly, this clause was too wide, for it would have prohibited the employee from working for non-competing employers in non-competing businesses, but the court modified the clause so as to prohibit him from working for the named competitor any time during the six months' notice period.

19.10 Similarly, the court can modify the length of the period of garden leave, and, if necessary, reduce it to a period of time which reflects the realities of the situation (*Provident Financial Group plc v Hayward*). Thus in *GFI Group Inc v Eaglestone* a garden leave period was cut down from 20 weeks to 13 weeks, although in *Euro Brokers Ltd v Rabey* a six-month garden leave period was upheld.

19.11 There is no reason in principle why a garden leave clause cannot be followed by a post-employment restrictive covenant, in effect lengthening the period of time when the employee is prevented from entering into competing employment. The one period cannot be set off against the other. But the existence of a garden leave clause may be a factor to take into account when determining the validity of the restrictive covenant and, if the garden leave clause is exceptionally long, the courts may, on grounds of public policy, refuse to enforce any further protection based on a restrictive covenant (*Credit Suisse Asset Management Ltd v Armstrong*).

Employees who have left the employment

19.12 During his employment, an employee will doubtless come across a considerable amount of information, some of which is likely to be of a confidential nature. Names and addresses of customers and suppliers, prices, production methods, secret processes, etc, are all likely to come his way. Thus when he leaves his employment, he does not leave with an empty mind, yet the disclosure of such information is capable of causing considerable harm to his former employer. To determine whether particular information falls into the category of information which ought not to be disclosed after the employment has ceased, regard must be had to all the circumstances, and, in particular, to:

(a) the nature of the employment;

(b) the nature of the information;

(c) whether the employer regarded the information as being confidential, and whether the employee was informed of this;

(d) whether the information could easily be isolated from other information which the employee is free to use (*Faccenda Chicken Ltd v Fowler*).

19.13 It appears that there are three classes of information which an employee may acquire during his employment. First, there is information which is trivial or easily available to the public at large. This clearly does not give rise to any implied term of confidentiality. Second, there is information which has been imparted to the employee, or which he learns during the course of his employment for the purpose of his employer's business. During the course of his employment this should not be the subject of unauthorised disclosure, but once the employment has ceased, it remains part of the employee's skill and knowledge, and can be used by him for his own benefit – if necessary in competition with his former employer. The law does not seek to prevent an employee from using his skill and know-how, even though these were obtained during his employment (*Stenhouse Australia Ltd v Phillips*) for to do so would amount to a restraint on competition per se. Thus in *Faccenda Chicken Ltd v Fowler* the employer sought an injunction to restrain two former employees from using their knowledge of sales and price information when they set up a competing business. It was held that this was not confidential information, and the application for an injunction was refused. Finally, there is information which has been imparted in confidence, or which clearly amounts to being a trade secret, such as secret processes, etc. This cannot be disclosed after the employment has ceased, unless there is a public interest in disclosure. A trade secret, as well as being specialised or technical information (such as chemical formulae or specialised processes), must be such that its disclosure would be liable to cause real or significant harm to the employer (*Lansing Linde Ltd v Kerr*). Whether information is to be treated as being confidential, or whether something is a trade secret will clearly depend on the facts of each case (*SBJ Stephenson Ltd v Mandy*), and the mere fact that the employer seeks to regard it as such is by no means conclusive (*Jack Allen (Sales and Service) Ltd v Smith*).

19.14 It will be obvious that the rule against disclosure is easier to state in theory than to enforce in practice, for it is not possible to wipe out from an employee's mind information which he has gained in the course of the employment and which he may properly place at the disposal of his new employer. A distinction must be drawn between trade secrets and confidential information on the one hand, and an employee's skill, knowledge and general familiarity with his former employer's business on the other hand (*Lock International plc v Beswick*). In *Printers and Finishers Ltd v Holloway* the claimants sought an injunction against their former works manager restraining him from disclosing certain confidential information which he had obtained during his employment. Some of this information was contained in documents which the defendant had taken with him, and an injunction was granted in respect of these and an enquiry was ordered to ascertain what damage, if any, had flowed from the defendant's breach of duty. So far as confidential matters which were in his memory were concerned, which related to the know-how and general processes of the claimant's business, these were not readily separable from his general knowledge of the whole trade, and it would not be unreasonable for him to recall particular skills of his former employer's business and use his skills for the benefit of his new employer. Consequently, an injunction relating to these matters was refused.

19.15 It is not necessary that the employer points out to the employee the precise nature or aspects of the production process for which protection as a trade secret is sought (*Lancashire Fires Ltd v SA Lyons & Co Ltd*).

19.16 However, if the information obtained, though confidential, relates to a breach of the law or wrongful act by the employer, then there is an entirely different situation, for 'there is no confidence as to the disclosure of an iniquity'. In *Initial Services Ltd v Putterill* the defendant was employed as a manager by the claimants. After leaving his employment he gave information to a newspaper concerning the conduct of the claimants' business, in particular alleging that they had violated the Restrictive Trade Practices Act 1956 by entering into agreements with other laundries which ought to have been registered under that Act, and that they had issued circulars which were misleading to the public. The newspaper proposed to publish an article which would have made detrimental allegations about the claimants' business, and an injunction was sought. It was held that the disclosure would be justified as being in the public interest, and there was no confidence attached thereto.

19.17 If an employee does disclose information relating to the commission of a fraud, crime or act of corruption by his former employer, he can rely on the defence of 'just cause' if the disclosure is made in the public interest. Thus in *Lion Laboratories Ltd v Evans* two ex-employees gave information to a newspaper which showed that there were doubts about the reliability of a breathalyser approved by the Home Office. It was held that the information disclosed was of grave public concern, and would not be restrained (see now para 10.70 for protected disclosures).

19.18 An ex-employee is not in breach of the implied term of confidentiality in disclosing information relating to his former employer's insolvency, because the duty of confidentiality is much more restricted in scope after the employment has ceased than that which is imposed by the general duty of good faith during the employment (*Brookes v Olyslager OMS (UK) Ltd*). Nor can an ex-employee be restrained from disclosing information to regulatory bodies (such as the Financial Services Authority) which have a duty to investigate matters within their remit (*Re a Company's Application*).

19.19 In the absence of an express covenant restricting post-employment activities, there can be no general restriction on an ex-employee canvassing or doing business with customers of his former employer, or competing with him in any way, and there is no implied term prohibiting this (*Wallace Bogan & Co v Cove*). An ex-employee is entitled to make use of the skill and knowledge he has acquired in his previous employment (*United Sterling Corpn v Felton*) and, although he can be restrained by a restrictive covenant not to disclose trade secrets or confidential information, or not to compete with his former employer, such a covenant can only give reasonable protection in limited circumstances (*Herbert Morris Ltd v Saxelby*).

Post-employment restraints

19.20 We have seen that an employer cannot prevent an ex-employee from competing with him, nor using the knowledge, skill and experience gained during the employment. The employer can, however, extract a promise that the ex-employee will not, for a limited period of time, use that knowledge etc to the disadvantage of the employer (*Spafax Ltd v Harrison*), provided the restriction is reasonably necessary for the protection of the employer's business. Thus if an employer has a genuine interest to protect, he can require the employee to sign a covenant, restricting the employee's future activities after the employment comes to an end. Normally, this covenant would be agreed at the commencement of the employment, but this is not essential. In *R S Components Ltd v Irwin* the employer asked a salesman, who was already in employment, to sign a covenant which would have prevented him from soliciting business from the firm's customers for a period of 12 months after leaving the employment. The employee refused to do so, and in consequence was dismissed. It was held that the dismissal was fair for 'some other substantial reason' (see para 17.144).

19.21 There are several limitations on the right of the employer to impose such restraints, for the courts will look with a critical eye on any agreement which has the effect of restraining a person from earning his livelihood in the future. The employer cannot take away the employee's skill, experience and fund of knowledge which he has obtained during the employment, and, in particular, the employer cannot protect himself against competition per se. For example, in *SW Strange Ltd v Mann* the defendant was employed by a firm of bookmakers as a manager. Most of the betting was done by telephone, and hence the defendant had little contact with customers. He agreed that after leaving his employment he would not engage in a similar business within a radius of 12 miles. After leaving his job, he set up as a bookmaker within the prohibited area. It was held that the restriction was void. The purpose of the covenant was not to give legitimate protection to the business interest of the employer, but was a naked attempt to prevent future competition.

19.22 The protection required by the employer must be contained in a restrictive covenant, agreed to by the employee prior to the end of the employment, and is subject to two general limitations. These are (a) the restraint must be designed to protect the legitimate interests of the employer, and (b) it must be reasonable, in terms of the activities prohibited, and in terms of time and area covered by the restraint. The fact that the employee is given a payment to enter into a restrictive covenant is a relevant factor to be taken into account, but it is not conclusive, and the restraint is still required to be justified (*Turner v Commonwealth and British Minerals Ltd*).

19.23 There are four legitimate interests in respect of which the employer is entitled to limited protection, namely (a) trade secrets and confidential information, (b) existing customers and connections, (c) working for competitors, and (d) enticing existing employees.

A. Trade secrets and confidential information

19.24 If an employer could not ensure that his employees would not pass on information concerning his secret processes, it might restrict the employment relationship to an extent where commercial initiative became impossible. The employer would not be able to trust the employee; furtive attempts would have to be made to disclose some information without disclosing all, industrial espionage would flourish, and employees would attempt to sell secrets by offering themselves on the labour market to the highest bidder. Research and development would be hampered and become unprofitable. So, at least, ran the economic theories of former ages, though with the advent of patent law the modern scene might be somewhat different. Nonetheless, the legal principles remain substantially the same. Thus if a trade secret, or a secret process, exists, the employer is entitled to have his employee's promise not to divulge that information to a future employer, at least, subject to possible limitations on time and area. In *Forster & Sons Ltd v Suggett* the defendant was a works engineer concerned with a secret process in the glass-making industry. He covenanted that he would not divulge any trade secret or manufacturing process, and would not be employed by a competitor anywhere in the United Kingdom for five years after leaving his employment with the plaintiffs. It was held that the covenant was reasonable and enforceable.

19.25 It is not possible to restrain an employee from disclosing to a future employer a special method of organisation, as opposed to a secret process, for one must draw a distinction between objective knowledge, such as trade secrets and lists of customers, which are part of the employer's property, and subjective knowledge which has been acquired by the employee, such as his general knowledge of the trade or industry, or his organisational ability. In *Herbert Morris Ltd v Saxelby* an engineer covenanted not to be engaged by a competitor for seven years after leaving his employment. This was held to be void, for it was a restraint on his technical skill and knowledge which he had acquired by his own industry, observation and intelligence, and this could not be taken away from him. On the other hand, in *SBJ Stephenson Ltd v Mandy*, a covenant against the disclosure of any information relating to the company's business affairs which had come into the employee's possession whilst employed by the company was held to be valid. The identity of customers, prices charged, renewal dates, market information and contractual arrangements were objective knowledge capable of being protected. But if an employer wishes to enforce a covenant against the disclosure of confidential information, he must be able to identify a perceived or actual harm from the disclosure which would justify the restraint (*Jack Allen Ltd v Smith*).

19.26 Another example is *Thomas Marshall Ltd v Guinle*, where the defendant was appointed managing director of the claimant company under a 10-year service contract, which contained clauses against disclosing confidential information relating to the affairs, customers or trade secrets of the company, during his employment or after it ceased. He resigned after five years and set up his own competing business. The court granted an injunction against him from acting in breach of the agreement.

B. Existing customers and connections

19.27 An employer is entitled to have a limited protection against an ex-employee dealing with existing customers, for this is part of the goodwill which has been built up over the years. A covenant can restrict the right to solicit or endeavour to entice away former customers, or to have post-employment dealing with such customers, but it is likely that such clauses should be limited to those customers with whom the ex-employee had some dealings, for otherwise the restraint is likely to be regarded as one designed to prevent competition (*Marley Tile Co Ltd v Johnson*). A clause prohibiting the ex-employee from approaching the employer's customers, or persons with whom the employer had been negotiating or who were in the habit of dealing with the employer may be reasonable, particularly if there is a relationship with potential customers which could be built up over a number of years, and the employee was in a position where he could form a bond with those customers (*International Consulting Services (UK) Ltd v Hart*). In *GW Plowman & Sons Ltd v Ash*, the defendant was employed as a sales representative. He covenanted not to canvass or solicit orders from any person who was a customer of the firm for a period of two years after leaving his employment. It was held that the restraint was valid, even though it extended to customers whom the employee did not know or with whom he had no contact during his period of employment. It was argued that the restraint was bad because it could apply to those customers who had ceased to do business with the firm, but the Court of Appeal thought that an employer was entitled not to abandon hope that such customers would return to do business once more.

19.28 On the other hand, if an employee does not come into contact with such customers, then it cannot be argued that he has built up a special relationship with them so as to entitle the employer to extract a covenant restraining the employee from approaching them with a view to taking business away from the employer. For example, if a firm is engaged mainly in trading in the south of England, and has few customers outside that area, a covenant restraining an employee from working in that type of business anywhere in the UK must of necessity be void, as being wider than legitimately required for the protection of the employer's business (*Dowden and Pook Ltd v Pook*). In *Attwood v Lamont* a tailor's cutter in a department store agreed not to be employed by another firm which competed with his employer. Since it can hardly be said that in his position he had gained the trust and confidence of the customers so that they would follow him if he left the firm, the covenant was void. Again, if the business is such that it is not of a recurring nature, then the employer's interest in the customer ceases on the conclusion of a particular transaction, and he is not entitled to protection against poaching. In *Bowler v Lovegrove* the defendant was a negotiating clerk who worked for a firm of estate agents. He covenanted not to enter into a similar business for one year within a restricted area, but it was held that as the business was of a non-recurring nature, the employer had no interest to protect, and the covenant was void.

19.29 The position held by the employee may be relevant, too. An employer can scarcely claim that he fears competition from an ex-employee if, during the period of employment, he pays him a low wage, for this reflects the regard he has for his services (*M and S Drapers v Reynolds*). Nor is an employer entitled to restrain competition by preventing the ex-employee from approaching persons who are not his customers. In *Gledhow Autoparts v Delaney* the claimants employed the defendant as a commercial traveller. It was agreed that after leaving his employment, the defendant would not seek orders from any firm within the area in which he had previously operated. The restraint was held to be void, for as worded, it would have prevented him from calling on firms who were not then customers of the claimants, and was therefore a covenant designed to restrain competition. Nor can a covenant restrain an ex-employee from dealing with businesses which were not in competition with the employer (*Scully UK Ltd v Lee*).

19.30 Moreover, the personality, temperament and general make-up of an employee is his own possession, and there is thus no proprietary right in an employee's own personality which the employer can keep to himself as part of his own business (*Cantor Fitzgerald (UK) Ltd v Wallace*).

19.31 The employer's 'connections' are also a legitimate object for protection. Thus an employment agency which supplied temporary staff to business clients was held to be entitled to extract and enforce a restrictive covenant from its own staff who dealt with the temporary staff (the connection) and the clients (*Office Angels Ltd v Rainer-Thomas*).

C. Working for competitors

19.32 We have seen (para 10.1) that the courts will not grant an injunction to compel a person to work for a particular employer, for this would amount to compulsory labour. Thus if an employee agrees that after leaving his employment, he will not work for anyone the courts will rarely enforce such an agreement because the employee will be faced with the alternative of being forced to work for his former employer or starve! But if the latter alternative does not exist, the courts may be more willing to enforce the agreement.

19.33 In *Littlewoods Organisation Ltd v Harris*, the claimants ran a mail order business, their chief rivals being Great Universal Stores (GUS). The defendant worked for the claimants in a senior position, and had access to confidential information about how the business was operated. He agreed that on leaving his employment, he would not work for GUS for a period of 12 months. He then resigned his position in order to take employment with GUS, and the claimants sought an injunction to restrain him. For the defendant it was argued that the covenant was too wide, and therefore void, for, as worded, it would have prevented him from being employed by GUS anywhere in the world, or by one of their companies which was not concerned with mail order. Nonetheless, the restriction was held to be valid by a majority of the Court of Appeal. It was held that where a covenant in restraint of trade was drafted in general terms, which, without alteration could be construed in a sense which was not unreasonably wide in relation to the relevant confidential information or trade secrets for which the covenantee was seeking protection, the court could construe the covenant in that sense, thereby rendering it valid and enforceable. Accordingly, the covenant should not be construed as applying to the whole range of business carried on by GUS throughout the world, but only to the mail order business carried on in the United Kingdom. So construed, it was no wider than was reasonably necessary to protect the confidential information about the mail order side of the claimants' business, and it was thus enforceable. There is little doubt that this case represents a major shift in the judicial approach to the interpretation of restrictive covenants, though it is arguable that the conclusion is warranted on the special facts.

19.34 But the protection taken out by the employer must be in respect of his specific interests, and if it is too wide for this purpose, it will be void. In *Commercial Plastics Ltd v Vincent*, the claimants employed the defendant to work on the production of PVC calendering sheeting for adhesive tape. The defendant agreed not to be employed by a competitor in the PVC calendering field for one year after leaving his employment. This restriction was held to be void. The protection legitimately required by the claimants could only be in respect of their own business, which was the production of adhesive tape. In fact, the covenant covered the whole field of calendering sheeting, and hence was too wide.

D. Enticing existing employees

19.35 A covenant which purports to restrict the right of an employee to solicit or entice other employees to leave the employer's employment and to work for another employer is generally void. Thus in *Hanover Insurance Brokers Ltd v Schapiro* the defendant entered into a restrictive covenant with his employers which provided, inter alia, that for a period of 12 months after leaving his employment he would not '... solicit or entice any employees of the company to the intent or effect that such employee terminates that employment.' When the defendant left his employment, the employers sought an injunction to restrain him from acting in breach of the clause quoted. It was held that an employee has the right to work for any employer who is willing to employ him. Thus employees are not part of the assets of an employer – like stock in trade or goodwill and customers. A restriction which sought to prevent a person from poaching employees – irrespective of their expertise, technical knowledge and/or juniority, and which could also apply to employees who were not in the particular employment when the defendant left, was clearly a restriction against competition, and therefore void (*TSC Europe UK Ltd v Massey*).

19.36 In *Hanover Insurance Brokers Ltd v Schapiro* (above) a non-solicitation clause was held to be unenforceable because it applied to all employees, irrespective of their position or experience, but different considerations may apply if the covenant purports to restrain the poaching of 'an executive' or a person 'in a senior capacity', and, if necessary, the court will identify those who fall within such categories (*Alliance Paper Group plc v Prestwich*). Further, the Court of Appeal has recently held that an employer has a legitimate interest in maintaining a stable, trained workforce in a highly competitive business (*Ingham v ABC Contract Services Ltd*) which can be protected within the limits of reasonableness by means of a non-solicitation clause (*Dawnay Day Ltd v de Braconier d'Alphen*).

19.37 Employers cannot agree to a restraint among themselves which would not be enforced if it was entered into by their employees. In *Kores Manufacturing Co Ltd v Kolok Manufacturing Co Ltd* two companies, both engaged in the selling of carbon paper, agreed that they would not employ any person who had been employed by the other party for a period of five years after that person had left the other's employment. Had the restraint been imposed by a company on the employees, it would have been void. It was equally void having been made by the employers themselves.

E. Reasonableness of the covenant

19.38 To assess whether or not a covenant in restraint of trade is reasonable, the courts will consider not only the subject-matter of the restraint, but the time and area within which it will operate. If the employer's business is worldwide, a worldwide restraint may be valid (*Nordenfelt v Maxim Nordenfelt Ltd*), but if the employer's business operates in a limited geographical area, a restraint which purports to operate outside that area will not be valid (*Office Angels Ltd v Rainer-Thomas*). A covenant with no geographical limitation will normally be unenforceable (*Commercial Plastics Ltd v Vincent*), as will a covenant which purports to operate in a densely populated area, which is not reasonably necessary for the protection of the employer's connections (*Office Angels Ltd v Rainer-Thomas*). In *Hollis & Co v Stocks* a covenant which restricted a solicitor from working within a 10-mile radius of Sutton-in-Ashfield in Nottinghamshire was upheld, but in *Mason v Provident Clothing and Supply Co Ltd* a covenant restraining a canvasser from competing with his former employer anywhere within 25 miles from the centre of London was held to be void.

19.39 The time element of a restrictive covenant must also be reasonable. In *Herbert Morris Ltd v Saxelby* a seven-year restraint on an engineer was not upheld, although in Nordenfelt's case (above) a 25-year restraint was held to be valid. In the latter case, the worldwide nature of the business, and the price paid for the employee's promise were significant factors in upholding the covenant. Time and area may be looked at together to assess the validity of the covenant. In *Fitch v Dewes* a solicitor's clerk was prohibited from entering into the employment of another solicitor within a radius of seven miles of Tamworth Town Hall. Although this was a lifetime restraint, the modest area enabled him to work quite openly outside the geographical limit, and it was held to be valid.

19.40 The restriction cannot be worded in a manner which prevents the employee from obtaining non-competing employment (*Commercial Plastics Ltd v Vincent* (above)). For example, in *Fellowes & Son v Fisher* the defendant was a conveyancing clerk employed by a firm of solicitors in Walthamstow. He agreed that for five years after leaving his employment, he would not (a) be employed or concerned in the legal profession anywhere within the postal districts of Walthamstow and Chingford, or (b) solicit any person who had been a client of the firm whilst he had been with them. After leaving his employment, he commenced work with another firm of solicitors who had offices in Walthamstow. The Court of Appeal refused to grant an injunction to restrain him. A restraint of five years which covered such a thickly populated area was undoubtedly too wide in the circumstances. Further, clause (a), as worded, would have prevented him from being employed as an assistant to a justices' clerk, or in the legal department of the local authority. In *Greer v Sketchley Ltd*, the activities of the company were confined to the Midlands and London area. The employee agreed that after leaving his employment he would not work for any similar business anywhere in the United Kingdom. This was held to be void; the fact that there was a problematical and possible expansion by the company into other areas of the country was too vague to justify such a wide restraint.

19.41 An area restriction will always be considered critically by the courts, since it will frequently amount to a covenant against competition, which would generally be unenforceable. Thus if such a restriction will do little to protect the employer (eg, because most of the orders are placed on the telephone), or if there is no functional connection with the area covered by the restriction and the areas associated with the employee's work, the restraint is likely to be void (*Office Angels Ltd v Rainer-Thomas*).

F. Interpreting a covenant in restraint of trade

19.42 If a covenant is too restrictive, it will be totally void, and the courts will not enforce it or any part of it. They will not normally validate the agreement by altering it, for the test is whether the parties have in fact made a valid agreement, not whether they could have done so, and it must stand or fall on its own merits. Thus in *Wincanton Ltd v Cranny* a non-competition clause prohibiting post-termination involvement 'in any capacity' with a competing firm was held to be void. The court refused to read into the covenant a reasonable coverage (see also *J A Mont Ltd v Mills*). Exceptionally, however, the courts may relax this strict interpretation by use of a device known as 'the blue pencil' rule.

19.43 The court must be satisfied that (a) the unenforceable provision is capable of being removed without the necessity of adding to or modifying the wording of what remains, (b) the remaining terms continue to be supported by adequate consideration, (c) the removal of the unenforceable provision does not so change the character of the contract that it becomes different from that which the parties entered into, and (d) the severance must be consistent with public policy underlying the avoidance of the offending term (*Marshall v NM Financial Management Ltd*).

19.44 If there are terms which are too wide, and others which are valid and reasonable, then the former may be struck out of the agreement altogether. If those terms which thus remain are valid, then they may be enforced. In *T Lucas & Co Ltd v Mitchell* the defendant was employed by the claimants as a sales representative. He agreed that after leaving his employment he would not (a) deal in any goods similar to those which he had previously sold, or (b) solicit orders from or supply any such goods to any customer of the firm within the Manchester area. The first part of the covenant was clearly void, for this was a restraint on competition. The second part was clearly reasonable. Because there were two separate restraints, capable of being enforced separately, the excision of the first was possible without affecting the second.

19.45 Severance is possible if there is no grammatical difficulty in removing the offending words (*Business Seating Ltd v Broad*). If that which remains is reasonable, the covenant will be enforced (*Rex Stewart Jeffries Parker Ginsberg Ltd v Parker*). The courts will prefer an interpretation which gives effect to the parties' intentions, rather than invalidate it by using a literal interpretation (*Turner v Commonwealth and British Minerals Ltd*).

19.46 If, in the particular circumstances of the case, there is 'a want of accuracy of expression' the court may be prepared to permit an interpretation which would give some sensible meaning to a covenant. Thus in *Business Seating (Renovations) Ltd v Broad*, a clause forbade a sales representative from canvassing, soliciting or endeavouring to take away from the company the business of any client or customers. The nature of 'the business' was not defined, but its meaning could be inferred from the nature of the defendant's employment, and, as a matter of construction, it meant the business carried out by the company.

19.47 It would appear that the courts are now taking a somewhat more relaxed view when construing a restrictive covenant, by seeking objectively to ascertain the intentions of the parties. Thus in *Hollis & Co v Stocks* a restrictive covenant contained a clause prohibiting an assistant solicitor from working for a period of 12 months within a 10-mile radius. This clause was clearly too wide, because it would have prevented him from doing any sort of work, but the Court of Appeal upheld an injunction, arguing that it was clear that the clause was designed to prevent him working as a solicitor. The balance of convenience was in favour of granting the injunction, because damages were not an appropriate remedy, and it was not possible for his former employers to quantify the loss.

19.48 There is a tendency in some cases for the courts to attempt to ascertain the true intentions of the parties and give effect to them, even though some redrafting of the covenant is involved (*GFI Group Inc v Eaglestone*), but the principle remains that the court will not rewrite the covenant so that it has a meaning which is different from that which it has when properly construed.

G. Breach of contract by the employer

19.49 There is a general rule that a party in breach of contract cannot rely on any of its terms in order to gain an advantage. Thus if an employer wrongfully dismisses an employee, he cannot enforce a restrictive covenant, for the whole of the contract will have been repudiated by him (*General Billposting Co Ltd v Atkinson*).

19.50 But in *Campbell v Frisbee* (a case which concerned a contract for services rather than a contract of employment) the High Court held that '. . . an employee's acceptance of an employer's repudiatory breach cannot displace the employer's established property rights, and these include his right in respect of confidential information.' There is no justification for granting as a windfall to a wrongfully dismissed employee a present of his employer's trade secrets or other secrets or confidences. The wrongful dismissal may arise because of a dismissal without notice, or with insufficient notice, or contrary to a con-tractual disciplinary procedure (*Dietmann v Brent London Borough Council*), or breach of a fixed-term contract consequence on the dissolution of a partnership (*Briggs v Oates*). It may even arise out of a constructive dismissal (*Cantor Fitzgerald International v Callaghan*). But if a contract provides that it may be terminated by an employer on giving six months' notice or six months' pay in lieu of notice, an employer who adopts the latter option is not acting in breach of contract (*Rex Stewart Jeffries Parker Ginsberg Ltd v Parker*).

19.51 To avoid this rule, some employers resorted to inserting into the covenant a clause which stated that it was to apply 'howsoever the employment is terminated' or if the contract was terminated 'for whatever reason' etc. Such phrases do not, by themselves, render the covenant unenforceable by virtue of being unreasonable. Not every stipulation in a contract falls when there has been a fundamental breach by one side which has been accepted by the innocent party. Thus if an employee is dismissed for reason of misconduct, or he resigns his employment, the restrictive covenant may still be enforced, despite the presence of the above phrases. The fact that the offending term may apply to some circumstances, but not to others, will not invalidate the convenant (*Rock Refrigeration Ltd v Jones*).

H. Restrictive covenants and transfers

19.52 It will be recalled (see Chapter 9) that if there is a transfer of an undertaking, the contracts of employment of the affected employees will pass automatically from the transferor to the transferee. It therefore follows that if the employee's terms and conditions include a restrictive covenant, then this will bind the employee if he subsequently leaves the transferee's employment. But the covenant needs to be considered in the light of the new situation, otherwise it may be unenforceable (see *Morris Angel & Son Ltd v Hollande*, para 9.27). Equally it is not possible to impose a restrictive convenant on an employee following a transfer, even though the employee agreed to it, if it was introduced by reason of the transfer (*Credit Suisse First Boston (Europe) Ltd v Padiachy*), because the employee is entitled to the terms and conditions which he enjoyed prior to the transfer, and it is irrelevant that he is better off as a result of the variation (*Credit Suisse First Boston (Europe) Ltd v Lister*). However, it does appear that any variation in a contract of employment which takes place unconnected with the transfer may well be valid.

I. Remedies for breach of contract

Injunctive relief

19.53 The prime remedy for the employer if the ex-employee acts in breach of the restrictive covenant is to seek an injunction restraining the breach.

19.54 In considering whether or not to grant an injunction, the court will take account of the 'balance of convenience' in accordance with the principles laid down in *American Cyanamid v Ethicon Ltd*. Three questions need to be asked: (a) is there a serious issue to be tried, (b) would damages be an appropriate remedy if the injunction is not granted, and (c) what is the likelihood of the plaintiff succeeding at a full trial. In *Lansing Linde Ltd v Kerr* it was alleged that the defendant was in breach of a covenant which was designed to prevent him from working for a competitior for a period of 12 months after leaving his employment. The Court of Appeal held that an application for an injunction was rightly refused. The trial of the action would not have taken place until most of the period for which the injunction was sought would have expired. Thus the question was not only whether there was a serious issue to be tried, but also an assessment of the plaintiff's prospect of succeeding at that hearing. The injunction, if granted, would have effectively determined the case in the claimant's favour, and therefore the judge had been correct in considering as an additional factor the strength of the plaintiff's claim.

19.55 Even though an employee is in breach of his covenant, the granting of an injunction to restrain him from working for a competitor is a discretionary remedy, and will only be granted if, on the balance of convenience, it is necessary to do so. In *GFI Group Inc v Eaglestone* the defendant was required by his employment contract to give 20 weeks' notice of termination. He, and two other highly paid employees, decided to resign and work for a competitor. The other two employees were only required to give four weeks' notice. The claimant sought an order to restrain the defendant from working in breach of his contract until the end of the 20-week notice period, but the court decided to uphold the restraint only for 13 weeks. The fact that two other employees had already commenced work for the competitor meant that the reality of the situation was that the damage had already been done. It was not necessary for the protection of the claimant's interests to hold the defendant to the full period of 20 weeks.

19.56 If there is a prima facie breach of a covenant not to deal with the employer's former customers, the employer is entitled to an injunction even though the customer has intimated that he will not do further business with the employer (*John Michael Design plc v Cooke*).

Search orders

19.57 In addition (or as an alternative) to obtaining an injunction, the aggrieved employer may seek a search order. This permits the employer to search the employee's premises or home etc, and to remove documents, drawings, records, prototypes or other specified matter. The purpose is to prevent a defendant from destroying, hiding or removing vital evidence, and to enable the claimant to obtain inspection of any relevant matter in the defendant's possession. A refusal to permit the search, and/or the removal, destruction etc of the evidence not only enables the courts to draw an adverse conclusion, but may also amount to a contempt of court (*Anton Piller KG v Manufacturing Processes Ltd*). Before granting the order, the court must be satisfied (a) that there is a strong prima facie case, (b) the actual or potential damage to the plaintiff would be very serious, and (c) that there is clear evidence that the defendant has in his possession incriminating matter, and that there is a real possibility that he would destroy, hide, remove or otherwise dispose of it (*Lock International plc v Beswick*).

19.58 Search orders are not available in Scotland, although there is a separate procedure by way of letters of request, under which a court may grant a commission and a diligence for the recovery of documents relevant to pending litigation.

Damages

19.59 If the employer can show that he has suffered damage as a result of the breach, he may bring an action accordingly. The amount of damages to be awarded will be such as to put the claimant in the position he would have been in had the contract been performed. Thus in *SBJ Stephenson Ltd v Mandy* the defendant signed a restrictive covenant preventing him from disclosing confidential information, engaging in competing activities and soliciting staff of the employer, for a period of 12 months from the end of the termination of his employment. He resigned his position, and subsequently acted in breach of the covenant. The employers were successful in obtaining an injunction, and were subsequently awarded substantial damages in respect of loss of income from former clients and for future loss.

Account of profits

19.60 An action for an account of profits is essentially based on the equitable principle of unjust enrichment, and is normally available only in those cases where there has been a breach of fiduciary duty or breach of the duty of confidence. Damages are assessed on the profits made by the defendant rather than on any proven loss by the claimant. Thus in *Nottingham University v Fishel* the defendant, a world-renowned fertility expert, was employed by the university. He carried out outside work for overseas clinics, from which he earned money. He also benefited financially from work performed by junior colleagues under his supervision. It was held that the university was entitled to an account of profits for this breach of fiduciary duty.

Actions against third parties

19.61 An action for inducing a breach of contract may be brought against someone who induces an employee to breach his contract of employment (*Bents Brewery Co Ltd* *v Hogan*) or to break the terms of a restrictive covenant. As well as obtaining an injunction (*Hivac v Park Royal Scientific Instruments Ltd*), the injured party may seek damages in tort (*British Industrial Plastics Ltd v Ferguson*).

Training agreements

19.62 An employer may permit an employee to go on a training course (possibly with paid leave of absence) under an agreement whereby the employee agrees to serve the employer for a specified period after completing the course. Clearly, such an agreement can be for the mutual benefit of both parties. The problem arises when the employee fails to serve the employer for the specified period. In *Strathclyde Regional Council v Neil*, the defendant was employed by the claimants as a trainee social worker. She was given paid leave of absence to go on a training course, and signed an agreement to serve the council for two years after completing the course. The agreement also specified that if she left her employment before completing two years' service she would refund to the council a sum of money, proportionate to the unexpired period of the contractual two years. After completing the course, she worked for the council for 15 months, and resigned her employment. It was held that the council could recover a proportion of their expenditure in respect of her salary, course fees, examination fees and book allowance. The terms of the contract were not extravagant or unconscionable.

20

Practice and Procedure

Making a claim to an employment tribunal

20.1 Subject to the provisions relating to the statutory disciplinary and dismissal and grievance procedures (see para 12.39), an employee who wishes to seek the enforcement of a statutory right, or to obtain a remedy for a breach of that right must present his claim to an employment tribunal within the appropriate time limit. An application for interim relief must be made within seven days of the dismissal, and a claim for a redundancy payment must be made within six months from the relevant date, although the employment tribunal has a discretion to extend the period for a further six months in certain circumstances if it is just and equitable to do so (ERA, s 164). Claims for equal pay must also be presented within six months from the termination of employment, as must a claim based on a dismissal connected with official industrial action (see para 21.104), and a claim against a trade union in respect of unlawful exclusion or expulsion.

20.2 The general principle is that all other claims must be presented within three months of the act complained of, unless it was not reasonably practicable to present the claim earlier, in which case it may be presented within such further period as the employment tribunal considers reasonable. So far as claims based on race or sex discrimination or disability are concerned, the employment tribunal must consider whether it is just and equitable to extend the time limit (*British Coal Corpn v Keeble*). If the statutory dismissal, disciplinary or grievance procedure is being followed, a further three months is allowed before the claim becomes out of time (see para 12.71).

20.3 Generally, there are two separate issues to consider. The first is whether or not it was reasonably practicable to present the claim within the time limits. If it was, that will usually be the end of the matter. The second is whether the employment tribunal should exercise its discretion so as to permit the claim to be admitted within such further period as it considers is reasonable. Thus, if a claimant makes a claim which is outside the three-month limit, but subsequently discovers facts which lead him to believe that he has a further legitimate complaint, the employment tribunal may still exercise its discretion to allow the latter complaint, even though there is no jurisdiction to consider the former (*Marley (UK) Ltd v Anderson*).

20.4 If the employee was not aware of the facts which gave rise to a potential complaint until after the three-month time limit has expired (eg the alleged acts of race or sex discrimination, see *Berry v Ravensbourne National Health Service Trust*), then it may be just and equitable or reasonable to allow the late submission of a claim, provided he acts expeditiously once he is aware of the true state of affairs (*Machine Tool Industry Research Association v Simpson*).

20.5 If the act complained of is a continuing act (eg race or sex or disability discrimination) which extends over a period, time will run from the end of the period (*Barclays Bank plc v Kapur*). The date on which the cause of the action crystallised will depend on the facts of each case (see *Clarke v Hampshire Electro-Plating Co Ltd*, para 4.147). If a claimant is ill during the three-month period, attention should be focused on whether the illness falls in the earlier weeks or in the far more critical weeks leading up to the expiry of the limitation period if the employment tribunal is considering whether to permit the claim outside the three-month period (*Schultz v Esso Petroleum*).

20.6 In deciding whether or not to allow a claim which is out of time, the employment tribunal must first enquire into the circumstances as to why it was not reasonably practicable to present it before the end of the relevant period. 'Practicable', in this connection, means 'feasible', and it is a question of fact for the employment tribunal to determine as to whether it was reasonably feasible to present the claim in time (*Palmer v Southend-on-Sea Borough Council*). Thus if the time limit expires on a non-working day (eg Sunday), an application will be out of time if it is presented on the following day (*Swainston v Hetton Victory Club Ltd*). However, the employment tribunal will consider whether to exercise their discretion to allow the complaint to be presented out of time, but this will only be permitted in exceptional circumstances (*Walls Meat Co v Khan*). If an employee is dismissed on the 14th day of the month, his claim must be presented on or before the 13th day of the third month following. If the month in question has no corresponding date (ie because it is a shorter month), the three-month period will expire at the end of the relevant month. Thus if an employee is dismissed on 30 November, his claim must be presented by 28 February (or 29th, if it is a leap year, see *Pruden v Cunard Ellerman Ltd*).

20.7 If an employee or his representatives (eg trade union official or solicitor) are at fault in not presenting the claim in time, then it is likely that the employment tribunal will refuse jurisdiction (*Times Newspapers v O'Regan*), but if an employee is blameless, it may be easier to infer that it was not reasonably practicable to present the claim in time (*Union Cartage Co Ltd v Blunden*). If the employer expressly requests that the application be delayed so that negotiations can take place with a view to reaching an amicable settlement, then it may not be practicable to present the claim within the time limit (*Owen v Crown House Engineering Ltd*). Ignorance of one's legal rights is not an excuse for not presenting the claim within the three-month period (*Avon County Council v Haywood-Hicks*), but mistaken advice given by a member of the staff of the employment tribunal may be a ground for extending the time limit (*London International College v Sen*). If a claimant knows of the time limits, or has been advised of them, or if he is capable of looking after his own affairs etc, it is for the employment tribunal to decide how much weight to place on all the factors which have led to the claim being presented out of time (*Robinson v Post Office*).

20.8 In a discrimination case, wrong advice by a legal adviser may be regarded as a valid excuse for not presenting a claim within the time limits, since it may be just and equitable to allow the claim to be presented out of time (*Chohan v Derby Law Centre*). However, this rule does not necessarily apply in the straightforward unfair dismissal case (or similar cases), where the test is that of reasonable practicability, not what is just and equitable.

There is no rule of law which states that if a claimant receives wrong advice from an advice bureau this will prevent him from asserting that it was not reasonably practicable to present the claim within the appropriate time limit (*Marks and Spencer plc v Williams Ryan*). The tribunal should balance the lack of real prejudice to the employer against the disadvantage to the claimant (*Baynton v South West Trains Ltd*). If, however, a claimant is held to be out of time because a skilled adviser has failed to ensure that the time limit was met, the claimant may sue for negligence or breach of contract (*Allen v Hammett*), although if it can be shown that the proposed claim had no prospect of success, the claimant is unlikely to recover damages (*Siraj-Eldin v Campbell Middleton Burness & Dickson*).

20.9 All complaints must actually be received (*Secretary of State for Employment v Banks*) by the Central Office of Employment Tribunals (COET) within the appropriate time limits (before midnight, see *Post Office v Moore*), although an application received by a Regional Office will be valid if presented in time (*Bengey v North Devon District Council*). If the application does not arrive in time because of an abnormal delay in the post, the claimant will have to rely on the escape clause (*Beanstalk Shelving Ltd v Horn*).

20.10 Documents or letters despatched by first class post are expected to arrive in the ordinary course of events on the second working day after posting; documents and letters sent by second class post are expected to arrive on the fourth working day after posting (*St Basil's Centre Ltd v McCrossan*). If there is a postal strike, appropriate allowances should be made (*Beanstalk Shelving Ltd v Horn*) although alternative means of delivery should be arranged. Working days are Monday to Friday but, technically, bank or public holidays are *dies non* (non-days), and time limits are accordingly extended (*Ford v Stakis Hotels and Inns Ltd*).

20.11 Thus if an application is posted, but arrives one day after the time limits have expired, it is open to the employment tribunal to decide if the claimant could have reasonably expected the application to be delivered in the ordinary course of the post. This is a question of fact for the employment tribunal to determine on the evidence (*St Basil's Centre v McCrossan*). On the post rules generally, see *Consignia plc v Sealy*.

20.12 But if, though posted in time, an application does not appear to have been received by COET, prudence requires that the claimant (or his representative) should make further enquiries, because it should be obvious from the failure to receive an acknowledgment that something is amiss, and therefore confirmation should be sought as to its arrival. It follows that if nothing is done to check the receipt of an application which has in fact never arrived, a fresh application may well be out of time (*Capital Foods Retail Ltd v Corrigan*). Indeed, a solicitor who submits an application on behalf of a client is expected to have a proper system operating which enables him to find out, contemporaneously, whether the conduct of business is taking a normal course, and to check, at or near the time, that replies which should have been received at a given date have in fact been received. Thus in *Camden and Islington Community Services NHS Trust v Kennedy*, the claimant's claim for unfair dismissal had to be presented by 27 December. Her solicitor posted her application on 19 December, but although he expected to receive an acknowledgment by 5 January, he delayed checking with the tribunal office until 30 January, when he was told that it had not been received. He posted another application the following day. It was held that the claim was out of time. Solicitors practising in the field of employment law must be aware of the need to comply strictly with the appropriate time limits, and ensure that they have in place systems which ensure that time limits are complied with.

20.13 If, in error, a claimant names the wrong employer in his application, an employment tribunal may, at the request of the claimant or on its own motion, add any other person to be joined in the proceedings, even though this is done outside the normal time limit for presenting a claim. The employment tribunal may exercise its discretion to join the other party not only when the claimant has misnamed or misdescribed the respondent, but also when he has failed to identify the 'correct' employer (eg where his contract has been transferred by virtue of the Transfer of Undertakings (Protection of Employment) Regulations; see *Drinkwater Sabey Ltd v Burnett*).

20.14 The general power to extend time limits on the ground that it is just and equitable to do so is to be used sparingly. The onus is on the applicant to show good reason, and the initial assumption is that an extension is to be the exception, not the rule (*Robertson v Bexley Community Centre*).

20.15 If the statutory disciplinary, dismissal or grievance procedures apply (see para 12.40), or if they are deemed to have been complied with (see para 12.47) the three-month time limit will be extended by a further three months in the following circumstances:

(a) In an express dismissal case, where the employee has reasonable grounds for believing that the disciplinary and dismissal procedure, whether statutory or otherwise, including the appeal procedure, was being followed, and had not been completed.

(b) In a constructive dismissal case, or, if the claim relates to one of the statutory claims listed in EA 2002, Sch 4 (see para 12.69), where the employee lodges a grievance in writing with the employer within the time limit of three months from the date of the action complained of, has waited 28 days for a response, and then issues tribunal proceedings.

(c) In a constructive dismissal claim, or where the claim relates to one of the statutory claims listed in EA 2002, Sch 4, where an employee issues a tribunal claim within the normal time limit of three months, but it is rejected under s 32 of the Act because no written grievance has been submitted to the employer, and the employee then submits a grievance and waits a further 28 days before reissuing the tribunal claim.

20.16 The statutory time limits go to the employment tribunal's jurisdiction, and if a claim is presented out of time, the tribunal will be unable to hear the claim even though the employer fails to take the point (*Rogers v Bodfari (Transport) Ltd*). But there is no time limit as such when it is proposed to add a new respondent, or substitute another one, to an application which has been lodged in time (*Drinkwater Sabey Ltd v Burnett*). If the claimant's claim is for breach of contract under the Employment Tribunals Extension of Jurisdiction Order, which is out of time, the employer's counterclaim, presented in time, can be proceeded with (*Patel v RCMS Ltd*).

A. Time limits for enforcing Community rights

20.17 European law (ie the Treaty of Rome or EC directives) does not specify any particular time limits for bringing proceedings when an employee is seeking to enforce a

Community right. The general principle to be adopted was laid down in *Fisscher v Voorhuis Hengelo BV* where the European Court held that national rules relating to time limits for bringing such actions were to be applied, providing that they are no less favourable than similar actions of a domestic nature, and do not render the exercise of rights conferred by Community law impossible in practice.

20.18 Thus, in principle, domestic time limits will apply, but the question arises, what are the time limits when it is discovered that UK law does not meet the requirements of EC law? Does time start to run from when the cause of action arose, or from when it is discovered that UK law is defective, or from when UK law is brought into line with EC law?

20.19 Part of the answer is to be found by considering the EC law which is being sought to enforce, bearing in mind that employment tribunals are creatures of statute, and may only exercise jurisdiction over matters specified in respective UK legislation. There have been a number of cases where the UK have failed to implement an EC requirement altogether, or failed to implement it fully or properly, and claimants have tried to re-open matters at a later date, arguing that time runs from when the UK should have implemented the article of the Treaty of Rome or Directive, as appropriate, or from when it was discovered that such a right existed. Generally speaking, these arguments will fail. Thus in *Biggs v Somerset County Council* the claimant worked for 14 hours per week as a teacher. She was dismissed in 1976, after having been employed for less than two years. As the law then stood, she had no right to bring a claim for unfair dismissal, but following the decision in *R v Secretary of State for Employment, ex p Equal Opportunities Commission* (decided in 1994), she immediately brought a claim for unfair dismissal, arguing that the qualifying threshold condition should be disapplied, as being contrary to EC law. The Court of Appeal held that her claim was not brought within the requisite time limit of three months from the date of her dismissal. Although in 1976, when she was dismissed, she would have been unaware of the impact of s 2 of the European Communities Act 1972 or the effect of the decision of the European Court of Justice in *Defrenne v Sabena*, her mistake was one of law, not of fact. There was no legal impediment to her bringing a claim and arguing that the restriction on part-time workers was indirectly discriminatory. The fact that she (and her advisers) did not fully understand the law at the time was not a ground for re-opening past transactions. The complaint was not presented within the time limit of three months, nor within a reasonable time after the expiry of that limit.

20.20 Similarly, in *Barber v Staffordshire County Council*, the Court of Appeal refused to permit a claimant to bring a new claim based on EU law when an earlier claim had already been dismissed by an employment tribunal. The doctrine of issue estoppel applies.

20.21 However, the decision in *Biggs v Somerset County Council* does not preclude all retrospective claims which are instituted as a result of a new interpretation of EC law. In *British Coal Corpn v Keeble* the EAT expressed the view that the decision in *Biggs* was only applicable to those cases where the claimant had failed to show that it was not reasonably practicable to bring the claim within the appropriate time limits. But, said the EAT, this did not apply to those cases where an extension of time is possible because it is 'just and equitable' to do so. Thus if a person is under a misapprehension of the law (eg due to some earlier legal ruling) a tribunal would still have a discretion to grant an extension of time. This discretion is only available in the areas of sex, race and disability discrimination. Thus in *DPP v Marshall* a transsexual made a claim for unlawful discrimination three years after the date when the cause of action arose, but within three months from the date of a decision of the European Court which had decided that gender re-assignment came within the scope of the EC Equal Treatment Directive. The EAT upheld a tribunal's finding that it was just and equitable to permit the claim to be heard on its merits.

B. Effective date of termination (s 97)

20.22 So far as unfair dismissals are concerned, the claim must be presented within three months from the effective date of termination (EDT) of employment. This date can be:

(a) if the employment is terminated with notice, the date on which that notice expires; or

(b) if the employment is terminated without notice, the date on which the termination takes effect; or

(c) in the case of a limited-term contract (ie a fixed-term or a task contract: see para 17.23) which terminated by virtue of the limiting event without being renewed under the same contract, the date on which the termination takes effect.

In other words, the effective date of termination is the actual date when the employment comes to an end (*Alboni v Ind Coope Retail*) and that date cannot be varied by any subsequent agreement between the parties. However, the notice that determines the effective date of termination can be varied, so that there can be a subsequent agreement that the effective date of termination can be brought forward or pushed backward, and time will start to run from the new date (*Palfrey v Transco plc*).

20.23 Certain problems have arisen out of this. In *Dixon v Stenor Ltd* Sir John Donaldson pointed out that there were four situations commonly met. The first is where the employee is given notice, and works to the end of that notice. The second is where there is a summary dismissal, and the third is where the employee is given money in lieu of notice. These cases are fairly straightforward, but the fourth situation presented a problem. This was where the employee is dismissed with notice, but is not required to work the period of that notice. In effect, he is on paid garden leave, and his employment does not effectively terminate until the notice expires, even though he may not be working during that time. If he were to submit an application during this period, in effect it would be premature. However, ERA, s 111(3) provides that if a dismissal is with notice, a tribunal may consider a complaint notwithstanding that it is presented before the effective date of termination of the employment. In other words, an employee may bring a complaint as soon as he receives his notice, or within three months from the effective date of termination of his employment.

20.24 If an employee is dismissed, and pursues an appeal through the domestic procedures, there are two possibilities. If the procedure provides for an immediate dismissal, with the possibility of reinstatement should the appeal be successful, the EDT is the date of dismissal (*J Sainsbury Ltd v Savage*). If the procedure provides for a suspension of the dismissal with the possibility of it being lifted following a successful appeal, the EDT is the date when the appeal was dismissed should the dismissal be confirmed (*Drage v Governors of Greenford High School*).

20.25 The fact that the employer retains the employee's P45 is irrelevant to the effective date of termination (*Newham London Borough v Ward*).

20.26 If an employer dismisses an employee without notice, but gives him a payment in lieu of notice, the effective date of termination is the date of dismissal (ERA, s 97(1)). Consequently, if on that date the employee does not have the requisite length of continuous employment, he cannot pursue his claim for unfair dismissal, unless, of course, he can add on his statutory notice 'to pull him past the post' (s 97(2), see para 15.26). If notice of termination is given orally, the period of notice commences the day after it has been given, and the effective date of termination is calculated accordingly (*West v Kneels Ltd*).

20.27 If an employee is dismissed with notice, he may bring his claim before the notice period expires, ie before the effective date of termination (ERA, s 111(3)), but a warning of a possible dismissal in the future is not a dismissal, and hence the presentation of a claim may be premature (*Rai v Somerfield Stores Ltd*, para 17.16 and see para 18.8).

20.28 The effective date of termination cannot be earlier than the date on which the employee receives notice of the dismissal. There is no room for a doctrine of 'presumed or constructive knowledge' of a dismissal (*McMaster v Manchester Airport plc*). Although the parties may agree a prospective date of termination, they cannot agree a retrospective date, because the EDT is dependent on what actually happened, and not what they may have agreed to treat as having happened. In any case, a consensual arrangement to antedate the date of termination would be a provision which purports to limit the operation of the Act, which would be void under s 203(1) (*Fitzgerald v University of Kent at Canterbury*).

20.29 It should be noted that s 97(2) will extend the effective date of termination by the requisite statutory notice for the purposes of s 92 (right to have written reasons for dismissal), s 94 (unfair dismissal), s 119(1) (calculation of the basic award) and s 227(3) (increases the maximum allowable week's pay), but not for the purpose of computing the time limit within which a claim must be brought under s 111(2).

20.30 If an employee's claim is based on constructive dismissal, time will run from when the resignation is actually communicated to the employer, whether by written or oral communication or by conduct (*Edwards v Surrey Police*), and this applies to claims based on race and sex and disability discrimination. In so far as the employer's conduct may have resulted in the employee suffering a detriment, the three-month time limit runs from the date of that conduct, not from when the employee decides to treat the repudiatory breach as putting an end to the contract of employment (*Metropolitan Police Comr v Harley*; but see para 12.66).

20.31 If the employee resigns with notice, he may present his claim before that notice has expired (*Presley v Llanelli Borough Council*), but if he resigns without notice, he can rely on the provisions of s 97(4) to 'pull him past the post' if he lacks the necessary period of continuous employment (see para 15.26).

C. Submitting a claim

20.32 All claims must now be presented to an employment tribunal office on the prescribed form (ET1), the only exceptions being certain claims brought under the National Minimum Wage Act, ss 19–21, proceedings brought by an employer under ERA, s 11, appeals against the industrial training levy, and appeals against a non-discrimination order. A claim must contain the prescribed information, which basically will be the name and address of the claimant and respondent, and details of the claim. The Secretary of Tribunals may refuse to accept the claim if it does not provide the requisite information, or if the tribunal does not have power to consider the claim (eg, because the claimant lacks the necessary qualifying conditions, or because the tribunal has no jurisdiction in the matter) or the employee has not raised a grievance with the employer as required by the Employment Act 2002, s 32(2)–(4) (but see para 12.72).

20.33 If the Secretary does refuse to accept the claim, he may refer the matter to a tribunal chairman who will decide whether the claim should be accepted. The chairman may invite the claimant to a pre-acceptance hearing, before he decides the matter.

20.34 It is the duty of the claimant to state (with as much precision as possible) the nature of the claim, but the employment tribunal will not investigate on its own motion every allegation made but not pursued by a party (*Mensah v East Hertfordshire NHS Trust*). Generally a claimant will be precluded from bringing fresh proceedings in respect of a matter which could and should have been litigated in earlier proceedings (*Divine-Bortey v Brent London Borough Council*).

D. Employer's response

20.35 A copy of the claim will be sent to the respondent employer, who must reply on the response form within 28 days of it being sent to him, although an application may be made before the 28 days have elapsed for an extension of time. A failure to present a response within the time limit will result in a default judgment being issued without a hearing, which can be on liability and/or quantum. To have the default judgment set aside, an application for review must be made within 14 days from when the default judgment was sent to the parties. In deciding whether or not to set the default judgment aside, the tribunal chairman must have regard to all the circumstances of the case, including the merits of the defence and any prejudice to either party (*Pendragon plc v Copus*).

The response should contain sufficient particulars to indicate the grounds on which the claim is to be resisted, and if it fails to do so, or if it is not presented in time, the Secretary may decline to accept it, or may refer the matter to a tribunal chairman, who will decide whether or not to accept it. If necessary, the chairman will invite the parties to a pre-hearing review (see para 20.69).

20.36 The 'label' which is attached to the response by the employer is generally irrelevant, as long as the response contains all the relevant information, for the actual legal position is a matter for the tribunal to determine on consideration of the factual evidence. Thus, if an employer submits that the reason for a dismissal was 'redundancy', and the facts are fully investigated by the tribunal, it is open to them to find that the reason was for 'some other substantial reason' (*Hannan v TNT-IPEC (UK) Ltd*). All relevant defences should be pleaded, if necessary in the alternative (*Church v West Lancashire NHS Trust*).

20.37 Once the claim has been made, a copy will be sent to the conciliation officer. The latter is under a statutory duty, either at the request of the parties or on his own initiative if he thinks he can be successful, to endeavour to promote a settlement without the matter going to a tribunal hearing, either by getting the parties to agree on reinstatement or re-engagement of the claimant, or securing agreement on the amount of compensation to be paid, or to get the claimant to withdraw his claim because it has little prospect of success (see para 1.7). There will be the standard or short periods of conciliation, as appropriate (see para 1.8).

20.38 From the available figures, it would appear that more than half of the complaints are settled without a tribunal hearing, though the confidential nature of the work of the conciliation officer is such that we have little knowledge of the terms or circumstances. About 70% of the cases referred to conciliation officers are settled on the basis of some form of monetary payment by the employer. The bulk of the remaining cases are settled because the claimant withdraws the claim, and in a few cases, there will be an agreement for reinstatement or re-engagement. Any communication to the conciliation officer is not admissible in evidence without the consent of the party who communicated it. In *M and W Grazebrook Ltd v Wallens* certain documents, which had been prepared by the personnel manager after the claimant had been dismissed, were shown to the conciliation officer. It was held that the documents were not covered by the privilege, for to find otherwise would enable a party to prevent disclosure of evidence by deliberately communicating it to the conciliation officer. On the other hand, if the documents had been specially prepared for the purpose of showing them to the conciliation officer then no disclosure can be ordered.

20.39 A claim under ERA, s 94 has two objects. First, the claimant will be seeking a finding that he has a statutory remedy and, second, he will be seeking compensation. Both those matters are justiciable before the employment tribunal. Thus, if the employers offer to pay the maximum compensation which would be payable, this does not prevent the claimant from proceeding with his claim in order to obtain a finding that the dismissal is unfair, where the employers are unwilling to concede this (*Telephone Information Services Ltd v Wilkinson*).

20.40 It will be seen (below) that an agreement reached whereby an employee agrees to waive his statutory rights is generally void, subject to certain exceptions, and hence the fact that the employee has accepted a sum in settlement (even though this may be in excess of the statutory compensation limits) does not preclude an employment tribunal from hearing the claim (*NRG Victory Reinsurance Ltd v Alexander*), and it is not vexatious or frivolous to pursue such a claim.

E. Restrictions on contracting out (ERA, s 203)

20.41 Subject to the exceptions noted below, an employee cannot voluntarily surrender or contract out of his statutory rights, and any statement or agreement to that effect is void. A private settlement between the parties, even one purporting to be in full and final settlement of all or any outstanding claims cannot prevent an employee from pursuing the matter further in the employment tribunal, for an employee cannot opt out of his statutory rights.

20.42 Thus in *Council of Engineering Institutions v Maddison* the employee accepted £1,600 in consideration that he would forgo any claim against his former employers. This was held to be void. The object of the legislation is to prevent hasty and imprudent agreements being entered into by the employee. On the other hand, such an agreement, whilst void, can be taken account of by the employment tribunal, and if it provides for compensation at a level not less than that which would have been awarded by the tribunal, then the employee will not have suffered any loss, and no further award will be made.

Further, it will be recalled (para 17.46) that an agreement for a financial settlement as a price for a resignation is not void under the Act (*Sheffield v Oxford Controls Co Ltd*). In practice, if an agreed settlement is reached, it is sound policy to call in the conciliation officer, thus turning the agreement into a binding one.

20.43 The exceptions to the rule are as follows:

(a) Any settlement made under the auspices of the conciliation office from ACAS acting under his statutory powers, whether the settlement is made orally or in writing, will be binding on the parties (*Gilbert v Kembridge Fibres Ltd*), and can be enforced. But the settlement, usually made on Form COT3, will only apply to the matters contained therein. Thus if a settlement is made to an unfair dismissal claim made under ERA, this will not bar a subsequent claim under other legislation, eg Sex Discrimination Act etc unless such claims have been specifically excluded (*Livingstone v Hepworth Refractories Ltd*). In the absence of precise language, sign-ing Form COT3 does not necessarily bar a further claim by an employee based on facts of which the employee was ignorant at the time the agreement was signed (*Bank of Credit and Commerce International SA v Ali*).

Where a counsel, solicitor, CAB adviser or member of a law centre, who has been named as a representative, holds himself out as having authority to negotiate and reach a settlement on behalf of a claimant, then, in the absence of any notice to the contrary, the other party is entitled to assume that the adviser has such authority. Thus an agreement reached between the adviser and the conciliation officer will be binding on the claimant whether or not the adviser has actual authority to enter into it. Thus the ostensible authority of the adviser extends beyond the pleadings and presentation of the case, but includes all the actual and potential issues which are known to the parties (*Freeman v Sovereign Chicken Ltd*).

(b) A collective agreement which provides for guaranteed remuneration where all parties have applied to the minister for an Order excluding the right to receive guarantee pay under s 35. About 30 such Orders have been made.

(c) A dismissal procedure agreement which provides for remedies at least as effective as ERA which has been designated by the minister by Order on an application by all the parties. However, such exclusion from statutory rights does not apply to failure to permit a woman to return to work after childbirth, dismissal for reason of pregnancy or childbirth, dismissal of protected shop or betting workers, dismissal for asserting a statutory right, and an inadmissible reason for redundancy.

(d) A collective agreement which provides for redundancy payments where all the parties have applied to the minister for an exemption Order. A few such Orders have been made under this provision.

(e) A fixed contract of two years or more where the employee has agreed in writing to exclude his right to a redundancy payment (this only applies to agreements entered into prior to 10 July 2002).

(f) A compromise agreement, which satisfied the following conditions:
   (i)   the agreement must be in writing;
   (ii) it must relate to particular proceedings;
   (iii) the employee must have received advice from a relevant independent adviser

as to the terms of the proposed agreement and its effect. An independent legal adviser is a qualified lawyer (barrister, solicitor, Fellow of the Institute of Legal Executives, or advocate), official, employee or member of an independent trade union who has been certified in writing as being competent and authorised to give advice on behalf of the trade union, a worker at an advice centre who has been certified in writing as being competent to give advice on behalf of the centre, or a person of a description specified in an order made by the Secretary of State;

(iv) the adviser must have a professional indemnity insurance policy or be covered by a contract of insurance;

(v) the agreement must identify the adviser; and

(vi) the agreement must state that the conditions regulating the compromise agreement under the Act are satisfied.

Compromise agreements may be made in respect of all those claims for which the employment tribunal has jurisdiction under the Employment Tribunals Act 1996, s 18(1), which covers most, though not all, of the rights contained in ERA, TULR(C)A (except a failure to consult with a trade union on redundancies), Sex Discrimination Act, Equal Pay Act, Race Relations Act and Disability Discrimination Act, Part-time Workers (Prevention of Less Favourable Treatment) Regulations 2000, Fixed-Term Employees (Prevention of Less Favourable Treatment) Regulations 2002, Employment Equality (Sexual Orientation) Regulations 2003 and Employment Equality (Religion or Belief) Regulations 2003. Compromise agreements are binding in respect of the particular complaints mentioned therein. A further claim may be made (within the appropriate time limits) in respect of matters not within the terms of the agreement (*Lunt v Merseyside TEC Ltd*). Thus the agreement should be drawn up in such a way that all matters which could be the subject of a complaint are effectively covered.

(g) An agreement to submit the dispute to arbitration under a scheme prepared by ACAS, which has been approved by the Secretary of State, under the provisions of TULR(C)A, s 212A (see para 1.12).

20.44 Strictly speaking, a compromise agreement can only settle those claims which have actually been raised (as a concern, not necessarily as a tribunal claim) at the date of the agreement (*Lunt v Merseyside TEC Ltd*). Thus very clear language must be used to ensure that a claimant releases claims or rights of which he is unaware or could not have been aware (*Hinton v University of London*).

20.45 One distinction between an ACAS COT3 and a compromise agreement is that the COT3 can be made in full and final settlement of all claims, whether actual or potential, whereas a compromise agreement 'must relate to the particular proceedings'. However, if the applicant (or his adviser) was aware of the possibility of further claims, the signing of a compromise agreement will be binding, because such additional claims would have been in contemplation when the agreement was signed (*Byrnell v British Telecommunications plc*).

20.46 A compromise agreement is a contract connected with employment, and as such it may be enforced in an employment tribunal under the provisions of the Employment Tribunals Extension of Jurisdictions Order (*Rock-It Cargo Ltd v Green*), and see para 1.31).

F. Death of the employer or employee

20.47 Where the employer dies, certain tribunal proceedings may be defended by the personal representative of the deceased employer (ERA, s 206). The relevant proceedings are those arising out of itemised pay statements, guarantee payments, protection from detriments, time off work (but not occupational pension scheme trustees), suspension from work on medical or maternity grounds, maternity and parental leave, written statements of reasons for dismissal, unfair dismissal, redundancy payments and rights on employer's insolvency. The personal representatives will have to perform all the obligations of the deceased, and any rights which accrue after death shall continue to devolve, and any liability which has not so accrued prior to death shall be treated as if it was a liability of the deceased employer immediately before death. For example, if an employer dies before or during a tribunal hearing, at the time of death, no liability has been incurred; once the tribunal makes an award, the liability shall be treated as if it had occurred prior to the death.

20.48 If the business does not carry on after the death of the employer, the employee will be deemed to have been dismissed for reason of redundancy, and will be entitled to the appropriate payment from the personal representatives. If the business does carry on functioning, and the employee continues to be employed by the personal representatives or trustees, there is no termination of employment, and continuity of employment is preserved (ERA, s 218(4)).

20.49 Similarly, where it is the employee who has died, the above tribunal proceedings may be instituted or continued by his personal representatives, or, if there is no such person, by any appropriate person appointed by the tribunal. On a claim for unfair dismissal, obviously the reinstatement or re-engagement provisions cannot apply, but the tribunal can nonetheless consider the question of compensation, and be enforced accordingly (Employment Tribunals Awards (Enforcement in case of Death) Regulations 1976).

20.50 There are no specific provisions which permit claims for sex, race or disability discrimination to be continued after the death of the employee, but apparently such claims may be brought under the provisions of the Law Reform (Miscellaneous Provisions) Act 1934 (see *Lewisham and Guy's Mental Health Trust v Andrews*). The 1934 Act does not apply to Scotland, but this was not necessary because Scottish common law always permitted an executor to pursue claims on behalf of a deceased person, and thus there is no reason why discrimination claims cannot be continued after the death of the claimant (*Executors of Soutar v James Murray & Co (Cupar) Ltd*).

Employment tribunal procedure

20.51 The Employment Tribunals (Constitution and Rules of Procedure) Regulations 2004 lay down the procedural rules for the various type of claims which may be brought before an employment tribunal. Schedule 1 lays down the general procedural rules, Sch 2 deals with national security issues, Sch 3 deals with appeals against the imposition of industrial levies, Sch 4 deals with appeals against the imposition of improvement and prohibition notices, Sch 5 deals with appeals against non-discrimination notices, and Sch 6 deals with equal value claims.

20.52 Although the procedural rules are detailed and precise, and are, in some respects, strictly construed, they should not be interpreted in such a way as to avoid injustice, or to drive away a possibly meritorious claimant or respondent (*Richardson v U Mole Ltd*). Regard must always be had to the interests of justice. The rules must not be interpreted so as to prevent an employment tribunal from entertaining jurisdiction to hear a claim for which primary legislation has provided an employment right, and a mandatory requirement in the rules must not be taken to the point of denying a claimant access to the tribunal system. Thus, in deciding under reg 1(4) whether the claimant has provided 'details of the claim' the test is whether, from the claim as presented, it is clear that the complainant is complaining about a breach of an employment right which falls within the jurisdiction of the employment tribunal. Thus if the claim appears to be defective on the face of it, the chairman should seek further and better particulars under reg 11 (*Grimmer v KLM Cityhopper UK*).

20.53 At the same time, it can be noted that the Employment Appeal Tribunal Rules were amended in 2004 so as to ensure harmony and consistency between the two jurisdictions, as well as a number of consequential improvements in procedures generally being made. In particular an attempt has been made to dispose of meritless appeals at the outset.

20.54 Generally speaking, the tribunal will regulate its own procedure. However, within that parameter, a tribunal must not only act fairly but be seen to act fairly. Thus, a tribunal chairman or member should not adjudicate on a case if s/he has some personal connection with either of the parties, or some knowledge of the facts (over and above those facts which are presented in evidence), or have an interest in the outcome of the case. In particular they must be careful not to show any animosity against a party or any form of bias, whether against a party to the proceedings or a representative. If there is any possibility of a conflict of interest arising, the tribunal chairman should first seek to ascertain whether there is another chairman (or tribunal member, as appropriate) who can hear the case. If not, he should give a full explanation (recorded or carefully noted, so as to avoid controversy about what was said), and, if there is a serious objection, as opposed to a fanciful one, give the party affected the option of having the hearing continued, or having it heard by a differently constituted tribunal (*Jones v DAS Legal Expenses Insurance Co Ltd*). But if a party is dissatisfied with the way the proceedings have been conducted, he can only succeed on an appeal if it can be shown that he has been prejudiced thereby (*Barnes v BPC (Business Forms) Ltd*).

20.55 Proceedings at the actual hearing are reasonably informal, for employment tribunals have the power to conduct them in whatever manner they consider to be most suitable. The parties may represent themselves, or be represented by a solicitor or barrister, or a representative of a trade union or employers' association, or any other person whom they desire to represent them.

A. Case management

20.56 In the original scheme of things, employment tribunals (formerly known as industrial tribunals) were intended to be a cheap, speedy and informal method of resolving employment disputes. The parties frequently represented themselves, and tribunal chairmen would assist them in presenting their respective cases. However, the growth of employment rights over the years and the tremendous increase in the number of claims made has resulted in more complex legal rules, frequently requiring the use of legal or other skilled representatives. In consequence, tribunal procedures became more formal and less flexible. The Employment Tribunals (Constitution and Rules of Procedure) Regulations 2004 contain a number of provisions designed to speed up hearings, concentrate on relevant facts and information, and discourage weak claims.

20.57 The overriding objective of the rules is to enable tribunals to deal with a case justly, including, so far as is practicable, ensuring that the parties are on an equal footing, saving expense, dealing with the case in ways which are proportionate to the complexity of the issues, and ensuring that the case is dealt with expeditiously and fairly. A chairman of tribunals has a general power to manage proceedings in order to achieve these objectives.

20.58 A chairman has wide powers to issue directions on any matter he considers to be appropriate, whether on his own volition or on an application by either party. Directions may be given as to the manner in which proceedings are to be conducted (witness statements prepared and exchanged, agreed bundles of relevant documents, statement of agreed facts, skeleton arguments etc), requiring additional information, extending time limits, provision of written answers to questions put, disclosure and/or production of documents, staying part of the proceedings, joining other respondents, postponing or adjourning proceedings, conducting a pre-hearing review, permitting an amendment to the claim or response, etc. If a direction is not complied with, a chairman may make an order in respect of costs or preparation time, and may, at a pre-hearing review or actual hearing, make an order to strike out the whole or part of the claim or response, as appropriate, but this punitive power should only be exercised if a fair trial is not possible due to the failure to comply. If there is a last-minute compliance, with an acceptable explanation, it is not appropriate to strike out the claim or defence (*National Grid Co plc v Virdee*). However, either party may apply for a review of directions given.

20.59 Either party may apply to a tribunal for an order for further particulars or disclosure of documents, but such orders are not made as a matter of routine, but only if the party requiring the information can show that he will be prejudiced without such information (*White v University of Manchester*). In particular, disclosure of documents will not be ordered to enable a party to indulge in a 'fishing expedition' ie to search for material in order to establish a case (*British Aerospace plc v Green*). An employment tribunal cannot order a party to produce 'evidence' or to create documentary evidence which was not in existence, because an order for discovery is limited to those documents which are in being (*Carrington v Helix Lighting Ltd*). The party against whom an order for discovery of documents is made is under a continuing duty to disclose all relevant documents, right up to the conclusion of the hearing (*Scott v Commissioners of Inland Revenue*).

20.60 Documents which are produced in order to comply with an order for discovery may only be used for the purpose of the hearing, and not for any other cause of action. In *Riddick v Thames Water Board Mills Ltd* an employee of the defendants wrote a confidential memorandum about the manner of the claimant's dismissal, which was allegedly defamatory. The claimant got to know about the document as a result of an order for discovery, made during the course of a legal action brought against the employer. The action was settled, but the claimant brought a further action for defamation. It was held that the public interest required that documents which were compulsorily disclosed on discovery should only be used for the purpose of the action in which they were disclosed, and that each party impliedly undertook not to use them for any other ulterior or improper motive.

20.61 In complex cases, such as those alleging race discrimination (*Martins v Marks & Spencer plc*), or disability discrimination (*Goodwin v Patents Office*), or protected disclosure claims (*ALM Medical Services Ltd v Bladon*), or where there are likely to be a large number of witnesses or a large number of documents, or many claimants (eg equal value claims), it is good practice to hold a meeting for preliminary directions, so as to ensure as far as possible that the parties and tribunal can identify the relevant issues to be determined.

20.62 If one party is seeking the disclosure of documents which the other side regards as being of a confidential nature, such as references, confidential assessments on the applicant or other employees, and so forth, the chairman of the employment tribunal should himself inspect the document to satisfy himself that discovery is essential in order to dispose fairly of the proceedings. If he does decide that they should be disclosed, the interests of third parties can be protected by 'covering up', substituting names, and, in rare cases, hearing the proceedings in camera (*Science Research Council v Nassé*).

20.63 If privilege is claimed from disclosure, a balance must be held between the public interest in non-disclosure and that of justice in the production of the documents (*Halford v Sharples*). Communications between parties headed 'without prejudice' should be excluded from the evidence submitted, unless the material was such that without them a dishonest case was being presented (*Independent Research Services Ltd v Catterall*).

20.64 Privilege from the disclosure of documents only applies to communications between clients and professional legal advisers, such as solicitors and barristers (*New Victoria Hospital v Ryan*).

20.65 There is no general duty on a party to disclose any documents in his possession or power, in the absence of any formal order to that effect. However, if he voluntarily discloses documents, there is a duty not to be selective in that disclosure, and he must not withhold other documents if there is a risk that the non-disclosure might convey a false or misleading impression as to the nature of any document disclosed (*Birds Eye Walls Ltd v Harrison*).

20.66 Attendance orders, compelling a person to attend as a witness, may also be made in appropriate circumstances. But a tribunal cannot direct that a representative chosen by a party to the proceedings shall not act as such (*Bache v Essex County Council*).

20.67 Case management discussions may take place in private, but an opportunity must be given for the parties to submit representations in writing or advance oral arguments if they so wish.

20.68 If there are High Court proceedings between the employer and employee in which there are issues in common with an application for unfair dismissal, the tribunal chairman has a discretion to order that the latter claim be postponed, pending the outcome of the High Court proceedings (*Carter v Credit Change Ltd*). He should take into account the convenience, expedition and cost when exercising his discretion (*First Castle Electronics Ltd v West*). The test to be applied is 'In which court is this action most conveniently and appropriate to be tried, bearing in mind all the surrounding circumstances, including the complexity of the issue, the amount involved, the technicality of the evidence and appropriateness of the procedure?' Thus, where a managing director was alleging a repudiatory breach of contract by the employers which was claimed to be a wrongful and unfair dismissal, the Employment Appeal Tribunal ordered that employment tribunal proceedings should be adjourned until after the hearing of the High Court action (*Bowater plc v Charlwood*).

B. Pre-hearing reviews

20.69 A pre-hearing review (PHR) must take place in public, and all parties must be given an opportunity to advance oral or written arguments. At such review, the chairman may determine interim or preliminary matters, issue directions, or, if the chairman considers that the contentions put forward in relation to a matter to be determined by the tribunal have little prospect of success but are nevertheless arguable, he may order that party to pay a deposit not exceeding £500 as a condition of being permitted to continue to take part in the proceedings. The chairman must first ascertain the ability of the party to comply with the order. If the deposit is not paid within 21 days, the claim may be struck out (unless the chairman gives a further 14 days in which to pay). If the deposit is paid it shall be refunded in full unless the tribunal makes a cost or preparation time order (see below) on the ground that the party has conducted the proceedings unreasonably in persisting in having the matter determined.

20.70 A chairman may also strike out the claim (or defence) if, at the PHR stage, it considered that the case is so weak that it has no reasonable prospect of success, and ought not to be permitted to proceed to a hearing. Since no evidence is called for at a PHR, the striking out option will be applicable in those cases where there is no conflict of evidence, or where the evidence presented is self-explanatory, or where the matter has already been litigated. The chairman may also strike out or amend any claim or response on the ground that it is scandalous, or vexatious, or has no reasonable prospect of success, or on the ground that the manner in which the proceedings have been conducted by or on behalf of the claimant or respondent has been scandalous, unreasonable or vexatious.

20.71 A restricted reporting order may be made in any case which involves an allegation of sexual misconduct or a disability case in which evidence of a personal nature is likely to be heard. The order will prohibit the publication of any identifying material, ie the names of the parties, until a decision on liability has been reached and entered into the register (*X v Metropolitan Police Comr*). Such order cannot be made to protect the identity of a corporate employer who may be vicariously liable for the acts of its employees, even though its commercial reputation may suffer (*Leicester University v A*). However, there is no power in such cases to exclude the press or members of the public (*R v Southampton Industrial Tribunal, ex p INS News Group Ltd*).

20.72 It is an offence punishable by a fine not exceeding level 5 on the standard scale to act in contravention of any such restricted reporting order.

C. The hearing

20.73 Hearings before an employment tribunal must be held in public (*Storer v British Gas plc*). An employment tribunal may only sit in private if:

(a) it would be against the interests of national security to allow evidence to be given in public;

(b) a person is giving evidence which he could not disclose without contravening a prohibition imposed by an enactment;

(c) the evidence has been communicated to a person in confidence; or

(d) the evidence is information which if disclosed in public, could cause substantial injury to an undertaking of the witness or in which he works for reasons other than its effect on collective bargaining (see rule 29, 1st Schedule).

20.74 However, it is permissible for a tribunal to hear certain evidence in private in order to protect the right to respect for private or family life, as required by Art 8 of the European Convention on Human Rights (*XXX v YYY*). If a private hearing is ordered, this does not preclude the presence of a party's representative (*Fry v Foreign and Commonwealth Office*).

20.75 If there is no prior settlement or withdrawal, the employment tribunal will hear the case. A date, time and place for the hearing will be notified to the parties, although applications for adjournments will be considered on appropriate grounds. At the hearing, as a general rule, the burden of proof is on the claimant, and he should therefore give evidence first in order to support his allegations. This is true of race or sex discrimination claims (but see Sex Discrimination (Indirect Discrimination and Burden of Proof) Regulations 2001, para 4.94), employment protection rights, claims made out of time, allegations by the respondent that the claimant was not an employee, or that he was not dismissed, etc.

20.76 If an employment tribunal is unable to come to a conclusion on a question of fact, they may apply the burden of proof. Thus in *Morris v London Iron and Steel Co Ltd* the tribunal could not decide whether an employee had been dismissed or resigned, and they held that he had not discharged the burden of proof which was on him to show that he was dismissed.

20.77 In unfair dismissal cases, if the dismissal is admitted, the employer will be required to give evidence first, and he must establish:

(a) the reason for the dismissal (or, if there is more than one reason, the principal reason, see *Smith v Glasgow City District Council*), and

(b) that it was a statutory reason.

He should then seek to show that he acted reasonably in the circumstances.

20.78 From a practical point of view, the employer should recognise that there are a number of matters within his knowledge about which the tribunal may wish to learn, and therefore should be prepared to give evidence on these matters. Thus it is not sufficient to show a reason for dismissal; the reasonableness of acting on that reason must also be shown. If an employee is dismissed because of redundancy, an employer should normally lead evidence to show that there was a fair selection system, full consultation with the individual concerned and trade union (if appropriate) and that efforts were made to find alternative employment, even if the applicant does not raise all these matters (*Langston v Cranfield University*). If the dismissal is for incompetence, the employer would need to show all those matters which a reasonable employer should have done before taking the decision to dismiss (see Chapter 17).

20.79 If one party is taken by surprise by the evidence of the other side, it will normally be possible to apply to introduce rebutting evidence, even if it is necessary to apply for an adjournment in order to produce the necessary evidence and/or witnesses. However, unreasonable applications for adjournments may be visited by an award of costs against the offending party although costs cannot be awarded as a pre-condition for resuming a hearing (*Cooper v Weatherwise (Roofing and Walling) Ltd*). An employment tribunal may permit a witness to be recalled for further examination, but should then give the other party an opportunity to make a further rebuttal (*Aberdeen Steak House Group v Ibrahim*).

20.80 If an employment tribunal, on its own volition, takes a point which was not taken by the parties, natural justice requires that the parties should be alerted to the fact, so that they can be given an opportunity to present further evidence on the matter, and/or make further submissions (*Laurie v Holloway*).

20.81 The standard of proof, ie the quantum of evidence which must be given in support of any particular allegation, must be sufficient to establish the balance of probabilities in that party's favour. The informality of tribunal procedure can sometimes mislead the parties into thinking that they can escape with a standard of proof which is in fact unacceptable. If the employer, for example, fails to prove the reason or the principal reason for the dismissal (*Smith v Glasgow City District Council*) or fails to show any reason, or gives a reason which the tribunal does not believe, then he will have failed to discharge the burden of proof which is placed on him, and the dismissal will be unfair. Although the tribunals will admit hearsay evidence in the proceedings, the weight which is given to such evidence is a matter for them to decide (*Coral Squash Clubs Ltd v Matthews*) and they will seldom base a decision in favour of an employer on such evidence, particularly if it is controverted by the direct evidence (or denials) of the claimant (*Mawson v Leadgate Engineering Ltd*). The tribunals will give such assistance as they can to a person who is not legally qualified or represented, but it is the duty of the parties to present all the relevant evidence before the tribunals, and applications of adjournments may be made if a party considers it necessary to call someone whose attendance was not thought necessary.

20.82 The evidential requirements in the employment tribunals are not the same as other courts. For example, in *Docherty v Reddy*, the claimant was dismissed for suspected theft. The tribunal permitted the employer to introduce evidence that the claimant had stolen on previous occasions. Such evidence would scarcely have been admissible in the criminal courts, as its probative value would have been exceeded by its prejudicial value, but the EAT held that the evidence was rightly admitted. The issues in the employment tribunals and the criminal courts are different; in this case, the tribunal had to decide if the employer had reasonable grounds for dismissing, and the claimant's previous conduct was a relevant factor to be taken into account.

20.83 Equally, whether a dismissal was fair or unfair can only be determined on the basis of the facts which were known to the employer at the time he dismissed the employee, and subsequent information which comes to light is only relevant if it confirms that reason. Such information cannot be admissible to show a separate and additional reason for dismissal, because when the employer dismissed the employee, he did not know of those facts. This can be illustrated by *W Devis & Sons Ltd v Atkins*, where the company dismissed a manager for failing to follow company directives. After he had left, it was alleged that facts were discovered which indicated that he had been guilty of gross misconduct, and that he had been taking secret commissions from customers, for which he could have been dismissed summarily. The employment tribunal refused to allow such evidence to be called on the issue of the fairness of the dismissal, and this was upheld on appeal to the House of Lords. It was permissible to adduce evidence which was discovered after the dismissal to prove the fairness of that reason, but not for the purpose of showing that the employers had discovered subsequently another reason which would have enabled them to dismiss fairly. However, if the dismissal is found to be unfair, the subsequent evidence can then be admitted for the purpose of determining the remedies which would be considered by the tribunal, whether by way of a refusal to make an order for reinstatement or re-engagement, a reduction in the amount of compensation to be paid, or an award of nil compensation (*Moncrieff v MacDonald*) or a reduction of the basic award (ERA, s 122).

20.84 If a claimant fails to attend the tribunal hearing, without good cause, the tribunal can dismiss the claim without having to be satisfied that the respondent could establish a good defence (*Roberts v Skelmersdale College*), or adjourn to another date (with or without an order for costs), but if the failure to attend was due to a medical reason, the decision whether to postpone is one within the discretion of the tribunal. Adequate reasons for taking this course of action must be given (*Teinaz v London Borough of Wandsworth*). If, having heard the claimant's case, the respondent makes a submission of no case to answer, on the ground that the claim is weak or misconceived, the tribunal should still continue to hear the respondent's evidence, for it is very rare that a submission of no case to answer can succeed (*Logan v Customs and Excise Comrs*). The tribunal should always be prepared to hear evidence from the other side, except perhaps in the most hopeless or frivolous cases (*Hackney London Borough Council v Usher*).

20.85 It can sometimes happen that during the course of the hearing, the tribunal may express a forcefully held opinion as to the merits of the case. This, by itself, does not indicate bias, as such views may well assist the parties in the manner in which they continue to conduct the proceedings. But the tribunal must indicate that the views expressed were only provisional, and that they remain open to persuasion to the opposite view (*Jininez v Southwark London Borough Council*).

20.86 A claim may be struck out on the ground that the manner in which the proceedings are conducted are scandalous, frivolous or vexatious, although before doing so an opportunity must be given to the party concerned to show cause why this should not be done.

Otherwise, after considering all the facts, hearing the witnesses, and studying any evidence tendered, the employment tribunal must determine the issue on the basis of the relevant legal requirement. Thus if the issue is whether or not the employer has acted reasonably, this does not mean that the tribunal must agree with the employer's decision, for in many cases more than one course of action is possible, and an employer is not to be criticised because he adopts one in preference to another. It is not the duty of the tribunal to decide if they would have come to the same conclusion as the employer based on the facts which were within the employer's knowledge (*Ferodo v Barnes*), nor should the tribunal substitute their own judgment for that of the employer (*Donn v Greater London Council*), and any temptation to interfere with management prerogatives should be resisted. In *St Anne's Board Mills Co Ltd v Brien* four employees refused to work with another employee, who they considered had been responsible for an accident. The employers investigated the matter, came to the conclusion that that employee was not to blame, and required the four to continue to work with him. They continued to refuse, and were dismissed. After considering the facts, the tribunal decided that the other employee had been responsible for the accident, and hence the four employees had not acted unreasonably in refusing to work with him. The dismissals were therefore unfair. On appeal, it was held that the question before the tribunal was not who was responsible for the accident, but whether the employers had acted reasonably in the circumstances. They had investigated the matter thoroughly and carefully, and come to certain conclusions. They had had the choice of dismissing an employee whom they considered to be blameless, or the four employees who were (in their view, wrongfully) refusing to work with him. In the circumstances, they had not acted unreasonably in dismissing the latter.

20.87 The paramount duty of the employment tribunal is to apply the law as laid down by Parliament. Account must be taken of the interpretation of that law as laid down by the EAT and other superior courts, but it is the statute which is paramount. In *Jowett v Earl of Bradford*, the employment tribunal refused to follow a test of selection for redundancy as laid down by the EAT in *Vickers v Smith*. It was held that this did not consititute an error of law on the part of the tribunal. When the language of a statute is unclear or ambiguous, then the duty of the courts is to interpret the statute and thus lay down binding precedents. But when the statute is clear and unambiguous, precedents are only guides, and do not bind (*Kearney & Trecker Marwin Ltd v Varndell*). The prime duty of the employment tribunal is to follow the words of the statute (*Anandarajah v Lord Chancellor's Department*).

20.88 About 95% of all the decisions of the employment tribunals are unanimous, the remainder being majority decisions of 2–1, sometimes with the two 'wingmen' joining together to outvote the legal chairman. An unusual case was *R v Industrial Tribunal, ex p Cotswold Collotype*, where one tribunal member thought that the claimant was unfairly dismissed, a second member thought the claimant was not unfairly dismissed but redundant, and the third member thought the claimant was neither unfairly dismissed nor redundant! It was held that if the voting was so inconclusive that no decision was reached, the tribunal had an inherent power to refer the matter to a differently constituted tribunal. If the members of the tribunal are unable to agree, it is preferable to reserve the decision. The views of the majority and minority should be set out clearly and distinctly in different paragraphs, and all efforts should be made to reach a unanimous decision *(Anglian Home Improvements Ltd v Kelly)*.

20.89 It is the practice of some employment tribunals to give an oral decision immediately the hearing finishes, and then promulgate the decision in writing at a later date. In rare cases it is possible for the chairman, before such written promulgation, to announce his intention to recall the tribunal in order to reconsider some point of law which he has omitted to notice, or which was not drawn to his attention. While such practice is unusual, there is no legal objection to it (*Hanks v Ace High Productions Ltd*). However, it is not possible for an employment tribunal to depart from their oral decision when it is reduced to writing (*Arthur Guinness Son & Co (Great Britain) Ltd v Green*).

20.90 If, at the end of the oral hearing, both sides agree to put their submissions in writing, the employment tribunal must send a copy of each party's submission to the other party, and give a specified time in which any response is to be made. Such comments should be limited to the correction of factual errors and legal submissions on any new points of law raised (*Barking and Dagenham London Borough Council v Oguoko*).

20.91 After all the evidence has been heard, and representations made, the tribunal will either give an oral judgment or reserve its decision to be given in writing at a later date. If an oral decision has been given, written reasons will only be provided if requested by one of the parties at the hearing or within 14 days of the judgment.

20.92 The written reasons should include the following information:

(a) the issues which the tribunal has determined;

(b) details of issues not determined, and the reason why;

(c) any findings of fact relevant to those issues;

(d) a concise statement of the relevant law;

(e) how the relevant findings of fact and applicable law have been applied in order to determine the issues; and

(f) where the judgment includes an award of compensation, a table of how the amount has been calculated.

D. Financial remedies

20.93 Monetary awards in respect of proceedings brought before an employment tribunal are subject to the special rules applicable in each case (see Appendix A). In particular, it should be noted that in race, sex and disability discrimination claims, there is no limit to the amount which may be awarded, and an award may also be made in respect of injury to feelings. Nor is there a limit to compensation awards in cases of health and safety and protected disclosure dismissals. Special rules are also applicable in claims brought under EU law (eg the Equal Treatment Directive) because 'full compensation' is required, and hence there is a difference in the stages at which percentage reductions are to be made for mitigation, contributory conduct, *ex gratia* payments, etc (see *Ministry of Defence v Hunt*).

Interest on awards

20.94 An award made by an employment tribunal will now attract interest, on a day-to-day basis, at the stipulated rate of interest, after 42 days from the date when the decision has been sent to the parties. Interest is not payable on costs awarded, nor on any part of the award which is subject to the recoupment provisions.

20.95 Interest is still payable if the tribunal's decision is subject to appeal or review, but if the amount of the award is subsequently varied, interest is payable on the amount as varied (Employment Tribunals (Interest) Order 1990).

20.96 In cases of sex, race and disability discrimination, and in equal pay claims, interest on awards will accrue from the date of the act of discrimination complained of (Employment Tribunals (Interest on Awards in Discrimination Cases) Regulations 1996.

E. Reviews by the employment tribunal

20.97 An application may be made to an employment tribunal within 14 days from the time the decision was sent to the parties, asking for a review of its decision. This is not an appeal, and there are limited circumstances in which the tribunal will accede to such a request. These are as follows:

(a) if the decision was wrongly made as a result of an error on the part of the tribunal's staff;

(b) if a party did not receive notice of the proceedings (*Hancock v Middleton*);

(c) if the decision was made in the absence of a party entitled to be heard. If an employer fails to reply to a complaint by not returning the appropriate defence within the stated time he may be denied the right to be heard unless he can show some valid reason for this. But if a party is prevented from attending a hearing through illness, then the tribunal should consider whether the absence was for a genuine reason, and if his story is believed, a review should be granted (*Morris v Griffiths*), In addition to seeking a review, the person applying should state in writing his reasons not only for the application, but also for contending that the decision of the employment tribunal was wrong. In *Drakard & Sons Ltd v Wilton*, the employers did not attend a tribunal hearing as they believed that once having made an offer of settlement to the conciliation officer, they thought that they would be contacted if any further steps were required. The EAT held that the tribunal should have granted a review. They should have enquired into the circumstances surrounding the failure to attend the hearing;

(d) new evidence comes to light, which could not have been discovered before. For example, if, after the claimant has been awarded compensation for unfair dismissal, new evidence comes to light that he had been defrauding the employer during the period of employment, so that it would have been possible to have dismissed him summarily, then this will be taken into account by the tribunal when it reviews the decision, and any previous award of compensation may be altered accordingly (*McGregor v Gibbings Amusements Ltd*). It must be shown that the new evidence which has now become available could not have been presented at the original hearing, and the application should be accompanied by the substance of that new evidence, including, if possible, proofs of witnesses (*Simmons v Medway Welding Ltd*);

(e) the interests of justice require a review. This general power can be illustrated by the case of *Berkeley Garage Ltd v Edmunds* where the employers were told by officers from the Department of Employment that the claimant was bringing his case out of time. Consequently, they did not bother to attend the hearing. The tribunal found that it was not practicable for the claimant to have presented the case earlier, and proceeded to hear the case on its merits. When the employers discovered this, they applied for a review and a rehearing, which the tribunal refused. On appeal this was reversed, for the interests of justice clearly required that the employers be given an opportunity to present their side of the story. Similarly, in *Help the Aged Housing Association (Scotland) Ltd v Vidler* the claimant was awarded £4,700 compensation for unfair dismissal, mainly on the basis that he was 60 years of age, and the tribunal thought that it would be a considerable length of time before he obtained further employment. Within two weeks of the tribunal's decision, he obtained employment. It was held on appeal that the tribunal should have exercised its powers of review and reviewed the compensation in the light of the new situation, for the original assessment was totally wrong. Because the claimant had obtained alternative employment so quickly, this altered the substratum of the tribunal's reasoning in computing the loss likely to be suffered, and hence it was in the interests of justice that there should be a review.

20.98 Before refusing an application for review, the employment tribunal should give the claimant an opportunity to elaborate in writing the grounds which he intends to put forward (*Drakard & Sons Ltd v Wilton*).

20.99 The power to review only applies when the employment tribunal has made a decision. There is no power to review an actual settlement reached during or at the end of proceedings, where the tribunal has not made a finding on liability (*Larkfield of Chepstow Ltd v Milne*).

20.100 An application for review may be made on the ground that there was an error in the proceedings, but not on the ground that the decision of the employment tribunal discloses an error of law, for that is a matter which must be dealt with on appeal to the EAT (*Trimble v Supertravel Ltd*).

20.101 An employment tribunal may also review its decision on its own motion.

F. Costs

20.102 In some circumstances, the tribunal may make an order that one party makes a payment to the other party in respect of costs incurred. Notice must be sent to the party against whom the order may be made to give him an opportunity of arguing why the order should not be made. A costs order may only be made if the other party was legally represented at the hearing, ie by a solicitor or barrister. The amount of costs is in the discretion of the tribunal, but any such order must not exceed £10,000, or other sum agreed between the parties, or costs assessed in accordance with the county court or sheriff's court rules, which may exceed £10,000.

20.103 A costs order must be made in an unfair dismissal case where the claimant has expressed a wish to be reinstated or re-engaged not less than seven days before the hearing, and the hearing has been adjourned or postponed because the respondent has failed, without a special reason, to adduce reasonable evidence as to the availability of a suitable job. A costs order may be made if a pre-hearing review is postponed, or if a party has, in bringing the proceedings, or he or his representative has, in conducting the proceedings, acted vexatiously, abusively, disruptively, or otherwise unreasonably, or the bringing or conducting of the proceedings has been misconceived (ie has no reasonable prospect of success). Costs may also be awarded against a party who has not complied with a practice direction.

20.104 If the employer makes an offer to settle the claim prior to the tribunal hearing, which is unreasonably rejected by the claimant, the tribunal is within its rights to exercise a discretion and make an award of costs (*Kopel v Safeway Stores plc*).

G. Preparation time order

20.105 A preparation time order may be made in favour of a party who was not legally represented at a hearing in order to compensate for the time spent on preparatory work directly relating to the proceedings, including time spent by legal or other advisers, but not in respect of time spent at the hearing. An application for a preparation time order must be made within 28 days from the issuing of the judgment. The amount of the order will be determined by the tribunal's assessment of the number of hours spent on preparation time by the party in whose favour the order is to be made, based on the information provided by that party, and the tribunal's own assessment of what it considers to be a reasonable and proportionate amount of time spent on such preparatory work with reference to the complexity of the proceedings and the number of witnesses and documentation required. A preparation time order may not exceed £10,000, and the ability of the party who is to pay must be taken into consideration.

20.106 A preparation time order must be made in unfair dismissal proceedings which have been postponed or adjourned and the claimant has expressed a wish to be reinstated or re-engaged but the respondent has failed, without a special reason, to adduce reasonable evidence as to the availability of a suitable job. An order may be made where a party has, in bringing the proceedings, or he or his representative has in conducting the proceedings, acted vexatiously, abusively, disruptively, or otherwise unreasonably, or the bringing or conducting of the proceedings has been misconceived, in that it has no reasonable prospect of success.

20.107 A tribunal cannot make a preparation time order and a cost order in favour of the same party in the same proceedings. If a deposit has been taken from a party as a condition of the claim going forward, that may be paid in part or full settlement of the costs or preparation time order.

H. Wasted costs order

20.108 A tribunal or chairman may make a wasted costs order against a party's representative to disallow or pay (or refund) to his client any wasted costs, which will cover any costs incurred by a party as a result of any improper, unreasonable or negligent act or omission by that representative. However, such an order cannot be made against a representative who is not acting in pursuit of profit with regard to the proceedings. Before making such an order the tribunal or chairman must give the representative a reasonable opportunity to make oral or written representations, and take into account his ability to pay.

I. Appeals

20.109 It has already been noted (see Chapter 1) that the Employment Appeal Tribunal will hear appeals on points of law from employment tribunals, and on points of law from the decisions of the certification officer. An appeal on a point of law from the employment tribunals must be made within 42 days from the date when the document recording the full reasons for the decision was sent to the appellant (*Hammersmith London Borough Council v Ladejobi*), not from the date which in the normal postal rules they might be deemed to have been received (*Mock v IRC*), although it is possible in exceptional circumstances to apply for an extension of time, but a good reason for the delay must be shown (*Duke v Prospect Training Services Ltd*). Legal aid is available in the EAT, but it should be noted that a delay in obtaining legal aid, or the fact that the assistance of the Equal Opportunities Commission or the Commission for Racial Equality is being sought for the purpose of pursuing an appeal are not reasons for not adhering to the 42-day time limit. In particular, a Practice Direction issued by the EAT makes it clear that if an application for a review is made to an employment tribunal, this does not prevent the time for appealing from running (although this obviously does not prevent an appeal against the refusal of the tribunal to grant the review), and further, if an employment tribunal makes a finding of liability, but adjourns the question of compensation, the time for appealing runs from the date of the decision, and is not suspended until the final matter of compensation has been dealt with. The EAT will also consider the motives of the appellant, the tactics used, whether the delay was intentional, the length of the delay, the merits of the appeal, and whether there would be any injustice or prejudice to the party who was successful before the employment tribunal (see *Aziz v Bethnal Green City Challenge Co Ltd*).

20.110 Once an appeal to the EAT has been lodged, a preliminary hearing/directions (PHD) will take place. The appellant will be required to satisfy the EAT that it is reasonably arguable that the employment tribunal made an error of law. If so satisfied, the appeal will be allowed to proceed, and the EAT will make any appropriate directions to ensure that the appeal may be determined efficiently and effectively. A special PHD form must be completed, enabling amendment to be made to the notice of appeal, giving time estimates for argument, and, if needed, requesting the chairman's notes of evidence. If the appeal does not raise an arguable point of law, it will be dismissed at the PHD stage. Only in very limited circumstances will an appellant be permitted to raise a point of law on appeal which was not canvassed before the employment tribunal (*Church v West Lancashire NHS Trust*).

20.111 An appeal from a decision of an employment tribunal can only hope to succeed if the employment tribunal have misdirected themselves in law, or entertained the wrong issue, or proceeded on a misapprehension or misconstruction of the evidence, or taken matters into account which were irrelevant to the decision, or reached a decision which no reasonable employment tribunal, properly directing themselves in law, could have arrived at. In *Neale v Hereford and Worcester County Council*, Lord Justice May propounded the so-called 'Biggles' test. He stated that the EAT should not interfere with the decision of the employment tribunal (except when they erred on a point of law) unless it was possible to say 'My goodness, that was certainly wrong!' Thus, if there is evidence to support their decision, the EAT will not normally interfere, particularly where the questions of fact and degree are at issue. The task of the EAT is to hear appeals only on points of law (*Spook Erection Ltd v Thackray*). It is not an error of law that the employment tribunal has misunderstood the facts (*British Telecommunications plc v Sheridan*).

20.112 In *Piggott Bros & Co Ltd v Jackson* the Court of Appeal stated that a decision of the employment tribunal can only be characterised as being perverse if it was not a permissible option. The EAT would have to identify a finding of fact which was unsupported by any evidence or a clear self-misdirection of law. However, in *East Berkshire Health Authority v Matadeen* the EAT held that in addition, 'perversity' was a free-standing basis for interfering with an employment tribunal's decision, if that decision 'was not a permissible option' or was 'a conclusion which offends reason' or 'so outrageous in its defiance of logic or of acceptable standards of industrial relations'. In particular, the EAT thought that the lay members were there to bring their experience and industrial judgment to the application of the law and to the decision to be reached on appeal. They were entitled to use that experience to ensure that employment tribunal decisions did not ignore generally acceptable standards. In *Yeboah v Crofton* the Court of Appeal gave some guidance on whether an appeal based on perversity should be brought.

20.113 The weight to be attached to the evidence is a matter for the employment tribunal, and it is not permissible for the EAT to substitute their own views on this (*Eclipse Blinds Ltd v Wright*). But an employment tribunal must consider whether a dismissal falls within the range of reasonable responses open to a reasonable employer, and not substitute their own judgment. A failure to adopt this approach may result in the decision not being a permissible option (*United Distillers v Conlin*).

20.114 The notice of appeal should state quite precisely what point of law is to be argued. It is not sufficient to make a bald statement that the employment tribunal misdirected itself on a point of law without specifying the error or misdirection to be appealed against. As Phillips J has pointed out, to say that something is an error of law does not, without further explanation, make it so. Indeed, if it turns out that there is in fact no arguable point of law involved in the appeal, the EAT is quite likely to make an award of costs against the unsuccessful party. Further, if no arguable point is disclosed in the notice of appeal, the notice itself can be rejected by the EAT, so that the appeal will never be heard.

20.115 In a Practice Direction issued in 2002 the EAT stated that copies of the notes taken by the chairman of the employment tribunal will only be made available if they are necessary for the purpose of arguing a point of law on appeal. More latitude will be allowed to applicants who were not legally represented at the tribunal hearing (*Webb v Anglian Water Authority*). The facts of the case will be found in the tribunal's decision, and any appeal must be based on the law as applied to those facts. However, it is permissible in argument to refer to the chairman's notes for the purpose of clarifying any ambiguity in the case. If an appeal is based on the actual conduct of the case by the chairman, or an allegation of bias by the chairman or members (*Facey v Midas Retail Security*), or some evidence contrary to that found by the tribunal, the claimant must first inform the Registrar of the EAT, so that this can be communicated to the respondent, and the views of the chairman sought. The EAT will not interfere with an award of compensation unless it is more than a trifling matter. If the question of the amount of compensation is alleged to be an error of law, it must be of a substantial nature for the EAT to interfere (*Fougère v Phoenix Motor Co Ltd*).

20.116 The EAT does have power to hear new evidence on appeal, but only if a reasonable explanation is produced as to why the evidence was not put before the employment tribunal. It must be shown that the existence of the new evidence could not have been known or foreseen, and that had it been available at the employment tribunal hearing, it would have had an important influence on either the outcome of the case or the award of compensation (*Photostatic Copiers (Southern) Ltd v Okuda*). The evidence must be credible, and of such a nature that it would have had a decisive effect on the tribunal's decision had they heard it (*International Aviation Services (UK) Ltd v Jones*). It is also possible to argue a new point of law, not canvassed before the employment tribunal, if the balance of justice so requires (*Russell v Elmdon Freight Terminal Ltd*).

20.117 If the decision of the employment tribunal is defective, because no reference or insufficient reference had been made to a particular aspect of the case, the EAT must not remit the case back to the employment tribunal for further amplification or clarification. The proper course is to allow the appeal and remit the case back for a further hearing (*Reuben v Brent London Borough Council*). However, there is no objection to remitting a matter back to the employment tribunal for fuller reasons or an amplification of the reasons (*Barke v SEETEC Business Technology Centre*) where the ground of appeal is the inadequate reasoning of the original decision (*Burns v Consignia plc (No 2)*). Where the EAT remits a case back to the employment tribunal to consider certain specific issues, the tribunal has no jurisdiction to hear or determine matters outside the scope of those issues. In particular, there is no power to permit one party to amend its case so as to raise issues which were not previously before the employment tribunal (*Aparau v Iceland Frozen Foods Ltd (No 2)*).

20.118 If there is a complaint about the actual conduct of the employment tribunal proceedings (eg that a member is falling asleep) this should be raised with the chairman at the time, and not after the tribunal has reached its conclusions (*Red Bank Manufacturing Co Ltd v Meadows*), although more serious matters, such as allegations of bias, can be raised at any time (*Peter Simper & Co Ltd v Cooke*). The procedure to be followed in such cases was outlined by the EAT in *Facey v Midas Security*.

20.119 An appeal may be brought on the ground that the promulgation of the decision of the employment tribunal has been delayed for an unconscionable length of time. In *Kwamin v Abbey National plc* it was suggested by the EAT that three and a half months should be the maximum time after the end of a case for the preparation and promulgation of all but the most complicated and lengthy judgments. If there is a delay beyond that time, the delay will be regarded as being culpable in the absence of a proper explanation. However, even though there is a delay, there is no automatic presumption that the decision will be set aside. It is for the party impugning the decision to show a material error or omission due to faulty recollection, so as to establish that the decision is unsafe by virtue of the delay.

J. Reviews by the Employment Appeal Tribunal

20.120 The EAT has power to review its own decision on the grounds (a) that the order was wrongly made as a result of an error on the part of the tribunal or its staff, (b) a party did not receive proper notice of the proceedings, and (c) the interests of justice require such review. However, the purpose of review is not to allow appeals to be reheard and, in particular, a review will not be granted if an appeal has been lodged to the Court of Appeal (*Blockleys plc v Miller*).

Vexatious litigants (Employment Tribunals Act 1996, s 33)

20.121 If the EAT is satisfied that any person has habitually and persistently and without reasonable grounds instituted vexatious proceedings or made vexatious applications before an employment tribunal or the EAT, then, on an application by the Attorney-General or the Lord Advocate, the EAT may make a restriction of proceedings order, the effect of which will be to debar that person from instituting proceedings or making applications without leave from the EAT. The hallmark of vexatious proceedings is that it has little or discernible basis in law, with the effect of subjecting the defendant to inconvenience, harassment and expense out of all proportion to any gain likely to accrue to the claimant (*A-G v Wheen*).

Further appeals

20.122 An appeal will lie from the EAT to the Court of Appeal (in Scotland the Court of Session). Leave to appeal must be given by the EAT, but if this is refused an application for leave to appeal must be made to the Court of Appeal or the Court of Session. It must be shown that there is a genuine point of law of practical consequence involved (*Campbell v Dunoon and Cowal Housing Association Ltd*). A further appeal will lie to the House of Lords (or to the Supreme Court when it is established).

21

Individual Trade Union Rights

21.1 In this chapter we shall consider the rights of an individual in respect of his trade union membership and/or non-membership. These rights exist vis-à-vis a trade union and against an actual or potential employer. The relevant statutory provisions are contained in the Trade Union and Labour Relations (Consolidation) Act 1992 (TULR(C)A), which has been amended by subsequent legislation, and reference will also be made to a number of legal decisions.

Rights vis-à-vis a trade union

A. Right not to be excluded from any trade union (TULR(C)A, s 174)

21.2 An individual cannot be excluded or expelled from any trade union unless:

(a) he does not satisfy an enforceable membership requirement contained in the rules of the union. Enforceable means the restriction of membership solely by reference to employment in a specified trade, industry or profession, or occupational description, or the possession of a specified trade, industrial or professional qualification or work experience;

(b) he does not qualify for membership by reason of the union operating only in a particular part of Great Britain;

(c) the union negotiates with one particular employer (or a number of particular employers who are associated) and the applicant is no longer employed by that employer;

(d) the exclusion or expulsion is entirely attributable to the applicant's conduct, and the conduct is neither 'excluded conduct' nor 'protected conduct'. Conduct is excluded if the individual ceases to be a member of a trade union, or being employed by a particular employer or at a particular place, or is conduct for which an individual may not be disciplined by a union by virtue of s 65 of the Act (see para 21.8). Conduct is protected if the individual is a member of a political party, or ceased to be a member, but conduct which consists of activities undertaken by an individual as a member of a political party is not protected. This means that although a trade union cannot expel or exclude a person from membership because he is a member of a political party, he can be excluded or expelled because of his activities as a member of that political party.

21.3 If a person's application for membership of a trade union is neither granted nor rejected within a reasonable period, he shall be treated as having been excluded from the union (s 177).

21.4 The significance of the law is two-fold. First, at common law a trade union was entitled to lay down the description of persons who were eligible to join, and could specify any qualification for membership it desired (see *Boulting v Association of Cinematograph, Television and Allied Technicians*), and exclude a person on any ground (see *Faramus v Film Artistes' Association*). The courts did take the view that a rule which operated arbitrarily and unreasonably was void as being against public policy (see *Nagle v Feilden*), but such cases were rare and, generally speaking, a trade union could control its own admissions, and the court had no power to order it to grant membership to any particular individual. Section 174 now overrides the common law in this respect. A trade union may lay down certain requirements for membership, as above, but otherwise must admit any person seeking to join.

21.5 The second significance of the law is that the Bridlington Agreement, which used to govern inter-union disputes arising from competition for members, and applied to TUC affiliated unions, can no longer be activated. Previously, if a trade union commenced recruitment in an area in which another union already had a substantial membership, the TUC could order the interloper to surrender the members gained in the recruitment drive (see *Rothwell v Association of Professional, Executive and Computer Staff and the Trade Union Congress*). This is no longer possible, because the individual has an indefeasible right to join whichever union he pleases, and cannot be expelled as a result of any award made by the TUC Disputes Committee.

21.6 A union may still specify who is entitled to join as a member within the limits specified above, but it is submitted that even these requirements cannot be exercised in an arbitrary and unreasonable manner (see *Nagle v Feilden*). But if an applicant needs a trade union card because an actual or prospective employer operates a 'closed shop' he cannot otherwise be excluded from membership (*Clark v NATSOPA (SOGAT '82)*). In any case, the aggrieved person would have a right against the actual or potential employer under the 'unfair recruitment' provisions (see para 21.27).

21.7 The remedy for a failure to admit or to expel an applicant to or from membership is dealt with at para 21.17.

B. Right not to be unjustifiably disciplined (TULR(C)A, ss 64–65)

21.8 The power of a trade union to take disciplinary action against a member, and the procedural rules which should be followed, is noted in Chapter 22. In addition, a member has the right not to be unjustifiably disciplined by the trade union. A member is unjustifiably disciplined if the reason for the disciplinary action was conduct by him which was:

(a) a failure to participate in or support a strike or other industrial action (whether by members of that union or by others) or indicate his opposition to or lack of support for any such strike or other industrial action; or

(b) something required from him by virtue of an obligation imposed by his contract of employment or other agreement made with his employer; or

(c) the making of an assertion that the union, or an official or representative or trustee of the union's property has contravened or is proposing to contravene a requirement of the union's rules or any other agreement or legal provision, or attempts to vindicate any such assertion; or

(d) the encouraging of any person to perform an obligation imposed by virtue of a contract of employment or any other agreement; or

(e) the contravention by him of any requirement imposed by a determination which itself constitutes an infringement of his rights or of the right of any other individual; or

(f) failing to agree to, or withdrawing from, a check-off agreement; or

(g) resigning from a union, becoming a member of another union, or refusing to join any other union; or

(h) working with individuals who are not members of the union or any other union; or

(i) working for an employer who employs individuals who are not members of the union, or who are or are not members of any other union; or

(j) requiring the union to do something which the union is required to do on the requisition of any member; or

(k) an approach to the certification officer for advice or assistance on any matter whatsoever, or involves any other person being asked for advice or assistance with respect to any assertion made under (c) above; or

(l) a proposal to engage in conduct outlined in paras (a) to (k) above, or preparatory conduct (s 65).

But a refusal to accept union policy that members should not take on additional work is not protected, because the policy is not 'other industrial action' (*Knowles v Fire Brigade Union*).

21.9 Discipline, for the purpose of this section, is a determination made under the union's rules by an official of the union, or by a number of persons including an official:

(a) that an individual shall be expelled from the union (or branch or section). In *Transport and General Workers' Union v Webber*, it was held that a recommendation that the claimant be expelled was not a determination for the purpose of s 174. Until an appeal against the recommendation had been heard, he was still a member of the union;

(b) that an individual shall pay any sum to the union (or branch or section) or to any other person whatsoever;

(c) that sums tendered by that individual in respect of any obligation to pay a subscription or other sums to the union (or branch or section) should be treated as unpaid or as paid for a different purpose;

(d) that that individual should be deprived of, or refused access to, benefits, services or facilities which would otherwise be available to him as a member of the union. Suspending a member involves depriving him of benefits which accrue from union membership (*National and Local Government Officers' Association v Killorn*);

(e) that another trade union (or branch or section) should be encouraged or advised not to accept that individual as a member; or

(f) that that individual should be subjected to any other detriment. Naming a person as a 'strike breaker' in a union circular, with the intention of causing him embarrassment is to subject that person to a detriment (*National and Local Government Officers' Association v Killorn*).

21.10 However, a member will not be unjustifiably disciplined if the reason for the disciplinary action was that he made an allegation that the union, an official, a representative or a trustee had contravened the union's rules or an agreement or an enactment or rule of law, and the assertion was false, and the member knew it was false or otherwise acted in bad faith.

21.11 If a complaint relating to an expulsion is brought under s 174, and is declared to be well founded, no further complaint relating to that matter can be brought under s 64 (unjustifiable discipline).

C. Complaints of unjustifiable discipline (TULR(C)A, ss 66–67)

21.12 An individual who believes that he has been unjustifiably disciplined by a trade union may present a complaint to an employment tribunal, alleging that his rights have been infringed. The complaint must be presented within three months of the alleged infringement, unless the employment tribunal is satisfied that it was not reasonably practicable to present the complaint earlier, and that any delay in making the complaint was wholly or partially attributable to any reasonable attempts to appeal against the decision or to have it reconsidered or reviewed.

21.13 If the employment tribunal find that the claimant has been unjustifiably disciplined contrary to s 64, they will make a declaration that the complaint is well founded. An application may then be made to an employment tribunal for an award of compensation, and an order that the union repay him any sum he has paid by way of a fine. The application must be made after four weeks but within six months of the declaration.

21.14 The amount of the award shall be such as the employment tribunal considers to be just and equitable in all the circumstances. The applicant is under a duty to mitigate against his loss, and the compensation award may be reduced if the infringement complained of was to any extent caused or contributed to by him. The amount of the award shall not exceed 30 times a week's pay (capped at £290 per week) plus £58,400. If on the date the application for compensation was made, the determination infringing the applicant's right not to be unjustifiably disciplined has not been revoked, or the union has failed to take steps to reverse anything done for the purpose of giving effect to the determination, the amount of compensation shall not be less than £5,900. An award of compensation for injury to feelings may be made (*Beaumont v Amicus MSF*).

D. Right to resign from a trade union (TULR(C)A, s 69)

21.15 In every contract of membership of a trade union, whether made before or after the passing of the Act, there shall be an implied term conferring a right on the member, on giving reasonable notice and complying with any reasonable conditions, to terminate his membership of the union. In *Ashford v Association of Scientific, Technical and Management Staffs* (decided under the provisions of the Industrial Relations Act 1971) the claimant wrote a letter of resignation to the union, which was to take immediate effect. This was not in accordance with the union rules, and subsequently expulsion proceedings were commenced. It was held by the NIRC that as the member had failed to give reasonable notice, he was bound by the union's rules. It was suggested that although it might be reasonable to invite members to state their reasons for resignation, it would not be reasonable to make such a statement a condition of resignation.

E. Right not to be expelled from the union (TULR(C)A, s 174)

21.16 The grounds upon which a person cannot be excluded from trade union membership (see para 21.2) apply equally to the right not to be expelled from a union. However, a person who resigns from the union because of dissatisfaction with the way the union is conducting its affairs cannot bring proceedings under s 174, for there is no such doctrine as 'constructive expulsion' (*McGhee v Transport and General Workers' Union*). If a member ceases to be a member of the union on the happening of an event specified in the rules of the union, he shall be treated as having been expelled from the union (s 177).

F. Remedies for wrongful exclusion or expulsion (TULR(C)A, ss 175–176)

21.17 A person who claims that he has been wrongly excluded or expelled from a trade union may present a complaint to an employment tribunal within six months from the date of the exclusion or expulsion, or, where it was not reasonably practicable to do so, within such further period as the tribunal considers reasonable. The fact that the internal appeal procedure has not been exhausted does not, by itself, render it not reasonably practicable to present the claim earlier (*GMB v Hamm*). If the tribunal find the complaint to be well founded, it shall make a declaration to that effect. If the tribunal find that the exclusion or expulsion was mainly attributable to 'protected conduct' (ie being or ceasing to be a member of a political party), it shall make a second declaration to that effect. A third declaration shall be made if the exclusion or expulsion was attributable to conduct which would have been contrary to the rules of the union.

21.18 If the application is declared to be well founded, and the applicant has been admitted or re-admitted to the union, an award of compensation shall be made which is just and equitable in the circumstances, and may be reduced if the applicant caused or contributed to the exclusion or expulsion. If on the date when the application was made the applicant has not been admitted or re-admitted to the union, the tribunal shall award compensation (see para 21.14), but this minimum award does not apply where either of the above second or third declarations have been made, when the just and equitable rule will apply.

G. Right of access to the courts (TULR(C)A, s 63)

21.19 A member who is seeking a determination or conciliation of a dispute under the union's rules should first pursue his case through the union's internal disputes procedure before seeking recourse to the courts (*White v Kuzych*). But irrespective of any provision in the union's rules, the member has an indefeasible right to apply to the courts any time after six months from when the union first receives his application to have the matter determined or conciliated. However, if the delay is attributable to the unreasonable conduct of the union member, the court can extend the six-month period (ie to give the union more time to deal with the complaint).

21.20 The right to apply to the court after six months is of course without prejudice to a member's right to apply to the court at any time when, for example, an appeal cannot cure a defect because the action complained against is ultra vires or otherwise contrary to law.

H. Right to a ballot before industrial action (TULR(C)A, s 62)

21.21 If a trade union calls on members to engage in a strike or other industrial action without the affirmative support of a ballot conducted in accordance with the stringent requirements of the Act, any member may apply to the court for an order seeking to have the authorisation or endorsement of the action withdrawn by the union. If the strike is not called by the specified person, or the Act's requirements relating to the functions of the independent scrutineer are not satisfied, or members have not been given an equal opportunity to vote, or a ballot has been held but a majority have not voted in favour, then the court will make such order as it considers appropriate for requiring the union to take steps for ensuring that there is no further inducement to take part in the action, and that no member engages in conduct after the making of the order by virtue of having been induced before the order to take part or continue to take part in the action.

21.22 The right to apply to the court for an order is thus available to an individual member of the union, whether or not the strike is actionable by anyone else (eg an employer, see para 23.47) and is additional to any right a member may have in respect of any breach which may have occurred of the trade union's rules. The right exists in respect of calls for any strike or other industrial action, whether or not the member is in breach of his contract of employment. Thus secondary action (see para 23.71) is covered.

21.23 A court may grant interlocutory or interim relief by ordering that the authorisation or endorsement of the industrial action is withdrawn, but it cannot order the union to hold a ballot. The right to bring an action under s 62 applies to self-employed persons, as well as to employees (s 62(8)).

21.24 Crown employees (who may not be employed under a contract of employment) are within the provisions of s 62 (see s 62(7)).

I. Other individual rights

21.25 A member of a trade union has the right to restrain the union from indemnifying unlawful conduct (see para 22.61), to bring an action against the union's trustees in respect of unlawful application of the union's property (see para 22.63), and to bring a complaint about the conduct of the ballot in respect of a political fund (see para 22.65). He has the right to inspect the register of members (see para 22.17) and examine the union's accounts, and can apply to the court if the union has failed to comply with the requirements relating to union elections, election addresses, appointment of a scrutineer, etc. These matters will be considered in Chapter 22.

Rights vis-à-vis an employer

21.26 An individual worker has a number of legal rights against an actual or potential employer, as follows.

A. Access to employment (TULR(C)A, s 137)

21.27 It is unlawful to refuse a person employment:

(a) because he is, or is not, a member of a trade union; or

(b) because he is unwilling to accept a requirement:
    (i)   to take steps to become or cease to be, or to remain or not to become, a member of a trade union; or
    (ii) to make payments or suffer deductions in the event of his not being a member of a trade union.

21.28 A person shall be taken to have been refused employment if the person to whom he is applying:

(a) refuses or deliberately omits to entertain and process his application or enquiry; or

(b) causes him to withdraw or cease to pursue his application or enquiry; or

(c) refuses or deliberately omits to offer him employment of that description; or

(d) makes him an offer of such employment the terms of which are such that no reasonable employer who wished to fill the post would offer, and which is not accepted; or

(e) makes him an offer of such employment but withdraws it or causes him not to accept it.

21.29 The law is aimed at preventing any form of discrimination against a worker on the ground of his trade union membership. The employer is quite entitled to refuse to employ someone because of that person's previous trade union activities (eg a well-known militant, see *Birmingham District Council v Beyer*), because the refusal is not based on trade union membership, but disruptive conduct in his previous employment. Whether the employer thus refuses employment because of past trade union membership or past trade union activities is a question of fact for the employment tribunal to determine in accordance with the evidence. However, once the worker has entered employment slightly different considerations may apply (see *Fitzpatrick v British Railways Board*, para 21.77).

21.30 The precise scope of s 137 is not clear. In *Harrison v Kent County Council* the claimant had previously been employed for some 14 years, during which time he was known to be the leader of a long and bitter industrial dispute. He then left the employment, and subsequently applied for an advertised vacancy. He was refused employment. He argued that the refusal was because of his trade union membership, and hence contrary to s 137. The employers argued that he was refused employment because of his uncooperative attitude and anti-management style. His claim failed before the employment tribunal, but this was reversed by the EAT, who held that there was an overlap between trade union membership and activities. If a person was refused employment because of his trade union activities, it was open to an employment tribunal to find that he was refused employment because of his trade union membership. However, it should be noted that the decision in this case was made prior to the House of Lords' decisions in *Associated Newspapers Ltd v Wilson* and *Associated British Ports v Palmer* where it was pointed out that there is a distinction between 'the purpose' and 'the effect' of an act, and thus the decision in *Harrison* must be regarded as being of doubtful authority.

Job advertisements (TULR(C)A, s 137(3))

21.31 Where a job advertisement (including every form of advertisement or notice, whether to the public or not), is published, which indicates (or might reasonably be understood as indicating) that the employment is only open to a person who is, or who is not, a member of a trade union, or make payments or suffer deductions (see para 21.27 above), then if a person applies for a job, and he is refused employment, it will be conclusively presumed that he was refused employment for that reason. Thus it is clear that all references to trade union membership or non-membership should be eliminated from job advertisements. However, the job advertisement per se is not unlawful (unlike advertisements which seek to discriminate on grounds of race or sex, see paras 4.140 and 4.83), and the only remedy is for an individual who has been refused employment to bring a personal complaint.

Unfair practices (TULR(C)A, s 137(4))

21.32 Where there is an arrangement or practice under which employment is only offered to persons put forward or approved by a trade union, a person who is not a member of the trade union, and who is refused employment because of that arrangement or practice, shall be taken to have been refused employment because he is not a member of the trade union.

Employment agencies (TULR(C)A, s 138)

21.33 The Act covers employment agencies, defined as any person who provides services for the purpose of finding employment for workers or for supplying employers with workers. In so far as the employment agency acts as an agent for an employer, the provisions of s 137 (above) apply. In so far as the agency is acting in its own right, the identical provisions apply, and a person who has been refused the services of an employment agency (on grounds on his membership or non-membership of a trade union) will have a right to complain against the agency to an employment tribunal. Advertisements by employment agencies are also covered by identical provisions (s 138(3)).

Exceptions to the Act

21.34 The Act only deals with employment under a contract of service or apprenticeship. Thus it cannot apply to self-employed persons. Further, if a person is being considered for appointment or election to an office in a trade union, then s 137 does not prevent anything done for the purpose of securing the compliance with a condition that he be or become a member of the trade union, even though this would constitute employment. Thus it is not unlawful to insist that a trade union official becomes a member of the union concerned.

21.35 The unfair recruitment provisions do not apply to members of the armed forces, police, share fishermen, employees who work outside Great Britain, seamen registered on ships registered at ports outside Great Britain, or who are not ordinarily resident in Great Britain, and when the minister issues an exemption certificate on the ground of national security.

Remedies under the Act (ss 139–142)

21.36 A person who considers that his rights have been violated under the Act may make a complaint to an employment tribunal within three months from the date of the act complained of, with the usual extension of time if it was not reasonably practicable to present it earlier. If the tribunal uphold the complaint, they must make a declaration to that effect, may award compensation, and may make a recommendation that the respondent takes action to obviate or reduce the effect on the complainant of the conduct which is the subject of the complaint. If the complaint is made against an employment agency and a prospective employer, there are provisions which permit the joinder of both parties, and any award of compensation may be apportioned between them, as the tribunal think just and equitable. It is also possible to join a third party (eg a trade union or shop steward) if the act complained of came about by virtue of industrial pressure.

21.37 The practical effect of legislation is that the pre-entry and post-entry closed shop is no longer lawful in Great Britain.

B. Inducements relating to union membership or activities (TULR(C)A, s 145A)

21.38 A worker has the right not to have an offer made to him by his employer for the sole or main purpose of inducing the worker:

(a) not to be or seek to become a member of an independent trade union;

(b) not to take part in the activities of an independent trade union at an appropriate time;

(c) to be or become a member of any trade union or of a particular trade union.

Inducements relating to collective bargaining (TULR(C)A, s 145B)

21.39 A worker who is a member of an independent trade union which is recognised by his employer has the right not to have an offer made to him by his employer if:

(a) acceptance of the offer (together with the other workers' acceptance of similar offers) would have the result that the workers' terms of employment will no longer be determined by collective agreement negotiated by or on behalf of the union; and

(b) the employer's sole or main purpose in making the offer is to achieve this result.

21.40 A worker has the right to make a complaint to an employment tribunal on the ground that his employer has made him an offer in contravention of ss 145A or 145B. It will be for the employer to show what his sole or main purpose was in making the offer. If the tribunal uphold the complaint, it shall make a declaration to that effect, and also award compensation to the worker of £2,500.

21.41 The purpose of ss 145A and 145B (which were inserted into TULR(C)A by the Employment Relations Act 2004) is to prohibit 'sweetener payments' as an inducement to workers not to belong to trade unions, such payments being held by the European Court of Human Rights to contravene Art 11 of the European Convention (see *Wilson v United Kingdom*, para 1.101).

C. Action short of dismissal (TULR(C)A, s 146, as amended)

21.42 Every worker has the right not to be subjected to any detriment as an individual by any act, or any deliberate failure to act, by his employer, if the act or failure takes place for the purpose of:

(a) preventing or deterring him from being a member of an independent trade union, or penalising him for being so; or

(b) preventing or deterring him from taking part in the activities of an independent trade union at an appropriate time, or penalising him for doing so; or

(c) preventing or deterring him making use of trade union services at an appropriate time, or penalising him for doing so; or

(d) compelling him to become a member of a trade union.

Detriment, for the purpose of this section, is detriment short of dismissal.

21.43 The first matter to be determined is whether the action was taken against the worker 'as an individual'. If action is taken against a trade union this may affect an individual worker, but the action was not necessarily taken against him as an individual. In *F W Farnsworth Ltd v McCoid*, a collective agreement provided that the employer had the right to derecognise a shop steward if his conduct was called into question. The employer notified the union that they intended to derecognise the claimant because his conduct was such that he was not suited to hold the office of shop steward. The claimant claimed that this derecognition constituted a breach of s 146(1). For the employer, it was argued that the action had not been taken against him as an individual, because it only affected his status as a shop steward, not as an employee. The argument was rejected. The Court of Appeal held that the purpose of s 146(1) was to allow an individual (in whatever capacity) to bring a complaint before an employment tribunal. However, it was thought that the employer could still successfully defend the action if they could show that the action taken was not for the purpose of preventing or deterring him from taking part in the activities of an independent trade union, but for the purpose of removing someone from the office of shop steward who was not fit for that role.

21.44 There is no breach of s 146 if the action taken (or omission) had the effect of so doing, if it was not done for that purpose. Thus in *Gallacher v Department of Transport*, the claimant was a civil servant, who spent most of his working time carrying out trade union duties. He put his name forward for promotion to a higher grade, but was turned down because of his lack of management skills. He was told that the only way he could acquire those skills was by taking a line job, and thus reduce the amount of time spent on trade union duties. He complained to an employment tribunal, who found that the advice given to him that he should spend more time gaining management experience was intended to deter him from spending time on trade union duties and activities. However, the EAT allowed the employer's appeal and that decision was upheld by the Court of Appeal. The employer's purpose was to ensure that only employees with sufficient line management experience were promoted. Thus any action taken was not for the purpose of deterring the applicant from exercising his statutory rights.

21.45 The 'appropriate time' for carrying out trade union activities or making use of trade union services means time which is outside his working hours, or at a time within his working hours at which, in accordance with arrangements agreed with or consent given by, his employer, it is permissible for him to take part in those activities. Such consent may be express, and will frequently be implied from the conduct of the parties. However, it would be rare that consent can be implied in the case of a shop steward who is not accredited (*Marley Tile Co Ltd v Shaw*). A worker cannot just engage in trade union activities in working hours when he feels like it. Thus in *Brennan and Ging v Ellward (Lancs) Ltd* the claimants left a site on which they were working to consult their trade union official, despite a warning that if they did so they would be dismissed. Although this may have amounted to trade union activities, it was not within the appropriate time for such activities.

21.46 In *Robb v Leon Motor Services* the claimant was a long distance coach driver. He was appointed shop steward. He was then told that he would have to drive other vehicles, because of all the trouble he was causing, and he claimed that by taking him off better paid and more important work, he was being deterred from carrying out his trade union activities at an appropriate time. It was held that even though this was action taken against him short of dismissal, and even though it was done for the purpose of deterring him from taking part in trade union activities, he could not succeed. There was no attempt to stop him from taking part in union activities outside his working hours, and the activities he was engaged in within working hours were not done with any arrangement or with the consent of the employers. Consequently, he was not being deterred from taking part in trade union activity at the appropriate time.

21.47 Whether the activities in question are the activities of an independent trade union is an issue of fact for the employment tribunal to determine (*Marley Tile Co Ltd v Shaw*). There must be some institutional link, with the union or an accredited shop steward being involved. Individual requests or complaints, or group meetings which have no union connection, are outside the statutory protections (*Dixon and Shaw v West Ella Developments Ltd*).

21.48 If there is a requirement (whether contractual or not) that in the event of a failure by the worker to become or remain a member of a trade union, he must make a payment (usually to charity), and a deduction is made from the worker's wages in consequence, this shall be treated as a detriment. Further, where a worker notifies the employer that he has ceased or will cease to be a member of a trade union as from a certain date, the employer will ensure that no amount representing his trade union subscription shall be deducted from the worker's pay (TULR(C)A, s 68, see below). If the employer fails to comply, the worker may seek a declaration in the county court. The court may make an order to ensure that the employer's actions are not repeated, but for any unlawful past deductions, the worker must seek a remedy in the employment tribunal under the provisions of s 23 of the Employment Rights Act 1996.

21.49 A complaint may be presented to a tribunal that an employer has taken action against a worker in violation of the above rights. The burden of proof is placed on the employer to show the purpose for which the action was taken. Moreover, no account is to be taken of any pressure which may have been exercised on the employer by way of strike or other industrial action (or threats of such), and the tribunal will determine the issue as if no such pressure has been exercised. But if the complaint is on the ground that the employer has taken action against the worker for the purpose of compelling him to be or become a member of a trade union, and the employer or worker claims that the employer was induced to take such action by such pressure, the employer or the worker may, before the hearing of the complaint, require the person who he claimed exercised the pressure to be joined as a party to the proceedings.

21.50 The employment tribunal may then make an award of compensation to the claimant either against the employer or the party who exercised the pressure, or partly against each of them as it thinks just and equitable in the circumstances (TULR(C)A, s 150).

21.51 The complaint must be presented within three months from the date of the last action complained of (see *Adlam v Salisbury and Wells Theological College*), with the usual extension of time in cases where it was not reasonably practicable to present it earlier. If the tribunal upholds the complaint, it may make a compensation award as it considers just and equitable having regard to the claimant's loss, and the infringement of his rights, including any expenses incurred and any benefits he might have received but for that action. There is no limit (in theory) on the amount of compensation which can be awarded. The claimant must mitigate against his loss, and compensation is subject to a reduction on the ground of contributory conduct.

21.52 The basis of the award is to compensate the worker for any loss suffered, not for the purpose of imposing a fine on the employer. In *Brassington v Cauldon Wholesale Ltd* an employer threatened to close his business down if he was forced to recognise a trade union. The claimant claimed this was action short of dismissal taken against him for the purpose of preventing or deterring him from joining an independent trade union, and with some hesitation, the EAT agreed that this was so and remitted the appeal back to an employment tribunal to assess compensation under TULR(C)A, s 149(2). Thus the infringement of a person's trade union rights will lead to an employment tribunal making a mandatory declaration, and compensation if the employee can show that he has suffered a loss. This could be, for example, stress causing ill-health (*Cheall v Vauxhall Motors Ltd*), injury to feelings as a result of being overlooked for promotion (*Cleveland Ambulance NHS Trust v Blane*), the loss of the benefit of trade union advice or assistance, and so on.

D. Detriment and dismissal in statutory recognition cases (TULR(C)A, Sch A1)

21.53 We shall see (Chapter 23) that the new Sch A1 inserted into TULR(C)A sets out a statutory procedure whereby a trade union may obtain recognition or suffer derecognition. The Schedule also (in Pt VIII) provides protection for any worker (see para 23.6) against suffering a detriment because he did or did not do any of a wide range of actions in connection with the statutory procedure for recognition or derecognition, including supporting or opposing the application, influencing others to support or oppose the application, voting in a ballot, and so on (see para 156 of the Schedule). However, there will be no protection if what the worker did was unreasonable (query whether a breach of contract by the worker, eg a strike, is unreasonable conduct on his part). A worker may make a complaint to an employment tribunal, which may make a declaration, and may also award compensation to be paid by the employer in respect of the act or omission complained of; the amount shall be such as the tribunal consider to be just and equitable.

21.54 If the detriment amounts to the termination of the worker's contract, but that contract is not a contract of employment, the amount awarded by the tribunal may be the equivalent of the normal basic and compensatory awards which can be made in unfair dismissal cases under ERA, ss 119 and 124(1).

21.55 So far as workers who are employees are concerned, if the detriment amounts to a dismissal, that dismissal shall be regarded as being automatically unfair under ERA, Pt X. It will also be unfair to select an employee for redundancy if the reason was any of the above specified reasons.

21.56 Similar protections are given to employees who are employed under a fixed-term contract, and the normal qualifying periods of employment and the age limits provisions do not apply to any of the above rights. Interim relief will also be available, as appropriate.

21.57 Workers who act or omit to act in circumstances which are outside the statutory procedure of Sch A1 must rely on those provisions which protect against detriment or dismissal in respect of trade union activities contained in TULR(C)A, ss 146 and 152 (see paras 21.42 and 21.77). Thus recruiting members, distributing literature, etc, with a view to obtaining recognition outside the statutory procedures, will constitute trade union activities under the existing TULR(C)A provisions, and are thus protected (*Lyon v St James Press Ltd*).

E. Time off work for trade union duties (TULR(C)A, s 168)

21.58 An employer shall permit an employee of his who is an official of a recognised independent trade union to take time off work during his working hours, for the purpose of carrying out any duties as such officially concerned with:

(a) negotiations with the employer related to or connected with collective bargaining; or

(b) the performance on behalf of the employees of functions in relation to or in connection with matters falling within collective bargaining which the employer has agreed may be performed by the union; or

(c) the receipt of information from the employer and consultations by the employer concerned with redundancies (see para 18.68) and the transfer of an undertaking (see para 9.58).

21.59 The employer will also permit the employee to have time off work during working hours to undergo training in aspects of industrial relations which is relevant to the carrying out of those duties, and which has been approved by the TUC or by his union.

21.60 Time off work for this purpose is not confined to face-to-face meetings with the employers, but can also include preparatory or co-ordinating meetings in order to discuss forthcoming negotiations, as long as these are in connection with the collective bargaining purposes outlined in s 178 (*London Ambulance Service v Charlton*).

21.61 A trade union official wishing to take time off work for training should show a copy of the syllabus to the employer. In *Menzies v Smith and McLaurin Ltd* the claimant wished to go on a course relating to job security. The union sent a copy of the syllabus to the employers, showing that topics to be covered included import controls, North Sea Oil, EEC policies, and so on. The company decided that all this was not relevant to his trade union duties, but agreed to give him time off work (without pay) for trade union activities. He went on the course and then claimed his pay. It was held that he was not entitled to be paid. The syllabus clearly indicated that the course was not relevant to his duties as a trade union official.

21.62 The amount of time off, the purposes for which, the occasions on which, and any conditions subject to which time off may be taken are those that are reasonable in all the circumstances having regard to the relevant provisions of the code of practice issued by ACAS. The employer shall pay an employee who has taken time off for these purposes in accordance with his usual rate of remuneration. A failure to permit an employee to have time off under this section, or a failure to pay him for time off, may be the subject of a complaint to an employment tribunal by the aggrieved employee. In *Blower v CEGB* the claimant, who was a night shift worker, was a member of a works committee which met during the day. His day shift colleagues were paid for attending, whereas he was not. It was held that he was not entitled to be paid. It was part of his union work that his leisure time would be eaten into; the law only requires time off to be paid for if it is during his normal working hours, not for time spent on trade union duties outside his working hours (see *Hairsine v Kingston upon Hull City Council*).

21.63 Whether it is reasonable to have time off under s 168 is a question of fact for the employment tribunal, and its findings cannot be challenged in the EAT unless it took into account matters which ought not to be taken into account (*Thomas Scott & Sons (Bakers) Ltd v Allen*).

F. Time off work for trade union activities (TULR(C)A, s 170)

21.64 An employer shall permit an employee who is a member of a recognised independent trade union to take time off during the employee's working hours for the purpose of taking part in:

(a) any activities of that trade union; and

(b) any activities in relation to which the employee is acting as a representative of that union. This might include, for example, attendance at a conference as a union delegate, etc, but the activities for which permission is to be granted do not include anything which involved the taking of industrial action, whether or not in contemplation or furtherance of a trade dispute. Nor does the lobbying of Parliament to protest against proposed legislation come within the definition of 'trade union activities', even if the lobby is organised by a trade union, because it is intended to convey political and ideological objections to the proposed legislation, and is not as such a trade union activity (*Luce v London Borough of Bexley*).

21.65 Again, the amount of time off, the purposes, the occasions and the conditions are those that are reasonable in all the circumstances having regard to the relevant provisions in the Code of Practice issued (see *Depledge v Pye Telecommunications Ltd*). When determining the reasonableness of time off to be taken for a particular purpose, the nature, extent and purpose of time off already taken by the employee may be taken into consideration (*Wignall v British Gas Corpn*). It will be noted that the employer does not have to pay an employee for time taken off for trade union activities. A failure to permit time off for these purposes may be the subject of a complaint to an employment tribunal by the aggrieved employee.

G. Time off work for trade union learning representatives (TULR(C)A, s 168A)

21.66 An employer shall permit an employee of his who is a member of an independent trade union recognised by the employer, and a learning representative of the trade union, to take time off work during his working hours, with pay, for the purpose of carrying on the following activities in relation to qualifying members of the trade union, ie members of the trade union who are employees of the employer of a description in respect of whom the union is recognised, and in relation to whom it is the function of the union learning representative to act as such.

21.67 The purposes in question are:

  (a) any of the following activities –
      (i)   analysing learning or training needs,
      (ii) providing information and advice about learning or training matters,
      (iii) arranging learning or training, and
      (iv) promoting the value of learning or training;
  (b) consulting with the employer about carrying on such activities; and
  (c) preparing for any of the above.

21.68 The trade union must give notice in writing to the employer that the employee is a learning representative of the trade union, and that he has undergone (or will be undergoing) sufficient training to enable him to carry on such activities. The training must be sufficient for the above purpose, having regard to any Code of Practice issued by ACAS or the Secretary of State. The amount of time off, the occasions on which, and any conditions subject to which time off may be taken are those that are reasonable having regard to any relevant provision of the Code of Practice.

21.69 An employee may present a complaint to an employment tribunal that his employer has failed to permit him to take time off as required by s 168A which, if the complaint is well founded, shall make a declaration, and may make an award of compensation.

21.70 A trade union member is entitled to reasonable time off work (without pay) for the purpose of having access to the services of his union learning representative. It will be unfair if an employee is dismissed because he brought proceedings to enforce his rights under s 168A.

H. Check-off arrangements (TULR(C)A, s 68)

21.71 If a trade union and an employer have an agreement whereby the employer will deduct the union subscriptions from the worker's wages and pay this direct to the union (ie a check-off agreement) the employer shall ensure that the worker has authorised the deduction in a document which is signed and dated, that the amount of the deduction does not exceed the permitted amount, and that the authorisation is current on the day of the deduction. An authorisation once made will be operative until the worker withdraws it in writing. The permitted amount to be deducted is the amount of the union subscription. It is no longer necessary for the employer to give one month's notice in writing before deducting an increase in the union subscription, but the amount of the deduction will still have to be shown on the regular itemised pay statement, and the worker is free to withdraw from the check-off arrangement at any time (Deregulation (Deduction from Pay of Union Subscriptions) Order 1998).

21.72 The fact that the worker has given his authorisation to the deductions does not give rise to any obligation on the part of the employer to continue to make the deductions (s 68(9)). That is clearly a matter between the employer and the trade union.

21.73 A worker may bring a complaint before an employment tribunal that his employer has made a deduction in contravention of s 68. The complaint must be presented within three months from the date of the last deduction, with the usual extension of time if it was not reasonably practicable to present the claim earlier.

21.74 If the tribunal find the complaint to be well founded, it shall make a declaration to that effect, and also order the employer to pay to the worker the unauthorised deduction (or unauthorised increase in subscription).

I. Deductions for the political fund of the union (s 86)

21.75 If a member of a trade union informs the employer in writing that he is exempt from paying the levy to the political fund of the union, the employer shall ensure that no amount representing the contribution to the political fund is deducted from the employee's wages.

21.76 If a person alleges that his employer has wrongly deducted a political fund contribution, or has refused to deduct union dues, he may make a complaint to an employment tribunal within three months, and the tribunal may make a declaration, order the employer to pay the applicant the amount deducted in contravention of s 87, or make an order requiring the employer to take steps specified in relation to emoluments payable. In the latter case, if there is still a failure to comply, there is an ultimate sanction of two weeks' pay (TULR(C)A, s 87).

J. Dismissal on the ground of trade union membership or non-membership, or trade union activities (TULR(C)A, s 152)

21.77 The dismissal of an employee will be unfair if the reason (or principal reason) was because the employee:

(a) was, or proposed to become, a member of an independent trade union; or

(b) had taken part, or proposed to take part, in the activities of an independent trade union at an appropriate time, or made use of trade union services at an appropriate time, or had failed to accept an offer made in contravention of ss 145A–145B (inducement relating to union membership or collective bargaining, see para 21.38). 'Appropriate time' means time which is outside his working hours, or time within his working hours at which, in accordance with arrangements agreed with or consent given by his employer it is permissible to take part in those activities. 'Working hours' means any time when the employee is required to work. A person is not taking part in trade union activities merely because he is a trade union activist, for one must distinguish between individual and trade union activities (*Chant v Aquaboats Ltd*). Nor do the activities of an unofficial strike committee constitute trade union activities. But enlisting the help of a trade union official to assist in negotiations of terms and conditions of employment may constitute trade union activities (*Discount Tobacco and Confectionery Ltd v Armitage*), (but see *Speciality Care plc v Pachela*). Going on strike does not constitute trade union activities, but leading an official strike will (*Britool Ltd v Roberts*).

If the employee is dismissed because the employer learns of his trade union activities in a previous employment (eg as a trade union activist), it would be inevitable that the employer was dismissing him because of the belief that he would be involved in trade union activities in his current employment, and thus the principal reason for the dismissal would be that the employee proposed to take part in trade union activities, and hence the dismissal is unfair (*Fitzpatrick v British Railways Board*). But if the trade union activist has obtained employment by deceit (eg by changing his name) then a dismissal for that deceit may be fair, and the reason is not because of past or proposed trade union activities (*Birmingham City District Council v Beyer*);

(c) was not a member of any trade union, or a particular trade union, or had refused or proposed to refuse to become or remain a member (*Crosville Motor Services Ltd v Ashfield*). This provision gives general rights to non-unionists not to be dismissed because of their non-membership of a trade union.

A distinction may be drawn between the fact of involvement in trade union activities and the manner of such involvement. Thus if, in the course of such activities, the trade unionist makes statements which are malicious, untruthful or irrelevant to the matter in hand, his manner of conducting those activities may take him outside the protection of s 152 (*Bass Taverns Ltd v Burgess*);

(d) had made use of trade union services at an appropriate time, or had failed to accept an offer which was made in contravention of ss 145A and 145B.

21.78 If a person is dismissed for any of the above reasons, it will be an unfair dismissal, and thus it is not necessary for him to have the normal qualifying period of employment of one year before he can bring his claim (TULR(C)A, s 154, and see *Carrington v Therm-A-Stor Ltd*). Nor does the upper age limit exclusion apply. Taking part in a strike may be trade union activity, but it is not at an appropriate time (see para 21.83).

21.79 It is also an unfair dismissal to select a person for redundancy because of his trade union membership/non-membership, or his trade union activities, or making use of trade union services (TULR(C)A, ss 152(1)–153).

21.80 To select an employee for redundancy because of his trade union membership or non-membership or trade union activities would, of course, be manifestly unfair, but it must be shown that the circumstances constituting the redundancy applied equally to other employees who held positions similar to that employee, and that they were not dismissed. Thus in *O'Dea v ISC Chemical Ltd*, the claimant, who was a senior shop steward, was paid as a technical services operator, although in fact he spent half of his working time working as a packaging operator and the other half on trade union activities. He was dismissed for reason of redundancy, although two other technical service operators were retained. It was held that his dismissal was not unfair. When considering his 'position' account had to be taken of his status as an employee, the nature of his work and his terms and conditions of employment. The claimant could not compare himself with technical service operators because he did not do that job.

21.81 It does not need to be shown that the employer acted maliciously or with a deliberate desire to get rid of a trade union activist. Thus if an employee spends a major part of his working hours on trade union duties, with the result that he is given a poor assessment when redundancy selection procedures are being implemented, 'the reason' for his selection is his trade union activities, carried out at an appropriate time with the consent (albeit reluctantly given) of the employer, and hence his dismissal falls within s 152(1) (*Dundon v GPT Ltd*).

21.82 Finally, it should be noted that the employment tribunal has no right to go into an investigation as to the reasons which have brought about the redundancies, or to require the employers to justify them on economic grounds. In *Moon v Homeworthy Furniture (Northern) Ltd*, a factory was closed down after a series of labour disputes. It was held that TULR(C)A had taken away any right of the courts or tribunals to interfere in industrial relations matters, and the tribunals refused to entertain an argument that the closure was unnecessary.

K. Dismissal in connection with industrial action (TULR(C)A, ss 237–239)

21.83 The law on dismissal for taking part in industrial action is somewhat complicated, and needs careful consideration. There are five different situations to consider.

21.84 The first situation arises when the employer conducts a lock-out. Here, the provisions of s 238(1)(a) apply, and if there is a dismissal, the 'no picking and choosing' rule applies.

21.85 The second situation arises when employees, who may be all union members, or some of whom are union members (and some are not), go on strike and the strike has not been authorised or endorsed by the trade union to which they belong. This is an unofficial strike, and the provisions of s 237 apply.

21.86 The third situation arises when none of those who go on strike or take industrial action are members of a trade union. This is not an unofficial industrial action, and clearly it is not official industrial action. Here, a dismissed employee can only complain of unfair dismissal if the 'no picking and choosing' rule has been violated (s 238(2)).

21.87 The fourth situation arises when a union authorises or endorses industrial action, but the action is not protected by virtue of s 219 because the balloting provisions have not been complied with, or secondary action, etc is being taken. This is official unprotected industrial action, and the 'no picking and choosing' rules in s 238(2) apply.

21.88 The fifth situation arises when a union calls a protected strike, ie one that is protected by TULR(C)A, s 219 (immunity from actions in tort, see para 23.41), and the union has not lost its immunity through a failure to comply with the legal rules which would lead to such loss, eg it has complied fully with the balloting provisions (see ss 222–235). Here, the provisions of s 238A apply, and dismissed employees enjoy much greater protection.

21.89 There is a further subtle distinction between ss 237–238 and 238A. Sections 237 and 238 are both concerned with a dismissal which takes place *while* an employee was taking part in industrial action, whereas 238A deals with a dismissal *for* taking part in industrial action. In other words, ss 237 and 238 apply whenever an employee is dismissed during the action industrial action, whereas s 238A will apply if the participation in the industrial action was the reason for the dismissal.

These situations can now be examined in more detail.

Dismissal in connection with a lock-out (TULR(C)A, s 238(I)(a))

21.90 A lock-out is the closing of a place of employment, or a suspension of the work, or the refusal by the employer to continue to employ his employees, done with a view to compelling those employees to accept terms and conditions of or affecting employment (ERA, s 235(4)). A lock-out by an employer is not necessarily a breach of contract by him (*Express and Star Ltd v Bunday*). If an employee claims that he has been dismissed by virtue of the lock-out, an employment tribunal is precluded from determining whether or not such dismissal is fair or unfair unless it can be shown that (a) one or more of the relevant employees were not dismissed, or (b) if they were dismissed, they were re-engaged within three months from the date of dismissal, but the applicant was not offered re-engagement. The relevant employees are those who were directly interested in the dispute on the day of the lock-out (*H Campey & Sons Ltd v Bellwood*).

Dismissal of unofficial strikers (TULR(C)A, s 237)

21.91 An employee has no right to claim that he has been unfairly dismissed if at the time of the dismissal he was taking part in an unofficial strike or other industrial action.

A strike or other industrial action will be unofficial unless:

(a) he is a member of the trade union, and the strike or other industrial action was authorised or endorsed by his trade union; or

(b) he is not a member of the trade union, but there are others who are taking part in the strike who are members of the trade union by which the strike or other industrial action has been authorised or endorsed.

21.92 In other words, if some or all of the employees who are taking industrial action are members of a trade union, and the union has not authorised or endorsed the industrial action, any employee who is consequently dismissed will have no claim for unfair dismissal, even if others who took part in the industrial action were not dismissed (s 237). If the trade union authorised or endorses the action, but then repudiates it, the action will become unofficial the next working day after the repudiation takes place. What amounts to a repudiation is set out in s 21 (see para 23.80). Thus an employer could dismiss the ringleaders of an unofficial strike without having to worry about the prospect of defending an unfair dismissal claim, subject to the exception in respect of protected reasons (see para 21.108).

Dismissal in connection with industrial action (s 238(1)(b), (2)(b))

21.93 The third situation applies when none of those who are taking industrial action are members of a trade union. This is not official industrial action, because they are not members of a trade union, nor is it unofficial industrial action, presumably because there is no-one to make it official. It is just industrial action. In these circumstances, if an employee is dismissed while taking part in industrial action, the tribunal shall not determine whether the dismissal was fair or unfair, unless it is shown that:

(i) one or more of the relevant employees (ie, those taking part in the industrial action) were not dismissed, or

(ii) that any such employee who was dismissed was offered re-engagement within three months of the claimant's dismissal, but that the claimant was not so offered.

There is no requirement that the offer to re-engage must be in writing (*Marsden v Fairey Stainless Ltd*).

21.94 Whether or not an employee is taking part in a strike or other industrial action must be determined as an objective fact. In other words, the test is 'what is the employee doing or omitting to do?' The subjective knowledge of the employer is not relevant (*Manifold Industries v Sims*).

21.95 An employee who is dismissed for taking part in a strike is not entitled to a redundancy payment, even though it can be shown that a subsequent redundancy situation is revealed. In *Baxter v Limb Group of Companies*, dock workers refused to work overtime following a dispute with the employers over bonus payments. They were dismissed, and subsequently the employers discontinued using direct labour and contracted the work out. The dismissed employees argued that the employers had decided to dispense with direct labour, and had manoeuvred the employees into a position where it appeared that they were dismissed for taking part in a strike or other industrial action, whereas the real reason for the dismissal was redundancy. The Court of Appeal dismissed their claim. The industrial action was the reason for the dismissal and for the decision to use contract labour. TULR(C)A, s 238 prohibits an employment tribunal from considering whether a dismissal is fair or unfair if, at the date of dismissal, the employee *was taking part* in a strike or other industrial action. It does not say that the employee was dismissed *because* he was taking part in such action. In other words, if the dismissals caused the redundancy, a redundancy payment cannot be made (*Sanders v Ernest A Neale Ltd*).

21.96 It will be recalled that a strike is a breach of contract by the employee which entitles the employer to dismiss him. Provided the employer dismisses all the strikers, or offers all of them re-engagement after the strike is over within three months, the employment tribunal has no jurisdiction to hear any complaint. This is the 'no picking and choosing' rule (see *McCormick v Horsepower Ltd*). But if an employer is selective in his dismissals or offers of re-engagement, those employees who have been excluded may bring claims in the employment tribunals. To avoid a finding of unfair dismissal, the employer must show that he has acted reasonably in not taking back those strikers who were not offered re-engagement. The question will be determined by the circumstances, having regard to the equity and substantial merits of the case (*Edwards v Cardiff City Council*).

21.97 Further, the employer can re-engage an employee who has been dismissed for striking any time after three months from the time another striker was dismissed without exposing himself to a claim for unfair dismissal from the latter.

21.98 But if the employer (or an associated employer) re-engages a striker by mistake (eg in ignorance of the fact that he had been on strike) this gives the employment tribunal jurisdiction to consider a claim from a striker who has not been offered re-engagement (*Bigham v GKN Kwikform Ltd*).

21.99 The three-month period is in the nature of a 'cooling off' period, designed to enable industrial disputes to be settled on honourable terms. As long as the offer of re-engagement is made within that period, the employment tribunal has no jurisdiction to hear a claim by a person who does not wish to accept that offer (*Highland Fabricators Ltd v McLaughlin*).

21.100 But the employer will lose the protection of s 238 if he seeks to dismiss before the strike has begun or after the strike is over. In *Heath v Longman (Meat Salesmen) Ltd* employees went out on strike, but subsequently decided to return to work. One of them informed the employer that the strike was over, but when they returned to work they were dismissed. The NIRC held that since they had returned to work, they were no longer on strike, and hence the dismissals were unfair. In *Midland Plastics Ltd v Till*, a letter was sent to the company management stating that unless certain demands were met, industrial action would commence at 11am. At 9.30am, the managing director spoke to four employees, who confirmed that they would abide by the decision, and they were immediately dismissed. It was held that the employment tribunal were not precluded by s 238 from entertaining a complaint of unfair dismissal. The threat to take part in a strike was a mere display of power by one side to a dispute which is a substantial feature of industrial relations negotiations. As the dismissals took place before the strike, s 238 did not apply.

21.101 The offer of re-engagement must be made to the striking employee. A general advertising campaign offering employment to those who apply does not amount to an offer of employment to any particular individual. Such a campaign merely makes available the opportunity to be offered employment (*Crosville Wales Ltd v Tracey*).

21.102 If a dismissal is unfair because the employer has re-engaged some of the strikers contrary to TULR(C)A, s 238, compensation is not to be reduced on the ground of contributory conduct merely because the employees who were not re-engaged took part in the strike. There must have been some other sufficiently blameworthy conduct which makes it just and equitable to reduce their compensation, for example if the strikers' leaders were over-hasty or indulged in inflammatory language. The circumstances of each claimant must be examined to see whether *his* compensation should be reduced because of *his* conduct other than the mere fact that he was on strike (*Tracey v Crosville Wales Ltd*).

Official unprotected industrial action

21.103 The fourth situation arises where a trade union calls a strike, but loses the protection of s 219 because:

(a) the strike was to enforce trade union membership (s 222); or

(b) because of the dismissal of unofficial strikers (s 223); or

(c) secondary action was taken (s 224); or

(d) the strike was to impose union recognition requirement (s 225); or

(e) the balloting provisions of ss 226–234 were not complied with; or

(f) notice was not given to the employer (s 234A).

In these circumstances the strike is no longer protected under s 238A (below), and hence the dismissal of employees on strike falls to be considered under the 'no picking and choosing' rule in s 238(2) (above). The action may be official, but it is not protected industrial action.

Protected industrial action (s 238A)

21.104 Finally, protected industrial action is industrial action in respect of which the trade union will be immune from liability in tort by virtue of TULR(C)A, s 219, and has not lost that immunity by virtue of the above matters. Those who take part in such industrial action have the protections conferred by s 238A, which will arise if the date of dismissal is:

(a) within the protected period, which is the basic period of 12 weeks beginning with the first day of protected industrial action, plus any extension period brought about by an employer lock-out; or

(b) after the end of the protected period, but the employee had ceased to take part in the industrial action before the end of that period; or

(c) after the end of the protected period, but the employer had not taken such procedural steps as would have been reasonable for the purposes of ending the dispute. The procedural steps include complying with agreed procedures, resuming negotiations, unreasonably refusing the use of conciliation or mediation services, etc (s 238A(6)).

21.105 Any such dismissal is automatically unfair, and there is no qualifying period of employment or upper age limit which would otherwise defeat a claim. A claim may be presented before the end of six months from the date of dismissal, with the usual extension of time provisions. It will be equally unfair to select an employee for redundancy if the selection was because the employee took part in protected industrial action as defined in the above three categories (ERA, s 105(7C)). The action taken must be an official strike called by a trade union which itself would be protected under TULR(C)A, s 219 (see Chapter 23). If the union repudiates the official action, and thus the strike changes from being official to unofficial, employees are given a day's grace in which to cease their action, ie if they continue to be on strike beyond the next working day after the day on which the repudiation took place, they will lose their protection of s 238A.

21.106 To determine whether the employer has taken reasonable steps to resolve the dispute, regard shall be had to:

(a) whether the employer or the union have complied with procedures established by any collective agreement or other agreement;

(b) whether the employer or the union offered or agreed to commence or resume negotiations after the start of the protected industrial action;

(c) whether the employer or the union unreasonably refused, after the start of the protected industrial action, a request for conciliation services to be used;

(d) whether the employer or the union unreasonably refused, after the start of the protected industrial action, a request that mediation services be used.

21.107 In determining whether the employer has taken those steps, no regard shall be had to the merits of the dispute. If there is a dismissal contrary to s 238A, an employment tribunal cannot make an order for reinstatement or re-engagement until after the conclusion of the protected industrial action. Additional powers are given to tribunals to carry out pre-hearing reviews and to adjourn proceedings if they become aware that legal actions are being brought challenging the legitimacy of the industrial action in question.

Exceptions in certain cases (ss 237–238)

21.108 The general principle is that an employee has no right to claim unfair dismissal if at the time of the dismissal he was taking part in an unofficial strike or other unofficial industrial action (s 237). However, this does not apply if the reason for the dismissal (or selection for redundancy) was a protected reason, ie a reason which violates an employee's rights with respect to pregnancy, maternity or parental leave, health and safety, working time, employee representative, jury service, dependants, protected disclosure or flexible working (s 237(1A)).

21.109 Similarly, if an employee claims that he was unable to claim that he was unfairly dismissed because at the date of the dismissal the employer did not act in violation of the 'picking and choosing' rule, then again, the employee's rights will revive if the reason for the dismissal was for one of the above reasons.

L. Dismissal due to industrial pressure (ERA, s 107)

21.110 If an employer is forced to dismiss an employee because of actual, or the threat of, industrial pressure by other employees, this may amount to an unfair dismissal. The reason is that ERA, s 107 provides that for the purpose of determining whether the employer has a statutory reason for dismissing, or whether the employer acted reasonably in dismissing, no account shall be taken of any industrial pressure (ie strike or other industrial action) which was put on the employer, and the question must be determined as if no such pressure had been exercised. In *Hazell Offsets v Luckett*, the claimant was dismissed from his managerial post after trade union representatives had indicated that they would not co-operate with him. Clearly, the principal reason for the dismissal was the industrial pressure, but this could not be advanced as a reason. Since there was no other reason, the dismissal was unfair. The tribunal thought that this did not seem right, nor fair, but it was clearly what Parliament had decided. But if the employee was partly responsible for the threat of industrial action, this could amount to contributory conduct so as to warrant a reduction in the compensation awarded. Thus if the industrial pressure is exercised because of some personal animosity, and the employee is unco-operative in a difficult situation, and, for example, refuses to move to another job, he may well have contributed to his dismissal (*Ford Motor Co Ltd v Hudson*).

21.111 However, if on a claim for unfair dismissal the employer or the claimant claims that the employer was induced to dismiss the claimant because of pressure which a trade union or other person exercised on him by way of calling, organising, procuring or financing a strike, or threatening to do so, and the pressure was exercised because the claimant was not a member of any trade union or a particular trade union, then the employer or the claimant may, before the hearing of the complaint, join that person as a party to the proceedings before the employment tribunal. If the latter decides to make an award of compensation in favour of the claimant, but also finds that the employer was induced to dismiss him because of the pressure, the tribunal may make an award against that person instead of the employer, or partly against that person and partly against the employer. The amount shall be such as the tribunal consider to be just and equitable in all the circumstances (TULR(C)A, s 160).

M. Selection for dismissal on grounds of redundancy (TULR(C)A, s 153)

21.112 We have seen that to select a person for dismissal on grounds of redundancy will be unfair if the reason for the selection was his membership or non-membership of a trade union. No qualifying period of continuous employment is required and the age limit does not apply.

N. Compensations for dismissals (TULR(C)A, ss 155–158)

21.113 In respect of compensation for dismissals for trade union membership or non-membership, there are rules relating to a minimum basic award, an additional award, as well as the usual compensation award (see Chapter 17).

O. Interim relief for dismissed trade unionists or non-unionists (TULR(C)A, ss 161–166)

21.114 If an employee considers that he was unfairly dismissed because he was, or proposed to become a member of an independent trade union, or had taken or proposed to take part in the activities of that union, or he was not a member of a trade union, he may present a complaint to an employment tribunal asking for an order that he be reinstated or re-engaged by the employer or, if this cannot be agreed upon, that he be suspended on full pay pending a settlement or a determination of the complaint. The employee must present the complaint before the end of seven days from the effective date of the termination of his employment, and must, if he is claiming he was dismissed because of his trade union membership or activities, accompany his complaint with a certificate signed by an authorised official of the trade union concerned, stating that the employee was or had proposed to become a member, and that there were reasonable grounds for believing that the reason for the dismissal was the one alleged in the complaint. The signature of a trade union official is prima facie evidence that he is duly authorised to sign the certificate, but if this is challenged, the onus is on the employee to show that the official had actual or implied authority to sign it (*Sulemany v Habib Bank Ltd*).

21.115 The tribunal will give the employer seven days' notice before the hearing, but shall thereupon hear the complaint as soon as is practicable. If the tribunal comes to the conclusion that it is likely that it would uphold a complaint of unfair dismissal on one of the above grounds, it shall announce this preliminary finding and explain to the parties its powers. It will then ask the employer if he is willing to reinstate the employee, or re-engage him on terms and conditions which are no less favourable than he formerly enjoyed, pending the determination or settlement of the complaint. If the employer is willing to re-engage the employee in another job, and specifies the terms and conditions, the tribunal will ask the employee if he is willing to accept, and if so, an order to that effect will be made. If the employee is unwilling to accept the job on those terms and conditions, then, if his refusal is reasonable, the tribunal will make an order for the continuation of his contract of employment, but if his refusal is regarded as being unreasonable, no order will be made. If the employer fails to attend the hearing, or states that he is unwilling to reinstate or re-engage the employee, the tribunal will make an order for the continuation of the employee's contract of employment.

21.116 The effect of an order for continuation of the contract of employment is that if the employment has ceased, it will continue in force, or if it has not yet ceased, it will continue when it does so cease, until, in either case, the determination or settlement of the complaint, for the purposes of pay, seniority, pension rights, and other similar rights, and for determining for any purpose the period for which the employee has been continuously employed. The tribunal will also specify the pay due to the employee from the time of dismissal until the complaint is finally settled, but it will take into account any lump sum received in lieu of wages. At any time after making the order and before the determination by the tribunal, the employer or the employee may apply for a revocation or variation of the order on the ground that there has been a relevant change in circumstances. Also, the employee may apply to the tribunal on the ground that the employer has not complied with the terms of the order. If his complaint is that the employer has not paid the amount specified, the tribunal will determine the amount due, and make it as a separate award for any other sum it gives by way of compensation. If the complaint relates to any other breach by the employer, then it shall make an award of compensation as it thinks just and equitable having regard to the loss suffered by the complainant.

21.117 An order for continuation of employment merely preserves the employee's rights; the employer does not have to permit him to come back to work, or to allow him on the premises.

21.118 On an application for interim relief, the employment tribunal must decide if the claimant can establish that he has a good chance of succeeding at a full hearing. This is a higher degree of certainty than a mere reasonable chance of success. 'Likely' means more than 'probable', and probable itself suggests more than an even chance (*Taplin v C Shippam Ltd*).

21.119 It will be extremely rare that an employer will admit that a person was dismissed because he engaged in trade union activity, and doubtless some other reason will be advanced. In *Forsyth v Fry's Metals Ltd* the tribunal considered the evidence under four headings: (a) the extent of the alleged behaviour, (b) the extent of the employer's dissatisfaction with the employee, (c) the coincidence in time between the alleged behaviour and the initial steps taken towards dismissal, and (d) the coincidence in time between the behaviour and the actual dismissal. In this case, the claimant was dismissed for alleged poor work performance. There was little direct evidence of this; on the other hand he had been instrumental in persuading most of the employees to join a trade union, and had been elected shop steward. On the facts, there was a likelihood that he would succeed in establishing his claim, and interim relief was granted.

21.120 On an application for interim relief, it is possible to join a person who is exercising pressure to bring about the dismissal (see TULR(C)A, s 160), and such a person shall be given notice of the time, date and place of the hearing as soon as reasonably practicable (s 162(3)).

22

The Law Relating to Trade Unions

22.1 In this chapter we shall concentrate on the law as it affects the running of a trade union. All the relevant law has now been consolidated by the Trade Union and Labour Relations (Consolidation) Act 1992, as amended. In so far as earlier reported decisions were based on provisions in earlier (now replaced) legislation, references to the relevant statutory provisions have, for the sake of convenience, been transposed to the corresponding provisions of the 1992 Act.

What constitutes a trade union?

A. Definition of a trade union (TULR(C)A, s 1)

22.2 A trade union is an organisation (whether permanent or temporary) which either:

(a) consists wholly or mainly of workers of one or more descriptions and whose principal purposes include the regulation of relations between workers and employers or employers' associations; or

(b) consists wholly or mainly of:
   (i) constituent or affiliated organisations which have those purposes; or
   (ii) representatives of such constituent or affiliated organisations, and in either case whose principal purposes include the regulation of relations between workers and employers or workers' and employers' associations, or include the regulation of relations between the constituent or affiliated organisations.

This definition discloses two functional bodies:

(a) a single trade union; and

(b) confederated organisations, such as the Trades Union Congress.

22.3 Whether or not a trade union has a 'legal personality' of its own was always a matter of some controversy. Section 10 provides that a trade union shall not be a body corporate, but shall nonetheless be capable of making contracts, suing and being sued in its own name, and capable of being prosecuted for any offences committed in its name. As, however, it has no 'legal' existence, property must be held by its trustees, and any judgment, order or award shall be enforced against the property held by the trustees. This does not apply to those organisations which were on the special register created by the Industrial Relations Act 1971 (see TULR(C)A, s 117) for these were professional organisations which engaged in collective bargaining on behalf of their members, and their legal personality stemmed from their charter of incorporation, or by virtue of incorporation under the Companies Acts. Such legal personality is to continue, but other than these, any registration by a trade union under the Companies Acts, or as a friendly society or an industrial and provident society, is void.

22.4 Between 1901 and 1971, a series of legal decisions had laid down that a trade union had some form of quasi-legal personality, but this status has been clearly removed by s 10. In *Electrical, Electronic Telecommunications and Plumbing Union v Times Newspapers*, it was held that a trade union, not having a legal personality, could not therefore sue for libel in respect of its reputation, for s 10 states that a trade union shall not be 'or treated as if it were', a body corporate, and hence the claimant trade union did not have the personality which could be protected by an action for defamation.

B. Listing of trade unions (TULR(C)A, s 2)

22.5 The certification officer (a post created in 1975 by the Employment Protection Act – see Chapter 1) has taken over and maintains a list of trade union organisations which were formerly held by the Registrar of Friendly Societies (s 257). On this list there will be organisations which were registered under the pre-1971 law (or formed as a result of an amalgamation of two or more bodies which were registered), all organisations registered under the Industrial Relations Act 1971, and all TUC affiliated trade unions. Any organisation (including employers' associations) which is not listed may apply for inclusion, submitting the appropriate fee, a copy of its rules, a list of officers, the address of its head office, and details of its name. The certification officer will refuse to enter on the list any organisation the name of which is the same as a previously registered or listed organisation, or a name which so closely resembles any such organisation as to be likely to deceive the public. If it appears to the certification officer that an organisation whose name is on the list is not a trade union he may remove it from the list, but not without giving notice of his intention to do so, and considering any representations which may be made. An organisation which is aggrieved by the decision of the certification officer to refuse to enter it on the list, or a decision to remove it from the list, may appeal either on a question of law or of fact, to the Employment Appeal Tribunal. Copies of the list shall be available for public inspection.

22.6 There are certain advantages of being a 'listed' trade union. First, it is evidence that the body concerned satisfied the statutory definition without further proof being required. Second, there are tax reliefs on income in the union's provident funds. Third, there are procedural advantages in connection with the passing of property consequent on the change of trustees. Fourth, and perhaps the most significant of all, only a listed trade union can apply for a certificate of independence.

C. Certification of trade unions (TULR(C)A, s 6)

22.7 Any trade union which is on the list may apply to the certification officer for a certificate that it is an independent trade union. A union is independent if:

  (a) it is not under the domination or control of an employer or groups of employers or an employers' association; and

(b) it is not liable to interference by an employer or any such group or association arising out of the provision of financial or material support or by any other means whatsoever tending towards such control (s 5).

If, after making enquiries the certification officer decides that the union is independent he will issue a certificate accordingly; otherwise he will refuse to do so, but must give reasons for his refusal. Even if he grants the certificate, he may withdraw it if he is of the opinion that the union is no longer independent, but he must notify the trade union concerned of his intention, and may take into account any relevant information supplied by any person. An appeal will lie on a point of law or fact to the Employment Appeal Tribunal against the decision of the certification officer to refuse to grant, or to withdraw, a certificate.

22.8 Only a trade union aggrieved by the decision not to grant a certificate may appeal. There is no general right of appeal by anyone who is aggrieved. In *General and Municipal Workers Union v Certification Officer*, a trade union objected to a decision of the Certification Officer to grant a certificate to another organisation, but it was held that the trade union had no right to appeal against that decision.

22.9 Once granted, the certificate is conclusive evidence of the independence of the trade union, and in any proceedings before any court, the Employment Appeal Tribunal, the Central Arbitration Committee, or an employment tribunal, where the independence of the trade union is in issue and there is no certificate in force and no refusal, withdrawal or cancellation recorded, the proceedings shall be stayed until a certificate has been issued or refused by the certification officer.

22.10 To understand the arguments about certification, it is necessary to make a short excursus into industrial relations. Some years ago there was an expansion of unionisation, particular among the so-called 'white collar' workers and management. A considerable number of staff associations have sprung up in order to exercise the sort of industrial pressure hitherto reserved for the blue collar workers. These staff associations are looked upon as not being 'proper' trade unions, and are sometimes referred to in a derogatory tone as being 'sweetheart unions' or 'house unions'. The test of independence for certification purposes is to permit through the net those unions which can demonstrate that they are truly independent, and not just the tame adjuncts of management. A considerable number of such staff associations have applied for and obtained certificates of independence; many have not bothered, on the ground that they can obtain by negotiation all the advantages which certification confers. Those that have succeeded in obtaining a certificate are criticised for bringing about a proliferation of trade unions (at a time when a reduction in the number of unions is thought to be desirable) and for not joining in with the existing established (ie TUC) trade unions.

22.11 The first case to be challenged under this branch of the law was *Blue Circle Staff Association v Certification Officer*. In 1971 the staff association was formed for salaried staff at the instigation of higher management. Subsequently, changes were made to the association's constitution and an application was made for certification. It was held by the EAT that the certification officer was right in his refusal to grant a certificate. The association had not yet attained the freedom from domination by the employer under which it had lived since its formation. There is a heavy burden to show that it had shaken off such paternal control.

22.12 A different view of the realities of the scene was taken in *Association of HSD (Hatfield) Employees v Certification Officer*, where the association was formed with the active encouragement of the employers, who shared the opposition of the association to proposals for nationalisation. After the decision to nationalise was taken, the new head of the industry visited the factory, and was met by a hostile demonstration organised by the association. A subsequent application for a certificate of independence was refused by the certification officer, and the association appealed to the EAT. It was held that the certificate should be granted. Under s 5(a) the organisation must show that it is not under the domination or control of the employer. This involves an examination of the factual situation, including finance, the extent (if any) of employer assistance or interference, the history, rules, organisation, membership base and general attitude. Under s 5(b) there is inevitably a degree of speculation, but the certification officer ought not to be unduly anxious about future possibilities as he always has the power to revoke the certificate if he thinks he should do so. On the facts of the case, the EAT was clearly impressed by the hostile demonstration, and held that as the association had demonstrated that it was 'fiercely independent of management' a certificate should be granted.

22.13 The fact that an association is company based is not fatal to the association's independence, for there are many trade unions in industry which negotiate with a single employer (eg the Post Office, or civil service unions). Nor is the fact that the employer makes facilities available to a trade union destructive of its independence, for this may be seen as good industrial relations practice, and is in accordance with the Code of Practice on Time Off for Trade Union Duties and Activities. In *Squibb UK Staff Association v Certification Officer*, a certificate of independence was refused because of fears of vulnerability to employer interference. This was based largely on the extensive facilities which were provided by the employer, which included time off with pay for the officials of the association when performing their duties, free use of office accommodation and rooms for meetings, the provision of free stationery, free use of the employer's telephone, photocopying and internal mailing system, and a free check-off system. In view of the obvious limited resources of the association, and its narrow membership base, the certification officer thought that it would be very difficult to function effectively if these were withdrawn by the employer. The EAT held that nonetheless the certificate should be granted, but this decision was reversed by the Court of Appeal, and the original ruling of the certification officer was confirmed. The test of 'liability to interference' by the employer, which would be fatal to the association's independence, meant vulnerable to, or at risk of, interference. The degree of the likelihood of the risk was irrelevant as long as it was not insignificant.

22.14 If the continued existence of the staff association is dependent on the approval of the employer, then it is 'liable to interference' and hence cannot be an independent trade union (*Government Communications Staff Federation v Certification Officer*).

Advantages of certification

22.15 There are a number of advantages in having a certificate of independence, which benefit the union, its officials (including shop stewards) and members, as follows:

(a) a member is entitled not to suffer a detriment (TULR(C)A, s 146(1)) or to be dismissed (s 152(1)) on grounds of trade union membership or activities, or making use of trade union services (s 152(1)). Interim relief is also available (s 161);

(b) an independent trade union may negotiate a dismissal procedure agreement which will replace individual statutory rights (ERA, s 110);

(c) an independent trade union may negotiate away the right of employees to strike (TULR(C)A, s 180);

(d) an independent trade union may negotiate a collective agreement modifying or derogating from rights contained in the Working Time Regulations, the Fixed-Term Employees (Prevention of Less Favourable Treatment) Regulations 2002, and replace the statutory default scheme on parental leave under the Maternity and Parental Leave etc Regulations 1999;

(e) an official or member of an independent trade union can act as an independent adviser for the purpose of compromise agreements (ERA, s 203(3A));

(f) an independent trade union will be able to receive money from the Secretary of State under the trade union modernisation scheme (see para 22.82).

22.16 If the independent trade union is recognised by the employer for collective bargaining purposes, then:

(a) it has the right to receive information for collective bargaining purposes (TULR-(C)A, s 181);

(b) it has the right to be consulted on redundancies (TULR(C)A, s 188) and proposed transfers (Transfer of Undertakings (Protection of Employment) Regulations 2006);

(c) an official of the union is entitled to paid time off work for trade union duties, and unpaid time off work for trade union activities and to act as a union learning representative (TULR(C)A, ss 168–170);

(d) the union can appoint safety representatives under the Health and Safety at Work Act 1974, s 2;

(e) representatives of an independent trade union can act as employee representatives for the purpose of the Transnational Information and Consultation of Employees Regulations 1999;

(f) the union is entitled to receive information from an employer concerning occupational pension schemes (Social Security Act 1975, s 56A);

(g) the union will be entitled to receive information on recent and probable development of the undertaking's activities under the Information and Consultation Regulations (see para 23.137).

D. Register of members (s 24)

22.17 A trade union shall maintain a register of the names and addresses of its members. The register shall be accurate, up to date, and may be kept by means of a computer.

22.18 A member is entitled to know whether there is an entry in the register relating to him, and be supplied with a copy of that entry. The person who has been appointed as an independent scrutineer for election purposes must also be permitted to inspect the register and be provided with an up-to-date copy of it (see para 22.48).

Confidentiality of the register of members (s 24A)

22.19 A trade union shall impose a duty of confidentiality on the independent scrutineer who has been appointed to oversee any ballot held on an election for office, political resolution or resolution to approve an instrument of amalgamation or transfer. The scrutineer or independent person must not disclose any name or address on the register (except in permitted circumstances), and must take all reasonable steps to ensure that no such disclosure takes place. Disclosure will be permitted (a) when the member consents, (b) where required for the purposes of the discharge of functions by the certification officer or of the scrutineer under the terms of his appointment, or (c) where required for the purpose of investigating crime or of criminal proceedings.

Remedies (ss 25–26)

22.20 A member of a trade union who claims that the union has failed to comply with ss 24 or 24A may apply to the certification officer for a declaration to that effect (s 25), or, in the alternative, to the court (s 26). The certification officer can make an enforcement order requiring the union to remedy the breach and/or abstain from acts which might lead to a future recurrence of the same breach. Any member of the union (who was a member at the time of the declared failure) may apply to the court to force the union to comply with the order. An appeal against the decision of the certification officer may be made to the EAT.

Membership of a trade union

22.21 In principle, it is for the trade union to lay down the description of persons who are eligible to join, and this will usually be laid down in the union's rules (*Boulting v Association of Cinematograph, Television and Allied Technicians*). It follows that it cannot accept for membership someone who is not within the prescribed class, and cannot create a category of membership not provided for in the rules (*Martin v Scottish Transport and General Workers' Union*). The rules may also specify a class of person who is not eligible to join (*Faramus v Film Artistes' Association*). However, a trade union cannot exclude a person from membership on arbitrary and unreasonable grounds (*Nagle v Feilden*). It is unlawful to discriminate against a woman in the terms on which it is prepared to accept her for membership, or by refusing or deliberately omitting to accept her application (Sex Discrimination Act 1975, s 12) or to discriminate against her in the way in which it affords her access to any benefits, facilities or other services, to deprive her of membership, or subject her to any other detriment (other than benefits on death or retirement). Similar provisions relating to unlawful discrimination on grounds of race etc are contained in the Race Relations Act 1976, s 12.

22.22 However, notwithstanding anything contained in the union's rules, a person cannot be excluded (or expelled) from a trade union unless this is permitted by the provisions of TULR(C)A, s 174 (see para 21.2), and a person who is so excluded or expelled has the right to bring a complaint before an industrial tribunal or the EAT as appropriate.

22.23 There is no statutory definition of who is a 'member' of a trade union, and the term has to be looked at in its context. Thus, if a trade union has a class of 'limited members', who have restricted rights, precisely defined in the union's rules, then they may not be 'members' for the purpose of voting in certain elections (eg on a proposal for the transfer of engagements, see *National Union of Mineworkers (Yorkshire Area) v Millward*).

Rules of a trade union

22.24 At common law, a trade union was tainted with illegality because its rules and/or objects were in 'restraint of trade'. In the nineteenth century this led to certain problems; the trade unionists were prosecuted for criminal conspiracy, and the rules of the unions were generally unenforceable. The effect of the doctrine against restraint of trade on trade unions, was nullified by the 1871 Trade Union Act (see now TULR(C)A, s 11), which provides that the purposes of a trade union or an employers' association shall not, by reason of being in restraint of trade, make any member liable for criminal conspiracy, or make any agreement or trust void or voidable, nor shall the rules be unlawful or unenforceable by virtue of their being in restraint of trade (see *Goring v British Actors Equity Association*). This also applies to incorporated employers' associations and special register bodies in so far as the purposes or rules relate to the regulation of relations between employers or employers' organisations and workers. It should be noted that Art 11 of the European Convention on Human Rights guarantees the right to freedom of association. Since the Convention now applies in the United Kingdom by virtue of the Human Rights Act 1998 (see para 1.97) it is arguable that the common law doctrine that trade unions are unlawful organisations (by virtue of having objects which are in restraint of trade) is no longer good law.

22.25 As long as a trade union complies with the various statutory requirements, there are no general restrictions on the rules which it may adopt. But the rules constitute a contract between the union and its members, and must be strictly observed.

A. Disciplinary action

22.26 If the trade union wishes to take disciplinary action, by way of fines or forfeitures, or wishes to expel a member, such powers must be contained in the rules, otherwise they cannot be exercised. In *Spring v National Amalgamated Stevedores and Dockers' Society* the plaintiff was enrolled as a member of the defendant union contrary to the Bridlington Agreement, which was designed to prevent poaching of members among TUC affiliated unions. The TUC ordered the union to expel the members, which it did, but the expulsion was held to be void when it was discovered that the union rules contained no power of expulsion.

22.27 However, it is possible for the court to imply into the union's rules a power to discipline a member, although since such a power is penal and could involve serious consequences which would affect the reputation and livelihood of the member, an implied disciplinary power would only arise when there are compelling circumstances to justify it. In *McVitae v UNISON* the claimant was a member of the National and Local Government Officers' Association (NALGO). Various complaints of intimidation, oppressive and sexist conduct were made against him and disciplinary proceedings were arranged. However, before they could take place, NALGO amalgamated with two other unions, to form Unison, and, following an investigation into the original complaints, Unison decided to re-institute the disciplinary proceedings. The claimant sought an injunction to prevent Unison from taking disciplinary action against him in respect of conduct which occurred prior to the union coming into existence.

There was no power in the instrument of amalgamation or the rules of the new union to discipline members in respect of conduct which occurred before its inception, but in the circumstances of the case, the court was prepared to imply such a power. The conduct in question was contrary to the rules of NALGO and Unison, and it could not have been intended that there should be a complete amnesty for conduct which occurred before the new union was created out of the amalgamation of the three unions.

22.28 If the rules specify the grounds on which disciplinary action may be taken, then the union must adhere to these grounds, and not proceed on others. Moreover, the courts have in the past exercised the power to interpret the rules of the union in accordance with the courts' understanding of the rules, not the union's. In *Lee v Showmen's Guild*, the claimant was expelled from the defendant guild for violating a rule designed to prevent 'unfair competition'. It was held that since the guild had misconstrued the meaning of this term, the court could substitute its own interpretation, and the expulsion was declared void. The interpretative power is particularly important in those cases where the rules are somewhat vague (eg 'conduct detrimental to the union' in *Kelly v National Society of Operative Printers' Assistants*), although the legitimate interests of the union will be upheld. In *Evans v National Union of Printing, Bookbinding and Paperworkers*, the rules provided that a member who acted contrary to the interests of the union might be expelled. The claimant absented himself from work on several occasions, contrary to an agreement between the union and the employers. As a result of such conduct, he was expelled. It was held that the expulsion was valid, for it was designed to uphold the success of the collective bargaining arrangements.

22.29 If the union rules provide for a procedure to be adopted in disciplinary cases, then that procedure must be strictly adhered to, and the smallest irregularity will be as fatal as the greatest. The rules cannot be so framed as to oust the jurisdiction of the courts by declaring that the decision of the union shall be final and binding (*Chapple v Electrical Trades Union*), and if there is an appeal procedure which is denied to the aggrieved member, the expulsion will be invalid (*Braithwaite v Electrical Electronics and Telecommunications Union*). If the expulsion is void because of lack of authority or some other reason, then, as the appeal procedure cannot cure the defect, the aggrieved member may apply to the courts nonetheless, without exhausting the internal machinery. In *Porter v National Union of Journalists*, the union called a strike of provincial journalists without holding a ballot as required by its rules. An injunction was granted to restrain the union from taking disciplinary action against those members who refused to comply with the instruction, for the strike call was unconstitutional.

22.30 Although the statutory requirements that a trade union must act in accordance with the rules of natural justice have been repealed, it is submitted that the common law position remains unchanged. This means that a trade union, in the exercise of what is essentially a quasi-judicial function, cannot expel a member without giving him a hearing, notifying him of the charges against him, and giving him an opportunity to rebut them (*Lawlor v Union of Post Office Workers*). It also means that the officials of the union should avoid being placed in the position of being prosecutor, judge and jury. In *Taylor v*

National Union of Seamen, the general secretary of the union dismissed the claimant for insubordination. When the claimant appealed to the executive council, the general secretary was the chairman of the meeting, and after the claimant had withdrawn, the meeting was treated to a long statement of matters which were not the subject of the charge, but which were prejudicial to him, and he had no opportunity of rebutting. It was held that the hearing of the appeal offended against the rules of natural justice.

22.31 However, the withdrawal of a privilege, granted outside the rules is not disciplinary action. In *Hudson v GMB*, a federated trade union nominated the claimant to attend a regional conference of the Labour Party. It was then alleged that she was a member of 'Militant', an organisation proscribed by the Labour Party, and so her nomination was withdrawn. She claimed that this was disciplinary action in violation of the rules of the union, as she had not been allowed to state her case. Further, she claimed that her nomination was a privilege which could not be withdrawn without proceedings taken in accordance with the principles of natural justice. Her claim failed. The withdrawal of the nomination was not a disciplinary measure relating to an office within the union's rules. Nor was the nomination made in respect of any permanent position which would involve a financial advantage. The union had no rules concerning such delegates, and the nomination could therefore be withdrawn at will.

22.32 A member who has been wrongfully expelled may apply for a declaration that he is still a member, an injunction restraining the union and its officials from acting on the purported expulsion, and damages for wrongful expulsion. In *Bonsor v Musicians' Union*, the appellant was expelled by the branch secretary, when this power could only be exercised by the branch committee. In consequence, he could not get work, and was reduced to earning a living by scraping rust off Brighton Pier. It was held that as the expulsion was void, he could recover damages for wrongful expulsion.

22.33 In addition (as already indicated) whatever the rules may or may not state, a member of a trade union has a statutory right not to be unjustifiably disciplined (see para 21.8) or expelled from a trade union (see para 21.2) unless the discipline or expulsion is not prohibited by the statute, and may seek an appropriate remedy before an employment tribunal.

B. Conduct of union affairs

22.34 Membership of a trade union confers certain rights and privileges on the members, and they are entitled to damages if these are not forthcoming. If the rules provide that members shall be entitled to legal advice, then a union which fails to provide that advice, or negligently provides incorrect advice, may be sued for the loss which flows from that breach. The tremendous increase in the statutory rights of employees is bound to throw an additional burden on trade union officials, who now need to be as familiar with those rights as management. Thus it is submitted that if a trade union fails to apply for a protective award in appropriate circumstances, or negligently delays the presentation of a claim to an employment tribunal so that it becomes out of time, the aggrieved member will have a right of action against that union for damages. No breach of contract arises if the member fails to show that his action had a reasonable prospect of success (*Buckley v National Union of General and Municipal Workers*), and in any case the union can fulfil the duty to use ordinary care and skill by handing over a potential claim to a firm of competent solicitors (*Friend v Institution of Professional Managers and Specialists*).

22.35 In the conduct of union affairs, the officials can only act within the confines of the rules. Thus in *Weakley v Amalgamated Union of Engineering Workers* the president of the union exercised a casting vote on a motion when the committee was equally divided. An injunction was granted restraining the union from acting on the motion, for, on a true construction of the rules, the president was not entitled to exercise a casting vote. But the officials may have implied power to do certain things which are in the interests of the union. In *Hill v Archbold*, two union officials brought an action in respect of matters which arose out of their employment. The actions were dismissed, but the union sought to pay the legal costs on behalf of the officials, though there was no provision in the rules for such expenditure. It was held that the union had implied power to do so, for the matter was incidental to their work as officials of the union.

22.36 A trade union which pays out strike pay which is not authorised by the rules (*Taylor v National Union of Mineworkers (Derbyshire Area)*) or imposes a levy for a purpose which is ultra vires (*Hopkins v National Union of Seamen*) can be restrained from so doing by an injunction. However, allegations of electoral irregularities can be pursued under the provisions of s 54 (see para 22.53).

C. Copy of the rules (s 27)

22.37 A trade union shall supply, at the request of any person, a copy of its rules, either free or on payment of a reasonable charge.

Executive committee (TULR(C)A, s 46)

22.38 Every member of the principal executive committee of a trade union (including those members who are members by virtue of holding an office) shall be elected by a ballot at least every five years. A person who holds his membership of the principal executive committee as a result of an election may continue as a member or official for such period as may be necessary (not exceeding six months) to give effect to an election result. In such a ballot, every member of the union shall be entitled to vote, except:

(a) those members who as a class are excluded by the rules from voting;

(b) members not in employment;

(c) members in arrears; and

(d) members who are students, trainees, apprentices or new members.

If the rules permit, it is possible to have voting restricted to special classes of membership, determined by reference to:

(a) trade or occupation;

(b) geographical area;

(c) separate sections of the union; or

(d) any combination of these.

Voting at an election must be made by the marking of a ballot paper by the person voting, and every person entitled to vote (a) must be allowed to do so without interference or constraint imposed by the union or any of its members, officials or employees, and (b) so far as is reasonably practicable, be able to do so without incurring any direct cost. So far as is reasonably practicable, voting papers must be sent to voters by post, containing or accompanied by a list of candidates, and the voter must be given a convenient opportunity to vote by post. So far as is reasonably practicable, voting shall be in secret, and the result shall be determined by the counting of the number of votes cast for each candidate (with or without the transferable vote) and votes shall be fairly and accurately counted.

22.39 The above provisions do not apply to trade unions which consist of representatives of constituent or affiliated organisations, merchant seamen who are ordinarily resident outside the United Kingdom, newly formed trade unions, or to members of the principal executive committee who are near retirement.

22.40 The president and general secretary (or persons who hold equivalent positions) shall be deemed to be members of the principal executive committee (and hence subject to the balloting provisions) as will be any other persons, notwithstanding anything in the rules of the union, if they are permitted to attend and speak at the meeting of that committee, other than for the purpose of providing the committee with factual information or technical or professional advice.

22.41 However, a person who is the president or general secretary of the union, and who is neither a voting member of the principal executive committee, nor an employee of the union, is not required to be elected in the above manner if he holds his office for a period of less than 13 months. Nor does the president need to be re-elected if he has been elected within the previous five years to the post of general secretary or member of the executive.

22.42 Elections for the members of the principal executive committee shall be by means of postal ballot, and no other method, except that there is no need to hold a ballot if the election is uncontested. If voting is done by means of a transferable vote system, and the same number of votes are cast for the final candidates, there is an implied term in the union's rules that the candidate with the most first-choice votes shall be declared the winner, especially if this method has been used as a tie-breaker in the past (*AB v CD*).

A. Election of candidates (TULR(C)A, s 47)

22.43 No member of a trade union may be unreasonably excluded from standing as a candidate for election to any position unless he belongs to a class of which all members are excluded by the rules of the union. The rules of the union may give the executive committee of the union a discretion to decide certain prescribed qualifications for a union post, but not having the confidence of the executive committee is not a qualification (*Ecclestone v National Union of Journalists*). No candidate shall be required to be a member of any political party.

If there is a tie between two candidates in a union election, and there is no express mechanism for resolving the tie, a tie-breaker must be implied into the union's rules (*AB v CD*).

B. Election addresses (TULR(C)A, s 48)

22.44 Every candidate in an election for the principal executive committee must be provided with an opportunity of preparing an election address, in his own words, and submitting it to the union to be distributed to those who are entitled to vote. Such election addresses are to be sent out with the voting paper, and the candidates are not required to bear any expense for the production of these copies. The election address shall be sent out without any modification except at the request of or with the consent of the candidate, or where the modification is necessarily incidental to the method adopted for the production of the copy. The same method of production is to be used for the election addresses of all candidates. A trade union may determine that election addresses may not exceed a certain length (but must permit a minimum of 100 words), and may incorporate only such photographs or other matter as the union may determine. So far as is reasonably practicable, the union must ensure that the same facilities and restrictions with respect to the preparation, submission, length and modifications, and the incorporation of photographs or other matter not in words are provided or applied equally to each of the candidates.

22.45 No person other than the candidate himself shall be subject to any criminal or civil liability in respect of the publication of a candidate's election address made under s 48.

C. Independent scrutineer (ss 49, 75, 100A, 226B)

22.46 Before an election is held for positions in the principal executive committee, or a ballot is held on the approval of a political fund, or approving an instrument of amalgamation or transfer, or a ballot on the holding of industrial action, the trade union must appoint a qualified independent person as a scrutineer, who will carry out his functions without interference. A person will be eligible for such appointment if he satisfies the conditions laid down in the Trade Union Ballots and Elections (Independent Scrutineers' Qualifications) Order 1988.

22.47 However, a scrutineer need not be appointed if there is a ballot on the holding of industrial action, and the number of members entitled to vote does not exceed 50 (s 226C).

22.48 The union will supply the scrutineer with a copy of the register of members, which he will inspect as appropriate, and in particular if requested to do so by a member or candidate who suspects that it was not accurate or up to date. The name of the independent scrutineer must be sent to every member of the union by notice, or communicated to members in the same manner as when matters of general interest are brought to their attention. His name must also appear on any ballot paper.

22.49 The storage, distribution and counting of ballot papers must be undertaken by an independent person, who may be the scrutineer or other person whose competence and independence is not in doubt (s 51A). The scrutineer must supervise the production and distribution of all voting papers, which are to be returned to him by those voting. He will retain them for one year after the announcement of the result of the election or ballot or, if the result is challenged before the certification officer or a court, until disposal is authorised.

22.50 As soon as is reasonably practicable after the last date for the return of the voting papers, the scrutineer shall make a report to the union, stating:

(a) the number of voting papers distributed;

(b) the number of voting papers returned to him;

(c) the number of valid votes cast in the election for each candidate, or, in a ballot, for each proposition;

(d) the number of invalid or spoiled votes returned; and

(e) the name of the person (if any) appointed as an independent person to count the votes.

22.51 The report will also state if he is satisfied that there was no contravention of any requirement imposed by law, that the arrangements for the ballot or election (including any security arrangements) minimised the risk of any unfairness or malpractice, and that he was able to carry out his functions without interference or anyone calling his independence into question. He will also state if he has inspected the register of members, and whether any such inspection has revealed any matter which should be brought to the attention of the union in order to ensure that it is accurate and up to date (s 52).

22.52 Within three months of receiving the scrutineer's report on an election (s 52(4)), on a political fund resolution (s 78(4)), or on an amalgamation or transfer resolution (s 100E(6)), the trade union shall send a copy to every member to whom it is reasonably practicable to send such a copy, or take all such steps for notifying the contents of the report to members of the union as it is the practice for the union to take when matters of general interest need to be brought to the members' attention. So far as ballots on industrial action are concerned, any person entitled to vote in the ballot, and the employer of any such person, is entitled to be supplied with a copy of the scrutineer's report on request. This may be supplied free of charge or on the payment of a reasonable fee.

D. Remedies (s 54)

22.53 Any member may apply to the High Court (or Court of Session) or the certification officer (but not both) for a declaration that the trade union has failed to comply with any requirement of the Act relating to secret ballots for trade union elections or relating to election addresses or to scrutineers. The court may make an enforcement order specifying the action which the trade union shall take in consequence of its failure to comply with the Act (s 56). The certification officer may grant the declaration, and, if necessary, make an enforcement order requiring the union to hold a fresh election (s 55). An appeal from the order of the Certification Officer may be made to the EAT.

Accounts, records, etc (TULR(C)A, s 28)

22.54 Every trade union and employers' association shall keep proper records, and establish a satisfactory system of control over its cash holdings, receipts and remittances. An annual return must be sent to the certification officer, with accounts duly audited. There are provisions in ss 32–42 detailing the matters which must be contained in the annual return including the salaries paid to, and the benefits provided for, the president, general secretary and members of the executive committee, together with the qualifications, appointment, functions, and removal of auditors, and for the control over members' superannuation schemes. Any person who refuses or wilfully neglects to perform a duty imposed by these provisions, or who alters a document required for those purposes, shall be guilty of an offence, punishable by a fine of up to level 3 and 5 on the standard scale respectively.

22.55 An annual statement must be sent to all members of the union (or otherwise communicated to them) giving details of the union's income and expenditure, salaries paid to the president, general secretary and executive members, and the income and expenditure of the political fund. The statement will also include prescribed information on the remedies to members who are concerned about any irregularities in the conduct of the union's affairs (s 32A).

A. Right to inspect accounts (ss 29–31)

22.56 A trade union shall keep its accounting records available for inspection for six years from 1 January following the end of the period to which those records relate.

22.57 Any member of a trade union may request to be permitted access to those records in respect of any period when he was a member. Such access shall be permitted within 28 days of the request and, unless otherwise agreed, at a reasonable hour and at the place where the records are normally kept. The member is entitled to take an accountant with him, and to take, or be supplied with, such copies or extracts from those records as he may require. The trade union may make a charge in respect of reasonable administrative expenses incurred (s 30).

22.58 If the trade union fails to comply with the member's request for access to the accounting records, the member may apply to the court or the certification officer (but not both), who may make such order as is considered appropriate for ensuring that that person:

(a) is allowed to inspect the records;

(b) is allowed to be accompanied by an accountant; and

(c) is allowed to take, or is supplied with, such copies of or extracts from those records as he may require (s 31).

22.59 The certification officer has the power to require the production of documents, take copies etc and appoint an inspector to investigate the financial affairs of the union, if he suspects that the financial affairs of the union have been conducted in a fraudulent manner, or a person managing its affairs has been guilty of fraud, or the union has failed to comply with a provision of the Act or its own rules with relation to the conduct of its financial affairs (TULR(C)A, s 37B). The inspector has wide powers of investigation, and will report back to the certification officer.

Offences (ss 45–45C)

22.60 If a trade union refuses to supply a copy of its rules (s 27), fails to keep accounting records (s 28), fails to keep records available for inspection (s 29), fails to give members access to the accounts (s 30), fails to make an annual return (s 32), make an annual statement to members (s 32A), breaches the auditing requirements (ss 33–37), or breaches the requirements relating to members' superannuation schemes (ss 38–42), it commits an offence. The offence will also be committed by every officer who is bound by the rules to discharge any of those duties, or, if there is no such officer, every member of the management committee. It will be a defence for the officer or member of the management committee to prove that he had reasonable cause to believe that some other competent person was authorised to discharge that duty. It is also an offence wilfully to alter a document, fail to produce a document, destroy, mutilate or falsify a document relating to the financial affairs of the union, or fraudulently alter or delete anything in such document, or to make a false statement. The offences may be punishable by a fine or, in some circumstances, up to six months' imprisonment. A person who has been convicted under these provisions shall not hold office as a member of the executive, president or general secretary for a period of five or ten years, depending on the offence.

A. Indemnifying unlawful conduct (s 15)

22.61 It is unlawful for any property of a trade union to be applied towards the payment for any individual, or towards the provision of anything for indemnifying an individual, in respect of any penalty which has been imposed on him for a relevant offence, or for contempt of court. A 'relevant offence' is any offence other than one which has been designated as an offence by the Secretary of State in relation to which s 15 does not apply.

22.62 If property has been so applied in contravention of this section, the equal amount of any payment is recoverable from the individual concerned by the trade union, and in the case of property, the individual shall be liable to account for its value. If the trade union unreasonably fails to make a claim against the individual, any member may apply to the court for authorisation to bring or continue proceedings on the union's behalf and at the union's expense.

B. Remedies against trustees (s 16)

22.63 If a member of a trade union considers that the trustees of the union's property are carrying out their functions so as to permit an unlawful application of the union's property, or are complying with an unlawful direction which has been given to them under the union's rules, he may apply to the court for an order. If the court is satisfied that the application is well founded, it may make such orders as it deems appropriate, including:

(a) requiring the trustees of the union to take all such steps as may be specified for the purpose of protecting or recovering the union's property;

(b) appointing a receiver (or judicial factor) of/on the union's property;

(c) the removal of one or more trustees.

22.64 Should the trustees act in contravention of the court's order, the court may remove all the trustees except those who can satisfy the court that there is good reason to allow them to remain a trustee.

Political fund and political objects (TULR(C)A, ss 71–74)

22.65 The Act lays down the necessary requirements before a trade union can have a political fund and pursue political objects. A resolution to establish a political fund must be passed at least every ten years by a ballot of all the union's members, and if approved, a separate political fund may be created. The ballot must be by the use of a voting paper, and every person entitled to vote must be allowed to do so without interference from or constraint imposed by the trade union or any of its members, officials or employees. The member must be able to vote without incurring any direct cost.

22.66 So far as is reasonably practicable, every person who is entitled to vote on a ballot concerning the establishment of a political fund must have the voting papers sent to him at his home or postal address, and be given a convenient opportunity to vote by post. The voting must be in secret, and the votes fairly and accurately counted (s 77).

22.67 If the political fund is established, no property of the trade union shall be added to that fund other than sums representing contributions made to the fund by the members or any other person and property accruing to the fund in the course of administering its assets. No liability of the political fund shall be met out of any other fund of the trade union. If there is no resolution in force establishing the political fund, no property shall be added to an existing fund (other than that which accrues in the course of administering the fund) and no union rule shall require any member to contribute towards the fund. The union may transfer the whole or part of the assets of an existing fund to such other fund of the trade union as it thinks fit. Where a resolution is passed rescinding an existing fund, the trade union may use the fund for a period of six months, but not so as to put the fund in deficit.

22.68 If a resolution to have a political fund ceases to have effect, the union shall take such steps to ensure that the collection of contributions to the fund is discontinued as soon as is reasonably practicable, and any contribution collected after the resolution ceases to have effect may be paid to any other fund of the trade union. If the trade union continues to collect contributions these are refundable at the members' request.

22.69 Any member of a trade union who wishes to contract out of a political fund must be free to do so, and if he does, he shall not in consequence be excluded from any benefit or disqualified from holding any office other than a position connected with the management of the political fund. Contributing towards the fund must not be a condition of membership.

22.70 The TUC has issued a 'Statement of Guidance' on political funds. It advises trade unions to draw up 'information sheets' about their political funds, and inform members why it has a fund, make clear members' legal rights to opt out, state the current amount of the levy, and provide information on how members may contract out.

22.71 The political fund may be used for the following purposes:

(a) any contribution to the funds of, or the payment of any expense incurred by, a political party;

(b) the provision of any services or property for the use by or on behalf of a political party;

(c) the registration of electors, the candidature of any person, the selection of any candidate, or the holding of a ballot by the union in connection with any election to a political office;

(d) the maintenance of any holder of a political office;

(e) the holding of any conference or meetings by or on behalf of a political party, or any other meetings the main purpose of which is the transaction of business in connection with a political party;

(f) the production, publication or distribution of any literature, document, film, sound recording or advertisement the main purpose of which is to persuade people to vote for a political party or candidate or not to vote for it or him.

22.72 An allegation that a trade union has broken a rule as to the use to which the political fund may be put may be the subject of an investigation by the certification officer. In *Richards v National Union of Mineworkers* a complaint was made that the union had spent money from the general fund sending members on a lobby of Parliament organised by the Labour Party, and had also paid money to a trade union consortium which was developing Labour Party headquarters. It was held by the certification officer that such expenditure was in furtherance of political objects, and he ordered that the money should come from the political funds of the union, not the general funds.

22.73 A member who claims that the union has applied its funds in breach of s 71 may apply to the certification officer for a declaration. After making the necessary enquiries, the certification officer may grant the declaration, specifying the amount of funds applied in breach of s 71 and any remedial action to be taken, and specify any steps to be taken to ensure that the same or similar breach does not take place in the future (s 72A).

A. Complaints over political fund ballots (TULR(C)A, ss 79–81)

22.74 A member of a trade union who complains that a ballot on the political fund was taken otherwise than in accordance with the rules approved by the certification officer, or that there has been a failure to comply with those rules, may apply to the certification officer or to the court (but not both) for a declaration. The application must be made within one year from the date when the result of the ballot was announced.

22.75 The court may make an enforcement order, specifying the action which the trade union shall take in consequence of its failure to comply with the Act.

Breach of union rules (ss 108A–108B)

22.76 A member of the union who claims that there has been a breach of other rules of the union may apply to the certification officer for a declaration. The rules in question are:

(a) the appointment or election of a person to, or the removal of a person from, any office;

(b) disciplinary proceedings by the union (including expulsion);

(c)   the balloting of members on any issue other than industrial action;

(d)   the constitution or proceedings of any executive committee or of any decision-making meeting;

(e)   such other matters as may be specified in an order made by the Secretary of State.

22.77 The application must be made within six months from the day when the breach occurred, or, if an internal complaints procedure was invoked, six months from when it was concluded. The certification officer is not entitled to consider a complaint about the discipline or dismissal of an employee of the union, as these are matters capable of being dealt with under the general law on individual employment rights.

22.78 The certification officer may refuse to consider the complaint unless reasonable steps were taken to resolve the issue by use of the internal complaints procedure, but if he hears the complaint he may make a declaration, and, if appropriate, an enforcement order, requiring the union to remedy the breach, or abstain from specified acts. An appeal from any proceedings under this section will lie to the EAT on a point of law.

Amalgamation and transfers (ss 97–105)

22.79 Two or more trade unions may decide to amalgamate into one union, or a union may wish to transfer its engagements to another union. In both cases, the instrument of amalgamation or transfer must first be submitted to the certification officer for approval, and then voted upon by the members of the amalgamating unions or transferor union, as the case may be. The union must give the members a notice in writing, which either sets out the instrument of amalgamation or transfer, or gives an account of it so as to enable the member to form a reasonable judgment of its main effects. Section 100 of the Act provides that the instrument may be approved by a simple majority of votes recorded, unless the rules of the union specifically exclude this provision, in which case some other specified proportion of members will be required to approve.

22.80 An independent scrutineer must be appointed, who will supervise the production and distribution of the voting papers, inspect the register of members, and generally report to the union after the ballot has been concluded. Voting in the ballot shall be accorded equally to all members of the union, the ballot papers will be numbered consecutively, and sent to members' homes or postal address. The notice sent to members shall not contain any statement making a recommendation or expressing an opinion about the proposed transfer or amalgamation. A copy of the scrutineer's report must be sent to every member or otherwise suitably published.

22.81 A complaint about the procedure relating to an amalgamation or transfer may be made to the certification officer, who may make a declaration, and an order specifying the steps to be taken before he will entertain the application (s 103).

Trade union modernisation (TULR(C)A, s 116A)

22.82 The Secretary of State is empowered to provide money to an independent trade union to enable or assist it to do any of the following:

(a) improve the carrying out of any of its existing functions;

(b) prepare to carry out new functions;

(c) increase the range of services it offers to its members;

(d) prepare for an amalgamation or transfer;

(e) ballot its members.

22.83 The money will be provided in such a way as the Secretary of State thinks fit, whether by grants or otherwise, and on such terms as he thinks fit, whether as to repayment or otherwise.

Employers' associations

A. Definition of employers' association (TULR(C)A, s 122)

22.84 An employers' association is defined as an organisation which either:

(a) consists wholly or mainly of employers or individual proprietors, and whose principal purposes include the regulation of relations between employers and workers or trade unions; or

(b) consists wholly or mainly of constituent or affiliated organisations with those purposes or representatives of such constituents or affiliated organisations, whose principal objects include the regulation of relations between employers and workers or between the constituent or affiliated organisations.

22.85 An employers' association may be incorporated under the Companies Acts, or may be an unincorporated association. In the latter case it shall nonetheless be capable of making contracts, or suing and being sued in its own name, and of being prosecuted in its own name. Its property, however, will have to be held by trustees, and any judgment, award or order would have to be enforced against that property. A trade association, which is largely concerned with the business interests of employers, is not an employers' association within the statutory definition, but if it did have as one of its purposes collective bargaining objectives, or if it regulated the relations between organisations which have such objectives, it could be an employers' association. This is because the Act requires the principal objects of an employers' association to 'include' the statutory objects, not that the principal objects 'shall be' the statutory objects.

B. Listing of employers' associations (TULR(C)A, s 123)

22.86 The Act permits the employers' associations to be entered on the appropriate list, but there are few advantages of doing so. Many employers' associations are incorporated under the Companies Act, and therefore do not require trustees to hold property. They do not have provident funds, and do not require certificates of independence. Not surprisingly, less than half of employers' associations have bothered to become listed.

23

Law Relating to Industrial Relations

Trade union recognition

23.1 Since 1871, when trade unions were legalised by the Trade Union Act of that year, the history of industrial relations in the United Kingdom has been somewhat turbulent. This is partly due to conflicting ideologies, sometimes of a political nature, but mainly due to a conflict between those who favour individual as opposed to collective bargaining arrangements. A consideration of the extent to which the law should play a role in the control of industrial relations, and the precise nature of that law, has always been a subject for political controversy. Various governments of differing political persuasions have made their impact throughout the years, but, mainly due to the reforms pushed through in the Thatcher era (see Appendix C) trade unions have now achieved a respectability and a role recognised by employers and confirmed by law. The whole story, though interesting from a legal and philosophical point of view, need not detain us in this book, but history has left its mark, and it is not possible to understand the present legal position without some reference to the previous law on this topic, though it is intended to keep such excursus to a minimum. In particular, it will be necessary to examine certain common law rules which, though they may now be only of historical importance, have shaped the legislative provisions.

23.2 Freedom of association, ie the right of an individual to join a trade union, is guaranteed by the European Convention on Human Rights (see para 1.97) and is now accepted in the United Kingdom as axiomatic. However, the right of a trade union to bargain and/or negotiate on behalf of its members is initially dependent on the willing co-operation of employers. Thus an employer may refuse to recognise a trade union, may recognise it for some purposes only (eg representation) or for all purposes (eg negotiations). Whether an employer recognises a trade union, and the extent of that recognition, are questions of fact; there need not be a formal agreement to confirm this (see para 23.4). Once recognition has been granted, various legal consequences will flow, including the right to receive information for collective bargaining purposes (para 23.15), the right to be consulted on redundancies (Chapter 18) and on transfers of the undertaking (Chapter 9) etc. Members of independent trade unions which are recognised by the employer are entitled to certain benefits, including time off work for union duties and activities, and have various protections from dismissal and detriment (Chapter 21).

23.3 One of the reasons for industrial unrest in the past was the reluctance of some employers to recognise a trade union for any purpose, for whatever reason. An attempt to force employers to recognise a trade union was made in the Employment Protection Act 1975, but this was not a success, and the provisions were subsequently repealed.

A. Voluntary recognition

23.4 Employment tribunals appear to operate under the general rule that it is for the trade union to show that there is some formal agreement (not necessarily in writing) that it is recognised for collective bargaining purposes (*T&GWU v Dyer*). The mere fact that there are employees who are trade union members, and that one of them negotiates, but without specific trade union authority, will not constitute recognition (*AUEW v Sefton Engineering*). Negotiations which may lead to recognition do not themselves constitute recognition (*T&GWU v Stanhope Engineering*). Nor can recognition be inferred if a full-time union official represents an individual in a disciplinary proceeding, for the purpose of collective bargaining (*T&GWU v Courtenham Products*). The fact that an employer is a member of an association which negotiates with a trade union does not mean that the individual employer recognises the union (*NUGSAT v Albury Bros Ltd*). Nor does recognition by a former employer by itself constitute recognition by a successor (*UCATT v Burrage*). In *NUTGW v Charles Ingram & Co Ltd* five propositions were established: (1) recognition is a mixed question of law and fact; (2) recognition requires mutuality; (3) there must be an express or implied agreement for recognition; (4) if the agreement was implied, there must be clear and unequivocal acts or conduct, usually over a period of time; (5) there may be partial recognition, for some, but not all purposes. Recognition for representation purposes only is not the same thing as recognition for negotiating purposes (*USDAW v Sketchley Ltd*).

B. Statutory recognition (TULR(C)A, Sch AI)

23.5 The Employment Relations Act 1999 lays down a new complex statutory procedure for recognition and derecongnition of trade unions, which can be found in TULR(C)A, Sch A1. The detailed provisions, including time limits and balloting procedures can be found in some 172 paragraphs of the Schedule (a further 23 paragraphs were added by the Employment Relations Act 2004), which additionally deal with semi-voluntary recognition, derecognition procedures, and protection of workers from detriments or dismissal on grounds relating to trade union membership or non-membership. However, the provisions do not apply where an employer employs fewer than 21 workers.

23.6 Schedule A1 is divided into nine parts, as follows:

Part I: statutory recognition;

Part II: voluntary recognition following a request for statutory recognition;

Part III: changes affecting the bargaining unit;

Part IV: derecognition, general;

Part V: automatic derecognition;

Part VI: derecognition of non-independent trade union;

Part VII: derecognition when a trade union loses its certificate of independence;

Part VIII: detriment and dismissal;

Part IX: general matters.

23.7 An independent trade union can apply to the Central Arbitration Committee (CAC) for a declaration requiring the employer to recognise it for collective bargaining purposes in respect of workers in a particular bargaining unit. CAC will grant the declaration if a majority of workers in the bargaining unit already belong to the trade union, or where the union obtains the support of a majority of those voting in a secret ballot, which consists of at least 40% of those entitled to vote. The employer and the union should then agree to a method of collective bargaining, although if they fail to do so, an application may be made by either party to CAC, who will impose one. Recognition, thus obtained, will last for a minimum of three years, and cannot be ended unilaterally by the employer even after the end of that time, unless the derecognition procedure has been followed (Pt I, paras 1–51). The manner in which collective bargaining is to be conducted is set out in the Trade Union Recognition (Method of Collective Bargaining) Order 2000, which is legally binding, and can be enforced by an order for specific performance.

23.8 An alternative method is an agreement for recognition, which will arise when the union makes an application to CAC for recognition, but then abandons it because the employer agrees voluntarily to recognise the union. Nonetheless, either side may still request CAC to impose a method of collective bargaining. An agreement for recognition will last for three years, but does not require the derecognition procedure to be followed to terminate it (Pt II, paras 52–63).

23.9 It should be noted that neither of the above two procedures in any way affects existing voluntary collective bargaining arrangements, which will no doubt continue without the necessity of being underpinned by a statutory procedure. Indeed, if there is a collective agreement in force a statutory claim for recognition cannot succeed (TULR(C)A, Sch A1, para 35, see *R(NUJ) v CAC*).

23.10 It is the task of CAC to determine the appropriateness of the bargaining unit. The employer has the right to make representations on such matters and, indeed, frame objections to the union's proposals. But as long as CAC takes such arguments into account, their function is to determine the appropriateness of the union's original proposals, and not to shop around seeking an alternative (*R (Kwik-Fit (GB) Ltd) v Central Arbitration Committee*).

23.11 If, for whatever reason, the original bargaining unit is no longer considered to be appropriate, either side may apply to CAC to select a new bargaining unit. There are provisions which are designed to ensure that the new unit does not overlap with an existing bargaining unit (including balloting if necessary), and CAC can make arrangements for workers who consequently fall outside the original unit into a residual unit (Pt III, paras 64–95).

23.12 An employer may derecognise the union if the number of workers falls below 21, or if an application is made to CAC (by the employer or by the workers) for a secret ballot to be held, at any time after three years from a CAC declaration. There is a further procedure for the workforce to apply for the derecognition of a non-independent trade union (which had achieved voluntary recognition), and for dealing with the situation which arises if a trade union loses its independent status (Pts 4, 5, 6, 7, paras 96–155).

C. Employers' training policies (TULR(C)A, s 70B)

23.13 If a trade union has obtained recognition for collective bargaining purposes under Sch A1, and CAC has imposed a method of collective bargaining (and the parties have not agreed that the imposed method should not be legally binding) a trade union will be entitled to be consulted about the employer's policy on training for workers within the bargaining unit, the plans for training those workers during the following six months, and to receive information about training provided since the previous meeting. Two weeks before a meeting is held for this purpose, the employer must provide the union with whatever information is required to ensure that the union's representative can participate meaningfully in the meeting, and which it would be in accordance with good industrial relations practice for the employer to disclose. The employer shall take account of any written representations made by the union within four weeks from the date of the meeting. If the employer fails to comply with s 70B, the trade union may present a complaint to an employment tribunal, which may make a declaration, and award compensation of up to two weeks' pay to each person who was a member of the bargaining unit.

Collective bargaining (TULR(C)A, Sch A1, para 94)

23.14 The existing definition of collective bargaining refers to negotiations between a trade union and an employer on a wide variety of matters, including terms and conditions of employment, termination and suspension of employment, allocation of work, discipline and physical conditions of work (TULR(C)A, s 178). However, for the purposes of Sch A1, the definition is more restrictive, with the following result:

(a) So far as existing voluntary arrangements are concerned, collective bargaining refers to those matters listed in TULR(C)A, s 178.

(b) Where statutory recognition is awarded under Pt I of Sch A1, collective bargaining refers to the three core issues of pay, hours and holidays.

(c) If the parties agree matters as the subject of collective bargaining (eg if there is an agreement for recognition under Pt II, or an agreement to change the agenda in relation to a new unit under Pt III), the matters referred to in the agreement.

(d) If there is a new unit, or a residual unit under Pt III (with certain exceptions, see para 94(2)), collective bargaining means negotiations on the matters which were the subject of collective bargaining in the corresponding or parent unit.

A. Disclosure of information (TULR(C)A, s 181)

23.15 For the purpose of all stages of collective bargaining it shall be the duty of the employer, on request, to disclose to representatives of a recognised independent trade union all such information relating to his undertaking as is in his possession, and is information without which the representatives would to a material extent be impeded in carrying on such bargaining, and is information which it would be in accordance with good industrial relations practice that he should disclose. In one of its earliest findings, the CAC held that the test of 'materially impeded' meant that the information should be both relevant and important (*Institute of Journalists v Daily Telegraph*). The employer need only make the disclosure to unions which are recognised by him. In determining what is good industrial relations practice, regard will be had to any Code of Practice issued by ACAS. If the trade union representatives so request the employer will disclose or confirm the information in writing, but he need not disclose:

(a) information the disclosure of which would be contrary to the national interest;

(b) any information which he could not disclose without breaking the law;

(c) information which he received in confidence;

(d) information relating to an individual, unless he has consented to the disclosure;

(e) information the disclosure of which would cause substantial injury to the employer's business for reasons other than its effect on collective bargaining;

(f) information obtained by the employer for the purpose of bringing or defending any legal proceedings.

23.16 The employer is not bound to produce, or allow the inspection of, any document, or to compile information where this would involve an amount of work or expenditure out of all reasonable proportion to its value in the conduct of collective bargaining.

23.17 If an independent trade union wishes to make a complaint that an employer has failed to disclose information which he is required to produce, it may report the matter to the CAC. If that body thinks that the complaint can be settled by conciliation it will refer the matter to ACAS, which will try to promote a settlement. If this does not prove possible, or if the complaint is not so referred, the committee will hear and determine the complaint. If it finds the complaint is wholly or partly well founded, it will issue a declaration, stating:

(a) the information in respect of which the complaint is well founded;

(b) the date on which the employer refused or failed to disclose the information; and

(c) a period (being more than one week from the date of the declaration) within which the employer ought to disclose the information. If, at the end of that period, the employer still fails to disclose, a further complaint may be made by the trade union.

23.18 The complaint may be accompanied by a claim relating to the terms and conditions of the employees, and if the employer still persists in his refusal, the committee may make an award that in respect of the employees of any description specified in the claim, the employer shall observe the terms and conditions demanded, or other terms and conditions which the committee considers to be appropriate. These will form part of the contracts of employment of those employees from a date specified in the award, until varied or superseded by a further award or a subsequent collective agreement, or an express or implied agreement made between the employer and the employees which is an improvement on the award. As a general rule, CAC would consider the likely loss which flows from the failure to give the union the relevant information, and make an award accordingly.

B. Legal liabilities and legal proceedings

23.19 At common law it is impossible for a trade union to engage in any effective industrial relations activity without falling foul of some well-established legal rule. An understanding of those liabilities is necessary in order to understand and appreciate the statutory protections which have been developed over the years.

Inducing or procuring a breach of contract

23.20 It is a tort (civil wrong) for a person to induce another to break a contract to which the other is a party, or to procure a breach of that contract. In *Lumley v Gye*, an opera singer contracted to sing at a theatre owned by the claimant. The defendant induced her to break that contract and sing for him instead. Clearly, the singer was liable for her own breach of contract, but it was held that the claimant could successfully sue the defendant for inducing her to break the contract. In terms of industrial relations, the tort is peculiarly appropriate (see, for example, the county court decision in *Falconer v ASLEF and NUR*). An employer has a contract (of employment) with an employee. If a trade union official calls upon that employee to strike, the employee is breaking the contract (for which he can be dismissed – but see Chapter 21) but the union official (and possibly the union also) could be held liable for inducing a breach of that contract. Equally, if a trade union was to call for a secondary boycott, it may be furthering strike action, but it is also inducing (or procuring) a breach of a commercial contract. In *Torquay Hotel Co Ltd v Cousins*, a trade union was in dispute with a hotel. A union official informed a company which was supplying oil to the hotel of the existence of the dispute, and instructed its members not to deliver oil supplies. It was held that an injunction would lie restraining the union officials from causing any fuel supplier to breach its contract to supply oil.

23.21 If a shop steward has express or implied authority to act on behalf of a trade union, then the union may be responsible for his actions unless it can shelter behind some legal protection (*Heatons Transport (St Helens) Ltd v Transport and General Workers' Union*). But a union cannot be responsible for activities of unofficial committees of shop stewards, particularly when they are pursuing policies which are contrary to those of the union, and where union officials are trying to solve problems through machinery for negotiation and conciliation, while the shop stewards are taking militant industrial action (*General Aviation Services (UK) Ltd v Transport and General Workers' Union*). However, in such a situation, the union must repudiate the activities in question (see para 23.80) if it wishes to retain its immunities.

23.22 For the tort of inducing or procuring or otherwise wrongfully interfering with contractual rights to be made out, five conditions must be satisfied: (1) it must be shown that the defendant persuaded or procured or induced a third party to break its contract with the claimant; (2) when the defendant so acted he had knowledge of the existence of the contract, if not its precise terms; (3) it must be shown that the defendant intended to persuade, induce or procure a breach of that contract; (4) the claimant must show more than nominal damage; (5) if the defendant puts forward the defence of justification, the claimant has to rebut that defence (*Timeplan Education Group Ltd v National Union of Teachers*).

Conspiracy

23.23 A conspiracy is a combination of two or more persons to do an unlawful act, or a lawful act by unlawful means. Such acts could lead to a prosecution for criminal conspiracy (ie where the conspirators combine in order to pursue criminal objects) or an action for civil conspiracy where the alleged act constitutes a tort. Since trade unions are by necessity combinations, it is not surprising that they are particularly vulnerable to this form of legal constraint. For example, in *Quinn v Leathem*, Leathem was a butcher who employed non-union labour. The union called upon him to dismiss them, but he refused to do so. Instead, he offered to pay the men's arrears of subscriptions if they were admitted into the union. This offer was rejected by the union officials, who wanted to teach the non-unionists a lesson 'and make them walk the streets for 12 months'. Munce supplied meat to Leathem, and the union threatened to call a strike of Munce's men unless supplies of meat to Leathem were cut off, and Munce complied with this request. It was held that the union officials had conspired together to cause harm to Leathem without lawful jurisdiction. Their legitimate trade union objectives could have been achieved by accepting Leathem's offer and admitting the men to membership, but in fact their subsequent conduct had been motivated by vindictiveness.

23.24 But the mere fact that an act causes harm does not, by itself, amount to a conspiracy. Clearly, a strike causes harm to an employer, but if the object is a legitimate one, eg obtaining higher wages, no actionable conspiracy exists (*Crofter Hand Woven Harris Tweed Co v Veitch*). In *Scala Ballroom (Wolverhampton) Ltd v Ratcliffe*, the claimants operated a colour bar at their dance hall. Officials of the Musicians' Union placed a boycott on the premises in protest. It was held that this was not a conspiracy to injure, for the combination was a legitimate furtherance of the union's interests.

Intimidation

23.25 This 'obscure and unfamiliar' tort was resurrected from oblivion in the controversial case of *Rookes v Barnard*, where a shop steward threatened to call a strike at Heathrow Airport unless the claimant, a non-unionist, was dismissed. This 'threat' constituted a breach of contract, which was held to be an unlawful act (ie in the same way that a threat to commit an act of violence would be unlawful) and the defendants were held liable for intimidation.

Other tort liabilities

23.26 There are a number of other possible headings of legal liabilities which trade unions may run up against, including such headings as unlawful interference with trade business or employment, interference with future contracts, and so forth. Such torts are to be found in judicial hints rather than actuality, and the fear was of their emergence rather than their existence. With the increased statutory control over the conduct of trade unions, it is unlikely that these obscure torts will be revived.

23.27 But if there are unlawful acts committed by a trade union, an injured party may apply for an injunction to restrain the commission of such acts, and sue for damages in respect of any loss suffered, including, if necessary, exemplary damages (*Messenger Newspapers Group Ltd v National Graphical Association*). A trade union can only defend itself if it can rely on the statutory protections.

Statutory protections

23.28 It is clear from the above that if trade unions are to carry out their legitimate functions in industrial relations, they require protection from these headings of common law liability, and arguably against judicial ingenuity in developing new case law which would restrict their activities. This has been the object of statute law since 1906; it was a process which was carried on by the Industrial Relations Act 1971, and has been continued in TULR(C)A. But the statutory immunities are not a licence to do anything; they only provide a protective cover for trade unions when legitimate objectives are being pursued. These objectives are limited to acts done in furtherance or contemplation of a trade dispute, and it is to the wide meaning of this phrase that we must now turn.

A. 'Trade dispute' (TULR(C)A, s 244)

23.29 A trade dispute means a dispute between workers and their employers which relates wholly or mainly to one or more of the following:

(a) terms and conditions of employment, or the physical conditions in which any workers are required to work;

(b) the engagement or non-engagement or termination or suspension of employment or the duties of employment, of one or more workers;

(c) the allocation of work or the duties of employment between workers or groups of workers;

(d) matters of discipline;

(e) membership or non-membership of a trade union on the part of a worker;

(f) facilities for officials of trade unions;

(g) machinery for negotiations or consultation, and other matters relating to the foregoing (ie (a)–(f) above), including recognition by employers or employers' associations of the right of a trade union to represent workers in any such negotiations or consultations or in the carrying out of such procedures.

23.30 The important change made by the Employment Act 1982 is that the dispute must relate 'wholly or mainly' to the above matters. In *Mercury Communications Ltd v Scott-Garner*, the claimants were granted a licence by the Government to run a telecommunications system (the 'liberalisation' agreement), which effectively broke the Post Office monopoly. The Government also proposed to privatise British Telecommunications. The Post Office Engineering Union opposed both the liberalisation and privatisation of the work, and gave instructions to its members not to do work which would enable the plaintiffs to connect to the British Telecommunications network. The claimants applied for an injunction to restrain the union from inducing a breach of contractual relations between themselves and British Telecommunications. The Court of Appeal granted the injunction. It was unlikely that the union would be able to establish at the trial that there was a trade dispute within the statutory definition. There was little evidence to support the union's contention that there was a dispute about the risk of loss of jobs. The reality was that the union was waging a campaign against the political decisions to liberalise and privatise the industry. But in *UNISON v Westminster County Council* a dispute between a local authority and employees about the proposed privatisation and contracting out of certain advisory services was held to be a dispute about terms and conditions of employment, and not a dispute about public policy. Similarly, a dispute about the reasonableness of an instruction from an employer can be a dispute about terms and conditions of employment within the meaning of s 244(1)(a) (*P v National Association of Schoolmasters/Union of Women Teachers*).

23.31 In addition, there are three other circumstances to consider. First, a trade dispute will exist between a minister of the Crown and a group of workers notwithstanding that the minister is not the employer of those workers, if the dispute relates to matters which have been referred for consideration to a joint body on which that minister is bound by statute to be represented, and which cannot be settled without the minister exercising a power.

23.32 For example, in *Wandsworth London Borough Council v National Association of Schoolmasters Union of Women Teachers*, the defendants wished to ballot their members to protest against the excessive workload caused by the assessment requirements of the national curriculum, which had been imposed by the Government. A local authority sought an injunction against the unions, arguing that the dispute was not about terms and conditions of employment, but about the very idea of the national assessment, and this was a matter which could only be resolved by the Secretary of State exercising a power conferred by statute. It was held that the dispute was wholly or mainly about the workload imposed on teachers and, therefore, since it was about the terms and conditions of employment, the statutory protection (see below) applied, and the application for an injunction was refused.

23.33 Second, there is a trade dispute even though it relates to matters occurring outside the United Kingdom as long as the persons who are taking action are likely to be affected in respect of one or more of the matters mentioned above. The third situation is more curious. In *Cory Lighterage Ltd v Transport and General Workers' Union*, a lighterman named Shute decided to leave the union, and the employers were informed that none of the crew would sail if he did not pay his union dues. The employers had no quarrel with the union, for they accepted the principle of 100% unionisation, but they could not dismiss Shute under the Dock Workers Employment Scheme, so they sent him home on full pay. It was held that as there was no dispute between the employers and the union, the statutory protections did not apply. The employers did not resist the demands of the union, but rather acceded to them by taking Shute off the lighter. In line with the policy of giving the widest possible protection to trade unions in all actual and potential conflict situations, TULR(C)A, s 244(4) provides that an act, threat or demand done or made by one party or organisation against another which, if resisted, would have led to a trade dispute with that other, shall, notwithstanding that because that other submits to the act or threat or accedes to the demand no dispute arises, be treated as done or made in contemplation or furtherance of a trade dispute.

23.34 There is no trade dispute if a strike is called about the terms and conditions of employment of employees of a third party who have never been employed by the employer with whom the union is in dispute, nor is there a trade dispute if it concerns the employment of the employees with a future unidentified employer. In *University College*

London Hospitals NHS Trust v UNISON the claimant entered into a contract with a consortium for the latter to build and run a new hospital. The union was opposed to the scheme, and sought to persuade the claimant to enter into a contractual agreement with the consortium whereby the terms and conditions of staff who were transferred to the new hospital would receive equivalent terms and conditions of employment to those who were not transferred. When the claimant refused to accede to the demand, the union called a strike, which was approved in a ballot of members. An injunction to restrain the strike was confirmed by the Court of Appeal. The dispute was about the terms and conditions which would apply to another employer, and in respect of employees who may at some future stage be employed by that other employer. The dispute was not between 'workers and their employer', because, at this stage, neither the future employer nor the workers employed by him could be identified.

23.35 But a strike called for political reasons is not a trade dispute. In *BBC v Hearn*, the Association of Broadcasting Staff threatened to stop a transmission of the Cup Final by satellite to South Africa, in protest of the alleged racist policies of the Government of that country. This would also have affected a number of other countries throughout the world. The Court of Appeal held that there was no trade dispute, and granted an injunction restraining the union from telling its members to break their contracts of employment, and from inducing the BBC to break its contracts with other countries. In *Express Newspapers v Keys*, three trade unions instructed their members to strike in response to a call sent out by the TUC for a one-day national stoppage in protest against Government policies. It was held that this was a political strike, not in connection with a trade dispute, and injunctions were granted restraining the unions from inducing or procuring breaches of contract between the claimants and their employees.

23.36 In *Examite Ltd v Whittaker*, a trade union called a strike against a firm called Baldwins Industrial Services, with the result that the company's business came to a stand-still. A new company called Examite was formed, with two shares being issued, and it took over the business of Baldwins and engaged some of its former employees. The union continued the strike against the new company, as it was considered to be a sham, and the company sought an injunction to restrain the union officials from intimidating the employees and to restrain them from procuring a breach of contract. It was held that a trade dispute existed between the union and Examite. There was sufficient evidence to show that the company had been formed to take over the business formerly carried on by Baldwins. The 'hat' worn by the employer was irrelevant. The truth was that the new company was carried on by the same people who ran the old one, and the legal form it took was irrelevant.

B. 'In contemplation of'

23.37 Having obtained the formula for a trade dispute, for an act to come within the statutory protection, it must be in contemplation of that dispute. The act may be so done if it is committed before the dispute arises, but is imminent. However, the dispute must be more than a mere possibility. In *Bents Brewery Co Ltd v Hogan* managers of a brewery were asked by a trade union official to obtain information about the firm's salaries, sales, etc. In providing this, the managers were in breach of their contract not to disclose confidential information to unauthorised persons (see Chapter 10). The union official was clearly

inducing a breach of that contract, and it was held that his action was not in contemplation of a trade dispute, even though one may well have arisen at some future date. His
actions may have been preparatory to the dispute, but were not in contemplation of one.

C. 'In furtherance of'

23.38 The act committed must also be in furtherance of the trade dispute, and not in
furtherance of some other issue. In *Conway v Wade* a union official informed employers
that unless a worker was dismissed there would be a strike. This was untrue, and the union
official's actions were prompted by his desire to get the worker to pay a fine which was due
to the union. It was held that although a trade dispute existed, the act was not done in
furtherance of that dispute, but for some other motive. A more difficult problem arises
when there is more than one motive for the acts in question, and some of the pre-1971
cases, which were decided on a much narrower definition of the term 'trade dispute' must
now be viewed with greater care. For example, in *Huntley v Thornton* the claimant was
recommended for expulsion by the branch committee of a trade union, but this was not
upheld by the national executive. Nonetheless, the local officials regarded him as being
expelled, and took steps to ensure that he did not obtain employment. The judge thought
that there was no trade dispute, but such conduct would nowadays clearly be covered by
the new, wider definition. More interesting was the finding that some of the officials were
not acting in furtherance of a trade dispute, but in furtherance of a personal grudge, and
their actions were in the nature of a vendetta. In other words, if protection is sought
for acts done in furtherance of a trade dispute, the predominant motive must be the
advancement of legitimate objects, and trade unionists cannot use the cover of the
statutory protection to pursue improper aims.

23.39 But not every action which flows from a trade dispute is necessarily in furtherance
of that dispute. In *Beaverbrook Newspapers Ltd v Keys*, a trade dispute existed between the
Daily Mirror newspaper and a trade union, which resulted in a complete stoppage of
production. The *Daily Express* decided to print more copies to cater for the increase in
demand, but the general secretary of the printing union told his members not to handle
the additional copies. The claimants applied for an injunction to restrain the union from
inducing their employees to break their contracts of employment. It was held that the
injunction would be granted. There was no trade dispute between the members of the
defendant's union and the claimants, and the action would not further the dispute
between the *Daily Mirror* and its employees.

23.40 Armed with the 'golden formula', we can now consider those statutory protections,
and consider when the immunities will be lost.

Statutory protection and loss of immunities

A. The provisions of TULR(C)A, s 219

23.41 Subsection (1) provides that an act done by a person in contemplation or furtherance of a trade dispute shall not be actionable in tort on the ground only (a) that it induces
another person to break a contract or interferes or induces any other person to interfere

with its performance; or (b) that it consists of his threatening that a contract (whether one to which he is party or not) will be broken or its performance interfered with, or that he will induce another person to break a contract or to interfere with its performance.

23.42 This subsection does three things. First, it gives immunity against legal action to anyone who calls a strike or other industrial action and thus induces a breach of contract (of employment) by the strikers, or a breach of a commercial contract by any other person. It also covers any inducement which interferes with the performance of a contract. A strike includes any refusal to work for specified periods when workers would normally work, provided it is concerted, ie mutually planned. It does not have to be a total stoppage (*Connex South Eastern Rly v National Union of Rail, Maritime and Transport Workers*). Whether an overtime ban is 'other industrial action' is a question of fact for the employment tribunal to determine (*Naylor v Orton & Smith Ltd*). Second, the subsection provides immunity where a threat of strike or other industrial action is made, whether this is done by the actual strikers or some other person, eg a trade union official. Thus, the threat to call a strike – the unlawful act in *Rookes v Barnard* – is no longer actionable. Third, it protects those who threaten to induce a breach of contract or to interfere with its performance.

23.43 Section 219(2) provides that an agreement or combination of two or more persons to do or procure the doing of an act in contemplation or furtherance of a trade dispute shall not be actionable in tort if the act is one which, if done without such agreement or combination, would not be so actionable. This subsection is designed to nullify the law of conspiracy as applied to trade disputes (above). If an act in contemplation or furtherance of a trade dispute would be actionable if done by one person, then a civil conspiracy would be committed if a group of persons did it. For example, if strikes commit a trespass by engaging in a sit-in, or commit a nuisance, or libel someone by picketing with defamatory placards, such conduct would be actionable if done by one person, and therefore no statutory protection exists.

23.44 Thus, in *News Group Newspapers Ltd v Society of Graphical and Allied Trades 1982* the defendants were responsible for organising mass picketing at the claimant's premises at Wapping. This was held to be a public nuisance, intimidation and an interference with commercial contracts, and injunctive relief was granted. But if the act was lawful if done by one person, it does not become an actionable conspiracy merely because a group of persons do it. Thus it is not unlawful for one person to threaten to strike or to go on strike. It therefore cannot be a conspiracy if more than one person does so. It is unlawful for one person to use violence; it will be a conspiracy for a group of persons to agree to use violence or actually to use it in a strike situation, and civil, as well as potential criminal liability, may arise.

23.45 However, it was suggested in *Meade v Haringey London Borough Council* that the immunity of a trade union from actions in tort based on conspiracy may not apply if there is an inducement to break a duty laid down by statute. Thus, if a local authority is forced to close a school (which it is under a statutory duty to keep open) because of trade union pressure, the union officials may be liable for inducing a breach of statutory duty and will not be protected by TULR(C)A. But if the statutory duty can be re-arranged so that it can still be carried out, injunctive relief will not be granted (*Barretts & Baird (Wholesale) Ltd v Institution of Professional Civil Servants*). Also, if there is no statutory obligation to break, a trade union cannot be liable for inducing an alleged breach (*Associated British Ports v Transport and General Workers' Union*).

B. Loss of immunities

23.46 In recent years, the tactics adopted by trade unions in industrial disputes have not always attracted universal approval, and Parliament has intervened to place restrictions on certain types of activities, by limiting the immunity conferred by TULR(C)A, s 219. The objects are twofold: first, to ensure greater democracy in trade unions by requiring secret ballots to be held before strikes or other industrial action are called, so as to negate decisions made at mass meetings by show of hands, or calls for action which may be unsupported by the rank and file; second, to prevent unnecessary hardship caused by industrial action to third parties who are in no way involved with or connected with the dispute. The primary purpose is to regulate official trade union action; unofficial action, though covered by the law, is seldom the subject of court proceedings (but see para 23.70).

Consequently, the immunity provided by TULR(C)A, s 219 will be lost unless the following legal hurdles can be surmounted.

Secret ballots before industrial action (TULR(C)A, ss 226–234A)

23.47 There is no legal requirement which insists that a ballot be called by the union before industrial action can be taken. However, a failure to do so will have the following legal consequences:

(a) industrial action which is authorised or endorsed by the union will not have the statutory immunity under s 219 from actions in tort, and an employer affected by the strike will be able to obtain an injunction and sue for damages;

(b) members of the trade union will be able to apply to the court for an order restraining the union from calling for strike action (TULR(C)A, s 62, see Chapter 21);

(c) any member of the public who suffers a reduction or delay in the quality or supply of goods or services may apply to the court for an injunction to restrain the strike (s 235A);

(d) employees who go on strike will not have the protection afforded by s 238A (para 21.104) although they will have the protection contained in s 238(1)(b) (para 21.93).

23.48 The balloting provisions contained in TULR(C)A, ss 226–235 have been amended by the Employment Relations Act 2004, and a new Code of Practice on Industrial Action Ballots and Notice to Employers has been issued (see Appendix D). The requirements apply only to official industrial action. It should be noted that for the purpose of the balloting provisions (as with secondary action, see para 23.71) any reference to a contract of employment also includes a contract under which a person personally does work or performs services for another. Thus self-employed workers who are union members are covered by the statutory provisions.

23.49 An act done by a trade union to induce a person to take part in industrial action will not be protected unless the industrial action has the support of a ballot, and the other detailed requirements of TULR(C)A are satisfied (s 226). These are that, not later than seven days before the opening day of the ballot, the union must take reasonable steps to notify the employer of persons who are entitled to vote:

(a) that a ballot is to be held;

(b) the date of the opening day of the ballot;

(c) a list of the categories of employee to which the employees concerned belong, a list of the workplaces of the employees concerned, the total number of employees, together with the figures of the total number of employees concerned, the number of employees in each category, and the number of employees concerned who work at each workplace. The list and figures supplied must be as accurate as is reasonably practicable in the light of the information which the union possesses (s 226A(3A)).

23.50 As an alternative, if there is a union subscription arrangement in force (see para 21.71) the union may send the list and figures containing the above information (s 226A(2)(c)(ii)). In either case, there is no need to name the actual employees who are to be ballotted.

23.51 A sample voting paper is to be sent to the employer at least three days before the opening day of the ballot. If the employees concerned are not all to be sent the same voting paper, a sample of each form of voting paper which is sent to any of them. Before the ballot is held, the union must appoint a scrutineer (see para 22.46), unless the number of those to be balloted is fewer than 50.

23.52 All those members of the trade union whom it is reasonable to believe (at the time of the ballot, see *London Underground Ltd v National Union of Rail Maritime and Transport Workers*) will be induced by the union to take part in the industrial action must be balloted, and no other person (s 227(1)). A union's policy of not balloting members who are in arrears of subscriptions does not satisfy s 227(1) because such persons might nonetheless be induced to take part in strike action as a gesture of solidarity, and therefore were entitled to vote on the matter (*National Union of Rail, Maritime and Transport Workers v Midland Mainline Ltd*). It is for the union to ensure that it has up-to-date information on the addresses of its members and their current job classifications. But if the union acquires new members, or if existing members transfer from employments which are not in dispute into the area of a dispute, immunity will not be lost, because it would hardly be reasonable for the union to believe that they would be induced to take part in the industrial action (s 232A).

23.53 So far as is reasonably practicable, a voting paper must be sent to the home address of the member, and he must be given a reasonable opportunity to vote by post (s 230(2)). If a member is denied the opportunity to vote, and is subsequently induced to take part in the industrial action, the trade union will lose its statutory immunity (s 232A), but the inadvertent failure to supply a ballot paper to union members will be disregarded for all purposes if the failure was accidental and not likely to affect the result of the ballot (s 232B). An inadvertent mistake which leads a member not to be accorded an opportunity to vote in a ballot does not mean that the union loses its immunity for failing to follow the correct balloting procedure. If the failure was accidental, and not likely to affect the result, it can be disregarded. Inadvertently failing to give a member the opportunity to vote is not the same thing as denying him an entitlement to vote (*P v National Association of Schoolmasters/Union of Women Teachers*).

Separate workplace ballots (TULR(C)A, ss 228–228A)

23.54 The general rule about balloting is that a separate ballot shall be held for each workplace (s 228(3)), and industrial action will not be protected unless a majority of workers at that workplace voted in favour (s 226(3)). A person's workplace is a single set of premises (if that is where he works) or premises with which the person's employment has the closest connection (s 228, and see *InterCity West Coast Ltd v National Union of Rail Maritime and Transport Workers*). This requirement does not apply where the union reasonably believes that all the members who are entitled to vote have the same workplace (s 228(2)).

23.55 If the union wishes to call an aggregate ballot of a genuine bargaining unit (instead of separate ballots), certain conditions must be satisfied. The entitlement to vote must be limited to all members of the union who, according to the union's reasonable belief, have an occupation of a particular kind, and are employed by a particular employer or any number of employers with whom the union is in dispute. There must be at least one of its members at each of the workplaces directly affected by the dispute, or the union must be balloting members of a particular occupational category who are employed by a particular employer or by a group of employers, or balloting all of its members who are so employed (s 228A).

Ballots for overseas members (TULR(C)A, s 232)

23.56 Generally, a trade union can elect whether or not to ballot overseas members (ie a person who is not a merchant seaman or offshore worker), who is outside Great Britain during the period of the ballot (s 232(3)) (Great Britain means England, Scotland and Wales). However, if the ballot relates to industrial action involving Great Britain and Northern Ireland, or if a member is temporarily seconded to Northern Ireland, members in both countries must be balloted. If a trade union reasonably believes that a merchant seaman will be at sea or a place outside Great Britain at the time of the ballot, then, if it is reasonably practicable, he is entitled to have a voting paper made available while on ship or at the place where the ship is.

Voting requirements (TULR(C)A, ss 229–231A)

23.57 Voting must be by means of marking a voting paper. This must state the name of the independent scrutineer, specify the address to which and the date by which it is to be returned, and be given one of a series of consecutive numbers, and marked with that number. The voting paper must contain the question (however framed) which requires the member to answer 'Yes' or 'No' whether he is prepared to take part in (or continue to take part in) a strike. A similar question must be posed if the issue is industrial action short of a strike, and for this purpose an overtime ban and a call-out ban will constitute industrial action short of a strike (*Connex South Eastern Ltd v National Union of Rail Maritime and Transport Workers* being thus overruled). The requisite majority must be on each of the relevant questions, not the combined voting figures on both ballots (if two questions are being posed) (*West Midlands Travel Ltd v Transport and General*

Workers' Union). After all, a member might be willing to take part in industrial action short of a strike, but not a strike, and vice versa (*Post Office v Union of Communication Workers*).

23.58 The question on the ballot paper must relate to a trade dispute (within the statutory definition) and not to matters in respect of which no statutory immunity applies (*London University Ltd v National Union of Railwaymen*).

23.59 The voting paper must also specify who, in the event of the vote being in favour of industrial action, is authorised to call upon members to take the industrial action. It is not necessary to name the individual in question, but he must be a person duly authorised either by the rules of the union, or the principal executive committee, or president or general secretary, or any other committee or official of the union (including shop stewards) (s 229(3), s 230(2)).

23.60 The ballot paper must contain the following statement 'If you take part in a strike or other industrial action, you may be in breach of your contract of employment. However, if you are dismissed for taking part in a strike or other industrial action which is called officially and is otherwise lawful, the dismissal will be unfair if it takes place fewer than 12 weeks after you started to take part in the action, and depending on the circumstances may be unfair if it takes place later.' There must be no further comment or qualification on this statement.

23.61 Every person who is entitled to vote must be allowed to do so without interference from, or constraint imposed by the union, or any of its members, officials or employees, and without direct cost. So far as is reasonably practicable, he must have the voting paper sent to his home address or other address as may be requested, and be given a convenient opportunity to vote by post (s 230(2)). The ballot shall be so conducted as to ensure that, so far as is reasonably practicable, voting is done in secret. The votes must be fairly and accurately counted, but accidental inaccuracies, which could not affect the result of the ballot, may be disregarded.

23.62 As soon as is reasonably practicable after the holding of the ballot, the trade union shall inform all persons entitled to vote of the number of:

    (a) votes cast;

    (b) individuals answering 'yes';

    (c) individuals answering 'no'; and

    (d) spoilt papers.

23.63 The union will also ensure that every relevant employer receives this information (s 231A), ie every employer who it is reasonable for the union to believe was the employer of any persons entitled to vote. A failure to do so would make subsequent industrial action unlawful.

23.64 A scrutineer's report will also be prepared, stating whether there were grounds for believing that the statutory grounds for holding the ballot were contravened, that the arrangements with respect to the production, storage, distribution return or handling of the voting papers, and the arrangements for the counting of the votes, including all security arrangements, were such as to minimise the risk of unfairness or malpractice, and that he was able to carry out his functions without interference from the trade union, or any of its members, officials or employees.

Effectiveness of the ballot (TULR(C)A, ss 233–234)

23.65 A ballot will not be effective in so far as it relates to a call for a strike or other industrial action before the date of the ballot, or any such call after the ballot ceases to be effective (s 233(3)). In other words, industrial action cannot be subsequently validated by a ballot. But this does not require a union to adopt a neutral stance on the matter, and urging members to vote in favour of strike action is not the same thing as calling them to strike (*Newham London Borough Council v National and Local Government Officers' Association*).

23.66 A ballot will also cease to be effective after the end of four weeks, or such longer period not exceeding eight weeks, from the date of the ballot, as may be agreed between the employer and the trade union. Industrial action which takes place after that time will not be supported by a ballot (*RJB Mining (UK) Ltd v National Union of Mineworkers*). If, during the four or eight-week period, industrial action is prohibited by a court order (eg on an application for a temporary injunction), and the order is subsequently discharged, or it lapses, the trade union may request the court to order that the period during which the prohibition took effect shall not count towards the four or eight-week period. Once industrial action has started, it may continue indefinitely if necessary, and if at any time it is suspended (eg to enable negotiations to take place), a new ballot will not be required if the resumption of industrial action was part of the original dispute (*Monsanto plc v Transport and General Workers' Union*), although if there is a fresh dispute a new ballot will be required (*Post Office v Union of Communication Workers*).

Notice of industrial action (TULR(C)A, s 234A)

23.67 An act done by a trade union to induce a person to take part in industrial action shall not be prevented from being actionable in tort by s 219 unless the union takes such steps as are reasonably necessary to ensure that the employer receives a relevant notice of the industrial action within the appropriate period, ie the period beginning with the day when the union informed the employer of the result of the ballot, and ending with the seventh day before the day specified in the notice for industrial action to commence. The notice must be in writing, and must contain a list of the categories of employee to which the affected employees belong, a list of the workplaces, the total number of affected employees, and the number of affected employees who work at each workplace or a list of employees in respect of whom a union subscription arrangement (see para 21.71) is in force (s 234A(3)(a)(ii)). The 'affected employees' are those employees of the employer who the union reasonably believes will be induced by the union to take part in the industrial action, but there is no need for the union to identify by name the employees concerned. The notice must state whether the industrial action is to be continuous or discontinuous, and if continuous, the date when it will commence, and if discontinuous, the dates when the action will take place.

23.68 Technically, if the union suspended industrial action (to enable negotiations to take place) a further seven days' notice would be required before the action could be resumed. However, s 234A(7B) now provides that if the union agrees with the employer that it will cease to authorise industrial action from a specified date (the suspension date) but that it may be again authorised with effect from a date not earlier than a specified date (the resumption date), then if the action is suspended, it may be resumed without the necessary notice being required.

Industrial action to enforce a closed shop (TULR(C)A, s 222)

23.69 Section 219 shall not provide an immunity in tort for acts done in furtherance or contemplation of a trade dispute if the reason for the act is that the employer is employing or proposes to employ a person who is not a member of a trade union or of a particular trade union. Immunity is also removed if the action is designed to put pressure on an employer into treating persons less favourably on grounds of their non-membership of a trade union.

Industrial action in support of unofficial strikers (TULR(C)A, s 223)

23.70 We have noted that if a person goes on unofficial strike, and is dismissed, he has no right to claim that he has been unfairly dismissed (see para 21.91). Section 223 provides that s 219 will not prevent an act from being actionable in tort, if the reason for the action was that an employer had lawfully dismissed unofficial strikers.

Secondary action (TULR(C)A, s 224)

23.71 The immunities conferred by s 219 will only apply when a trade union takes industrial action (supported by the appropriate ballot) vis-à-vis an employer with whom there is a trade dispute. In recent years, it became an increasingly popular technique to strengthen the effectiveness of such action by extending it to employers who were not themselves parties to the dispute, in the hope that pressure (direct or indirect) would be thereby exerted on the employer with whom there was a dispute. This is known as secondary action (see, eg *Duport Steels Ltd v Sirs*).

23.72 Secondary action is defined as when a person:

(a) induces another to break a contract of employment; or

(b) interferes or induces another to interfere with its performance; or

(c) threatens that a contract of employment under which he or another is employed will be broken, or its performance interfered with; or

(d) threatens that he will induce another to break a contract of employment, or to interfere with its performance;

and the employer under the contract of employment is not the employer party to the dispute (s 224(2)).

23.73 In these circumstances, nothing in s 219 shall prevent an act from being actionable in tort where one of the facts relied upon for the purpose of establishing such liability amounts to secondary action which is not lawful picketing.

23.74 The current definition of secondary action is wider than the original definition contained in the Employment Act 1980, and thus there are greater pitfalls for those who engage in such action. Secondary action must result in a breach of a contract of employment, whether or not there is a breach of a commercial contract. Further, the present definition extends the meaning of contract of employment to include the contract of a self-employed person who contracts personally to do work or perform services for another, thus closing a loophole revealed in *Shipping Co Uniform Inc v International Transport Workers' Federation* (see TULR(C)A, s 224(6)).

23.75 The only type of secondary action which now remains lawful is peaceful picketing, as laid down in TULR(C)A, s 220 (see para 23.101), ie by workers who are (or were) employed by the employer who is a party to the dispute, and by a trade union official whose attendance is lawful by virtue of s 220(4) of the Act. Secondary picketing (ie at the gate of an employer who is a customer or supplier to the employer who is a party to the dispute) is not lawful.

Pressure to impose union recognition requirement (s 225)

23.76 An act will not be protected by s 219 if it constitutes an inducement of a person to incorporate into a contract a term requiring a party to a contract for goods or services to recognise a trade union for the purpose of negotiating on behalf of workers employed by him, or to negotiate or consult with an official of a trade union (such a contract term would be avoid by reason of s 186, see para 23.116). Nor will an act be protected if it interferes with the supply of goods or services, by inducing another person to break a contract of employment, and the reason being that the supplier does not recognise or negotiate or consult with a trade union (see para 23.113).

C. Immunity of trade unions (TULR(C)A, s 20)

23.77 Section 14 of TULRA 1974 (which re-enacted provisions dating from the Trade Disputes Act 1906) conferred total legal immunity on trade unions in respect of most actions in tort. This immunity was repealed by the Employment Act 1982, and nowadays a trade union will be liable in tort if the protection of TULR(C)A, s 219 is not available. However, a trade union cannot be responsible for everything which is done in its name by its members, shop stewards or officers, but only for those actions which have been authorised or endorsed.

23.78 A trade union will only be liable for inducing breaches of contract, or threatening that a contract will be broken, or for actions for conspiracy, if the act in question is authorised or endorsed by the union. An act shall be taken to have been endorsed or authorised by the trade union if it was done or authorised or endorsed by:

(a) any person empowered by the rules to do, authorise or endorse the act; or

(b) the principal executive committee or the president or general secretary of the union; or

(c) by any other committee of the union, or any other official of the union (whether employed by the union or not).

23.79 Thus, under the current law, a trade union may be held to be legally liable not only for the acts of its full-time officials, but also for its shop stewards if they are authorised to do an act. Further, the liability arises for the acts of any committee (set up in accordance with the union's rules) and also for the acts of any group of members of which a shop steward was a member, and the purpose of which included the organising or co-ordinating of industrial action (TULR(C) A, s 20(4)). This is so notwithstanding anything in the rules of the union, or any contract or rule of law subject to the repudiation provisions, below.

23.80 However, the union will not be liable if the act was repudiated by the principal executive committee or president or general secretary as soon as was reasonably practicable. Written notice must be given to the committee or official in question, without delay, and the union must do its best to give written notice of the fact and date of repudiation, without delay, to every member whom the union believes is taking part in the industrial action, and to the employer of every such member (s 21).

23.81 The written notice must be in the following form: 'Your union has repudiated the call (or calls) for industrial action to which this notice relates and will give no support to unofficial industrial action taken in response to it (or them). If you are dismissed while taking industrial action, you will have no right to complain of unfair dismissal.'

23.82 The repudiation will not be effective if the principal executive, president or general secretary behave in a manner inconsistent with the repudiation (see *Richard Read (Transport) Ltd v National Union of Mineworkers (South Wales Area)*). If, within three months of the purported repudiation, a person who is a party to a commercial contract which has been interfered with by the unofficial industrial action so requests, the union must confirm the repudiation in writing.

D. The effect of the Act

23.83 If a trade union calls for a strike or other industrial action in violation of the balloting provisions of the Act, or for a reason which is not permitted by the Act, it can be sued, and will not have the immunity conferred by s 219. An application may be made by an aggrieved person to the court for an injunction (*Solihull Metropolitan Borough Council v National Union of Teachers*) and a failure to comply constitutes contempt of court, which would lead to a fine or imprisonment being imposed (*Express and Star Ltd v National Graphical Association*) or sequestration of property (*Kent Free Press v National Geographical Association*). Additionally, an action for damages could be brought against the trade union, subject to the limits on the amount which can be awarded, depending on the size of the trade union.

Amount of damages (TULR(C)A, s 22)

23.84 If a trade union is sued successfully in tort, there are limits to the amount of damages which may be awarded. These limits are dependent on the size of the union's membership and are as follows:

fewer than 5,000 members, the limit is £10,000

5,000 or more, but less than 25,000, the limit is £50,000

25,000 or more, but less than 100,000, the limit is £125,000

100,000 or more, the limit is £250,000.

23.85 These limits are applicable in each claim brought against the union, and are not global limits on each incident. Thus, if a trade union calls a strike in circumstances where it lacks legal immunity under s 219, each employee who has suffered damage may sue the union for the maximum sum, depending on the number of members it has. In addition, interest may be added to the award (*Boxfoldia Ltd v National Graphical Association*). For example, in *Willerby Holiday Homes Ltd v Union of Construction, Allied Trades and Technicians*, a trade union called a strike despite the fact that the pre-ballot notice did not conform to s 226A, the actual ballot did not conform to s 227(1), and the notice of strike action did not conform to s 234A. An award of damages amounting to £130,000 was made.

23.86 The limits do not apply to any action in tort in respect of personal injury caused by negligence, nuisance or breach of statutory duty, nor to any breach of duty in connection with the ownership, occupation, possession, control or use of property.

23.87 If damages, costs or expenses are awarded against a trade union, these cannot be enforced against the 'protected property' ie property which belongs to trustees other than in their capacity as trustees of the union, property owned by members in association with other members (ie common property), the property of an official who is not a member or trustee, political funds and provident benefit funds.

Injunctions and interdicts (TULR(C)A, s 221)

23.88 An injunction without notice is an application for a temporary injunction to restrain the commission of some act. It is usually made in great haste, and thus only the party applying will have the time and opportunity to argue the case and be represented. Section 221 states that the court shall not grant such an application if the party against whom the injunction is sought claims, or the court thinks he might claim, that the act was done in contemplation or furtherance of a trade dispute, unless all reasonable steps have been taken to give that person notice of the hearing and an opportunity has been given for that party to be heard.

23.89 If an application is made for an interlocutory injunction (ie restraining an act until the matter comes to trial), and the party against whom the injunction is sought claims that he acted in contemplation or furtherance of a trade dispute, the court shall, in exercising its discretion whether or not to grant the injunction, assess the likelihood of success of any defence which may be raised that the act complained of will be protected by the statutory immunities (s 221(2)). For the procedure in Scotland, see *NWL Ltd v Nelson and Laughton*).

A. Injunctive relief (TULR(C)A, s 20(6))

23.90 If a trade union is responsible for official or unofficial strike action under the provisions of s 20 then in any court proceedings arising out of the act in question, the court may grant an injunction requiring the trade union to take such steps as the court thinks appropriate for ensuring:

(a) that there is no, or no further, inducement of persons to take part in industrial action; and

(b) that no person engage in any conduct after the granting of the injunction because he was induced to take part in industrial action before the injunction was granted.

23.91 This appears to give the court power to order a trade union to take disciplinary action against those who continue to induce or take part in industrial action after it has been repudiated by the union. However, no court shall make an order of specific performance or grant an injunction if the effect is to compel an employee to work or attend any place for the doing of any work (s 236).

23.92 A failure by a trade union (or any other person) to observe the terms of an injunction amounts to contempt of court, in respect of which a fine and/or imprisonment or sequestration of property may be ordered (*Kent Free Press v National Geographical Association*).

B. Industrial action affecting an individual (s 235A)

23.93 Any individual, who claims that industrial action has been called by a trade union which is actionable in tort or which has not been supported by a ballot under s 226, and the effect of which is to prevent or delay the supply of goods or services, or reduce their quality, may make an application to the High Court or Court of Session. It is immaterial that the individual in question is entitled to be supplied with the goods or services in question. If the court is satisfied that the claim is well founded, it shall make such order as it considers appropriate for requiring the union to take steps for ensuring that no further act is done by him to induce any person to take part in the industrial action, and that no person engages in any conduct before the making of the order because he has been induced before the making of the order to take part in industrial action. This section also applies to Crown employment even though no contract of employment may exist.

23.94 The situation may sometimes arise where a trade union calls for industrial action which would otherwise be actionable in tort because the various statutory provisions have not been complied with, but (for whatever reason) the employer (or union members) are unwilling to seek to restrain the industrial action. In such circumstances, any individual, whether affected by the industrial action or not, can bring an application to the court, seeking an appropriate order.

Legal effect of collective agreements (TULR(C)A, ss 178–179)

23.95 A collective agreement is any agreement or arrangement made by or on behalf of a trade union on the one part, and one or more employers or employers' associations on the other part, relating to one or more of the matters contained above in the definition of a trade dispute. In essence, a collective agreement performs two functions. First, it lays down the guiding procedures which will govern the relationship between the signatory parties, by providing, for example, for the constitution of any joint body, or the procedure to be adopted in the event of a dispute or disagreement. Second, it will lay down patterns of terms and conditions of employment which are to cover union members, and possibly others as well, and which are to be observed by all federated and some assenting non-federated firms. Such terms and conditions are usually the minimum, not the maximum rate, so if national bargaining results in a particular award, this may frequently be supplemented at a local level by a further bout of negotiations.

23.96 So far as legal enforceability of these agreements is concerned, s 179 provides that any agreement shall be conclusively presumed not to have been intended by the parties to be a legally enforceable contract, unless the agreement is in writing, and contains a provision stating that the parties do intend the agreement to be legally binding (*Universe Tankships Inc of Monrovia v International Transport Workers' Federation*). It is possible for the parties to state expressly that only part of the agreement is intended to be legally binding, and part not, in which case the parties' intentions will be given effect to, though it is possible to look at a non-legally binding part for the purpose of interpreting a part which is legally binding.

23.97 There must be an express statement to the effect that the parties intend the collective agreement to be legally enforceable (*Prison Service v Bewley*). If the agreement states that the parties intend to be bound by it, this may indicate that it is intended to be binding in honour only, which would not satisfy the provisions of TULR(C)A, s 179 (*National Coal Board v National Union of Mineworkers*).

23.98 The extent to which, and the circumstances in which, the terms of a collective agreement can be incorporated into the contract of employment of an individual employee have already been examined in Chapter 3. Section 180 lays down one further important rule. If a collective agreement, whether legally binding or not, contains a clause prohibiting or restricting the right of workers to engage in a strike or other industrial action, this particular clause shall not be incorporated into the individual contract of employment of any worker, unless the collective agreement:

(a) is in writing;

(b) contains a provision expressly stating that such term shall be or may be incorporated into such contract;

(c) is reasonably accessible at the place of work of such a worker, and is available for him to consult during working hours; and

(d) is one made by an independent trade union.

It should have been noted that this rule applies notwithstanding any agreement to the contrary, whether contained in a collective agreement or an individual contract of employment.

23.99 Thus, if a collective agreement provides that 'the union will not call a strike until the disputes procedure is exhausted', a breach of this clause would be governed by the law relating to the legal effect of the agreement, as mentioned above. If the collective agreement states: 'The employees will not go on strike until the disputes procedure is exhausted', then this clause will only form part of the individual contract of employment if the above conditions are fulfilled. The matter, however, is not really important, for a strike is likely to be a breach of most individuals' contracts of employment (whether or not it is in breach of the terms of a collective agreement) as it is a breach of the duty of faithful service (see Chapter 10) and a breach of contract of such importance that a striker may be dismissed.

23.100 However, if CAC grants a declaration imposing a statutory collective bargaining framework (see para 23.7) the procedure to be followed is legally binding, and can be enforced by specific performance (Trade Union Recognition (Method of Collective Bargaining) Order 2000).

Peaceful picketing (TULR(C)A, s 220)

23.101 It shall be lawful for a person in contemplation or furtherance of a trade dispute to attend:

(a) at or near his own place of work; or

(b) if he is an official of a trade union, at or near the place of work of a member of that union whom he is accompanying and whom he represents;

for the purpose only of peacefully obtaining or communicating information, or peacefully persuading any person to work or to abstain from working. If a person works at more than one place, or at a place where it is impracticable to picket because of its location, his place of work shall be any premises from which he works, or from which his work is administered. A person whose employment has been terminated because of a trade dispute is allowed to picket at his former place of work.

23.102 A trade union official who has been elected or appointed to represent some of the members shall be regarded as representing only those members. Otherwise, a union official shall be regarded as representing all its members (s 220(4)). The purpose of this provision is to draw a distinction between officials who are shop stewards and full-time officials.

23.103 An employee's 'place of work' means his principal place of work or base. It does not refer to premises which, during his work, he may visit from time to time (*Union Traffic Ltd v Transport and General Workers' Union*).

23.104 Whether the picketing has taken place at or near the place of work is a question of fact and degree. In *Rayware Ltd v Transport and General Workers' Union*, pickets stood at the entrance of a private estate, about three-tenths of a mile from the employers' premises. An application by the employers for an injunction to restrain unlawful picketing failed. The pickets could not get any nearer to their place of work without trespassing, and thus they were picketing lawfully near their place of work.

23.105 Section 220 only makes lawful the above acts. If something else is done, the section provides no protection. Thus in *Piddington v Bates*, a policeman wished to restrict the number of pickets who were outside a factory. When a striker tried to join the picket line, he was arrested, and charged with obstructing the policeman in the course of his duty. A conviction was upheld, for the policeman had acted on reasonable grounds that a breach of the peace might have occurred. In *Tynan v Balmer*, a group of pickets walked in a circle at the entrance of a factory in order to prevent traffic from entering and this was held to be an obstruction of the highway and a nuisance.

23.106 Nor do pickets have the power to stop vehicles, for traffic control is a matter for the police. In *Broome v DPP* a trade union official stood in front of a lorry and attempted to persuade the driver not to deliver goods to a factory where a dispute was on. The police told him to get out of the way, but he refused, and he was arrested and charged with obstructing the highway, an offence under the Highways Act 1959. It was held that he was guilty of the offence. Views were expressed in *Broome's* case that the law gave no right to pickets to stop persons or vehicles, for that would indicate that those persons were under a duty to stop and listen. The purpose of the statute was to make attendance at a picket line lawful, and then only for the statutory purposes of peacefully communicating information, etc.

23.107 Mass picketing can also amount to the tort of public nuisance (unreasonable obstruction of the highway), private nuisance (interference with access to the highway) and intimidation (see *News Group Newspapers Ltd v Society of Graphical and Allied Trades 1982*). Thus under the new law, 'flying pickets' and mass demonstrations are clearly unlawful, the former because they will not normally be picketing at their own place of work, the latter because it is unlikely that it is for the purpose of peacefully persuading. In *Thomas v National Union of Mineworkers (South Wales Area)*, it was held that mass picketing constituted a common law nuisance (as well as an offence under TULR(C)A, s 241(1)), for all citizens had the right to use the highway without harassment or unreasonable interference. Accordingly, injunctions were granted against various trade union officials to prevent them from organising, encouraging, etc, members of the union congregating at coal mines, other than for the statutory purpose of peacefully communicating information, numbers in such cases being restricted to six.

23.108 Section 219(3) of TULR(C)A now provides that if an act is done in the course of picketing which is not lawful then s 219 will not provide a defence to any action which may be brought. Thus, if a picket induces workers to break their contracts of employment, and he is picketing at some place other than his own place of work, he can be sued in tort, and the statutory immunity of s 219 will not be available to him. Thus, unlawful picketing may now attract civil, as well as criminal liabilities. A Code of Practice on picketing has been approved by Parliament laying down the parameters for peaceful picketing (see Appendix D).

23.109 If a tort is committed by picketing, s 220 will provide a trade union with legal protection provided the picketing is lawful within that section. But if no tort has been committed, the statutory rules are basically irrelevant. Thus, in *Middlebrook Mushrooms Ltd v Transport and General Workers' Union*, the employers were mushroom producers, employing some 300 workers. They wished to introduce certain cost-saving measures, but these were not agreed to, and the union called a strike. The employer then dismissed all those employees who went on strike.

The union then urged its members to attend at supermarkets which were supplied with the mushrooms by the employers, and hand out leaflets to members of the public, asking them not to buy the employers' mushrooms. The employers brought an action for an interlocutory injunction restraining the union and its officials from organising the 'pickets' outside the supermarkets. The judge held that there was a direct interference with the contracts between the employers and the supermarkets, and granted the injunction.

However, the Court of Appeal reversed the decision. There was nothing in the leaflets which were handed out to members of the public which was aimed at the managers of the supermarket who placed orders with the employers. Thus the union was not seeking to persuade a party to the contract (ie the employers and the supermarkets) but members of the public, who, of course, had no contractual relations with the employers. It may well be that the managers of the supermarket might react to the reaction of the public (not to the picketing), but this, at most, would amount to an indirect inducement not to enter into future contracts, and, as no unlawful means had been used, the application for an injunction was dismissed.

23.110 If the industrial action is unofficial, and a trade union representative is routinely present when picketing is taking place, it will be presumed that he had sufficient know-ledge of the unlawful element of the picketing to have endorsed those actions, and possibly to have, in practice, organised the unlawful activity which the union has not repudiated (*Gate Gourmet London Ltd v TGWU*).

A. Sit-in

23.111 Workers who engage in a sit-in or work-in are in breach of their contractual licence to remain on the employers' premises (*City and Hackney Health Authority v National Union of Public Employees*), and as such, if they refuse to leave after being given reasonable notice to do so are committing the tort of trespass and interfering with busi-ness by unlawful means (*Norbrook Laboratories Ltd v King*). It is possible to obtain an injunction against those involved, and also an employer may use the special expedited procedure to obtain possession of the property (see Ord 113 of the Rules of the Supreme Court).

23.112 If a trade union called for or authorised the sit-in or work-in, it would not be protected by the immunity conferred by s 219, even if a ballot was held, because the immunity in respect of interference with business by unlawful means was removed with the repeal of earlier legislation.

Union recognition

A. Union or non-union members only contracts (TULR(C)A, s 144)

23.113 Any term or condition in a contract for the supply of goods or services shall be void in so far as it purports to require that the whole or part of the work shall be done by persons who are not members of a trade union (or a particular trade union), or who are members of a trade union (or a particular trade union).

23.114 It will be a tort of breach of statutory duty if, on the grounds of union member-ship or non-membership, a person:

  (a) fails to include a particular person's name on a list of approved suppliers of goods or services;

  (b) terminates a contract for the supply of goods or services;

  (c) excludes a person from tendering for the supply of goods or services;

  (d) fails to permit a person to submit a tender; or

  (e) otherwise determines not to enter into a contract for the supply of goods or services.

23.115 Thus any person who suffers damage through the failure or refusal of another to enter into a contract with him for the supply of goods or services on the grounds of union membership or non-membership may sue for breach of statutory duty, and will be able to recover damages (subject to any general defences which may exist to such an action). Further, if there is pressure from any person to induce another to incorporate into a contract to which that other is a party any term or condition which would be void by the above provisions then s 219 shall not be a defence. Nor will s 219 be a defence if a person induces or threatens to induce another person to break a duty imposed by s 144. Thus if trade unionists threaten to strike unless an employer enters into a union labour only contract, or unless he removes non-union sub-contractors from a site, such acts will be actionable despite the general immunity of s 219 (see s 222(3)).

B. Prohibition on union recognition requirements (TULR(C)A, s 186)

23.116 Any term or condition of a contract for the supply of goods or services shall be void in so far as it purports to require any party to the contract:

(a) to recognise one or more trade unions; or

(b) to negotiate or consult with any official of a trade union.

C. Refusal to deal on union exclusion grounds (TULR(C)A, s 187)

23.117 If a person maintains a list of approved suppliers of goods or services, or list of persons from whom tenders may be invited, and fails to include on that list a person who does not recognise trade unions, or terminates a contract for the supply of goods or services on that ground, or does other acts which prevent a person from being able to enter into a contract for the supply of goods or services because he does not recognise trade unions, such action will amount to a breach of statutory duty, and is actionable accordingly (subject to any relevant defences) by the person against whom the action was taken or by any other person adversely affected.

23.118 An act will not be protected by s 219 if it consists of inducing a person to impose a union recognition requirement contrary to ss 186–187 (see s 225).

Criminal liabilities

23.119 Members of the armed forces and policemen have no right to strike, and it is unlawful to induce a member of the prison service to strike or commit a breach of discipline, which effectively prevents them from taking part in an official strike (Criminal Justice and Public Order Act 1994, s 127). Merchant seaman may lawfully terminate their contracts and give 48 hours' notice of strike action provided their ship is in a safe berth in the United Kingdom. Industrial action by post office workers may involve criminal liability (see *Gouriet v Union of Post Office Workers*) and there are restrictions on aliens who promote industrial action.

23.120 Sections 240–241 of TULR(C)A enact two provisions which may be relevant in trade disputes generally. The first is contained in s 240 of the Act, which provides that where any person wilfully and maliciously breaks a contract of service of hiring, knowing or having reasonable cause to believe that the probable consequences of his doing so, either alone or in combination with others, will be to endanger human life, or cause serious bodily injury, or to expose valuable property whether real or personal to destruction or serious injury, he shall, on conviction, be liable to a fine or to imprisonment for a term not exceeding three months.

23.121 The second provision is contained in s 241 of the Act. This states that every person who, with a view to compelling any person to abstain from doing an act which he has a legal right to do:

(a) uses violence to or intimidates such other person or his wife or children, or injures his property; or

(b) persistently follows such other persons from place to place; or

(c) hides any tools, clothes or other property owned or used by such other person, or deprives him of or hinders him in the use thereof; or

(d) watches or besets the house or other place where such person resides, or works, or carries on business, or happens to be, or the approach to such house or place; or

(e) follows such other person with two or more other persons in a disorderly manner along any street or road,

then he shall be liable to a fine not exceeding level 5 on the standard scale or a term of imprisonment not exceeding six months, or both.

23.122 Section 241 was considered in the recent case of *Galt v Philp*, where workers engaged in a 'sit-in', during which they locked and barricaded laboratories, thus preventing other employees from entering the rooms. This was held to be 'besetting' within the meaning of s 241(1)(a) and the individuals concerned were found guilty of an offence under the Act.

23.123 It must be remembered that TULR(C)A, s 219 only protects a person from civil liability, and does not give any immunity in respect of criminal acts.

A. Public Order Act 1986

23.124 This Act abolished the common law offences of riot, rout, unlawful assembly and affray, and repealed the provisions of the Public Order Act 1936, relating to threatening behaviour likely to provoke a breach of the peace. A number of statutory criminal offences have been introduced by the new Act, which may be invoked when the conduct of industrial disputes gets out of hand. These are:

(a) *Riot* (s 1). This is where 12 or more people use or threaten to use violence for a common purpose which would cause a person of reasonable firmness to fear for his personal safety;

(b) *Violent disorder* (s 2). This has the same elements as *riot*, except that it applies when three or more persons are taking part;

(c) *Affray* (s 3). This also has the same elements as *riot*, except that only one person need be involved, and threats, by themselves, would not be sufficient;

(d) *Fear or provocation of violence* (s 4). It is an offence to use threatening, abusive or insulting words or behaviour or to distribute or display any visual representation which is threatening, abusive or insulting, where the act is intended or likely to make a person fear immediate violence, or to provoke immediate violence;

(e) *Harassment, alarm or distress* (s 5). This has almost the same elements as *fear or provocation of violence*, but the accused may defend himself by arguing that he had no reason to believe that a person alarmed was within his hearing or sight, or that his conduct was reasonable.

23.125 The Act also lays down new rules for marches, processions, demonstrations and public assemblies.

B. Intentional harassment

23.126 The Criminal Justice and Public Order Act 1994, s 154 creates a new criminal offence of intentional harassment. This is committed if a person, with intent to cause another person harassment, alarm or distress:

(a) uses threatening, abusive or insulting behaviour, or disorderly behaviour;

(b) displays any writing, sign or visible representation which is threatening, abusive or insulting

so that the other person feels harassment, alarm or distress.

23.127 It is believed that this offence could be committed in a number of employment situations, including verbal or written abuse etc to those who cross picket lines, and harassment on grounds of race, sex, sexual orientation, disabilities, religion, and so on.

European Works Councils

23.128 The Transnational Information and Consultation of Employees Regulations 1999 came into force in January 2000, and implement the European Works Council Directive 94/45/EC. The regulations apply to undertakings and groups of undertakings with at least 1,000 employees in the European Economic Area (ie, the 15 member states of the EU and Norway, Liechtenstein and Iceland), and at least 150 employees in each of two or more states. Employee numbers are calculated by adding together the number of employees in each month in a two-year period, and dividing the total by 24 (reg 6). An employee (or employee representative) may request information from the management for the purpose of determining whether the establishment or undertaking is part of a European-scale undertaking, and if there is a failure to supply the information, a complaint may be made to the Central Arbitration Committee, which can order the disclosure of the relevant information (reg 8), or, if it considers the matter to be beyond doubt, declare that the undertaking is a Community-scale organisation, ie within the scope of the Regulations.

23.129 If there is a valid request by employees or their representatives (see reg 9) management shall set up a special negotiating body, charged with the task of determining the scope, composition, functions, and term of office of a European Works Council, or, as an alternative, the arrangements for an information and consultation procedure (regs 11–17).

The members of the special negotiating body must be elected by ballot, organised by management, and an employee or employee representative may complain to CAC if there is dissatisfaction with the balloting plans. CAC can require that the ballot arrangements be modified so as to reflect the interests of UK employees. However, if there is already in existence a consultative committee which has been elected by ballot and represents all UK employees, that committee may nominate its own members to be members of the special negotiating body.

23.130 Negotiations between management and the special negotiating body must be carried out in a spirit of co-operation, with a view to reaching agreement, either by establishing a European Works Council or an information and consultation procedure. If necessary, one or more experts may be engaged to assist. If a Works Council is established, the agreement will determine the undertakings covered, the composition of the Works Council, its functions, venue, frequency and duration of meetings, financial and material resources to be allocated, and the duration of the agreement and procedure for renegotiation. If an information and consultation procedure is adopted, the agreement will specify a method by which the representatives are to meet to discuss the information conveyed to them, which must in particular relate to transnational questions which significantly affect the interests of the employees (reg 17).

23.131 If management fails to establish a European Works Council or an information and consultation procedure, or if the terms of the agreement are not complied with by management, a complaint may be made to the EAT, which can make an order specifying the steps which central management shall take, with the ultimate sanction of a penalty notice (up to £75,000) if there is a failure to take the required steps.

23.132 A person who is or was a member of the European Works Council or information and consultation representative (or an expert who was assisting) shall not disclose any information or document which has been in his possession by virtue of his position as such, which central management has entrusted to him on terms requiring it to be held in confidence. A breach of this duty is actionable, although not in respect of a protected disclosure (see para 10.68). Disputes as to whether it was reasonable for management to impose a requirement of confidentiality, as well as complaints that management have improperly withheld information which ought to be disclosed, may be referred for settlement to CAC.

A. Time off work for members of a European Works Council (regs 25–27)

23.133 An employee who is:

(a) a member of a special negotiating body;

(b) a member of a European Works Council;

(c) an information and consultation representative; or

(d) a candidate for election as a member or representative

is entitled to take reasonable time off work, with pay (at the appropriate hourly rate), during working hours, in order to perform his functions as a member, representative or candidate. He may bring a claim to an employment tribunal, that:

(a) his employer has unreasonably refused to permit him to take time off work; or

(b) has failed to pay him for taking time off work.

The complaint must be made within the usual time limit of three months (with the usual extension if it was not reasonably practicable to present it earlier). If the complaint is well founded, the tribunal will make a declaration, and order the employer to pay the amount to which the employee was entitled, or would have been had he taken the time off work.

B. Protection from detriment and dismissal (regs 28–33)

23.134 An employee who is:

(a) a member of a special negotiating body;

(b) a member of a European Works Council;

(c) an information and consultation representative; or

(d) a candidate for election as a member or representative

has the right not to be subjected to any detriment by an act or deliberate failure to act, or to be dismissed, on the ground that the employee performed any functions or activities as a member, representative or candidate, or made a request for time off work or for pay for time off work to perform those functions or activities.

23.135 Any employee (whether or not he is one of the above categories) has the right not to be subjected to any detriment, or to be dismissed because:

(a) he took proceedings before an employment tribunal to enforce a right or secure an entitlement under the regulations;

(b) he exercised an entitlement to complain to an appeal tribunal or CAC;

(c) he requested information from management to ascertain whether the establishment is part of a Community-scale undertaking (see reg 7);

(d) acted with a view of securing that a special negotiating body, or European Works Council or an information and consultation procedure, did or did not come into existence;

(e) indicated that he supported or did not support any of those institutions;

(f) stood as a candidate for membership of a special negotiating body, or European Works Council or as an information and consultation representative;

(g) influenced the way in which votes were to be cast by other employees in a ballot under the regulations;

(h) voted in such ballot;

(i) expressed doubts as to whether the ballot was properly conducted; or

(j) proposed to do or declined to do any of the things mentioned in paras (d)–(i) above.

23.136 A complaint may be made to an employment tribunal by a person who alleges that he has suffered a detriment or been dismissed on any of the above grounds. The complaint must be made within the usual time limits. If the complaint relates to a detriment, and is well founded, the tribunal will make a declaration, and may award compensation, as it thinks just and equitable. If the complaint relates to a dismissal, reinstatement or re-engagement can be ordered, or the usual basic and compensation awards will be made (see Chapter 20).

C. Information and Consultation of Employees Regulations 2004

23.137 These regulations give effect to EC Directive 2002/14/EC and are designed to create a framework for informing and consulting with employees. They apply from 2005 to all undertakings which employ more that 150 employees; from April 2007, the regulations will apply to undertakings which employ more than 100 employees, and from April 2008, all undertakings with more than 50 employees will be covered. However, they only apply to undertakings which have a registered office or a principal place of business in Great Britain.

23.138 An 'undertaking' is a public or private undertaking which carries out an economic activity, whether or not operating for gain (see reg 2). This can be an incorporated legal entity, or an unincorporated body such as a partnership, co-operative, charity, mutual society, building society, etc. An undertaking does not include a group of companies, and therefore each company within a group must make its own arrangements. However, certain parts of the public sector will not come within the scope of the regulations, although a Cabinet Office Code of Practice will apply to such bodies, and local authorities will be encouraged to adopt similar arrangements.

23.139 To determine how many employees are employed in the undertaking, an average is taken in respect of the previous 12 months. The monthly total of number of employees employed in each calendar month is added together, and that total is divided by 12. Part-time employees can be counted provided they work for a certain number of hours (see reg 4(3)).

D. Pre-existing agreements (regs 8–9)

23.140 Many undertakings will already have a pre-existing agreement, which has been voluntarily negotiated outside of, or prior to, the regulations. If so, there is no requirement to enter into a new arrangement unless at least 40% of existing employees make a request, and this request is endorsed by a majority of those voting and 40% of those eligible to vote in a ballot. To be a valid pre-existing agreement, certain conditions must be met:

(a) The pre-existing agreement must be in writing. Thus, existing informal or customary arrangements will have to be formalised.

(b) All employees in the undertaking must be covered. This requirement may cause difficulties in practice, either in respect of members of senior management who are outside formal arrangements, or parts of the workforce not covered by a formal collective agreement.

(c) It must set out the manner in which the employer will give information to the employees or their representatives. This is the 'what', 'where' and 'how' requirement, which must be satisfied.

(d) It must have been approved by the employees. There can be an express approval, or an approval given by representatives of an independent trade union or other appropriate representatives.

E. Negotiated agreements (reg 7)

23.141 In the absence of any such pre-existing agreements, there is no obligation on an employer to do anything. However, the statutory procedure may be triggered by a request from 10% of the employees to commence negotiations about the establishment of an information and consultation procedure. (If 10% would amount to fewer that 15 employees, or more than 2,500 employees, a valid request occurs if there is a request by 15 or 2,500 employees respectively). Employees (or their representatives) may request data from the employer to determine the number of employees employed so as to ascertain whether or not the regulations apply. There are certain formalities to be observed when making the request.

23.142 The employer may, at this stage, seek a declaration from CAC that the request is not valid (eg because it lacks the relevant support from the employees, or because there is an insufficient number of employees employed in the undertaking, etc). If this is upheld by CAC, that will be the end of the matter, although there is nothing to prevent a further request being made once any apparent defect in the earlier request has been remedied. A request will not be valid if it is made within three years of a previous agreement having been made, or the standard provisions (see below) are deemed to apply.

23.143 Otherwise, the employer must enter into negotiations to reach a negotiated agreement. The regulations provide for the election or appointment of negotiating representatives, ensuring that they represent all the employees. Both parties should 'work in a spirit of cooperation and with due regard for the reciprocal rights and obligations, taking into account the interests of both the undertaking and the employees' (reg 21). Negotiations for an agreement should not last more than six months, although there is a certain flexibility with regard to the timetable. There may be a single agreement covering all the employees, but there may be separate consultation arrangements for different parts of the undertaking, because parts of an undertaking may have little in common with other sectors and have different activities. The agreement will provide for the appointment or election of information and consultation representatives. It must be signed on behalf of the employer and by all the negotiating representatives, or signed by a majority of them and either approved in writing by 50% of the employees or approved in a ballot of all the affected employees.

23.144 The agreement may provide that consultation will take place through representatives or provide for information and consultation to be provided or undertaken directly with the employees. A Guidance Note issued by the DTI makes certain suggestions about the contents of the agreement, but the employer and employee representatives are free to agree different arrangements about the coverage of the agreement, the methods chosen for providing information and consultation arrangements, the frequency with which information is provided, the subject-matter to be covered, and the methods adopted for the exchange of views and opinions. Statutory consultation requirements such as handling redundancies, TUPE transfers, health and safety consultations, etc may be included or excluded in the agreement, although if they are excluded they must still be observed in the usual manner. The agreement should consider how confidential information is to be handled, the resolution of disputes, and the circumstances in which the agreement can be reviewed, revised or terminated.

23.145 It must be stressed that consultation is not collective bargaining. It is about the exchange of views and the establishment of a dialogue with the workforce. However, where the Standard Information and Consultation Provisions apply (see below), consultation about changing work organisation or contractual relations must be conducted with a view to reaching agreement, although employers will still be free to make the final decisions if there is disagreement within the consultation arrangements.

F. Statutory default provisions (reg 18)

23.146 If the employer fails to initiate negotiations following a valid employee request, or if they fail to reach a negotiated agreement, the Standard Information and Consultation Provisions (SICP) will come into effect. The employer must hold a ballot, under the supervision of a ballot supervisor, to ensure the election of the relevant number of information and consultation representatives (one representative for each 50 employees, subject to a maximum of 50 representatives). Thereafter, there are specific issues in respect of which the employer is to provide information and on which to consult with the representatives so elected. These are:

(a) the recent and probable development of the undertaking's activities and economic situation;

(b) the situation, structure and probable development of employment within the undertaking and any anticipatory measures envisaged, in particular where there is a threat to employment within the undertaking;

(c) decisions which are likely to lead to substantial changes in work organisation or in contractual relations, including business transfers and collective redundancies.

23.147 The information provided must be given at such time, in such fashion and with such content as to enable the representatives to conduct an adequate study, and to prepare for consultation.

23.148 There is a general requirement that if the employer provides information or documents in confidence, the recipient must not breach that confidence, unless he reasonably believes that the disclosure would be protected by virtue of ERA, s 43A (see Chapter 10). Additionally, the employer may withhold information the disclosure of which would seriously harm the functioning of, or would be prejudicial to, the undertaking. A representative who disputes that the information is confidential, or that disclosure would be harmful or prejudicial may apply to CAC for a ruling.

23.149 An employee who is a negotiating representative, or a SICP representative has the usual right to have time off work (with pay) to perform his duties as such. He will have the statutory protection against dismissal or detriment because he performed his functions as such or exercised his right to have time off work to do so. However, a dismissal will not be automatically unfair if the reason was that he disclosed information or documents in breach of his duty of confidentiality, unless he reasonably believed that the disclosure was a protected disclosure (see Chapter 10). An individual employee also has protection against dismissal or detriment if he took action to enforce his rights under the regulations (eg, by acting to secure a negotiated agreement, etc).

23.150 There is no such statutory protection for employees or representatives who have a pre-existing agreement, as these fall outside the scope of the regulations. Such rights as they have will be determined within the existing legal provisions (see especially Chapter 17).

G. Enforcement (reg 22)

23.151 Most of the rights contained in the regulations may be enforced by way of a complaint to the Central Arbitration Committee (CAC) (rights in respect of time off work, detriment and dismissal may be enforced in the employment tribunal). There are some 14 types of complaints which can be made, ranging from a breach of the employer's obligation to provide information on the numbers of employees employed, through to a declaration as to whether the disclosure of certain information is covered by the confidence provisions. In most cases, CAC will issue a declaration, which will have effect as if made by the High Court (or Court of Session). There is a right of appeal to the EAT.

23.152 If the employer fails to hold a ballot for the election of SCIP representatives, or if he fails to comply with the terms of a negotiated agreement or the SICP, and CAC finds the complaint well founded, the applicant may apply to EAT for a penalty notice. Unless the EAT is satisfied that the failure was beyond the employer's control, or there was some other reasonable excuse, EAT may set a penalty of up to £75,000, depending on its gravity or other factors, including the reason for the failure, etc.

23.153 The DTI has issued Guidance Notes to the regulations. ACAS has issued 'Good practice advice'. CAC has issued 'A Guide for Employers and Employees to the role of the Central Arbitration Committee (CAC)'.

Appendices

APPENDIX A

Monetary awards (as at 1 February 2006)

Statutory reference	Statutory right	Maximum rate	Maximum award
1. ERA s 12(4)	Itemised pay statement	none	Unnotified deduction for 13 weeks prior to application to an employment tribunal
2. ERA s 31(1)	Guarantee pay	£18.90 per day	£94.50 in any period of three months
3. ERA s 69(1)	Medical suspension pay	none	26 weeks' pay
4. TULR(C) A 1992 s 149(2)	Action short of dismissal	none	Just and equitable
5. TULR(C) A 1992 s 172(2)	Time off work	none	Just and equitable (refusal to allow) or normal pay or average hourly earnings (failure to pay)
6. ERA s 54(3)	Time off to look for work or arrange for retraining	none	Two fifths of a week's pay
7. ERA s 93(2)	Written reasons for dismissal	none	Two weeks' pay
8. ERA ss 118–124	Unfair dismissal	£290 per week	Basic award £8,700 Compensation award £58,400 Additional award £7,540–£15,080
9. TULR(C) A 1992 s 158(1) and (2)	Unfair dismissal for trade union membership or non-membership		(a) Re-instatement/ re-engagement not sought
		£290 per week	(i) Basic award £8,700 (minimum £4,000) (ii) Compensation award £58,400
			(b) Re-instatement/ re-engagement sought, but IT makes no order
		£290 per week	(i) Basic award £8,700 (minimum £4,000) (ii) Compensation award £58,400 (c) Re-instatement/ re-engagement ordered but not complied with
		£290 per week	(i) Basic award £8,700 (minimum £4,000) (ii) Compensation award £58,400

Statutory reference	Statutory right	Maximum rate	Maximum award
		£290 per week	(iii) Additional award £7,540–£15,080 (d) Re-instatement/ re-engagement ordered and complied with Compensation award – loss made good
10. ERA s 162	Redundancy pay	£290 per week	£8,700
11. ERA s 184	Rights on employer's insolvency	£290 per week	Arrears of pay £2,320
		£290 per week	Statutory notice £3,480
		£290 per week	Holiday pay £1,740
		£290 per week	Basic award £8,700
12. Sex Discrimination Act 1975 s 65	Sex discrimination	none	Just and equitable
13. Race Relations Act 1976 s 56	Race discrimination	none	Just and equitable
14. Disability Discrimination Act 1996 s 8	Disability discrimination	none	Just and equitable
15. TULR(C)A 1992 s 67(8)	Right not to be unjustifiably disciplined	£290 per week	£67,100
16. TULR(C)A 1992 s 176(6)	Unreasonable expulsion/ exclusion from trade union membership	£290 per week	£67,100
17. TULR(C)A 1992 s 189(4)	Protective award	none	Up to 90 days' pay
18. ET Extension of Jurisdiction Order 1994	Breach of contract	none	£25,000
19. TULR(C)A s 140(4)	Refusal to employ on TU grounds		£58,400
20. TULR(C)A s 70C	Consultation with union on training	£290	£580
21. ERelA s 11(2)	Right to be accompanied	£290	£580

APPENDIX B
Names and addresses

Advisory, Conciliation and Arbitration Service
Brandon House
180 Borough High Street
London SE1 1LW

020 7210 3000

www.acas.org.uk/

(Regional offices can be found in Newcastle-upon-Tyne, Leeds, London, Bristol, Nottingham, Liverpool, Thetford, Kent, Birmingham, Fleet, Manchester, Glasgow and Cardiff)

Employment Tribunal Service Head Office
Ground Floor
19–29 Woburn Place
London WC1H 0LU

020 7273 8603
Fax: 020 7273 8686

Employment Tribunal Service (Scotland)
Eagle Building
215 Bothwell Street
Glasgow G2 7 TS

0141 204 0730
Fax: 0141 204 0732

Central Arbitration Committee
PO Box 51547
London SE1 1ZG

020 7904 2300
www.cac.gov.uk/

Certification Officer
Brandon House
180 Borough High Street
London SE1 1LW

020 7210 3734

Commission for Racial Equality
St Dunstan's House
201–211 Borough High Street
London SE1 1GZ

020 7939 0000

www.cre.gov.uk/

Department of Trade and Industry
Caxton House
Tothill Street
London SW1H 9NA

020 7273 3000

www.dti.gov.uk/

Disability Rights Commission
DRC Helpline
Freepost
MID02164
Stratford-upon-Avon CV37 9BR

08457 622 633

Employment Appeal Tribunal
58 Victoria Embankment
London EC4Y 0DS

020 7273 1041
Fax: 020 7273 1045

Email: Londoneat@ets.gsi.gov.uk/

52 Melville Street
Edinburgh EH3 7HF

0131 225 3963
Fax: 0131 220 6694

Equal Opportunities Commission
Arndale House
Arndale Centre
Manchester M4 3EQ

Email: information@eog.org.uk.html

Health and Safety Commission
Rose Court
2–10 Southwark Bridge Road
London SE1 9HS

020 7273 3000

APPENDIX C

Main legislative provisions 1980–2006

1. Employment Act 1980

Enabled the payment of public funds to be made for ballots held by trade unions (since repealed); independent trade unions were entitled to hold ballots on an employer's premises; the Secretary of State was empowered to issue codes of practice (Codes on Picketing and Trade Union Ballots have been issued; the Code on Closed Shop Agreements and Arrangements has been revoked); there is a right not to be unreasonably excluded or expelled from a trade union, but this applied only where there was a union membership agreement in force – somewhat limited because of the provisions of the Employment Act 1990, see below; the burden of proof in unfair dismissal cases was neutralised as between the parties; a dismissal for non-membership of a trade union where there was a union membership agreement was to be unfair unless a ballot was held, or if the employee objected to joining on grounds of conscience or deeply held conviction (this provision has since been repealed); minor changes were made to the provisions on unfair dismissal and maternity leave of absence and guarantee payments; the Act provided for time off work for antenatal care, redefined peaceful picketing, and dealt with liability in tort for secondary action (since repealed).

2. Employment Act 1982

Companies were required to deal with the employee involvement in their annual reports; new rules were laid down when a person was dismissed because of union or non-union membership, and on ballots for union membership agreement (since repealed); the Act provided for a minimum basic award and a special award and for a contribution against third parties when dismissal was on the ground of trade union membership or non-membership; changes were made when dismissal was in connection with a strike or other industrial action, and terms in contracts requiring work to be done by union or non-union workers were stated to be void; the immunity of trade unions from actions in tort was removed, but a trade union would only be liable if the act was authorised or endorsed by a responsible person (since amended); the Act provided for limits on damages awarded against trade unions, and the definition of 'trade dispute' was altered.

3. Trade Union Act 1984

Trade unions are required to hold ballots for certain posts, and the immunity of trade unions from actions in tort was removed unless the industrial action was supported by a secret ballot (since amended); ballots have to be held to establish the political fund.

4. Sex Discrimination Act 1986

The first six sections of this Act altered the Sex Discrimination Act 1975 and the Equal Pay Act 1970 in consequence of rulings by the European Court of Justice to the effect that UK law did not comply with the Equal Treatment Directive (76/207/EEC). The exemption in favour of an employer who employed five or fewer employees was repealed, and the definition of genuine occupational qualification for private household employment was altered; the upper age limit for unfair dismissal was equalised; discriminatory terms of employment in collective agreements were declared to be void, and certain restrictions on working hours and conditions of employment of women were removed.

5. Wages Act 1986

Repealed the Truck Acts 1831–1940 and other legislation relating to the payment of wages. The Act provides for a remedy in respect of unlawful deductions from wages, with special provisions for retail employment; the functions of Wages Councils were restricted; redundancy rebates were limited to employers who employed less than 10 employees (since repealed).

6. Employment Act 1988

A trade union member can obtain a court order restraining the union from calling a strike without holding a ballot; he also has the right not to be unjustifiably disciplined by the union; other provisions gave greater control to members of the affairs of the union; it became thus automatically unfair to dismiss a person because he was not a member of a trade union; industrial action to enforce a closed shop would no longer attract immunity; changes were made to the law on trade union ballots and elections; the post of Commissioner for the Rights of Trade Union Members was created, and given power to provide assistance to trade union members in taking certain legal actions; there must be an independent scrutineer appointed for certain ballots, and mandatory postal ballots for union elections and political fund ballots.

7. Employment Act 1989

This Act further amended the Sex Discrimination Act, so as to bring UK law in line with the European directive on the implementation of the principle of equal treatment for men and women as regards access to employment, vocational training, promotion and working conditions; it repealed many provisions of protective legislation which laid down different treatment for men and women, and removed restrictions relating to the employment of young persons; Sikhs were exempted from the requirement to wear safety helmets on construction sites; minor changes were made to the Employment Protection (Consolidation) Act (written statement under s 1, time off for trade union duties, two years' qualifying employment for written reasons for dismissal), and the age up to which women and men could receive redundancy payment was assimilated; the redundancy rebate was abolished altogether; the Secretary of State was given power to provide for pre-hearing assessment); the Training Commission was dissolved.

8. Employment Act 1990

This Act made it unlawful to refuse a person employment because he was or was not a member of a trade union (being the final nail in the coffin of the closed shop); immunity in respect of secondary action was abolished, minor amendments were made to the law on trade union ballots and the responsibility of a trade union for the acts of its officials; a ballot on industrial action ceases to be effective after four weeks, though this period is extended if there are court proceedings; unofficial strikers lost their right to bring a claim for unfair dismissal, the powers of the Commissioner for the Rights of Trade Union Members were increased; the Act made provision for the revision of codes of practice.

9. Trade Union and Labour Relations (Consolidation) Act 1992

This Act consolidates all the relevant law on trade unions and labour relations, including provisions from the Conspiracy and Protection of Property Act 1875, Trade Union Act 1913, Trade Union (Amalgamations etc) Act 1964, Trade Union and Labour Relations Act 1974, Employment Protection Act 1975, Trade Union and Labour Relations (Amendment) Act 1976, Employment Protection (Consolidation) Act 1978, Trade Union Act 1984, and the Employment Acts of 1980, 1982, 1988, 1989 and 1990.

10. Trade Union Reform and Employment Rights Act 1993

This Act amends the Employment Protection (Consolidation) Act 1978 and the Trade Union and Labour Relations (Consolidation) Act 1992, and makes further changes in the law. The independent scrutineer appointed for trade union elections and ballots is given more powers, voting is to be fully postal, funds for trade union ballots are to be phased out, and ballots may no longer be carried out on employers' premises. An individual cannot be excluded or expelled from a trade union except on specific grounds, employers must not make unauthorised deductions from a worker's pay in respect of union subscriptions, and the right not to be unjustifiably disciplined is extended. To be protected from being sued in respect of industrial action, a trade union must send a copy of the ballot paper to the employer before the date of the ballot, and inform the employer of the result. Notice of industrial action must be given to an employer. Any individual may apply to the High Court claiming that industrial action is unlawful, and he may receive assistance from a new Commissioner for Protection against Unlawful Industrial Action. There is a new general right to maternity leave for pregnant employees, and a woman dismissed on grounds connected with pregnancy or childbirth no longer requires two years' qualifying employment before she can present a claim of unfair dismissal. Protection is given to persons in health and safety cases, consultations with trade unions on redundancies must be carried out with a view to reaching agreement. Amendments are made to the written statement to be given to every employee within eight weeks of commencing employment. Wages Councils are abolished. The constitution and jurisdiction of industrial tribunals and the Employment Appeal Tribunal is altered. ACAS is given power to make charges for advice, women dismissed on grounds of pregnancy or childbirth are to be given written reasons for their dismissal without the need to request them, certain compensation awards are increased, and interim relief will apply in health and safety cases. It is unfair to dismiss an employee on the ground that he asserted a statutory right.

11. Disability Discrimination Act 1995

This Act makes it unlawful to discriminate against a person who has a physical or mental disability as defined. A National Disability Council is created to advise the Secretary of State on related matters. Codes of practice are to be produced. The Act will be brought into force by stages, and will be subject to regulations to be made.

12. Employment Rights Act 1996

This Act consolidates all the main statutory provisions on employment law, including those provisions which were formerly contained in the Employment Protection (Consolidation) Act 1978, Wages Act 1986, Sunday Trading Act 1994, and the relevant parts of other legislation.

13. Industrial Tribunals Act 1996

This Act consolidates those earlier legislative provisions which deal with the constitution and procedures of industrial tribunals and the Employment Appeal Tribunal. The Act has now been renamed the 'Employment Tribunals Act 1996'.

14. Employment Rights (Dispute Resolution) Act 1998

This Act renamed industrial tribunals 'employment tribunals', and makes certain provisions designed to speed up the hearing of complaints before them (eg cases which can be heard by a chairman alone, interlocutory matters to be dealt with by a legal officer). Non-lawyers (duly insured) can enter into compromise agreements. Empowers ACAS to draw up an arbitration scheme.

15. National Minimum Wage Act 1998

Creates the Low Pay Commission, and sets out the procedures for ensuring and enforcing a national minimum wage for all workers.

16. Employment Relations Act 1999

This Act made a number of changes in the law relating to trade unions, by introducing a new statutory framework for collective bargaining, alterations in the balloting procedures, and increased protections for trade union members, in particular when taking part in official industrial action. The maternity leave provisions were simplified, and new provisions on time off work for domestic emergencies, to care for dependants and parental leave were introduced. An employee has the right to be accompanied in grievance or disciplinary proceedings, the service qualification was reduced to one year for unfair dismissal claims etc, and the compensation limit for unfair dismissal claims was raised to £50,000. The offices of Commissioner for the Rights of Trade Union Members and Commissioner for Protection against Unlawful Industrial Action were abolished.

17. Employment Act 2002

This Act made changes in the law relating to maternity leave, and introduced paid paternity and adoption leave. Employment Tribunal procedures were reformed, and ACAS was required to operate within fixed periods of conciliation. Statutory dismissal, disciplinary and grievance procedures were implied into all contracts of employment, with various sanctions against those who fail or refuse to follow those procedures. Changes were made to the written statement of terms and conditions of employment, and equal pay questionnaires introduced. Union learning representatives were given the right to have time off with pay to perform their functions. The Act gave employees the right to request flexible working hours in order to care for a child, and the Secretary of State was empowered to introduce regulations covering a number of topics in the Act.

18. Employment Relations Act 2004

This Act made a number of changes to the statutory recognition procedures, and made amendments to the law relating to industrial action, trade union membership, and other rights of workers and employees.

19. Equality Act 2006

This Act created the Commission for Equality and Human Rights.

APPENDIX D

Codes of Practice

The following Codes of Practice may be obtained from HMSO (St. Clements House, 2–16 Colegate, Norwich, NR3 1BQ1 Tel: 01603 723011; http:// www.hmso.gov.uk/)

1 Disciplinary and Grievance Procedures in Employment (ACAS)
2 Disclosure of Information to Trade Unions for Collective Bargaining Purposes (ACAS)
3 Time off for Trade Union Duties and Activities (ACAS)
4 For the elimination of discrimination on grounds of sex and marriage (EOC)
5 Race Relations in Employment (CRE)
6 Equal Pay (EOC)
7 Employment and Occupation (DRC)
8 Picketing (SoS)
9 Industrial Action Ballots and Notice to Employers (SoS)
10 Access to Workers during Recognition and Derecognition Ballots (SoS)
11 Safety Representatives and Safety Committees (HSC)
12 Time off for the Training of Safety Representatives (HSC)
13 The Employment Practices Data Protection Code (IC)
14 Avoidance of Race Discrimination in Recruitment Practices While Seeking to Prevent Illegal Working (SoS)

Index